Israel Smith Clare

The World's History Illuminated - Vol. 02

Israel Smith Clare

The World's History Illuminated - Vol. 02

ISBN/EAN: 9783744651516

Printed in Europe, USA, Canada, Australia, Japan

Cover: Foto ©ninafisch / pixelio.de

More available books at **www.hansebooks.com**

EXTERIOR OF THE COLOSSEUM, ROME.

THE WORLD'S HISTORY
ILLUMINATED

CONTAINING A RECORD OF THE HUMAN RACE FROM THE EARLIEST HISTORICAL PERIOD TO THE PRESENT TIME. EMBRACING A GENERAL SURVEY OF THE PROGRESS OF MANKIND IN NATIONAL AND SOCIAL LIFE, CIVIL GOVERNMENT, RELIGION, LITERATURE, SCIENCE AND ART 🙢 🙢 🙢 🙢 🙢 🙢

COMPLETE IN EIGHT VOLUMES

Compiled, Arranged and Written by........ ISRAEL SMITH CLARE Author of "THE WORLD'S HISTORY ILLUMINATED," and "COMPLETE HISTORICAL COMPENDIUM."

REVIEWED, VERIFIED AND ENDORSED BY THE PROFESSORS OF HISTORY IN FIVE AMERICAN UNIVERSITIES, WITH AN INTRODUCTION ON THE EDUCATIONAL VALUE OF HISTORICAL STUDY

By MOSES COIT TYLER, A.M., L.H.D.

PROFESSOR OF AMERICAN HISTORY IN CORNELL UNIVERSITY.

"NOT TO KNOW WHAT HAPPENED BEFORE WE WERE BORN IS TO REMAIN ALWAYS A CHILD; FOR WHAT WERE THE LIFE OF MAN DID WE NOT COMBINE PRESENT EVENTS WITH THE RECOLLECTIONS OF PAST AGES?"—*CICERO.*

Volume II.—Ancient Oriental Nations and Greece

ILLUMINATED WITH MAPS, PORTRAITS AND VIEWS.

ST. LOUIS
WESTERN NEWSPAPER SYNDICATE

COPYRIGHT, 1897,
BY
R. S. PEALE AND J. A. HILL.

Lib. Univ. Mus.

TABLE OF CONTENTS.

PART I.—ANCIENT HISTORY.—VOL. II.

CHAPTER IX.—REPUBLIC OF CARTHAGE.

SECTION I.

GEOGRAPHY OF NORTHERN AFRICA, ... 387-388
Northern Africa.—Small Rivers.—Political Divisions.—Carthage.—Her Territory.—Foreign Possessions.

SECTION II.

THE REPUBLIC OF CARTHAGE, ... 388-391
Founding of Carthage by Queen Dido of Tyre.—Growth of Carthage.—Carthaginian Colonies.—Extension of the Carthaginian Dominion.—Employment of Foreign Mercenaries.—Carthaginian Navy.—Constitution of Carthage.—Her Revenue.—Religion.—Horrible Human Sacrifices.

SECTION III.

CARTHAGINIAN COMMERCE, ... 391-392
Extent of Carthaginian Commerce.—Exports.—Imports.—Commerce by Sea.—Caravan Trade.

SECTION IV.

WARS OF CARTHAGE IN SICILY, ... 392-396
War with Cyrênê.—Supremacy of Carthage in the West.—Wars with the Phocæans.—Commercial Treaty with Rome.—Wars with the Greeks in Sicily.—Wars with Syracuse.—Carthaginian Defeat at Himéra.—Later Carthaginian Successes.—Syracusan Treachery.—Carthaginian Defeats.—Conspiracy of Hanno.—Siege of Syracuse.—Invasion of Africa by Agathocles.—His Victories.—Pyrrhus, King of Epirus, in Sicily.—Final Defeat of the Carthaginians.

SECTION V.

CARTHAGE'S STRUGGLE WITH ROME, . . . 396-398
The Three Punic Wars.—Carthaginian Conquest of Spain.—Losses of Carthage.—Hannibal's Reforms.—His Exile and Suicide.—Destruction of Carthage.

CHAPTER X.—THE MEDO-PERSIAN EMPIRE.

SECTION I.

EXTENT AND PRODUCTIONS, ... 403-411
Extent of the Empire.—Its Character.—Countries Included in the Empire.—Persia Proper.—Its Cities.—Climate.—Animals.—Plateau of Iran.—The Northern and Eastern Provinces of the Empire.—Rivers.—Lakes.—Cities of the Empire.—Neighboring Countries.—Climate of the Empire.—Animals.—Vegetable Productions.—Minerals.—Stones.—Gems.

SECTION II.

POLITICAL HISTORY, ... 411-446
Earliest Mention of the Persians.—Their Migration to and Settlement in Persia Proper.—Archæmenes.—Connection of Persia with Media.—Founding of the Medo-Persian Empire by Cyrus the Great.—His Conquest of Lydia.—His Northern and Eastern Conquests.—Conquest of Babylon.—His Last War and Death.—His Character.—Cambyses.—His Conquest of Egypt.—His Grand Projects.—Revolution in Persia and Suicide of Cambyses.—His Character.—The Pseudo-Smerdis.—Discovery of the Imposture.—Death of the Usurper.—Darius Hystaspes.—Six Great Noble Houses.—Revolts against Darius Hystaspes.—Punishment of the Rebellious Governors.—Organization of the Empire.—Twenty Satrapies.—Standing Army.—Garrisons.—New Arrangement of the Revenue.—Taxation.—System of Checks.—"King's Eyes" and "King's Ears"—Satraps, Commandants and Secretaries.—Posts.—Coinage.—Royal Palace at Susa.—Chehl Minar at Persepolis.—Rock-tomb at Nakhsh-i-Rustam.—Rock Inscription of Behistun.—Expedition of Darius Hystaspes to India.—His Great Scythian Expedition.—Conquests of Megabazus.—Return of Darius to Susa.—Ionian Revolt and Its Suppression.—Expedition against Greece.

—Battle of Marathon.—Death of Darius Hystaspes. —His Character.—Xerxes the Great.—His Expedition against Greece.—Battles of Thermopylæ, Salamis, Platæa and Mycale.—Battle of Eurymedon. —Assassination of Xerxes.—His Character.—Artaxerxes Longimanus.—Revolt of Egypt.—Peace of Callias with Greece.—Rebellion in Syria.—Character of Artaxerxes Longimanus.—His Death. —Xerxes II.—Darius Nothus,—Revolts against Him.—Persia's Alliance with Sparta.—Terituchmes.—Character of Darius Nothus.—His Death.— Artaxerxes Mnemon.—Rebellion of His Brother, Cyrus the Younger.—Battle of Cunaxa and Death of Cyrus the Younger.—His Character.—Revelation of Persian Weakness.—Retreat of the Ten Thousand Greeks.—War between Persia and Sparta. —Peace of Antalcidas. Revolt of the Evagoras in Cyprus and Its Suppression.—Revolt of the Cadusians.—Schemes of Artaxerxes Mnemon.—Occupation of Samos.—Expedition against Egypt.— Revolts.—Decay of the Medo-Persian Empire.— Death of Artaxerxes Mnemon.—His Private Life. —His Character.—Artaxerxes Ochus.—His First Expedition against Egypt.—Revolts.—Expedition against Phœnicia.—Destruction of Sidon.—Phœnicia Recovered. — Second Expedition against Egypt.—Mentor and Bagôas.—Rise of Macedon under Philip the Great.—Artaxerxes Ochus Poisoned by Bagôas.—Bagôas Places Arses upon the Throne and Assassinates Him.—Darius Codomannus, the last Medo-Persian King.—His Character. —Alexander the Great of Macedon.—His Invasion of the Medo-Persian Empire. — Battles of the Granicus, Issus and Arbéla. — End of the Medo-Persian Empire. — Assassination of Darius Codomannus by His Own Officers. — His Magnificent Burial by Alexander.

SECTION III.

MEDO-PERSIAN CIVILIZATION, ... 446–478

The Medes and Persians of Kindred Aryan Race. —Persian Physiognomy.—Character of the Persian Intellect. — Courage, Energy and Truthfulness of the Persians.—Their Hatred of Debt.—Their Unreserve and Openness.—Their Loyalty.—Offensive Arms.—War-Chariots.—Tactics.—Rare Use of Military Engines. — Commanders. — Motley Appearance of a Persian Army.—Order of March.—Manner of Encamping.—Commissariat.—Treatment of Prisoners. — Punishments for Rebellion. — Persian Fleets.—Rank and Position of the Persian King.— His Costume.—The Throne.—Attendant Officers. — Other Court Officers. — The King's Food and Drink.—Royal Festivals and Banquets.—Furniture of the Palace.—Royal Harem, or Seraglio.—Employment of the Eunuchs.—Privileged Families.— Court Etiquette. — The King's Luxuries. — His Amusements. — His Serious Occupations. — Royal Tombs.—Ten Persian Tribes.—Dress of the Poor, —Costume of the Rich.—Food and Drink.—Early Temperance and Sobriety.—Later Luxury and Self-Indulgence. — Meats. — Etiquette. — Plurality of Wives and Concubines.—Education of Boys.—Serious Occupations of the Persians.—Their Contempt for Trade and Commerce.—General Advance of Luxury.—Uncertain Tenure of Happiness.— Severity of Legal Punishments.—Persian Architecture.—Great Palace at Persepolis.—Staircases at Persepolis.—Palace of Darius Hystaspes.—Palace of Xerxes.—Propylæa.—Hall of a Hundred Columns.—Chehl Minar.—Ruins of Pasargadæ.— Palaces at Istakr and Susa.—Tomb of Cyrus the Great. — Tomb of Darius Hystaspes. — Tower at Nakhsh-i-Rustam. — Gateway at Istakr. — Characteristics of Persian Architecture.—Origin of Persian Architecture.—Mimetic Art.—Figures in High Relief. — Processional Scenes.—Animal Representations.—Gem-Engravings.—Coins.—Fabrics.

SECTION IV.

ZOROASTER AND THE ZEND-AVESTA, . . 478–483

Character of the Persian Worship.—Symbol of Ahura-Mazda. — Of Mithra. — Spirits of Good and Evil.—Contempt and Hatred of Idolatry.—Religious Sympathy of the Persians and the Jews.— Magism.—Human Sacrifices.—Other Corruptions. —The Mithraic Worship. — Later Worship of Other Gods.—Last Stage of the Persian Religion.—Median and Persian Language and Writing.—Aryan Character of the Words.

CHAPTER XI.—THE SANSKRITIC HINDOOS.

SECTION I.

GEOGRAPHY OF INDIA, ... 484–486

Area and Location of Hindoostan.—Its Divisions. —Boundaries.— Mountains. — Rivers.— Soil.— Climate.—Vegetable Products.—Animals.—Minerals. —Adjacent Islands.—Petty Kingdoms.—The Hindoos One Nationality.

SECTION II.

HINDOO ORIGIN AND CIVILIZATION, . . . 486–490

India a Land of Mystery.—The Hindoos have no History. — Their Ultra-Spiritualism. — Aids from Comparative Philology.—The Aryans in Central Asia.—The Aryans in India.—The Native Races.— Hindoo Castes.—Religious Character of Hindoo Literature and Art.

SECTION III.

BRAHMANISM, ... 490–510

Theology of the Vedas.—The Laws of Manu.— The Brahmans.—The Three Systems of Hindoo Philosophy, the Sánkhya, the Vedanta and the Nyasa.—The Hindoo Triad and Its Origin.—The Epics of the Mahabharata and the Ramayana.— The Puranas.—The Modern Hindoo Worship.— Universality of Idolatry in India.—Religious Festivals.—The Idol of Juggernaut.—Krishna.—Profound and Subtle Character of Hindoo Philosophy. —Extreme Hindoo Idealism and Spiritualism.

SECTION IV.

BUDDHISM, ... 510–524

Gautama the Buddha.—Buddhist Councils.—Missionary Spirit of Buddhism.—Its Extent.—The Grand Lama in Thibet.—Buddhist Scriptures.— Buddhist Inscriptions.—Leading Buddhist Doctrines.—Buddhist Worship.—Karma and Nirvana. —Buddhism Rational and Humane. — Buddhist Monasticism. — Ancient Buddhist Architecture.— Rock-cut Temples and Monasteries of India.— Buddhism a Religion of Human Equality and Freedom.—Good and Evil of Buddhism.

TABLE OF CONTENTS.

CHAPTER XII.—ANCIENT CHINA.

SECTION I.

GEOGRAPHY OF CHINA, ... 525–526
Area and Population of the Chinese Empire.—China Proper.—Chinese Islands.—Climate.—Tea and Rice Culture.—Silk Manufacture.—Political Divisions of the Empire.—Provinces of China Proper.

SECTION II.

POLITICAL HISTORY, ... 526–530
Antiquity of China.—Its Permanence.—Chinese Chronology.—Aborigines of China.—Settlement of Chinese in the Country.—Their Early History.—Fohi, the Founder of the Chinese Monarchy.—His Successors.—Yu the Great and the Hia Dynasty.—The Shang Dynasty.—Wu-Wang and the Chow Dynasty.—Confucius, the Great Moral Philosopher.—The Tsin Dynasty.—Ching-Wang and the Great Wall.—The Han Dynasty.—Introduction of Buddhism.—Tradition of St. Thomas.—China Divided into Three Kingdoms.—Second Tsin Dynasty.—Tartar Inroads.—China Reunited by the Prince of Sui.—The Hang Dynasty.—Christianity Preached in China.—The Sung Dynasty.—Tartar Conquest of China.

SECTION III.

CHINESE CIVILIZATION, ... 530–534
The Chinese a Mongolian People.—Antiquity and Permanence of Chinese Civilization.—Great Works and Inventions.—Peculiarities of Chinese Civilization.—Chinese Government Based on Education.—Civil Service Examinations.—Chinese Industry.

SECTION IV.

CONFUCIUS AND HIS RELIGION, ... 534–539
Life and Character of Confucius.—His Teachings.—Philosophy and Subsequent Development of Confucianism.—Religious Character of the Book of Kings.

SECTION V.

LAO-TSE AND TAO-ISM, ... 539–540
Forms of Tao-ism.—Its Obscurity.—Its Philosophy.

CHAPTER XIII.—ANCIENT GREECE.

SECTION I.

GEOGRAPHY OF GREECE, ... 543–549
Location and Extent.—Boundaries.—Physical Features.—Mountains.—Rivers.—Lakes.—Littoral Islands.—Sections.—Political Divisions.

SECTION II.

EARLY LEGENDS AND TRADITIONS, . . . 549–557
Sources of Early Grecian History.—The Hellenes.—Foreign Colonies in Greece.—Hercules.—Argonautic Expedition.—Trojan War.—Social and Political Condition of Greece During the Heroic Age.—Hellenic Migrations.—Return of the Heraclidæ.—Devotion of Codrus.—Hellenic Colonization of the Ægean Islands, Asia Minor, Thrace and Southern Italy.

SECTION III.

GRECIAN MYTHOLOGY AND RELIGION, . 558–579
Grecian Theogony.—The Twelve Great Deities.—Zeus.—Poseidon.—Apollo.—Arês.—Hephaistos.—Hermês.—Hèrê.—Athênê.—Artemis.—Aphroditê.—Dêmêtêr.—Hestia.—Other Gods.—Triton.—Oceanus.—Nereus.—Infernal Deities.—Pluto.—Plutus.—Somnus.—Terrestrial Deities.—Dionysus.—Latona.—Eos, or Aurora.—Pan.—Flora.—Comus.—Pomona.—Æolus.—Zephyr.—Momus.—Astrea.—Terminus.—Nemesis.—Dryads and Hamadryads.—The Oread.—Naiad.—Satyr.—Nereides.—The Muses.—The Graces.—The Sirens.—The Furies.—The Fates.—The Harpies.—The Gorgons.—The Lares, or Penates.—The Manes.—Demi-gods and Heroes.—The Centaurs.—Castor and Pollux.—Perseus.—Pegasus.—Esculapius.—Promêtheus.—Atlas.—Orpheus.—Amphion.—Manifestations of the Deities.—Belief in a Future Life.—Judgment of the Dead.—Tartarus, or Hades.—Elysium.—Greek Worship.—Temples.—Idols.—Altars.—Priests.—Eleusinian Mysteries.—Oracles.—The Oracle of Apollo at Delphi.—Amphictyonic Council.—Olympic Games.—Other National Games.

SECTION IV.

THE SMALLER GRECIAN STATES, ... 579–581
Gradual Growth of the New Grecian Civilization.—Growth and Political Character of the City.—Greek Love of Independence.—Its Effects.—Common Ties of the Greek States.—Growth of Argos.—Bœotia.—Acarnania, Ætolia and Locris.—Thessaly.—Corinth.—Sicyon.—Arcadia.—Elis.

SECTION V.

THE GREEK ISLANDS, ... 581–582
Revolutions in the Greek Islands.—Corcyra.—Ægina.—Eubœa.—TheCyclades.—Creté.—Cyprus.—Rhodes.

SECTION VI.

GREEK COLONIES, ... 582–592
Number and Diffusion of Greek Colonies.—Causes.—Relation of the Colonies to the Mother Country.—Geographical Classification.—Greek Colonies in Asia Minor.—Æolis.—Ionia.—Dorian Hexapolis.—Milesian Colonies on the Propontis and the Euxine.—Milesian Colonies in Thrace.—Athenian and Corinthian Colonies in Thrace and Macedon.—Lampsacus.—Cyzicus.—Perinthus.—Heracléa.—Sinôpé.—Amisus.—Colonies on the Eastern Euxine Coast and in the Crimean Peninsula.—Cyrêné, in North Africa.—Magna Græcia in Southern Italy.—Cumæ.—Tarentum.—Croton.—Sybaris.—Locri·Epizephyrii.—Rhegium.—Greek Colonies in Sicily.—Syracuse.—Her Wars with Carthage.—Roman Conquest of Sicily.—Greek Colonies in Gaul, Spain and Corsica.

SECTION VII.

SPARTA UNDER THE LAWS OF LYCURGUS, 592–601
Description of Sparta.—Early Spartan History.—Early Spartan Conquests.—Political Condition of Sparta.—Lycurgus.—His Civil and Political Code.—His Social Institutions.—Objects of the Lycurgan Constitution.—Its Effects.—The Spartan

Character.—Fate of Lycurgus.—Spartan Conquests.
—First Messenian War.—Second Messenian War.
—Wars with Arcadia and Argos.—Sparta Supreme
in the Peloponnesus.—Sparta's Alliance with Cyrus
the Great of Persia.

SECTION VIII.

ATHENS UNDER THE LAWS OF SOLON, . 601–609

The Aristocratic Government of Athens.—Draco's Code.—Cylon's Attempt at Usurpation.—Sacrilege of Megacles.—Expulsion of the Alcmæonidæ.—Plague at Athens.—Purification of Epimenides.—Political Troubles at Athens.—Solon's Code.—His Reforms Adopted.—Quarrels of the Athenian Factions.—Solon's Travels.—His Return.—Usurpation of Pisistratus.—Solon's Voluntary Exile and Death.—Pisistratus Driven Away.—Recalled.—His Quarrel with Megacles.—Pisistratus Driven Away a Second Time.—Again Recalled.—His Liberality.—He Causes Homer's Poems to be Collected.—His Death.—Hippias and Hipparchus.—Assassination of Hipparchus.—Tyranny of Hippias.—His Expulsion from Athens.—Return of the Alcmæondiæ.—Administration of Clisthenes.—His Reforms.—Ostracism.—Clisthenes Expelled, but Recalled.—Quarrels of Athens with Sparta.—Conquest of Eubœa.—Athens a Pure Democracy.

SECTION IX.

EARLY GREEK POETRY AND PHILOSOPHY, 609–619

Homer.—Hesiod.—Lyric Poetry.—Archilochus.—Tyrtæus.—Alcman.— Terpander.— Sappho.—Alcæus.—Mimnermus—Theognis.—Anacreon.—Dramatic Poetry.—Thespis.—Phrynicus and Chœrilus.—Greek Philosophy.—Thales.— Anaximander.—Anaximenes.— Pythagoras.— Æsop, the Fabulist.—The Seven Wise Men of Greece.

SECTION X.

THE PERSIAN WAR. 620–636

Revolt of the Ionian Greeks of Asia Minor against Darius Hystaspes, King of Persia.—They are Aided by Athens.—Capture and Burning of Sardis.—Persian Expedition under Mardonius Sent against Greece.—Its Failure.—Darius Hystaspes Demands Submission from the Greek States.—Invasion of Greece by the Persians under Datis and Artaphernes.—Capture of Eretria by the Persians.—Landing of the Persians at Marathon.—Miltiades, the Athenian Commander.—Battle of Marathon.—Importance of the Athenian Victory over the Persians.—Failure of Datis in his Attempt to Surprise Athens.—Glory of Miltiades.—His Unsuccessful Expedition against Paros.—His Melancholy End.—Ingratitude of his Countrymen.—Aristides and Themistocles.—Banishment of Aristides. Administration of Themistocles.—War with Ægina.—Foresight of Themistocles.—He Induces the Athenians to Increase Their Navy.—Gigantic Expedition of Xerxes into Greece.—Battle of Thermopylæ.—Heroism of Leonidas and his Spartan Band.—Athens Deserted by its Inhabitants and Burned by the Persians.—Battle of Salamis.—Retreat of Xerxes.—His Return to Asia.—Mardonius Renews the Attempt to Conquer Greece.—Battle of Platæa.—Destruction of the Persian Army.—Battle of Mycale.—Greece Freed from her Invaders.—Importance of Greece's Triumph.

SECTION XI.

SUPREMACY OF ATHENS, ... 636–655

The Greeks now on the Offensive; the Persians on the Defensive.—Capture of Cyprus and Byzantium.—Athens Conquers Sestos.—Athens Becomes More Democratic.—Athens Rebuilt upon a Better Plan.—Themistocles Fortifies the City.—Jealousy of the Spartans.—They are Baffled by Themistocles.—Piræus, the Harbor of Athens.—Banishment of Themistocles.—Treason of Pausanias.— His Banishment and Death.—Athens the Leading State of Greece.—Confederacy of Delos.—Death of Aristides.—Athens under Cimon.—Cimon's Conquests.—Battle of the Eurymedon.—Cimon's Continued Successes.—Changes in the Confederacy of Delos.—Splendor of Athens.—Suicide of Themistocles.—Revolt of Thasos.—Subdued by Cimon.—Sparta Destroyed by an Earthquake.—Revolt of the Spartan Helots and the Messenians.—Sparta Solicits Aid of Athens.—Insults the Athenian Army.—Banishment of Cimon.—Rise of the Democratic Party at Athens.—Administration of Pericles.—Height of Athenian Glory and Greatness.—Plans of Pericles.—His Measures against Sparta.—Completion of the Long Walls of Athens.—Athenian Expedition to Egypt.—Athenian Victories over Corinth, Epidaurus and Ægina.—War between Doris and Phocis.—Athenian Defeat at Tanagra.—Victory at Œnophyta.—Athenian Successes.—Capture of Ithomé and End of the Helot Revolt and the Third Messenian War.—Destruction of the Athenian Fleet in Egypt by the Persians.—Cimon Recalled to Athens.—Peace between Athens and Sparta.—Cimon's Expedition against Cyprus.—His Death.—Athenian Victory off the Cyprian Salamis.—Peace with Persia.— Quarrel about the Delphic Oracle.—War Renewed between Athens and Sparta.—Athenian Defeat at Coronæa.—Athens Loses Bœotia.—Revolt of Eubœa and Megara against Athens.—The Revolts Subdued by Pericles.—Peace between Athens and Sparta.—Greatness of Athens under Pericles.—He Beautifies the City.—Erection of the Parthenon.— Intellectual Supremacy of Athens.—Athenian Expeditions against Samos.—Reduction of Samos and Byzantium.—Supremacy of Athens.—Rebellion of Corcyra against Corinth.—Corcyra Aided by Athens.—Revolt of Potidæa against Athens.—Peloponnesian Congress at Sparta.—Sparta's Demands Rejected by Athens.—Treacherous Theban Attack on Platæa.—Treacherous Massacre of the Thebans.—Persecution of Pericles.—Trial and Acquittal of Aspasia.—Vindication of Pericles.

SECTION XII.

THE PELOPONNESIAN WAR, ... 656–675

Commencement of the Peloponnesian War.—The Ten Years' War.—Spartan Invasion of Attica.—Overcrowding of Athens.—Wisdom of Pericles.—His Countrymen Exasperated at him.—Devastation of the Peloponnesus by the Athenian Navy.—Retreat of the Spartans from Attica.—Another Spartan Invasion of Attica.—Plague at Athens.—Indignation against Pericles.—His Defense.—Cleon the Tanner.—Pericles Dismissed from Office.—His Domestic Bereavements.—His Vindication and Reinstatement.—His Death.—His Greatness.—Spartan Ravages.—Reduction of Potidæa by the Athenians.—Of Platæa by the Spartans.—Progress of the War.—Revolt of Mitylené.—Cleon Causes the Inhabitants to be Sentenced to Death.—The Decree Reversed.— Revolutions in Corcyra.— Second Plague at Athens.—Purification.—Athenian Naval Victory at Pylos.—Sparta Solicits Peace.—Cleon Prevents a Settlement.—The Tanner's Good Fortune.—His Victory over the Spartans at Sphacteria.—Other Athenian Successes.—Athenian Invasion of Bœotia.—Defeat at Delium.—Capture of Amphipolis by Brasidas the Spartan.—Athens Sues for Peace.—Death of Cleon and Brasidas.—Peace of Nicias.—Alcibiades.—Argos Submits to Sparta.—Athenian Expedition to Sicily.—Siege of Syracuse.—Destruction of the Athenian Fleet and Army.—Consternation at Athens.—The Decelian War.—Treachery of Alcibiades.—The Athenians Rise Superior to their Reverses.—Fidelity of Samos.—Athenian Successes in the East.—Alcibiades Seeks to Return to Athens.—He Assists his Countrymen.—Vigorous Efforts of Athens.—Persian Alliance with Sparta.—Athens under the Council of Four Hundred.—Revolt of Eubœa and Loss of the Athenian Fleet.—Democracy Restored in Athens.—Persian Aid to Sparta.—Athenian Naval Victories.—Destruction of the Spartan and Persian Fleets at Cyzicus.—Alcibiades takes Chalcedon, Selymbria and Byzantium.—Return of Alcibiades to Athens.—His Welcome by his Countrymen.—Cyrus the Younger and Lysander the Spartan.—Defeat of the Athenian Fleet.—Second Disgrace and Death of Alcibiades.—Conon the Athenian.—Callicratides the Spartan.—Conon's Defeat near Mityléné.—Athenian Naval Victory near Lesbos.—Lysander's Victory over Conon at Ægos-Potamos.—Its Disastrous Consequences.—End of the Athenian Supremacy.—Surrender of Athens to Lysander.—Her Humiliation.

SECTION XIII.

SUPREMACIES OF SPARTA AND ATHENS, 675–704

Spartan Supremacy.—Athens under the Thirty Tyrants.—Their Overthrow by Thrasybulus.—The Council of Ten in Athens.—Their Overthrow.—Athenian Democracy Restored.—Socrates.—His Condemnation and Death.—Elis Overrun and Plundered by the Spartans.—Spartan Aid to Cyrus the Younger against his Brother, Artaxerxes Mnemon.—Battle of Cunaxa.—Retreat of the Ten Thousand under Xenophon.—War between Persia and Sparta.—Victories of Agesilaüs over the Persians in Asia Minor.—Thebes, Corinth, Argos and Athens Make War on Sparta.—Lysander Defeated by the Thebans at Haliartus.—Other Greek States Join the Allies.—Spartan Victory at Corinth.—Victory of Agesilaüs at Coronæa.—Conon the Athenian Secures Persian Aid.—The Walls of Athens Rebuilt by Means of Persian Gold.—Conon Defeats the Spartan Fleet off Cnidus.—The War in Corinthian Territory.—Spartan Disasters.—Peace of Antalcidas.—Persia the Arbiter of Grecian Affairs.—Sparta's Supremacy in Greece.—Sparta's Aggressions on Mantinéa and Olynthus.—Spartan Seizure of the Cadmæa.—Recovery of the Cadmæa by the Thebans.—War between Sparta and Thebes.—League against Sparta.—Pelopidas and Epaminondas.—Progress of the War.—Spartan Disasters.—Congress at Sparta.—Peace of Callias.—Thebes Deserted.—Her Danger.—The Sacred Band of Thebes.—Spartan Invasion of Bœotia.—Battle of Leuctra.—Effects of the Theban Victory.—Sparta's Peril.—Supremacy of Thebes.—Jason of Pheræ.—Truce.—Assassination of Jason.—Renewal of the War.—Invasion of Laconia by Epaminondas.—The Arcadian League.—Mantinéa Rebuilt.—Epaminondas Restores the Messenians.—Alliance of Athens and Sparta.—Successes of Epaminondas in the Peloponnesus.—He is Accused but Vindicated.—His Continued Triumphs.—The Tearless Battle.—Alexander of Thessaly Humbled by Pelopidas.—Alliance of Thebes and Persia.—Grecian Congress at Thebes.—Captivity and Release of Pelopidas in Thessaly.—Renewed Triumphs of Epaminondas in the Peloponnesus.—Alliance of Athens and Arcadia.—Negotiations for Peace.—Victory and Death of Pelopidas in a War with Alexander of Thessaly.—Violation of the Sanctity of the Olympic Games by the Arcadians.—Treachery of a Theban Captain.—Its Effects.—Alliance of Sparta and Arcadia.—Invasion of the Peloponnesus by Epaminondas.—Battle at Sparta.—Battle of Mantinéa.—Victory and Death of Epaminondas.—End of Theban Glory.—Agesilaüs in Egypt.—His Reception there.—His Revenge and Death.—Wars of Athens with Alexander of Thessaly and with Macedon and Thrace.—The Social War.—Decline of Athens.

SECTION XIV.

RISE OF MACEDON UNDER PHILIP, . . . 704–721

Description of Macedon.—Origin of the Nation.—Founding of the Macedonian Kingdom.—Tributary to Persia.—Recovery of its Independence.—Early History of Macedon.—Philip II.—His Conquest of the Illyrians.—His Plans for the Subjugation of Greece.—His Vigorous Measures at Home.—His Encroachments on the Possessions of Athens.—His Capture of Amphipolis.—His Marriage.—Proceedings of the Amphictyons.—Beginning of the Phocian or Sacred War.—Philip's Intervention in the Sacred War.—The Phocians Routed by Philip.—Thermopylæ Closed against Philip.—Demosthenes the Orator.—His Philippics.—Philip Attacks and Captures Olynthus.—Athenian Embassy to Pella.—Macedon Becomes an Amphictyonic State.—Cessation of War in Greece.—The Locrian or Second Sacred War.—Philip's Capture of Elatéa.—Alliance of Athens and Thebes against Philip.—Battle of Chæronéa.—End of Grecian Independence.—Supremacy of Macedon.—Grecian Congress at Corinth.—Philip Induces the Grecian States to Declare War against Persia.—Humiliation of Sparta.—Assassination of Philip.—His Character.

SECTION XV.

LITERATURE, PHILOSOPHY AND ART, . . 721–741

Simonides, the Elegiac Poet.—Pindar the Lyric Poet.—The Three Great Athenian Tragic Poets, Æschylus, Sophocles and Euripides.—Comedy.—Aristophanes the Great Athenian Comic Poet.—The Three Great Historians, Herodotus, Thucydides and Xenophon.—Ctesias.—Athenian Oratory.—Pericles, Alcibiades, Lysias and Isæus.—Hyperides, Phocion, Lycurgus and Dinarchus.—Isocrates.—Æschines.—Demosthenes.—New Systems of Grecian Philosophy.—Xenóphanes.—Parmenides.—Zeno the Eleatic.—Leucippus.—Demócritus.—Heraclitus.—Empedocles.—Anaxagoras.—Archelaüs.—Socrates.—Plato.—Aristotle.—Antisthenes.—Diogenes.—Zeno the Stoic.—Aristippus.—Epicurus.—Pyrrho.—Carneades and Arcesilas.—The Fine Arts.—The Parthenon at Athens.—Glory of Athenian Architecture and Sculpture.—Phidias and his Great Works.—The Doric, Ionic and Corinthian Styles of Architecture.—Grecian Sculpture and Painting.

SECTION XVI.

GENERAL VIEW OF CIVILIZATION, ... 741–753

The Greeks an Aryan People.—Their Characteristics.—The First People to Develop Democracy.—Greek Armies.—Warfare.—Fortified Towns.—Battering-Ram.—Moving-Tower.—Tortoise.—Greek Ships of War.—Houses and Furniture.—Meals and Banquets.—Dress.—Greek Women.—The Hetæræ.—Freemen and Slaves.—Occupations.—Writing.—Education. — Gymnasia. — Music. — Marriages. — Funerals.—The Academy and the Lyceum at Athens.—Walls and Ports of Athens.—The Acropolis and its Edifices.—The Ceramicus.

SECTION XVII.

CONQUESTS OF ALEXANDER THE GREAT, 753-770

Alexander's Accession. — His Qualities. — His War Horse Bucephalus.—His Appointment of Generalissimo.—His Suppression of the Illyrian Revolt.—Revolt of the Greek States.—Its Suppression by Alexander.—Destruction of Thebes.—Alexander's Invasion of the Medo-Persian Empire.—Battle of the Granicus.—Siege and Capture of Miletus and Halicarnassus.—Alexander's Progress in Asia Minor.—Cutting of the Gordian Knot.—Preparations of King Darius Codomannus.—Battle of the Issus.—Siege and Capture of Tyre and Gaza.—Alexander in Egypt.—Founding of Alexandria.—Alexander's Return to Asia.—Battle of Arbéla.—End of the Medo-Persian Empire.—Alexander at Babylon, Susia and Persepolis.—Assassination of King Darius Codomannus.—Alexander in Scythia.—Execution of Philotas and Parmenio.—Murder of Clitus.—Peloponnesian Revolt Suppressed by Antipater.—Oratorical Contest at Athens between Demosthenes and Æschines.—Banishment of Demosthenes.—Recall of Grecian Exiles.—Alexander's Invasion of India.—Porus, King of the Punjab.—Alexander's Return to Persia.—His Last Actions and Measures.—His Illness and Death.—His Remains.—His Character.—Results of His Conquests.

MAPS IN VOLUME II.

Medo-Persian Empire 400, 401
Ancient Greece. 541
Homeric Greece.. 542
Ancient Athens.. 743
Ancient Greece and Her Colonies..................... 744, 745

CHAPTER IX.

REPUBLIC OF CARTHAGE.

SECTION I.—GEOGRAPHY OF NORTHERN AFRICA.

LTHOUGH Africa was circumnavigated in very early times, the interior yet remains unexplored; and the southern part, because of the difficulty of navigation in the ocean, was neglected until all knowledge of its discovery had been forgotten. But the northern coast bordering on the Mediterranean became lined with Greek and Phœnician colonies. This vast region was naturally divided into three strips, differing in width, almost parallel with the sea-line—1, the maritime country, which consisted mainly of very fertile tracts, whence it was called Inhabited Africa, is now styled Barbary; 2, a rugged mountain district, whose loftiest peaks form the chain of Mount Atlas, in which abound wild horses and palm-groves, whence the ancients called it the land of lions, and the moderns Beled el Gerid, or the Land of Dates, while the Romans generally called it Gætulia; 3, a vast sandy desert, called Sahara by the Arabs.

Several small rivers flow north into the Mediterranean from the chain of Mount Atlas, but there are no important streams on the south side of these mountains, and there is no great river in the interior north of the distant Niger, of which the ancients knew very little or nothing; and nothing was actually known of its real course until the present century, when the Lander brothers first explored it along its entire course.

The Mediterranean coast of Africa west of Egypt embraced six political divisions. Of these, Marmarica, the most eastern division, bordering on Egypt, was a sandy tract occupied by nomad tribes. Cyrenaica, west of Marmarica, was a fertile district planted with Greek colonies, extending to the greater Syrtis, and its chief cities were Cyrênê and Barca. Both Marmarica and Cyrenaica embrace the territory of the modern Barca. Regio Syrtica, the modern Beylik of Tripoli, was a sandy region subject to the Carthaginians, but principally occupied by nomad hordes. The domestic territory of Carthage embraced that of the modern Beylik of Tunis. West of this section was a very fruitful country subject to Carthage, the northern part being called Byzacéna, and the southern Zeugitána. Numidia embraced the eastern part of the territory of the present Algeria. Mauritania comprised the middle and western portion of the present Algeria and the northern part of the domain included in the present empire of Morocco. Numidia and Mauritania were both occupied by nomad hordes, the ancestors of the present Moors and Berbers; but both these countries had some Carthaginian colonies along the coasts.

The mighty city of Carthage—for a long time the mistress of the Mediterranean—was built on a peninsula in the interior of a large bay, now known as the Gulf of Tunis, formed by the projection of the Hermæan promontory (now Cape Bon) on the east, and the promontory of Apollo (now Cape Zebid) on the west. The peninsula was about midway between Utica and Tunis, both these cities being visible from the walls of Carthage; Utica being about nine miles distant, and Tunis only six miles. This peninsula was connected with the mainland by an isthmus with an average of about three miles in length; and on the seaside was a narrow neck of land projecting westward, forming a double harbor, and serving as a mole or breakwater to protect the shipping. Towards the sea the city was fortified only by a single wall; but the isthmus was guarded by the citadel Byrsa, and by a triple wall eighty feet high and about thirty feet wide.

The African territory of Carthage extended westward along the coast of the Pillars of Hercules (now Straits of Gibraltar); eastward to the altars of Philæni, which marked the frontier between the territories of Cyrênê and Carthage; and southward to the Tritonian lake, but many of the nomad tribes beyond these limits were nominally subject to the great commercial republic.

The fertile provinces of Carthage were occupied by a people who tilled the soil, and extended in a direct line from Cape Bon to the most eastern angle of the Triton lake, a distance of almost two hundred geographical miles, with an average breadth of one hundred and fifty miles.

The foreign possessions of Carthage embraced the Balearic Isles, Corsica, Sardinia and the smaller islands in the Mediterranean, the southern portions of Sicily and Spain, some settlements on the western coast of Africa, and the Fortunate Isles in the Atlantic, supposed to be the Canaries and the fertile Madeira.

SECTION II.—THE REPUBLIC OF CARTHAGE.

HEN Queen Dido and the aristocratic party fled from Tyre to escape the tyranny of the queen's brother Pygmalion, they sailed for the coast of Northern Africa, in the modern Beylik of Tunis, upon which several flourishing Phœnician colonies had already been established, such as Utica, Hadrumetum, Leptis and others. The Tyrian fugitives under Dido selected as the site for the new colony the head of a peninsula projecting eastward into the Gulf of Tunis, on the tenth meridian of longitude, and joined with the mainland by an isthmus three miles wide. Here were several excellent land-locked harbors, a position easily defended, and a fairly fertile soil. The settlement was made with the good will of the natives, who understood the benefits of commerce, and willingly gave the new colonies a part of the soil at a certain specified rent. Thus Carthage was founded B. C. 869.

The growth of Carthage was slow, but gradually it grew into importance; and within one or two centuries from the date of her foundation Carthage had become a considerable power, far outstripping all the other Phœnician colonies in that region, and had acquired a rich and extensive dominion. The native tribes in the vicinity of the new city, who had originally been nomads, were induced to adopt agricultural pursuits. Carthaginian colonies were thickly planted among them, intermarriages between the colonists and the natives were encouraged, and a mixed population arose in the fertile tract south and south-west of Carthage, known as Liby-Phœnices, and these adopted the language and habits of the settlers and became faithful and attached subjects. Beyond this occupied territory Carthaginian influence was extended over numerous pure African tribes, most of which were nomads, while a few were agricultural. The tribes were held in loose and nominal subjection, as are the Arab tribes of modern Algeria by the French; but they were still considered Carthaginian subjects, and doubtless contributed to the resources of Carthage.

The proper territory of Carthage was regarded as extending southward to Lake Triton, and westward to the river Tusca, which separated Zeugitána from Numidia, thus almost corresponding to the modern Beylik of Tunis. From this compact and valuable territory the Carthaginians proceeded to extend their supremacy or influence over all Northern Africa from the Cyrenaica (the modern Barca) on the east to the Atlantic on the west; and their authority came to be gradually acknowledged by all the coast tribes between the Tusca and the Pillars of Hercules, and also by the numerous nomad races between Lake Triton and Cyrenaica. In the former region numerous Carthaginian settlements were made, while Carthage claimed and exercised the right to march troops along the shore. From the latter tract only commercial advantages were obtained, but these were very important.

We have already observed that the Phœnicians had established numerous settlements on the northern coast of Africa long before the founding of Carthage, but Carthage soon eclipsed all these in power and importance. Utica, Hadrumetum, Leptis Magna and other cities were at first independent Phœnician colonies, as free of the authority of Carthage as she was of their dominion. But by degrees Carthage extended her sway over these cities. Yet to the very last Utica and several others of these Phœnician communities maintained a certain degree of independence, being only members of a confederacy under the leadership of Carthage. These confederates of Carthage were unable to resist her, or to exercise much check upon her policy, but she was not absolute mistress upon all places within her territory.

Carthage even extended her dominion beyond the limits of Northern Africa. She established her influence in the West of Sicily at an early date, and superseded the more ancient influence of Phœnicia in that island. The Carthaginians conquered Sardinia near the end of the sixth century before Christ, after long and sanguinary wars. They had already occupied the Balearic Isles—Majorca, Minorca and Ivica. They subsequently made settlements in Corsica and in Spain, and subjugated the smaller islands of Malta, Gaulos (now Gozo) and Cercina in the Mediterranean, and those of Madeira and the Canaries in the Atlantic. By the end of the sixth century before Christ, Carthage had extended her power from the Greater Syrtis on the east to the Fortunate Isles (the Canaries) on the coast, and from Corsica on the north to the Atlas mountain chain on the south.

The great commercial city effected her extensive conquests by the employment of foreign mercenaries. Besides the disciplined force which. Carthage obtained from her own native citizens and from the mixed race of Liby-Phœnices, and besides the irregular troops which she drew from her other subjects, she employed large bodies of hired troops, derived partly from the independent African nations, such as the Numidians and the Mauritanians, and partly from the warlike European races brought into contact with her by her foreign trade, such as the Iberians of Spain, the Gauls of Gaul (now France), and the Ligurians of Northern Italy. We have evidence that this practice existed as early as the year B. C. 480, and there are abundant reasons for believing that it began at a considerably earlier period.

The naval power of Carthage must have dated from the very founding of the city. As the sea in ancient times swarmed with pirates, an extensive commerce required the possession of a powerful navy to protect it.

For several centuries Carthage must have been undisputed mistress of the Western Mediterranean. The officers and sailors in her fleets were mainly native Carthaginians, while the rowers were principally slaves, bred or bought by the state for the purpose.

Carthage was an aristocratic republic, and its constitution vested the political power in a privileged class. The native element, located at Carthage, and in its immediate vicinity, were the ruling element, and virtually governed all the rest of the Carthaginian dominion. This native element itself was divided by class distinctions, according to wealth. The two *Suffetes*, who stood at the head of the state, were chosen only from certain families, but all native Carthaginians were eligible to all other offices. Still, as no office was salaried, the poor man could not afford to serve the state in any civil or political capacity, and thus the offices virtually fell into the hands of the rich. Public opinion was likewise strongly on the side of wealth. Candidates for office were expected to expend large sums of money in treating on the most extensive scale, if not in actual bribery. Thus office and political power practically became the heritage of a circle of wealthy families.

At the head of the state were two *Suffetes*, or Judges, who, in early times, were Captains-general, as well as civil chief magistrates, but whose offices by degrees came to be regarded as only civil and not military. These Suffetes were chosen by the citizens from certain wealthy families, perhaps for life. Next to these magistrates was the *Council*, consisting of several hundred men, and from this body almost all the officers of the government were appointed, either directly or indirectly—as the *Senate of One Hundred*, a select committee of the Council, which directed all its proceedings; and the *Pentarchies*, commissions of five members each, which managed the different departments of state and filled vacancies in the Senate. The Council of One Hundred Judges (or with the two Suffetes and the two High Priests, 104), a high court of judicature chosen by the people, was the most popular element in the constitution of Carthage; but the members of the court were virtually selected from the upper classes, and their power was rather employed to check the excessive ambition of individul members of the aristocracy than to enlarge the civil rights or improve the social condition of the masses. The people were contented, however, as they elected the Suffetes under certain limitations, and usually, freely. The people may have filled vacancies in the Great Council; and when the Suffetes and the Council disagreed on public measures the people discussed and took action, and their decision was final. Questions of peace or war were frequently brought before them, though not necessarily so. The aristocratical features of the constitution were upheld by the weight of popular sentiment, which favored the vesting of political power in the hands of the rich. The openings which trade gave to enterprise enabled any one to become rich, and abject poverty was scarcely known, because as soon as it made an appearance it was relieved by the planting of colonies and the allotment of waste lands to all such as applied for them.

It was necessary for Carthage to have a large and secure revenue, since her power mainly depended upon her maintenance of vast armies of foreign mercenaries. This revenue was partly drawn from state property, especially rich mines in Spain and elsewhere; partly from the tribute which was paid by the confederated cities, such as Utica, Hadrumetum and others, as well as by the Liby-Phœnices, the dependent African nomads, and the provinces, such as Sardinia, Sicily, etc.; and partly from customs rigorously exacted from all the Carthaginian dominions. The tribute was the most elastic of all these sources of revenue, which was increased or diminished as the demands of the state required, and is reputed to have sometimes amounted to fifty per cent. on the income of those subject to it.

A curious kind of banking was established at Carthage. Pieces of a compound metal, the secret of whose composition was strictly preserved, so as to prevent forgery, were sewed up in leather coverings and marked with a government seal declaring the nominal value. This money was only current in Carthage itself.

The religion of Carthage was that of her mother Tyre, and was therefore polluted by obscene rites and sanguinary human sacrifices. But the Carthaginians also introduced foreign gods into their pantheon, as they adopted the worship of Ceres from the Sicilians, and sent embassadors to Greece to consult the oracle of Delphi. There does seem to have been a distinct priestly caste, or even order, in Carthage, the sacerdotal functions being exercised by the magistrates. Diodorus informs us that in the temple of Saturn at Carthage the brazen image of the god stood with outstretched hands to receive the bodies of children offered to it. Mothers brought their infants in their arms; and as any indications of reluctance would have rendered the sacrifice unacceptable to the image, they caressed them to keep them quiet until the moment when they were handed over to the image, which was contrived so as to consign whatever it received to a fiery furnace beneath it. Inscriptions have been discovered at Carthage recording the offering of such sacrifices. They continued after the Roman conquest of Carthage, until the Roman Proconsul Tiberius suppressed these bloody rites by hanging the priests who conducted them on the trees of their own sacred grove. Thenceforth the public exhibitions of the sacrifice ceased, but they continued in secret to the time of Tertullian, in the third century of the Christian era. In the history of Phœnicia we have given accounts of these sacrifices.

SECTION III.—CARTHAGINIAN COMMERCE.

THE commerce of Carthage extended in the north as far as Cornwall in Britain and the Scilly Isles, in the east to Phœnicia, in the west to Madeira and the Canaries, in the south by sea to the coast of Guinea, and by caravans across the Great Desert to Fezzan and to Central Africa. Carthage obtained the commodities that she needed mainly by trade, exchanging for them her own manufactures, such as textile fabrics, hardware, pottery, personal ornaments, harness for horses, tools, etc. But it was likewise to a great extent a carrying trade, by which Carthage enabled the nations of Western Europe, Western Asia and Central Africa respectively to obtain each other's products. Carthaginian commerce was partly a sea and partly a land traffic. By sea this commerce was mainly with her mother Tyre, with her own colonies, with the nations along the Western Mediterranean, with the tribes along the Alantic coast of Africa from the Pillars of Hercules to the coast of Guinea, and with the savage Britons of Cornwall and the Scilly Isles. But while Carthaginian merchants scoured the sea in every direction in their trading ships, caravans directed by Carthaginian enterprise crossed the Great Desert and brought to Carthage from Central Africa the products of those remote regions, such as gold-dust and negro slaves, while from the districts north of the desert were obtained dates and salt. Upper Egypt, Cyrêné, the oases of the Sahara, Fezzan, and probably Ethiopia and Bornou carried on this traffic with the famous commercial republic.

The principal commerce of the Carthaginians in the Western Mediterranean was with the Greek colonies in Sicily and Southern Italy, from which they obtained wine and oil in exchange for negro slaves, precious stones and gold, procured from the interior of Africa, and also for cotton cloths manufactured at Carthage and in the island of Malta. From Corsica they procured honey, wax and slaves; from Sardinia, corn; from the Balearic Isles, the best breed of mules; from the Lipari Isles, resin, sulphur and pumice-stone; from Southern Spain, the precious metals. Beyond the Pillars of Hercules the Carthaginians superseded the Phœnicians in the tin trade with the British Isles and the amber traffic with the nations along the Baltic. On the western coast of Africa, Carthaginian colonies lined the shores of the present Morocco and Fez, but their chief mart in this region was the island of Cerne, now Suána, in the Atlantic Ocean, which was the great depot of merchandise, and from which goods were transported in light barks to the opposite coast, where they were bartered with the natives. The Carthaginians exported trinkets, saddlery, cotton webs, linen, pottery and arms; receiving in exchange undressed hides and elephants' teeth. Besides this trade there was a very lucrative fishery; the tunny fish (*thynnus scomber*), still abundant on the north-western coast of Africa, being regarded as a great luxury by the Carthaginians.

SECTION IV.—WARS OF CARTHAGE IN SICILY.

YRENE, the Greek colony which had attained great commercial prosperity, regarded the Carthaginians with jealousy, and war soon broke out between the rival commercial cities.

While the great Medo-Persian Empire was making itself master of the East, the Republic of Carthage was fast becoming supreme in the West, under the family of Mágo—a family which possessed the chief power for more than a century. But just as they were rising into importance they had to meet a powerful enemy in the Western Mediterranean, whose recognized skill and valor threatened a dangerous rivalry.

The enterprising inhabitants of Phocæa, a great maritime city of Iona, in Grecian Asia Minor, unable to resist the conquering Persians, abandoned their country and settled in the island of Corsica, a portion of which was already occupied by the Carthaginians. The Carthaginians and Tyrrhenians, or Tuscans, of Italy, jealous of the rivalry of the Phocæans, entered into an alliance to exterminate them, and sent a fleet of one hundred and twenty sail to drive them from Corsica; but this allied fleet was defeated by a Phocæan fleet half as large, after which, however, they abandoned Corsica for the southern shores of Gaul, where they founded the city of Massilia, now Marseilles.

In B. C. 508, just after Rome had become a republic by the expulsion of Tarquin the Proud, a commercial treaty was concluded between the republics of Rome and Carthage, from the terms of which it is shown that Carthage was already mistress of the Western Mediterranean, being supreme on the northern coast of Africa and the island of Sardinia, and also holding possession of the Balearic Isles and a large part of Sicily and Spain.

Carthage, jealous of Grecian valor and enterprise, and alarmed at the rapidly-increasing wealth and power of the Greek colonies in Sicily and Southern Italy, entered into an alliance with Xerxes the Great, King of Persia, when that famous monarch led his gigantic expedition into Greece, and agreed to assail the Grecian colonies while he waged war with Greece itself. Accordingly a Carthaginian armament was prepared, consisting of two thousand ships of war, three thousand transports and vessels of burden, and an army of three hundred thousand men; the command of the entire expedition being assigned to Hamilcar, the head of the celebrated family of Mágo. This vast host consisted mainly of African mercenaries, and was composed of light troops, wholly undisciplined. This immense expedition landed in Sicily at Panormus (now Palermo); and, after a short rest, Hamilcar advanced and besieged Himéra. The governor of the city, Théron, made a heroic defense, and sorely pressed by famine and the overwhelming force of the besiegers, urgently requested aid from Syracuse.

Thereupon Gelo, King of Syracuse, led a force of five thousand horse and fifteen thousand foot against the Carthaginians. On the way he captured a messenger from the Selinuntines to Hamilcar, promising on a certain day to join the Carthaginians with the auxiliary force of cavalry that he had requested. Hamilcar had offered large bribes to win over some of the Greek colonies in Sicily to the side of the Carthaginians; but the Selinuntines, the old foes of the Syracusans, alone agreed to aid him. Gelo sent the letter to Hamilcar; and having taken steps to intercept the treacherous Selinuntines, he sent a select body of his own troops to the Carthaginian camp in their stead at the stated time. The Syracusans being admitted without being suspected, suddenly galloped to Hamilcar's tent, killed the general and his principal officers, and set fire to the Carthaginian fleet in the harbor. The blaze of the burning ships, the cries of Hamilcar's servants, and the triumphant shout of the Syracusans, threw the entire Carthaginian army into confusion, in the midst of which it was attacked by Gelo with the remainder of his forces. Having lost their leaders, the Carthaginians could make no successful resistance, and lost more than half their number in the field; while the remainder, without arms or provisions, sought refuge in the interior of the island, where most of them perished. This great victory of the Greek race in Sicily was won on the same day that the Greeks in the mother country resisted the Persian hosts at Thermopylæ and defeated the Persian fleet at Artimisium—three of the grandest triumphs won in the gigantic struggle for Hellenic freedom, B. C. 480. The miserable remnant of the mighty Carthaginian hosts under Gisgon, Hamilcar's son, was obliged to surrender at discretion.

For the next seventy years Carthage made no further effort to conquer Sicily from the Greeks, but greatly extended her power over the native tribes of Northern Africa, and made important conquests from the Cyrenians.

After an Athenian fleet had been destroyed in an attack upon Syracuse, B. C. 416, the Carthaginians again had their attention directed to Sicily by an embassy from the city of Segesta, asking their protection against the Syracusans, whose anger it had incurred by its alliance with the Athenians.

The Carthaginians readily seized the pretext afforded them by the Segestan embassy, and sent another expedition against Sicily under the command of Hannibal, the son of Gisgon. This invasion was successful. Selinuntum and Himéra were taken by storm, and their inhabitants were massacred. The Sicilian Greeks requested a truce, which was granted them on conditions exceedingly favorable to the Carthaginians.

Elated with this success the Carthaginians now aimed at the complete conquest of Sicily. Inules, the son of Hanno and Hannibal, at the head of a large armament, besieged Agrigentum, the second city of the island. The siege lasted eight months, during which the besiegers suffered severely from pestilence, and the garrison from famine. The Agrigentines finally sallied from the city, forced their way through the Carthaginian lines by night, and retreated to Gela, leaving the aged, the sick and the wounded to the mercy of the Carthaginians. Himilco, who had succeeded to the chief command of the Carthaginians on the death of his father Hannibal, ordered the massacre of these helpless victims. Gela soon shared the fate of Agrigentum; and Dionysius I., King of Syracuse, who had assumed the command of the confederated Sicilians, negotiated for peace; whereupon a treaty was concluded, which neither party sincerely desired to observe any longer than would be necessary to prepare for a more decisive struggle, B. C. 405. As soon as the Carthaginians had retired, Dionysius I. sent deputies to all the Greek states of Sicily, requesting them to make a simultaneous attempt to drive the Carthaginians from the island, and secure their independence from any danger in the future. He succeeded in his plans. The Carthaginian merchants who had settled in the chief towns, on the faith of the late treaty of peace, were treacherously massacred; while Dionysius, at the head of a formidable army, took several important Carthaginian fortresses, B. C. 397.

Carthage sent a gigantic force to punish this treachery, and Himilco advanced against Syracuse and besieged the city, but a violent plague carried off a large part of the Carthaginian army; while Dionysius sallied from the city with all his forces, and assailed the camp of the besiegers with such success that Himilco found himself obliged to surrender on terms sparing the lives of himself and his Carthaginians, but abandoning all his auxiliaries to the vengeance of the Syracusans.

The Carthaginians sent another armament under Mágo, a nobleman of high rank, to repair their losses in Sicily, but these forces were routed with terrible slaughter, Mágo himself being slain. His son, the younger Mágo, being reinforced from Africa, won a great victory over the Syracusans; and Dionysius was obliged to sue for peace, which was concluded on terms honorable to both parties.

After this war in Sicily, a frightful plague carried off multitudes of the inhabitants of Carthage, B. C. 347. Immediately after this, insurrections broke out in the African provinces of Carthage and in the Carthaginian colonies of Sicily and Sardinia; but the Carthaginian Senate by a policy of firmness, tempered by conciliation, overcame these threatened dangers, and the state recovered its former vigor and prosperity.

Meanwhile Syracuse was torn by domestic troubles following the death of Dionysius I., who, though called a tyrant by the Greek historians, was a wise and prudent monarch. Says Scipio Africanus: "No one ever concerted his schemes with more wisdom, or executed them with more energy than the elder Dionysius." His son and successor, Dionysius II., was a profligate sovereign, whose excesses were a cause of tumult and distraction to the state. The Carthaginians took advantage of the internal dissensions in Syracuse with great eagerness, to execute their favorite design of conquering Sicily; and a large armament was equipped for the purpose and placed under the chief command of Mágo, B. C. 346.

In his first attack Mágo made himself master of the harbor of Syracuse. The Syracusans, destitute of money, solicited the aid of the Corinthians, and Timóleon, one of the greatest generals and purest patriots of antiquity, was sent to their aid. A large portion of the Carthaginian army had been levied in the Greek colonies. Timó-leon, appealing to their patriotism, addressed letters to the leaders of these mercenaries, remonstrating with them on the disgrace of bearing arms against their kindred. Hearing of these intrigues of Timóleon, and thus distrusting his Greek mercenaries, Mágo returned to Carthage. The Carthaginians were aroused to the highest pitch of indignation at the unexpected termination of the campaign, and Mágo committed suicide to escape their wrath. New forces were raised to retrieve their losses in Sicily. Hannibal and Hamilcar were appointed to the command, and were entrusted with an army of seventy thousand men, and a fleet of two hundred war-galleys and a thousand ships of burden. Timóleon hastened to meet the invaders, though his forces scarcely numbered seven thousand men. He unexpectedly attacked the Carthaginian army on its march, near the river Crinísus, and the Carthaginians, completely surprised, were routed in confusion. The Syracusans took one town after another, until finally the Carthaginian Senate was obliged to solicit peace and to accept the terms dictated by the triumphant Syracusans.

While Carthage was thus unsuccessful abroad her liberties were menaced with destruction. Hanno, one of the chief men of the state, determined to make himself master of his country by poisoning the leading men of the Senate at a banquet. This nefarious plot was foiled by its timely discovery, and the chagrined traitor determined to openly rebel. Arming his slaves, twenty thousand in number, Hanno took the field, inviting the native African tribes to join his standard, but this appeal was disregarded. Before Hanno could collect fresh forces, he was surrounded by an army hastily gathered, his followers were routed, and Hanno himself was made prisoner. He was put to death with the most cruel tortures, and, in accordance with the barbarian custom of Carthage, his children and nearest relatives shared his fate.

Fresh dissensions in Syracuse gave the Carthaginians a new pretext for interfering in Sicilian affairs. Agathocles, an intrigu-

WARS OF CARTHAGE IN SICILY.

ing demagogue of low extraction, had acquired great influence among his countrymen, and, finally, by the secret aid of the Carthaginians, became master of the state. But he displayed so little gratitude that he announced his intention to drive the Carthaginians from the island. The Carthaginian Senate at once sent Hamilcar with a formidable army against Agathocles, who was utterly defeated and forced to shut himself up within the walls of Syracuse. The city was soon besieged, but Agathocles assembled the Syracusans and declared that he would save them from all dangers if an army and a small sum of money were placed at his disposal, saying that his plan would completely fail if he disclosed its nature. Thereupon an army of liberated slaves was hastily levied, the sum of fifty talents was intrusted to his discretion, and a fleet was raised secretly. When all was ready Agathocles declared his design of transporting his forces into Africa, and alarming the Carthaginians into the evacuation of Sicily.

Eluding the vigilance of the blockading squadron, Agathocles safely arrived in Africa before the Carthaginians were aware of his designs, B. C. 309. He cut off all opportunity of retreat by burning his transports, for the purpose of inspiring his soldiers with a resolution to conquer or die. He then boldly advanced, stormed Tunis and several other cities, dividing their plunder among his soldiers, and instigated the native African princes to revolt against Carthage. Hanno and Bomilcar were sent to check the progress of this bold invader, with forces four times the size of the Sicilian army; but they were decisively defeated by Agathocles, who followed up his success by storming the Carthaginian camp, where he found heaps of fetters and chains, which the Carthaginians, in proud confidence of victory, had prepared for the Sicilian invaders.

This unexpected defeat produced dreadful consternation at Carthage. Hamilcar, who was prosecuting the siege of Syracuse with vigor, was surprised by the unexpected order to return home to defend his own country. He raised the siege and sent five thousand of his best troops, and, after supplying their place with fresh mercenaries, he again invaded the territories of Syracuse, but was unexpectedly attacked, defeated and slain.

Ophellas, King of Cyrêné, had joined Agathocles with all his forces; but the King of Syracuse, jealous of his influence, caused him to be privately poisoned. Having thus rid himself of his rival, Agathocles thought he could safely return to Sicily and leave his army in Africa under the command of his son. But in his absence all the results of his former victory were lost; as the army threw off all restraint and discipline, while the Greeks, indignant at the murder of Ophellas, withheld their contingents, and the African princes returned to their allegiance to Carthage. Hearing of these disorders, Agathocles hastened to remedy them, but utterly failed and fled back to Sicily, leaving both his sons and his soldiers to their fate. Indignant at this desertion, the Syracusan army surrendered to the Carthaginians; and Agathocles soon afterward died either from grief or poison.

After the death of Agathocles the Carthaginians renewed their intrigues in Sicily and soon gained a controlling influence in the island. The Greek colonies, in alarm, solicited the aid of Pyrrhus, King of Epirus, who had married a daughter of Agathocles, and who was then in Italy defending the colonies of Magna Græcia against the Romans (B. C. 277). Pyrrhus took every Carthaginian town in Sicily, except Lilybæum, but soon returned to Italy; and the fruits of his victories were lost, notwithstanding the efforts of Hiero, King of Syracuse.

The result of the wars in Sicily was not encouraging to the Carthaginians. Carthage had only succeeded in keeping possession of one third of the island at the cost of several hundred thousand lives, of large fleets, and of a vast treasure; but she had not advanced her possessions a single mile. Her armies had been generally beaten, when they encountered their foes on equal terms. The Carthaginian generals were usually inferior to those of the Greeks. Carthage had also discovered that descents could be made upon her own shores, and that her African subjects could not always be relied upon. Yet she did not abandon her purpose. After the death of Agathocles the power of the Greeks in Sicily rapidly declined.

SECTION V.—CARTHAGE'S STRUGGLE WITH ROME.

CARTHAGE was now about to enter a struggle with a new enemy—Rome. This gigantic struggle embraced three long wars covering more than a century, and included the three *Punic Wars*, the details of which will be related in the history of Rome. Pyrrhus, upon leaving Sicily, exclaimed to his attendants: "What a fine field of battle we are leaving to the Carthaginians and the Romans!" His prediction was soon fulfilled. A body of mercenaries called Mamertines, in the pay of Agathocles, after the death of that king, treacherously seized the city of Messina and massacred all the inhabitants. Hiero, King of Syracuse, took the field against the Mamertines and defeated them in battle. Half the Mamertines invoked the aid of the Carthaginians and gave the citadel in their possession, while the other half sought the protection of Rome. The Romans granted the aid required, invaded Sicily, took Messina by siege and routed the Carthaginians with terrible slaughter. This was the beginning of the *First Punic War*, which lasted twenty-three years (B. C. 264-241), the details of which will be found in our account of Roman history. In this war Carthage lost Sicily and her supremacy in the Western Mediterranean, and in consequence all her other insular possessions. The mercenaries mutinied and besieged Tunis. They then marched against Utica, while the light African cavalry, that had also mutinied, ravaged the country to the very gates of Carthage. The mutineers were only subdued after they had reduced the fairest provinces of the republic to a desert waste. The mercenaries in Sardinia had likewise revolted; and the Romans, in violation of the late peace, seized the island, and Carthage was not in a position to resent this injury.

Hamilcar Barca, grieved at the evident decline of his country, formed a plan to elevate it again to an equality with its insolent rival by completely conquering the Spanish peninsula. His son Hannibal, then only a boy of nine years, earnestly requested permission to accompany his father on this expedition; but before granting the request, Hamilcar led the boy to the altar and made him swear eternal enmity to Rome.

For nine years Hamilcar commanded the Carthaginian forces in Spain, and conquered the whole peninsula by force or negotiation. He used the treasures he acquired to strengthen his family's influence in the state, depending mainly on the democracy for support against his powerful rival, Hanno, who had the chief influence among the aristocracy.

Hasdrubal, Hamilcar's son-in-law, inherited his power and his projects. It is thought that he designed founding an independent kingdom in Spain after failing to make himself absolute in Carthage. He founded a magnificent new capital in that country, naming it Carthago Nova (new Carthage)—now called Carthagena—in a region where the richest silver-mines were opened; and large bribes were sent to Carthage to allay jealousy or stifle inquiry. He exerted himself to his utmost to conciliate the native Spaniards, and married a daughter of a Spanish king. The Romans, alarmed at his success, at length forced him to sign a treaty, by which he agreed not to cross the Iberus (now Ebro), nor to attack the territory of the Greek city of Saguntum, an ally of Rome.

When Hasdrubal fell a victim to an as-

ATTACK ON CARTHAGE.

sassin's dagger, the family of Barca was sufficiently influential to obtain Hannibal's appointment as his successor, though he had scarcely reached his legal majority, B. C. 221. The youthful commander, after gaining several victories over the Spaniards, besieged and captured Saguntum, thus causing the second war with Rome, whose details will be found in our account of Roman history.

During this *Second Punic War* (B. C. 218 –201), the Carthaginian navy, the source of the greatness and security of the state, was neglected; and party spirit also distracted Carthage with violence. At the close of the war Carthage was deprived of all her foreign possessions outside of Africa, and her fleet was surrendered to the Romans. Thenceforth Carthage was virtually only a commercial city under the protection of Rome. The Romans, by entering into an alliance with Massinissa, King of Numidia, raised up a powerful rival against Carthage in Africa itself, and that monarch seized most of the western Carthaginian colonies.

Notwithstanding his recent reverses, Hannibal yet remained at the head of the state in Carthage, and reformed several abuses that had crept into the management of the public finances and the administration of justice. By these wise reforms Hannibal aroused the antagonism of the factious nobility who had previously fattened on public plunder. They united with the old rivals of the Barcan family, and even went so far as to act as spies for the Romans, who still feared the abilities of Hannibal. As a result of their machinations, the old general who had made Rome tremble for her existence was forced to flee from the country he had so long and so faithfully served; and after some years of exile the old victor of Trasimenus and Cannæ poisoned himself to escape the malignant enmity of the Romans, who even persecuted him in exile and by threats forced the King of Bithynia to deny him protection. The mound marking his last resting-place is a remarkable object to this day.

The Carthaginians soon had cause to lament the loss of their greatest leader. The Romans were not conciliated by his exile; and Massinissa, depending upon their support, made frequent raids into the Carthaginian territories. Both parties accused each other of aggression before the Roman Senate (B. C. 162); and though both received an equal hearing, the decision had long before been settled in Massinissa's interest. During the progress of these negotiations Carthage was distracted by political dissensions. The popular party ascribed the low condition into which the republic had sunk to the animosity shown by the aristocratic faction to the Barcan family, and particularly to Hannibal, because of his financial and judicial reforms; and a tumultuous assembly of the people banished forty of the leading Senators, exacting an oath from the citizens that they would never allow them to return. The exiles sought refuge with Massinissa, who sent his sons to intercede with the Carthaginian populace in their favor. The Numidian princes were denied permission to enter the city, and were even driven from the Carthaginian territory. This insult caused another war between Carthage and Numidia, in which Carthage was defeated and forced to accept a humiliating peace.

The Roman Senate, under the constant solicitations of the elder Cato, at length determined upon the complete destruction of Carthage. To provoke Carthage into a war, the Romans made one arrogant demand after another, all of which the Carthaginians, conscious of their weakness, readily obeyed. The Carthaginians gave three hundred noble children as hostages, surrendered their ships of war and their magazines of arms; but when the Romans finally demanded that they should abandon their city and consent to its destruction, they took courage from despair and absolutely refused to obey, making the most vigorous exertions to defend their city to the last. War at once resulted. The Romans were almost uniformly successful; and after a struggle of four years (B. C. 149–146), the *Third Punic War* ended in the fall of Carthage, which was taken by storm and completely destroyed, the city being set on fire and many of its inhabitants perishing in the flames rather than survive the ruin of their city, B. C. 149.

trolled the destinies of the West, while Persia ruled supreme in the East—this great maritime power which had once made Rome tremble for her own national existence—

ANCIENT UTICA

Thus perished the mighty commercial republic of ancient Africa, after an existence of more than seven centuries. This great power which had for several centuries controlled, now fell a helpless victim to her powerful and merciless enemy, and forever ceased to live except in the memory of her glory and greatness.

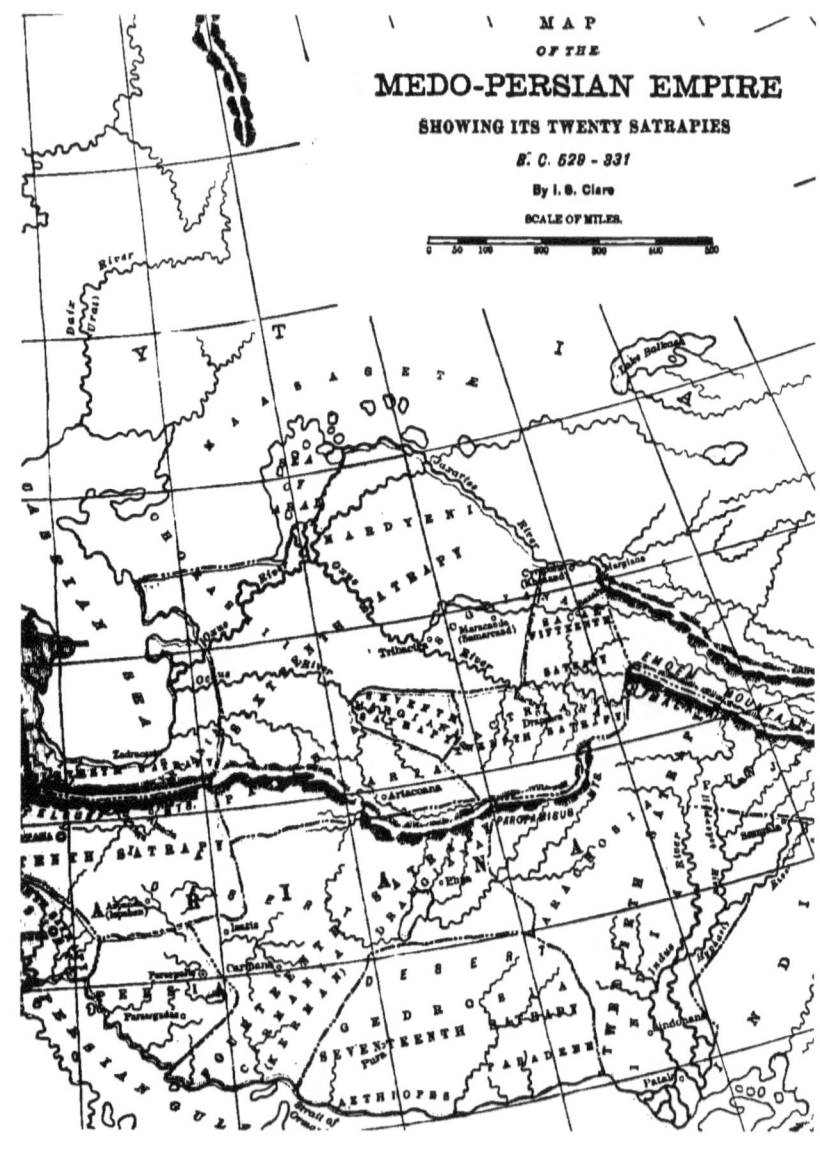

CHAPTER X.

THE MEDO-PERSIAN EMPIRE.

SECTION I.—EXTENT AND PRODUCTIONS.

THE great Medo-Persian Empire was the first of the three greatest empires of antiquity; the other two being those of Alexander the Great, which comprehended very near the same regions and territories, and the Roman. The Medo-Persian was thus the first of the great ancient Asiatic empires, covering the widest territorial area, and was four times as large as the Assyrian had been; being about three thousand miles in extent from east to west, and from five hundred to fifteen hundred miles from north to south, covering an area of about two million square miles. It extended from the Hyphasis and the Sutlej on the east to the African desert, the Mediterranean, the Ægean and the Euxine on the west; and from the Euxine, the Caucasus, the Caspian, the Oxus and the Jaxartes on the north to the frontiers of Ethiopia, Arabia, the Persian Gulf and the Erythræan Sea (now Arabian Sea) on the south. In this vast domain were various races and many tribes and nations, likewise every variety of soil and climate, and different kinds of animal, vegetable and mineral productions. The Medo-Persian Empire was the first of the great ancient Oriental monarchies which really *was* an empire; being more compact and centralized than any of those which had preceded it, such as the Assyrian, Median and Babylonian, which were mere collections of kingdoms, each with its own sovereign, its own laws and institutions, acknowledging the supremacy of the great monarch whose arms had triumphed over their kingdom; while the empire now under consideration was a vast dominion comprising many nations whose kings had been dethroned, and which all formed provinces ruled by satraps appointed by the Medo-Persian monarch.

The countries included as provinces, or satrapies, in the Medo-Persian Empire may be divided, for the sake of convenience, into the central, western and eastern. The central provinces were Persia proper, Media, Susiana, Babylonia, Assyria, the Caspian coast tract, and Sagartia, or the great desert. The western provinces were Pæonia, Thrace, Asia Minor, Armenia, Iberia, Syria and Phœnicia, Palestine, Egypt and the Cyrenaica. The eastern provinces were Hyrcania, Parthia, Aria, Chorasmia, Sogdiana, Bactria, Scythia, Gandaria, Sattagydia, India, Paricania, the Eastern Ethiopia and Mycia. Many of these countries have been described in previous portions of this book; such as Susiana, Babylonia, Assyria, Media, the Caspian coast district, Armenia, Syria, Phœnicia and Palestine. We will confine our geographical description to Persia proper, the home of the dominant race, and the other regions which have not yet occupied our attention, beginning with Persia proper itself.

Persia proper was a comparatively small country, and corresponded to the modern Persian province of Iran, Farsistan, or Fars. It lay upon the gulf bearing its name, extending from the mouth of the Tab (Oroates) to a point where the gulf connects with the Indian Ocean. It was bounded on the north by Media Magna, on the east by Mycia, on the south by the Erythræan, or Arabian Sea, and on the west by Susiana. It was about four hundred and fifty miles in length, and about two hundred and fifty miles in width, having an area of over one hundred thousand square miles.

Persia embraced two distinct regions, which modern geographers term the "warm district" and the "cold region." The "warm district" occupied about one-eighth of the country, and was a tract of sandy plain, in many places impregnated with salt, extending between the mountains and the sea the entire length of the kingdom. The soil is poor and badly watered. The other seven-eighths of the country embraced the "cold region," and was a mountainous tract, "consisting of alternate mountain, plain, and narrow valley, curiously intermixed, and as yet very incompletely mapped." It has taken altogether an aspect of sternness and sterility, although it has numerous spots of rare beauty and fertility. It has a scant water supply, and very few lakes have any outlets. Numerous lakes, some of which are salt, abound in Persia, and these receive the waters of most of the streams.

"The most remarkable feature of the country consists in the extraordinary gorges which pierce the great mountain chain, and render possible the establishment of routes across that tremendous barrier. Scarped rocks rise almost perpendicularly on either side of the mountain streams, which descend rapidly, with frequent cascades and falls. Along the slight irregularities of these rocks the roads are carried in zigzags, often crossing the streams from side to side by bridges of a single arch, which are thrown over profound chasms where the waters chafe and roar many hundred feet below. The roads have for the most part been artificially cut in the sides of the precipices, which rise from the streams sometimes to the height of two thousand feet. In order to cross from the Persian Gulf to the high plateau of Iran, no fewer than three or four of these *kotuls*, or strange gorge passes, have to be traversed successively. Thus the country towards the edge of the plateau is peculiarly safe from attack, being defended on the north and east by vast deserts, and on the south by a mountain barrier of unusual strength and difficulty."

In these regions, which combined facility for defense with pleasantness of climate, the principal cities of the country have always been located. The earliest known capital of Persia was Pasargadæ, or Persagadæ, whose ruins yet exist at Murgab, in latitude 30° 15' north and longitude 50° 17' east. Here are the famous tomb of Cyrus the Great and other interesting remains of ancient Persian architecture. About thirty miles south from Pasargadæ, or more than forty by the ordinary road, was Persepolis, the second capital, situated towards the edge of the plateau, having the mountain barrier to the south-west and the desert at no great distance to the north-east. Like Pasargadæ, Persepolis was situated in a plain, but in a larger and more fertile one. The plain of Merdasht is one of the most productive in Persia, being watered by the Bendamir and Pulwar rivers, which unite a few miles above the site of the ancient city. "From these two copious and never-failing rivers a plentiful supply of the precious fluid can at all times be obtained; and in Persia such a supply will always create the loveliest verdure, the most abundant crops, and the richest and thickest foliage. The site of Persepolis, is naturally far superior to that in which the modern provincial capital, Shiraz, has grown up, at about the same distance from Persepolis as that is from Pasargadæ, and in the same—*i. e.* in a southwest—direction."

Besides Pasargadæ and Persepolis, Persia proper had few important cities. The capital of Carmania was Carmana, a town of some consequence, mentioned by Ptolemy and Ammianus, and may be identified with the modern Kerman, the capital of the province of the same name, and one of the chief cities of modern Persia. "Situated, like Pasargadæ and Persepolis, in a capacious plain, surrounded by mountains which furnish sufficient water for cultivation to be carried on by means of *kanats* in most parts of the tract enclosed by them, and occupying a site through which the trade of the country almost of necessity passes, Kerman must always be a town of no little consequence. Its inland and remote position, however, caused it to be little known to the Greeks; and, apparently, the great Alexandrian geographer was the first who made them acquainted with its existence and locality."

The chief Persian towns, or villages, upon the coast of the Gulf were Armuza, in the province of Armuzia, opposite the modern island of Ormuz; Sisidona, near Cape Jerd; Apostana, probably about Shewar; Gogana, perhaps the modern Kongoon; and Taöce, on the Granis, celebrated for the royal palace in its vicinity. The most important inland towns, after Persepolis, Pasargadæ and Carmana, were Gabæ, near Pasargadæ, likewise the site of a palace; Uxia, or the Uxian city, whose site can not be definitely identified.

Persia proper had a twofold climate; being hot and enervating in the low country, and cold in the mountain region in winter, but pleasant during the remainder of the year. The vegetable productions were neither numerous nor remarkable. The low country produced dates in moderate quantities; and in a few localities corn, the vine and various kinds of fruit-trees were cultivated. The mountain region furnished an abundance of rich pasture; an admirable quality of grapes flourishing in those parts, and most of the fruits being abundant. Persia is believed to be the native country of the peach and the citron. The grains chiefly raised in Persia were wheat, barley, millet and rice. Indian corn, introduced from America, has been successfully grown there in modern times. Pulse, beans, sesame, madder, henna and cotton were cultivated in ancient times.

The wild animals of Persia proper were the lion, the bear, the wild ass, the stag, the antelope, the ibex, or wild goat, the wild boar, the hyena, the jackal, the wolf, the fox, the hare, the porcupine, the otter, the jerboa, the ichneumon and the marmot. The domestic animals were the camel, the horse, the mule, the ass, the buffalo, the cow, the goat, the sheep, the dog and the cat.

The western and central provinces of the Medo-Persian Empire have been described in our accounts of the other ancient empires, and therefore we will confine ourselves to the eastern provinces. Between the Elburz and Zagros mountains on the north and west, the Suliman and Hala ranges on the east, and the coast-chain running from Persia proper almost to the Indus on the south, is the great plateau of Iran, from three thousand to five thousand feet above the sea-level; being eleven hundred miles long, and from five hundred to seven hundred miles wide. Two-thirds of this tableland is a desert. The rivers flowing from the mountains, except the Etymandrus, or Helmend, are insignificant, and their waters lose themselves in the sands of the interior. Only the Helmend and the Ghuzni form lakes, the others being absorbed by irrigation, or sucked up by the desert. A few rivers force their way through the mountain barriers and reach the sea, especially in the south; while the Heri-rud, or river of Herat, in the north, makes its escape from the plateau in a similar way, but is absorbed in the sands of Kharesm, after passing through two mountain-chains. Thus most of this region is desert throughout the year, "while as the summer advances, large tracts, which in the spring were green, are burnt up—the rivers shrink back towards their sources—the whole plateau becomes dry and parched —and the traveler wonders that any portion of the land should be inhabited."

The great plateau is not a single unbroken plain. In the western portion are "brown irregular rocky ridges."

Having now described Persia proper, we will notice briefly the various provinces of the Medo-Persian Empire. Media, Susiana, Assyria, Babylonia, Syria, Palestine, Asia Minor and Egypt have already been described in other portions of this volume. We will therefore devote our attention to the eastern provinces not yet described.

Besides Persia proper the great plateau of Iran embraced the following countries, which formed a part of the empire, and which will now be described:

Mycia was a small tract south-east of Persia, on the shores of the Persian Gulf, opposite the island of Kishm and the promontory of Ras Mussendum. It was ultimately absorbed in Persia proper.

Carmania was east of Persia proper and corresponded to the modern Kerman. It was a very fertile region, and was often regarded as forming a part of Persia proper. Its capital was Carmana, now Kerman.

Sagartia was the largest and the most populous of the plateau countries. It comprised the entire desert of Iran, reaching from Kashan and Koum on the west to Sarawan and Quettah towards the east, a distance of nine hundred miles. It was bounded on the north by Media, Parthia and Aria; on the east by Sarangia and Sattagydia; on the south by Mycia and the Eastern Ethiopia; on the west by Media and Persia. It contained no important city in ancient times, the people being nomads, whose flocks and herds found a scanty pasturage on the less barren parts of the vast table-land.

Cadusia was a thin strip of country along the south-eastern and southern shores of the Caspian, corresponding to the modern Ghilan and Mazanderan. It hardly belonged to the great plateau, as it lay outside the Elburz mountain range, on the southern slopes of the chain, and between them and the Caspian Sea. It contained no important city, but was fertile, well-wooded and well-watered; and had a large population.

Hyrcania lay east of Cadusia, at the south-eastern corner of the Caspian, where the name yet exists in the modern river Gurgan. The Elburz chain here widens to two hundred miles, and a fertile region is formed containing many rich valleys and lofty mountain pastures, together with some considerable plains. The principal city of Hyrcania was Zadracarta.

Parthia lay south and south-east of Hyrcania, including the sunny flank of the Elburz mountain-chain and the low country at the northern edge of the desert, where it bordered on Sagartia. It was a narrow but fertile territory, watered by many streams which here flow from the mountains.

Aria, the modern territory of Herat, adjoined Parthia on the east. It was a small but fertile region on the river Arius (the modern Heri-rud), with a capital city called Aria, or Artacoano (the modern Herat).

Arachosia, east of Aria, embraced most of Western and Central Afghanistan. Its rivers were the Etymandrus (the modern Helmend) and the Arachotus (the modern Arghand-ab). The capital was Arachotus (now Candahar). It was an extensive country, mountainous and mainly barren, but containing a fair amount of good pasturage and a few fertile valleys.

Sattagydia adjoined Arachosia on the east, corresponding to South-eastern Afghanistan, or the tract between Candahar and the Indus valley. It closely resembled Arachosia in character, but was on the whole wilder and more rugged.

Gandaria lay north of Sattagydia, and embraced the modern Cabul and Kaferistan. It consisted of a mass of tangled mountain-chains, with fertile valleys between them, frequently, however, narrowing to gorges difficult to penetrate. Its chief stream was the Cophen (or river of Cabul), a tributary of the Indus; and its principal town was Caspatyrus (now Cabul).

Sarangia was the region lying about the salt lake (Hamoon), into which the Etymandrus (Helmend) river empties itself. This tract is flat, and generally desert, except along the courses of the numerous streams which flow into the Hamoon from the north and the east.

Gedrosia corresponded to the modern Beloochistan. It lay south of Sarangia, Arachosia and Sattagydia, and east of Sagartia and Mycia. It was bounded on the east by the Indus valley, and on the south by the Erythræan Sea (now Arabian Sea).

The following countries of Central Asia —in the region of the modern Turkestan—

also formed a part of the Medo-Persian Empire, and will now be noticed. There were three countries of some importance:

Chorasmia, to the extreme west, between the Caspian and the Lower Oxus river, was a desolate region, except close along the river-bank, known yet as *K'haresm*, and forming a portion of the Khanate of Khiva.

Sogdiana, between the Lower Oxus and the Lower Jaxartes, resembled Chorasmia in its western portion, but towards the east was traversed by spurs of the Bolor and the Thian-Chan mountains, and was watered by many streams descending from them. The chief of these rivers was the Polytimetus of the Greeks, on which was Maracanda (now Samarcand), the capital.

Bactria, on the Upper Oxus, between Sogdiana and the Paropamisus (now Hindoo-Koosh) mountains, was mountainous, fertile, and well watered towards the east, but towards the west descending into the desert. The principal cities were Bactra (now Balkh), the capital, a little south of the Oxus and Margus (now Merv), on a stream of its own, in the western desert. According to tradition Bactria was a country of very great importance in primitive or prehistoric times. Philologists believe this country to have been the primeval seat of the Aryan nations before their migration into India, Media and Persia, and Europe. Bactra, the capital of the country, is believed to have been the first great capital of the Aryan race. Some moderns have reported that the bricks of Balkh bear cuneiform inscriptions; but as yet the sight has been but partially explored.

In the North-west were the following provinces of the empire, which have not yet been described:

Armenia lay east of Asia Minor, north of Assyria, and north-west of Media. It was a lofty region, consisting almost wholly of mountains, and has been termed "the Switzerland of Western Asia." The mountain system culminates in Mount Ararat, which has an elevation of seventeen thousand feet. Therefore all the great rivers of Western Asia here take their rise, namely, the Tigris, the Euphrates, the Halys, the Araxes and the Cyrus. In the highest part of this lofty region are the elevated lake-basins of Urumiyeh and Van, each of which has a distinct and separate water-system of its own. The only important ancient town in this section occupied the site of the modern Van, on the east coast of the lake of the same name.

Colchis, or the valley of the Phasis, between the Caucasus and Western Iberia, corresponded to the modern districts of Imeritia, Mingrelia and Guriel. Its main importance lay in its commanding one of the principal routes of early commerce, which passed by way of the Oxus, the Caspian, the Aras and the Phasis, to the Euxine. The chief town of Colchis was Phasis, a Greek settlement at the mouth of the Rion river. The natives of Colchis were black and believed to be Egyptians.

Iberia, or Sapeiria, adjoined Armenia to the north-east. It embraced all of the modern Georgia, together with some portions of Russian and Turkish Armenia, especially the tract about Kars, Ispir and Akhaltsik. Its rivers were the Cyrus (now Kur) and the Araxes (now Aras), which flow together into the Caspian. Its one lake was Goutcha, in the mountain region north-east of Mount Ararat.

East of the plateau of Iran lay the valley of the Indus, called *India* from that river. The region was cut off from the rest of Hindoostan by a wide belt of desert, and comprised two regions. The region of the modern Punjab, abutting on the Himalaya mountain-chain, and containing fifty thousand square miles, was a vast triangular plain, intersected by the courses of five great rivers (whence Punjab—five rivers) the Indus, the Hydaspes (now Jelum), the Acesinus (now Chenab), the Hydraotes (now Ravee), and the Hyphasis (now Sutlej)—fertile along their course, but otherwise barren. The region now known as Scinde, or the Indus valley below the Punjab, was a tract about the same size, including the rich plain of Cutchi Gandava on the west bank of the river, and the broad delta of the Indus towards the south. The chief town of the upper region was Taxila (now Attock). The principal town of the lower region was Pattala (now Tatta).

Such was the extent of the vast Medo-Persian Empire. Territorially the great mass of the empire lay towards the east, between the Zagros mountains and the Indian desert; but its most important provinces were its western ones. The only regions of much value east of Persepolis were the valleys of the Indus and the Oxus. Westward were Susiana, Babylonia, Assyria, Media, Armenia, Iberia, Colchis, Cappadocia, Asia Minor, Cyprus, Syria, Palestine, Egypt, Cyrenaica—all of them great, and mainly productive countries. The two richest grain tracts of the ancient world, the best pasture regions, the districts producing the most valuable horses, the most abundant of known gold fields of antiquity, were within the limits of this vast empire, which was self-sufficing, containing within it all that man required in those times, for his most highly cherished luxuries, as well as for his absolute necessities.

The productiveness of the empire is to be attributed to its many large streams. The six great rivers of the empire, which contributed to fertilize the lands through which they flowed, were the Nile, the Tigris, the Euphrates, the Indus, the Oxus and the Jaxartes. The first three have already been described in other parts of this work. The Indus rises north of the Himalayas, and flows in a south-westerly direction into the Arabian Sea, being nineteen hundred and sixty miles long, of which twelve hundred and sixty were through Persian territory. The Oxus (now Amoo) rises at a lake west of the Bolor mountains and flows north-westerly through the great desert of modern Turkestan into the Sea of Aral, and is at present fourteen hundred miles long; but anciently, after reaching the Sea of Aral, it flowed westward into the Caspian Sea, thus increasing its length by four hundred and fifty miles, making the entire stream at that time eighteen hundred and fifty miles long. The Jaxartes (now Shion, or Sir Daria) rises from two sources in the Thian-Chan mountains, and flows first west, then north, and finally north-west into the Sea of Aral; its entire length being fourteen hundred and fifty-eight miles.

There were numerous lakes in the empire; but of these only the Caspian and Aral seas, Lakes Van and Urumiyeh in Armenia, the Dead Sea in Palestine, and Lake Mœris in Egypt, are of any note.

The principal cities of the empire, besides Pasargadæ and Persepolis in Persia, were Susa, the capital of Susiana; Babylon; Ecbatana, Rhages, and Zadracarta, in Media; Bactra (now Balkh), in Bactria; Maracanda (now Samarcand), in Sogdiana; Aria, or Artacoana (now Herat), in Ariana; Caspatyrus on the Upper Indus; Taxila (now Attock), on the Lower Indus; Pura, in Gedrosia (the modern Beloochistan); Carmana (now Kerman), in Carmania (now Kerman); Arbela, in Assyria; Amida (now Diarbekr), in Armenia; Mazaca, in Cappadocia; Trapezus (now Trebizond), in Pontus; Perga and Tarsus, in Asia Minor; Damascus, in Syria; Jerusalem, in Palestine; Tyre and Sidon, in Phœnicia; Azotus, or Ashdod, and Gaza, in Philistia; Sardis, in Lydia; Memphis and Thebes, in Egypt; and Cyrêné and Barca, in Cyrenaica. The cool Ecbatana became the summer capital of the empire; Susa, the spring capital, and Babylon, the winter capital; so that the Persian court moved with the seasons.

The countries bordering on the empire were India on the east; Arabia on the south; the African desert and Greece on the west; and the vast Scythian countries of Europe and Asia on the north.

Having described the soil, climate, animals, vegetables and minerals of Persia proper, we will now briefly note those of the provinces of the empire, not previously described in other portions of this volume.

The climate of the whole southern coast of the empire, from the mouth of the Tigris to that of the Indus, in the lower valleys of the great streams, was a damp, close heat, intolerably stifling and oppressive. The upper valleys of these streams and the plains into which they expanded were less hot and less moist, but were subject to violent storms, on account of the nearness of the mountains. In the mountains of Armenia, in the Zagros region and in the Elburz, the climate was more rigorous, being intensely cold in winter, but pleasant in summer. Asia Minor had a warmer climate than the high mountain districts, and its western and southern coasts, fanned by fresh sea-breezes or mountain-breezes from the Amanus and the Taurus, and cooled by frequent showers during the summer, were particularly delightful. In Syria and Egypt the heats of summer were oppressive, especially in the *Ghor*, or depressed Jordan valley, and in those portions of Egypt bordering on Ethiopia; but the winters were mild and the springs and autumns delightful. In the Cyrenaica there was a cool, delicious summer climate—an entire absence of rain, as in Egypt, with cool sea-breezes, cloudy skies and heavy dews at night, which, in the place of moisture, covered the ground with the freshest and loveliest verdure during the entire summer. The autumn and winter rains were violent, and terrific storms frequently occurred. "The natives regarded it as a blessing that over this part of Africa the sky was 'pierced,' and allowed moisture to fall from the great reservoir of water 'above the firmament.'" In the northern and north-eastern portions of the empire, "in Azerbijan, on the plateau of Iran, in the Afghan plains, in the high flat region east of the Bolor, and again in the low plain about Aral lake and the Caspian, a severe climate prevailed during the winter; while the summer combined intense heat during the day with extraordinary cold—the result of radiation—at night." In the mountain regions of the Bolor, the Thian-Chan, the Himalaya, and the Paropamisus, or Hindoo-Koosh, the winters lasted over half the year, with deep snow covering the ground almost all that time, while the summers were moderate. In the Indus valley the climate was hot and dry, with oppressive tornadoes of dust; or close and moist, swept by heavy storms which make the region more unhealthful. Altogether the climate of the empire belonged to the class of warmer temperate climates. In the Indus valley, along the coast from the mouth of the Indus to that of the Tigris, in Chaldæa and parts of Susiana, in the South of Palestine, and in Egypt frost was entirely unknown; while in the high mountain regions the winters were intensely cold. In the more elevated regions—in Phrygia and Cappadocia, in Azerbijan, on the great plateau of Iran, in the district about Kashgar and Yarkand—there was a long period of sharp and bracing weather. Nevertheless the summer heat of the whole empire was great. The springs and autumns were mostly mild and agreeable. There were few unhealthy localities within the empire. Although the variations of temperature in the course of a single day and night were uncommonly great, there was on the whole a healthy and agreeable climate.

The animals of the empire in general were the tiger, the elephant, the hippopotamus, the crocodile, the monitor, the two-humped camel, the Angora goat, the elk, the monkey and the spotted hyena. The tiger is found in the low tract between the Elburz and the Caspian, in the low flat region about the Sea of Aral, and in the Indus valley. The elephant was found in the Indus valley. The hippopotamus was found in Egypt, where it was a sacred animal. The crocodile—another sacred Egyptian animal—frequented the Nile and Indus valleys. The two-humped camel belonged to Bactria. The elk was found in Armenia, in the modern Afghan region, and in the Indus valley. The spotted hyena was an Egyptian animal. The rarer birds of the empire were the ostrich in Mesopotamia, the parrot in the Indus valley, the ibis in Egypt, the great vulture in the Taurus region in Asia Minor, the Indian owl, the spoonbill, the benno and sicsac. The most valuable fish of the Persian seas were the pearl-oyster of the Persian Gulf, and the murex of the Mediterranean, which furnished the celebrated *purple dye* of Tyre. There were all kinds of fish found in the rivers, lakes and seas of the empire; while various reptiles, as turtles, snakes and lizards, abounded. The Egyptian asp was a dangerous reptile. The chameleon was found in Egypt, in the Caucasus region and in India.

The vegetable productions of the empire were numerous. In the northern portions were such trees as pines, firs, larches, oaks, birch, beech, ash, ilax and junipers; while shrubs and flowers also flourished, as in the more temperate regions. The southern tracts grew various kinds of palms, mangoes, tamarind-trees, lemons, oranges, jujubes, mimosas and sensitive plants. The empire embraced a variety of trees, shrubs and flowers. The walnut and the Oriental pine grew to a vast size in many places. Poplars, willows, fig-mulberries, konars, cedars, cypresses and acacias were common. Bananas, egg-plants, locust-trees, banyans, terebinths, the gum-styrax, the gum-tragacanth, the assafœtida plant, the arbor vitæ, the castor-oil plant, the Judas tree, the pomegranate, the oleander, the pistachio-nut, the myrtle, the bay, the laurel, the mulberry, the rhododendron and the arbutus also prevailed in luxuriant abundance. The empire produced all the known kinds of grain and nearly all the known fruits. The excellent and rare kinds were the famous wheat of Æolis, the dates of Babylonia, the citrons of Media, the Persian peach, the grapes of Carmania, the Hyrcanian fig, the plum of Damascus, the cherries of Pontus, the mulberries of Egypt and of Cyprus, the silphium of Cyrêné, the wine of Helbon, the wild grape of Syria and the papyrus of Egypt. Altogether the Medo-Persian Empire produced as excellent a variety of vegetable products as any other state or community of ancient or modern times.

The mineral treasures of the empire were various and abundant. Persia proper and Carmania possessed mines of gold, silver, copper, iron, red lead, orpiment, salt, bitumen, naphtha, sulphur, and lead. Drangiana, or Sarangia, furnished rare and valuable mineral tin, with which copper could be hardened into bronze. Armenia yielded emery, so essential for the polishing of gems. The mountains and mines of the empire supplied almost all kinds of useful and precious stones. Gold was also supplied by the mountains and desert of Thibet and India, from the rivers of Lydia, from the mountains of Armenia, from the regions in the vicinity of the modern Cabul and Meshed. Silver, the great medium of exchange in Persia, was also abundant, and was found in the mines of Carmania, Armenia, Asia Minor, and the Elburz. Copper was abundant in Cyprus and Carmania, and, perhaps was also, as now, found in Armenia. Iron was found within the empire in the form of immense boulders and also in ironstone. Lead was procured from Bactria, Armenia, Carmania and many portions of the present Afghanistan. Orpiment was obtained from Bactria, Carmania and the Hazareh country. Antimony was found in Armenia, Media and the modern Afghanistan. Hornblende, quartz, talc and asbestos were obtained from various places in the Taurus mountain region in Asia Minor. Salt was widely diffused, being abundant in Persia proper, in Carmania, in Media, in Chaldæa and Palestine, in India and in North Africa. In Carmania and Palestine it was found in large masses called "mountains." In India it was the chief production of a long mountain-range, which is capable of furnishing the entire world with salt for thousands of years. Bitumen and naphtha were also widely diffused; being found at the eastern foot of the Caucasus, in Mesopotamia, in the low country of Persia proper, in the Bakhtiyari mountains, and in the Jordan valley in Palestine. Sulphur was found in Persia proper, in Carmania, on the coast of Mekran, in Azerbijan, in the Elburz mountain region, on the plateau of Iran, in the vicinity of the Dead Sea in Palestine, and very abundantly near the site of Nineveh.

Excellent building stone was found in various portions of the empire. Egypt furnished granite, various marbles, sandstone, limestone, etc. Basalt was obtained from the Taurus region. Gray alabaster was procured in great abundance in the vicinity of Nineveh, and a better quality was quarried near Damascus. Mill-stones were supplied by a gritty silicious rock on the banks of the Euphrates, above Hit.

The various provinces of the empire furnished numerous gems, such as the emerald, the green ruby, the red ruby, the opal, the sapphire, the amethyst, the carbuncle, the jasper, the lapis-lazuli, the agate and the topaz. Emeralds were found in Egypt, Media and Cyprus; green rubies in Bactria; red rubies in Caria; opals in Egypt, Cyprus and Asia Minor; amethysts in Egypt, Cyprus, Galatia and Armenia; sapphires in Cyprus; carbuncles in Caria; jaspers in Cyprus, Asia Minor and Persia; sard in Babylonia; agates in Carmania, Susiana and Armenia; topaz in Upper Egypt; jet in Lycia; garnets and the beryl in Armenia, and lapis-lazuli in Egypt, Media and Cyprus. Lapis-lazuli existed in huge masses. Whole cliffs of this gem overhang the river Kashkar in Kaferistan. The myrrhine vases of antiquity, supposed to be of agate, came from Carmania, and seem to have been of great size.

SECTION II.—POLITICAL HISTORY.

HE history of the Medo-Persian Empire begins with the overthrow of Astyages, the last King of Media, by CYRUS THE GREAT. But in the present narrative we must go considerably farther back; because in this instance, as in most other cases, the empire grew out of a previously-existing monarchy. Darius Hystaspes reckoned eight Persian kings before himself. The inscriptions of the Assyrian kings begin to notice the Persians about the middle of the ninth century before Christ. At that time Shalmaneser II., the Black Obelisk King of Assyria, found them in South-western Armenia, where they were in close contact with their Aryan kinsmen, the Medes, but of whom they appear to have been then entirely independent. Like the modern Kurds in the same region, they were not subject to a single head, but were governed by many petty chieftains, each of whom was the lord of a single town or a small mountain district. Shalmaneser II. says in his inscription that he took tribute from twenty-five such chiefs. His son and grandson received similar tokens of submission from this people. For almost a century thereafter the Assyrian records say nothing of the Persians, until the reign of Sennacherib, when they are found to be no longer in Armenia, but to have migrated beyond the Zagros, into the regions north and northeast of Susiana, where they established their permanent home.

The Persians thus did not finish their migrations until near the end of the Assyrian period, and perhaps did not form an organized monarchy until near the fall of Nineveh. The establishment of a powerful monarchy in the neighboring country of Media about B. C. 660, or a little later, doubtless induced the Persians to follow the example of their kindred.

According to the native Persian tradition, the first Persian king was ACHÆMENES, (Hakhamanish), from whom all the later Persian monarchs were descended, excepting probably the last, Darius Codomannus, who, some writers say, was not a member of the royal clan. The name of the first Persian king, Achæmenes, was derived from the royal clan of the Achæmenidæ. Certain writers have doubted the existence of Achæmenes, but he may have been a real king, who founded the original Persian monarchy by uniting the scattered tribes into one nation, and raised Persia into a power of some importance.

The successor of Achæmenes was his son TEISPES, according to the Behistun Inscription. Little is known of him and the next three monarchs, and the names of two are quite uncertain. One tradition ascribes either to the second or to the fourth king the establishment of friendly relations with a certain Pharnaces, King of Cappadocia, by the intermarriage of Atossa, a Persian princess, with the Cappadocian monarch.

According to Herodotus, Persia, under these early kings, was absolutely subject to the dominion of the Medes, who conquered Persia and imposed their yoke upon its people before B. C. 634. But the native Persian records and the accounts of Xenophon represent Persia as being at this time a separate and powerful kingdom, either entirely independent of Media, or only nominally dependent. In the Behistun Inscription, Darius Hystaspes says: "There are eight kings of my race before me; I am the ninth. For a length of time we have been kings." The political condition of Persia as represented to us by Xenophon and the Behistun Inscription is perhaps the true one, and it may be doubted if there ever was a Median conquest of Persia; but Persia, being weaker and less developed, may have acknowledged the suzerainty of the more powerful Media, while being left undisturbed in the control of her own domestic affairs, and perhaps not much interfered with in her relations with foreign nations. Persia may have occupied the same relation toward Media that Egypt now does toward Turkey. This position was irksome to the Persian kings and unpleasant to their subjects. It detracted from the dignity of the Persian monarchs as independent sovereigns, and perhaps sometimes hampered them, as they would from time to time have to pay court to their suzerain. Towards the close of the Median period the Persian monarch was obliged to send his eldest son, the heir and crown-prince, to Ecbatana, to reside at the Median court as a hostage for the faithful discharge of the duties of his father as a vassal king. The Persian crown-prince was thus kept in a sort of honorable captivity, not being permitted to leave the Median court and return home without the consent of the Median king, though otherwise well treated.

Xenophon and Nicolas of Damascus represent this as the actual condition of Persia at that time. CAMBYSES, the father of Cyrus the Great—called Atradates by the latter writer—was King of Persia, and resided at Pasargadæ, while his son Cyrus was a resident at the Median court at Ecbatana, where he was in high favor with the reigning sovereign, Astyages. Xenophon and Herodotus represent Cyrus as the grandson of Astyages, whose daughter was the wife of Cambyses and the mother of Cyrus; but Nicolas of Damascus and Ctesias assert that there was no relationship between them, the Median monarch simply retaining the young Persian prince at his capital because he was attached to him.

According to Ctesias, Cyrus, while at the Median court, resolved to liberate his country by a revolt, and secretly communicated with his father for this purpose. His father assented reluctantly, and preparations were made which led to the escape of Cyrus and the beginning of the war of Persian independence. The detailed account of the struggle has already been given in the history of Media, and need not be repeated here. After repeated defeats, the Persians made a final stand at Pasargadæ, their capital, where, in two great battles, they destroyed the power of Astyages, who was himself taken prisoner; and thus was inflicted the death-blow upon the Median Empire.

Cambyses lost his life during the struggle, and the Persian triumph gave the sovereignty of the great Aryan empire to the youthful Cyrus, who thus became the founder of the great Medo-Persian Empire, which was the dominant power in Western Asia for the next two centuries (B. C. 558–B.C. 331). The greater portion of Astyages's subjects quietly submitted to the young conqueror, who was to rule them from Pasargadæ as the Median monarchs had previously governed them from Ecbatana. Fate had destined a single lord for the many tribes and nations occupying the vast domain situated between the Persian Gulf and the Euxine, or Black Sea; and the arbitrament of the sword had decided that

Cyrus should be that single lord. The statement of Nicolas of Damascus, that the nations previously subject to the Medes vied with each other in the readiness and zeal which they displayed in making their submission to the triumphant Persian prince, seems altogether probable. Cyrus immediately succeeded to the undisputed inheritance of which he deprived Astyages, and was recognized as king by all the tribes between the Halys and the desert of Khorassan. Nicolas even represents the Parthians, the Bactrians and the Sacæ as submitting at once to the young conqueror.

Cyrus is said to have been exactly forty years of age when, by his triumph over Astyages, he transferred the supremacy of the Aryan race from the Medes to their Persian kinsmen. With dominion came riches; the wealth of the Assyrian kings—the gold, the silver, and the "pleasant furniture" of those mighty monarchs, of which there was "none end"—along with all the additions made to those immense stores by the Median sovereigns, had come into his possession; so that from comparative poverty he had suddenly become one of the wealthiest—if not the very wealthiest—of princes. With an insatiable ambition and more than ordinary ability, Cyrus aimed at universal dominion. Ctesias tells us that as soon as he was seated on his throne he led an expedition against the renowned Bactrians and Sacans of the distant North-east; but the quarter which really received his first attention was the North-west, where the powerful empire of Lydia had absorbed all the kingdoms of Asia Minor west of the Halys.

Having become master of all Asia Minor except Lycia, Cilicia and Cappadocia, Crœsus, the famed wealthy King of Lydia, had for some years surrendered himself to the enjoyment of his immense riches and to an ostentatious display of his magnificence. But the revolution in the East which had overthrown his ally, Astyages, and transferred the sovereignty in that quarter to the enterprising Persian prince, roused the indolent and self-complacent Crœsus from his lethargy. He at once made preparations for the inevitable struggle which was to decide the lordship of this part of Asia. After consulting the Grecian oracles he sent ambassadors to Babylon and Memphis, and the result was an alliance of the Kings of Lydia, Babylonia and Egypt, along with Sparta, against the growing power of the Medo-Persian monarch.

Cyrus in the meantime sent emissaries into Asia Minor to incite revolt amongst the Asiatic Greeks and other subjects of the Lydian king, but in this he was disappointed, as the Ionian Greeks remained loyal to their master. Cyrus then led a large army into Cappadocia, into which country Crœsus had advanced to meet him. In the district of Pteria an indecisive engagement occurred, and the next day Crœsus retreated, and was not pursued by Cyrus until he had retired across the Halys into his own dominions. Herodotus, our main authority for the account of this war, states that Crœsus raised a new army from the contingents of his allies to renew the struggle. Cyrus, biding his time, crossed the Halys and advanced directly toward Sardis. Upon reaching his capital Crœsus had dismissed most of his troops to their homes for the winter, giving orders for their return in the spring, when he expected auxiliaries from Sparta, Babylon and Egypt. Thus left defenseless, he suddenly learned that his intrepid enemy had followed him into the heart of his own kingdom and had approached almost to his capital. Hastily collecting an army of native Lydians, Crœsus encountered the advancing foe in the rich plain a few miles east of Sardis. Cyrus, aware of the merits of the Lydian cavalry, put his camels in front of his army, thus frightening the Lydian horses so that they fled from the field. The riders dismounted and fought bravely on foot, but their valor was unavailing. After a long and sanguinary conflict the Lydian army was utterly defeated and obliged to seek refuge behind the walls of Sardis.

Crœsus hastily sent fresh messengers to his allies, soliciting them to come immediately to his aid, hoping to maintain himself until their arrival, as his capital was defended by walls of such strength as to be considered impregnable by the Lydians themselves. An unsuccessful attempt was made to take the city by storm, and the siege would have become a blockade but for an accidental discovery. A Persian soldier having approached to reconnoiter the citadel on the side which was naturally strongest, and therefore the least guarded, perceived one of the garrison descending the rock after his helmet, which had dropped from his head over the precipice, and picking it up and returning with it. Being an expert in climbing, he succeeded in ascending the same rock to the summit, and was followed by several of his comrades. Thus the citadel was surprised, and the city was taken and plundered.

Thus the chief city of Asia Minor fell into the hands of the Persians after a siege of fourteen days. The Lydian king narrowly escaped with his life from the confusion of the sack; but, being recognized in time, was made prisoner and brought into the presence of the victorious Persian monarch. Herodotus and Nicolas of Damascus tell us that Cyrus condemned his captive to be burned alive, but relented after Crœsus had been on the funeral pile, and ever afterward treated him with clemency, assigning him a territory for his maintenance and giving him an honorable position at court, where he passed thirty years in high favor with Cyrus and his son and successor, Cambyses.

With the fall of Sardis, Lydia and its dependencies were absorbed into the Medo-Persian Empire; but the Greek cities upon the coast of Lydia were not permitted quietly to become tributaries, and the Carians in the south-western corner of Asia Minor refused to submit to the new conqueror without a struggle. For several weeks after the capture of Sardis, Cyrus remained in that city, receiving during that time an insulting message from Sparta, to which he made a threatening response; and after arranging the government of the newly-conquered province and transmitting its treasures to Ecbatana, he left Lydia for the Median capital, taking Crœsus along with him.

Cyrus was contemplating schemes of conquest in other quarters, but no sooner had he left Sardis than an insurrection broke out in that city. Pactyas, a Lydian, who had been assigned the task of conveying the treasures of Crœsus and his wealthiest subjects to Ecbatana, revolted against Tabalus, the Persian commandant of the city, and, being joined by the inhabitants and by Greek and other mercenaries whom he had hired with the treasures entrusted to his care, besieged Tabalus in the citadel. Cyrus heard of this revolt while on his march, but sending Mazares, a Mede, with a strong body of troops to suppress it, proceeded eastward. When Mazares reached Sardis, Pactyas had fled to the coast, and the revolt was ended. The rebellious Lydians were disarmed; and Pactyas, relentlessly pursued, and demanded successively of the Cymæans, the Mitylenæans and the Chians, was finally surrendered by the last-named people. The Greek cities which had supplied Pactyas with auxiliaries were next attacked; and the inhabitants of Priêné, the first of these cities which was taken, were all sold into slavery.

Mazares died shortly afterward, and was succeeded by Harpagus, also a Mede, who dealt less harshly with the unfortunate Greeks. Besieging their cities one after another, and gaining possession of them by means of banks or mounds piled up against the walls, Harpagus sometimes connived at the escape of the inhabitants to their ships, while in other cases he permitted them to become Persian subjects, liable to tribute and military service, though not disturbed otherwise. The Ionians, even those of the islands, excepting the Samians, voluntarily accepted the same position and also became subjects of Cyrus the Great.

Only one Greek continental town suffered nothing during this troublesome time. When Cyrus refused the offers of submission from the Ionian and Æolian Greeks after he had taken Sardis, he excepted Miletus, the most important and the most powerful Greek city of Asia Minor. Four Lydian kings had failed to subdue Miletus, and Crœsus, the last, only succeeded in the attempt.

Thales, the great Milesian philosopher, suggested that the Ionian Greeks of Asia Minor should unite in a confederation to be governed by a congress which should meet at Teos, each city retaining its own laws and domestic independence, but uniting for military purposes into a federal union. But the advice of Thales was disregarded, and the Asiatic Greeks were reduced under the Persian dominion.

After the conquest of the Ionian cities Harpagus subdued the nations of Southwestern Asia Minor—the Carians, the Dorian Greeks, the Caunians and the Lycians. The Carians readily submitted on the approach of Harpagus, who had impressed the newly-conquered Ionians and Æolians into his service. The Dorian cities of Myndus, Halicarnassus and Cnidus submitted without resistance; but the Caunians and Lycians, animated by a love of freedom, and having never before submitted to any conqueror, made a heroic defense. After being defeated in the field they retired within the walls of their chief cities, Caunus and Xanthus; and, finding defense impossible, they set fire to these cities, their women, children, slaves and valuables perishing in the flames; after which they sallied forth from the burning cities sword in hand, attacked the besiegers' lines, and fought until every one of their number had fallen.

In the meantime Cyrus was pursuing a career of conquest in the far East. Herodotus, who is undoubtedly a better authority than Ctesias for the events of the reign of Cyrus the Great, states that the conqueror now subdued the Bactrians and the Sacans in that part of Central Asia now called Turkestan. Bactria enjoyed the reputation of having been a great and glorious country in primeval times, and is considered the prehistoric home of the Aryan, or Indo-European, branch of the Caucasian race—the Bactrians, the Medes and Persians, the Brahmanic or Sanskritic Hindoos, and the European nations. In the oldest portion of the Zend-Avesta it was celebrated as "*Bakhdi credhwô-drafsha*," or "Bactria with the lofty banner;" and certain traditions point to it as the native country of Zoroaster. There is good reason for believing that it had maintained its independence until it was conquered by Cyrus, or that it had been unmolested by the great monarchies which had swayed the destinies of Western Asia for over seven centuries. The Bactrians were an Iranic, or Aryan nation, and retained in their remote and comparatively-savage country the simple habits of the primitive Aryans. They were among the best soldiers of the East, though armed with weapons of a different character, and they always proved themselves to be a dangerous foe. Ctesias tells us that when Cyrus invaded their country they fought an indecisive pitched battle with his troops, and that they were not subdued by force of arms, but that they submitted voluntarily when they learned that Cyrus had married a Median princess. Herodotus, however, states that the Bactrians were among the Central Asian nations conquered by Cyrus. The account of Herodotus is the more probable, as so warlike a nation as the Bactrians is not likely to have quietly submitted, and as the marriage of a Median princess, if he had contracted one, would not have rendered him any more acceptable to the Bactrians, especially as Bactria had not constituted any part of the Median Empire.

After the conquest of Bactria, Cyrus attacked the Sacæ, whose country is believed to have bordered on Bactria, and who occupied the region of the modern Kashgar and Yarkand. The Sacæ were considered good soldiers. Their weapons were the bow and arrow, the dagger and the battle-ax. They were formidable enemies either on foot or on horseback. They were probably Tartars, or Turanians, in race, and were in all likelihood the ancestors of the modern inhabitants of those regions. Ctesias says that their women went to the field in nearly equal numbers with their men, and that the mixed army which resisted Cyrus consisted of half a million, comprising both sexes, three hundred thousand men and two hundred thousand women. They were commanded by a king named Amorges, whose wife was called

Sparethra. This king was taken prisoner in a battle with the Persians, whereupon his wife took command of the Sacan forces, defeated Cyrus, and took so many prisoners of rank that the Persian monarch gladly released Amorges in exchange for them. Herodotus tells us that the Sacæ were, however, finally conquered, and that they became subjects and tributaries of Persia.

Herodotus informs us that Cyrus about this time also subdued a number of other countries in this part of Asia, namely, Hyrcania, Parthia, Chorasmia, Sogdiana, Aria (now Herat), Drangiana, or Sarangia, Arachosia, Sattagydia and Gandaria. Arrian, a later Greek historian, states that Cyrus founded a city named Cyropolis, located on the Jaxartes, in Sogdiana—a town of great strength defended by high walls. Pliny tells us that Cyrus destroyed Capisa, the chief city of Capisēnē, near the Upper Indus, probably on the site of the modern Kafshan, a little north of Cabul. Diodorus, Strabo and Arrian say that the Ariaspæ, a people in Drangiana, supplied Cyrus with provisions when he was warring in their vicinity, and that he gave them in return a new name, which the Greeks translated as "Euergetæ," meaning *benefactors*. The Ariaspæ are believed to have had their abode near the Hamoon, or Lake of Seistan. Thus we find traces of the presence of the Persian conqueror in the remote North on the Jaxartes, in the distant East in the modern Afghanistan, and as far South as Seistan and the Helmend; and there is reason to believe that he reduced under his dominion the entire region between the Caspian on the west and the desert of Tartary and the Indus valley on the east, and between the Jaxartes on the north and the deserts of Seistan and Khorassan on the south.

Tradition states that Cyrus on one occasion penetrated Gedrosia, the modern Beloochistan, on an expedition against the Hindoos, or Indians, and that he had lost his whole army in the waterless and trackless desert of that region; but we have no evidence that he reduced the country to subjection. Gedrosia, however, seems to have been a part of the Medo-Persian Empire in the reign of Darius Hystaspes, but it is not known whether he, or Cambyses, or the great founder of the empire conquered it.

The conquest of the immense region between the Caspian and the Indus, occupied by a numerous, valiant and freedom-loving population, may very likely have employed Cyrus about thirteen or fourteen years. Alexander the Great, two centuries later, was occupied five years in reducing the same region, when the inhabitants had entirely lost their warlike character.

In the history of the Babylonian Empire we have described the conquest of Babylon by Cyrus the Great, and need not repeat our account of that great event here. The capture of the city of Babylon by the Persian conqueror was the death-blow to the Babylonian Empire, as the capture and destruction of Nineveh by the Medes and Babylonians had been the death-stroke to the Assyrian. Thus the rich and fertile provinces of Babylonia, Susiana, Syria, Phœnicia and Palestine, together embracing about a quarter of a million square miles, were added to the immense empire which Cyrus had already built up.

In the conquest of Babylon the last formidable Asiatic rival of Persia was wiped out of existence, and with its extinction perished the old Semitic civilization of Asia, which, represented in succession by early Chaldæa, Assyria and later Babylonia, had a history of almost two thousand years. Thus the fall of Babylon, and with it the old Semitic civilization, is one of the most important landmarks in the history of the world, as it at once transferred the supremacy in the civilized world from the Semitic to the Aryan race; and ever since that time the Aryan nations have entirely swayed the destinies of mankind in every sphere of human activity—in politics, in social life, in science, art and literature; and the human race entered upon a new era—a career of activity and progress which it had never before known.

Says Rawlinson: "So long as Babylon, 'the glory of kingdoms,' 'The praise of the whole earth,' retained her independence, with her vast buildings, her prestige of antiquity, her wealth, her learning, her ancient and grand religious system, she could scarcely fail to be, in the eyes of her neighbors, the first power in the world, if not in mere strength, yet in honor, dignity, and reputation. Haughty and contemptuous herself to the very last, she naturally imposed on men's minds, alike by her past history and her present pretensions; nor was it possible for the Persian monarch to feel that he stood before his subjects as indisputably the foremost man upon the earth until he had humbled in the dust the pride and arrogance of Babylon. But, with the fall of the Great City, the whole fabric of Semitic greatness was shattered. Babylon became 'an astonishment and a hissing'—all her prestige vanished—and Persia stepped manifestly into the place, which Assyria had occupied for so many centuries, of absolute and unrivaled mistress of Western Asia."

With the fall of Babylon perished "an ancient, widely-spread, and deeply venerated religious system," as represented in the Assyro-Babylonian polytheism. Although this religion retained its votaries for some time, it was no longer a prevailing system, supported by the resources of a state and enforced by civil authority over a wide expanse of territory, but "it became simply one of the many tolerated beliefs, exposed to frequent rebuffs and insults, and at all times overshadowed by a new and rival system—the comparatively pure creed of Zoroaster." The Persian conquest of Babylon was a mortal wound to the sensuous idolatry which for more than twenty centuries had been universally prevalent in the countries between the Mediterranean and the Zagros mountain range. This idol-worship only survived in places, and slightly corrupted pure Zoroastrianism; but on the whole it rapidly declined from the date of the fall of Babylon. Says the prophet Isaiah: "Bel boweth down; Nebo stoopeth." Says Jeremiah: "Merodach is broken in pieces." It was then that judgment was done upon the Babylonian graven image. The system of which they constituted an essential feature, "having once fallen from its proud preëminence, gradually decayed and vanished."

As the old Semitic idolatrous polytheism declined, pure spiritual monotheism advanced. "The same blow which laid the Babylonian religion in the dust struck off the fetters from Judaism." The Jewish monotheism—purified and refined by the hard discipline of adversity, and protected, upheld and reinstated in its own home by Cyrus the Great, who felt towards it a natural sympathy, because of its resemblance to the monotheism of Zoroaster—advanced thenceforth in influence and importance, "leaving little by little the foul mass of superstition and impurity which came in contact with it." Proselytism became more general, and the Jews spread themselves wider. Their return to their own land from the Babylonian Captivity, which Cyrus authorized soon after he had taken Babylon, was the first step in the gradual enlightenment of heathen nations by the diffusion of Jewish beliefs and practices, aided and facilitated by the high esteem in which the Jewish religion was held by the civil power, both under the Medo-Persians and subsequently under the Macedonian Greeks.

When Babylon fell, all its dependencies submitted to the Persian conqueror, excepting Phœnicia, which had always sullenly and reluctantly yielded to either the Assyrian or the Babylonian sway, and which now thought the opportune moment had arrived for recovering its independence. Therefore upon the destruction of her Babylonian suzerain, Phœnicia quietly resumed her independent position, making no act of submission to the conquering Cyrus, but establishing friendly commercial relations with one of the conquering king's vassals, the Jewish leader, Ezra, who had been sent into Palestine to reëstablish his countrymen in Jerusalem.

Herodotus tells us that Cyrus, in the year B. C. 529, after reigning twenty-nine years, led an expedition against the Massagetæ, a Scythian tribe whose country lay on the north-eastern border of his empire, to the north-east of the Caspian Sea. Leading his army across the Jaxartes, he defeated the Massagetæ in a great battle by stratagem, but was himself afterwards defeated and killed, his body falling into the enemy's possession. Herodotus further says that Thomyris, the queen of the Massagetæ, in revenge for the death of her son, who had fallen in the battle, caused the head of the mighty Persian king to be cut off from the body and to be thrown into a skin filled with the blood of Persian soldiers, saying, as she thus insulted the corpse: "I live, and have conquered thee in fight; and yet by thee am I ruined, for thou tookest my son with guile; but thus I make good my threat, and give thee thy fill of blood."

Ctesias tells us that the people against whom he led his last expedition were the Derbices, a nation on the borders of India. Aided by their Indian allies, who furnished them with elephants, the Derbices encountered Cyrus, who was defeated and mortally wounded in the battle; but reinforced by a body of Sacæ, the Persians renewed the struggle, gaining a decisive victory, which obliged the Derbices to submit to the Persian dominion. Cyrus, however, died of his wound the third day after the first battle.

Xenophon tells us that Cyrus the Great died peacefully in his bed. This conflict of testimony on the part of the three eminent Greek historians throws a veil of uncertainty over the closing scene of the life of the great founder of the Medo-Persian Empire. While it is probable that he lost his life in an expedition against a nation on the north-eastern frontier of his empire, B. C. 529, after he had reigned twenty-nine years, it is certain that his body did not fall into the enemy's possession from the fact that it was conveyed into Persia proper and buried at Pasargadæ. His tomb may yet be seen at Murgab, on the site of the early Persian capital.

The last expedition of Cyrus may not have been prompted by mere ambition and thirst for conquest. The nomadic nations of Central Asia have at all times been turbulent, and have been with difficulty held in check by the civilized nations to the south and west of them; and the invasion of that region by the Persian monarch may have been for the purpose of striking terror into the barbarians, and to protect his own dominions from a possible savage inroad.

The Greek writers give us a more favorable view of Cyrus the Great than of any other ancient Oriental monarch. Herodotus and Nicolas of Damascus represent him as brave, active, energetic, a great strategist, and as thus possessing all the characteristics of a successful warrior. Herodotus also tells us that he conciliated his subjects by friendly and familiar treatment, but refused to indulge them by yielding to their desires when they conflicted with their own welfare. He was also credited with having had a ready humor, which displayed itself in witty sayings and repartees, as illustrated in the case of the Ionian Greeks, who just before the fall of Sardis had refused his overtures, but who after the capture of the city came to offer their submission, when Cyrus replied to them thus: "A fisherman wanted the fish to dance for him, so he played a tune on his flute, but the fish kept still. Then he took his net and drew them out on the shore, and they all began to leap and dance. But the fisherman said, 'A truce to your dancing now, since you would not dance when I wanted you.'"

Berosus and Herodotus both bear testimony to the fact that Cyrus treated his captives with mildness, and readily forgave even the heinous crime of rebellion. Herodotus also tells us that he was devoid of the usual pride of the ordinary Oriental despot, but conversed familiarly with those about him. Such being his virtues, it is not surprising that the Persians, comparing him with their later sovereigns, cherished his memory with the highest veneration, as attested by Xenophon; and that their affection for his person induced them to take his type of countenance as their standard of physical beauty, of which fact we are informed by Plutarch.

Cyrus possessed the genius of a conqueror,

but lacked that of a statesman. We have no vestige of any uniform system for the government of the provinces which he had conquered. In Lydia he set up a Persian governor, but vested some important functions in a native Lydian; says Herodotus. In Babylonia he entrusted the control of public affairs to "Darius the Mede," whom he permitted to assume the title of king; says Daniel. In Judæa he appointed a native Jew, Ezra, governor. In Sacia he allowed the king who had resisted his arms to reign as a tributary monarch. This want of uniformity in the government of the empire, which may have been dictated by policy or circumstances, was an obstacle to the consolidation of the vast dominion which Cyrus had acquired by conquest; and the Medo-Persian Empire at his death had no more cohesion than any of the other preceding Asiatic empires.

Though originally a rude mountain chief, Cyrus proved his ability to appreciate the dignity and value of art, after he had built up an empire. His edifices at Pasargadæ united massiveness with elegance, and exhibited a simple but refined taste. He ornamented his structures with reliefs ideal in their nature. If, as seems probable, he constructed at Persepolis the Great Central Propylæa, the South-eastern Palace and the Hall of a Hundred Columns, he originated the entire system of arrangement subsequently pursued in the erection of all Persian palaces.

In his domestic life Cyrus seems to have displayed the same moderation and simplicity which marked his conduct in public affairs. Herodotus tells us that he had but one wife, Cassandané, the daughter of Pharnaspes, a member of the royal family. His sons were Cambyses and Smerdis, on the authority of Herodotus and the Behistun Inscription. According to Herodotus, his daughters were Atossa, Artystoné and a third whose name is not known. The wife of Cyrus died before her husband, who greatly mourned for her. Xenophon and Ctesias state that just before his own death he sought to guard against a disputed succession by leaving the inheritance of his great empire to his elder son, Cambyses, and entrusting the actual government of several large and important provinces to his younger son, Smerdis. But his plan subjected both his sons to untimely ends, as we shall presently see.

No sooner was CAMBYSES seated upon the throne, B. C. 529, than he grew jealous of his brother; and the Behistun Inscription informs us that he ordered him to be privately put to death, and so secretly was this done that the manner, and even the fact, of his death was known to only a few. Smerdis was generally thought to be still living, and this belief furnished an opportunity for a personation, as will be noticed.

Meanwhile Cambyses set about executing his father's plans for the conquest of Egypt. Seeking a pretext for a quarrel, he demanded that a daughter of Amasis, King of Egypt, should be sent him as a secondary wife. Amasis, fearing to refuse, sent him a damsel named Nitetes, whom he falsely represented as his daughter, and who informed Cambyses of the deception soon after her arrival. This, according to Herodotus, was the ground for a quarrel. Cambyses at once set about making his preparations for an expedition. Egypt was almost inaccessible on account of her situation, being protected on all sides by seas and deserts. Herodotus states that the Persian monarch made a treaty with the Arab sheik who had most influence over the desert tribes, and obtained the aid of a powerful navy by intimidating the Phœnicians into accepting his yoke and by wresting from Egypt the island of Cyprus. The Egyptian navy was unable to withstand the united fleets of Phœnicia, Cyprus, Ionia and Æolis. Being thus deprived of the supremacy of the seas, Egypt lost one of the chief elements of her defense.

Cambyses entered Egypt in B. C. 525, after preparing four years for the invasion, and he at once defeated the Egyptian king Psammenitus, who had just succeeded his father Amasis, in the bloody battle of Pelusium. Psammenitus was aided by a large body of mercenaries, consisting of Greeks and Carians. The enthusiasm of these allies in the cause of the Egyptian monarch was fully attested by their treatment of one of their own number who had deserted to the Persians just before the battle, and was believed to have given important information to the invaders. His children, whom he had left behind him in Egypt, were seized and put to death before their father's eyes by his former comrades, who mixed their blood in a bowl with water and wine, and then drank the mixture. Ctesias says that the Egyptians and their allies lost fifty thousand men in the decisive battle of Pelusium, while the triumphant Persians lost only seven thousand. After his disastrous defeat Psammenitus threw himself into Memphis, where, being closely besieged by land, while the Persian fleet cut off all supplies from the sea by occupying the Nile, he was forced to surrender after a desperate resistance. Herodotus informs us that the captive Egyptian monarch was at first treated with clemency. The date of this conquest of Egypt is fixed at B. C. 525 by the concurrent testimony of Diodorus, Eusebius and Manetho.

Herodotus and Diodorus state that the Libyans of the desert bordering upon the west side of the Nile, and even the Greeks of Cyrenaica, offered their submission to the conqueror, sending him presents and agreeing to become his tributaries. Being lord of Asia, Cambyses now aspired to become also master of Africa. The only two African powers which could offer any serious resistance to his arms after the conquest of Egypt were Ethiopia and Carthage. Ethiopia—the only great power of the South—was at least the equal, and perhaps the superior, of Egypt. Carthage—the great power of the West—was remote and but little known, but had begun to attract attention on account of her rapidly-rising maritime supremacy and her increasing wealth. Cambyses desired to conquer both these powers, and also the oasis of Siwah. As a good Zoroastrian he desired to show the superiority of Ormazd to all the "gods of the nations;" and the temple of Amun on the oasis of Siwah being the most famed of all African shrines, he designed pillaging and destroying this sanctuary. But he was forced to forego his designs against Carthage by the peremptory refusal of the Phœnicians, who furnished his main naval strength, to aid in an attack upon their colonists, with whom they had always maintained friendly relations.

An army of fifty thousand men sent by Cambyses against the oasis of Siwah perished to a man in a simoom amid the sands of the Libyan desert. A larger force led by Cambyses himself against Ethiopia, after marching across the Nubian desert, was forced to return for want of supplies, after a large portion of his troops had perished from famine. The abilities and resources of the Persian king were not equal to his ambition.

Observing symptoms of a disposition to revolt after his return to Egypt, Cambyses, who had hitherto treated the captive Psammenitus with mildness and magnanimity, caused him to be condemned for his part in a conspiracy to recover his lost crown. The native Egyptian officers who had been left in charge of the city of Memphis were also capitally punished for their part in the incipient rebellion. These harsh measures entirely nipped the threatened revolt in the bud, but no reconciliation between the conqueror and the conquered followed. Cambyses being aware that his severity had produced an implacable hatred of Persian rule in the hearts of the Egyptians, and suspecting the people, and especially their leaders, the priests, he resolved upon a departure from his usual policy of clemency and toleration toward his subjects, and sought to bring the Egyptian priesthood and religion into contempt. He therefore stabbed the sacred bull, believed to be the incarnate Apis, ordered the priests to be publicly scourged, put a stop to the Apis festival by making it a capital offense to participate in it, opened the tombs and curiously examined the mummies, intruded himself into the chief sanctuary at Memphis and publicly scoffed at the image of

Phthah, doing the same in the inviolable temple of the Cabeiri, and capped the climax of his insults by ordering the burning of the images. These injuries and indignities produced an implacable hatred of the Persian yoke in the hearts of the Egyptians—a hatred which did not become extinct with the lapse of time, and which manifested itself frequently in rebellion during the two centuries of Persian dominion. But for the time the iron policy of Cambyses was successful; and the Egyptians, with their faith in their gods rudely shaken, their proud spirits humbled and their hopes shattered, then quietly submitted and remained obsequious and sycophantic for an entire generation.

Having completed the subjection of Egypt, Cambyses started on his return to Persia. When he had reached Syria he received the startling intelligence that a revolution had occurred in Persia. A herald suddenly burst into his camp and proclaimed to his entire army that Cambyses, son of Cyrus, had ceased to reign and that all Persian subjects must thereafter pay their allegiance to Smerdis, son of Cyrus. At first Cambyses supposed that the person he employed to put Smerdis to death had deceived him, and that his brother was still living; but the suspected person, who was a nobleman named Prexaspes, succeeded in reassuring him of the death of Smerdis. Prexaspes knew that the pretended Smerdis must be an impostor, and suggested his identity with a certain Magus, whose brother had been assigned by Cambyses the management of his household and the care of his palace. This suggestion was made because of his knowledge of the resemblance which the pretender bore to the murdered Smerdis. Herodotus says that the Magus was really named Smerdis, but this is disproved by the Behistun Inscription, which informs us that his real name was Gomates. Cambyses, in his momentary despondency at the unexpected event, committed suicide, by inflicting upon himself a wound with his own sword, which caused his death in a few days, B. C. 522. This is the account from Herodotus. The Behistun Inscription states that the self-inflicted wound was intentional. Ctesias says that Cambyses died of a wound which he accidentally inflicted upon himself while carving wood for his amusement at Babylon.

Cambyses, although returning from Egypt a substantial conqueror, was discouraged by the fact that his army had become dispirited by its losses and its failures, and could not therefore be depended upon to fight with enthusiasm in his interest against the revolutionists who had dethroned him. The other reasons for the king's suicide may have been his unpopularity on account of his haughty and tyrannical temper, and his disregard for law and custom when they stood in the way of the gratification of his desires. His incestuous marriage with his sister Atossa was utterly repugnant to the religious feelings of the Persian people. Herodotus tells us that Atossa afterwards married the false Smerdis, and still later Darius Hystaspes. We can not, however, accept all the stories told of the crimes of Cambyses, as they mainly come from his enemies, the Egyptians; nor the accounts given by Herodotus of the escape of Cyrus, the murder of the son of Prexaspes, and the execution of twelve noble Persians on a trivial charge in Egypt. Herodotus says that the Persians themselves called Cambyses a "despot," or "master," and considered him "harsh and reckless," in comparing him with Cyrus, whom they considered a "father," because he was mild and beneficent. Cambyses may have doubted whether the many Magians in his army would have fought zealously for the Zoroastrian cause.

Cambyses was brave, active and energetic, like his illustrious father, but he did not possess his father's strategic genius, his discretion, or his fertility in resources. Born to the inheritance of a great empire, he was proud and haughty, regardless of the feelings of others, and impatient of admonition or remonstrance. His pride rendered him obstinate when he had committed an error; and his contempt for others led him at times to harsh and cruel measures, as the execution of his brother Smerdis, his repressive proceedings after the revolt in Egypt, and his orders to his troops to enslave the Ammonians of the oasis of Siwah. Herodotus accuses him of "habitual drunkenness." The "madness of Cambyses" was reported to Herodotus by the Egyptian priests, his inveterate enemies, who desired it to be believed that their gods had thus punished his impiety and sacrilege.

The death of Cambyses, B. C. 522, left the conspirators who had inaugurated the revolution at the capital at liberty to perfect their plans, and to secure themselves and perpetuate their power. The Magi doubtless desired to change the national Persian religion by subverting pure Zoroastrianism, but prudence dictated that they must move with caution and be careful not to offend the zealous and sincere Zoroastrians. To conciliate the people and acquire popularity for the newly-proclaimed king, there was a general remission of tribute and military service for three years—a measure the priests knew would give great satisfaction to all the tribes and nations in the empire outside of Persia proper itself. The Persians being always exempt from tribute, were not affected by this measure, while military service was popular with the dominant nation, for whose glory the conquests had been made.

To further strengthen his tenure of royalty the PSEUDO-SMERDIS married all the widows of Cambyses—a common practice in the East. To prevent the detection of his imposture through the free intercourse of his wives, the usurper isolated them by assigning each wife her own portion of the palace, and allowed no one of his wives to visit the others, nor permitted them to be visited by any of their relatives, thus cutting off all communication between them and the outside world.

The usurping Magus grew bolder with the progress of time, and then began the religious reformation which he and his fellow Magi so much desired. The Behistun Inscription states that he destroyed the Zoroastrian temples in different places and suppressed the Zoroastrian worship with its hymns in praise of Ahura-Mazda. He replaced the old ceremonies with the Magian rites, and constituted his fellow Magi as the priest-caste of Persia. These changes were agreeable to the Medes and other subject nations of the empire, and also to that portion of the Persian people who desired a more material worship and a more gorgeous ceremonial than that of the Zoroastrian system.

In Judæa the religious change gave a fresh impetus to a religious struggle then in progress in that distant province of the empire, and strengthened the side of intolerance. The Jews had been occupied for fifteen or sixteen years in rebuilding the great Temple at Jerusalem, in accordance with the permission granted them by Cyrus the Great. The Samaritans, who disliked their enterprise, had vainly tried to induce Cambyses to stop the work; but they succeeded with the Pseudo-Smerdis, who issued an edict reversing the decree of Cyrus and authorizing the Samaritans to stop the work by force, if necessary. In accordance with this decree, the Samaritan authorities proceeded to Jerusalem, and, in the language of Ezra, "made the Jews to cease by force and power."

Herodotus, whose account of the imposture of the Pseudo-Smerdis is that thus far given, states as the causes leading to the discovery of the imposture the religious changes inaugurated by the usurper, and the seclusion of the king's seraglio and of himself from the rest of mankind, the usurping monarch never leaving the palace nor permitting any of the Persian nobles to enter it. In consequence of this isolation, the previous suspicion developed into a general national belief that the king who occupied the throne was not Smerdis, the son of Cyrus, but a usurper and an impostor. Still there was no outbreak for a time, and no dissatisfaction except in Persia proper and in the north-eastern provinces, where the Zoroastrian faith remained pure and uncorrupted.

Rumors which arose among the chief Persians were sternly repressed at the beginning, and all discontent was for a time smothered by a systematic reign of terror. Finally some of the leading nobles, convinced of the imposture, met in secret council and deliberated upon what action should be taken under the circumstances. The arrival of Darius, the son of Hystaspes, a prince of the blood royal, at the capital, was a signal for the rising which was to hurl the pretender from the throne. Herodotus and the Behistun Inscription both tell us that at the age of twenty he had been suspected by Cyrus the Great of a design to seize the throne. He was now twenty-eight years of age. Upon arriving at the capital, Darius was placed at the head of the plot against the Pseudo-Smerdis. He at once armed his partisans and began the attack. Herodotus and Ctesias tell us that Darius and his adherents entered the palace in a body, and, surprising the Magus in his private apartments, killed him after a short struggle. The two Greek writers differ as to the details of the struggle. Darius himself in the Behistun Inscription gives a different version of the affair. According to this source of information the Magus was not killed in his palace at Susa, or Ecbatana, but was slain with some of his adherents in a struggle with Darius and six Persian nobles of high rank at the small fort of Sictachotes, in "the Nisæan plain," in Media, whither he had fled with a body of his followers.

The victorious conspirators hastened to the capital, carrying with them the head of the dead Magus and displaying it everywhere in evidence of the death of the late impostor, after which they caused a general massacre of the Magian priests, who had abetted the late usurpation. The exasperated Persians poniarded every Magus they could find, and only the approach of night saved the caste from extermination. The carnage ceased when darkness came on. The day was appointed to be observed as a solemn festival, under the name of Magophonia; and a law was made forbidding any Magus to leave his house on that day.

DARIUS HYSTASPES ascended the Persian throne B. C. 521. Herodotus tells us that before his accession, the Seven—Darius and the six nobles—discussed the choice of king and the form of government, but this statement is utterly unworthy of credit. Darius was supported by the other six conspirators, his "faithful men," as they are called in the Behistun Inscription, from the very beginning. While the six acquiesced in Darius's right to the throne, they exacted a guarantee of certain privileges for themselves. The king bound himself to select his wives from among the families of the conspirators only, and sanctioned their claim to have free access to his person at all times without asking his permission. One of them, Otanes, exacted a guaranty that he and his house were to remain "free," and were to receive an annual magnificent *kaftan*, or royal present.

Thus a check was placed upon absolute despotism. A hereditary nobility was acknowledged. The monarch became somewhat dependent upon his grandees. He could not consider himself the sole fountain of honor. The six great nobles stood round the throne as its supports, but they occupied a position so near the king as to detract to some extent from his prestige and dignity.

As soon as he was firmly established on the throne Darius Hystaspes proceeded to restore the old Zoroastrian religion. He rebuilt the Zoroastrian temples which his usurping predecessor had destroyed, and perhaps also restored the old sacred chants and the other Zoroastrian ceremonies. In the Behistun Inscription, Darius exhorts his successors in the strongest terms to put to death all "liars," by whom are meant all apostates from the Zoroastrian faith. His zeal for Zoroastrianism was soon known in the provinces.

The Jews at once resumed the rebuilding of the Temple at Jerusalem; and when the Samaritans sought to induce Darius to stop the work, the only result was an edict confirming the old decree of Cyrus the Great, forbidding the interference of the Samaritans, and granting the Jews more money, cattle, corn, etc., from the royal stores, for the accomplishment of the great enterprise, which was declared to be for the advantage of the king and his house, because when the Temple was finished sacrifices would be offered in it to "the God of Heaven," and prayers would be uttered "for the life of the king and of his sons," as we are told in the Book of Ezra. Thus there was a mutual sympathy between the religion of Zoroaster and the worship of Jehovah.

The reign of Darius Hystaspes was soon disturbed by revolts in different portions of the empire. The governors of Lydia and Egypt rose in rebellion, and insurrection raised its head everywhere, even in the heart of the empire itself. For six long years was Darius employed in reducing province after province to obedience. Susiana, Babylonia, Persia itself, Media, Assyria, Armenia, Hyrcania, Parthia, Margiana, Sagartia and Sacia, all revolted during this period and were successively reduced to submission. From the Behistum Inscription it would appear that religion entered largely as an element into these rebellions, which were in some cases connected with the overthrow of Magism and the restoration of the pure Zoroastrian faith which Darius seemed determined upon effecting. In some parts of his inscription Darius protests against the crime of "lying"—false religion—and not against that of rebellion. The accounts of these rebellions are from the Behistun Inscription.

In Susiana a certain Atrines assumed the title of king, and the people revolted in his favor. About the same time a pretender in Babylon assumed to be the son of the last Babylonian king, Nabonadius, and bore the famous name of Nebuchadnezzar. Darius sent a force to subdue the Susianians, while he himself led an army against the Babylonian pretender. A Babylonian naval force vainly endeavored to prevent Darius from crossing the Tigris, after which Darius defeated the pretender's troops, and advanced toward Babylon and gained a second victory at a small town on the banks of the Euphrates, many of the rebels being drowned in the river, into which they had been driven. The pretender, Nebuchadnezzar, escaped with a few horsemen and took refuge in Babylon, which was soon taken, the pretender himself being made prisoner and executed.

In the meantime Atrines, the original leader of the rebellion in Susiana, had been taken prisoner by the troops sent against him, and, being brought before Darius while he was on his march against Babylon, was put to death. But a new leader named Martes, who was a Persian, appeared in Susiana and assumed a name connecting him with the old Susianian kings. On the approach of Darius, after he had suppressed the Babylonian revolt, the revolted Susianians, in great alarm, submitted and put the pretender to death, hoping thus to propitiate their sovereign.

A far more formidable and important rebellion was that of Media, Armenia and Assyria, which three provinces revolted in concert. A Median pretender, who called himself Xathrites and claimed descent from Cyaxares, was acknowledged by the revolted countries as their king. Darius, settling himself in Babylon, sent his generals against the rebels to test their strength. Hydarnes, one of the Seven conspirators, was sent into Media with an army; while Dadarses, an Armenian, was dispatched into Armenia; and Vomises, a Persian, was ordered to march through Assyria into Armenia also. These three generals were encountered by the pretender's forces, and several indecisive battles were fought. Hyrcania and Parthia soon revolted and acknowledged Xathrites as their king. Darius thereupon left Babylon and took the field against the insurgents himself, marched into Media, defeated the pretender at Kûdrûs, and entered Ecbatana in triumph. The Median pretender, becoming a fugitive and an outcast, fled towards the East, but was overtaken in the district of Rhages and made a prisoner by the troops of Darius. The king cut off the captive pretender's nose, ears and tongue, and then kept him for some time chained to the door of his palace, so that his capture would not be doubted, after which he caused him to be crucified in his capital, Ecbatana, in the presence of those who had beheld his former glory.

The great Median rebellion was thus crushed in its original seat; but it remained to be put down in the countries to which it had extended—Parthia and Hyrcania—which still resisted their former governor, Hystaspes, the father of Darius. The king marched as far as Rhages to his father's aid, and thence sent a body of troops to reinforce him. With this assistance, Hystaspes won so great a victory over the rebels that they at once submitted, and the rebellion was at an end.

In the meantime a revolt had broken out in Sagartia, where a native chief claimed to rule as a descendant and heir of Cyaxares, and was recognized by the Sagartians as their king; but Darius easily suppressed this revolt by means of an army of Medes and Persians, who were commanded by a Median leader named Tachamaspates. The pretender was captured, and, like the Median pretender, had his nose and ears cut off, and, after being chained for a while at the palace door, was finally crucified at Arbela.

A feeble revolt also occurred in Margiana about this time, the Margians acknowledging a native named Phraätes as their king; but the satrap of Bactriana, whose jurisdiction extended over Margiana, quelled this revolt in its incipiency.

Thus far Darius had contended with the rebellions of foreign and alien nations which had been brought under the Persian dominion by the great Cyrus. But now, in his absence in the north-eastern provinces of his empire, Persia itself rose in revolt against his authority and acknowledged for their king an impostor, who, unwarned by the fate of the former impostor, the Pseudo-Smerdis, and relying upon the obscurity still overhanging the disappearance of the real Smerdis, assumed his name and claimed to be the legitimate heir to the throne. But Darius, with his army of Medes and Persians, reëstablished his authority, after a struggle of some duration. Artabardes, one of his generals, defeated the impostor in two engagements; and the force which he had sent to excite rebellion in Arachosia was routed by the satrap of that province. The pretended Smerdis himself was captured and crucified.

In the meantime Babylon had again revolted. An Armenian named Aracus, settled in Babylonia, headed this insurrection and called himself "Nebuchadnezzar, son of Nabonadius." Darius sent a Median general named Intaphres with an army against the new pretender. Intaphres soon crushed the revolt, capturing Babylon and taking Aracus prisoner. This rebel pretender was also crucified.

The Medo-Persian Empire now enjoyed a season of tranquillity, and Darius proceeded to chastise the governors of the more remote provinces for their acts savoring of rebellion. Orœtes, the governor of Sardis, had not been fully loyal even under Cambyses, as he had endeavored to entrap and put to death one of that king's allies, Polycrates of Samos, and had assumed a disloyal attitude from the time of the Magian revolution. He quarreled with Mitrobates, the governor of a neighboring province, murdered him, and seized his territory. A courier who had been sent by Darius with a message which Orœtes did not like was waylaid and murdered by assassins sent by the disloyal governor. Darius could not overlook such disloyalty; and one of his nobles, armed with written orders bearing the king's seal, tested the guards kept about the satrap's person; and upon finding them ready to obey the king's commands, he presented an order for the governor's execution, which they carried into effect at once.

Aryandes, the governor of Egypt, had also assumed a disloyal attitude in a different way. When he learned that Darius had issued a gold coinage of remarkable purity, he issued a silver coinage of similar character, on his own authority and without consulting the king. It is believed that he even put his name on these silver coins—an act which implied a claim to independent sovereignty. Darius had him put to death on the charge of a design to revolt, although he had excited no disturbance.

According to Herodotus this affair occurred in the latter part of Darius's reign.

But the empire was not yet fully tranquilized. The Behistun Inscription records a revolt in Susiana, suppressed by Gobryas, one of the Seven; and another among the Sacæ of the Tigris, quelled by Darius himself. The erection of the Behistun Inscription appears to have occurred about B. C. 516-515—that is about the fifth or sixth year of Darius's reign; and marks the close of the first period of his reign, or the period of disturbance, and the beginning of the second period, or the period of tranquillity, internal progress, and patronage of the fine arts by the king.

Having had so much trouble in restoring tranquillity to his empire by the reduction of so many revolts, Darius naturally considered plans for the prevention of similar occurrences in the future. The past revolts showed him the weakness of the ties hitherto regarded as sufficient to bind the component parts of the empire together, and how easily any obstacle might tend to the disruption of the greatest empire. All the great empires which had existed in Western Asia during the seven centuries previous to the Medo-Persian had more or less been subject to the inherent weakness of chronic rebellion, and no remedy had yet been found to avert these frequent perils. Darius Hystaspes was the first who designed and carried into execution an entirely new system of government. Thirlwall deservedly styled him "the first true founder of the Persian state." He found the Medo-Persian Empire a conglomerate mass of heterogeneous elements, held together loosely by the solitary tie of subjection to a general head; he left it a compact, consolidated and well-organized body, bound together by the bonds of a well-regulated, compact and homogeneous system, permanently established in every province. Thus Darius Hystaspes established the first *real* empire in all history.

To establish a uniform system of governing his vast dominions, Darius divided his empire into twenty provinces, called *satrapies*, the governors of which were styled *satraps*. To perfect this uniformity, he substituted fixed and definite burthens, instead of variable and uncertain calls, and established a variety of checks and counterpoises among the officials to whom the king delegated his powers; thus tending vastly to the security of the monarch and to the stability of the empire.

Uniformity was secured by establishing the same machinery of administration in all portions of the empire, and not by abolishing all national differences, or assimilating all the various nations of the empire to one type. The nations were permitted, and even encouraged, to retain their respective languages, customs, manners, religion, laws and modes of local government. Care was only taken to subordinate all these to the supreme power of the empire, which was one and the same over all the provinces, which were dependent upon the imperial government.

Herodotus tells us that the number of satrapies into which Darius divided his empire was twenty, but the number may have varied at different times. The satrap, or supreme civil governor, of each of these political divisions, was entrusted with the collection and transmission of the revenue, the administration of justice, the preservation of order, and the general supervision of the affairs of the satrapy. Thucydides and Xenophon tell us that the satraps were appointed or dismissed by the king at his pleasure and held their offices for no definite period, being subject to removal or death at any moment, simply on the presentation of the royal *firman*, without any other formality. These satraps, as representatives of the Great King, were despotic, being vested with a portion of his majesty. Xenophon and Herodotus tell us that they had palaces, courts, body-guards, parks or "paradises," large numbers of eunuchs and attendants, and seraglios, or harems, well supplied with wives and concubines. Xenophon says that they exercised the power of life and death over those under their jurisdiction, and that they assessed the tribute on the towns and villages in their respective satrapies at their pleasure, and appointed deputies, also sometimes called satraps, over cities or districts within their respective provinces. They exacted from the provincials whatever amount they considered them capable of furnishing above the tribute due to the crown for the support of royal and satrapial courts. Favors and justice were purchased from them by gifts. They sometimes committed flagrant outrages on the persons and honor of those whom they governed. Fear of removal or execution, if complaint reached the Great King, was generally the only restraint upon their tyranny.

The empire also had a uniform military system. The services of the subject nations were declined, except in a few instances, in which, according to Herodotus and Arrian, a levy *en masse* of the subject populations was ordered. Order was maintained by numerous large garrisons of Median and Persian troops quartered on the inhabitants. All strong places were thus occupied; and the great capitals, which were likely to be centers of disaffection, were specially watched. Thus a large standing army, composed of the conquering and governing race, guarded the peace of the empire throughout, and rendered a native revolt hopeless, under ordinary circumstances.

Sometimes exceptions were made to the general uniformity of the civil administration, and occasionally it was considered wise to permit a native dynasty to rule in a province, the satrap sharing a divided authority with the native prince, as Herodotus informs us was the case in Cilicia, and may have been so in Paphlagonia and Phœnicia. Sometimes also tribes within the limits of a satrapy were recognized as independent, and Xenophon tells us that petty wars were carried on between these hordes and their neighbors. Bands of robbers infested the mountains in many places, owning no allegiance to any one, and defying both the satrap and the standing army.

Persia proper occupied an exceptional position. It paid no tribute and was not counted as a satrapy; but the inhabitants were obliged to bring gifts, according to their means, to the king, whenever he passed through their country. Nicolas of Damascus says that the king was bound, whenever he visited Pasargadæ, to present to each Persian woman appearing before him a sum equal to twenty Attic drachmas, equal to about five dollars of our money. This custom was designed to commemorate the service rendered by the female sex in the battle in which Cyrus the Great repulsed the forces of Astyages.

The new arrangement of the revenue inaugurated by Darius Hystaspes aimed at the substitution of definite burdens instead of variable and uncertain charges. The amount of tribute was everywhere fixed in money and in kind, which each satrap was required to furnish to the crown. A specified payment in money, varying, in ordinary satrapies, from 170 to 1,000 Babylonian silver talents, or from forty-two thousand pounds to a quarter of a million sterling, and amounting in the case of the Indian satrapy to over a million sterling, was required yearly by the sovereign and had to be remitted by the satrap to the capital. Each satrapy was also required to furnish such commodity, or commodities, for which it was most noted. Herodotus says that Assyria and Babylonia paid one-third of this burden. He also says that Egypt was required to supply grain sufficient for the nourishment of one hundred and twenty thousand Persian troops quartered in the country. Media had to contribute one hundred thousand sheep, four thousand mules and three thousand horses. Cappadocia had to furnish half that number of sheep, mules and horses. Strabo says that Armenia furnished twenty thousand colts. Herodotus says that Cilicia gave three hundred and sixty white horses, and one hundred and forty talents in money (equal to thirty-five thousand pounds sterling), in place of further tribute in kind. He also states that Babylonia was required to furnish five hundred boy eunuchs, besides corn. These charges were all fixed by the crown, and the chief object of the system was to tax each province in proportion to its wealth and resources.

The satrap was vested with the power of assessing the taxation of different portions of his province. The mode of exaction and collection in some places, according to Herodotus, was by land-tax. Herodotus informs us that Persian subjects in many portions of the empire had to pay a water rate. The rivers of the empire were considered the king's property; and when water was needed for irrigation, a government official superintended the opening of the sluices, and regulated the quantity of water which might be drawn off by each tribe or district. A large sum of money was paid the officer for opening the sluices, and this sum was transmitted to the imperial treasury. Herodotus also says that fisheries, salt-works, mines and quarries were regarded as crown property and contributed largely to the revenue. They were rented to responsible individuals, who paid a certain fixed rate and made what profit was possible by the transaction.

While the amounts of taxation and tribute exacted by the crown were fixed and definite, the satraps were allowed to make what exactions they desired beyond them. Like a Roman proconsul, a Persian satrap was to pay himself out of the pockets of those under his jurisdiction, and he was usually careful to pay himself very well. One satrap of Babylonia drew from his province yearly in money a sum equal to one hundred thousand pounds sterling.

To check the rapacity or greed of the officials, Darius established in each province three officers holding their authority directly from the crown, and responsible to it only. These were the satrap, the military commandant, and the secretary. The satrap was vested with the civil administration, and particularly with the finances. The commandant had charge of the troops. The secretary informed the court, by dispatches, of occurrences in the province; and Xenophon tells us that he was called the "King's Eye" and the "King's Ear." These three officials acted as checks and counterpoises upon each other, and rebellion was thus made extremely difficult and hazardous.

Xenophon states that, as a further precaution against revolt, an officer, commissioned by the crown, inspected each province yearly, or at stated intervals. These inspectors were generally of royal rank, sons or brothers of the sovereign. They were accompanied by an armed force, and were authorized to correct anything amiss in the province, and, if necessary, to inform the crown of any official insubordination or incompetency.

Herodotus informs us that to still further secure the fidelity of satraps and commandants, these officials were chosen from among the monarch's blood relations, or were attached to the crown by marriage with one of the princesses. This policy was extensively pursued by Darius and yielded excellent results.

The system of checks, while it was a security against revolt, had the corresponding disadvantage of weakening the hands of authority in times of danger and difficulty. When internal or external dangers menaced the empire the powers of government were weakened by division, the civil authority being vested in one officer, and the military in another. Thus the concentration of power necessary for quick and decisive action, for unity of purpose, and for secrecy of plan and execution, was wanting. These considerations led to a modification of the original plan of satrapial government; and thus the offices of satrap, or civil administrator, and commandant, or commander of the troops, were vested in the same individual, who thus had as much power as have the Turkish pashas and the modern Persian khans, or beys—an authority virtually unlimited. This system was an advantage in the defense of the provinces against foreign foes, but it endangered the stability of the empire, as it naturally led to formidable rebellions.

Herodotus and Xenophon give us full accounts of the system of posts, instituted by Darius Hystaspes for rapidity of communication. Darius considered it of the utmost importance that the orders of the court should be speedily transmitted to the satraps, and that their reports and those of their royal secretaries should be received without unnecessary delay. He established on the routes already in existence between the leading cities of the empire a number of post-houses at regular intervals, in accordance with the distance that it was estimated that a horse could gallop at his best speed without stopping. A number of couriers and several relays of horses were maintained at each post-house at the expense of the government. When a dispatch was to be sent it was carried to the nearest post-house along the route, where it was taken by a courier, who immediately mounted on horseback and galloped with it to the next station. There it was handed to a new courier, who at once mounted a fresh horse and took it to the next station, and thus it was transmitted from hand to hand until it arrived at its destination. Xenophon states that the messengers traveled by night as well as by day, and that the conveyance was so rapid that it was often compared to the flight of birds. Herodotus says that at every station were excellent inns or caravanseries, that bridges or ferries were established upon all the streams, that guard-houses were found here and there, and that the whole route was securely protected against brigands who infested the empire. Ordinary travelers followed so convenient a route, but they were not allowed the use of post-horses, even when the government did not need them.

Herodotus also describes the system of coinage adopted by Darius Hystaspes. It is believed by some that the term *daric* is derived from his name. It is certain that he was the first Persian monarch who coined on a large scale, and it is likewise certain that his gold coinage was considered in later times as of extraordinary value because of its purity. His gold darics seem to have contained, on an average, little less than one hundred and twenty-four grains of pure metal, which would be equal to twenty-two shillings of English money. They were of the type then common in Lycia and Greece, being fluted, flattened lumps of metal, very thick compared with the size of their surface, irregular and rudely stamped. The silver darics were similar in general character, but were larger than the gold, and weighed from two hundred and twenty-four to two hundred and thirty grains, or little less than three shillings of English money.

We will now proceed with the events of the second period of the reign of Darius Hystaspes, for which we are mainly dependent upon Herodotus, but for which we have also some notices from Xenophon, Thucydides and Ctesias. The political history of an Oriental monarchy must always necessarily consist chiefly of a series of biographies, as the sovereign is all in all in those countries, his sayings, doings and character shaping and constituting the annals of the state.

In the second period of his reign, that of the era of internal tranquillity, Darius Hystaspes pursued chiefly the arts of peace, and, as we have seen, consolidated and secured his empire by inaugurating the satrapial government in all its provinces, by establishing a system of posts, by issuing his coinage, by supervising the administration of justice, and in various other ways in which he displayed a love of order and method and a genius for systematic arrangement. He also devoted some attention to ornamental and architectural works, to sculpture and to literature. He founded the royal library at Susa, the chief residence of the later Persian monarchs. He erected a very important edifice at Persepolis; and he certainly designed, if he did not execute, the *Chehl Minar*, the principal one of the splendid structures upon the great central platform. The great platform itself, with its grand and stately steps, was erected by him, as his name is inscribed upon it. The immense blocks of hard material attest the solidity and strength of his works. He was the first Persian king to ornament the steps approaching a palace with elaborate bas-reliefs. He designed and constructed the rock-tomb at Nakhsh-i-Rustam, where his remains were interred. The great rock-inscription at Behistun was his immortal work. He surpassed all his predecessors and all his successors in attention to the creation of permanent historical records. The Behistun Inscription is unparalleled in ancient times for its length, finish and delicacy of execution, at least outside of Egypt or Assyria. Darius also set up the only really historical inscription at Perscepolis. He was one of the only two Persian kings who placed inscriptions upon their tombs. He alone gives the historian interesting geographical and historical notices.

During this epoch of general peace, extending from B. C. 516 to B. C. 508 or 507, Darius undertook one important expedition towards the East, in the region of the Upper Indus, famed for its fertility, its gold and its ingenious but warlike people. After exploring the course of the Indus from Attock by means of boats, he led or sent an expedition into the Punjab, which speedily conquered that rich region and probably the entire Indus valley, thus adding to the empire a brave and warlike race, an immense revenue, and a vast gold-producing district, which suddenly sent a large influx of the precious metal into Persia, thus probably leading to the introduction of the gold coinage and the establishment of commercial relations with the natives, which inaugurated a regular trade conducted by coasting-vessels between the mouths of the Indus and the Persian Gulf.

For the history of all these great expeditions of Darius we are also mainly indebted to Herodotus. The next great expedition was led by Darius across the Hellespont (now Dardanelles), the narrow strait which partly separates Asia Minor from Europe. The story of the voyage and escape of Democedes, as related by Herodotus and partially confirmed from other sources, was not a mere myth. If a vessel was fitted out at Sidon by order of the Persian king, and placed under the guidance of Democedes to explore the coasts of Greece, and if it proceeded as far as Crotona, in Magna Græcia, we may infer that Darius Hystaspes already meditates the conquest of Greece. But for the time the king's attention was directed to another quarter; and in order to secure Western Asia from attack, Darius resolved to strike terror into the barbarian Scythian hordes of the steppe region of the present Southern Russia. He therefore ordered Ariaramnes, satrap of Cappadocia, to cross the Euxine with a small fleet, descend suddenly upon the Scythian coast, and carry off a number of captives. Ariaramnes skillfully executed his commission, and captured a Scythian chief's brother, from whom the Persian king derived all the information he wanted. Darius then collected a fleet of six hundred ships, mainly from the Greeks of Asia Minor, and an army, consisting of seven hundred thousand men according to Herodotus, and eight hundred thousand according to Ctesias, composed of contingents from all the nations under his dominion. With this army he crossed the Bosphorus on a bridge of boats constructed by Mandrocles of Samos, and marched through Thrace along the line of the Little Balkan, receiving the submission of the tribes along the route; crossed the Great Balkan; conquered the Getæ, who occupied the region between the Balkans and the Danube; crossed the Danube by means of a bridge, which the Ionian Greeks had made with their vessels just above the apex of the Delta, and thus invaded Scythia. The Scythians retired as the Medo-Persian army advanced, and destroyed the forage, drove off the cattle, and filled in the wells, so that the invaders would be forced to retire for want of the means of subsistence. But the admirable condition of the Persian commissariat enabled Darius to remain in Scythia for two months without incurring much loss. Herodotus tells us that Darius marched eastward to the Tanais (now Don) river, and thence north to the country of the Budini, where he burnt the town of Gelonus, probably near the present Voronej. He returned with the bulk of his army, leaving the impress of his name and power upon the Scythian hordes. Ctesias states that Darius lost eighty thousand men in this inroad. Vain efforts had been made to induce the Greeks guarding the bridge over the Danube to break it, and thus hinder his return. Darius recrossed the river after an interval of more than two months, and thenceforth enumerated "the Scyths beyond the sea" among the subject nations of his vast empire. He was unopposed on his return march through Thrace. Before crossing the Bosphorus he commissioned Megabazus, one of his generals, to complete the conquest of Thrace, assigning him eighty thousand men for this purpose. These remained in Europe, while Darius with the remainder of his army passed over into Asia. In one campaign, B. C. 506, Megabazus overran and subjugated the whole region between the Propontis (now Sea of Marmora) and the Strymon river, thus extending the Medo-Persian dominion westward to the frontier of Macedonia. He conquered the Greek colonies in that section, the Thracians and a number of other tribes. One of these tribes, the Pæonians, was transported into Asia. The Thracian tribes who submitted were those of the coast, no effort being made to subdue those of the interior.

At this time an ancestor of Alexander the Great occupied the throne of Macedon. With a contempt for the insignificance of this kingdom, Megabazus sent an embassy demanding earth and water as tokens of submission, according to the Persian custom. Amyntas yielded at once to the Persian demand; but the insolence of the Persian ambassadors caused them to be assassinated with their entire retinue. When a second embassy was sent to inquire into the fate of the first, Alexander, the son of Amyntas, who had planned the massacre, managed to have the matter kept silent by bribing one of the envoys with a large sum of money and with the hand of his sister, Gygæa. Macedonia became a subject kingdom and accepted the suzerainty of the Medo-Persian monarch.

After the conquest of Macedonia, Megabazus proceeded to Sardis, where Darius had remained for about a year. He was superseded by Otanes, the son of Sisamnes —not the conspirator of that name—who reduced the Greek cities of Byzantium (now Constantinople), Chalcedon, Antandrus and Lamponium, with the two neighboring islands of Lemnos and Imbrus. The inhabitants of these cities were accused of having failed to furnish contingents for the expedition into Scythia, or of molesting it on its return, which were crimes deserving enslavement, in the estimation of Otanes.

Darius then proceeded to Susa, his capital, where he had built the great palace whose remains have been recently uncovered by English enterprise. Susa was thereafter the chief capital of the Medo-Persian Empire. It had a softer climate than that of Ecbatana and Persepolis, and less sultry than that of Babylon. It occupied a central point for communication with the East and the West. Its people were more yielding and submissive than either the Medes or the Persians. The king gladly rested for awhile from the fatigues of his warlike efforts, and recruited himself at Susa in the quiet life of the court. For some years he conceived no aggressive projects, until his designs upon Greece were revived by an extraordinary provocation.

Simultaneously with the expedition into Scythia, Aryandes, the satrap of Egypt, marched against the Greek town of Barca, in Cyrenaica, to avenge the murder of a king who was a tributary of Persia. Barca was taken and its inhabitants were transported to Asia, but the satrap's army was attacked on its return by the semi-independent nomad tribes and suffered considerable loss.

From this time forth the history of the Medo-Persian Empire is closely connected with that of Greece. We therefore confine ourselves to a mere sketch of the remaining portion of Medo-Persian history, and give a full account of the Græco-Persian wars and the conquest of the Medo-Persian Empire by Alexander the Great in that portion of this volume relating to the history of Greece, to which these great events more properly belong.

The Greeks of Asia Minor, exasperated at the support which Darius Hystaspes gave their tyrants, and probably made sensible of their power by the circumstances attending the Scythian campaign, rose in rebellion against the Persian power at the instigation of Miletus, the most important of Asiatic Greek cities, murdered or expelled their tyrants, and set the power of Persia at defiance. Two states of European Greece—Athens and Eretria—aided the rebels. Bold action was taken. Sardis, the capital of the satrapy of Western Asia Minor, was taken and burned. The rebel invaders were driven into retreat, overtaken and defeated in the battle of Ephesus, whereupon the Athenians and Eretrians deserted their Asiatic kinsmen. But many Greek states of Europe and Asia, encouraged by the fall of Sardis, declared their independence; and the rebellion spread like lightning along the whole coast of Asia Minor from the Sea of Marmora to the Gulf of Issus. The Ionian, Dorian and Hellespontine Greeks, the Carians and Caunians of the south-western corner of Asia Minor, and the Cyprians, Greek and native, rose simultaneously in revolt; but after several battles with various results, Persia triumphed and the insurrection was quelled. The confederate fleet was defeated in the battle of Ladé, and Miletus was taken soon afterwards. The rebellious states were severely punished, and the authority of the Great King was again firmly established in all the revolted countries.

The Persian monarch prepared to take vengeance on the European Greeks for the aid given their revolted Asiatic brethren, his own rebellious subjects. But aside from this a Medo-Persian expedition against Greece was only a question of time, as Darius had never relinquished his ambitious designs against the land of the Hellenes. An expedition was therefore set on foot in B. C. 493, under Mardonius, which followed the coast-line through Thrace and Macedonia. A storm at Mount Athos shattered the Medo-Persian fleet, and the land-force was crippled by a night attack of the Brygi. Mardonius therefore abandoned his enterprise and returned to Asia. His fleet, however, reduced Thasos; and his army reduced the Macedonians to complete subjection to Persia.

Two years after the failure of Mardonius a second great Medo-Persian expedition was led against Greece. This expedition, conducted by Datis, proceeded by sea, crossing the Ægean by way of the Cyclades, and fell upon Eretria, which was besieged and taken by treachery. A landing was made upon the Greek continent at Marathon, in Attica; but the decisive defeat of the great Medo-Persian host by the Athenians under Miltiades in the ever-memorable battle of Marathon, B. C. 490, compelled the invaders to return to Asia. This was the first great check received by the Medo-Persians, and showed how completely powerless were the huge masses of an Oriental army against Grecian valor and discipline. The entire history of the struggle between Greece and Persia is only a repetition of this early lesson.

Undaunted by his two signal failures against Greece, Darius began to prepare for a third attack, but his designs were cut short by his death, B. C. 486. Darius Hystaspes was, next to Cyrus the Great, the greatest of the Persian kings, and he was far the superior of Cyrus as a statesman. Cyrus founded the Medo-Persian Empire; Darius consolidated it. Though inferior to Cyrus as a military leader, he displayed energy, vigor, foresight and judicious management in his military expeditions. He also showed promptness in resolving and ability in executing, also discrimination in the selection of generals, and a power of combination rarely seen in Oriental commanders. He was individually brave, and ready to expose himself to dangers and hardships, though he did not recklessly throw himself into peril. He was satisfied to employ generals when the object to be achieved appeared to be beyond his capacity, and he was not envious of their military successes. He was kind and warm-hearted—strongly attached to his friends, and magnanimous toward conquered foes. He could be severe when occasion required it, but he was disposed to be mild and indulgent. He surpassed all the other Persian monarchs in the arts of peace. To him only was the Medo-Persian Empire indebted for its organization. He was a skillful executive, a good financier, and a wise and far-sighted ruler. He was the only many-sided one of all the Persian princes. He was at the same time an organizer, a general, a statesman, an executive, an architect, a patron of art and literature. Had he never reigned Persia would have sunk as rapidly as she arose, and would have had as brief an existence as many of the other short-lived powers of the East.

Darius Hystaspes was succeeded on the Medo-Persian throne by his eldest son, XERXES, the son of his favorite wife, Atossa, and therefore a direct descendant of Cyrus the Great. In the second year of his reign, B. C. 485, Xerxes crushed the revolt in Egypt and punished the Egyptians with increased burdens. Ctesias tells us that he then provoked a rebellion of the Babylonians by acts regarded by them as impious, and which they avenged by killing their satrap, Zopyrus, and declaring their independence. Megabyzus, the son of Zopyrus, reconquered the revolted city, whose famous temple was plundered and ruined and many of whose shrines were desolated in punishment for the revolt.

Xerxes next directed his attention to the conquest of Greece. After careful preparations for four years, from B. C. 484 to B. C. 481, he set out for the invasion of Greece at the head of an immense host, said to number two millions of fighting men. A part of the expedition consisted of a large and well-equipped fleet. The expedition marched in three columns along the coast, B. C. 480, and the passage of the Hellespont was made on a double bridge of boats. There was a grand review at Doriscus, and the advance through Thessaly was unopposed. The Persian fleet passed through the canal of Athos, and two hundred ships were lost in a storm off Cape Sepias. The Persian land-forces were repulsed in attempting to force the narrow pass of Thermopylæ, but the pass was finally flanked and its handful of heroic defenders. under the Spartan king Leonidas, were slain. At the same time there was an indecisive sea-fight off Artemisium. Two hundred Persian ships were lost off the coast of Eubœa. The invaders advanced through Phocis and Bœotia, and failed in an attack on Delphi. They then advanced into Attica, and took and burned Athens, causing general alarm throughout Greece. In the great sea-fight of Salamis the Medo-Persian fleet was destroyed, whereupon Xerxes fled from Greece, B. C. 480. A Medo-Persian army under Mardonius wintered in Thessaly, and reoccupied Attica the next spring, but was annihilated by the Greeks in the great battle of Platæa, B. C. 479, while the Medo-Persian fleet was broken up in the sea-fight off Mycalé, in Asia Minor, the protecting land force being defeated and the ships burned. The Persians then abandoned European Greece and never renewed their projects for its conquest.

The Greeks now retaliated on their fallen foe. They delivered the isles of the Ægean sea from the Persian yoke, expelled the Persian garrisons from Europe, and ravaged the coast of Asia Minor, making descents upon it at will. For twelve years no Medo-Persian fleet ventured to contest with them for the mastery of the seas, and a Persian land and naval force collected for the protection of Cilicia and Cyprus was thoroughly annihilated at the river Eurymedon, in Asia Minor, by the Greeks commanded by the Athenian Cimon, B. C. 466.

In the year after the battle of Eurymedon, B. C. 465, the reign of Xerxes came to an abrupt end. With him began those internal disorders of the seraglio which made the court a constant scene of intrigues, assassinations, executions and conspiracies for a period of a century and a half. Xerxes had only one wife, Amestris, whom Herodotus calls the daughter, and Ctesias, the granddaughter, of Otanes, one of the Seven conspirators. He surrendered himself to the free indulgence of illicit passion among the princesses of the court, the wives of his near relations. The most horrible consequences resulted. The jealous spite of

Amestris was vented on such as she blamed for alienating from her her husband's affections. Her barbarities threatened to drive those whom she provoked into rebellion, and it was found necessary to execute them in order to preserve tranquillity. Among those executed, Herodotus tells us, were Masistes, a brother of Xerxes, and some of his sons, nephews of Xerxes. The king's example was followed by members of the royal family; and Amytis, a daughter of Xerxes and also wife of Megabyzus, the grandson of Megabyzus, one of the Seven conspirators, became notorious for her licentiousness. Eunuchs advanced to power and incited the disorders which distracted the court. The king created for himself deadly enemies among his courtiers and guards. Finally Artabanus, captain of the guard, a courtier of high rank, and Aspamitres, a eunuch, the king's chamberlain, conspired against their sovereign and assassinated him in his sleeping apartment, after he had reigned twenty years (B. C. 486-465). For the account of this court tragedy we are indebted to Plutarch and Diodorus Siculus.

The character of Xerxes was below that of any of his predecessors. Herodotus ascribes him the virtue of a kind of magnanimity, which induced him to bear patiently such as opposed his views or gave him disagreeable advice, and which deterred him from reeking vengeance under some circumstances. He was devoid of any other commendable traits. He was weak and easily controlled, and utterly surrendered himself to his gusts of passion. He was selfish, fickle, boastful, cruel, superstitious, licentious. We see in him the Oriental despot in that contemptible aspect in which the mental and moral qualities are alike defective, and in which the entire reign is a constant course of vice and folly. The decline of the Medo-Persian Empire in territorial greatness and military strength, and its decay of administrative vigor and national spirit, commenced with the reign of Xerxes. The corruption of the court—the evil which weakens and destroys almost all Oriental dynasties—also began in his reign. His expeditions against Greece exhausted and depopulated the empire, and the losses incurred in those expeditions were not repaired in his lifetime.

Xerxes displayed grandeur of conception as an architect. His Propylæa and the sculptured staircase in front of the Chehl Minar are splendid erections upon the platform of Persepolis, and rank him high among Oriental builders.

The three sons left by Xerxes were Darius, Hystaspes and Artaxerxes. His two daughters were Amytis and Rhodoguné. Hystaspes was satrap of Bactria, and Darius and Artaxerxes were only at court at the time of their father's assassination. Fearing the eldest son most, Artabanus persuaded Artaxerxes that Xerxes was murdered by his brother; whereupon Artaxerxes caused Darius to be put to death and himself seized the throne, B. C. 465, according to Ctesias and Diodorus Siculus.

ARTAXERXES LONGIMANUS—"the Longhanded"—was no sooner seated upon the throne than Artabanus aimed at removing the young monarch and making himself king; but his designs being betrayed to Artaxerxes by Megabyzus, and his previous crimes being exposed, he was killed along with his instrument, Aspamitres, seven months after the assassination of Xerxes. The sons of Artabanus, seeking to avenge their father's death, were defeated and slain in battle by the royal army under Megabyzus. Ctesias is our best authority for the events of this reign, as he was the court physician of Artaxerxes Mnemon.

In the meantime Hystaspes unfurled the standard of rebellion in Bactria, considering himself the rightful successor of his father. Artaxerxes himself took the field against his rebel brother; and, after an indecisive engagement, defeated him in a second battle, in which, according to Ctesias, the wind blew with violence into the faces of the Bactrians. So decisive was the victory of Artaxerxes that the Bactrian revolt was quelled. The fate of Hystaspes is not known.

Soon afterward Egypt suddenly asserted

her independence, B. C. 460. Inarus, a Libyan king, headed a revolt against the Persian rule, and was aided by Amyrtæus, an Egyptian. In the battle of Papremis, in the Delta, the Persians were defeated, and their commander, Achæmenes, was killed by Inarus himself. The revolt now became general throughout Egypt, and the remnant of the Persian army was shut up in Memphis. Athens responded to the request of Inarus for help by sending a fleet of two hundred ships to his aid. This fleet sailed up the Nile, defeated a Persian squadron, and assisted in the capture of Memphis and the siege of its citadel (White Castle). Herodotus, Ctesias, Thucydides and Diodorus are our authorities for the events of this Egyptian revolt. A large Persian army under Megabyzus entered Egypt, defeated the Egyptians and their Athenian allies in a great battle, relieved the citadel of Memphis from its siege, and recovered the city. The defeated Athenians fled to the tract called the Prosôpitis, in the Delta, where they were besieged for a year and a half, until Megabyzus turned the water from one of the streams, whereby the Athenian ships were stranded, when the Persians marched across the river bed and overwhelmed the Athenians with their superior numbers. Inarus was betrayed to Megabyzus by his own men, carried a captive to Persia and there crucified. Amyrtæus escaped to the fens, where he maintained his independence for some time, but the remainder of Egypt was reduced to submission to Persian sway (B. C. 455); while Athens was taught a severe lesson for her interference between the Great King and his revolted subjects.

Six years later B. C. 449, Athens, bent on recovering her lost prestige, sent a fleet of two hundred ships under Cimon to the Levant. This fleet sailed to Cyprus and besieged Citium. Cimon died there, but his fleet attacked and utterly defeated a Persian fleet of three hundred ships off Salamis, and sent sixty ships to aid Amyrtæus, who still maintained himself in the Delta. The King of Persia, fearing the loss of Cyprus and Egypt, sued for peace, and agreed to the inglorious " Peace of Callias," whereby the independence of the Asiatic Greeks was acknowledged, and Persia stipulated not to send any fleet or army to the coasts of Western Asia Minor, while Athens promised to relinquish Cyprus and recall her squadron from Egypt. The Peace of Callias ended the first great war between Persia and Greece after lasting exactly half a century, from B. C. 499 to B. C. 449.

Soon afterward Megabyzus, the satrap of Syria, offended at the crucifixion of Inarus, contrary to the pledge he had himself given to him, rose in revolt against his sovereign, defeated every army sent against him, and so alarmed Artaxerxes that he was permitted to dictate the conditions on which he would return to his allegiance. This example of a successful rebellion on the part of a satrap naturally had the most disastrous consequences for the stability of the empire. The prestige of the imperial government was shaken, and satraps were permitted to defy the authority of their sovereign whenever a fair opportunity presented itself, because, if successful, they had nothing to fear, and might expect pardon in any case.

Though Plutarch and Diodorus commended the character of Artaxerxes Longimanus, he was on the whole a weak and contemptible prince. He was mild and possessed several other good qualities, but the weakness of his character led to a rapid decline of the empire during his reign. The disorders of the court continued; and Artaxerxes allowed his mother Amestris and his sister Amytis, who was the wife of Megabyzus, to indulge without hindrance their cruel and licentious dispositions.

Like his father, Artaxerxes Longimanus had only one legitimate wife. All that is known of this woman, whose name was Damaspia, is that she died on the same day as her husband, and that she was the mother of his only legitimate son, Xerxes. Artaxerxes had seventeen other sons with various concubines, mostly Babylonians. All these sons survived their father. Ctesias is the authority for the facts concerning the domestic relations of Artaxerxes Longimanus, who died B. C. 425.

XERXES II. succeeded his father on the Persian throne, but after a reign of forty-five days he was murdered by his half-brother, called Secydianus by Ctesias and Sogdianus by Herodotus, after a festival in which he had indulged too freely. SOGDIANUS usurped the throne, but was himself murdered after a reign of six months by another half-brother named Ochus, who usurped the throne under the name of DARIUS, and is known in history as DARIUS NOTHUS, so called by the Greeks.

Darius Nothus had been satrap of Hyrcania and had married his aunt Parysatis, a daughter of Xerxes. He had two children before his accession—a daughter named Amestris and a son named Arsaces, who succeeded his father on the throne as Artaxerxes. Darius Nothus reigned nineteen years, and was disturbed by a constant succession of revolts. The first revolt was that of his full brother, Arsites, who was aided by a son of Megabyzus. After gaining two victories over the royal army, Persian gold corrupted the mercenaries, and the rebels were obliged to surrender on condition that their lives should be spared. Parysatis caused her husband to violate the pledges given the rebels, and Arsites and his fellow conspirator were executed; thus showing the world that perfidy was essential to a proper dealing with such as defied its authority.

Pissuthnes, satrap of Lydia, the son of Hystaspes, next rebelled. His immense wealth—accumulated during the twenty years while he was satrap—gave him the means for hiring the services of Greek mercenaries, who were commanded by Lycon, an Athenian. Tissaphernes, the Persian general sent against him, bribed Lycon and his followers to desert Pissuthnes and join his enemies; and the unfortunate satrap was obliged to surrender on conditions and to accompany Tissaphernes to the court. Darius, in violation of the pledge made by his general, executed the fallen rebel and bestowed his satrapy on Tissaphernes in reward for his success. Lycon, the Athenian, was rewarded for his treachery by being assigned the revenues of several cities and districts under the dominion of the Great King. Amorges, a bastard son of Pissuthnes, still maintained himself in Caria, where he held the strong city of Iasus and defied the power of Tissaphernes. By hiring Grecian mercenaries he maintained himself as an independent sovereign for some years.

The terrible disasters to the Athenian arms in Sicily in B. C. 414 encouraged the Persian king to treat the Peace of Callias as a dead letter, and he ordered the satraps of Asia Minor to collect tribute from the Greek cities, B. C. 413. The satraps, Tissaphernes and Pharnabazus, both made tempting offers to Sparta; and in B. C. 412 three treaties were concluded between Sparta and Persia, by which the two powers united in a war against Athens. Thenceforth the King of Persia was always able by means of his gold to secure an ally among leading Grecian states. At one time he could purchase the alliance of Sparta, at another time that of Athens, at another time that of Thebes. The Persian armies were commanded by Greek generals; the Persian fleets were conducted by Greek captains; while, according to Arrian, the very rank and file of the Persian standing army was at least half Greek. By keeping up the dissensions in Greece, Persia prolonged her tottering empire for eighty years.

The policy of the court of Susa, well executed by the satraps of Asia Minor, was to preserve the counterpoise among the leading states of Greece by permitting neither Athens nor Sparta to become too powerful at the expense of its rival, to assist each by turns as occasion required, and to encourage them to waste each others' strength, but to change sides whenever it was necessary to strike an effective blow against either side. The cunning Tissaphernes adroitly pursued his policy, which was more clumsily executed by the more sincere Pharnabazus, until the younger Cyrus came upon the scene. The younger Cyrus had selfish aims of his own, which conflicted with the true interests of the empire. As he needed a powerful land-force for the accomplishment of his designs he preferred the aid of Sparta to that of Athens, and gave the former such effectual help that in two years from the time he appeared on the coast the war was ended. Persian gold manned and partly built the Spartan fleet which defeated the Athenian navy at Ægos-Potami; and by placing his entire stores at the command of Lysander, the Spartan leader, Cyrus secured the good will of Sparta and her allies. Our sources of information concerning these relations between the Greeks and the Persians are the works of Ctesias, Xenophon, Thucydides and Arrian.

In B. C. 409 or 408, according to Xenophon, the Medes made an unsuccessful effort to recover their independence. In B. C. 405, according to Manetho, Egypt again revolted and enjoyed a short spasm of independence under Nepherites, or Nefaorot, who established himself on the throne of the Pharaohs, and under his three successors.

The story of Terituchmes, as told us by Ctesias, illustrates the dreadful corruption, cruelty and dissoluteness of the Persian court at this period. Terituchmes was the son of Idernes, a Persian noble of high rank. When his father died, he succeeded to his satrapy as if it were a hereditary fief, and as he enjoyed the favor of Darius Nothus he obtained that king's daughter, Amestris, for a wife. He afterwards became enamored of his own half-sister, Roxana, and grew tired of his wife. To rid himself of his wife he entered into a conspiracy with three hundred others and projected a revolt. The conspirators were bound to each other by the ties of a common, cruel and detestable crime. Amestris was to be placed in a sack, and each conspirator was to stab her body with his sword. To prevent this diabolical plot, Darius commissioned Udiastes, who served Terituchmes, to save his daughter by all means. Accordingly Udiastes, at the head of a band, slew Terituchmes after a desperate struggle. Parysatis, the queen, afterwards caused Roxana to be hewn in pieces, and the mother, brothers and sisters of Terituchmes to be buried alive. Arsaces, heir-apparent, afterwards Artaxerxes Mnemon, had great trouble in saving his own wife, Statira, the sister of Terituchmes, from the general massacre, by begging her life with tears and entreaties. The son of Terituchmes maintained himself in his father's government for some time, but the wicked Parysatis finally caused him to be poisoned.

Darius Nothus was at once weak and wicked in character. He violated his own pledges in murdering his brothers, Sogdianus and Arsites. He likewise disregarded his plighted word with Pissuthnes. He sanctioned the general massacre of the relatives of Terituchmes. During his reign the eunuchs of the palace became so powerful that one of them aspired to the throne itself. Darius was controlled by his cruel and vindictive wife, Parysatis. Although he gained some tracts in Asia Minor, he lost Egypt and Cyrenaica, the entire Persian territory in Africa. In his reign checks, which were designed to hold the great officers of the empire in restraint, were gradually relaxed. Satraps became virtually uncontrolled in their provinces, their lawless proceedings being connived at or condoned; and gradually the satrapies became hereditary fiefs, the sons of satraps being allowed to succeed their fathers in their governments—a custom dangerous to the peace and stability of the empire. Another dangerous step was the union of the offices of satrap and military commander in the same individual, and the appointment of a single satrap for several satrapies. Bribery, intrigue and treachery, instead of force, were the means employed to suppress rebellions, and pledges given to rebel leaders to obtain their submission were openly violated. Corruption, cunning and treachery were also the weapons employed against Persia's foreign foes. Warlike habits were cast aside, and the Medo-Persian armies began to be supplied by degrees with mercenaries. Ctesias and Xenophon are the chief sources of our information concerning the decline of the empire and the frightful corruption of the court.

Darius Nothus died B. C. 405, after appointing as his successor his eldest son, Arsaces, who took the name of Artaxerxes, and is known in history as ARTAXERXES MNEMON—a name given him by the Greeks because of his excellent memory.

Artaxerxes Mnemon had from the first a rival and competitor for the throne in his brother, the younger Cyrus. Their mother, Parysatis, the wife of Darius Nothus, had vainly endeavored to induce her husband to bequeath his crown to Cyrus, the younger son, her favorite. The Persian monarchs were installed with religious ceremonies in a temple at Pasargadæ, the original capital of Persia, which was yet considered as having a special sanctity. Just as Artaxerxes Mnemon was about to engage in the ceremonies attending his royal inauguration, Tissaphernes informed him that his life was menaced by Cyrus, who intended to conceal himself in the temple and assassinate him while he changed his dress. One of the officiating Magi confirmed the charge; whereupon Cyrus was arrested, and his life was only spared through the interference of his mother, who embraced him in her arms and thus prevented the executioner from performing his task. Her intercessions induced Artaxerxes to spare his brother's life and to permit him to return to his satrapial government in Asia Minor, assuring him that the accusations made against her favorite son were utterly groundless. Plutarch is our authority for the account of these circumstances connected with the accession of Artaxerxes Mnemon.

Xenophon, Ctesias and Plutarch are our sources of information concerning the struggle between Artaxerxes and his brother. After returning to Asia Minor, Cyrus collected an army of Greek mercenaries, and made open war on Tissaphernes, who had been sent with him to watch his movements. When Cyrus had raised a force of eleven thousand heavy-armed and two thousand light-armed Greek mercenaries Tissaphernes hastened to the capital to inform Artaxerxes of the proceedings and designs of Cyrus, whose purpose of dethroning his brother and placing the royal diadem of his illustrious namesake upon his own brow could no longer be mistaken.

Cyrus, placing entire reliance upon his personal following, consisting of his Greek mercenaries, at once began his rebellion by suddenly assuming the offensive, and boldly advancing toward the heart of the empire, with the intention of surprising his brother while he was unprepared. Cyrus started from Sardis in B. C. 401, and marched through Lydia, Phrygia and Cilicia, with an army consisting of thirteen thousand Greek mercenaries and almost a hundred thousand native troops. The Greek mercenaries now for the first time learned the true object of the expedition, and were with the utmost difficulty prevailed upon to remain with the army of Cyrus in its onward march. The expedition entered Syria by the mountain passes near Issus, crossed the Euphrates at Thapsacus, and marched rapidly through Mesopotamia to the plain of Cunaxa, about fifty-seven miles from Babylon. On this plain of Cunaxa, Cyrus encountered the vast army of Artaxerxes, numbering four hundred thousand men according to Ctesias, and nine hundred thousand according to Plutarch. The Greek allies of Cyrus sustained their ancient military renown by completely routing the troops of the Great King opposed to them; and Cyrus dashed with rash impetuosity into the center of his brother's army, where Artaxerxes commanded in person, and hurled his javelin at Artaxerxes, striking him upon the breast with such force as to pierce the cuirass and inflict a slight flesh wound, causing the king to fall from his horse; but at the same instant Cyrus himself received a wound under the eye from a Persian javelin, and in the struggle which ensued was slain with eight of his followers. Artaxerxes ordered his traitorous brother's head and right hand to be cut off. The death of Cyrus virtually decided the victory for Artaxerxes, though the conflict was maintained till nightfall. The Persian troops under Tissaphernes, who attacked the Greek mercenaries under Clearchus, were utterly routed, and dispersed over the plain in all directions.

The battle of Cunaxa was a two-fold blow to the power of Persia. Had Cyrus lived the empire might have been infused with new vigor. The younger Cyrus was certainly by far the superior of his brother. He was active, energetic, prompt in deed, ready in speech, faithful in observing his engagements, brave and liberal. He possessed more foresight and self-control than most Orientals. He understood how to deal with most classes of men. He knew how to inspire affection and retain it. He was devoid of national prejudice, and was able to appreciate the character and institutions of foreigners at their full value. Possessing more talents of statesmanship than any King of Persia since Darius Hystaspes, he would have raised the empire to some of its former vigor and power.

Cyrus had some grievous defects; and his external polish of Grecian manners and habits of thought and action, and his admiration for the Greek race, did not wholly conceal his native Asiatic barbarism, as is fully exemplified in his slaying of his cousin for what he regarded as disrespect; in his secret and silent execution of Orontes for intended desertion; in the fit of jealous rage with which he rushed recklessly and wildly upon his brother, disconcerting all his well-arranged plans and thus ruining his cause. Although the younger Cyrus had more method, more foresight, more power of combination, more breadth of mind than other Orientals of his time, or than most Asiatics of any time, he lacked some of the essentials of a great statesman, or of a great general. His civil administration of three years in Asia Minor was mainly distinguished for his barbarous severity towards criminals, and by a squandering of the resources of his government, so as to reduce him to actual necessity when he was about to begin his expedition. His generalship was sadly at fault at Cunaxa, as displayed in the reckless impetuosity which cost him his life and his cause, and in his failure to provide against probable and possible contingencies.

A more fatal result of the rebellion of Cyrus the younger than his death was its revelation of Persian weakness, and of the ease with which a Greek army could penetrate to the very heart of the empire, defeat the largest army which might take the field against it, and remain in the country or retire, as it might choose. Hitherto Grecian statesmen regarded Babylon, Susa, Ecbatana and Persepolis as distant places which it would be sheer recklessness to attempt to reach by force of arms, and from which it would be the height of folly to think a single individual would be able to return alive without the Great King's permission. Thenceforth the Greeks considered the occupation of these great cities as only a question of time. The general belief of Persia's inaccessibility gave place to a conviction that the heart of the empire could be penetrated with great ease.

Not only the march to Cunaxa, but the skillful and safe retreat of the Greek allies of Cyrus from that memorable field—"the Retreat of the Ten Thousand"—contributed to this wonderful change of opinion in the Hellenic mind. The safe return to Greece of ten thousand men, who had routed the hosts of the Great King in the center of his vast dominions, and fought their way back to the sea for a thousand miles without any further loss than the ordinary casualties of war, was at once an evidence of the vulnerability of the Medo-Persian Empire and of the incalculable superiority of Grecian to Asiatic soldiers. If a small Greek army, without maps or guides, might make its way for a thousand miles through Asia without meeting an enemy whom it could not vanquish with ease, it was evident that the whole fabric of Persian power was so rotten that it would topple over if exposed to a formidable attack. Thus this famous retreat was as important as the battle of Cunaxa itself. The fact of this safe retreat, and not the manner in which it was accomplished, had an important bearing on the subsequent history of Persia. The retreat was safely conducted, in spite of the military power of the empire, and notwithstanding the basest and most cruel treachery. The Greeks, though deprived of their leaders by a treacherous massacre, deceived, surprised, and hemmed in by superior numbers, amid terrific mountains, precipices and snows, under the skillful leadership of Xenophon, forced their way to Trapezus (now Trebizond) on the Euxine, losing less than a fourth of their number during the retreat.

The Greeks made another discovery concerning Persia's weakness. They now learned that the vast domain extending from the Ægean to the Indus, instead of being consolidated into one centralized monarchy with all its resources wielded by a single arm, had within its heart and center, on the confines of Media and Assyria, independent tribes which defied the Persian arms; while toward the verge of the old dominion entire provinces, once held under sway, had recovered their independence. In place of the nineteenth satrapy mentioned by Herodotus there now existed a collection of warlike independent tribes whose services the Great King had to purchase if he wanted them, and who usually were on hostile terms with him. Thus the Greeks saw that the great empire built up by Cyrus the Great, by Cambyses and Darius Hystaspes, had fallen from its high estate, and that both its dimensions and its resources had been seriously diminished.

The Grecian aid given to the younger Cyrus in his rebellion against Artaxerxes Mnemon produced a rupture between Sparta and Persia, as Sparta would neither apologize nor recede. With the services of the Ten Thousand, Sparta undertook to protect the Greeks of Asia Minor against Persia, and waged war for six years in Asia Minor against the satraps of Lydia and Phrygia (B. C. 399–B. C. 394). The disorganization of the Medo-Persian Empire was clearly manifested during this war. The two satraps just alluded to were so jealous of each other that neither hesitated to make a truce with the Spartans provided they attacked the other, and one satrap paid thirty talents of silver for the transfer of the war from his own government to that of his rival. The native tribes were also becoming rebellious. The Mysians and Pisidians had for some time been virtually independent. The Bithynians seemed inclined to revolt, while the native kings in Paphlagonia asserted their independence. The Spartan king, Agesilaüs, took full advantage of these troubles of the Persians in Asia Minor; but Persian gold, and jealousy of Sparta among the other Grecian states, soon gave the Spartans sufficient employment at home by stirring up a league of Athens, Thebes, Corinth and Argos against the power of Sparta. Agesilaüs was therefore recalled from Asia, and Conon the Athenian, in alliance with the satrap Pharnabazus, defeated the Spartan navy in the battle of Cnidus, thus weakening the prestige of Sparta in Asia Minor (B. C. 394). The victorious allies then crossed the Ægean Sea, ravaged the coasts of the Peloponnesus, and seized and occupied the island of Cythera. Persian gold rebuilt the long walls of Athens and liberally subsidized all the enemies of Sparta. With the Persian fleet in her waters and the leading states of Greece leagued against her, Sparta saw that she must succumb if the contest continued, and therefore proposed a general peace, by the terms of which all the Greek cities of Asia Minor were relinquished to the Persians and the balance of power among the Greek states in Europe was maintained. These terms were not accepted until six years later (B. C. 387), when the Spartan Antalcidas had explained them at the court of the Great King; whereupon Artaxerxes Mnemon issued an *ultimatum* to the belligerents, slightly modifying the terms in regard to Athens, extending them in regard to himself so as to include the islands of Clazomenæ and Cyprus, and forcing their acceptance by a threat. Thus the Great King recovered the territory which Persia had lost by the "Peace of Callias" more than sixty years before.

Artaxerxes Mnemon needed peace with

the Greeks, as all the resources of his empire were required to suppress the revolt which had for some years disturbed Cyprus. The precise date of the Cyprian revolt under Evagoras, the Greek tyrant of Salamis, is uncertain; but it is known that as early as B. C. 391 he was openly at war with Persia and had entered into an alliance with the Athenians, who in that year and in B. C. 388 sent him assistance. Aided likewise by Achôris, independent sovereign of Egypt, and Hecatomnus, vassal king of Caria, Evagoras was enabled to assume the offensive, to reconquer Tyre, and to extend his revolt into Cilicia and Edom. Autophradates, satrap of Lydia, undertook an unsuccessful expedition against him. After concluding the "Peace of Antalcidas" with Sparta in B. C. 387, Persia collected a fleet of three hundred vessels, partly from the Greeks of Asia Minor, and an army of three hundred thousand men, to crush the revolt of Evagoras. Evagoras with a fleet of two hundred triremes attacked the Persian fleet, but was utterly defeated by Tiribazus, who shut him up in Salamis, and reduced him to submission after a struggle of six years, B. C. 380 or 379. Our chief authorities for this struggle are Diodorus Siculus, Isocrates and Theopompus. The promise of pardon made to Evagoras was faithfully observed, and he was allowed to remain in his government with a recognition of his title, but was required to pay an annual tribute to the Great King.

During the Cyprian revolt Artaxerxes Mnemon was personally employed in a campaign against the Cadusians, the inhabitants of the low and fertile district between the Elburz mountain-range and the Caspian sea, who had also revolted against the Great King. Artaxerxes led an army estimated by Plutarch to number three hundred thousand foot and ten thousand horse. The land was not much cultivated, rugged, and covered with thick fogs. The Cadusians were brave and warlike. Having admitted Artaxerxes into their country, they waylaid and intercepted his convoys; and his army was soon reduced to extreme distress, being obliged to subsist on the cavalry-horses and the baggage animals. Cornelius Nepos tells us that many thousands of the royal army were slain, and that the army was only saved from greater disasters by the military talent of Datames. The most disastrous consequences were only averted by Tiribazus, who having been recalled from Cyprus on charges preferred against him by Orontes, the commander of the land force, managed by cunning to induce the two Cadusian kings to submit. This enabled Artaxerxes to retire from the country without serious disaster.

A period of tranquillity followed the campaign against the Cadusians. Artaxerxes strengthened his power among the Greeks of Asia Minor by razing some of their cities and garrisoning others with Persian troops. His satraps began to absorb the islands off the coasts; and, according to Isocrates, Samos was annexed to the empire. Cilicia, Phœnicia and Edom were recovered after the defeat of Evagoras. But Egypt had now remained independent under its native kings for over thirty years, since its revolt during the reign of Darius Nothus. In B. C. 375, Artaxerxes applied to Athens for the services of her great general, Iphicrates, to reconquer Egypt. His request was granted; and in the following year an armament was collected at Acre, the Persian army under Pharnabazus numbering, according to Diodorus Siculus, two hundred thousand men, and the Greek mercenaries under Iphicrates numbering twenty thousand men, but according to Cornelius Nepos twelve thousand. This expedition landed at the Mendesian mouth of the Nile and stormed the city commanding this branch of the river; but the inactivity of Pharnabazus, until the Delta had been flooded by the rising of the Nile, obliged the expedition to return; and Egypt remained independent for over a quarter of a century longer.

Artaxerxes Mnemon remained the supreme arbiter of Grecian affairs from the time of the "Peace of Antalcidas" in B. C. 387. In B. C. 372 Antalcidas was sent by Sparta to Susa a second time to procure an imperial rescript, prescribing the conditions on which the hostilities then raging in Greece should cease. In B. C. 367 Pelopidas and Ismenias were sent by Thebes to the Persian capital on the same errand. The next year a rescript was obtained by Athens more favorable than preceding ones. Thus all the leading states of Greece applied in turn to the Great King for his royal decree, thus mutually recognizing him as a master of the destinies of Greece, whose decision was to be binding upon all the Grecian states in every contest that distracted the Hellenic race.

Still the progress of internal decay and the tendency to disintegration was threatening the speedy dissolution of the empire. The long reign of Artaxerxes Mnemon was now nearing its end. He was venerable in years, and feeble, mentally and physically. He suspected his sons and nobles, particularly those who displayed more than ordinary ability. The empire was now constantly shaken by revolts. The first of these was that of Ariobarzanes, satrap of Phrygia, whom Autophradates, satrap of Lydia, and Mausôlus, the native King of Caria, under the suzerainty of Persia, failed to reduce to submission. The next revolt was that of Aspis, satrap of a portion of Cappadocia, and was aided by the Pisidians, but was finally subdued by Datames, the satrap of the remainder of Cappadocia. Then Datames himself rebelled and made an alliance with Ariobarzanes, the rebellious satrap of Phrygia, and defended himself so successfully against Autophradates that Artaxerxes first made a treaty with him and then removed him by treachery. Finally, in B. C. 362, the flames of revolt spread over the western provinces of the empire; and in this rebellion the satraps of Mysia, Phrygia and Lydia, Mausôlus, the tributary King of Caria, and the people of Lycia, Pamphylia, Cilicia, Syria and Phœnicia participated. Tachos, King of Egypt, incited these disturbances, and the Spartans likewise secretly encouraged them. A desperate struggle was only averted by the usual resources of bribery and treachery. Orontes, satrap of Phrygria, and Rheomithras, one of the rebel generals, being bribed, deserted and betrayed their confederates. By this means the insurrection was quelled in Asia Minor; but Tachos, the native King of Egypt, whose army was commanded by the Spartan king Agesilaüs, and whose fleet was commanded by the Athenian admiral Chabrias, advanced into Syria, was welcomed by the Phœnicians, and laid siege to some of the Syrian cities. But Persia was saved considerable loss in this quarter by the dissensions which broke out among the Egyptians, and Tachos was obliged to return to Egypt to uphold his throne against two pretenders who had risen in his absence. Thus the empire was again saved by the internal division of its enemies. For the accounts of these revolts we are indebted to Xenophon, Diodorus Siculus and Cornelius Nepos.

A year later, B. C. 359, Artaxerxes Mnemon died, after a reign of forty-six years, and, according to Plutarch, at the age of ninety-four. His private life was unhappy, like that of most of the later Persian kings; though he and his first wife, Statira, a deserving woman, were fondly attached to each other. His mother, Parysatis, was the cause of all the trouble. This cruel woman was the master of Artaxerxes during his long reign, and acted as if she were the real sovereign of the empire. She encouraged Cyrus in his rebellion, and was instrumental in bringing those responsible for frustrating it to the most horrible deaths. Hatred and jealousy induced her to poison Statira, because she exercised some influence over her husband. She encouraged Artaxerxes to contract an incestuous marriage with his daughter, Atossa—a marriage which led to additional unfortunate' consequences. Artaxerxes had three sons by Statira—Darius, Ariaspes and Ochus. Darius, the eldest, was formally declared the heir to the throne; but Ochus intrigued with Atossa to obtain the succession to the crown for himself. To prevent the success of his brother's designs, Darius conspired against his father's life; but, being detected, was seized and executed. Ariaspes, as the eldest living son, was then the natural heir. Ochus then persuaded Ariaspes that his father had become offended at him and was about to put him to a cruel and ignominious death; whereupon Ariaspes, in despair, committed suicide. Ochus, now the legitimate heir to the throne, resorted to assassination to get rid of his only remaining rival, Arsames, one of his half-brothers, a favorite illegitimate son of Artaxerxes—a crime which caused the death of the aged and unhappy king from grief. Plutarch has given us the full account of the domestic life of this unhappy sovereign. Artaxerxes Mnemon was the weakest of all the Persian monarchs. He was mild, affable, good-natured, affectionate and well-meaning; but his lack of a strong will prevented those about him from committing the most atrocious cruelties. He could not save his wife and son, whom he fondly loved, against those who plotted their destruction; and lacked the will or courage to avenge their fate. Powerless to resist entreaty and importunity, he granted favors which should have been refused, and condoned offenses which deserved punishment. Unable to long retain the most just resentment, he remitted the mildest and most merited punishments. He fairly succeeded in his foreign relations and in suppressing revolts in his own dominions, but could not infuse vigor in the tottering empire. His good fortune and the mistakes of his enemies only enabled him to transmit his entire inheritance to his successor.

The next king, known as ARTAXERXES OCHUS, was the most cruel and sanguinary of all the Persian monarchs. Upon his accession, in B. C. 359, he rid himself of rivals by destroying all the princes of the blood royal as far as he was able to. Justin tells us that he even cruelly put to death the most innocent princesses. He attempted to reconquer Egypt, which had successfully maintained its independence for almost a half-century under its native kings, against all the attempts of Persia to reduce it to submission. Notwithstanding a serious rebellion had broken out in Asia Minor, Artaxerxes Ochus led a vast army into Egypt, against its native king, Nectanebo, whose forces were commanded by two Greek generals, Diophantus, an Athenian, and Lamius, a Spartan. Diodorus and Isocrates inform us that Ochus was defeated and his army utterly repulsed; that Phœnicia rose in revolt and asserted her independence under the leadership of Sidon, expelled or massacred the Persian garrisons in her cities, and entered into an alliance with Egypt; and that Cyprus also rebelled, the kings of its nine principal towns assuming independent sovereignty. Cyprus was reduced to submission by Idrieus, prince of Caria, with eight thousand Greek mercenaries under Phocion, the Athenian, and Evagoras, son of the former Evagoras, the Cyprian monarch. But Belesys, satrap of Syria, and Mazæus, satrap of Cilicia, were defeated by Tennes, the Sidonian king, who was assisted by four thousand Greek mercenaries sent by Nectanebo, King of Egypt, and commanded by Mentor the Rhodian. The Persians were driven out of Phœnicia; but when Ochus himself approached with three hundred and thirty thousand men, the Phœnician monarch sought to secure his own safety by delivering a hundred of the leading citizens of Sidon into the hands of the Persian king, whom he then admitted into the city. Ochus cruelly caused the hundred citizens to be speared to death, and the five hundred more who came to entreat his mercy were consigned to the same horrible fate. The cowardly king, Tennes, failed to save his own life by his treachery, as Ochus also put him to death. The Sidonians, in despair, set fire to their city, perishing with it in the flames, after having previously burned their own ships to prevent any of their number escaping. Forty thousand thus perished, each having shut himself up in his own dwelling, to which he set fire. The city became a heap of ruins, and these were sold by Ochus for a vast sum. Upon the end of the Phœnician revolt, Mentor the Rhodian, the ablest of the Greek mercenary leaders, transferred his services to the Persian king.

The accounts of these Phœnician and Egyptian revolts are derived from Didorus Siculus, the great ancient authority for the events of the reign of Artaxerxes Ochus.

After the fall of Sidon, Ochus invaded Egypt with a Persian army of three hundred and thirty thousand men, assisted by fourteen thousand Greek mercenaries, six thousand of whom were furnished by the Greek cities of Asia Minor, four thousand under Mentor consisting of the troops which he had brought from Egypt to assist the Phœnicians, three thousand being sent from Argos, and four thousand from Thebes. He divided his expedition into three portions, over each of which he placed a Persian and also a Greek general. The Greek commanders were Lacrates of Thebes, Mentor of Rhodes, and Nicostratus of Argos; the latter a man of such enormous physical strength that he regarded himself as a second Hercules, and adopted the traditional costume of that fabulous hero—a club and a lion's skin. The Persian generals were Rhœsaces, Aristazanes and Bagôas, the chief of the eunuchs. The Egyptian king had only one hundred thousand men to oppose to the vast host of Ochus, and twenty thousand of these were Greek mercenaries. He occupied the Nile and its various branches with a powerful navy. The Greek generals in the Persian service outmaneuvered Nectanebo, who hastily retreated to Memphis, leaving the fortified towns to the defense of their garrisons. The Persian leaders excited jealousies and suspicions between the Greek and Egyptian troops composing these garrisons, and thus reduced the secondary cities of Lower Egypt, after which they advanced on Memphis, Nectanebo fleeing in despair to Ethiopia. Thereupon all Egypt submitted to Artaxerxes Ochus, who demolished the walls of the cities, plundered the temples, and after fully rewarding his mercenaries, returned triumphantly to his capital with a vast booty.

Grote has truly said that "the reconquest of Egypt by Ochus must have been one of the most impressive events of the age," and that it "exalted the Persian Empire in force and credit to a point nearly as high as it had ever occupied before." Ochus thus raised himself to a degree of prestige and glory above that of any Persian king since the time of Darius Hystaspes. Revolts or rebellions did not again disturb the empire. Mentor and Bagôas, the two generals who had borne the most conspicuous part in the Egyptian campaign, were rewarded by Ochus with the most important posts. Mentor, as governor of the whole sea-coast of Asia Minor, reduced the many chiefs who had assumed an independent sovereignty to submission within a few years. Bagôas, as the king's minister at the capital, maintained tranquillity throughout the empire. The last six years of the reign of Ochus formed the most tranquil and prosperous period of the later Medo-Persian history; and this happy state of affairs must be ascribed to the talents of Bagôas and Mentor, and reflect credit upon the king himself who selected such able officials and retained them permanently in office.

But while the Medo-Persian Empire seemed to have been thus reinvigorated with new life and strength, and when it seemed to have started on a new career of power and glory, its existence was menaced by a new power which had suddenly risen into prominence on its north-western frontier. Artaxerxes Ochus and his counselors perceived the future danger. A Persian force was sent to aid the Thracian prince, Cersobleptes, to maintain his independence; and the city of Perinthus, with Persian aid, made a successful defense against the besieging army of Philip of Macedon (B. C. 340). Thus before Philip had subdued Greece, Persian statesmen saw a formidable rival in the rapidly-rising Macedonian moharchy.

While the empire was thus threatened from without, conspiracy and revolution again distracted the court and paralyzed the action of the government. The violence and cruelty of Artaxerxes Ochus made him unpopular with his subjects. Bagôas himself grew so suspicious of his sovereign that he poisoned him in B. C. 338, and placed the king's youngest son, ARSES, upon the throne, while he likewise assassinated all the new monarch's brothers. Bagôas was now virtual ruler, but in the course of a year Arses began to assert himself and uttered threats against Bagôas, who thereupon caused Arses and his infant children to be assassinated, and placed Codomannus, the son of Arsanes, upon the throne, B. C. 336. The new king assumed the name of Darius, and is known in history as DARIUS CODO-MANNUS. The account of these events has been transmitted to us from ancient times by Diodorus, Arrian, Strabo and Quintus Curtius. According to Strabo, Darius Codomannus did not belong to the royal house; but according to Diodorus, he was the grandson of Ostanes, a brother of Artaxerxes Mnemon. In the very year that Darius became King of Persia (B. C. 336), Alexander the Great became King of Macedon upon the assassination of his father, Philip, by Pausanius, a Macedonian nobleman.

Darius Codomannus, the last of the Medo-Persian kings, was morally superior to most of his predecessors, but he was destitute of sufficient intellectual ability to enable him to wrestle with the difficult circumstances of his situation. He was personally brave, tall and handsome, amiable in disposition, capable of great exertion, and possessed of some military capacity. The invasion of Asia Minor by Alexander the Great, which occurred in B. C. 334, did not alarm Darius, who seemed to have no full comprehension of the peril which thus threatened the existence of his empire. He seems to have despised the youth and inexperience of Alexander, who was then but twenty years of age; and he made no sufficient preparation to resist this formidable attack upon the Medo-Persian Empire. Since the battle of Marathon the final struggle between Greece and Persia was only a question of time, but the liberal employment of Persian gold had delayed the inevitable contest for more than a century and a half. The Greeks now had a leader more ambitious than Cyrus and more able than Xerxes.

The satraps and generals of Persia shared the confidence of their sovereign, and though a large army was collected in Mysia and a powerful fleet was sent to the coast, no effort was made to prevent the passage of the Hellespont by Alexander's army. In the spring of B. C. 334 Alexander with his thirty-five thousand Græco-Macedonian troops crossed the strait which Xerxes had passed with his hosts of five millions less than a century and a half before. The inferiority of the Greek army in numbers was far overbalanced by its superior efficiency. It consisted of veteran troops in the highest possible condition of discipline and equipment, and every Macedonian and Grecian soldier was animated by the most enthusiastic devotion to his youthful leader and confident of victory.

Had the Persian leaders made any serious opposition Alexander's invasion of Asia Minor might have been prevented. The first earnest effort to stay the progress of the invader was made in the attempt to prevent the passage of the Granicus, a little river in Mysia flowing into the Propontis (now Sea of Marmora). In the battle which ensued the Persians were defeated, and Alexander succeeded in crossing the stream. In consequence of this defeat, the Persians were thrown on the defensive, and Alexander's conquest of Asia Minor was the immediate result. The death of Memnon, the brother of Mentor, deprived the King of Persia of his ablest general, who had already collected a large fleet, captured many islands in the Ægean, and prepared to carry the war into Greece and thus compel Alexander to withdraw from Asia Minor. After besieging and capturing Miletus and Halicarnassus, Alexander's triumphant progress through Asia Minor was unopposed, and by the spring of B. C. 333 he was at the gates of Syria.

Darius Codomannus assembled a vast army in the spring of B. C. 333, and, now obliged to act wholly on the defensive, endeavored to stop the further advance of the invader. With seven hundred thousand men, Darius encountered Alexander on the plain of Issus; but hemmed in in a narrow defile between the mountain, the river and the sea, the immense Persian hosts were routed, and Darius himself was obliged to flee for his own life. His wife, mother and children were made prisoners by Alexander, who treated them with the utmost respect, and honored Darius's wife, who died soon afterward, with a most magnificent burial. The defeat of Darius Codomannus at Issus was followed by the conquest of Syria, Phœnicia and Egypt by Alexander, who captured Tyre and Gaza, after vigorous sieges.

In the spring of B. C. 331 Alexander retraced his triumphant march through Syria, and, directing his course toward the heart of the Medo-Persian Empire, crossed the Euphrates at Thapsacus, traversed Mesopotamia and encountered Darius Codomannus a second time near the Assyrian city of Arbela, on the plain of Gaugamela, east of the Tigris. The Persian king, since his defeat in the battle of Issus twenty months before, had collected the entire force of his vast dominion for the final struggle, which was to decide the fate of his empire. With only forty-seven thousand men Alexander totally defeated and routed the immense hosts of Darius, said to number over a million men, in the great battle of Arbela, which was the death-blow to the Medo-Persian Empire.

Darius Codomannus fled to the city of Arbela, about twenty miles distant from the battle-field. Here the unfortunate monarch was seized by his own officers, headed by the treacherous Bessus, satrap of Bactriana, who, seeing their master's fortunes ruined, had contrived a plan to deliver him to Alexander and thereby advance their own interests. They loaded him with chains and forced him to accompany them in their flight toward Hyrcania, on the approach of Alexander to Arbela. The next day Alexander arrived at Arbela and took possession of the king's treasures; after which he went in hot pursuit of Darius and his fleeing officers. Hemmed in on all sides and finding escape impossible, the treacherous Bessus and his fellow-conspirators basely turned upon their king, mortally wounding him and leaving him to die by the roadside in the mountains. A Macedonian soldier discovered the former lord of Asia in his dying condition, and, in response to his appeal, brought him a cup of cold water. Darius sincerely thanked his generous enemy, expressing sorrow at his inability to reward him for this kindness to him in his dying moments. He commended the soldier to the notice of Alexander, who he said had sufficient magnanimity to grant his dying request, and then expired. Alexander arrived shortly after his death, and, deeply affected, covered the dead body of the last Medo-Persian king with his own royal mantle, and directed that a magnificent funeral procession should convey it to Pasargadæ, where it was interred in the tombs of his illustrious ancestors, with royal honors. The conqueror also provided for the fitting education of the children of his fallen adversary.

Although the battle of Arbela sealed the fate of the Medo-Persian Empire, the reduction of its north-eastern and eastern provinces occupied the conqueror several years longer; but their final conquest made Alexander lord of Asia, and master of the vast empire founded by Cyrus the Great.

SECTION III.—MEDO-PERSIAN CIVILIZATION.

ALREADY we have alluded to the ethnic identity of the Persians with the Medes; and we have seen that their primeval home was in Bactria, and that in prehistoric times they migrated to the southwest. The Medes and Persians were a kindred branch of the great Iranic, or Aryan family—the Indo-European division of the Caucasian race. The name Aryan has been assigned to this portion of the Caucasian race on grounds of actual tradition and his-

ALEXANDER DISCOVERING THE DEAD BODY OF DARIUS.

tory. In the Zend-Avesta, "the first best of regions and countries," the original home of Ahura-Mazda's peculiar people was *Aryanem vaejo*—"the source of the Aryans." Herodotus states that in his time the Medes were known as *Aryans* by all the surrounding nations. The sculptor employed by Darius Hystaspes at Behistun explained to the Scythian aborigines of the Zagros mountain region, in a note of his own, that *Ahura-Mazda*, of whom so much was said in the inscription, was "the God of the Aryans." Darius Hystaspes, in another inscription, boasted that he was a "Persian, the son of a Persian, an Aryan of Aryan descent." Eudemus, the disciple of Aristotle, called the people whose priests were the Magi "the Aryan nation." Strabo introduced the term *Ariana* into geography, and assigned it a meaning almost identical with that of the modern Iran. The Sassanian kings divided the world into *Airan* and *Aniran*, and claimed to be sovereigns of both the Aryan and non-Aryan nations. The term *Iran* is the only name by which a modern Persian knows his country.

Obscure in their early annals, the Medes and Persians became the most important Aryan tribes towards the eighth or seventh century before Christ. They were close kindred, united together, each wielding the superiority by turns. They claimed and exercised supremacy over all the other Aryan tribes, and likewise over certain alien races. Their distinguishing characteristics gave them the superiority over other nations, and had developed a civilization of their own. The character, mode of living, habits, customs, manners, etc., of the Persians were the same as those of the Medes, already described in the history of Media; but we have more copious information concerning the Persians, and we can therefore add considerable in this connection to what has been already said.

The Aryan physiognomy, as revealed to us by the Persian monuments, characterized both the Medes and the Persians. There is a uniformity in the type of the face and head in all of these monuments, and this type contrasts remarkably with the Semite type assigned to themselves by the Assyrians, from whom the Aryans seem to have derived the general idea of bas-reliefs, and likewise their general manner of dealing with subjects upon them. The peculiarity of the physiognomy bears strong evidence to its truthfulness, which is also attested by the fact that the Persian artists endeavored to represent the varieties of mankind and were fairly successful in rendering them. Varieties of physiognomy are represented with great care, and often with wonderful success, upon the bas-reliefs.

Herodotus tells us that the skulls of the Persians were uncommonly thin and weak, which he ascribed to the national habit of always covering the head. The Persians were quick and lively, keen-witted, capable of repartee, ingenious, and especially far-sighted for Orientals. They possessed fancy and imagination, were fond of poetry and art, and had a certain power of political combination. The religious ideas of the Medes and Persians were more elevated than those of other ancient nations besides the Hebrews; and these ideas, as entertained by all Iranic nations, were inherited by the Persians from a remote ancestry. Persian architecture and sculpture did not display any remarkable genius. The Persians were distinguished for their courage, energy and honesty. The valor of the Persian troops at Thermopylæ and Platæa won the admiration of their foes; and Herodotus expressed the belief that, "in boldness and warlike spirit, the Persians were not a whit behind the Greeks," and that the sole reason for their defeat was the inferiority of their equipment and discipline. Having no proper shields and little defensive armor, and wielding only short swords and lances, they dashed upon the serried ranks of the Spartans, whose large spear-shafts they seized and tried to break. Grote compares their valor with the brilliant deeds of the Romans and the Swiss. Æschylus very deservedly called the Persians a "valiant-minded people." They were bold, dashing, tenacious and stubborn. No nation of Asia or Africa could withstand them. The Greeks were superior to them because of the superiority of Grecian arms, equipment and discipline.

During the earlier years of their ascendency the Persians were as much distinguished for their energy as for their courage. Æschylus alludes to a strange fate which obliged them to engage constantly in a long series of wars, to delight in combats of horse, and in the siege and capture of cities. Herodotus represents Xerxes as bound by the examples of his ancestors to engage his people in some great enterprise, and not to allow their military spirit to decay on account of lack of employment. We have already seen that for eighty years, under the first four monarchs, wars and expeditions did not cease, that the activity and energy of the king and people carried them on, without rest or cessation, in a career of conquest almost unparalleled in Oriental history. In the later period this spirit was less marked, but at all times the Persians were characterized by a certain vigor and activity, which has distinguished them particularly from "the dreamy and listless Hindoos upon the one hand and the apathetic Turks upon the other."

The Greeks praised the Persians especially for their love of the truth. Herodotus states that the Persian youth were taught three principal things: "To ride, to draw the bow, and to speak the truth." In the Zend-Avesta, particularly in the earliest and purest portions of it, truth is strongly inculcated. Ahura-Mazda himself is "true," "the father of truth," and his worshipers must conform themselves to his image. In the Behistun Inscription, Darius Hystaspes protests against "lies," which he appears to consider the embodiment of evil. A love of intrigue is characteristic of Orientals; and in their later history the Persians seem to have given way to this natural inclination, and to have made a free use of cunning and deception in their wars with the Greeks; but in their earlier period they considered lying as the most shameful thing of which a person could be guilty. Truth was then admired and practiced. Persian kings strictly observed their promises, no matter how inconvenient may have been their fulfillment, and never gave foreign nations any reason to complain that they had violated the terms of a treaty. Thus the Persians were an honorable exception to the usual Asiatic character, and compared favorably with the Greeks and Romans for general truthfulness and a faithful observance of their engagements.

Herodotus also tells us that the Persians endeavored to keep out of debt. They had a keen sense of the difficulty which a debtor found to avoid subterfuge and equivocation —forms of falsehood, slightly disguised. They disliked to buy and sell wares in the market-place, or to haggle over prices, as they thought that it involved falsity and unfairness. They were frank and open in speech, bold in act, generous, warm-hearted, hospitable. Their principal faults were an addiction to self-indulgence and luxury, a passionate yielding to the feelings of the moment, and a sycophancy and subservience toward their sovereign so great as to destroy their self-respect and manliness. They were alike immoderate in joy or sorrow, according to Herodotus; and Æschylus's tragedy of the "Persæ" correctly illustrates the real habits of the Persian people. The Persians were unreserved, and laughed and wept, shouted and shrieked, in the presence of others without the least restraint. Lively and excitable, they gave full vent to every passion, and did not care who witnessed their rejoicings or lamentations.

In Persia the king was so much the state that patriotism was absorbed in loyalty to royalty; and an unquestioned submission to the will and caprice of the monarch was by habit and education implanted in the very nature of the Persian people. Herodotus states that in war the concern of all was the personal safety of the sovereign. Such a value was attached to the royal person that it was thought the public safety depended upon his escape from danger and suffering. All the decisions of the sovereign were received with the most unquestioned acquiescence; his will, whatever it might be, was cheerfully submitted to. Their loyalty degenerated into a parasitical passiveness, and became a defect instead of a virtue. No remonstrance, reproof or warning was ever heard of at court; and tyranny encountered no restraint in the wildest caprices and extravagances. Herodotus tells us that the father whose innocent son the king shot in pure wantonness before his eyes, congratulated his majesty upon the excellence of his archery, instead of protesting with indignation against the crime. Unfortunates, bastinadoed by the king's orders, expressed themselves as delighted because his majesty had condescended to remember them. The tone of sycophancy and servility thus engendered sapped the self-respect of the people, and tended to fatally corrupt their whole character.

The Persian monuments throw considerable light upon the warlike customs of the people. The Medes and Persians looked unfavorably upon the chariots, and their armies consisted almost wholly of foot and horse. Herodotus says that in the earlier times the footman usually dressed in a close-fitting leather tunic with long sleeves, reaching from the neck to the knee. Below this was worn a pair of tight-fitting leather trousers, reaching to the ankles. The feet were covered by a high shoe or low boot. The head was protected by a loose, round felt cap, projecting a little in front, and rising considerably above the head. A double belt or girdle was worn around the waist, and a short sword was suspended from it.

The offensive weapons of a Persian footman were a short sword, a short spear and a bow. The sword was carried in a sheath, suspended from the girdle on the right side. The Persepolitan sculptures represent it as attached to the right thigh by a thong passing round the knee. The representations of the guardsmen on the Persepolitan sculptures would seem to indicate that the Persian spear was about seven feet long. The Grecian spear was sometimes twenty-two feet long. Herodotus and Xenophon represented the Persian bow as uncommonly large, while the sculptures represent it as not more than four feet long. It appears to have been carried, strung on the left shoulder with the arm passing through it, or in a bow-case slung on the left side. The arrows were made of reed, tipped with metal and feathered, and were carried in a quiver hung at the back near the left shoulder. From the sculptures these would appear to have been about two and a half feet long. The arrow-heads were either of bronze or iron, and seem to have been of various shapes, the most common closely resembling those of the Assyrians. Other offensive weapons of the Persians were sometimes a battle-ax, a sling and a knife. Xenophon declares the battle-ax to have been the common Persian weapon, but it only appears in the sculptures in one or two instances. Xenophon, Strabo and Quintus Curtius mention the use of the sling by the Persian light-armed troops. Xenophon witnessed the effect of this weapon during the Retreat of the Ten Thousand, which he conducted. Persian slingers only threw stones, and not small lumps of lead, as did the Rhodians. The Persian footman also carried a knife, worn in a sheath, and probably suspended from the girdle.

The defensive armor of the Persians were shields of wicker-work, which protected them almost from head to foot, and probably closely resembled the Assyrian wicker shields. The Persian soldier usually planted his shield on the ground while discharging his arrows at the foe. Sometimes the Persian footmen also wore coats of mail, consisting of scale armor, or of quilted linen, like the Egyptian corselets. Scale armor could scarcely be penetrated; as the scales, which were of iron, bronze or gold, overlaped one another like the scales of a fish.

Herodotus says that in the earlier times the Persian cavalry were armed exactly like the infantry, except that the horsemen sometimes wore bronze or iron helmets. In the time of the younger Cyrus cavalry soldiers were very fully protected, wearing helmets on their heads, coats of mail about their bodies, and greaves on their legs.

Their principal offensive arms then seem to have been the short sword, the javelin and the knife. The sculptures give us no representations of the Persian cavalry soldiers. The Persian cavalry appear to have sometimes worn a round shield. Each horseman usually carried two javelins, which were short spears, or pikes, with shafts of cornel-wood and iron points. He used one of these weapons as a missile, and retained the other for use in a hand-to-hand combat with the foe. Xenophon preferred this weapon to the weak reed-lance generally carried by cavalry soldiers in his day, though it was no match for the longer and equally-strong spear of the Macedonian cavalry.

The later Persians protected the horse, as well as the horseman. They selected large and powerful animals, principally of the Nisæan breed, for the cavalry service, and cased them almost entirely in mail. The head was guarded by a frontlet, and the neck and chest by a breast-piece; the sides and flanks having their own special covering, while the thighs were defended by cuirasses. This armor, like that of the riders, consisted of felt or leather covered with metal scales. The cavalry had thus to bear considerable weight, and was encumbered in flight or retreat, the weaker horses often sinking beneath their burdens and being trampled to death by the stronger ones.

Besides the heavy horsemen, the Persians employed a light-cavalry force, as in the case of the troops which, under Tissaphernes, harassed the Ten Thousand in their retreat. The Persians were educated in habits of quickness and agility in mounting and managing horses, which were very valuable for the light-cavalry service. Besides Herodotus and Xenophon, the ancient authorities on the infantry and cavalry services of the Persians are Strabo, Arrian and Quintus Curtius.

The Persians did not often use chariots in their armies, as we have already said. None were employed against the Greeks by Darius or Xerxes, and none were used at the Granicus nor at Issus; the only two occasions in which we are told that they were used by the Persians being in the battles of Cunaxa and Arbela. The kings and princes, however, always directed the movements of their armies, when commanding in person, from the war-chariot, either in battle or on the march. Diodorus, Arrian and Quintus Curtius tell us that the Persians had two hundred war-chariots in the battle of Arbela, but the number at Cunaxa is not mentioned. The wheels of the Persian war-chariots were armed with scythes, according to Xenophon, Diodorus Siculus and Quintus Curtius. Neither at Cunaxa nor Arbela did the scythed chariots perform any important service.

The Persian war-chariot was perhaps higher than the Assyrian. The wheels seem to have been from three to four feet in diameter, and the body rose above them to an elevation of almost five feet from the ground. The person of the chariot-warrior was thus protected by the curved board which enclosed the chariot on three sides. The axle-tree is said to have been broad, and the whole chariot was solid and strong in its construction. The wheels had twelve spokes radiating from a nave of more than ordinary size. The felloes, though narrower than those of the Assyrian war-chariot, were, like them, composed of three distinct layers of wood. The tires were probably of metal, and were indented like the edge of a saw.

The Persian war-chariot does not seem to have been ornamented. The body was sometimes patterned with a chequer-work, in Assyrian style, and the spokes were often very elegant, but the workmanship was massive and plain in its general character. The pole was short and ended with a simple curve. The sculptures represent the chariots as drawn by only two horses; but Xenophon, Diodorus Siculus and Quintus Curtius inform us that the usual custom was to have four horses. The harness consisted of a yoke, a belly-band, a narrow collar, a headstall, a bit and reins. When the charioteer left his seat, the reins could be attached to a loop or bar projecting from the front of the chariot-board.

The Persian chariots usually contained

but two persons, the driver, or charioteer, and the warrior. Sometimes there was also an attendant whose duty was to open and shut the chariot-doors. The charioteer wore a visor and a coat of mail, only his eyes being exposed to the foe. Arrian states that the last Medo-Persian king used fifteen elephants in the battle of Arbela.

In battle the chariots were placed in front of the cavalry and infantry. The cavalry were usually massed upon the two wings. The infantry were placed in the middle, drawn up according to nations, in a number of oblong squares almost touching one another. The bravest and best-armed troops were placed in front. The ranks were generally very deep. When the battle commenced the chariots were first hurled against the foe, it being hoped that they would throw their ranks into confusion. The main line then advanced to the attack. The Persian heavy-armed troops planted their shields in front of them and discharged their arrows at the enemy, while the slingers and other light-armed troops in the rear hurled missiles over the heads of their comrades into the enemy's ranks beyond them. The enemy by pressing forward brought on a hand-to-hand struggle, and the conflict was then usually decided in a very few minutes. If the Persian line of battle was broken, all was at once considered lost, and rout and flight ensued. The efforts of the Persian cavalry to stay the progress of the advancing foe by desperately charging on their flanks was generally unavailing. When its line of battle was broken a Persian army became utterly discouraged and demoralized, and the example of flight set by its commander was followed by the rank and file.

The Persians chiefly relied for success on their numbers, which enabled them to renew the attack repeatedly with fresh troops, or to outflank and surround the enemy. The cavalry were their best troops. The heavy horse armed in the early times with the bow, and in the later with the javelin, greatly distinguished themselves on many famous fields, as related to us by Herodotus, Arrian and others. The light cavalry was celebrated for quickness and dexterity of maneuver. It was loosely organized like the modern Bashi-Bazouks and Cossacks. It fell on an enemy in huge masses; it assailed, retreated, rallied, again advanced, and was formidable even in flight and rout, as each rider discharged his arrows backwards with unerring aim at the pursuing foe. The Persians thus originated the practice followed so skillfully by their Parthian successors. The Persians sometimes resorted to stratagem. At Arbela, Darius Codomannus had spiked balls scattered over the ground where he expected that the Greek cavalry would make its attacks; and at Sardis, Cyrus was indebted for his victory to the frightening of the Lydian horse with his camels.

Xenophon tells us that military engines were used by the Persians; but no other ancient writer says anything about them, and we may conclude that they were rarely employed. According to Herodotus they relied on the bank or mound in ordinary sieges, and they sometimes drove mines under the walls to effect a breach. Where the place was strongly fortified they generally resorted to stratagem, or to the blockade. Sometimes they used fire to reduce towns, and perhaps often succeeded by escalade. They were usually successful in their sieges, displaying courage, activity and fertility of resource in conducting them.

A Persian army was generally under a single commander, who was the king, if he was present, or, if he was not present, a Persian or a Mede appointed by him. Under the commander-in-chief were a number of general officers, leaders of corps and divisions. Next in rank below these were the chiefs of the various ethnic contingents constituting the army, who were usually the satraps of the various provinces. The appointments thus far were made directly by the crown; but the satrapial commanders appointed the officers next below themselves, the captain over a thousand, or the captains over ten thousand, according to the size of the contingent. The officers appointed subordinates, commanders of a hundred and commanders of ten. Thus we see that a decimal system principally prevailed. The lowest rank of officers each commanded ten men, the next above them commanded a hundred, the next above the last a thousand, and the next ten thousand. The officer commanding ten thousand was a divisional chief, or was subject to the commander of the ethnic contingent, who was himself under the orders of the divisional commander. There were thus six ranks of officers below the commander-in-chief.

The proper place for the commander-in-chief was considered to be in the center of the line of battle, where he would be safer, and where his orders could be most rapidly carried to every part of the battle-field. He was expected to take part in the conflict, and was thus often exposed to imminent peril of his life. The death or flight of the chief commander often caused a general panic, stopping the issue of any further general order, and thus paralyzing the entire army.

Herodotus and Arrian tell us that a Persian army contained sometimes over a million men. These writers, and Xenophon and Quintus Curtius, state that the troops were drawn from the whole empire, and were marshaled in the field according to nationalities, each tribe or nation being accoutered in its own style. Thus might be seen the gilded breastplates and the scarlet kilts of the Medes and Persians, the woolen shirt of the Arabs, the leathern jerkin of the Berbers, or the cotton dress of the Hindoos. Savage Ethiopians from the Upper Nile, ornamented with a war paint of red and white, and clad scantily with the skins of leopards or lions, could be seen in one place, with their large clubs, arrows pointed with stone, and spears ending in the horns of an antelope. In other places were wild Scyths, with their spangled trousers and their tall pointed caps, with battle-axes and clubs. Near them were the Assyrians, with their helmets and quilted linen corselets, and with their spears and iron maces. Cane bows, arrows without feathers, and stakes hardened at one end by fire, were seen side by side with the best steel swords and daggers from the workshops of Phœnicia and Greece. In one place the bronze helmet was surmounted with the ears and horns of an ox. In another its place was supplied by a fox-skin, a leathern or wooden skull-cap, or a head-dress made of a horse's scalp. The animals belonging to a Persian army were horses, mules, wild asses, camels and elephants. One large body of cavalry was armed only with the dagger and a long leathern thong which they used as a lasso; and the unfortunate caught in its noose had little chance of escape.

The Persians, like the Assyrians, generally avoided fighting during the winter and marched their armies against the foe in early spring. Their vast hosts were moved with a fixed order. In marching through their own country the baggage and the sumpter-beasts were sent in advance. About half the troops came next, moving slowly in a continuous column along the appointed line of the route. At this point there was a break, in order for the most important portion of the army to follow next. A guard composed of a thousand horse and a thousand foot, selected specially from among the Persian people, opened the way for what was most sacred in the estimation of all Persians—the emblems of their religion and of their sovereign. The sacred emblems consisted of the sacred horses and chariots, and probably also in later times of silver altars bearing the ever-burning and heaven-kindled fire. Behind these emblems followed the Great King seated on a chariot drawn by Nisæan steeds, and, according to Quintus Curtius, protected on either side by a chosen number of his relations. Behind the royal chariot was a second guard, which consisted of a thousand foot and horse, like the first guard. After these followed ten thousand picked infantry, probably the celebrated "Immortals" mentioned by Herodotus. Then came a body of ten thousand select Persian horsemen. After a vacant space of almost a quarter of a mile marched the remainder of the vast army.

Upon entering an enemy's territory, or

upon approaching a hostile force in their own country, the Persians withdrew their baggage-train, which followed some distance in the rear of the army. Horsemen were sent out in front to look for the enemy. If the army was large it was sometimes divided into several corps, which advanced simultaneously by several different routes, the commander-in-chief accompanying the central force.

The Persians marched from sunrise to sunset, according to Xenophon and Quintus Curtius. They seldom marched more than twenty-five miles a day, and if a faster rate was attempted it was found necessary to allow the men intervals of three days' rest. The baggage-train, consisting of a great multitude of camels, horses, asses, mules, oxen, etc., carrying burdens on their backs, impeded the movement of a Persian army. The wives or female companions of the chief men were often conveyed in litters, amid a multitude of eunuchs and attendants, and with all the cumbersome paraphernalia of female wardrobes. There were no roads, and no bridges over rivers, except such as were sometimes made of boats. They marched by an established route. The carts and litters sometimes stuck fast in the mud almost to the axles. Rivers along the line of march had to be forded or crossed by means of boats or rafts.

In the evening, according to Xenophon, a Persian army would encamp in the open plain in the vicinity of water. If an enemy was believed to be near, a ditch was hastily dug and an embankment thrown up inside. If the soil was sandy, sacks were filled with it, and the camp was protected by means of sand-bags. The *gerrhophori*, or Persians carrying large wicker shields, were placed just inside the rampart. The remainder of the army had their proper places, the commander-in-chief being in the center. All the soldiers had tents, according to Xenophon, and these were pitched so as to face the east. The cavalry-horses were tethered and hobbled in front of their owner's tents.

The Persians did not like to camp nearer an enemy than seven or eight miles, as a precaution against surprise or a night attack. They had no special corps of pioneers, the work of felling trees or removing brushwood being assigned to a certain number of regular soldiers whenever necessary. The construction of bridges was assigned to skillful workmen, or to the crews of ships.

A large baggage-train conveyed corn sufficient to supply the army for months. Ships laden with corn accompanied the expedition as closely as possible to supply any necessary demand. Sometimes magazines were established at points along the line of march for the stores of provisions which might be needed. Requisitions for supplies were likewise made upon the inhabitants of towns and villages along the line of march. According to Herodotus, whenever a Persian army rested for the night the inhabitants were required to furnish bread sufficient for a meal for each man, and to provide a banquet for the king, or general, and his numerous suite. The provision here included, in addition to various kinds of meats, poultry and water-fowl, a full service for the table, including much gold and silver plate, which were all carried off by the guests after the meal. The only instance recorded in which a Persian army suffered from want of supplies was during the invasion of Ethiopia by Cambyses, when, according to Herodotus, the army was reduced to such straits that the soldiers began to eat each other.

The Persians readily gave quarter when an enemy asked for it, and usually treated prisoners of war very kindly. Important personages, such as kings or princes, were allowed to retain either their titles and their freedom with even a nominal authority, or received appendages in other portions of the Persian dominions, or were kept about the court as friends and table-companions of the Great King, as in the case of Crœsus. Prisoners of less rank were usually allowed land and houses in some provinces far from their own country, and thereafter were in the condition of subject nations, according to Herodotus, Strabo and Quintus Curtius. Prisoners were never exchanged. In a few instances only, as in the case of the Thebans taken prisoners at Thermopylæ, were prisoners treated with severity; but here they were regarded as rebels, because they had previously given "earth and water" as tokens of submission. The Greek captives who met Alexander after the battle of Arbela, some of them branded and others mutilated, may have been Greeks of Asia Minor who had been guilty of rebellion. Rebels were liable to any punishment which the king thought proper to inflict upon them; and in some cases, after a rebellion, sentences of extreme severity were passed upon the persons regarded as having been most in fault. Herodotus tells us that three thousand Babylonians were crucified by order of Darius Hystaspes, in punishment for their revolt. The Behistun Inscription informs us that, where an example was needed, the leader of a rebellion and his chief adherents were crucified. In some cases a rebel was chained to the king's door before he was executed. Minor punishments for rebellion were branding, and deportation of the rebels *en masse* from their own country to some distant region. In the former case they perhaps became royal slaves attached to the king's household. In the latter case they were treated as prisoners of war in general.

The conquest of Phœnicia, Cyprus, Egypt and the Greek islands gave the Persians the use of skilled seamen, vessels and dockyards, from which the Great King derived an almost inexhaustible supply of war-ships and transports. At times Persia held absolute command of the Mediterranean sea—as from B. C. 525 to B. C. 480, and again from B. C. 354 to B. C. 332; and she bore full sway over the Levant during the whole period of her empire, except during the short period of seventeen years from the battle of Eurymedon in B. C. 466 to the "Peace of Callias" in B. C. 449.

The war-ship most in favor during the period of Persian supremacy was the *trireme*, a decked galley impelled by rowers sitting in three tiers, or banks, one above another. This vessel had been invented by the Corinthians, according to Thucydides, and had been generally adopted by the nations bordering on the Mediterranean during the period from B. C. 700 to B. C. 525, when the Persians got control of the sea by the reduction of Phœnicia, Cyprus and Egypt. The Persian fleets principally consisted of triremes during the whole period of the empire.

The trireme carried a crew of two hundred persons, most of them rowers, and thirty men-at-arms, or marines. The rowers occupied small seats attached to the side of the vessel, arranged in three tiers obliquely, the second above and behind the first, and the third above and behind the second. Each rower managed an oar, working it through a hole pierced in the side of the vessel. He prevented his oar from slipping by a leathern strap, which he twisted around it and fastened to the thole, perhaps by means of a button. Besides the rowers the crew consisted of the captain, the steersman, the petty officers, and the sailors who trimmed the sails and looked to the rigging. The Persian trireme had a mast, and at least one square-shaped sail, hung across the mast by means of a yard or spar, like the square sails of modern vessels. The rudder was composed of two wide-bladed oars, one on each side of the stern, united by a cross-bar, and managed by one steersman. The middle portion of the trireme always had a deck, which was usually level with the bulwarks, and on which the men-at-arms stood when they engaged the enemy.

The trireme had a beak projecting from its prow, either above or below the water-line, strongly shod with an iron casting and ending in one or more sharp points, or in the head of an animal. Like a modern ram, a trireme used its beak against the side of an enemy's ship, and if it struck with full force it crushed in the vessel, and thus sunk the ship and crew. To secure itself against damage, the whole prow of a trireme was made very strong, and was supported at the side with beams to prevent the timbers from starting.

The description of the trireme is minutely

given by Herodotus, who says that the Persian fleet consisted also of other kinds of vessels, such as *triaconters, penteconters, cercuri* and others. Triaconters were long ships with sharp keels, shaped much like a trireme, rowed by thirty rowers sitting upon a level, like the rowers of modern boats, fifteen on each side of the vessel. Penteconters were much the same, but had more oars and oarsmen. Triaconters and Penteconters often had no sails. Cercuri were light boats, very long and swift; and were, according to Pliny, invented by the Cyprians.

The Persians used transports to convey horses or food. The horse-transports were large, clumsy vessels. Corn-transports were somewhat lighter. The ships of war were used to carry troops and to construct bridges, as well as for naval battles. The Persians constructed bridges of boats across unfordable streams, and also over the Bosphorus and the Hellespont during their invasions of Europe when they carried their arms against Scythia and Greece. Over these floating bridges, they safely passed their men, horses, camels, chariots and carts from one continent to the other. The bridge erected across the Hellespont by Xerxes was broken by the violence of the elements; and his army, which had passed into Europe over this bridge, had to return on board ships to Asia.

The Persian fleets were manned by subject nations—Phœnicians, Syrians, Egyptians, Cypriots, Cilicians, Lycians, Pamphylians, Carians, Greeks. These were equipped in their respective national costumes and served side by side in their several contingents of ships, thus giving the fleet of the Persians the same motley appearance exhibited by their army. The marines, or fighting force of the navy, was an almost homogeneous body, composed of only the kindred Medes and Persians, and the Sacæ. Each ship carried thirty of these.

A Persian fleet and army constituting one expedition were generally placed under one commander, who, however, entrusted the direction of the fleet in a sea-fight to such officer, or officers, as he named; while he conducted the operations on land. The fleet and army were sometimes assigned to different commanders of coördinate authority, and this arrangement caused misunderstanding and quarrel.

In battle a Persian fleet endeavored to enclose the enemy in the form of a crescent, or detached squadrons to cut off their retreat. They formed their line several ships deep, and advanced directly at their best possible speed against the foe just before the battle began, seeking to sink the enemy's ships by main force. If met by a skillful adversary, who avoided or withstood their first onset, they were likely to be thrown into confusion because of their vast numbers, and were placed at the mercy of their antagonist, who was thus able to shatter or sink their vessels. In such an event the Persians would lose very heavily, as most of their sailors could not swim.

When the Persian naval commanders desired to avoid an engagement, the ships were run upon the shore, a rampart was thrown up around them and defended by sailors. The crews of Persian vessels were always armed, so as to act as soldiers on shore behind a rampart when occasion demanded. Under such circumstances they were also assisted by such of their army as might happen to be in the vicinity.

The Asiatic Greeks furnished the largest number of ships in the Persian navy; the Phœnicians the next largest number; the Egyptians third; next the Cypriots; then the Cilicians; then the Carians; then the Lycians; and the Pamphylians the least. The best ships and the best sailors were the Phœnicians, particularly those of Sidon. In later times ships were furnished by Phœnicia, and also by Cilicia and Cyprus. Xenophon and Arrian mention the Phœnicians only. Thucydides mentions Phœnicians and Cilicians. Diodorus Siculus mentions Phœnicians, Cilicians and Cypriots. Herodotus states that in the fleet of Xerxes the combined Greek contingents numbered three hundred and seven ships; the Phœnicians and Syrians furnishing three hundred, the

Egyptians two hundred, the Cypriots one hundred and fifty, the Cilicians one hundred, the Carians seventy, the Lycians fifty, and the Pamphylians thirty.

Having considered the warlike usages of the Persians, we now come to their peaceful habits, manners and customs. The Persian king was what all other Asiatic monarchs have ever been—an absolute despot. Says Rawlinson: "The Persian king held the same rank and position in the eyes of his subjects which the great monarch of Western Asia, whoever he might be, had always occupied from time immemorial. He was their lord and master, absolute disposer of their lives, liberties, and property; the sole fountain of law and right, incapable himself of doing wrong, irresponsible, irresistible—a sort of God upon earth; one whose favor was happiness, at whose frown men trembled, before whom all bowed themselves down with the lowest and humblest obeisance."

The Persian monarch displayed a state and pomp of the utmost magnificence. His ordinary dress in time of peace was the long flowing "Median garment," or *candys*, mentioned by Xenophon, which was probably made of the most costly silk, and "which, with its ample folds, its wide hanging sleeves, and its close fit about the neck and chest, gave dignity to almost any figure, and excellently set off the noble presence of an Achæmenian prince." The royal robe was either altogether of purple, or sometimes of purple embroidered with gold. It extended below the ankles, and was fastened to the waist by a broad girdle. A tunic or shirt was worn under it, reaching from the neck to the knee, and its tight-fitting sleeves covered the entire arm as far as the waist. This tunic is spoken of by Xenophon, Diodorus Siculus and Strabo. The tunic was of a purple color, like the *candys*, or royal robe, but was also striped or mixed with white. The lower limbs were covered by trousers of a crimson color. He wore shoes on his feet like those of the Medes, long and tapering at the toe, buttoned in front, and reaching far up the instep; their color being deep yellow or saffron, according to Æschylus.

So far the Persian king's costume was very much like that of the higher class of his subjects. His head-dress, called *kitaris*, or *kidaris*, was a tall stiff cap, becoming slightly wider as it ascended to the top, and ending in a ring or circle projecting beyond the lines of the sides. A fillet, or band—the *diadem* proper—which was blue, spotted with white, was worn around the *kidaris* near the bottom. The *kidaris*, or tiara, of the Persian monarchs, was made perhaps of cloth or felt, and was high and stiff. Other Persians wore only soft, rounded fillets and low caps around their heads.

The Persian king was likewise distinguished by his golden scepter and his parasol. The scepter was a plain rod, five feet long, ornamented with a ball at its upper end, and tapering to nearly a point at its lower end. The king held it in his right hand near the thick end, resting the thin end on the ground in front of him. When walking he planted it upright before him. When sitting he sloped it outwards with its point on the ground. The parasol was confined to the king in Persia, as it was in Assyria. The Persian parasol had no tassels or flaps like the Assyrian, but otherwise resembled it. It was held over the king's head on state occasions by an attendant who followed next behind him.

The Persian monarch's throne was an elevated seat with a high back, but no arms, and was cushioned and adorned with a fringe and with mouldings or carvings along the back and legs. The legs ended in lions' feet, resting on half balls which were ribbed or fluted. The sides of the chair below the seat were paneled, like the Assyrian thrones, but had no carvings. The seat was so high above the ground that a footstool was required for the monarch's feet. The legs of this plain footstool ended in bulls' feet.

The king wore gold ear-rings inlaid with precious stones. He also wore golden bracelets around his wrists, a golden collar around his neck, and a golden girdle around his waist. In this girdle he carried a short sword, and Quintus Curtius says that the sheath was formed of a single precious stone.

The Persian monarch was attended in war by his charioteer, his stool-bearer, his bow-bearer, and his quiver-bearer; in peace by his parasol-bearer and his fan-bearer, who also carried the royal pocket-handkerchief. Other officers of the court were the steward of the household; the groom, or master of the horse; the eunuch, or keeper of the women; the "King's Eyes and Ears," who informed the sovereign on all important matters; the scribes, or secretaries, who wrote the king's letters and edicts; the messengers, who went his errands; the ushers, who introduced strangers to the king; the "tasters," who tried the various dishes set before the monarch to see if they contained poison; the cup-bearers, who handed the king his wine and tasted it; the chamberlains, who helped him to bed; and the musicians, who entertained him with song and harp. The court also embraced guards, doorkeepers, huntsmen, grooms, cooks and many other domestic servants, along with a great number of visitors and guests, princes, nobles, captives of rank, foreign refugees, ambassadors, travelers, etc. Ctesias tells us that the king fed daily within the precincts of his palace no less than fifteen thousand persons, and that each day's food cost four hundred talents. A thousand beasts, such as sheep, goats, oxen, stags, horses, asses and camels, were slaughtered for each repast, in addition to an abundance of fowl, such as ordinary poultry and ostriches.

The Persian king himself did not often dine with his guests. Sometimes he admitted his queen and several of his children. Sometimes some of his privileged companions were received at a banquet of wine, where they drank in the royal presence, but of a different wine and on different terms. The king reclined on a golden couch, and drank the red wine of Helbon. The guests drank an inferior wine, seated on the floor. The guests were divided into two classes at a great banquet. Those of lower rank were entertained in an outer court of the chamber to which the public were admitted. Those of the higher class entered the private apartments, and were feasted in a chamber opposite to the king's chamber, the monarch being concealed from view by a curtain hung across the door. On a royal birthday or other great festival the king presided openly at the banquet, drinking and conversing with his lords and showing himself to many of the guests. Gold and silver couches were spread for all, and "royal wine in abundance" was served in goblets of gold. The guests often carried home such food as was set before them and they did not eat.

The pillared courts and halls of the great palaces of the Achæmenian kings at Susa and Persepolis were well furnished and fitted internally. The floors were paved with stones of different colors, blue, red, white and black; and Athenæus tells us that carpets from the looms of Sardis were spread in some of the courts for the king to walk upon. The spaces between the pillars were filled with elegant hangings of several colors, white, green and violet, which were fastened with fine linen cords to silver rings and marble pillars, so as to screen the guests from view, while not excluding the pleasant summer breeze. The walls of the apartments were covered with plates of gold. The furniture was rich and elegant. The king's golden throne stood under an embroidered canopy or awning held up by four golden pillars inlaid with precious stones. Gold and silver couches filled the rooms. The king's private chamber was adorned with rich and elegant objects. The golden vine impending over the monarch's bed was the work of Theodore of Samos, and here costly precious stones were used to imitate grapes. Here perhaps was also the golden plane-tree, and also a bowl of solid gold, likewise the work of the great Samian metallurgist and distinguished for its artistic workmanship.

Like other Asiatic monarchs, the Medo-Persian kings had a royal harem, or seraglio. The earlier monarchs had only three or four wives and a moderate number of concubines. Herodotus says Darius Hystaspes had four wives. Three wives of Cambyses are only mentioned. One of the wives held the highest station and was alone entitled *queen*, being considered wife in a different sense from the others. Such was Atossa to Darius Hystaspes, Amestris to Xerxes, Statira to Artaxerxes Mnemon. The chief wife, or queen-consort, wore on her head a royal crown, or tiara. She was the recognized head of the female apartments, or Gynæceum, and the concubines acknowledged her dignity by prostrating themselves before her presence. When the king entertained the male courtiers on great occasions, she feasted all the females in her own portion of the palace. She had a large revenue assigned her, mainly by an established law or custom, as Herodotus informs us. Her dress was magnificent and she displayed great love of ornament. Herodotus also tells us of the influence and power wielded by some of the queen-consorts.

The other wives of the monarch—daughters of the chief nobles—occupied an inferior status; having none of the privileges of the chief wife, and only saw the king when summoned to share his apartment by turns. They occupied that part of the Gynæceum called "the first house of the women." The concubines occupied the portion of the Gynæceum designated "the second house of the women." They were in the special charge of a eunuch. Fair damsels were constantly brought from various parts of the empire to supply the harem; a continual succession being required, as none shared the royal couch more than once, unless she won the sovereign's special regard. In the later period of the empire the concubines became so numerous that they amounted, according to Quintus Curtius, to three hundred and sixty. The king took them along in his wars and in his hunting expeditions. A part of their duty was to sing and play for the king's entertainment, and Athenæus tells us that they had to perform this task during all of each night.

The Gynæceum—at least in the palace at Susa—was a building distinct from the general structure, separated from the "king's house" by a court; and comprised at least three sets of apartments—those for the virgins who had not yet seen the monarch, those for the concubines, and those for the queen-consort and the other royal wives. Two eunuchs of distinction had charge respectively of the apartment of the wives and that of the concubines. The queen-consort exercised authority over all the male and female inmates of the apartment for the wives.

The monarch's mother, if she outlived his father, held a higher position at her son's court than that of his chief wife. As queen-mother, she retained the ensigns of royalty which she had worn during her husband's reign, and exercised far more authority or influence than she had wielded as queen-consort. The habits of veneration and obedience to which the monarch had been reared when a boy, he retained when a man; and the sovereign who tyrannized over millions of subjects yielded in the seraglio to the power of a woman whose influence he was not strong enough to cast off. The queen-mother sat at the royal table whenever the king dined with his wife, and occupied a seat above him, while the wife occupied a seat below. She had a suite of eunuchs distinct from those of her son, according to Plutarch. She was supplied with ample revenues. She virtually exercised a power of life and death, though she could not legally claim this power. She screened offenders from punishment, obtaining for them the royal pardon, or giving them a refuge in her own apartments; and she poisoned, or openly executed, such as excited her jealousy or resentment; as Plutarch tells us was the case with Parysatis, the mother of Artaxerxes Mnemon.

The man-servants about the harem were all eunuchs. Each wife of the king—as well as the queen-mother—had a number of eunuchs among her attendants; while the king employed a certain number of this class of unfortunates to have charge of the apartment of the concubines and that of the virgins. His own attendants appear also to have been mainly eunuchs. In the later times of the empire eunuchs seem to have wielded great political power, and to have held the principal offices of state. They were the king's counselors in the palace and his generals in the field. They had control of the education of the young princes, and had no difficulty in making them their tools. Their intrigues and ambition led to the plots and conspiracies, the executions and assassinations, which disgrace the later history of the Medo-Persian Empire. Little is mentioned of the eunuchs before the reign of Xerxes. The Persepolitan sculptures give us no representations of eunuchs. The Persian sculptures give us no representation of a female, and the inscriptions make no reference to the gentler sex—a reserve which has always characterized Asiatics with regard to women. Even now it is considered highly improper in Persia to ask a man about his wife. Plutarch states that in ancient Persia it was a capital crime to address a royal concubine, or even to pass her litter upon the road. The litters conveying women were always curtained. Queen Statira, consort of Artaxerxes Mnemon, attracted general attention by relaxing the ordinary etiquette in riding in her litter with her curtains drawn, though only females were permitted to approach her. Married women could not see even their fathers or brothers, according to Herodotus. Eunuchs were expected to confine themselves to their proper place in the seraglio, or to attend its female inmates when they traveled in their litters, or when they took the air; but were not to be seen in the throne-room, the ante-chambers, or the outer courts of the palace. This seclusion of the women and eunuchs of the harem accounts for their non-representation upon the Persian sculptures.

The six privileged families of ancient Persia ranked next to the royal family, or clan of the Achæmenidæ, and held a rank above that of all the other grandees. Herodotus informs us that these six families derived their special dignity from the circumstance that they had been the accomplices of Darius Hystaspes in the conspiracy which overthrew the Pseudo-Smerdis; and from the time of Darius Hystaspes there were, besides the royal clan of the Achæmenidæ, six great Persian families, whose chiefs had the privilege of free access to the king, and from which he was obliged to select his legitimate wives. The chiefs were known as "the Seven Princes," or "the Seven Counselors." They occupied seats next to the monarch at public festivals. They had the privilege of tendering him their advice at any time. They recommended great public measures, and were partially responsible for them. They could ask admittance to the king's presence whenever they chose, unless he were in the seraglio. They had precedence in all ceremonies and had a rank entirely distinct from office. Occasionally they held office. They wore no special insignia.

Officers of the court always carried wands about three feet long, or an ornament resembling a lotus blossom, which the king himself sometimes held in his hand. These officers wore the long Median robe and the fluted cap, or the close-fitting Persian tunic and trowsers. All wore girdles, in which a dagger was frequently placed; and all wore gold collars and gold ear-rings. The Median robes were of different colors—crimson, scarlet, purple, dark grey, etc. A sleeved cloak, or coat, extending to the feet, was sometimes worn over the Persian tunic; and was fastened in front by strings and hung loosely from the shoulders, the sleeves generally hanging empty at the side.

None, excepting the "Seven Princes," could approach the king without being introduced by the usher. Herodotus, Justin and Plutarch state that all who entered the royal presence were required to prostrate themselves. The hands of those introduced had to be hidden in their sleeves during the audience. None were permitted to touch the carpets laid for the king to walk upon in the palace courts. It was a capital offense to enter the monarch's presence without being summoned, the person so offending being put to death by the attendants, unless the king held out his golden scepter towards the offender, as a sign that he pardoned the intrusion. It was likewise a capital crime to sit down, even ignorantly, upon the royal throne; and it was a serious offense to wear any of the monarch's cast-off garments. The king was bound by an iron-clad etiquette, as well as were his subjects. He was required to live mainly in seclusion; to eat his meals mostly alone; to never go on foot outside the palace walls; to never revoke an order once given, although he might intensely regret it; to never disregard a promise, no matter what evil results he might fear from its observance. It was essential that he should appear infallible, immutable, entirely free from repentance, to uphold the quasi-divine character ascribed to him.

The king only was allowed the enjoyment of certain luxuries. The wheat of Assos was sent to court to furnish him with bread, and the vines of Helbon were cultivated solely to supply him with wine. Water was conveyed to Susa, from distant streams considered specially sweet and pure, for his own use. In his expeditions he was accompanied by a train of wagons laden with silver flasks filled with water from the clear stream of the Choaspes. The salt used to season his food was brought from the oasis of Siwah. Every province showed pride in supplying him with its best and choicest products.

Hunting and playing at dice were the chief amusements of the Great King. Darius Hystaspes was represented on his signet-cylinder as engaged in a lion-hunt. This cylinder—which has a trilingual inscription reading, "Darius, the Great King" —informs us that the Persian kings, like the Assyrian, pursued the lions in their chariots and usually slew them by means of arrows. Seated in a light chariot, and attended by an unarmed charioteer, they roused the king of beasts from his lair, and chased him at full speed if he fled, or, if he boldly faced his pursuers, attacked him with arrows or with the javelin. Sometimes the king indulged in this sport alone, but usually he was accompanied by some of his courtiers, who participated in the chase on condition that they did not shoot off their arrows before he had discharged his. If they disregarded this law they might subject themselves to capital punishment, or at least to exile.

The Persian monarchs may also have chased stags, antelopes, bears, leopards, wild asses, wild boars and wild sheep—animals found in the vicinity of the royal palaces, and mentioned by Xenophon among the beasts hunted by Cyrus the Great. In chasing the wild ass the horsemen scattered themselves over the plain and pursued the animal by turns. As the wild ass could outrun any horse with a rider on his back, relays of horses were needed to tire him out, and thus enable the hunters to bring him within range of their weapons.

Sometimes the kings hunted in their parks, or "paradises," which were vast walled enclosures, well wooded, and watered with sparkling streams, in which were kept various kinds of wild beasts, mainly such harmless ones as stags, antelopes and wild sheep, which the monarchs pursued and dispatched with their arrows, or with the javelin; but this sport was regarded as tame in comparison with hunting in the open field.

Inside the palace the Persian kings amused themselves by playing at dice, the stakes sometimes running as high as a thousand darics, equal to almost eleven hundred pounds sterling, on a single throw. Plutarch tells us that the kings played for the persons of their slaves, eunuchs, or others, who, when lost, became the absolute property of the winner in the game.

Carving or planing wood was another favorite royal amusement. Ælian states that when the Persian monarch went on a journey he diverted himself in his carriage in this way; and Ctesias says that he amused himself thus inside the palace.

A Persian king seldom found any pleasure in literature. The letters, edicts, and perhaps also the inscriptions of the king, were the work of the scribes, who received their orders from the king or his ministers, and clothed them in their own language. The scribes never asked their royal master to place his signature on a parchment, his seal with his name engraved upon it sufficiently authenticating all edicts and proclamations.

Herodotus, Xenophon and Josephus give us accounts of the serious occupations of the Persian sovereigns; such as the holding of councils, the reviewing of troops, the hearing of complaints, the granting or refusing of redress, the bestowing of rewards, perhaps the hearing of causes, and, above all, the direction of the civil administration of the empire. An enterprising monarch carefully heard all the reports from the officials of the different satrapies, and those from the persons appointed occasionally by the crown to inspect the condition of the various satrapies. The king's secretaries dispatched his answers to these reports, after he had duly deliberated upon them and affixed his seal to them. A Persian sovereign who resolved to govern as well as reign found ample employment in giving attention to the concerns of his vast empire; but few of these monarchs possessed energy and self-denial sufficient to give their constant attention to the serious duties of their royal station; the cares of government usually devolving upon some favorite adviser, either a relative or a eunuch, to whom the king entrusted the whole direction of public affairs, in order that he might abandon himself to sensual pleasures, to the sports of the chase, or to light and frivolous amusements.

Some of the Persian kings had the same passion for building which characterized the Assyrian and Babylonian monarchs. Herodotus says that the Persians had no temples. In architecture the kings devoted their chief efforts to the construction of palaces and tombs. The dead body of a Persian monarch was laid in a golden coffin, which was covered with a close-fitting lid, and placed in a massive structure built to serve both for a tomb and a monument, as in the case of Cyrus the Great; or in a chamber cut out of the side of some great mass of solid rock, as in the case of the later Persian sovereigns. In both cases the entrances to the tombs were carefully closed after the bodies had been placed in them. Aristobulus, Arrian and Strabo tell us that a number of objects, such as rich cloaks and tunics, trowsers, purple robes, gold collars, gold ear-rings set with gems, daggers, carpets, goblets and hangings, were placed inside the tomb with the coffin, for the king's use in the other world. The tombs were generally ornamented with sculptures, but out of the eight royal tombs discovered that of Darius Hystaspes alone is seen to have an inscription. If the tomb was built, and not cut out of the rock, the ground in its vicinity was formed into a park or garden, which Aristobolus and Arrian tell us was planted with all kinds of trees. A dwelling-house for the priests who watched over the royal sepulcher was in the park near the tomb.

We will now notice briefly the manners and customs of the Persian people. Herodotus tells us that the Persians were divided into ten tribes, four of which were nomadic and three agricultural. The nomadic tribes were the Dai, the Mardi, the Dropici and the Sagartii; the agricultural were the Panthialæi, the Derusiæi, and the Germanii, or Carmanians. The Pasargadæ, one of the three remaining tribes, were the ruling class in the Medo-Persian Empire.

Strabo and Xenophon carefully described the dress of the Persians. The poorer classes wore the leather tunic and trowsers, the national costume of ancient Persia; a loose felt cap on the head, a strap or belt around the waist, and high shoes on the feet, in early times; but a linen or muslin rag on the head and a longer tunic in later times. The richer classes generally adopted the Median costume prevailing at the court, wearing long purple or flowered robes with loose hanging sleeves, flowered tunics with sleeves extending to the knees, embroidered trowsers and elegant shoes. They also wore drawers under the trowsers, shirts under their tunics, gloves on their hands, and socks or stockings under their shoes; all of which were rare luxuries in ancient times. Like most other Orientals, the ancient Persians were very fond of ornaments. Xenophon and Herodotus described these fully. Men of rank wore gold chains or gold collars around their necks, and gold bracelets around their wrists. The sheaths and handles of their swords and daggers were usually of gold. Many of them wore ear-rings. The trappings of their horses were elegant and costly, the bits of the bridles being frequently of solid gold. They also wore costly gems, and necklaces, bracelets and anklets of pearl. Strabo says that even children wore ornaments of reddish gold.

Herodotus and Xenophon also described the furniture of the better class of houses as elegant and costly. The tables were plated or inlaid with silver and gold. The magnificent couches for the repose of the inmates had gorgeous coverlets, and the legs of the couches rested on carpets so elastic as to act as a kind of spring. All wealthy mansions could make a rich display of gold and silver plate, especially drinking cups.

In the earlier times all Persians were noted for their temperance and sobriety. Their ordinary food was wheat bread, barley cakes, and roasted or broiled meat, seasoned with salt and with bruised cress-seed, a substitute for mustard. Herodotus, Xenophon and Strabo say that the earlier Persians drank only water; and Xenophon says that they ate only one meal each day. The poorer classes subsisted on the natural products of the soil. Strabo says that they were fed on acorns and wild pears. Ælian says that the poorer class lived on milk, cheese, dates and wild fruits.

But these simple habits of the earlier Persians soon gave way to luxury and self-indulgence when their conquests enabled them to gratify all their desires and propensities. Xenophon tells us that they then began their one meal a day early in the morning and made it last till night. Only on grand occasions were many kinds of meat set upon the board; but there was a continual succession of the lighter kinds of food, with intervals between the courses. Wine was now substituted for water, each man priding himself on the quantity he was able to drink, and the banquets usually ending in general intoxication. Drunkenness actually became a kind of institution; as at the yearly feast of Mithras, the King of Persia, according to Duris, was bound to be drunk; and Herodotus and Strabo say that it became a common custom to deliberate on all important matters under the influence of wine, and intoxication was a family duty when a crisis impended in any household.

Besides the meats we consume, the Persians ate the flesh of goats, horses, asses and camels. Poultry, such as geese and chickens, formed a part of the diet of the wealthy; as did various kinds of game, such as wild boars, stags, antelopes, bustards and perhaps partridges. The inhabitants of the coast-region largely used oysters and fish.

The strictest etiquette prevailed among all classes of Persians. Each man saluted his equal, his superior or his inferior according to well-known rules, which were universally observed. Inferiors prostrated themselves on the ground when they met superiors. Equals kissed each other on the lips. Persons almost equal kissed each other's cheeks, according to Herodotus. Wives lived secluded in the Gynæceum, or went out in litters, seeing no males except their husbands, their sons, and their husband's eunuchs. Concubines sometimes danced, sang and played at banquets to entertain their master's guests.

According to Herodotus and Strabo, a Persian was permitted to have several wives and as many concubines as he desired. Most of the wealthy class had vast numbers of each, as every Persian prided himself on the number of his sons; and the king gave an annual prize to the Persian who was able to show the most sons living. According to Xenophon, the younger Cyrus took two Greek concubines with him in his expedition against his brother. In the earlier times Persians took their concubines with them in military expeditions, but left their wives at home. Each concubine had a litter at her disposal, and a number of female attendants to wait upon her and execute her orders. In the later period of the empire, according to Quintus Curtius, wives accompanied their husbands with the army.

Herodotus, Xenophon, Plato and Strabo all inform us that the Persians—at least those of the leading clans—carefully educated their sons. During their first five years the boys remained entirely with the women; seldom, if ever, seeing their fathers. After that time their training began. They were expected to rise before daybreak, and to appear at a certain place where they were exercised with other boys of their age in running, slinging stones, shooting with the bow and throwing the javelin. At seven they were taught to ride, and soon afterwards they were permitted to begin to hunt. They were taught not only to manage the horse, but to jump on and off his back when he was at speed, and to shoot with the bow and throw the javelin with unerring aim while the horse was at full gallop. State-officers conducted the hunting, and they endeavored to thus create in the youths under their care all the qualities essential in war. The boys were taught to endure the extremes of heat and cold, to perform long marches, to cross rivers without wetting their weapons, to sleep at night in the open air, to be satisfied with one meal in two days, and to subsist at times on the wild products of the country, such as acorns, wild pears and the fruit of the terebinth-tree. On such days when they did no hunting they engaged in athletic exercises and contests with the bow or the javelin during the morning, after which they dined simply on the plain food already mentioned as that of the men in the earlier times, and occupied the afternoon in such employments as agriculture, planting, digging for roots, etc., or in manufacturing arms and hunting implements, such as nets and springs. By this kind of training the Persian youth acquired hardy and temperate habits. In the inculcation of morals, their teachers chiefly insisted on the strictest regard for the truth. They received very little intellectual education, and learning to read was no part of their regular training. They received religious teaching and moral knowledge in the form of legendary poems, which made them familiar with the deeds of gods and heroes, which the teachers sung or recited to them, afterwards requiring them to repeat what they had heard, or, at least, to give some account of it. This education, commencing when the boy was five years old, continued fifteen years, and ended when he was twenty.

This training made the Persians excellent soldiers and accomplished horsemen. Having acquired from early boyhood the habit of passing the greater portion of each day in the saddle, they felt most at home when they were on horseback. When thus mounted they pursued the stag, the wild boar, the antelope, even sometimes the bear or the lion; and discharged their arrows, or slung stones, or threw their javelins at these animals with deadly aim. They only sometimes dismounted from their steeds when the beast angrily turned on its pursuers and stood at bay or attacked them in its furious despair, in which case they received the attack or slew the brute on foot with a short but strong hunting-spear. Hunting was the chief pastime of the higher class of Persians as long as the ancient manners continued in vogue, and the bolder spirits indulged in this amusement long after the decay of the empire commenced and the advance of luxury had altered the character of the people.

A Persian was regarded as having reached manhood at the age of fifteen, when he was enrolled in the army. He remained subject to military service thenceforth until he was fifty. Those of the highest rank became the king's body-guard and constituted the garrison of the capital. They numbered about fourteen or fifteen thousand men. Others, though subject to military duty, attached themselves to the court, and expected civil employment as satraps, secretaries, attendants, ushers, judges, inspectors, messengers. A portion engaged in those agricultural employments which the Zoroastrian religion regarded as most honorable. But the greater part of the nation, like the legionaries of imperial Rome, engaged in garrison duty in the provinces of the empire. Persia could not have had a population of more than two millions. Only one-fourth of these could have been males between the ages of fifteen and fifty. This half a million men not only supplied the official class at court and throughout the provinces, and furnished those who tilled the soil for Persia proper, but also supplied the whole empire with those many large garrisons which upheld the Medo-Persian dominion in all the conquered provinces. Herodotus states that in his day Egypt alone contained a standing army of one hundred and twenty thousand Persians; and Persia proper furnished the bulk of the standing army performing garrison duty in all the provinces.

Herodotus informs us that the Persians detested commerce, because shopping and bargaining involved temptations to deceit and falsehood. Strabo tells us that the richer classes boasted that they did not buy or sell, and they were doubtless supplied with all the necessaries of life from their estates, and by their slaves and dependents. The middle class would buy, but not sell; while the lowest and poorest were traders and artisans. Xenophon says that shops were banished from the public portions of the towns.

Quintus Curtius states that the Persian ladies regarded it beneath their dignity to soil their hands with work, and despised the labors of the loom, which no Grecian princess considered as unbecoming her rank.

According to Xenophon, some effeminate and demoralizing customs were introduced into the Medo-Persia Empire during the general advance of luxury under Xerxes. The Persians were very careful with their beards and hair from the very earliest period, curling both, and making the beard to partly hang straight from the chin. They at length began to wear false hair, used cosmetics to beautify their complexions, and colored the eyelids to make the eyes appear larger and more beautiful. They had special servants to perform the operations of the toilet, and these were called "adorners" by the Greeks. Their furniture became more soft and elegant. Their floors were covered with beautiful carpets, and their beds with many delicate coverlets. A cloth was spread upon the ground for them to sit upon. They would not mount a horse unless he was so richly caparisoned that the seat of his back was softer than their couches. They also increased the number and variety of their viands and of their sauces, always seeking for strange delicacies and offering rewards for the invention of "new pleasures." An unnecessary number of indolent menials were kept in all wealthy familes, each servant being confined strictly to one duty; and porters, bread-makers, cooks, cup-bearers, water-bearers, table-waiters, chamberlains, "awakers," "adorners," were all distinct from one another, and filled each noble mansion, advancing the general demoralization. According to Herodotus, the vice of pæderasty was learned from the Greeks, and the licentious worship of Beltis, with its religious prostitution, from the Assyrians.

The laws of the Medes and Persians, which the Hebrew Scriptures tell us were unchangeable, were of the most barbarous cruelty and severity. Herodotus, Plutarch, Xenophon, Ctesias and Nicolas of Damascus describe these. Not only were murder, rape, treason and rebellion punished with death; but also such offenses as deciding a case wrongfully for a bribe, intruding on the king's privacy without permission, coming near to one of his concubines, seating one's self upon the throne, even accidentally, and the like. The modes of execution were also cruel. Poisoners had their heads placed upon a broad stone, and had their faces crushed and their brains beaten out by repeated blows from another stone. Ravishers and rebels were crucified. Two legal forms of execution were burying alive, as mentioned by Herodotus, and the lingering death resulting from placing the victim's body between two boats in such a way that only the head and hands projected at one end and the feet at the other, as related by Plutarch. Xenophon states that the younger Cyrus maintained good order in his satrapy by cutting off the hands and feet, or putting out the eyes, of those guilty of theft or rascality; persons thus maimed being seen along all the most frequented roads. Other writers and the Behistun Inscription mention similar punishments inflicted on rebels, and Quintus Curtius states that captives taken in war were also thus dealt with. According to Nicolas of Damascus, mutilation and scourging were the ordinary methods of punishment for secondary offenses. Herodotus states that the Persians imprisoned only accused persons for safe keeping before the time of arrest and that of execution; and Ctesias tell us that political offenders were exiled to the small islands in the Persian Gulf.

Says Professor Rawlinson concerning the uncertain tenure of happiness: "On the whole the Persians may seem to have enjoyed an existence free from care, and only too prosperous to result in the formation of a high and noble character. They were the foremost Asiatic people of their time, and were fully conscious of their preëminency. A small ruling class in a vast Empire, they enjoyed almost a monopoly of office, and were able to draw to themselves much of the wealth of the provinces. Allowed the use of arms, and accustomed to lord it over the provincials, they themselves maintained their self-respect, and showed, even towards the close of their Empire, a spirit and an energy seldom exhibited by any but a free people. But there was nevertheless a dark side to the picture—a lurking danger which must have thrown a shadow over the lives of all the nobler and richer of the nation, unless they were utterly thoughtless. The irresponsible authority and cruel dispositions of the kings, joined to the recklessness with which they delegated the power of life and death to their favorites, made it impossible for any person of eminence in the whole Empire to feel sure that he might not any day be seized and accused of a crime, or even without the form of an accusation be taken and put to death, after suffering the most excruciating tortures. To produce this result, it was enough to have failed through any cause whatever in the performance of a set task, or to have offended, even by doing him too great a service, the monarch or one of his favorites. Nay, it was enough to have provoked, through a relation or a connection, the anger or jealousy of one in favor at Court; for the caprice of an Oriental would sometimes pass over the real culprit and exact vengeance from one quite guiltless—even, it may be, unconscious—of the offense given. Theoretically, the Persian was never to be put to death for a single crime; or at least he was not to suffer until the king had formally considered the whole tenor of his life, and struck a balance between his good and evil deeds to see which outweighed the other. Practically, the monarch slew with his own hand any one whom he chose, or, if he preferred it, ordered him to instant execution, without trial or inquiry. His wife and his mother indulged themselves in the same pleasing liberty of slaughter, sometimes obtaining his tacit consent to their proceedings, sometimes without consulting him. It may be said that the sufferers could at no time be very many in number, and that therefore no very wide-spread alarm can have been commonly felt; but the horrible nature of many of the punishments, and the impossibility of conjecturing on whom they might next fall, must be set against their infrequency; and it must be remembered that an awful horror, from which no precautions can save a man, though it happen to few, is more terrible than a score of minor perils, against which it is possible to guard. Noble Persians were liable to be beheaded, to be stoned to death, to be suffocated with ashes, to have their tongues torn out by the roots, to be buried alive, to be shot in mere wantonness, to be flayed and then crucified, to be buried all but the head, and to perish by the lingering agony of 'the boat.' If they escaped these modes of execution, they might be secretly poisoned, or they might be exiled, or transported for life. Their wives and daughters might be seized and horribly mutilated, or buried alive, or cut into a number of fragments. With these perils constantly impending over their heads, the happiness of the nobles can scarcely have been more real than that of Damocles upon the throne of Dionysius."

In the ancient world the Persians did not possess as great a fame as architects and artists as did their instructors in art, science and letters, the Assyrians and Babylonians; because their works, being less ancient and less original, did not in the same way strike the lively imagination of the Greeks, who were also jealous of a contemporary and rival nation, and who could not have the same access to the Persian masterpieces as they had to the Babylonian, and therefore possessed less knowledge about the former. Herodotus and Xenophon, who impressed their countrymen with the grandeur and magnificence of the great structures of Assyria and Babylonia, never visited Persia proper. Ctesias, who resided at the Persian court for seventeen years, must have seen Susa, Ecbatana and Persepolis, and must therefore have been familiar with the character of the palaces, but he seems to have said little about these edifices. Only after Alexander had led his conquering army through the vast Medo-Persian Empire was a proper estimate made of the great Persian structures; and the most magnificent one of them—that of Persepolis—was burned to the ground through a barbarous act of the Macedonian conqueror as soon as it was seen, thus depriving the Greeks of an opportunity to fully recognize the true greatness of Persian architecture, even after they had occupied the country. Nevertheless we observe thereafter, as in the works of Polybius and Strabo, an acknowledgment of the merits of Persian art, of its grandeur and magnificence.

The moderns, on the other hand, for the last three centuries have exaggerated the greatness of Persian architecture. Ever since Europeans first began to visit the East, the ruins of Persepolis and those of other portions of Persia attracted the special attention of travelers; while the site of Babylon received but slight notice, and that of Nineveh and the other great Assyrian cities was scarcely known. English, French and German *savans* measured, described and figured the Persian ruins with the utmost precision and minuteness. Ker Porter, Chardin, Le Brun, Ouseley and the elder Niebuhr zealously endeavored to represent fully and faithfully the wonders of the *Chehl Minar;* and the exhaustive literary descriptions of the remains of Persepolis by Baron Texier and MM. Flandin and Coste soon appeared.

Persian architecture was displayed in the palace and the tomb. Temples were insignificant before the time of Artaxerxes Mnemon; and therefore did not attract the attention of contemporaries, and were not of a character to leave traces of themselves to subsequent times. But the palaces and sepulchers of the Persian monarchs are noticed by Ctesias, Arrian and Diodorus Siculus as interesting works; and the remains of these structures are to be identified with the ruins still seen in Persia.

There are now remaining vestiges of four great Persian palaces—that of Ecbatana, the Median capital; that of Darius and Xerxes on the great mound of Susa; that within the walls of Persepolis; and the Great Palace, in the vicinity of the same city. The last of these—the chief residence of the later Medo-Persian monarchs—was the one burned by Alexander the Great; and its remains have been described by Mr. Fergusson, in his *Handbook of Architecture*, as "by far the most remarkable group of buildings now existing in this part of Asia."

This edifice, or group of edifices, constituted the greatest of the architectural works of the Medo-Persian kings, and these have suffered less from the ravages of time and barbarism than the other structures of ancient Persia; while modern research and excavation have brought more to light concerning these magnificent Persepolitan buildings than the other remains of this famous ancient land.

The structures at Persepolis are situated on an immense mound like the Assyrian and Babylonian palaces. The mound or platform at Persepolis is raised at the foot of a high range of rocky hills, on which it abuts toward the east. It consists of solid masses of hewn stone united by metal clamps, and laid so as to form a smooth perpendicular wall, the least height of which above the plain below is twenty feet. The platform is an oblong square, two-thirds as broad as long. The north side is not parallel to the south side, and forms an angle of about eighty degrees with the western side. On the three sides of the platform are numerous angular projections and indentations. The platform is not uniformly high, but consists of several distinct terraces, three of which yet remain. The southern terrace is the lowest, extending about eight hundred feet from east to west and about one hundred and seventy-five feet from north to south. The northern terrace is more than thrice as wide as the southern one, and is elevated about thirty-five feet above the plain. The central or upper terrace is forty-five feet above the plain, and is seven hundred and seventy feet long on the west side of the platform, and about four hundred feet wide. On this central terrace were located most of the great and important buildings.

The ascents to these terraces were made by means of broad and solid staircases, which constitute a remarkable feature of the place. The staircase on the west front of the platform and leading from the plain to the top of the northern terrace is twenty-two feet wide, and Fergusson calls it "the noblest example of a flight of stairs to be found in any part of the world." It constitutes the only remaining ascent to the platform. "It consists of two distinct sets of steps, each composed of two flights, with a broad landing-place between them, the steps themselves running at right angles to the platform wall, and the two lower flights diverging, while the two upper ones converge to a common landing-place on the top. The slope of the stairs is so gentle that, though each step has a convenient width, the height of a step is in no case more than from three to four inches. It is thus easy to ride horses up and down the staircase, and travelers are constantly in the habit of ascending and descending it in this way."

Another remarkable staircase leads from the level of the northern terrace to that of the central. This staircase fronts to the north, and consists of four single flights of steps; two being central and facing each other, and leading to a projecting landing-place about twenty feet wide; while the other two are on each side of the central flights, about twenty-one yards from them. This staircase is two hundred and twelve feet long, its greatest projection being in front of the line of the terrace-on which it abuts, which is thirty-six feet. The steps are sixteen feet broad, and rise gently like those of the lower or platform staircase Each step is less than four inches, and so there are thirty-one steps in an ascent of ten feet.

This second staircase is elaborately ornamented, while the platform staircase is perfectly plain. The whole face of this second platform is covered with sculptures. The central projection, divided perpendicularly into three compartments, contains representations in the spandrels on each side, such as a lion devouring a bull; and in the compartment between the spandrels are eight colossal Persian guardsmen, armed with spears and with a sword or shield. Above the lion and bull, towards the edge of the spandrel where it slopes, forming a parapet to the steps, was a row of cypress trees; while at the end of the parapet and along its entire inner face were a set of small figures, guardsmen like those in the central compartment, but carrying mainly a bow and quiver instead of a shield. Along the extreme edge of the parapet on the outside was a narrow border thickly set with rosettes. In the long spaces between the central stairs and those on each side of them, the spandrels contained representations of the lion and bull similar to that of the first compartment; while between them and the central stairs the face of the wall is divided horizontally into three bands, each ornamented with a continuous row of figures. The highest row is mutilated. The middle row has some artistic merit. The whole scene represented on the right side illustrates the bringing of tribute or presents to the Great King by the subject nations. This subject was continued to some extent on the left side, but most of the space was occupied by representations of guards

1—29.-U. H.

and court officers; the guards being placed towards the center, keeping the principal stairs, while the officers were farther away. The three rows of figures were separated from one another by narrow bands, set thickly with rosettes. In the front of the middle staircase, the precise center of the entire work, and the space next to the spandrels to the extreme right and the extreme left, were marble slabs designed to bear inscriptions to commemorate the builder of the work, but only one of these inscriptions was completed. On the western end of the staircase was the following inscription in the ancient Persian language: "Xerxes the Great King, the King of Kings, the son of King Darius, the Achæmenian." The central and eastern tablets were never inscribed.

There were six other staircases, most of them consisting of a double flight of steps, resembling the central part of the staircase just described. Two of these belonged to the Palace of Darius, which was entered by their means from the central terrace, above which it is elevated about fourteen or fifteen feet. Two others belonged to the Palace of Xerxes, and led up to a wide paved space in front of that edifice, at an elevation of about ten feet above the general level of the central terrace. They were located at the two ends of the terrace opposite each other. The eastern one consisted of two double flights of steps, and in general arrangement resembled the staircase which led to the platform from the plain, excepting that it had no recess, but extended its full width across the line of the terrace. It was the more elegant of the two, and was adorned with representations of bull and lion combats, with figures of guardsmen, and with attendants conveying articles for the table or the toilet. The inscriptions upon it describe it as the work of Xerxes. The western staircase was composed only of two single flights of steps, facing each other, and having a narrow landing-place between them. Its ornamentation was similar to that of the eastern, though not so elaborate.

A staircase resembling the one just described, but still somewhat peculiar, was erected by Artaxerxes Ochus, at the western side of the Palace of Darius, so as to give it a second entrance. The spandrels there have the usual figures of the lion and bull, but the space between is arranged somewhat unusually. It is divided vertically and horizontally into eight square compartments, three on each side and two in the middle. The upper of these two contains only a winged circle, the emblem of Divinity. The lower compartment, twice as large as the upper, had an inscription of Artaxerxes Ochus, religious in tone, but barbarous in language. The other six compartments had each four figures, representing tribute-bearers introduced to the Great King by a court officer.

The other and original staircase to the Palace of Darius was at its northern side, and led up to the great portico, which was its only entrance in ancient times. Two flights of steps, facing each other, led to a paved space of the same extent as the portico and extending in front of it about five feet. On the base of the staircase were sculptures in one line, the lion and the bull being in each spandrel; and between the spandrels were eighteen colossal guardsmen, nine facing each way towards a central inscription, which was repeated in other languages on slabs set between the guardsmen and the bulls. Above the spandrels, on the parapet facing the stairs, was a line of figures representing attendants bringing materials for the banquet into the palace. A similar line embellished the inside wall of the staircase.

Opposite the staircase just described, and about thirty-two yards distant from it, was another almost similar staircase, leading up to the portico of another edifice, seemingly erected by Artaxerxes Ochus, and occupying the south-western corner of the upper terrace. Here were apparently the usual sculptures, but they are so mutilated as to be scarcely recognized.

Finally, there was a peculiar staircase, consisting of a flight of steps cut in the solid rock, leading up from the southern terrace to the central or upper one, at a point intervening between the south-western structure, or the Palace of Artaxerxes Ochus, and the Palace of Xerxes, or central southern building. These steps are singular in facing the terrace to which they lead; and are of rude construction, without a parapet, and entirely without sculpture or other ornamentation. They afford the only means of communication between the central and southern terraces.

The Persepolitan ruins present the appearance of a number of distinct buildings. The platform or mound contains ten of these structures, five being of vast size, the others insignificant. Four of the five large edifices are located upon the central or upper terrace, the fifth lying east of that terrace,

The "Palace of Darius" is located near the western edge of the central or upper terrace, midway between the Great Hall of Audience and the Palace of Artaxerxes Ochus. It is about one hundred and thirty-five feet long, and almost a hundred feet wide. It occupies the most lofty position of all the structures on the platform, and is elevated from fourteen to fifteen feet above the general level of the central terrace, being four or five feet higher than the "Palace of Xerxes." Its front was toward the south, where it was approached by the usual kind of double staircase, which conducted to a deep portico of eight pillars placed in two rows of four each. On each side of the portico were guard-rooms, opening into it,

RUINS OF PERSEPOLIS.

between it and the mountains. The four structures upon the central terrace consist of three buildings composed of several sets of chambers, along with one great open pillared hall. The three edifices made up of several sets of chambers are known as *palaces* and are named after their respective founders—Darius Hystaspes, Xerxes and Artaxerxes Ochus. The fourth is called the *Chehl Minar*, or "Great Hall of Audience." The building situated between the central or upper terrace and the mountains is termed the "Great Eastern Edifice."

twenty-three feet long and thirteen feet wide. The main chamber was behind the portico, and was a square of fifty feet, with a roof resting on sixteen pillars, placed in rows of four, in line with the pillars of the portico. Only the bases of the pillars remain, and it is not known whether the pillars were of wood or stone. The walls of the hall were from four to five feet thick, and were pierced by doors, windows and recesses. The hall was entered from the portico by a door exactly in the center of the front wall, and on each side of the door were two windows, which looked into the portico. The opposite, or back, wall was pierced by two doors, facing the intercolumniations of the side rows of pillars, as the front door faced the intercolumniation of the central rows. A square recess was between the two doors which pierced the back wall, and similar recesses adorned the same wall on each side of the doors. A single doorway originally pierced each of the side walls, and a square recess was between each doorway and the front wall, while two similar recesses were between the two doorways and the back wall. These side doorways and recesses fronted the pillars.

The doorways were ornamented with sculpture, those in the back wall displaying on their jamb figures of the king followed by two attendants, one of whom holds a cloth and the other a fly-chaser. These figures all had their faces turned towards the apartment. The front doorway exhibited the monarch followed by his parasol-bearer and the bearer of the fly-chaser, with his back turned to the apartment, seeming to issue forth from it. On the jambs of the doors of the side apartments were representations of the king in combat with a lion or a monster; the king in all cases facing outwards and appearing to guard the entrances to the side chambers.

Moderate-sized chambers were at the back of the hall and at either side. The largest were in the back of the edifice, where there appears to have been one about forty feet by twenty-three, and another twenty-eight feet by twenty. The doorways here had sculptures representing attendants bearing napkins and perfumes. The five side chambers were much smaller than those back of the great hall, the largest being only thirty-four feet by thirteen.

Artaxerxes Ochus cut a doorway in the outer western wall, and another opposite to it in the western wall of the great hall. He also added a second staircase to the edifice, thus giving the palace access from the west as well as from the south.

The two grand palaces erected on the same terrace—one by Xerxes and the other by Artaxerxes Ochus—will next be briefly noticed. The "Palace of Xerxes" resembled that of Darius Hystaspes, but was larger, having two rows of six pillars each in the portico; while the great hall behind was a square of eighty feet, with its roof resting on thirty-six pillars. On each side of the hall and on each side of the portico were apartments similar to those already described as abutting on the same parts of the Palace of Darius, but being larger and more numerous. The largest two were thirty-one feet square, and had roofs each resting on four pillars. The Palace of Xerxes had no apartments back of the great hall, as the edifice was so close to the edge of the upper terrace. The ornamentation of this palace much resembled that of Darius, only that instead of the combats between the king and lions or mythological monsters are representations of attendants bringing articles for the king's table or his toilet, like the figures which adorn the principal staircase of the Palace of Darius. The same kind of figures likewise ornament all the windows in the Palace of Xerxes. Says Rawlinson: "A tone of mere sensual enjoyment is thus given to the later edifice, which is very far from characterizing the earlier; and the decline of morals at the Court, which history indicates as rapid about this period, is seen to have stamped itself, as such changes usually do, upon the national architecture."

The "Palace of Artaxerxes Ochus" is in so ruined a condition that no fair description of it can be given. About twenty yards east of the Palace of Xerxes are the ruins of a small building, consisting of a hall and a portico almost similar to the corresponding portions of the Palace of Darius, but entirely without a vestige of circumjacent chambers or any inscriptions. The building is low and on the level of the northern terrace, and is half buried in the rubbish accumulated at its base. Its fragments display grandeur and massiveness, and its sculptures are in strong and bold relief. The building faces toward the north. It may have been originally surrounded on its eastern, southern and western sides by chambers, like the hall and portico of the Palace of Darius. It is supposed to have been the palace of Cyrus the Great or Cambyses. Artaxarxes Ochus made some additions to the Palace of Darius on its western side, and also added a staircase and a doorway to the Palace of Xerxes. Thus the Persepolitan palaces occupied the southeu half of the central or upper terrace, and covered a space five hundred feet long by three hundred and seventy-five feet wide.

The Persepolitan platform also contains the remains of propylæa, or gateways, and halls of immense size. There seem to have been four propylæa on the platform. The largest was directly opposite the center of the landing-place at the top of the great stairs which led to the platform from the plain. This gateway consisted of an apartment eighty-two feet square, with a roof resting on four magnificent pillars, each sixty feet high. The walls of the apartment were from sixteen to seventeen feet thick. Two grand portals, each twelve feet wide by thirty-six feet high, led into this apartment; one facing the head of the stairs, and the other opposite to it, towards the east. Both portals were flanked with colossal bulls, those toward the staircase representing the real animal, while the pair opposite resemble the famous winged man-headed bulls of the Assyrian palaces. The walls which enclosed this chamber have almost wholly disappeared, the only vestiges of them being on the southern side, where there appears to have been an unornamented doorway. The walls are supposed to have been brick, either sun-dried or kiln-baked.

A smaller gateway, but very closely resembling the one just noticed, occupied a position to the east of the Palace of Darius, and a little to the north of the Palace of Xerxes. There only remain the bases of two pillars and the jambs of three doorways. A third gateway of the same description was located in front of the great eastern hall, about seventy yards from its portico. It is so utterly ruined that little can be said about it, but the remains of a colossal bull indicate that it must have been ornamented.

The fourth gateway was on the terrace on which was built the Palace of Xerxes, and directly fronting the landing-place at the head of its principal stairs, in the same manner as the propylæa just described, fronted the great stairs leading up from the plain. This gateway was less than one-fourth as large as the great propylæa, and about half as large as the propylæa standing nearest to it. The bases of the pillars only remain in good condition.

We will now briefly describe the two other great edifices erected on the Persepolitan platform, alluded to as "the most magnificent of the Persepolitan buildings—the Great Pillared Halls—which constitute the glory of Aryan architecture, and which, even in their ruins, provoke the wonder and admiration of modern Europeans, familiar with all the triumphs of Western art, with Grecian temples, Roman baths and amphitheaters, Moorish palaces, Turkish mosques and Christian cathedrals." Says Fergusson, concerning the *Chehl Minar*, or "Great Hall of Xerxes:" "We have no cathedral in Eugland that at all comes near it in dimensions; nor indeed in France or Germany is there one that covers so much ground."

The "Hall of a Hundred Columns" stood midway in the platform between its northern and its southern edges, and near the rocky mountain on which the platform abuts towards the east. This immense edifice was the largest structure on the platform, and consisted of a single magnificent chamber, with a portico, and perhaps also guard-rooms, in front. The portico was one hundred and eighty-three feet long by fifty-two feet deep, aud had sixteen pillars, about thirty-five feet high, arranged in two rows of eight pillars each. The great chamber behind the portico was a square of two hundred and twenty-seven feet, and thus had an area of fifty-one thousand five hundred and twenty-four square feet. Over this immense square were one hundred columns, arranged in rows of ten columns each; each column being thirty-five feet high, and standing at a distance of almost twenty feet from any other. Each of the four walls enclosing this vast hall was ten and a half feet thick, and each was pierced at equal intervals by two doorways, the doorways of the one wall being exactly opposite to those of the other, and "each looking down on an avenue of columns." In the spaces of the wall on each side of the doorways, eastward, westward and southward, were three square-topped, ornamented niches. The front, or northern, wall was pierced by windows, looking upon the portico, excepting towards the corners of the edifice, where there were niches instead. The portico was forty-four feet narrower than the structure which it fronted, and its *antæ* projected from the front wall, about eleven feet from each corner. The portico thus had only eight pillars in each row instead of ten, and space was left on each side for a narrow guard-room opening to the porch, which is indicated by the doorways placed at right angles to the front wall, which are ornamented with figures of soldiers armed with spear and shield. The doors are ornamented with figures of the king, either in the act of destroying symbolical monsters, or seated upon his throne under a canopy, with the tiara on his head and the golden scepter in his right hand. On the jambs of the great doors opening to the porch are seen, in the top compartment, the king seated under the canopy, accompanied by five attendants; while below him are his guards, arranged in five rows of ten each, some armed with spears and shields, others with spears, short swords, bows and quivers. Both portals together have figures of two hundred Persian guardsmen, attending on the king's person. The doors at the back of the edifice display sculptures representing the throne elevated on a high platform, with three stages upheld by figures in various costumes, seemingly representing the natives of the different provinces of the Medo-Persian Empire.

The portico of the Hall of a Hundred Columns was flanked on each side by a colossal bull, which stood at the inner angle of the *antæ*, thus somewhat reducing the width of the entrance. Its columns were fluted, and each had the complex capital seen in the great propylæa and in the Hall of Xerxes. It was built of the same kind of immense blocks as the south-eastern edifice, or Ancient Palace—blocks frequently ten feet square by seven feet thick. It is situated somewhat low, and has no staircase nor any inscription.

The most remarkable of all the Persepolitan structures was the famous *Chehl Minar*, whose ruins cover a space of almost three hundred and fifty feet in one direction, and almost two hundred and fifty in another. These ruins consist almost wholly of stone pillars, divided into four groups, the largest of which was a square of thirty-six pillars, arranged in six rows of six pillars each, all equally distant from one another and covering an area of over twenty thousand square feet. On the northern, eastern and western sides of this square were magnificent porches each having twelve columns, arranged in two rows of six columns each, in line with the pillars of the central cluster. The porches were located seventy feet from the main edifice and seem to be wholly separate from it. They are one hundred and forty-two feet long by thirty feet wide, each thus covering an area of four thousand two hundred and sixty feet. All the pillars in the edifice were each sixty-four feet high. Even in their ruined condition, they tower above all the other ruins of Persepolis, still retaining a height of over sixty feet.

The pillars had three kinds of capitals, those of the colonnades being comparatively simple and consisting each of one member; those of the eastern colonnade consisting of two half-griffins with their heads looking in opposite directions, and those of the western colonnade being composed of two half-bulls similarly arranged. The capitals of the pillars in the northern colonnade, which faced the great sculptured staircase, and which constituted the real front of the edifice, were exceedingly complex and consisted of three members; the lower representing a lotus-bud accompanied by pendent leaves, the middle representing volutes of the Ionic order placed perpendicularly, and the upper composed of a figure of two half-bulls resembling that forming the complete capital of the western group of pillars. The pillars of the great central cluster had capitals similar to those of the northern colonnade.

The bases of the colonnade pillars are remarkably elegant, being bell-shaped and ornamented with a double or triple row of pendent lotus-leaves, some rounded and others pointed. The columns resting on the bases taper gently as they ascend, and consist of several masses of stone carefully joined, and secured at the joints by an iron clamp in the direction of the axis of the column. All the columns are elegantly fluted along their whole length, each pillar having from forty-eight to fifty-two incisions, or flutings. The flutes are arcs of circles smaller than semi-circles, thus resembling those of the Doric order, the cutting of all being very exact and regular.

Having described the ruins of Persepolis, we will next notice those at Murgab, the ancient Pasargadæ, and those at Istakr, which were carefully examined by the celebrated French explorers, MM. Coste and Flandin.

The ruins of Pasargadæ, considered the most ancient in Persia, include the well-known "Tomb of Cyrus" and two chief edifices. The largest of these edifices had an oblong-square shape, about one hundred and forty-seven feet long by one hundred and sixteen feet wide; and appears to have been surrounded by a high wall, which had huge portals, consisting of large stone blocks, partly hollowed out, to make them movable. The jamb of each portal had the following inscription: "I am Cyrus, the King, the Achæmenian." Inside the walled enclosure was evidently a pillared structure much higher than the surrounding walls, as there is still a plain pillar remaining, which is thirty-six feet long, and three feet four inches thick at the base. On the paved area around are the bases of seven similar pillars, arranged in lines and so located as to indicate an oblong hall, having twelve pillars, in three rows of four pillars each. The intercolumniations measure twenty-seven feet ten inches in one direction, and but twenty-one feet in the other.

The smaller edifice, situated near the larger, covers a space of one hundred and twenty-five feet by fifty, and consists of twelve pillar bases, arranged in two rows of six pillars each, the pillars being somewhat thicker than those of the larger edifice and placed somewhat nearer to one another. The base is shaped at the side in the form of a semi-circular bulge, ornamented with a series of nine flutings, carried entirely around the base in parallel horizontal lines. In front of the pillar bases, at the distance of about twenty-three feet from the nearest, is a square column, still upright, which has a strange mythological figure sculptured upon it, with the same inscription as that on the larger edifice: "I am Cyrus, the King, the Achæmenian."

Two other buildings at Murgab are remarkable for their masonry; one being a square tower with slightly-projected corners, and built of hewn stone blocks laid very regularly and raised to a height of forty-two feet; the other being a massive and elegant platform built wholly of square stone blocks, faced with blocks eight or ten feet long, laid in horizontal courses and rusticated throughout in an ornamental style, resembling that of the substructions of the Temple of Jerusalem, and occasionally occurring in Greece.

The palace at Istakr is better preserved than either of the two pillared structures at Murgab, though not in a condition sufficient to form an idea of its ground-plan. One pillar remains erect, but the bases of eight others have been discovered perfect, while the walls can be partially traced, and the jambs of several doorways and niches yet remain. These remains show that the Istakr palace resembled the Persepolitan edifices in having fluted pillars with capitals, massive doors and window-jambs, and thick walls; while its plan was entirely different.

The palace at Susa—exhumed by those diligent and enterprising Englishmen, Mr. Loftus and General Williams—consisted of a great hall, or throne-room, closely resembling the Chehl Minar at Persepolis and several smaller edifices. It was located at the summit of the great mound or quadrilateral platform composed of burned bricks, and which supported the palace of the old Susian kings from a very remote antiquity. It fronted a little west of north, and commanded a splendid view over the Susianian plains to the mountains of Luristan. Four of its pillar-bases bore similar inscriptions showing that it was originally built by Darius Hystaspes and subsequently repaired by Artaxerxes Longimanus. It bore such an exact resemblance to the Chehl Minar that it need not be described.

The tombs of the Persian kings were remarkable works, which attracted the attention of the ancients and have been very carefully examined in modern times. There are eight of these tombs, but only of two types, so that only two need be described.

The most ancient and remarkable of the Persian royal tombs is that of Cyrus the Great at Murgab, the ancient Pasargadæ. Its design is unique, and it is entirely different from all the other royal sepulchers. The Greek historian Arrian called it "a house upon a pedestal"—a very appropriate description. The entire structure is built of huge blocks of elegant white marble. The base rises in the form of a pyramid of seven steps differing in height. The small "house" on top of the base is crowned with a stone roof, formed in front and rear into a pediment like that of a Greek temple. The "house" is without any window, but one of the end walls was pierced by a low and narrow doorway leading into a small chamber or cell, about eleven feet long, seven feet wide, and seven feet high. Here, we are told by Strabo and Arrian, the body of Cyrus the Great was laid in a golden coffin. Inside the chamber is perfectly plain and has no inscription. On the outside there is an elegant cornice below the pediment and a good moulding over the doorway, which also has two recesses, while there is a slight moulding at the base of the "house," and another at the bottom of the second step. Otherwise the entire structure is perfectly plain. It is at present thirty-six feet high from the ground, the top of the roof being somewhat worn away. At the base it measures forty-seven feet by forty-three feet nine inches.

The tomb stands within a rectangular area, marked out by pillars, the bases or broken shafts of these yet remaining. There appear to have been about twenty-four of these pillars, all of them circular and smooth; and each side of the rectangle had six of them, about fourteen feet apart.

The seven other Persian royal sepulchers are rock-tombs, executed in mountain sides, at a considerable height, and placed so as to be easily seen but almost inaccessible to approach. There are four such tombs in the side of the mountain bounding the Pulwar valley on the north-west, and three in the immediate vicinity of the Persepolitan platform, two of these being in the side of the mountain overhanging the platform, and one in the rocks a little farther south. In general shape these excavations apparently resemble a Greek cross. This is divided into three compartments by horizontal lines; the upper compartment containing a curious sculptured representation of the king worshiping Ormazd; the middle compartment, comprising the two side limbs with the space between them, being so carved as to represent a portico; and the lower portion being perfectly plain. In the center of the middle compartment is a sculptured representation of a doorway resembling closely those yet standing on the great platform, being doubly recessed and ornamented with lily-work at the top. The upper part of this doorway is filled with the solid rock, smoothed to a flat surface and crossed by three horizontal bars. The lower part is cut away to the height of four or five feet, so as to give entrance to the tomb itself, which is hollowed out of the rock behind.

So far the rock-tombs are similar in almost every respect; but the excavations back of their ornamented fronts exhibit some curious differences. In the simplest case there is seen, on entering, an arched chamber, thirteen feet five inches long by seven feet two inches wide, out of which a deep horizontal recess opens opposite the door, the recess being about four feet above the ground and arched like the chamber. In the tomb of Darius Hystaspes and some other early royal sepulchers there is no arch, both the internal chamber and the recess being square at the top. Near the front of the recess is another perpendicular excavation, six feet ten inches long, three feet three inches wide, and three feet three inches deep. This second excavation was the receptacle for the body, and was either covered or designed to be covered with a stone slab. In the deeper portion of the recess is place for two similar sarcophagi, but these have not been excavated, and apparently only one body was interred in this tomb. Other sepulchers exhibit similar general features, but contain three, six or nine sarcophagi. In the tomb of Darius Hystaspes the sepulchral chamber has three distinct recesses, each containing three sarcophagi; the tomb thus holding nine bodies. It seems to have been originally cut for a solitary recess, precisely on the plan of the tomb just described, but has been elongated towards the left. Two of the tombs at Nakhsh-i-Rustam exhibit a yet more elaborate ground-plan, in which are curved lines instead of straight ones. The tombs above the Persepolitan platform are more profusely and elegantly ornamented than the others, the lintels and side-posts of the doorways being covered with rosettes, and the entablature above the cornice having a row of lions facing on each side towards the center.

There is a peculiar square tower, built of large marble blocks, cut very exactly and joined together without any kind of mortar or cement, just in front of the four royal tombs at Nakhsh-i-Rustam. This curious structure is thirty-six feet high, and each side measures about twenty-four feet. The edifice is ornamented with pilasters at the corners and with six recessed niches, in three rows, one above the other, on three of its four sides. On the fourth face are only two niches, one above the other, and below them is a doorway with a cornice. The surface of the walls between the pilasters is ornamented with rectangular depressions resembling the sunken ends of beams. The doorway looking north toward the tombs is halfway up the side of the building, and leads into a chamber twelve feet square by nearly eighteen feet high, reaching to the top of the building and roofed in with four large stone slabs, which reach entirely across from one side to the other, and are more than twenty-four feet long, six feet wide, and from a foot and a half to three feet thick. These slabs are so cut on the top that the roof inclines very slightly every way, and at their edges they are fashioned between the pilasters into a dentated cornice like that on the tombs. They were clamped together on the outside as carefully as those at Persepolis and Pasargadæ. The edifice appears to have been originally closed by two massive stone doors.

There is a remarkable gateway at Istakr, constructed of vast stone blocks, and situated in the gorge between the town wall and the opposite mountain, and across the road from Pasargadæ to the plain of Merdasht. On each side of this structure were thick walls, one abutting on the mountain and the other perhaps connecting with the town wall, while between them were three huge pillars.

We have now described all the more important architectural works of the ancient Persians, as far as the data at our command have made it possible. Concerning the characteristics of Persian architecture, Professor Rawlinsons says:

"First, then, simplicity and regularity of the style are worthy of remark. In the ground-plans of buildings the straight line only is used; all the angles are right angles; all the pillars fall into line; the intervals between pillar and pillar are regular, and generally equal; doorways are commonly placed opposite intercolumniations; where there is but one doorway, it is in the middle of the wall which it pierces; where there are two, they correspond to one another. Correspondence is the general law. Nor only does door correspond to door, and pillar to pillar, but room to room, window to window, and even niche to niche. Most of the buildings are so contrived that one half is the exact duplicate of the other; and where this is not the case, the irregularity is generally either slight, or the result of an alteration, made probably for convenience sake. Travelers are impressed with the Grecian character of what they behold, though there is an almost entire absence of Greek forms. The regularity is not confined to single buildings, but extends to the relations of different edifices to one another. The sides of buildings standing on one platform, at whatever distance they may be, are parallel. There is, however, less consideration paid than we should have expected to the exact position, with respect to a main building, in which a subordinate one shall be placed. Propylæa, for instance, are not opposite the center of the edifice to which they conduct, but on one side of the center. And generally, excepting in the parallelism of their sides, buildings seem placed with but slight regard to neighboring ones."

Having described their architecture, we will now notice the other arts of the ancient Persians. There are but few specimens of their mimetic art remaining, and these consist of reliefs executed on the natural rock or on large slabs of hewn stone used in building, of impressions on coins, and of intaglios cut upon gems. There remain no Persian statues, no modeled figures, no metal castings, no carvings in ivory or wood, no enamelings, no pottery. Modern excavations in Persia have not yielded traces of the furniture, domestic implements, or wall ornamentation of the ancient inhabitants, as have the excavations in Mesopotamia concerning the ancient Assyrians and Babylonians. The only small objects discovered are a few cylinders and some spear and arrow heads.

The nearest approach to statuary in Persian ruins are the figures of colossal bulls guarding portals or porticoes, which are only sculptures in high relief, carved in front as well as at the side. There are two such specimens, one representing the real animal, the other a monster in the form of a winged man-headed bull.

The other Persian reliefs may be classed under four heads—1, mythological figures, representing the king in combat with a lion, a bull or a monster; 2, processional scenes, representing guards, courtiers, attendants, or tribute-bearers; 3, representations of the king walking, sitting on his throne, or engaged in worship; 4, representations of lions and bulls, either singly or engaged in combat.

On the jambs of doorways in three of the Persepolitan edifices are represented a human figure dressed in the Median robe, with the sleeve thrown back from the right arm, in the act of killing a lion, a bull or some grotesque monster; the animal in each instance attacking his assailant with three of his feet, while he stands on the fourth. One monster has the head of griffins already described as represented on the capitals of columns, a feathered head and crest, the wings of a bird, the tail of a scorpion, and legs ending in eagle's claws. The other monster has the head of an eagle, the ears of an ass, feathers on the neck, breast and back, with a lion's body, legs and tail. We have observed similarly grotesque figures in Assyria; but the Persian form was original, not borrowed from the Assyrian.

Persian gem-engravings represent monstrous forms of greater grotesqueness, symbolizing the powers of Darkness or of various kinds of evil. The gems and cylinders represent the king in conflict with a great variety of monsters, some resembling the Persepolitan, while others have strange forms not seen elsewhere, such as winged lions with two tails and with the horns of a ram or an antelope, a half dozen different kinds of sphinxes and griffins, and various other nondescript creatures.

Persian artists represented three kinds of processional subjects—1, lines of royal guards or officers of the court; 2, royal purveyors arriving at the palace with a train of attendants and with provisions for the king's table; 3, the conquered nations bringing as a present to the Great King the precious products of their respective countries. The second kind represented curious varieties of costume and Persian utensils, also animal forms, such as kids. The third kind represented a remarkable variety of costume and equipment; also many human and animal forms; horses, asses, camels, cattle, sheep, being found interspersed among men and chariots and groups of cyprus-trees. Processional scenes of this class are found on the Persepolitan staircase, but the fullest and most elaborate is seen on the grand step in front of the Chehl Minar, or Great Hall of Audience, where there are twenty such groups of figures.

There are three kinds of representations of the king upon the relief—1, those in which he is on foot, attended by the parasol-bearer and the napkin-bearer, or by the latter only; 2, those in the palaces representing the king on a throne supported by many *caryatid* figures; 3, those on tombs representing the king on a platform upheld by the same kind of figures, worshiping before an altar. The supporting figures are numerous in both the second and third representations, and we observe different ethnic types, as that of a negro and those of Scyths or Tartars.

There are few animal scenes represented on the bas-reliefs, and these differ but little in type, the most curious being one several times repeated at Persepolis, where it constitutes the usual ornamentation of the triangular spaces on the façades of stairs, such as the combat between a lion and a bull, or a lion seizing and devouring a bull; the bull in his agony rearing up his fore-parts and turning his head towards his powerful assailant, whose strong limbs and jaws have a firm hold of his powerless and unhappy victim.

Figures of bulls and lions are seen upon the friezes of some of the tombs, and upon the representations of canopies over the royal throne, reproducing well-known Assyrian forms. A figure of a sitting lion appears on some of the façades of staircases, being found in the central compartment of the parapet-wall at the top.

The Persian gem-engravings are found on various kinds of hard stone, such as cornelian, onyx, rock-crystal, sapphirine, sardonyx, chalcedony, etc.; and are generally executed with wonderful skill and delicacy. The designs which they represent are usually mythological; but scenes of real life frequently appear upon them, such as the hunting-scene in which the king struggles with two lions roused from their lairs, and the gem-engraving representing a combat of two Persians with two Scythians. The Persians are represented as fighting with the bow and the sword; the Scythians, marked by their peaked cap and their loose trowsers, use the bow and the battle-ax. One Scyth receives a death-wound, while the other seems about to discharge an arrow, but also on the point of flight.

Gem-engravings likewise embrace graceful and elegant vegetable forms, such as delineations of palm-trees, with their feathery leaves, their dependent fruit, and the rough bark of their stems. The lion-hunt represented on the signet-cylinder of Darius Hystaspes occurs in a palm-grove. One gem contains a portrait supposed to represent a satrap of Salamis, in Cyprus, and is very neatly executed.

There are three principal types of Persian coins. The earliest have on one side the figure of a king crowned with a diadem and armed with a bow and javelin, while there is an irregular indentation on the other side. The later coins have other designs, such as horsemen, the fore part of a ship, or the king drawing an arrow from his quiver. Another style shows on one side the king in combat with a lion; while the other side exhibits a galley, or a towered and battlemented city, with two lions standing below it, back to back. The third style has on one side the king in his chariot, with his charioteer in front of him, and usually an attendant carrying a fly-chaser behind; while the other side has a trireme or a battlemented city.

The king's throne and footstool are the only articles of furniture represented in the Persian sculptures. There are likewise few utensils represented, the most elaborate being the censer already mentioned, and with which is usually seen a kind of pail or basket, shaped like a lady's reticule, in which the aromatic gums for burning were perhaps kept. A covered dish and goblet, with an inverted saucer over it, are likewise often seen in the hands of the royal attendants; while the tribute-bearers frequently carry, with other offerings, bowls or basins.

The Persians had a peculiarly simple taste in regard to personal ornaments. Ear-rings were generally plain rings of gold. Bracelets were golden bands. Collars were golden circlets twisted in a very inartificial manner. Sword hilts or sheaths were not artistic, but spear-shafts were sometimes adorned with the figure of an apple or a pomegranate. Dresses were not often patterned, but depended on make and color for their effect. Thus extreme simplicity characterized the Aryan races, while the Semitic nations affected the most elaborate ornamentation.

Professor Rawlinson says: "Persia was not celebrated in antiquity for the production of any special fabrics. The arts of weaving and dyeing were undoubtedly practiced in the dominant country, as well as in most of the subject provinces, and the Persian dyes seem even to have had a certain reputation; but none of the productions of their looms acquired a name among foreign nations. Their skill, indeed, in the mechanical arts generally was, it is probable, not more than moderate. It was their boast that they were soldiers, and had won a position by their good swords which gave them the command of all that was most exquisite and admirable, whether in the natural world or among the products of human industry. So long as the carpets of Babylon and Sardis, the shawls of Kashmir and India, the fine linen of Borsippa and Egypt, the ornamental metal-work of Greece, the coverlets of Damascus, the muslins of Babylonia, the multiform manufactures of the Phœnician towns, poured continually into Persia proper in the way of tribute, gifts, or merchandise, it was needless for the native population to engage largely in industrial enterprise."

The same authority also says: "To science the ancient Persians contributed absolutely nothing. The genius of the nation was averse to that patient study and those laborious investigations from which alone scientific progress ensues. Too light and frivolous, too vivacious, too sensuous for such pursuits, they left them to the patient Babylonians, and the thoughtful, many-sided Greeks. The schools of Orchoë, Borsippa and Miletus flourished under their sway, but without provoking their emulation, possibly without so much as attracting their attention. From the first to the last, from the dawn to the final close of their power, they abstained wholly from scientific studies. It would seem that they thought it enough to place before the world, as signs of their intellectual vigor, the fabric of their Empire and the buildings of Susa and Persepolis."

SECTION IV.—ZOROASTER AND THE ZEND-AVESTA.

ALREADY have we described the original form of the Persian religion in our account of Media, where we have endeavored to give a clear and concise statement concerning the system of Zoroaster and the doctrines taught by the Zend-Avesta, the sacred book of that system. The religion of the Persians was identical with that of the Medes in its earliest form, consisting chiefly of the worship of Ahura-Mazda, the belief in Angra-Mainyus as the principle of evil, and complete observance of the teachings of Zoroaster. When the Medes established their sway over the nations long professing Magism, their faith became corrupted by the creed of the subject nations, and they accepted the Magi as their priests; and thus arose the mixed religion described in the section on Zoroastrianism and Magism in our chapter on the history of Media. But the Persians in their wilder country, not so easily exposed to corrupting influences, adhered zealously to the original Zoroastrian faith in its primitive purity and remained true to its traditions. Their political dependence on Media during the period of the Median Empire did not influence them away from this pure faith; and the Medes, being tolerant, did not attempt to interfere with the creed of their subjects. The simple Zoroastrian faith and worship, corrupted by Magism in the then-luxurious Media, was maintained in its pure state in the rugged uplands of Persia, among the hardy shepherds and cultivators of that uninviting region, and was professed by the early Achæmenian princes and accepted by their subjects.

The principal feature of the Zoroastrian religion during the first period was the acknowledgment and worship of One Supreme God, Ahura-Mazda, or Ormazd, "the Lord of Heaven," "the Giver of heaven and earth," "He who disposed of thrones and dispensed happiness." The first place in Persian inscriptions and decrees is assigned to the "Great God, Ormazd." Every Persian monarch of whom we have inscriptions, each more than two lines long, mentions Ahura-Mazda as his upholder; and the early Achæmenian kings did not name any other god. All rule "by the grace of Ahura-Mazda." From Ahura-Mazda proceed victory, conquest, safety, prosperity, blessings of all kinds. The "law of Ahura-Mazda" is the rule of life. The protection of Ahura-Mazda is the precious blessing for which prayer is constantly offered.

Still "other gods," inferior to Ahura-Mazda, are recognized in a general way. The usual prayer is to ask the protection of Ahura-Mazda along with that of the inferior divinities (*bada bagiabish*). Sometimes a special protection is asked for a particular class of deities—*Dii familiares*—or "deities who guard the house."

The Persian inscriptions do not allude to the worship of Mithra, or the Sun, until the reign of Artaxerxes Mnemon, the victor of Cunaxa. Neither do the inscriptions refer to the Dualism between the good and evil beings or principles, Ahura-Mazda and Angra-Mainyus—a belief which was a distinguishing feature of the Zoroastrian religion long before the rise of the Median Empire. Neither Herodotus nor Xenophon has transmitted to us any account of this part of the Persian creed, and Plutarch was the first Greek writer to give it notice.

Persian worship in the early times was that required by the Zend-Avesta, consisting of prayer and thanksgiving to Ahura-Mazda and the good spirits of his creation, the recital of the Gâthâs, or hymns, the offering of sacrifice, and the participation in the Soma ceremony. Worship appears to have occurred in the temples, which most cuneiform scholars believe are mentioned in the Behistun Inscription.

Darius Hystaspes and other early Persian kings represented themselves on their tombs in the act of worship. A few feet before them is an altar set on three steps and crowned with the sacrificial fire. It has a square shape, and is ornamented only with a sunken square recess and a strongly-projecting cornice at the top. The altar, with the steps, seems about four and a half feet high. The horse was the Persians' favorite victim for sacrifice, though they also offered cattle, sheep and goats. Human sacrifices were almost, if not wholly, unknown to them, and are mentioned by no other authority than Herodotus, who alludes to two occasions on which human victims were sacrificed by the Persians. Human sacrifices were certainly not in accordance with the spirit of pure Zoroastrianism.

Idolatry is entirely repugnant to the spirit of the Zend-Avesta, and Herodotus says that the Persians knew nothing of images of gods. Nevertheless they had symbolic representations of their deities, and they adopted the forms of their religious symbolism from idolatrous nations. The winged circle, with or without the human figure—used by the Assyrians as the emblem of their supreme god, Asshur—was employed by the Persians as the symbol of their Great God, Ahura-Mazda, and as such, was assigned conspicuous places on their rock-tombs and on their great edifices. All the details of the Assyrian model were followed, with but a single exception. The human figure of the Assyrian original wore a close-fitting tunic, with short sleeves, in accordance with the ordinary Assyrian costume, and was crowned with the horned cap marking a god or a genius. In the Persian imitation the Median robe and a tiara, sometimes that worn by the king and sometimes that of the court officers, took the place of the Assyrian costume.

The plain disk or orb represented on the Persian sculptures is the symbol of Mithra, the Sun. In sculptures in which the emblem of Mithra occurs with that of Ahura-Mazda, the latter occurs in the center and the former to the right. The solar emblem appears on all the sculptured tombs, but is seldom found elsewhere.

The Persians represented the spirits of good and evil—the Ahuras and the Devas of their mythology—under human, animal and monstrous forms. The figure of a good genius, which is seen on one of the square pillars erected by Cyrus the Great at Pasargadæ, is believed to symbolize "the well-formed, swift, tall Serosh," mentioned in the nineteenth Fargard of the Vendidad. The figure is that of a colossal man, with four wings issuing from his shoulders, two of which spread upwards above his head, while the other two droop downwards, reaching almost to the feet. The figure stands erect, in profile, having both arms raised and both hands open. The costume of the figure consists of a long fringed robe extending from the neck down to the ankles, and of a very remarkable head-dress. The latter is a striped cap, fitting the head closely, and overshadowed by an elaborate ornament of a purely Egyptian character. From the top of the cap are seen rising two twisted horns, which spread right and left, and which support two grotesque human-headed figures, one on each side, and a complicated triple ornament between them, unskillfully copied from a very much more elegant Egyptian model.

The winged man-headed bulls, adopted by the Persians from the Assyrians, with slight modifications, were perhaps likewise regarded as emblems of some good genius, as they are represented on Persian cylinders as upholding the symbol of Ahura-Mazda in the same manner that the man-headed bulls on the Assyrian cylinders appear as upholding the symbol of Asshur. Their position at Persepolis, where they guarded the entrance to the palace, coincides with the idea that they represented guardian spirits, objects specially regarded by the Persians. But the bull is represented in the bas-reliefs of Persepolis among the evil or hostile powers, which the king fights and destroys, though the bull here represented is not winged or human-headed; yet on some cylinders seemingly Persian, the king combats bulls of precisely the same type as that assigned in other cylinders to the upholders of Ahura-Mazda. Apparently in this case the bull in certain combinations and positions symbolized a good spirit, while in others he was the emblem of a *deva*, or evil genius.

The usual emblems of the evil powers of mythology were winged or unwinged lions and various grotesque monsters. At Persepolis the lions stabbed or strangled are of the natural form, and this type likewise occurs upon gems and cylinders, but on these last the king's adversary is frequently a winged lion, while sometimes he is both winged and horned. The monsters are of two main types, in both of which the forms of a bird and those of a beast are commingled, the bird predominating in the one, and the beast in the other.

During the prevalence of the purer and earlier form of the Persian religion, the Persian kings, animated by a fierce iconoclastic spirit, seized every opportunity to show their hatred and contempt for the idolatries of the surrounding nations, burning temples, confiscating or destroying images, scourging or slaying idolatrous priests, stopping festivals, disturbing tombs, smiting with the sword such animals as were believed to be divine incarnations. Fearing to stir up religious wars, they were somewhat tolerant within their own dominions, except after a rebellion, when a province was at their mercy. But when they invaded foreign lands they displayed their hostility toward idolatrous and materialistic religions in the most forcible manner. During their invasion of Greece they burned every temple they came near, and in their first invasion and conquest of Egypt they outraged all the religious feelings of the people.

This period, when pure Zoroastrianism prevailed, was the time when a religious sympathy drew together the Persian and Jewish nations. Cyrus the Great seems to have identified Jehovah with Ahura-Mazda; and, accepting the prophecy of Isaiah as a Divine command, undertook the rebuilding of their Temple for a people, who, like his own, permitted no image to defile their sanctuary. Darius Hystaspes likewise encouraged the completion of the enterprise, after it had been interrupted by the troubles following the death of Cambyses. Thus was laid the foundation for that intimate friendship between the two nations, as shown us so abundantly in the books of Ezra, Nehemiah and Esther—a friendship which induced the Jews to remain loyal to Persia to the very last, and to brave the conquering Alexander the Great after his victory of Issus, rather than desert masters who had treated them with so much kindness and sympathy.

The first effort made to corrupt the original pure Zoroastrian faith was during the reign of the Pseudo-Smerdis. Horodotus states that when Cambyses started on his expedition against Egypt, he left a Magus named Patizeithes at the capital as controller of the royal household. The appointment of the priest of an alien religion to such an important office is the first evidence we possess of a decline of zeal on the part of the Achæmenian kings, and the first historical proof of the existence of Magism within the limits of Persia proper. It is likely that Magism was a more ancient creed than that of Zoroaster in the country in which the Persians had become settled; but now, for the first time since the Persian conquest of Media, Magism began to make a show of its strength, to force itself into exalted official stations, and to attract general attention. Originally the religion of the old Scythic tribes conquered by the Persians and held in subjection by them, it had acquired many votaries among the Persians themselves. The very causes which had corrupted Zoroastrianism in Media soon after the rise of her empire were slowly at work in Persia, where Magism had made many converts before Cambyses started for Egypt. His long stay in that land hurried on the politico-religious crisis in Persia under the Pseudo-Smerdis, when the Magi attempted to substitute Magism for Zoroastrianism as the state religion. The miserable failure of this attempt was immediately followed by a reaction, and it appeared as if Zoroastrianism had won a final triumph. But Magism, defeated in this effort to establish itself by force, began to work more quietly and insidiously, and by degrees and apparently almost imperceptibly grew into favor, mingling itself with the Zoroastrian creed, simply adding to it, but not displacing it. The later Persian system was a union of the Magian elemental worship and the Dualism of Zoroaster; the Magi became the national priesthood; the rites and ceremonies of the two religions were commingled; and two originally separate and distinct, but not wholly antagonistic, creeds were blended into one system. The name of Zoroaster was still cherished in fond remembrance by the Persian nation, while practically Magian rites predominated, and the later Greeks called the mixed religion "the Magism of Zoroaster."

We have described the Magian rites in our account of Media, and repetition is unnecessary. Their predominant feature was the fire-worship still cherished by those descendants of the ancient Persians who did not accept the Mohammedan religion. On lofty mountain peaks in the chains traversing both Media and Persia, fire-altars were erected, on which burned a perpetual flame constantly watched lest it be extinguished, and believed to have been kindled from heaven. A shrine or temple was reared over the altar in most cases, and on these spots the Magi daily chanted their incantations, exhibited their barsoms, or divining-rods, and performed their strange ceremonies. Victims were offered on these fire-altars. On the occasion of a sacrifice, fires were kindled near by with logs of dry wood, from which the bark had been stripped, and which was lighted from a flame which burned from the fire-altar. A small quantity of the victim's fat was consumed in this sacrificial fire, but the remainder of the victim was cut into joints, boiled, and then eaten or sold by the worshiper. According to the Magi, the animal's *soul* was the true offering, which the god accepted.

If the Persians ever offered human victims, as Herodotus says they did on two occasions, this horrid practice must be ascribed to Magian influence, as it is wholly antagonistic to the entire spirit of Zoroaster's teaching. The first instance of this practice is said to have occurred during the reign of Xerxes, when Magism, which had been sternly repressed by Darius Hystaspes, endeavored again to show its power, grew into favor at court, and secured a permanent standing. Herodotus tells us that the Persians, during their invasion of Greece, sacrificed at Ennea Hodoi, on the Strymon river, nine youths and nine maidens by burying them alive.

Having accepted a fusion of Magism with their original Zoroastrian creed, the Persians thereafter gradually adopted such portions of other religious systems as attracted them and with which they had been brought into close contact. Before the time of Herodotus they had adopted the Babylonian worship of a Nature-goddess, identified by the Greeks at one time with their Aphrodité, at another time with Artemis, at another time with Heré; thus compromising with one of the grossest of the idolatries which they despised and detested in theory. Thus the Babylonian goddess Nana—the counterpart of the Grecian Aphrodité and the Roman Venus—was accepted by the Persians under the name of Nanæa, Anæa, Anaitis, or Tanata, and soon became one of the chief objects of Persian worship. Actual idolatry was at first avoided, but Artaxerxes Mnemon, the victor of Cunaxa and a zealous devotee of the goddess, not satisfied with the mutilated worship which then prevailed, sought to introduce images of this goddess into all the chief cities of the empire—Susa, Persepolis, Babylon, Ecbatana, Damascus, Sardis, Bactria.

The introduction of this idolatry was soon followed by another. Mithra, the Sun—so long reverenced, if not actually worshiped by the Zoroastrians—was likewise honored with a statue and accepted as a god of the first rank, during the reign of Artaxerxes Mnemon.

Towards the close of the empire two hitherto inferior and obscure deities—Vohumano, or Bahman, and Amerdad, counselors of Ahura-Mazda—became the objects of an idolatrous worship; shrines being erected in their honor, and being ofter visited by companies of Magi, who chanted their incantations and performed their rights of divination in these new edifices as readily as before the old fire-altars. The image of Vohu-mano was of wood and was carried in procession on certain occasions.

Thus, in the progress of time, the Persian religion became more and more assimilated to the systems of belief and worship prevalent among the neighboring Asiatic nations. Several kinds of idolatry came into vogue, some borrowed from other nations, others evolved out of the Persian itself. Magnificent temples were reared to the worship of various deities; "and the degenerate descendants of pure Zoroastrian spiritualists bowed down to images, and entangled themselves in the meshes of a sensualistic and most debasing Nature-worship." Nevertheless, the Dualistic faith maintained itself amid all the corruptions. Ahura-Mazda, or Ormazd, was from first to last acknowledged as the Supreme God. Angra-Mainyus, or Ahriman, was from first to last recognized as the great evil principle or spirit, neither becoming an object of worship, nor a mere personification of evil. Aristotle's inquiries near the close of the empire still showed Ormazd and Ahriman admitted to be "Principles" of good and evil, "still standing in the same hostile and antithetical attitude, one towards the other, which they occupied when the first Fargard of the Vendidad was written, long anterior to the rise of the Persian power."

The Zend-Avesta was written in the ancient sacred Zend language. The language of the Medes and Persians belonged to the form of speech known to moderns as the Aryan, or Indo-European. The peculiarities of the Indo-European forms of speech are a certain number of common, or widely-spread, roots. The old roots of the Medo-Persian language are almost universally kindred forms familiar to the philologist through the Sanskrit or the Zend, or both, while many of them are forms common to all, or most, of the varieties of the Indo-European stock. Thus *father* in the old Persian, as in Sanskrit, is *pitar*, and in Zend is *pater;* in Greek *patar;* in Latin *pater;* in Gothic *fader;* in German *vater;* in English *father;* and in Erse or native Irish *athair*. *Name* is in old Persian, Zend and Sanskrit, *nāna;* in Greek *onoma;* in Latin *nomen;* in German *nahme,* or *name;* in English *name*. The word *house* in Greek is *domos;* in Latin *domus;* in Sanskrit, or ancient Hindoo, *dama;* in Zend and Medo-Persian, *demana;* in Irish *dahm;* in Slavonic *domu,* and our English word *domestic* comes from the same root.

The ordinary writing of the Medes and Persians—as their race origin, their language, institutions and religion—was identical; and its characters were found in a cuneiform alphabet of thirty-six or thirty-seven forms, representing twenty-three distinct sounds. The writing was from left to right, as with the Aryan nations in general. Words were separated from one another by an oblique wedge, and were divided at any point where the writer reached the end of a line. Enclitics were joined without any break in the words which they accompanied.

The Persian writing has been transmitted to us almost entirely upon stone. It includes many rock-tablets, inscriptions upon buildings, and several brief legends upon vases and cylinders. It is incised or cut into the material in every instance. The letters differ in size; some being two inches long; those of vases about a sixth of an inch. The inscriptions cover a space of no less than a hundred and eighty years, beginning with Cyrus the Great, and ending with Artaxerxes Ochus. It is believed that the Persians also employed a cursive writing for ordinary literary purposes. Ctesias says that the royal archives were written on parchment, and there is sufficient evidence that the educated Persians were thoroughly familiar with the art of writing, as attested by Herodotus and Thucydides. Says Professor Rawlinson: "It might have been supposed that the Pehlevi, as the lineal descendant of the Old Persian language, would have furnished valuable assistance towards solving the question of what character the Persians employed commonly; but the alphabetic type of the Pehlevi inscriptions is evidently Semitic; and it would thus seem that the old national modes of writing had been completely lost before the establishment by Ardeshir, son of Babek, of the New Persian Empire."

CHAPTER XI.

THE SANSKRITIC HINDOOS.

SECTION I.—GEOGRAPHY OF INDIA.

THE peninsula of Hindoostan contains almost a million and a quarter square miles. This great domain of Southern Asia is divided physically into three very distinct tracts, one towards the north-west, consisting of the basin drained by the Indus; one towards the east, or the basin drained by the Ganges; and one towards the south, or the peninsula proper. The north-western division, or the Indus valley, is the only one connected with ancient history. This region has already been described in our geographical account of the provinces of the Medo-Persian Empire. The portion of India north of the Vindya mountains was anciently called *Hindoostan*, and the region south of that range was designated as the *Deccan*.

Hindoostan is bounded on the north by the Chinese Empire; on the east by Burmah, Siam and the Bay of Bengal; on the south by the Indian Ocean; and on the west by the Arabian Sea, Beloochistan and Afghanistan. It is about eighteen hundred miles in extent from north to south, and in its widest part about fifteen hundred miles from east to west. Its area is one million four hundred thousand square miles, and it contains about two hundred and fifty million inhabitants.

The Himalaya mountains, which extend along its northern border, divide it from Thibet, and are the highest in the world; one of its peaks, Mt. Everest, almost six miles high, being the loftiest mountain peak on the globe. These mountains rise in successive stages from the plains, forming several parallel ridges, their tops being covered with perpetual snow. The Western Ghauts are a mountain range along the western shore of Hindoostan, reaching an elevation of almost two miles. The Eastern Ghauts are a less lofty mountain chain along the eastern coast.

The Ganges is the principal river of Hindoostan. It rises in the Himalaya mountains; and, after a winding course of eight hundred miles among these chains, flows through the delightful plains for thirteen hundred miles, reaching the sea by many channels. A triangular island, two hundred miles long, is formed and intersected by several currents. The western branch, called the Hoogly river, is navigable by ships. The Ganges is the sacred river of the Hindoos, who believe that it has the power to cleanse them from all sin if they bathe in its waters, and therefore it is the object of their highest veneration. The entire navigable portion of this river, and the magnificent region which it drains, with its millions of people, are now under the dominion of Great Britain, which rules the entire peninsula of Hindoostan from the Himalayas on the north to Cape Comorin on the south, and from the frontiers of Burmah on the east to the confines of Afghanistan on the west.

The Ganges receives the waters of eleven considerable rivers. It has annual inundations in July and August, caused by the rains and melting snows of the North. The Indus, or river of the Punjab and Scinde in the extreme west, is the second great river of Hindoostan; and rises on the northern slope of the Himalaya mountains in Thibet, and, turning southward, breaks through the mountains and flows south-west into the Arabian Sea. The Indus and its tributaries drain a fertile region called the Punjab, meaning *five rivers*. The principal tributaries of the Indus are the Chenab, the Sutlej and the Jhelum. The chief rivers of Southern India are the Nerbudda, the Godavery and the Kistna.

The extreme northern part of Hindoostan is mountainous and rugged. The valley of the Ganges, embracing the chief part of India, consists of a plain of unrivaled fertility, twelve hundred miles long and four hundred miles wide; over which flow large rivers with a tranquil and even current. To the westward is the great Indian desert, six hundred miles long. To the north-west is the extremely-fertile region of the Punjab. Around the Nerbudda is the plateau of Central India, twelve hundred feet above the level of the sea. Farther south is the plateau of the Deccan, still more elevated. Beyond this, on the east and west, the land sinks into a low, flat region.

The climate of Hindoostan varies greatly in different parts of the country. The vast plains have an almost continual summer, yielding double harvests, with the luxuriant foliage and the parching heat of the torrid zone. The plateaus of Central India exhibit the products of temperate climates. The elevated mountain region to the extreme north displays immense forests of fir, and the mountain summits have the stern features of perpetual winter. The flat region to the south is hot and unhealthy. The year consists of three seasons—the rainy, the cold and the hot. The rainy season lasts from June to October, the cold from November to February, and the hot from March to May.

No country in the world is richer in the variety of its vegetable products. Among its trees are the teak, almug, cocoa, betel, banian, jaca, etc. There is an infinite variety of the most delicious fruits, such as oranges, lemons, citrons, dates, almonds, mangos, pineapples, melons, pomegranates, etc. Spices and aromatic plants abound. In some portions of the country are extensive tracts covered with impenetrable thickets of prickly shrubs and canes, called *jungles*, which are the retreat of wild beasts.

There are a great variety of animals found in India. There are numerous wild and tame elephants, which have been trained to the service of man from time immemorial, for war and the chase, as well as for beasts of burden and travel. The royal Bengal tiger is almost equal to the lion in strength, and is peculiar to India. The rhinoceros, the lion, the bear, the leopard, the chetah, or hunting leopard, the panther, the fox, the antelope, various kinds of deer, the nylghau, the wild buffalo, the yak, or grunting ox, are among the more important quadrupeds. The forests abound in monkeys, and huge crocodiles and venomous serpents of large size are found in the marshes. An infinite variety of birds of rich plumage are found in the jungles and the forests.

Hindoostan produces an abundance of minerals, such as iron, copper and lead. Dimonds are produced by washing in several places on the Kistna and Godavery. Golconda has long been renowned for its diamonds and other precious gems.

Off the southern coast of Hindoostan is the fine island of Ceylon, about three hundred miles long and about one hundred wide. The coast is low and flat, and the interior abounds in mountains of moderate height. The island produces fine fruits, and is celebrated for its cinnamon. The chief town is Colombo. The natives are the Cingalese and the Candians. The island belongs to Great Britain. Missionaries have been successful in converting the natives, and many English have settled in the country, and have introduced European improvements. The Hindoos are nearly black, though belonging to the Caucasian race, and to the Aryan branch. The Greeks had not heard of the country until Alexander the Great had invaded it. It was then and long afterwards called *India*, the term being applied to the entire region between China and the Arabian Sea. Afterward geographers divided it into *India beyond the Ganges, and India within the Ganges.* The former is at present termed *Farther India*, and the latter *Hindoostan.*

In ancient times Hindoostan was divided into many petty kingdoms of which we know nothing; and so it has remained for ages, except that the Mogul empire several centuries ago comprehended the entire country, as does the British dominion at the present time. Though divided into many tribes and casts, the Hindoos are one people. Hindoostan has been invaded by the world's great conquerors, such as Alexander the Great, Mahmoud of Ghiznee, Zingis Khan and Tamerlane; and was the seat of the great empire of Aurungzebe several centuries ago.

SECTION II.—HINDOO ORIGIN AND CIVILIZATION.

INDIA has been a land of mystery from the most remote antiquity. From the most ancient times it has been known as one of the most populous regions of the globe, "full of barbaric wealth and a strange wisdom." This celebrated land has attracted many of the great conquerors of the world's history, and has been overrun and subdued by the armies of Darius Hystaspes, of Alexander the Great, of Mahmoud of Ghiznee, of Zingis Khan, of Tamerlane, of Nadir Shah, of Lord Clive and Sir Arthur Wellesley. These conquerors, from the Persian king to the British East-India Company, have overrun and plundered India; "but have left it the same unintelligible, unchangeable and marvelous country as before. It is the same land now which the soldiers of Alexander described—the land of grotto temples dug out of solid porphyry; of one of the most ancient pagan religions of the world; of social distinctions fixed and permanent as the earth itself; of the sacred Ganges; of the idols of Juggernaut, with its bloody worship; the land of elephants and tigers; of fields of rice and groves of palm; of treasuries filled with chests of gold, heaps of pearls, diamonds and incense. But, above all, it is the land of unintelligible systems of belief, of puzzling incongruities, and irreconcilable contradictions."

The sacred books of the Hindoos are of the greatest antiquity, and their literature is one of the richest that has ever been produced, extending back twenty or thirty centuries. Yet the Hindoos have no history, no annals, no authentic chronology, for history belongs to this world, and chronology belongs to time. But the Hindoos take no interest in this world or in time. The ancient Egyptians considered events so important that they wrote on stone and upon the imperishable records of the land the most trifling occurrences and affairs of everyday life, inscribing them upon tombs and obelisks. But the Hindoos regarded this world and human events of so little account in comparison with the infinite world beyond this life that they made no record of even the most important events, and were thus the most unhistoric people on earth, caring more "for the minutiæ of grammar, or the subtilties of metaphysics, than for the whole of their past." The only certain date which has escaped the general obscurity shrouding ancient India is that of the Hindoo prince Chandragupta, a contemporary of Alexander the Great, and called Sandracottus by the Greek historians. He became king B. C. 315, when Gautama the Buddha had been dead, according to the Hindoo account, one hundred and sixty years. According to this account Buddha must have died B. C. 477. This is the only date transmitted to us by the ancient Hindoos.

But in recent years light has dawned upon us from an unexpected source. While we can derive no knowledge concerning the history of India from its literature, or from its inscriptions or carved temples, the science of language comes to our assistance. "The fugitive sounds, which seem so fleeting and so changeable, prove to be more durable monuments than brass or granite." The study of the Sanskrit language—the sacred, and now obsolete, language of the ancient Brahmanic Hindoos—has given us light concerning the ethnic origin of this people and their migration from their primeval home to the land of the Indus and the Ganges. "It has rectified the ethnology of Blumenbach, has taught us who were the ancestors of the nations of Europe, and has given us the information that one great family, the Indo-European, has done most of the work of the world." It informs us that this family, the Aryan, or Indo-European, consists of seven races—the Hindoos, the Medo-Persians, the Greeks, the Romans, who all migrated from their prehistoric ancestral home in Central Asia to the South of Asia and Europe; and the Kelts, the Teutons and the Slavs, who entered Europe to the north of the Caucasus and the Caspian. This light has been furnished us by the new science of comparative philology. The comparison of the languages of the seven races just mentioned has made it clear that all these races were originally one; that they migrated from a region of Central Asia east of the Caspian and north-west of India; that they were originally a pastoral or nomad people and gradually adopted agricultural habits as they descended from the plains of the modern Turkestan into the valleys of the Indus and the Ganges and overspread the plateau of Iran. In these seven linguistic families the roots of the most common names are the same, the grammatical constructions are also the same, thus furnishing abundant evidence that the seven languages are descended from one common mother-tongue.

The original stock of the great Indo-European race in Central Asia before its dispersion has likewise been conjectured from the linguistic evidence before us. The original stock has been called *Aryan*, a designation which is found in Manu, who says: "As far as the eastern and western oceans, between the mountains, lies the land which the wise have named Arya-vesta, or *inhabited by honorable men.*" The people of Iran are thus named in the Zend-Avesta, with the same meaning of *honorable*. Herodotus says that the Medes were originally called *Aryans*. Strabo states that in the time of Alexander the Great the entire region about the Indus was called *Ariana*. In modern times the name *Iran* for Persia and *Erin* for Ireland are perhaps linguistic vestiges of the original family designation.

Long before the epoch of the Vedas, or the Zend-Avesta, the Aryans were living as a pastoral people on the great plains east of the Caspian Sea, in the region of the modern Turkestan. The condition of the undivided Aryans in Central Asia is deduced from the circumstance that the name of any fact is the same in two or more of the seven Indo-European languages, as we have seen in our account of the Zend and old Persian language. We have seen that the names for father, house and for boat were almost similar in the seven languages, from which we must infer that the prehistoric Aryans lived in houses, and that they had made some progress in navigation, and that they sailed in boats on the Jaxartes and the Oxus.

That the Aryans were originally a pastoral people is implied in the very word *pastoral*, as *pa* in Sanskrit means to watch, to guard, as men guard cattle—from which an entire series of words has been derived in all the Aryan languages.

According to Pictet, the prehistoric Aryans—the ancestors of the Hindoos, Medo-Persians, Greeks, Latins, Kelts, Teutons and Slavs—were dwelling in Central Asia, in the region of Bactria, some three thousand years before Christ. They must have dwelt there long enough to develop a language which became the mother-tongue of all the Indo-European languages. They were a pastoral people, but not nomads, as they had fixed habitations. They had oxen, horses, sheep, goats, hogs and domestic fowls. Herds of cows fed in pastures, each owned by a community, and each having a cluster of stables in the center. The daughters of the house were the dairy-maids. The food was mainly the products of the dairy and the flesh of the cattle. The cow was the most important animal, and its name was given to many plants, and even to the clouds and stars, wherein many fancied heavenly herds to be passing over the firmament.

The Aryans were likewise an agricultural people, as they certainly had barley, and perhaps other cereals before their separation into the three branches which spread over India, Media and Persia, and Europe. They possessed the plow, also mills for grinding grain. They had hatchets, hammers and augurs. They were acquainted with gold, silver, copper and tin. They could spin and weave, and were acquainted with pottery. Their houses had doors, windows and fireplaces. They had cloaks or mantles. They boiled and roasted meat, and used soup. They had lances, swords, bows and arrows, and shields. They had family life, some simple laws, games, dances, and wind instruments. They were acquainted with the decimal notation, and their year had three hundred and sixty days. They worshiped the heaven, the earth, the sun, fire, water, wind; but this Nature-worship was developed out of an earlier monotheism.

It is believed to have been three thousand years before Christ when the Aryan ancestors of the Hindoos crossed the Indus and settled in the Hindoo peninsula, which they eventually overspread, conquering the original dark-skinned races of the peninsula and intermingling with them. After the Aryan emigrants had settled in the region between the Punjab and the Ganges, they became transformed from warlike shepherds into tillers of the soil and builders of cities. India became one of the most ancient seats of civilization, the Hindoos attaining a high degree of advancement in art, literature and philosophy; but their civilization at length became stationary, and they made no further progress. Their literature was immense; and their works were all written in the very ancient and sacred Sanskrit language, now obsolete; and many of these works are about four thousand years old. The oldest works in the Hindoo literature are the *Vedas*, the early sacred writings.

M. Saint Martin says that the last hymn of the Vedas was written when the Hindoos had arrived at the Ganges from the Indus, and were building their oldest city at the confluence of the river with the Jumna. They then had a white complexion, and called the race whom they conquered *blacks*, who subsequently became *Sudras*, or the lowest caste of India.

After conquering the original dark-skinned natives of the country, the Aryan immigrants imposed a system of castes in the severest form upon the population. The number of castes was four, and the members of each were not allowed to intermarry or associate with those of any other caste. This rule has been strictly adhered to by the Hindoos to the present time. The first caste was that of the priests, or Brahmans, who were a wealthy, honorable and privileged class, possessing the chief political and ecclesiastical power, and were held in greater respect and veneration than the princes. They were regarded as sacred and inviolable. They were not subject to corporeal punishment for any crime, were exempt from all taxation, and constituted the king's chief council and held all the offices. The next caste was that of the warriors, who were responsible for the security and defense of the state, in return for their compensation and certain privileges. But the peaceful character of the people and the remoteness of the country from powerful enemies furnished little occasion for military duty; and thus the soldiers soon became slothful and degenerate, thus making it easy for the priests, or Brahmans, to maintain their political ascendency. The kings belonged to the soldier caste. The third caste was composed of the tillers of the soil, merchants, tradesmen and mechanics, who were heavily burdened with taxes and held the land only in right of occupancy, not ownership. The fourth caste was that of the servants and laborers, called *Sudras*, and were descended from the dark-skinned aborigines conquered by the Aryan immigrants. Every man was obliged to follow his father's occupation; and those who violated the rules of caste—a crime considered worse than death—became *Pariahs*, or outcasts. They were regarded by the other Hindoos as the refuse of mankind, and were treated with the deepest contempt. "They do not venture to dwell in the towns, cities or villages, or even in their neighborhood; everything they touch is looked upon as unclean, and it is pollution even to have seen them."

The rigorous division of Hindoo society into castes, laid down by the Brahmans as a divine ordinance, checked the progress of civilization after it had reached a certain point, and caused it to lapse into a state of repose and stagnation. The sensibility and creative imagination of the Hindoos appears in their copious literature, which relates intimately to their theology and religion. The most important of their literary productions are the four books of the *Vedas*, which are held in the most profound respect by all classes of Hindoos, as their religion. They include religious hymns and prayers, directions respecting sacrifices, and moral proverbs and maxims. The laws of Manu are most highly reverenced after the Vedas. The Hindoos possessed many other poetical works, distinguished for highly figurative language and for deep sensibility and religious feeling. Many of these have been brought to Europe by the English since their conquest of the country, and have been translated by scholars into the modern European languages. In the first century after Christ—many ages before Copernicus lived—Aryabhatta, a Hindoo, taught that the earth is a sphere, and that it revolves on its own axis.

The vast realm of Sanskrit literature was unknown to Europe until a century ago, when Sir William Jones, the great English scholar and Orientalist, introduced it to the knowledge of the West. "The vast realm of Hindoo, Chinese and Persian genius was as much a new continent to Europe, when discovered by Sir William Jones, as America was when made known by Columbus. Its riches had been accumulating during thousands of years, waiting till the fortunate man should arrive, destined to reveal to our age the barbaric pearl and gold of the gorgeous East—the true wealth of Ormus and of Ind."

Sir William Jones translated the laws of Manu, extracts from the Vedas, and other works, from the Sanskrit into English. Since his time wonderful progress has been made in the study of Sanskrit literature, especially within the last half century, since the time when the Schlegels led the way in this field. Professors of Sanskrit are now found in all the great European universities, and this country has produced one eminent Sanskrit scholar in Professor William D. Whitney, of Yale College. Among the leading European Sanskrit scholars is Professor Max Müller, of the university of Oxford, in England, a native of Germany. The system of Brahmanism, which until recently was only known to Western readers through the works of Colebrooke, Wilkins, Wilson and a few others, has now become accessible through the writings of Max Müller, Lassen, Bopp, Weber, Windischmann, Burnouf, Muir, Vivien de Saint-Martin, and a host of other distinguished writers in Germany, France and England.

Hindoo art, as well as literature, was intimately connected with religion. Especially worthy of attention are the rock-hewn temples and grottoes, the most renowned of which are those found at Ellora, in the middle of Lower India, at Salsette, near Bombay, and on the island of Elephanta, in the bay of Bombay. In these places we see temples, grottoes, dwellings and passages, covered with images and inscriptions cut one above another in the solid rock, and extending for miles. These grottoes contain a vast quantity of works executed artistically and elaborately, which must have required the labors of many thousands of men for countless ages, and the greatest diligence and perseverance for their completion.

The great abundance of the productions of nature and art in India, such as pearls, precious stones, ivory, spices, frankincense and silks, has made that country famous from an early period, as the great center of the maritime and caravan trade, and has likewise made it a constant prey to foreign invasion and conquest. Disunited, and divided into many petty kingdoms, and weakened by the system of castes and other institutions, enervated by the lack of individual freedom, the Hindoos were easily subdued by foreign invaders.

SECTION III.—BRAHMANISM.

THE theology taught by the Vedas embraced such chief gods as Indra, god of the air; Varuna, god of light, or heaven; Agni, god of fire; Savitri, god of the Sun; and Soma, god of the moon. Yama was the god of death. All the powers of Nature were personified in turn, as earth, food, wine, seasons, months, day, night and dawn. Indra and Agni were the chief of all the divinities, but an original monotheism lurks behind this incipient polytheism, as each god in turn becomes the Supreme Being. The Universal Deity appears first in one form of Nature, then in another. Colebrooke says that "the ancient Hindoo religion recognizes but one God, not yet sufficiently discriminating the creature from the Creator." And Professor Max Müller says: "The hymns celebrate Varuna, Indra, Agni, etc., and each in turn is called supreme. The whole mythology is fluent. The powers of nature become moral beings."

Max Müller adds: "It would be easy to find, in the numerous hymns of the Veda, passages in which almost every single god is represented as supreme and absolute. Agni is called 'Ruler of the Universe;' Indra is celebrated as the strongest god, and in one hymn it is said, 'Indra is stronger than all.' It is said of Soma that he 'conquers every one.'"

But clearer traces of monotheism than these are found in the Vedas. In one hymn of the Rig-Veda it is said: "They call him Indra, Mitra, Varuna, Agni; then he is the well-winged heavenly Garutmat; that which is One, the wise call it many ways; they call it Agni, Yama, Matarisvan."

The following from the Rig-Veda, the oldest of the Vedic hymns, clearly expresses the unity of God:

"In the beginning there arose the Source of golden light. He was the only born Lord of all that is. He established the earth, and this sky. Who is the God to whom we shall offer our sacrifice?

"He who gives life. He who gives strength; whose blessing all the bright gods desire; whose shadow is immortality, whose shadow is death. Who is the God to whom we shall offer our sacrifice?

"He who through his power is the only king of the breathing and awakening world. He who governs all, man and beast. Who is the god to whom we shall offer our sacrifice?

"He whose power these snowy mountains, whose power the sea proclaims, with the distant river. He whose these regions are, as it were his two arms. Who is the god to whom we shall offer our sacrifice?

"He through whom the sky is bright and the earth firm. He through whom heaven was established; nay, the highest heaven. He who measured out the light in the air. Who is the god to whom we shall offer our sacrifice?

"He to whom heaven and earth, standing firm by his will, look up, trembling inwardly. He over whom the rising sun shines forth. Who is the god to whom we shall offer our sacrifice?

"Wherever the mighty water-clouds went, where they placed the seed and lit the fire, thence arose he who is the only life of the bright gods. Who is the god to whom we shall offer our sacrifice?

"He who by his might looked even over the water-clouds, the clouds which gave strength and lit the sacrifice; *he who is God above all gods*. Who is the god to whom we shall offer our sacrifice?

"May he not destroy us—he the creator of the earth—or he, the righteous, who created heaven; he who also created the bright and mighty waters. Who is the god to whom we shall offer our sacrifices?"

This is one of many hymns to Agni:

"Agni, accept this log which I offer to thee, accept this my service; listen well to these my songs.

"With this log, O Agni, may we worship thee, thou son of strength, conqueror of horses! and with this hymn, thou high-born!

"May we thy servants serve thee with songs, O granter of riches, thou who lovest songs and delightest in riches.

"Thou lord of wealth and giver of wealth, be thou wise and powerful; drive away from us the enemies!

"He gives us rain from heaven, he gives us inviolable strength, he gives us food a thousandfold.

"Youngest of the gods, their messenger, their invoker, most deserving of worship, come at our praise, to him who worships thee and longs for thy help.

"For thou, O sage, goest wisely between these two creations (heaven and earth, gods and men), like a friendly messenger between two hamlets.

"Thou art wise, and thou hast been pleased; perform thou intelligent Agni, the sacrifice without interruption, sit down on this sacred grass!"

Indra is praised thus in the Rig-Veda:

"He who as soon as born is the first of the deities, who has done honor to the gods by his deeds; he at whose might heaven and earth are alarmed and who is known by the greatness of his strength; he, men, is Indra.

"He who fixed firm the moving earth, who spread the spacious firmament; he, men, is Indra.

"He who having destroyed Vritra, set free the seven rivers; who recovered the cows; who generated fire in the clouds; who is invincible in battle; he, men, is Indra.

"He to whom heaven and earth bow down; he at whose might the mountains are appalled; he who is drinker of the Soma juice, the firm of frame, the adamant armed, the wielder of the thunderbolt; he, men, is Indra. May we envelope thee with acceptable praises as husbands are embraced by their wives"

Some of the verses in this hymn bear a strong likeness to one of the grandest Psalms in the Bible, the 139th:

"The great lord of these worlds sees as if he were near. If a man thinks he is walking by stealth, the gods know it all.

"If a man stands or walks or hides, if he goes to lie down or to get up, what two people sitting together whisper, King Varuna knows it, he is there as the third."

(So the Psalmist says: "Thou compassest my path and my lying down and art acquainted with all my ways." Verse 3.)

"This earth, too, belongs to Varuna the king, and this wide sky with its ends far apart. The two seas (the sky and the ocean) are Varuna's loins; he is also contained in this drop of water.

"He who should flee far beyond the sky, even he would not be rid of Varuna the king. His spies proceed from heaven toward this world; with thousand eyes they overlook this earth. (Compare with this verse 7 to 12 of the same psalm.)

"King Varuna sees all this, what is between heaven and earth, and what is beyond. He has counted the twinklings of the eyes of men. As a player throws the dice, he settles all things.

"May all thy fatal nooses, which stand spread out seven by seven and threefold, catch the man who tells a lie, may they pass by him who tells the truth."

We must not omit a few verses from prayers in which pardon for sin is sought:

"However we break thy laws from day to day, men as we are, O god Varuna,

"Do not deliver us unto death, nor to the blow of the furious, nor to the wrath of the spiteful!"

Again:

"Wise and mighty are the works of him who stemmed asunder the wide firmaments (heaven and earth). He lifted on high the bright and glorious heaven; he stretched out apart the starry sky and the earth.

"I ask, O Varuna! wishing to know this my sin. I go to ask the wise. The sages all tell me the same: Varuna it is who is angry with thee. . . .

"Absolve us from the sins of our fathers, and from those which we committed with our own bodies."

The following contains some of the finest verses in the Veda:

"Let me not yet, O Varuna! enter into the house of clay; have mercy, almighty, have mercy!

"If I go along trembling, like a cloud driven by the wind; have mercy, almighty, have mercy!

"Through want of strength, thou strong and bright god, have I gone wrong; have mercy, almighty, have mercy!

"Thirst came upon the worshiper, though he stood in the midst of the waters; have mercy, almighty, have mercy!

"Whenever we men, O Varuna! commit an offence before the heavenly host, whenever we break the law through thoughtlessness; punish us not, O god, for that offence!"

Max Müller divides the Vedic age into four periods, thus: Sutra period, from B. C. 200 to B. C. 600. Brahmana period, from B. C. 600 to B. C. 800. Mantra period, from B. C. 800 to B. C. 1000. Chandas period, from B. C. 1000 to B. C. 1200. Dr. Haug considers the Vedic period as extending from B. C. 1200 to B. C. 2000, and the very oldest hymns to have been composed B. C. 2400.

Indra, the god of the air, is the chief deity in the oldest Vedas. He becomes Zeus in Greek, and Jupiter in Latin. The hymns to Indra sound very much like the Psalms of David. Indra is invoked as the most ancient god whom the fathers worshiped. Next to Indra comes Agni, the god of fire. Fire is worshiped as the principal motion on earth, as Indra was the moving power above the earth. The forms of the flame and all belonging to it are worshiped, as well as the fire itself. All nature is called Aditi, whose children are named Adityas. M. Maury quotes from Gautama these words: "Aditi is heaven; Aditi is air; Aditi is mother, father and son; Aditi is all the gods and the five races; Aditi is whatever is born and will be born: in short the heavens and the earth, the heavens being the father and the earth the mother of all things. "This closely resembles the Greek Zeus-pateer and Gee-mêteer. Varuna is the vault of heaven. Mitra is frequently associated with Varuna in the Vedic hymns. Mitra is the sun illuminating the day, while Varuna was the sun with an obscure face going back in the darkness from west to east to again take his luminous disk. From Mitra the Persian Mithra appears to be derived. In the Veda there are no invocations to the stars, but the Aurora, or Dawn, is greatly admired; as are likewise the Aswins, or twin gods, who in Greece become the Dioscuri. Rudra, the god of storms, is supposed by some writers to be the same as Siva. But the two antagonistic worships of Vishnu and Siva do not appear until long after this period. Vishnu appears frequently in the Veda, and his three steps are often alluded to. These steps of Vishnu measure the heavens, but his actual worship appeared at a much later period.

The religion of the Vedas consisted of odes and hymns—a religion of worship simply by adoration. There were sometimes prayers for temporal blessings, sometimes only for sacrifices and libations. There are scarcely any traces of human sacrifices.

Brahmanism began long after the age of the Vedas, and its text-book is the Laws of

Manu. Siva and Vishnu are yet unknown. Vishnu is named but once, Siva not at all. The writer knows only three of the Vedas. The Atharva-Veda is later. As Siva is named in the oldest Buddhist writings, the Laws of Manu must have been more ancient than these. In the time of Manu the Aryans were dwelling in the valley of the Ganges. The caste-system was then completely established, and the Brahmans' authority was supreme. The Indus and the Punjab were then wholly forgotten. The Laws of Manu were established somewhere from B. C. 1200 to B. C. 700. Wilson, Max Müller, Lassen and Saint-Martin believed them to have been written about B. C. 900 or B. C. 1000. Brahma has now become acknowledged as the Supreme Deity, and one still comes into relation with him thorough sacrifice. Nothing is said about widow-burning in Manu; but it is mentioned in the Mahabharata, one of the great epics, which appears later.

In the region of the Sarasvati, a holy river, formerly emptying into the Indus, but now lost in the desert, the Aryan race in India was transformed from a people of nomads into a settled community. They there received their laws, built their first cities, and founded the Solar and Lunar monarchies.

The Manu of the Vedas and the Manu of the Brahmans are very different personages. In the Vedas the first Manu is called the father of mankind. He also—like Xisuthrus, Sisit or Noah—escapes destruction from a deluge by building a ship, which a fish advised him to do. He preserved the fish, which grew to a vast size, and when the flood came it acted as a tow-boat to drag the ship of Manu to a mountain, as we are told in a Brahmana.

The Brahmans appear afterward to have given the name of Manu to their code of laws. Sir William Jones first translated these.

The following is from the First Book of the Laws of Manu on Creation:

"The universe existed in darkness, imperceptible, undefinable, undiscoverable, and undiscovered; as if immersed in sleep."

"Then the self-existing power, undiscovered himself, but making the world discernible, with the five elements and other principles, appeared in undiminished glory, dispelling the gloom."

"He, whom the mind alone can perceive, whose essence eludes the external organs, who has no visible parts, who exists from eternity, even he, the soul of all beings, shone forth in person.

"He having willed to produce various beings from his own divine substance, first with a thought created the waters, and placed in them a productive seed."

"The seed became an egg bright as gold, blazing like the luminary with a thousand beams; and in that egg he was born himself, in the form of Brahma, the great forefather of all spirits.

"The waters are called Nárá, because they were the production of Nara, or the spirit of God; and hence they were his first ayana, or place of motion; he hence is named Nara yana, or moving on the waters.

"In that egg the great power sat inactive a whole year of the creator, at the close of which, by his thought alone, he caused the egg to divide itself.

"And from its two divisions he framed the heaven above and the earth beneath; in the midst he placed the subtile ether, the eight regions, and the permanent receptacle of waters.

"From the supreme soul he drew forth mind, existing substantially though unperceived by sense, immaterial; and before mind, or the reasoning power, he produced consciousness, the internal monitor, the ruler.

"And before them both he produced the great principle of the soul, or first expansion of the divine idea; and all vital forms endued with the three qualities of goodness, passion, and darkness, and the five perceptions of sense, and the five organs of sensation.

"Thus, having at once pervaded with emanations from the Supreme Spirit the minutest portions of fixed principles immensely operative, consciousness and the five perceptions, he framed all creatures.

"Thence proceed the great elements, endued with peculiar powers, and mind with operations infinitely subtile, the unperishable cause of all apparent forms.

"This universe, therefore, is compacted from the minute portions of those seven divine and active principles, the great soul, or first emanation, consciousness, and five perceptions; a mutable universe from immutable ideas.

"Of created things, the most excellent are those which are animated; of the animated, those which subsist by intelligence; of the intelligent, mankind; and of men, the sacerdotal class.

"Of priests, those eminent in learning; of the learned, those who know their duty: of those who know it, such as perform it virtuously; and of the virtuous, those who seek beatitude from a perfect acquaintance with scriptural doctrine.

"The very birth of Brahmans is a constant incarnation of Dharma, God of justice, for the Brahman is born to promote justice, and to procure ultimate happiness.

"When a Brahman springs to light, he is born above the world, the chief of all creatures, assigned to guard the treasury of duties, religious and civil.

"The Brahman who studies this book, having performed sacred rites, is perpetually free from offence in thought, in word and in deed.

"He confers purity on his living family, on his ancestors, and on his descendants as far as the seventh person, and he alone deserves to possess this whole earth."

The Second Book of Manu treats of education and the priesthood. It condemns self-love as an unworthy motive, also the performance of sacrifices and the practice of penances and austerities for the sake of a reward. It enjoins upon priests to beg their food, first of their mothers, sisters, or mother's whole sisters, then of some other female who will not disgrace them. A priest who knows the Veda, and is able to pronounce to himself, both morning and evening, the syllable *óm* attains the sanctity conferred by the Veda. The book condemns sensuality and declares no man thus contaminated ever able to procure felicity either from the Vedas, or from liberality, sacrifices, strict observances, or pious austerities. It declares that a student who humbly follows his teacher will attain knowledge, the means of salvation. Sensual indulgence is to be repented of by fasts, the performance of ablutions, and the reading of texts from the Vedas.

The Fourth Book treats on private morals, enjoining upon Brahmans the strict observance of truth as the primal rule, and condemning falsehood in the severest terms, declaring that sacrifice becomes vain by falsehood. It declares that in one's passage to the next world, no one, not even of his family or relatives, remains in his company, his virtue only adhering to him.

The Fifth Book relates to diet. It requires entire abstinence from animal flesh of any kind, because it involves the taking of animal life, which is totally prohibited. It also commands total abstinence from all intoxicating drink. It enjoins its devotees to subsistence on pure fruit and roots, and such grains as are eaten by hermits. Sacred learning, austere devotion, fire, holy aliment, earth, the wind, water, air, the sun, time, and prescribed acts of religion, are mentioned as purifiers of embodied spirits. Of all pure things purity in acquiring wealth is pronounced the most excellent. The learned are declared purified by forgiving injuries; those who are negligent by liberality; those with secret faults by pious meditation; those who best know the Veda by devout austerity. Bodies are declared cleansed by water; the mind is pronounced purified by truth; the vital spirit by theology and devotion; the understanding by clear knowledge. Women are allowed no sacrifice separate from their husbands, nor any religious rite, nor fasting; "as far only as a wife honors her lord, so far is she exalted in heaven." "A faithful wife, who wishes to attain in heaven the mission of her husband, must do nothing unkind to him, be he living or dead." She is enjoined to emaciate her body by living voluntarily on pure flowers, roots and fruit; and when her lord is deceased she is not to pronounce the name of another man. She is enjoined to continue until death forgiving all injuries, performing harsh duties, avoiding all sensual pleasures, and cheerfully practicing the strictest rules of virtue, followed by those women who are devoted to their husbands.

The Sixth Book of the Laws of Manu relates to devotion. It appears that the Brahmans were accustomed to becoming ascetics, or entering religion, as the Roman Catholics would say. A Brahman, or twice-born man, who desires to become an ascetic, must relinquish his home and family and go to live in the forest. He must subsist on roots and fruit, and clothe himself in a bark garment or a skin. He must bathe in the morning and in the evening, and allow his hair to grow. He must spend his time in reading the Vedas, with his thoughts intent on the Supreme Being. He must be "a perpetual giver but no receiver of gifts; with tender affection for all animated bodies." He must perform various sacrifices with offerings of fruits and flowers. He must practice austerities by exposing himself to heat and cold, and "for the purpose of uniting his soul with the Divine Spirit he must study the Upanishads."

"A Brahman, having shuffled off his body by these modes, which great sages practice, and becoming void of sorrow and fear, is exalted into the Divine essence."

"Let him not wish for death. Let him not wish for life. Let him expect his appointed time, as the hired servant expects his wages."

"Meditating on the Supreme Spirit, without any earthly desire, with no companion but his own soul, let him live in this world seeking the bliss of the next."

The anchorite is to beg his food, but only once a day. If it is refused him, he must not be sorrowful; and if he receives it, he must not be glad. He must meditate on the "subtle indivisible essence of the Supreme Being." He must be careful not to destroy the life of even the smallest insect.

He must make atonement for the death of those which he has unknowingly destroyed, by making six suppressions of his breath, repeating at the same time the triliteral syllable A U M. In this way he will finally become united with the Eternal Spirit, "and his good deeds will be inherited by those who love him, and his evil deeds by those who hate him."

The Seventh Book relates to the duties of rulers. One of these duties is to reward the good and to punish the wicked. "The genius of punishment is a son of Brahma, and has a body of pure light." Punishment is considered an active ruler. It governs the human race, it dispenses laws, it preserves mankind, and it is the perfection of justice. If it were not inflicted, all classes of mankind would become corrupt, all barriers would be cast away, and complete confusion would be the result. Kings must respect the Brahmans, must shun vices, must choose good counselors and brave soldiers. A king must be a father to his people. When going to war he must observe the rules of honorable warfare, must not use poisoned arrows, must not strike a fallen foe, nor one who begs for life, nor one unarmed, nor one who surrenders. He must not take too little revenue, and thus "cut up his own root;" nor too much, and thus "cut up the root of others." He must be severe when necessary, and mild when necessary.

The Eighth Book relates to civil and criminal law. The Raja is required to hold his court daily, aided by his Brahmans, and to decide causes respecting debts and loans, sales, wages, contracts, boundaries, slander, assaults, theft, robbery, and other crimes. The Raja, "understanding what is expedient or inexpedient, but considering only what is law or not law," is expected to investigate all disputes. He must protect unprotected women, restore property to its rightful owner, must not encourage litigation, and must decide in accordance with rules of law. The rules correspond almost exactly to our law of evidence. Witnesses are warned to tell the truth in every case by considering that, though they may think that no one sees them, the gods clearly see them and likewise the spirits in their own breasts.

"The soul itself is its own witness, the soul itself is its own refuge; offend not thy conscious soul, the supreme internal witness of men."

"The fruit of every virtuous act which thou hast done, O good man, since thy birth, shall depart from thee to the dogs, if thou deviate from the truth."

"O friend to virtue, the Supreme Spirit, which is the same with thyself, resides in thy bosom perpetually, and is an all-knowing inspector of thy goodness or wickedness."

The law then describes the punishments which the gods would inflict upon false witnesses; but strangely permits false witness to be given for benevolent reasons, to save an innocent man from a tyrant. This is styled "the venial sin of benevolent falsehood." The book then describes weights and measures, also the rate of usury, which is set down at five per cent. Compound interest is forbidden. The law of deposits takes considerable space, as in all Asiatic lands, where investments are not easy. Much is said concerning the wages of servants, particularly such as are employed to watch cattle, and the responsibilities devolving upon them. The law of slander is carefully defined. Crimes of violence are likewise described in detail. If a man strikes a human or animal creature so as to cause pain, he shall himself be struck in the same manner. A man is permitted to chastise with a small stick his wife, his son or his servant, but not the head or any noble part of the body. But the Brahmans have the protection of special laws.

"Never shall the king flay a Brahman, though convicted of all possible crimes; let him banish the offender from his realm, but with all his property secure and his body unhurt."

"No greater crime is known on earth than flaying a Brahman; and the king, therefore, must not even form in his mind the idea of killing a priest."

The Ninth Book relates to women, to families, and to the law of castes. It says that women must be kept in a dependent condition.

"Their fathers protect them in childhood; their husbands protect them in youth; their sons protect them in age. A woman is never fit for independence."

It is said to be men's duty to watch and guard women, and not very flattering views are expressed regarding the female character.

"Women have no business with the text of the Veda; this is fully settled; therefore having no knowledge of expiatory texts, sinful women must be as foul as falsehood itself. This is a fixed law."

It is said, however, that good women become like goddesses, and shall be joined to their husbands in heaven, and that a man is only perfect when he consists of three persons united—himself, his wife and his son. Manu likewise ascribes to ancient Brahmans a maxim almost literally like one of the Bible, namely, "The husband is even one person with his wife." Manu says nothing about the burning of widows, but gives minute directions for the conduct of widows during their life, and also directions regarding the marriage of sons and daughters and their inheritance of property. The remainder of the Ninth Book further describes crimes and punishments.

The Tenth Book of Manu relates to mixed classes and times of distress; the Eleventh to penance and expiation. In the Eleventh Book is mentioned the strange rite consisting in drinking the fermented juice of the moon-plant, or acid asclepias, with religious ceremonies. This Hindoo sacrament began in the Vedic age, and the Sanhita of the Sama-Veda consists of hymns to be sung at the moon-plant sacrifices. This ceremony is yet occasionally practiced in India, and Dr. Haug has tasted this sacred beverage, which he says is bitter, unpleasant and intoxicating. Manu says that no one has a right to drink this sacred juice who does not properly provide for his own family. He encourages sacrifices by asserting that they are highly meritorious and will expiate sin. Involuntary sins do not require as heavy a penance as those committed with knowledge. Crimes committed by Brahmans do not require as heavy a penance as those committed by others; but those committed against Brahmans carry a much deeper guilt and require a much severer penance. The law declares:

"From his high birth alone a Brahman is an object of veneration, even to deities, and his declarations are decisive evidence."

"A Brahman, who has performed an expiation with his whole mind fixed on God, purifies his soul."

The Law of Manu strictly prohibits the drinking of intoxicating liquor, except in the Soma sacrifice, already alluded to, and it declares that a Brahman who tastes intoxicating liquor sinks to the low caste of a Sudra. If a Brahman who has tasted the Soma juice even smells the breath of a man who has been drinking ardent spirits, he must do penance by repeating the Gayatri, suppressing his breath, and eating clarified butter. Cows are objects of reverence next to the Brahmans, perhaps because the Aryan race were originally nomads and depended on this animal for food. He who kills a cow must perform severe penances, among which are the following:

"All day he must wait on a herd of cows and stand quaffing the dust raised by their hoofs; at night, having servilely attended them, he may sit near and guard them."

"Free from passion, he must stand while they stand, follow when they move, and lie down near them when they lie down."

"By this waiting on a herd for three months, he who has killed a cow atones for his guilt."

Such offenses as cutting down fruit-trees or grasses, or killing insects, or injuring sentient creatures, require as a penance the repeating of a number of texts from the Vedas, the eating of clarified butter, or the holding of the breath. A low-born man who treats a Brahman with disrespect, or who even gets the better of him in an argument, is required to fast all day and to prostrate himself before him. He who strikes a Brahman shall remain in hell a thousand years. The power of sincere devotion is nevertheless very great. Any one is freed from all guilt by reading the Vedas, open confession, repentance, reformation and alms giving. It is said that devotion is equal to the performance of all duties. Even the souls of worms, insects and vegetables reach heaven by the power of devotion. But the sanctifying influence of the Vedas is particularly great. He who is able to repeat all of the Rig-Veda would be free from guilt, even if he had killed the inhabitants of three worlds.

The last book of Manu relates to the doctrine of the metempsychosis, or transmigration of the soul and final beatitude. Here it is declared that every human action, word and thought bears its good or evil fruit.

From the heart come three sins of thought, four of the tongue, and three of the body, namely, covetous, disobedient and atheistic thoughts; scurrilous, false, frivolous and unkind words; and actions of theft, bodily injury and licentiousness. He who controls his thoughts, words and actions is called a triple commander. The three qualities of the soul are giving it a tendency to goodness, to passion and to darkness. The first leads to knowledge, the second to desire, the third to sensuality. To the first belong the study of the Vedas, devotion, purity, self-control and obedience. From the second proceed hypocritical actions, anxiety, disobedience and self-indulgence. The third produces avarice, atheism, indolence, and all acts for which a man is ashamed. Virtue is the object of the first quality, worldly success of the second, and pleasure of the third. The souls in which the first quality predominates rise after death to the condition of deities. Those controlled by the second quality pass into the bodies of other men. Those dominated by the third quality become animals and vegetables. Manu expounds this law of the soul's transmigration very minutely. For great sins any one is condemned to pass many times into the bodies of dogs, insects, spiders, snakes or grasses. This change relates to the crime. One who steals grain shall be born a rat. One who steals meat shall become a vulture. One who indulges in forbidden pleasures of the senses shall have his senses rendered acute to endure intense pain.

The highest virtue is doing good because it is right goodness done from the love of God and based on the knowledge of the Vedas. A religious act performed simply with the expectation of reward in the next world, will only give one a place in the lowest heaven. But one doing good deeds without the hope of reward, "perceiving the supreme soul in all beings, and all beings in the supreme soul, fixing his mind on God approaches the Divine Nature."

"Let every Brahman, with fixed attention, consider all nature as existing in the Divine Spirit; all worlds as seated in him; he alone as the whole assemblage of gods; and he the author of all human actions."

"Let him consider the supreme omnipresent intelligence as the sovereign lord of the universe, by whom alone it exists, an incomprehensible spirit; pervading all beings in five elemental forms, and causing them to pass through birth. growth and decay, and so to solve like the wheels of a car."

"Thus the man who perceives in his own soul the supreme soul present in all creatures, acquires equanimity toward them all, and shall be absolved at last in the highest essence, even that of the Almighty himself."

We now come to the three systems of Hindoo philosophy—Sánkhya, Vedanta and Nyaya. Duncker says that the Hindoo system of philosophy arose in the sixth or seventh century before Christ. As the Buddhist religion implies the existence of the Sánkhya philosophy, this philosophy must have existed prior to Buddhism. Kapila and his two principles are likewise mentioned in the Laws of Manu and in the later Upanishads. This would bring it to the Brahmana period, according to Max Müller, from B. C. 800 or B. C. 600, and perhaps earlier. Colebrooke says that Kapila is mentioned in the Veda. Kapila was even regarded as an incarnation of Vishnu, or of Agni. Lassen says that the Vedanta philosophy is mentioned in the Laws of Manu. This philosophy is based on the Upanishads, and would appear to be later than that of Kapila, as it criticises his philosophy. Nevertheless Duncker regards it as the oldest system, and as already commencing in the Upanishads of the Vedas.

The Sánkhya philosophy of Kapila is contained in numerous works, particularly in the Sánkhya-Káriká by Iswara-Krishna, which consists of eighty-two memorial verses with a commentary. The Vedanta philosophy is contained in the Sutras, the Upanishads, and especially in the Brahma-Sutra ascribed to Nyaya. The Nyaya philosophy is found in the Sutras of Gautama and Canade.

It is not known when the three systems of Hindoo philosophy arose, or who were their founders. They agree in some points, but differ in others. They all three agree in having for their object deliverance from the evils of time, change, sorrow, into an everlasting rest and peace. Their aim is practical, not speculative. All agree in regarding existence as an evil, meaning by existence a life in time and space. All are idealistic, in which the world of matter and time is a delusion and a snare, and in which ideas are considered the only substance. All agree in accepting the doctrine of the metempsychosis, or transmigration of the soul, the end of which transmigration only brings final rest and deliverance. All agree that the means of this deliverance is to be found in knowledge, in a perfect knowledge in reality and not in appearance. All three systems are held by Brahmans who regard themselves as orthodox, who esteem the Vedas above all other books, who pay complete respect to the Brahmanism of the day, who perform the daily ceremonies and observe the usual rules of caste. The three systems of philosophy supplement the religious worship, but are not designed to destroy it. The Vedantists maintain that while there is really only one God, the various forms of worship in the Vedas, of Indra, Agni, the Maruts, etc., were all designed for those who could not comprehend this sublime monotheism. Those who believe in the Sánkhya hold that though their system entirely ignores God, and is called "the system without a God," it simply ignores, but does not deny the Divine existence.

Each of the three philosophies has a speculative and a practical side. The speculative is, How did the Universe come into existence? The practical is, How is man to be delivered from evil?

The Vedanta, or Mimansa, doctrine reasons from a single eternal and uncreated principle, and asserts that there is only being in the universe, God or Brahm, and that everything else is *Maya*, or illusion. The Sánkhya teaches that there are two eternal and uncreated substances, Soul and Nature. The Nyaya asserts that there are three eternal and uncreated substances—Atoms, Souls and God.

The three philosophies agree that only by knowledge can the soul be freed from the body or matter or nature. Worship is not sufficent, though it must not be despised. Action is injurious, because it implies desire. Only knowledge can lead to complete rest and peace.

The three philosophies teach that the soul's transmigration through different bodies is an evil resulting from desire. So long as the soul desires anything, it will continue to migrate and suffer in consequence. When it attains clear insight, it ceases to wander and finds repose.

Duncker supposed the Vedanta, or Mimansa, philosophy to be referred to in Manu. Mimansa means searching. In its logical forms, after stating the question, giving the objection and the answer to the objection, it gives the conclusion. The first portion of the Vedanta relates to worship and to the ceremonies and the ritual of the Vedas. The second portion teaches the doctrine of Brahma. Brahma is the one, eternal, absolute, unchangeable Being. He first be-

comes ether, then air, then fire, then water, then earth. All bodily existence proceeds from these five elements. "Souls are sparks from the central fire of Brahma, separated for a time, to be absorbed again at last."

"Brahma, in his highest form as Para-Brahm, stands for the Absolute Being." Haug has translated the following from the Sáma-Veda: "The generation of Brahma was before all ages, unfolding himself evermore in a beautiful glory; everything which is highest and everything which is deepest belongs to him. Being and Not Being are unveiled through Brahma."

Windischmann has translated the following passage from a Upanishad: "How can any one teach concerning Brahma? He is neither the known nor the unknown. That which cannot be expressed by words, but through which all expression comes, this I know to be Brahma. That which cannot be thought by the mind, but by which all thinking comes, this I know is Brahma. That which cannot be seen by the eye, but which the eye sees, is Brahma. If thou thinkest that thou canst know it, then in truth thou knowest it very little. To whom it is unknown, he knows it; but to whom it is known, he knows it not."

Windischmann has also translated the following from the Kathaka-Upanishad: "One cannot attain to it through the word, through the mind, or through the eye. It is only reached by him who says, 'It is! It is!' He perceives it in its essence. Its essence appears when one perceives it as it is."

According to Bunsen, the old German expression *Istigkeit* corresponds to this. This is also the name of Jehovah given by Moses from the burning bush, thus: "And God said unto Moses, I AM THE I AM. Thus shalt thou say unto the children of Israel, I AM hath sent me unto you." The idea here is that only God really exists, and that He is the origin of all being. The same is expressed in another Upanishad thus: "HE WHO EXISTS is the root of all creatures; HE WHO EXISTS is their foundation, and in him they rest."

This speculative pantheism is carried still

farther in the Vedanta philosophy. Thus says Sankara, the principal teacher of this philosophy: "I am the great Brahma, eternal, pure, free, one, constant, happy, existing without end. He who ceases to contemplate other things, who retires into solitude, annihilates his desires, and subjects his passions, he understands that Spirit is the One and the Eternal. The wise man annihilates all sensible things, and contemplates that one spirit who resembles pure space. Brahma is without size, quality, character, or division."

According to this philosophy, says Bunsen, the world is the Not-Being. It is, says Sankara, "appearance without Being; it is like the deception of a dream." He says further: "The soul itself has no actual being."

According to a Hindoo authority, Shoshee Chunder Dutt: "Dissatisfied with his own solitude, Brahma feels a desire to create worlds, and then the volition ceases so far as he is concerned, and he sinks again into his apathetic happiness, while the desire, thus willed into existence, assumes an active character. It becomes Maya, and by this was the universe created, without exertion on the part of Brahma. This passing wish of Brahma carried, however, no reality with it. And the creation proceeding from it is only an illusion. There is only one absolute Unity really existing, and existing without plurality. But he is like one asleep. Krishna, in the Gita, says: 'These works (the universe) confine not me, for I am like one who sitteth aloof uninterested in them all.' The universe is therefore all illusion, holding a position between something and nothing. It is real as an illusion, but unreal as being. It is not true, because it has no essence; but not false, because its existence, even as illusion, is from God. The Vedanta declares: 'From the highest state of Brahma to the lowest condition of a straw all things are delusion.'"

Shoshee Chunder Dutt, however, contradicts Bunsen's assertion that the soul also is an illusion according to the Vedanta. He says: "The soul is not subject to birth or death, but is in its substance, from Brahma himself." The truth appears to be that the Vedanta considers the individuality of the soul as from Maya and illusive, but regards the substance of the soul as from Brahma, and as destined to be absorbed into him. As the body of man is to be resolved into its material elements, so the soul of man is to be resolved into Brahma. This substance of the soul is neither born nor dies, nor is it a thing of which it can be said: "It was, is, or shall be." In the Gita, Krishna tells Arjun that he and the other princes of the world "never were not."

The Vedantist philosopher, nevertheless that he regards all souls as emanations from God, does not believe that all of them will be absorbed into God at death. Only such as have obtained a knowledge of God are rewarded by absorption into Deity, the others continuing to migrate from one body to another as long as they remain unfit for absorption. "The knower of God becomes God." This union with Deity is the complete loss of all personal identity, and is the attainment of the highest bliss, in which there are no grades, and from which there is no return. This absorption does not come from good works or penances, as these confine the soul and do not free it. "The confinement of fetters is the same whether the chain be of gold or iron." "The knowledge which realizes that everything is Brahm alone liberates the soul. It annuls the effect both of our virtues and vices. We traverse thereby both merit and demerit, the heart's knot is broken, all doubts are split, and all our works perish. Only by perfect abstraction, not merely from the senses, but also from the thinking intellect and by remaining in the knowing intellect, does the devotee become identified with Brahm. He then remains as pure glass when the shadow has left. He lives destitute of passions and affections. He lives sinless; for as water wets not the leaf of the lotus, so sin touches not him who knows God." He needs no more of virtue, for "of what use can be a winnowing fan when the sweet southern wind is blowing."

His meditations are of this kind: "I am Brahm, I am life. I am everlasting, perfect, self-existent, undivided, joyful."

Virtue, penance, sacrifices, worship, effect a happy transmigration from lower forms of bodily life to higher ones; but do not accomplish the end which is the soul's great aim and desire—absorption into the Universal Supreme Being. They simply prepare the way for such absorption by causing one to be born in a higher state of being.

The Sánkhya philosophy of Kapila is founded on two principles, not on simply one, as is the Vedanta. According to the seventy aphorisms, Nature is one of these principles. Nature is uncreated and eternal; being one, active, creating, non-intelligent. Souls are the other of the two principles, and are likewise uncreated and eternal. Souls are many, passive, not creative, intelligent, and the opposite of Nature in everything. But the union of the two is that from which all nature proceeds, in accordance with the law of cause and effect.

This system is frequently called atheism, as God is not recognized in it. It thus argues that no one perfect being could create the universe. Desire implies want, or imperfection. Then if God wished to create, He would not be able to do so. If He were able, He would have no desire to do it. Therefore, in neither case, could God have created the universe. The gods are generally spoken of by the well-known names of Brahma, Indra, etc.; but all are finite beings, belonging to the order of human souls, though of a superior kind.

"Every soul is clothed in two bodies—the interior original body, the individualizing force, which is eternal as itself and accompanies it through all its migrations; and the material, secondary body, made of the five elements—ether, air, fire, water and earth. The original body is subtile and spiritual. It is the office of Nature to liberate the Soul. Nature is not what we perceive by the senses, but an invisible plastic principle behind, which must be known by the intellect. As the Soul ascends by goodness, it is freed by knowledge. The final result of this emancipation is the certainty of non-existence—'neither I am, nor is aught mine, nor do I exist,'—which seems to be the same result as that of Hegel, Being=Not-Being."

The result of knowledge is to put an end to creation, leaving the Soul freed from desire, from change, from the material body, in a state which is Being, but not Existence.

The Sánkhya philosophy was very important as it was the source of Buddhism, and the doctrine thus described was the basis of Buddhism.

M. Cousin has called it the sensualism of India. But it is as purely an ideal doctrine as that of the Vedas. Both its eternal principles are ideal. Kapila asserts that the one which is a plastic force can not be perceived by the senses. Soul, the other eternal and uncreated principle, who "is witness, solitary, bystander, spectator and passive," is itself spiritual, and clothed with a spiritual body, within a material body. The Karika declares the material universe to be the result of the contact of the Soul with Nature, and consists in chains with which Nature binds herself, for the purpose of freeing the Soul. When through knowledge the Soul looks through these, and sees the final principle beyond, the material universe is at an end; both Soul and Nature are freed.

Scotus Erigena, the great Irish philosopher of the ninth century of our era, made a fourfold division of the universe—1, a Nature which creates and is not created; 2, a Nature which is created and creates; 3, a Nature which is created and does not create; 4, a Nature which neither creates nor is created. In the same way Kapila says: "Nature, the root of all things, is productive but not a production. Seven principles are productions and productive. Sixteen are productions but not productive. Soul is neither a production nor productive."

The Sánkhya philosophy is often likewise noticed in the Mahabharata. The Nyaya philosophy differs from that of Kapila in assuming that there is a third eternal and indestructible principle as the basis of matter, namely, Atoms. It likewise assumes the existence of a Supreme Soul, Brahma, who is almighty and allwise. It agrees with Kapila in making all souls eternal, and distinct from the body. It has the same evil to overcome —transmigration. It has the same method of release—Buddhi, or knowledge. It is a more dialectic system than the others, and is more of a logic than a philosophy.

The Nyaya philosophy has been compared to the Buddhist system. The Buddhist Nirvana has been regarded as equivalent to the emancipation of the Nyaya philosophy. Apavarga, or emancipation, is asserted in the Nyaya system to be ultimate deliverance from pain, birth, activity, fault and death. So the Pali doctrinal books of Buddhism refer to Nirvana as an exemption from old age, disease and death. "In it desire, anger and ignorance are consumed by the fire of knowledge. Here all selfish distinctions of mine and thine, all evil thoughts, all slander and jealousy, are cut down by the weapon of knowledge. Here we have an experience of immortality which is cessation of all trouble and perfect felicity."

We now come to the origin of the Hindoo Triad. A worship founded on that of the ancient Vedas had gradually risen among the Hindoos. In the West of India the god Rudra, mentioned in the Vedic hymns, had become transformed into Siva. In the Rig-Veda, Rudra is sometimes the name for Agni. He is described as father of the winds. He is the same as Maha-deva. He is at the same time fierce and benevolent. He presides over medicinal plants. Weber and Professor Whitney consider him the Storm-god. But his worship extended by degrees, until under the name of Siva, the Destroyer, he became one of the chief deities of the Hindoos. In the meantime, in the Ganges valley, a similar devotion had risen for the Vedic God, Vishnu, who in the same way had been elevated to the front rank in the Hindoo pantheon. He had been raised to the character of a Friend and Protector, "gifted with mild attributes and worshiped as the life of Nature." By accepting the popular worship, the Brahmans were enabled to successfully oppose Buddhism.

It is believed that the Hindoo Triad arose from the efforts of the Brahmans to unite all the Hindoos under one system of religion, and it may have succeeded for a time. Images of the Trimurtti, or three-faced God, are often seen in India, and this is yet the object of Brahmanical worship. Thought invariably tends toward a triad of law, force or elemental substance, as the best explanation of the universe. For this reason there have been triads in so many religions. In Egypt there was the Triad of Osiris the Creator, Typhon the Destroyer, and Horus the Preserver. In Persia was the Triad of Ormazd the Creator, Ahriman the Destroyer, and Mithra the Restorer. In Buddhism is the Triad of Buddha, the Divine Man, Dharmma the Word, and Sangha the Communion of Saints. Pure monotheism is not long satisfactory to the speculative mind, because it does not explain the discords of the universe, though it accounts for its harmonies. A dualism of antagonistic forces does not afford any better satisfaction, because the world does not seem to be such a scene of complete discord and warfare as is here assumed. Therefore the mind is ready to accept a Triad, in which the unities of life and development proceed from one element, the antagonisms from a second, and the harmonies of reconciled oppositions from a third. In this very manner arose the Brahmanical Triad.

Thus arose from the spiritual pantheism into which all Hindoo religion appeared to settle, another system, that of the Trimurtti, or Divine Triad—the Hindoo Trinity of Brahma the Creator, Vishnu the Preserver, and Siva the Destroyer. A foundation for the unity of Creation, Preservation and Destruction already existed in a Vedic saying, that the highest being exists in three states—creation, preservation and destruction.

None of these three supreme deities of Brahmanism ranked very highly in the Vedas. Siva is not named once therein. Lassen says that Brahma is not noticed in any Vedic hymn, but first in a Upanishad. Vishnu is mentioned in the Rig-Veda as one of the names for the sun. He is therefore the Sun-god of the Hindoos. Sunrise, noon and sunset are his three steps. He is spoken of as one of the sons of Aditi. He is styled "the wide-stepping," "the strong," "measurer of the world," "the deliverer," "renewer of life," "who sets in motion the revolutions of time," "a protector," "preserving the highest heaven." He seems to begin his career in this mythology as the sun.

Brahma, a word first signifying prayer and devotion, became the primal God in the Laws of Manu, wherein he was recognized as the first born of the creation, from the self-existent being, in the form of a golden egg. He became the creator of all things by the power of prayer. Brahma very naturally became the god of the priests in their struggle for ascendency over the warriors. In the meantime the worship of Vishnu the Preserver had been growing in the Ganges valley, while at the same time the worship of Siva the Destroyer was making rapid progress in the Indus valley. Then occurred those mysterious wars between the kings of the Solar and Lunar races, mentioned in the great epics. These wars were ended by a compromise, by which Brahma, Vishnu and Siva were united into one Supreme Deity as Creator, Preserver and Destroyer—three in one.

This Hindoo Triad resulted apparently from an ingenious and successful effort, on the part of the Brahmans, to unite all classes of Hindoo worshipers against the Buddhists. In this sense the Brahmans edited afresh the epic of the Mahabharata, into which they inserted passages praising Vishnu in the form of Krishna. The Greek accounts of India after its invasion by Alexander the Great speak of the worship of Hercules as prevailing in the East, and Colebrooke and Lassen think that by Hercules they refer to Krishna. Brahmanism struggled with Buddhism nine centuries for the mastery in India, from B. C. 500 to A. D. 400, and the struggle ended in the final triumph of Brahmanism and the total expulsion of Buddhism from India.

Before this Triad, or Trimurtti, of Brahma, Vishnu and Siva, there appears to have been another Triad of Agni, Indra and Surya. This may have furnished the example for the second Triad, which vested Brahma, Vishnu and Siva respectively with the attributes of Creation, Preservation and Destruction. Brahma, the Creator, did not long remain popular, but the worship of Vishnu and Siva as Krishna are to this day the popular Hindoo religion.

A strange feature of the worship of Vishnu is the doctrine of the Avatars, or incarnations of the Deity. The number of these Avatars is ten—nine of whom have passed, while one is to come. The object of Vishnu each time is to save the gods from destruction threatened them because of the vast power acquired by some king, giant or demon, by greater acts of austerity and piety. For here, as elsewhere, extreme spiritualism is separated from morality; and thus these extremely pious, spiritual and self-denying giants are the most cruel and tyrannical monsters, who must be destroyed at every hazard. By force or fraud, Vishnu overcomes all of them.

His first Avatar is of the Fish, as stated in the Mahabharata, the object being to recover the Vedas, which had been stolen by a demon from Brahma while asleep. Because of this loss mankind became corrupt, and were destroyed by a deluge, except a pious prince and seven holy men who were saved in a ship. Vishnu, in the form of a large fish, drew the ship in safety over the water, killed the demon, and recovered the Vedas. The second Avatar was in a Turtle, to make him drink of immortality. The third Avatar was in a Boar, the fourth in a Man-lion, the fifth in the dwarf who deceived Bali, who had become so powerful by austerities as to conquer the gods and take possession of Heaven. In the eighth Avatar he appears as Krishna, and in the ninth as Buddha.

This system of Avatars is so strange and so firmly implanted in the Hindoo system that it apparently indicates some law of Hindoo thought. Vishnu does not mediate between Brahma and Siva, but between the deities and the lower races of men or demons. This danger arises from a certain fate or necessity superior to gods and men. There are laws enabling a Brahman to get away from the power of Brahma and Siva. This necessity is the nature of things, the laws of the external world of active existences. Only when essence becomes existence does spirit pass into action and become subject to law. The danger is then from the world of nature. The gods are pure spirit, and the spirit is everything. But now and then nature appears to be something, as it will not be ignored or absorbed in Deity. Personality, activity, or human nature revolt against this ideal pantheism, this abstract spiritualism of the Hindoo system. To conquer body, Vishnu or spirit enters into body repeatedly. Spirit must appear as body to destroy Nature. This shows that spirit cannot be excluded from anything— that it is able to descend into the lowest forms of life, and work *in* law no less than above law.

But every effort of Brahmanism was not able to arrest the natural development of the religious system, and it passed into polytheism and idolatry. For many centuries the worship of the Hindoos has been divided into numerous sects. Though most of the Brahmans yet profess to recognize Brahma, Vishnu and Siva as equally divine, the great mass of the nation worship Krishna, Rama and Lingam, and numerous other gods and idols. There are Hindoo atheists who revile the Vedas. There are the Kabirs, a kind of Hindoo Quakers, who oppose all worship; also Ramanujas, an ancient sect of worshipers of Vishnu; the Ramavats, who live in monasteries; the Panthis, who oppose all austerities; the Maharajas, whose religion is very licentious. Most of these worship Vishnu or Siva, as the worship of Brahma has entirely disappeared.

We now come to the epics, the Puranas and the modern Hindoo worship. The two great and popular Hindoo epics are the Mahabharata and the Ramayana. The whole ancient life of India appears in these two remarkable epic poems. According to Lassen, these epics refer to a period following the Vedic age. But they embrace passages inserted at a much later epoch, perhaps after the war which drove the Buddhists from India. Mr. Talboys Wheeler regards the war of Rama and the Monkeys against Ravena as alluding to this struggle, thus making Ramayana later than the Mahabharata, but most writers differ with him on this point. The writers of the Mahabharata appear to have been Brahmans educated under the Laws of Manu; but the date of neither poem can be accurately established. Lassen has demonstrated that most of the Mahabharata was written before Buddhism had been the state religion of India. These epics were originally transmitted from age to age by oral tradition. As their doctrine is that of the priesthood they must have been brought to their present forms by the Brahmans. If these poems had been composed after the reign of King Asoka, when Buddhism became the state religion of India, it must have been frequently alluded to, but no such allusions appear in the epics, except a few passages which seem to be modern additions. The epics must therefore have been composed long anterior to the time of Buddhism. Lassen's view is accepted by Max Müller.

The Vedas are now read by very few Hindoos, whose sacred books are the Puranas and the two great epics. The Ramayana contains fifty thousand lines, and is regarded with great veneration by the Hindoos. It describes the use of Rama, who is an incarnation of Vishnu, his banishment and residence in Central India, and his war with the giants and demons of the South, to recover his wife, Sita. It perhaps is founded on some actual war between the early Aryan invaders and settlers of Hindoostan with the aborigines of the country.

The Mahabharata, probably of later date, contains about two hundred and twenty thousand lines, embraced in eighteen books, each of which would constitute a large volume. It is supposed to have been collected by Vyasa, who likewise collected the Vedas and the Puranas. These legends are of great antiquity, and apparently allude to the early history of India. There seem to have been two Aryan dynasties in ancient India—the Solar and the Lunar. Rama belonged to the former and Bharata to the latter. Pandu, a descendant of the latter, has five brave sons, who are the heroes of this book. Arjuna, one of these sons, is particularly distinguished. One of the episodes is the celebrated Bhagavat-gita. Another is known as the Brahman's Lament. Another describes the deluge, showing the tradition of a great flood existing in India many centuries before the time of Christ. Another relates the story of Savitri and Satyavan. These episodes take up three-fourths of the poem, and most of the legends of the Puranas are derived from them. A supplement, itself a longer poem than Homer's Iliad and Odyssey combined (which contain about thirty thousand lines), is the source of the modern worship of the Krishna. The entire poem represents the multilateral character of the Hindoo religious system. It indicates a higher degree of civilization than that of the Homeric poems, and describes a great variety of fruits and flowers existing under culture. The characters are likewise nobler and purer than those of Homer. The pictures of social and domestic life are very touching. Children are represented as obedient to their parents, parents as watchful of their children, wives as loyal and obedient to their husbands, but independent in their opinions, and peace as prevailing in the household.

The various works of the Puranas are derived from the same source as the two epics. They contain the cosmogony of the poems, and relate their mythological legends more fully. Vishnu and Siva are almost the only objects of worship in the Puranas. There is a sectarian element in their devotion to these gods, showing their partiality and preventing them from being authority for Hindoo religious faith in its entirety.

According to Mr. Wilson, the Puranas, in their original form, belong to a period about a century before Christ. They arose out of the struggle between Brahmanism and Buddhism. The Brahmanic system had given the Hindoos no personal deities and no external worship, and the masses took no interest in the abstract view of Deity as held by the Brahmans. According to Mr. Wilson, the common class of Hindoos now read eighteen Puranas. Women read them considerably. Some of the Puranas are very ancient, or contain fragments of still more ancient Puranas. The very word Purana means *antiquity*. Most of them are devoted to the worship of Vishnu. According to the Bhagavat-Purana, the only true object of life is to meditate on Vishnu. Brahma, styled in one place "the cause of causes," declares Vishnu to be the only pure absolute essence, of which the universe is the manifestation. In the Vishnu-Purana, Brahma, as the first of the gods, adores Vishnu as the Supreme Being whom he himself is not able to understand.

The power of ascetic penances is highly spoken of in the Puranas, as well as in the epics. In the Bhagavat-Purana it is stated that Brahma created the universe by a penitence of sixteen thousand years. The Ramayana tells us that a sage of a lower caste became a Brahman by practicing austerities, in spite of the gods, who regarded such a breach of castes as a breach of Hindoo etiquette. They tried to stop his devotions by sending a beautiful nymph to tempt him, and the famous Sakuntala was their daughter. But the resolute ascetic finally conquered the gods, and as they persisted in their refusal to make a Brahman of him, he commenced the creation of new heavens and new gods, but the deities only succumbed after he had made several stars, and permitted him to become a Brahman. It is likewise stated that the Ganges, the sacred river, in the course of her wanderings, overflowed the sacrificial ground of another powerful ascetic, who drank up all its waters in his anger, but the persuasions of the gods eventually induced him to discharge the waters of the river through his ears into its channel.

These theories contain the most complete

examples of piety separated from morality. By devout asceticism the most wicked demons obtained power over gods and men. In the epic poems this principle is seen already fully developed. "The plot of the Ramayana turns around this idea." A Rajah, Ravana, had acquired such power by means of sacrifice and devotion that he tyrannized over the gods; forcing Yama, the Death-god, to retire from his realm, forcing the sun to shine there the entire year and the moon to be always full above his Raj. Agni, the Fire-god, is not permitted to burn in his presence. Maruts, the Wind-god, is to blow just as he desires. Neither gods nor demons can harm him. Thus Vishnu becomes incarnate as Rama, while the gods become incarnate as Monkeys, so as to destroy him. Piety and morality were believed to confer such wonderful power.

The Puranas are derived from the same source as the epic poems, and teach the same ideas more extensively. There are here scarcely any gods worshiped besides Vishnu and Siva, and these are worshiped with a sectarian zeal not known to the epics. Most of the Puranas embrace these five subjects—Creation, Destruction and Preservation, the Genealogy of the gods, the Reigns of the Manus, and the History of the Solar and Lunar races. They derive their philosophy of creation from the Sánkhya philosophy. They are invariably characterized by pantheism, as they always identify God with Nature; wherein they differ from Kapila. The Puranas are always in the form of a dialogue. There are eighteen Puranas, and they are said to contain altogether one million six hundred thousand lines.

The present Hindoo religion is quite different from that of the Vedas or Manu. Idolatry is now universal throughout India, and every month has its special worship—the most sacred being April, October and January. The Hindoo year begins with April. During this sacred month bands of singers go from house to house, early in the morning, singing hymns to the gods. On the first of April, Hindoos of all castes dedicate pitchers to the shades of their ancestors. The girls bring flowers with which to worship little ponds of water dedicated to Siva. Women worship the river Ganges, bathing in it and offering it flowers. They also walk in procession around the banyan or sacred tree. They then worship the cow, pouring water over her feet, and putting oil on her forehead. They sometimes take a vow to feed some particular Brahman in a luxurious manner during the entire month. They bathe their idols daily with religious care and offer them food. This continues during the entire month of April only.

In May the Hindoos worship a goddess called Shusty, who is friendly to infants. They bring their babes to be blessed before the image of the goddess by some aged women. The messenger of the goddess is a cat. On these occasions social parties are also given, though the lower castes are kept distinct at four separate tables. The women have a perfect entertainment by themselves, as they are not permitted to meet the men at such times.

The month of June is devoted to the bath of Juggernaut, who was one of the incarnations of Vishnu. The name Juggernaut implies Lord of the Universe. The worship of this deity is somewhat recent, and his idols are very repulsive in appearance. But for the time the worship of this god puts an end to the distinctions of caste. Inside the temple Hindoos of every caste may eat of the same dish, but as soon as they leave the sacred edifice this equality ceases. The ceremony of the bath had its origin in a legend. The idol Juggernaut, wishing to bathe in the Ganges, appeared in the form of a boy at the river, and then gave one of his golden ornaments to a confectioner for something to eat. The following day the ornament was missing, and the priests were unable to find it anywhere. But during the night the god revealed to a priest in a dream that he had given it to a certain confectioner in payment for his lunch; and such being found to be the case, a festival was established on the spot, where the idol is bathed every year.

The other festival of June is the worship

of the Ganges, the sacred river of the Hindoos. The people come to bathe and offer sacrifices, consisting of flowers, incense and clothes. The place where the river enters the sea is the most sacred spot. Before plunging into the stream, each one confesses his sins to the goddess. On the surface of this river all differences of caste likewise cease for the time, the holiness of the river making the low-caste man holy also.

In the month of July the famous ceremony of the car of Juggernaut is celebrated. This ceremony was instituted to commemorate the departure of Krishna from his native land. The car of Juggernaut is shaped like a pyramid, consisting of several stories, some as high as fifty feet. These cars, found in all parts of India, are the offerings of the rich, and some of them have costly statues of the god. They are drawn by hundreds of men, as it is believed that each one who pulls the rope will assuredly go to the heaven of Krishna at death. Vast multitudes accordingly crowd around the rope so as to pull, and in the general excitement they often fall under the wheels of the car and are crushed to death. This, however, is simply accidental, as Krishna does not wish his worshipers to suffer. He is a mild deity, and unlike the fierce Siva, who delights in self-torture.

In the month of August the Hindoos celebrate the nativity of Krishna, the account of whose birth resembles that of Christ in one particular. The tyrant whom he came to destroy endeavored to kill him, but a voice from heaven told the father to flee with the infant across the Jumna; and the tyrant, like Herod, killed the infants in the village. In August there is also a feast upon which no fire must be kindled and no food cooked, and on which the cactus-tree and serpents are worshiped.

In September the great festival of the worship of Doorga, the wife of Siva, occurs. It begins on the seventh day of the full moon and continues three days. It commemorates a visit of the goddess to her parents. The idol has three eyes and ten hands. The ceremony is very costly, and can therefore only be celebrated by rich people, who also give presents to the poor on this occasion. The image is placed in the middle of the hall of the rich man's house. One Brahman sits before the idol with flowers, holy water and incense. Near the idol are trays laden with rice, fruit, and other kinds of food, which are given to the Brahmans. Goats and sheep are then sacrificed to the image on the altar in the yard of the house. When the victim's head falls the people shout: "Victory to thee, O mother!" The bells are then rung, the trumpets sounded, and the people shout for joy. The lamps are waved before the idol, and a Brahman reads aloud from the Vedas. A dinner follows on each of the three days, to which the poor and the low-caste Hindoos are invited with the others, and are served by the Brahmans. The people visit house after house, and in the evening are entertained with music and dancing, and public shows. Thus the worship of the Hindoos, especially in Bengal, is social and joyful.

In October, November and December there are not so many ceremonies. January is devoted to religious bathing. In the same month the religious Hindoos invite Brahmans to read and expound the sacred books in their houses, which are open to all who wish to hear. In February there are festivals to Krishna.

The month of March is devoted to ascetic exercises, particularly the well-known one of swinging suspended by hooks, which is a festival in honor of Siva. A procession marches through the streets, enlisting followers by putting a thread around their necks. Every one so enlisted is required to join the party and go with it until the end of the ceremony under the penalty of losing caste. On the day before swinging, men are required to thrust iron or bamboo sticks through their arms or tongues. The day following they go in procession to the swinging tree, where the men are suspended by hooks and whirled round the tree four or five times.

The Hindoos regard building temples, digging tanks, or planting trees by the roadside as pious acts. The wealthy have idols in the houses, and pay a priest who appears every morning to wake up the idols, washes and dresses them, and offers them food. He comes again in the evening to give them their supper and put them to bed.

Mr. Gangooly, in his book on the Hindoos, denies most emphatically the oft-repeated statement that Hindoo mothers cast their infants into the Ganges as a religious sacrifice. He says that the motherly instinct is as strong with them as with others; and also that their religion teaches them to offer sacrifices for the life and health of their children.

The Hindoo philosophy is as acute, as profound and as spiritual, as any other that has ever been developed, yet it exists side by side with the grossest of superstitions. "With a belief so abstract as to escape the grasp of the most speculative intellect," the people cherish the idea that they can atone for sin by bathing in the Ganges, or by reciting a text from the Veda. With an ideal pantheism resembling that of Hegel, they believe that Brahma and Siva can be driven from the throne of the universe by any one who will sacrifice a sufficient number of wild horses.

The true road to felicity is supposed to be abstracting one's self from matter, the renunciation of all gratification of the senses, the maceration of the body; yet luxury, licentiousness and the gratification of the appetites are carried farther in India than in any other part of the world. A code of laws and a system of jurisprudence older than the Christian era, and an object of universal reverence, fixes every right and privilege of ruler and subject, but the application of these laws depends upon the arbitrary decisions of the priests, and their execution upon the will of the sovereign: "The constitution of India is therefore like a house without a foundation and without a roof." Not to kill a worm or to tread on a blade of grass for fear of destroying or endangering animal life is a principle of the Hindoo religion; "but the torments, cruelties and bloodshed inflicted by Indian tyrants would shock a Nero or a Borgia." About half the best-informed writers on India call the Brahmanical religion a pure monotheism, while the other half declare that it is a polytheism of a million gods. Some say that the Hindoos are spiritualists and pantheists, while others contend that their idolatry is more gross than that of any other living people.

Thus it will be seen that the prevailing belief which pervades the whole system of Brahmanism is an ideal pantheism, which conceives of God as the soul of the universe, or as the universe itself. "In Him the whole universe is absorbed; from Him it issues; He is intwined and interwoven with all creation." "All that exists is God; whatever we smell, or taste, or see, or hear, or feel, is the Supreme Being." We have also seen that the Invisible Supreme Being manifests himself under the three forms of Brahma the Creator, Vishnu the Preserver, and Siva the Destroyer. We have likewise seen that the central point of Hindoo theology is the doctrine of *metempsychosis*, or transmigration of souls; according to which the human soul is joined to earthly bodies for purposes of punishment, and the soul's aim and effort are to reunite itself with the Divine Spirit of the universe. The Hindoos therefore take a very pessimistic view of this earthly life, which they regard as a time of trial and punishment, from which man can only be released by a holy life, by prayer and sacrifice, by penance and purification. If a person neglects these duties and sinks deeper into vice and sin, the soul after death will enter the body of an inferior animal and will have to commence its wanderings afresh.

Although the Hindoos have sacred books of great antiquity, and a copious literature reaching back twenty or thirty centuries, they have no history, no chronology, no annals.

In India the entire tendency of thought is ideal; the whole religion is a pure spiritualism. An extreme one-sided idealism is the central tendency of the Hindoo mind. "The God of Brahmanism is an intelligence absorbed in the rest of profound comtemplation. The good man of this religion is the one who retires from an evil world into abstract thought."

The Hindoos are a very religious people, but their one-sided spiritualism, their extreme idealism is the cause of all their incongruities, their irreconcilable inconsistencies. They have no history and no authentic chronology; because history belongs to this world and chronology to time, and this world and time do not interest them, God and eternity being all in all.

The Hindoos, from religious motives, are extremely given to asceticism. They torture their bodies with self-inflicted torments, because the body is the soul's great enemy, and they must keep it down by ascetic mortifications. But in India, as everywhere else, ultra asceticism leads to extreme self-indulgence, as one extreme tends to produce another. Thus in one portion of India religious devotees swing on hooks in honor of Siva; hang themselves by the feet, head downwards, over a fire; roll on a bed of prickly thorns; jump on a couch filled with sharp knives; bore holes in their tongues, and stick their bodies full of pins and needles, etc. In the meantime in other places entire regions are given to self-indulgences, and companies of 'abandoned women connected with different temples consecrate their gains to the support of their worship.

A one-sided spiritualism displays itself in morals in the extremes of austerity and sensuality, and it exhibits itself in religion in the opposites of an ideal pantheism and a gross idolatry.

The Brahmanic spiritualism fills the world full of God, and, denying the real existence of this world, degenerates into a false pantheism. It declares that there is nothing *without* God, and that there is nothing *but* God. This second view was the result of the doctrine of *Maya*, or *Illusion*. *Maya* signifies the delusive appearance assumed by spirit. It is maintained that there is nothing but spirit, which neither creates nor is created, which neither acts nor suffers, which can not change, and into which all souls are absorbed when they liberate themselves by meditation from the belief that they suffer or are happy, that they are able to experience pleasure or pain.

This spiritualism leads to polytheism. Because if God does not really create or destroy, but only appears to do so, these appearances are not combined as the acts of one Being, but are distinct, independent phenomena. The removal of will and personality from the conception of God involves the removal of unity. If creation is an illusion and there is really no creation, the *appearance* of creation is nevertheless a fact. There being no substance, only spirit, this *appearance* of creation necessarily has its cause in spirit, being a *divine* appearance, God. In the same way, destruction is an appearance of God, and reproduction is an appearance of God, and every other appearance in nature is a manifestation of God. But as the unity of will and person is taken away, there is a plurality of gods, not only one God, and thus we have polytheism.

An ultra spiritualism tends to pantheism, and pantheism degenerates into polytheism. Thus, in India there exists a spiritualism denying the existence of everything but motionless spirit, or Brahm, and a polytheism which believes in and worships Brahma the Creator, Vishnu the Preserver, Siva the Destroyer, Indra the God of the Sky, the Sactis or energies of the gods, Krishna the Hindoo Apollo, Doorga, and a multitude of other deities as countless as the changes and appearances of things.

This system necessarily tends to idolatry. Men are so constituted that they must worship something. If they believe in one Being, the Absolute Spirit, the Supreme and Only God—Para Brahm—they cannot worship him, because he is literally an unknown God. He possesses no qualities, no attributes, no activity. He is not the object of hope, fear, love or aversion. All things in the universe except spirit are illusive appearances, which are nevertheless *divine* appearances; and which, having some traits, qualities and character, *are* objects of hope and fear. They cannot, however, worship them as apppearances, and must therefore worship them as persons. If they possess an outward personality or soul, they become real beings, distinct from Brahm, though they are his appearances. Consequently they must have an outward personality—a body, a form, symbolical and characteristic—they become idols.

As a result, idol-worship is universal in India. The most horrible and grotesque images are carved in the stone of the grottos, stand in rude, black statues in the temples, or are roughly painted on the walls. Figures of men with heads of elephants or other animals, or with six or seven human heads—often rising in a pyramid, one out of the other, frequently with six hands joined to one shoulder—"grisly and uncouth monsters, like nothing in nature, yet too grotesque for symbols—such are the objects of the Hindoo worship."

SECTION IV.—BUDDHISM.

 WISE and good king reigned in his capital city, Kapilavastu, north of Central India and of the Kingdom of Oude, near the borders of Nepaul, at the end of the seventh century before Christ. He was one of the last of the great Solar race, so celebrated in the ancient epics of India. His wife, called Maya on account of her great beauty, became the mother of a prince named Siddârtha, Sakya-muni, or Gautama, and afterwards known as the Buddha. Buddha is not a proper name, but an official title. As we should always say Jesus *the* Christ, and not Jesus Christ, so we should always say *Siddârtha* the Buddha, or *Sakya-muni* the Buddha, or *Gautama* the Buddha. The name Siddârtha (contracted from Sarvârtha-siddha) was the baptismal name given him by his father, and means "The fulfillment of every wish." Sakyamuni means "The hermit of the race of Sakya"—Sakya being the ancestral name of his father's race. Gautama is the name by which he is most generally known.

This young prince's mother died seven days after he was born, and the child was brought up by his maternal aunt. He distinguished himself by his personal and intellectual qualities, but yet more by his early piety. The Laws of Manu make it apparent that occasionally in the earliest periods of Brahmanism those desiring greater piety became hermits, living alone in the forests, there engaging in acts of prayer, meditation, abstinence and the study of the Vedas. The Brahmans, however, were only devoted to this practice. The King therefore grieved when his son began to cherish thoughts of becoming an anchorite, in the bloom of his youth and highly accomplished in all kingly qualities of mind and body. The young Siddârtha appears to have passed through the deep experience out of which the great prophets of the human race have ever risen. His heart and mind became impressed with the evils of this world. "The very universe seemed full of mortality; all things were passing away." Nothing appeared permanent or stable. Only truth; only the absolute, eternal law of things seems immutable. Said he: "Let me see that, and I can give lasting peace to mankind. Then shall I become their deliverer." Thus against the strong entreaties of his father, his wife and his friends, he left the palace one night, and became a mendicant. Said he: "I will never return to the palace till I have attained to the sight of the divine law, and so become Buddha" (meaning "to know," from the Sanskrit root, whence our English words "bode" and "forbode").

He first visited the Brahmans and listened to their doctrines, but found no satisfaction in them. The wisest of the Brahmans were not able to teach him true peace—the profound inward rest already known as Nirvana. He was then twenty-nine years of age.

He practiced the Brahmanic austerities for six years to conquer the senses, although he disapproved of them as an end. He became fully convinced that therein did not lie the road to perfection. Accordingly he resumed his former diet and a more comfortable manner of living, and thus lost many disciples whom he had attracted by his wonderful austerity. Alone in his hermitage he finally arrived at that solid faith that the only real basis of a truly free life was to be found in *knowledge* unshaken. The place where he reached this beatific vision, after a week of constant meditation, is one of the most sacred places of India. When he attained the knowledge that was to deliver the human race from its woes, he was seated under a tree, with his face toward the east, having remained unmoved for a day and a night. Twelve centuries after his death, a Chinese pilgrim was shown what then passed for the sacred tree. It was enclosed by high brick walls, with an opening to the east, and close by were numerous topes and monasteries. Saint-Hilaire thinks that these ruins and the site of the tree may again be discovered. On that retired spot began a movement which altogether has been a source of happiness and improvement to many millions of mankind for twenty-four centuries.

After himself reaching this inward certainty of vision, Gautama decided to instruct the human race in this truth. He was very well aware that he would be subjected to opposition, insult, scorn, neglect. But he sought three classes of men—those already on the right road to truth, and who did not need him; those settled in error and whom he was unable to rescue; and the poor doubters who were uncertain of their way. The Buddha went forth to preach to deliver these doubters. On his way to Benares, the holy city of India, he was confronted with a serious difficulty—the want of money to pay the boatman for his passage over the Ganges. At Benares he made his first converts, for the first time "turning the wheel of the law." The Buddhist sacred books contain his discourses. Among his numerous converts was his father. He was fiercely opposed by the leading Brahmins, "the Hindoo Scribes and Pharisees." After thus living and teaching, he died at the age of eighty years.

As soon as Gautama was dead he was highly honored by all. His remains were cremated with great pomp, and his followers contended for the unconsumed fragments of bone. These were finally divided into eight parts, and each of these fortunate possessors erected a tope over the relics which he had obtained. The ancient books of the North and the South agree in regard to the places where they were built. Gautama the Buddha, who believed with Jesus the Christ that "the flesh profiteth nothing," would perhaps have been the very first to condemn this idolatry; but fetish-worship remains in the purest systems of religion.

Like most Oriental dates, the time of Sakya-muni's death is not certain. The Northern Buddhists, in Nepaul, Thibet, etc., differ much among themselves. The Chinese Buddhists are just as uncertain. Lassen and most other scholars regard the date fixed upon by all the Buddhist authorities of the South, especially those of Ceylon, B. C. 543, as the correct date. Westergaard a few years ago wrote a monograph on the subject, in which he tries to prove that the correct date was about two centuries later.

A general council of Siddârtha's followers was held immediately after his death to settle upon the doctrine and discipline of the new religion. According to the legend, three of the disciples were selected to recite from memory the teachings of the sage. The first was appointed to repeat his teaching and discipline; "for discipline is the soul of law," they said. Thereupon Upali ascended the pulpit and repeated all of the precepts relating to morals and the ritual. Next Ananda was chosen to recite his master's discourses respecting faith or doctrine. At last Kasyapa announced the philosophy and metaphysics of the new religious system. The council sat seven months, and the result of their work was the triple division of the Tripitaka, the sacred books of the Buddhists. Like Socrates and Jesus, Sakya-muni himself left nothing in writing. He simply taught by personal conversation.

The second general council of Buddhism was held about a century after Siddârtha's death, to correct some abuses which had commenced to creep into the church. A large brotherhood of monks proposed the relaxation of conventional discipline, permitting more liberty in regard to food, intoxicating drinks, and the taking of gold and silver when offered as alms. Ten thousand schismatic monks were degraded, but they founded a new sect. The third general council was held during the reign of Asoka, the great Buddhist king in Northern India, and degraded and expelled the sixty thousand heretics. Missionaries were then sent to preach Buddhism in different lands of Eastern and South-eastern Asia. The *Mahawanso*, or Sacred History of Buddhism, translated from the Cingalese by Mr. George Turnour, records the name and success of these missionaries. The relics of some of them have been found recently in the Sanchi topes, and in other sacred buildings, contained in caskets, with inscriptions of their names. These inscribed names correspond with those given to the same missionaries by the historical books of Ceylon. Thus, according to the Mahawanso, two missionaries, Kassapo, or Kasyapa, and Majjhima, or Madhyama, proceeded to preach in the region of the Himalaya mountains. The ancient account, and a Ceylonese history of the fifth century of the Christian era, say that these missionaries journeyed, preached, suffered, and toiled, side by side; and in 1851, Major Cunningham found the relics of these missionaries in the second Sanchi tope, where they had remained concealed during all these centuries. When Captain Fell visited the tope in 1819, it was perfect, "not a stone fallen." And though injured in 1822 by some relic-hunters, its contents were not touched. The tope is a structure built of rough stones without mortar, thirty-nine feet in diameter, in the shape of a solid hemisphere, with a basement six feet high, projecting five feet all around, so as to make a terrace. It is surrounded by a stone enclosure, with carved figures. A small enclosure was found in the center of the tope, constructed of six stones, containing the relic-box of white sandstone, about ten inches square. Inside this box were four caskets of steatite, a sacred stone among the Buddhists, each of these caskets containing small parts of burnt human bone. On the outside of one of these caskets was the following inscription: "Relics of the emancipated Kasyapa Gotra, missionary to the whole Hemawanta." On the inside of the same lid was carved this inscription: "Relics of the emancipated Madhyama." These relics and those of eight other leading Buddhists had reposed in this monumental sepulcher since the time of King Asoka, and must have been deposited there at least as early as B. C. 220.

Buddhism manifested a missionary spirit which distinguishes it from all other religions preceding Christianity. The religion of Confucius never tried to extend itself beyond China. Brahmanism never attempted to go outside of India. The system of Zoroaster confined itself to the Medes, Persians, Bactrians, and a few other Aryan races. The religion of Egypt remained only in the Nile valley. That of Greece confined itself to the Hellenic race. But Buddhism was inspired with a desire to make its teachings known and accepted by the whole human race. Buddhism spread rapidly throughout India, and its teachings of love, charity and human equality, exerted a wonderful influence. Its ardent missionaries succeeded in converting vast multitudes in Nepaul, Thibet, Burmah, Ceylon, Farther India and China; and although driven from India after wrestling nine centuries with Brahmanism, Buddhism spread over all Eastern Asia—that is, among the Mongolian nations; and is to-day the religion of one-third of the human race, having more adherents than any other faith. It is the popular religion of China. It is the state religion of Thibet and Burmah. It is the religion of Japan, Siam, Anam, Assam, Nepaul, Ceylon, Mongolia and Manchooria. Like Christianity, Buddhism has its monkish orders; and its monasteries in all the countries in which it prevails are yet the chief sources of knowledge and the centers of instruction to the people.

The sovereign head of the Buddhist religion in Thibet is the Grand Lama, who resides in a magnificent temple at Pootala, near Lassa, the capital of Thibet. All the priests are called Lamas, and are under the Grand Lama, who is a sort of pope. He is regarded as the Buddha, the Deity himself, residing in a human form, and is therefore divine and human. When the human body of the Grand Lama dies, the priests, guided by certain signs, and proceeding in accordance with established forms, name the child into whose body the Grand Lama must enter, and there the Buddha accordingly becomes installed. The Buddha thus becomes incarnate in the Grand Lama, and divine emanations fill the priesthood, while the masses of the people practice the grossest idolatry. Although the Grand Lama has no temporal power, he is the head of the entire Buddhist church, as the Pope is of the whole Roman Catholic church. He is so exalted in the eyes of his more ignorant worshipers that, it is said, a divine odor is exhaled from his body, flowers spring up from his footsteps, and at his word parched deserts are refreshed with flowing rivulets, while his very excrements are considered sacred.

We have had few sources of information concerning Buddhism until a recent period; but within the last half century, so many sources have been opened that we can now study this great religion in its original features and its subsequent development. The sacred books of Buddhism have been preserved independently in Ceylon, Nepaul, China and Thibet. Eminent English scholars, such as G. Turnour, R. Spence Hardy and Georgely, devoted themselves to the study of the Pitakas, or the Buddhist sacred books in the Pali language, preserved in Ceylon. Mr. Hodgson collected and studied the Sanskrit sacred books found in Nepaul. In 1825 he transmitted to the Asiatic Society in Bengal sixty works in Sanskrit, and two hundred and fifty in the language of Thibet. M. Csoma, an Hungarian physician, discovered in the Buddhist monasteries in Thibet a vast mass of sacred books translated from the Sanskrit works previously studied by Mr. Hodgson. In 1829 M. Schmidt found the same works in the Mongolian language. M. Stanislas Julien translated Buddhist works from the Chinese language. Still more recently, inscriptions cut upon rocks, columns and other monuments in the North of India have been transcribed and translated. These inscriptions were deciphered by Mr. James Prinsep, who discovered them to be in the ancient language of the province of Magadha, where Buddhism made its first appearance. They contain the decrees of a king, or rajah, named Pyadasi, shown by Mr. Turnour to be the same as the renowned Asoka, who seems to have ascended the throne at some time from B. C. 319 to B. C. 260. Similar inscriptions have been discovered in other portions of India, demonstrating to the satisfaction of such eminent scholars as Burnouf, Prinsep, Turnour, Lassen, Weber, Max Müller, Saint-Hilaire and others, that Buddhism had almost become the state religion of India, in the fourth century before Christ.

The power of Buddhism was based on the strength of conviction inspiring its apostles. We often are told that Buddhism is atheism, that it denies God and immortality. Sakyamuni was induced to take his departure from two profound convictions—the evil of constant change and the possibility of something more settled and permanent. In the language of the Book of Ecclesiastes he might have exclaimed: "Vanity of vanities! all is vanity!" The gloomy character of that book is founded on the very same style of reasoning as that of Siddârtha, "that everything goes round and round in a circle; that nothing moves forward; that there is no new thing under the sun; that the sun rises and sets, and rises again; that the wind blows north and south, and east and west, and then returns according to its circuits." Gautama was young, and he desired to know where rest and peace could be found. He beheld age coming on. He was in good health, but knew that sickness and death would some day come upon him. He saw no means of escaping from the sight of this continual round of origin, development and decay, life and death, joy and sorrow, happiness and misery. He earnestly and intensely yearned for something real, something stable, something lasting.

He was convinced that all existence is an evil, and that release from this state of change and decay could only be attained through knowledge. He did not, however, mean by knowledge the observation and remembrance of external facts. He did not mean learning. He did not mean speculative knowledge, or the faculty of reasoning. He meant intuitive knowledge, the sight of everlasting truth, the power of perceiving the immutable laws of the universe. This knowledge could only be acquired by moral training, by purity of heart and life, and not by any mental process. For this reason he renounced the world and became a hermit in the forest.

He thus separated himself from the Brahmans. They likewise believed in the efficacy of asceticism, of self-mortification, abnegation and penance. They also had hermits in his time. They, however, believed in the value of penance as an additional merit. They practiced self-denial for its own sake. Gautama practiced it as a means to a higher end, namely, release from the miseries of existence, purification and intuition. He believed that he had finally attained that end. He ultimately perceived the truth. He grew "wide awake." Illusions passed away. He saw the reality. He had become the Buddah—*the Enlightened—the Man who knew.*

In another point he departed from Brahmanism. He was yet only a man, not a God. In Brahmanism devotion ultimately resulted in absorption in the Divine essence, in Deity. The Brahmanic doctrine is divine absorption. The Buddhistic is human development. Brahmanism considers God everything, and man nothing. Buddhism regards man as everything, and God as nothing. Thus Buddhism makes so much of man as to forget God. But while it is "without God in the world" it does not deny him. It believes in the three worlds —the eternal world of absolute being; the celestial world of the gods, Brahma, Vishnu, Siva, Indra, Agni, Varuna, etc.; and the infinite world composed of individual souls and the laws of nature. It only says that we know nothing of the world of absolute being, Nirvana, which is our aim and end. But it is directly opposite to all that we know, and is consequently nothing to us. We know the everlasting laws of nature, and if we obey these we will rise, but if we disobey we will fall. By perfect obedience to these eternal and unchangeable laws of nature we shall finally reach Nirvana and everlasting repose.

The Buddha looked upon the world as consisting of two orders of existence—souls and laws. He perceived an infinite multitude of souls, in men, animals and insects. He observed that they were surrounded by immutable laws—the laws of nature. Knowledge of, and obedience to, these laws freed one from the miseries of existence, and brought him into the happy state of Nirvana.

The fundamental doctrine of Buddhism, as taught by its founder and accepted by all Buddhists, in the North and in the South, in Burmah and Thibet, in Ceylon and China, in Nepaul and Japan, is the doctrine of what they regard as the four great "sublime truths."

They say that there is pain; that pain comes through the desire or passion for things that can not long be ours; that both pain and desire can be ended in Nirvana, the way to which is shown by the fourth truth of the Buddha.

The four paths to this way are the following: He has entered the first path who sees the evils arising from separate existence, and who believes in the Buddha and in the power of his system only to attain salvation, which is release from the miseries of existence.

He has entered the second path who, in addition to the above, is free from lust and evil to others.

He has entered the third path who is further free from all kinds of evil desires, from ignorance, doubt, wrong belief and hatred.

He has arrived at the fourth path who is wholly free from sin and passions, by which are meant the lust of the flesh, the love of existence and the defilements of wrong belief and ignorance.

The four paths have also been summed up in eight steps or divisions, as follows: Right views, right thoughts, right speech, right actions, right living, right exertion, right recollection, right meditation.

Then follow ten commandments. Five of these apply to all men, and are as follows: Do not steal; do not kill; do not commit adultery; do not lie; do not become intoxicated. The other five are directed to monks, and are the following: Take no solid food after noon; do not visit dances, singing, or theatrical entertainments; use no ornaments or perfumery in dress; use no luxurious beds; accept neither gold nor silver.

A countless number of commentaries and expositions have been made upon these doctrines and precepts. Everything has been commented upon, explained and elucidated. Voluminous works upon the Buddhist system fill the monastic libraries of Thibet and Ceylon. The monks have their Golden Legends, their Lives of Saints, full of miracles and wonders. "On this simple basis of a few rules and convictions has arisen a vast fabric of metaphysics. Much of this literature is instructive and entertaining. Some of it is profound. Baur, who had made a special study of the intricate speculations of the Gnostics, compares them with the vast abstractions of Buddhism."

The Buddhist scriptures are called the Pitakas, or the Tripitaka—"three baskets" —so called because they are in three parts. The first Pitaka contains rules of discipline; the second, the discourses of the Buddha; while the third deals with philosophy and the subtle doctrines of the religion. The

1—32.-U. H.

Buddha's sayings, transmitted from generation to generation and preserved in men's memories, were finally set down in writing. They grew as the Christian Scriptures grew, and all the writings were at last accepted as the sacred records of Gautama's teachings.

Among the many traditions relating to the Buddha is one telling of a young mother whose child had died, and who, in her great love and sorrow, clasped the dead body to her bosom, going about from house to house and asking if any one could give her medicine for it. The neighbors considered the woman mad, but a wise man, seeing that she was unable or unwilling to comprehend the law of death, said to her: "My good girl, I cannot myself give medicine for it, but I know of a doctor who can attend to it." She asked who the doctor was, and was sent by the wise man to the Buddha. After she had done homage to him, she said: "Lord and master, do you know any medicine that will be good for my boy?" The Buddha answered that he did, and told her to bring a handful of mustard seed which must be taken from a house where no son, husband, parent or slave had died. The woman then went to look for such mustard seed, but could find no such house, for when she inquired if any son, husband, parent or slave had died there, one would reply, "I have lost a son;" another would say, "I have lost both parents;" while all answered, "Lady, the living are few, but the dead are many." Finally, unable to find any house which had not been visited by death, she became impressed with the truth, whereupon she left her dead boy in the forest, and returned to the Buddha and told him her story. He said to her: "You thought that you alone had lost a son; the law of death is that among all living creatures there is nothing that abides." When he had finished preaching the law the woman became one of his disciples.

"Once upon a time Buddha lived in a village, and in the sowing season, went with his bowl in hand to the place where food was being given by a Brahman, who, seeing him, spoke thus:

"'O priest, I both plough and sow, and having ploughed and sown, I eat; you also, O priest, should plough and sow, and having ploughed and sown, you should eat.'

"'I too, O Brahman, plough and sow, and having ploughed and sown, I eat,' said Buddha.

"'But we see neither the yoke, nor plough, nor ploughshare, nor goad, nor oxen, of the venerable Gautama. . . .

"'Being questioned by us as to your ploughing, speak in such a manner as we may know of your ploughing.'

"The Buddha replied: 'For my cultivation, faith is the seed; penance the rain; wisdom my yoke and plough; modesty the shaft for the plough; mind the string; presence of mind my ploughshare and goad.'

"Then the Brahman offered him rice boiled in milk from a golden vessel.

"In a chapter very popular among the Buddhists of Ceylon, the demon Alavaka is said to have asked Buddha, 'What is the best wealth to a man in this world? What thing well done produces happiness? Of savory things, which is indeed the most savory? The life of one who lives in what manner, do they say, is the best?'

"Buddha answered: 'Faith is the best wealth to a man here. The observing well the law produces happiness. Truth is indeed the most savory of all savory things. The living endowed with wisdom, they say, is the best of all modes of living.'

"On another occasion, when asked what was the greatest blessing, Buddha said:

"'The succoring of mother and father, the cherishing of child and wife, and the following of a lawful calling, this is the greatest blessing.'

"'The giving alms, a religious life, aid rendered to relations, blameless acts, this is the greatest blessing.'

"'The abstaining from sins and the avoiding them, the eschewing of intoxicating drink, diligence in good deeds, reverence and humility, contentment and gratefulness, this is the greatest blessing.

. . . 'Those who having done these things, become invincible on all sides, attain happiness on all sides. This is the greatest blessing.'

"There is a discourse of Buddha's which some have called, from the place where it was preached, his 'sermon on the mount,' but it lacks clearness, nor could it be set down in language easy to grasp. The extracts from Buddhist sacred books just given show how forcefully Buddha could put much meaning into few words, and of this there is rich proof in a book called the 'Dhammapada,' or 'Path of Virtue,' which is believed to contain his sayings. For example:

"'He who lives looking for pleasures only, his senses uncontrolled, idle and weak, Mâra (the tempter) will certainly overcome him, as the wind throws down a weak tree.'

"'Let the wise man guard his thoughts; they are difficult to perceive, very artful, and they rush wherever they list; thoughts well guarded bring happiness.'

"'As the bee collects nectar, and departs without injuring the flower, or its color and scent, so let the sage dwell on earth.'

"'Like a beautiful flower, full of color but without scent, are the fine but fruitless words of him who does not act accordingly. But like a beautiful flower full of color and full of scent, are the fine and fruitful words of him who acts accordingly.'

"'He who lives a hundred years, vicious and unrestrained, a life of one day is better if a man is virtuous and reflecting.'

"'Let no man think lightly of evil, saying in his heart, It will not come near unto me. Even by the falling of water-drops a water-pot is filled; the fool becomes full of evil even if he gathers it little by little.'

"'Not to commit any sin, to do good, and to purify one's mind, that is the teaching of the Awakened.' (This is one of the most solemn verses among the Buddhists).

"'Let us live happily then, not hating those who hate us! Let us dwell free from hatred among men who hate!'

"'Let us live happily then, free from greed among the greedy! Let us dwell free from greed among men who are greedy!

"'Let us live happily then, though we

call nothing our own! We shall be like the bright gods, feeding on happiness!'"

The Buddhist God is the Buddha himself, the deified man, who has become an infinite being by entering Nirvana. Prayer is addressed to him, as man must pray to something. In Thibet prayer meetings are held even in the streets. Father Huc says: "There is a very touching custom at Lassa. In the evening, just before sundown, all the people leave their work, and meet in groups in the public streets and squares. All kneel and begin to chant their prayers in a low and musical tone. The concert of song which rises from all these numerous reunions produces an immense and solemn harmony, which deeply impresses the mind. We could not help sadly comparing the Pagan city, where all the people prayed together, with our European cities, where men would blush to be seen making the sign of the cross."

This confession was early enjoined in Thibet, and public worship in that country is a solemn confession before the assembled priests. It confers an absolution from all sin. It consists in a public confession of sin, and a promise to cease sinning. In the pagodas, or temples, holy water is used in the service.

The Thirty-five Buddhas who have preceded Gautama are regarded as the chief powers for taking away all sins. These are styled the "Thirty-five Buddhas of Confession." Gautama has been included in the number. In the sacred pictures some lamas are likewise joined with them, one of these being Tsonkhapa, a lama who was born A. D. 1555, and others. The mendicant priests of Buddha must confess twice a month, at the new and full moon.

There are Buddhist nunneries for women. It is said that Gautama agreed to their establishment at the urgent request of his aunt and nurse, and of his favorite disciple, Ananda. These nuns take the same vows as the monks. Their rules require them to treat even the youngest monk with reverence, and utter no angry or harsh words towards a priest. The nun is required to be willing to be instructed, and must go to a virtuous teacher for this purpose once in every fortnight. She must devote only two weeks at a time to spiritual retirement, and must not go out simply for amusement. She can only be initiated after two years preparation, and must attend the closing ceremonies of the rainy season.

The two chief metaphysical doctrines of Buddhism are *Karma* and *Nirvana*. Karma is the law of consequences, by which every act performed in this life receives its full recompense in the next world, where the soul is born again, but such recompense is only possible if the soul passes on. Said the Buddha: "Karma is the most essential property of all beings; it is inherited from previous births, it is the cause of all good and evil, and the reason why some are mean and some exalted when they come into the world. It is like the shadow which always accompanies the body." The Buddha himself reached all his elevation by means of a Karma obtained in previous states. None can obtain Karma or merit except such as hear the Buddha's discourses.

Eminent scholars have not agreed respecting the meaning of Nirvana, the end which all Buddhists desire to attain. Some have supposed it to mean utter annihilation, entire cessation of existence. Others have believed it to signify absorption into Deity —the same as the Brahmanical doctrine of the ultimate aim and end of the human soul. The weight of authority supports the first view. Burnouf says: "For Buddhist theists, it is the absorption of the individual life in God; for atheists, absorption of this individual life in the nothing. But for both, it is the deliverance from all evil, it is supreme affranchisement." Max Müller, Turnour, Schmidt and Hardy all agree that it is annihilation. M. Saint-Hilaire holds the same view, calling it a "hideous faith," but saying that it is the doctrine of one-third of the human race.

But some of the most distinguished scholars hold the opposite view, among them Bunsen, who alludes to the fact that in the most ancient monuments of Buddhism, the earliest Sutras, Nirvana is mentioned as a state attained in this life, being a condition in which all desires cease, all passions die. Bunsen maintains that the Buddha never denied or questioned the existence of God or the doctrine of immortality.

The Pali Sacred Books give the following account of Nirvana:

"Again the King of Ságal said to Nágaséna: 'Is the joy of Nirvana unmixed, or is it associated with sorrow?' The priest replied that it was unmixed satisfaction, entirely free from sorrow.

"Again the King of Ságal said to Nágasèna: 'Is Nirvana in the east, west, south or north; above or below? Is there such a place as Nirvana? If so, where is it?' Nágaséna replied: 'Neither in the east, south, west or north; neither in the sky above, nor in the earth below, nor in any of the infinite sakwalas, is there such a place as Nirvana.' Milinda asked: 'Then if Nirvana have no locality, there can be no such thing; and when it is said that any one attains Nirvana, the declaration is false.' Nágaséna replied: 'There is no such place as Nirvana, and yet it exists; the priest who seeks it in the right manner will attain it.' Milinda asked: 'When Nirvana is attained is there such a place?' Nágaséna replied: 'When a priest attains Nirvana there is such a place?' Milinda asked: 'Where is that place?' Nágaséna replied: 'Wherever the precepts can be observed; it may be anywhere; just as he who has two eyes can see the sky from any or all places; or as all places may have an eastern side.'"

The Buddhists regarded Nirvana as the object of all their hope, but if you ask them what it is, they may answer: "Nothing." This would apparently imply that utter annihilation is the highest good—the most desirable end. Such a doctrine would be the most extreme pessimism.

When a Buddhist says that Nirvana is *nothing*, he means that it is *no thing;* that it is nothing that we can at present perceive; that it is the contrary of all we know, of what we now call life, a condition so entirely different from what we know or are able to know at present that it is just the same as nothing to us. All present life is subject to constant change; *that* is permanent. All present life goes up and down; *that* is stable. All present life is the life of sense; *that* is spirit.

In the same way the Buddhist denies God. He regards Him as unknowable—as impossible to be conceived of. The Buddhist regards the element of time and the finite as all, in the same way that the Brahman regards the element of eternity as all. It is the most extreme opposite of Brahmanism.

It seems as though the Oriental mind could not at the same time conceive of God and nature, the finite and the infinite, eternity and time. Brahmanism believes only in the reality of God, the infinite and the eternal, and ignores the reality of the finite, of nature, history, time and the world. The Buddhist, on the contrary, accepts the last and ignores the first.

Buddhism is a system of rationalism. It appeals to man's reason. It proposes to save man by knowledge, from a present hell, and not a future one. The Buddha preached numberless sermons, while his missionaries preached abroad. Buddhism extended itself by peaceful means—by its rational appeal to the human mind. It never propagated its doctrines by the sword, even when it had the power of rajas to uphold it. Buddhism has won all triumphs peacefully, not depending on the sword of the conqueror or the frauds of priestcraft. It has its superstitions and errors, but it has not deceived. It is the most tolerant of all religions. It has not persecuted, and has no prejudices against the adherents of other religions. Buddhism has had no Inquisition. It has not burned alive or imprisoned or excommunicated heretics. Though extremely zealous in extending their faith, Buddhists have all the time displayed a spirit of toleration truly remarkable. But one religious war has obscured their peaceful history during twenty-three centuries. That war occurred in Thibet, but little is known about it. A Buddhist in Siam told Mr. Crawford that he believed all the religions of the world to be branches of the true religion. A Buddhist in Ceylon sent his son to a Christian school, and said to the missionary: "I respect Christianity as much as Buddhism, for I regard it a help to Buddhism." The French Roman Catholic missionaries, MM. Huc and Gabet, were told by a Buddhist in Thibet that he considered himself both a good Buddhist and a good Christian.

Buddhism is also humane in spirit, and therein lay the cause of its wonderful success. In its origin it was a protest against the power of the Brahmanic priesthood. It broke down all castes by asserting the doctrine of human equality, and by allowing any one wishing to lead a holy life to become a priest. It displays an unbounded charity for all souls, and considers it a duty to make sacrifices for all. Said the Buddha: "Not from birth does one become a Vasala (slave), not from birth does one become a Brahman. By bad conduct does one become a Vasala, by good conduct does one become a Brahman." One legend says that the Buddha gave his body for food to a starving tigress, which was too weak to nurse her young. An incident is on record concerning the Buddha, who asked a woman of low caste for water, and who, when she expressd surprise, said: "Give me drink, and I will give you truth." The commandment, "Thou shalt not kill," which applies directly to all living creatures, has exerted a wonderful influence in softening the manners of the Mongol nations, whose history has not been filled with constant wars and bloodshed as has the history of Christian and other nations.

The commandment not to kill is closely related with the doctrine of the metempsychosis, or transmigration of souls, which is one of the leading doctrines of Buddhism, as well as of Brahmanism. Buddhism has abolished all human and animal sacrifices; and its altars, free from innocent blood, are crowned only with flowers and leaves. It likewise teaches a practical humanity consisting of good actions. It made it the duty of children to obey and honor their parents, and of parents to care for their children. It also made it a duty of all to forgive their enemies, to return good for evil, to do unto others as they would have others do unto them, to be kind to the sick and the poor and the sorrowing. It diffused a spirit of charity abroad which encompassed the life of the lowest, as well as that of the highest. All the priests of Buddhism are supported by daily alms. It is a duty of Buddhists to be hospitable to strangers, to establish hospitals for the sick and the poor, and even for sick animals, to plant shade trees and to erect houses for travelers.

Mr. Malcolm, the Baptist missionary, says that as he sat down to rest one day in a small village in Burmah, a woman brought a nice mat for him to lie on. Another brought some cool water for him, while a man brought him a half dozen good oranges. None expected or desired the least reward, but went away, leaving him to his repose. He says: "None can ascend the river without being struck with the hardihood, skill, energy, and good humor of the Burmese boatmen. In point of temper and morality, they are infinitely superior to the boatmen of our Western waters. In my various trips, I have seen no quarrel nor heard a hard word."

Mr. Malcolm says further: "Many of these people have never seen a white man before, but I am constantly struck with their politeness. They desist from anything on the slightest intimation; never crowd around to be troublesome; and if on my showing them my watch or pencil-case, or anything which particularly attracts them, there are more than can get a sight the outer ones stand aloof and wait till their turn comes . . . . . .

"I saw no intemperance in Burmah, though an intoxicating liquor is made easily of the juice of a palm. . . . .

"A man may travel from one end of the kingdom to the other without money, feeding and lodging as well as the people."

"I have seen thousands together, for hours, on public occasions, rejoicing in all ardor, and no act of violence or case of intoxication. . . . . .

"During my whole residence in the country I never saw an indecent act or immodest gesture in man or woman. . . . I have seen hundreds of men and women bathing, and no immodest or careless act. .

"Children are treated with great kindness, not only by the mother but by the father, who, when unemployed, takes the young child in his arms, and seems pleased to attend to it, while the mother cleans the rice or sits unemployed at his side. I have as often seen fathers caressing female infants as male. A widow with male and female children is more likely to be sought in marriage than if she has none. . . . . .

"Children are almost as reverent to parents as among the Chinese. The aged are treated with great care and tenderness, and occupy the best places in all assemblies."

According to Saint-Hilaire, the Buddhist morality is one of endurance, patience, submission and abstinence, instead of one of action, energy or enterprise. It is based on love for all things, every animal being possibly our relative. The virtues of Buddhists are to love their enemies, to offer their lives for animals, to abstain from even defensive warfare, to govern themselves, to shun vices, to obey superiors, to reverence age, to provide food and shelter for men and animals, to dig wells and plant trees, to despise no religion, to show no intolerance and not to persecute. Polygamy, though tolerated, is not sanctioned. Monogamy generally prevails in Ceylon, Siam and Burmah; but is less prevalent in Thibet and Mongolia. Buddhism affords women better treatment than any other Oriental religion.

Buddhism has regular priests but no secular ones; and all its clergy are monks, who take the three vows of poverty, chastity and obedience, as did the Christian monks of the middle ages. The vows of the Buddhists are not irrevocable, and they can be relinquished at any time, and return into the world if they desire to do so. The first Roman Catholic missionaries who met the Buddhist priests were struck with wonder at the many resemblances between the customs of Buddhism and those of Roman Catholicism, and thought that Satan had been mocking their sacred rites. Father Bury, a Portuguese missionary, on beholding Chinese bonzes tonsured, using rosaries, praying in an unknown language, and kneeling before images, exclaimed in astonishment: "There is not a piece of dress, not a sacerdotal function, not a ceremony of the court of Rome, which the Devil has not copied in this country." Mr. Davis, an English authority, alludes to "the celibacy of the Buddhist clergy, and the monastic life of the societies of both sexes; to which might be added their strings of beads, their manner of chanting prayers, their incense, and their candles." Mr. Medhurst, another English authority, speaks of the images of a virgin, called the "queen of heaven," having an infant in her arms, and holding a cross. Confession of sins is practiced regularly. Father Huc, the French missionary, says of the Buddhists in China, Thibet and Tartary: "The cross, the miter, the dalmatica, the cope, which the Grand Lamas wear on their journeys, or when they are performing some ceremony out of the temple—the service with double choirs, the psalmody, the exorcisms, the censer suspended from five chains, and which you can open or close at pleasure—the benedictions given by the lamas by extending the right hand over the heads of the faithful—the chaplet, ecclesiastical celibacy, religious retirement, the worship of the saints, the fasts, the processions, the litanies, the holy water —all these are analogies between the Buddhists and ourselves." He might have also said that in Thibet is the Dalai Lama (Grand Lama), a sort of Buddhist Pope.

The Roman Catholic missionaries next thought that the Buddhists had learned these customs from the Nestorian missionaries who visited China in the early centuries of the Christian era. But Wilson translated plays from written works before the time of Christ, in which Buddhist monks appear as mendicants. The worship of relics is no less ancient. Fergusson describes topes, or shrines of relics, of exceeding antiquity, in

India, Ceylon, Burmah and Java; many of them belonging to the time of King Asoka, the great Buddhist sovereign who ruled all India about B. C. 250, and in whose reign Buddhism was made the state religion of India and held its third church council.

The ancient Buddhist architecture, very curious and some of it very elegant, includes topes, rock-cut temples and monasteries. Some of the topes are monolithic columns, over forty feet high, and having ornamented capitals; while others are enormous domes of brick and stone, containing sacred relics. The tooth of Buddha was once preserved in a magnificent shrine in India, but was taken to Ceylon in A. D. 311, where it yet remains an object of universal reverence. It is a piece of ivory or bone two inches long, and is kept in six cases, the largest being of solid silver, five feet high. The other cases are inlaid with rubies and precious stones. Ceylon likewise has the "left collar-bone relic," in a bell-shaped tope, fifty feet high, and the thorax bone, in a tope erected by a Hindoo rajah, B. C. 250. Besides these topes there are two others, which were afterwards built, the last being eighty cubits high. The Sanchi tope is the finest in India, and is a solid stone dome, one hundred and six feet in diameter and forty-two feet high, with a basement and terrace having a colonnade, now fallen, of sixty pillars, with elegantly-carved stone railing and gateway.

The numerous rock-cut temples of the Buddhists in India are of great antiquity. Fergusson believes that over nine hundred yet remain, most of which are within the Presidency of Bombay. Many of these date back two centuries before Christ. They resemble the earliest Roman Catholic churches in form. They are excavated out of solid rock, and have a nave and side aisles, ending in an apse, or semi-dome, round which the aisle is carried. One of the excavated rock temples at Karli, built in this style, is one hundred and twenty-six feet long and forty-five feet wide, having fifteen elegantly-carved columns on each side, which separate the nave from the aisles. The façade of this temple is likewise profusely ornamented, and has a large open window to light the inside, below a beautiful gallery of rood loft.

The numerous rock-cut monasteries of the Buddhists in India have now been deserted for centuries. Between seven and eight hundred are known to remain, most of which were excavated between B. C. 200 and A. D. 500. Buddhist monks at that early period, as well as at the present time, took the three vows of celibacy, poverty and obedience, which are taken by the members of Roman Catholic orders. Besides this, *all* the Buddhist priests are mendicants. They shave their heads, wear a friar's robe tied round the waist with a rope, and beg from house to house, carrying their wooden bowls for boiled rice. The old monasteries of India have chapels and cells for the monks; but the largest could accommodate only thirty or forty; while one monastery in Thibet visited by MM. Huc and Gabet (the lamasery of Kounboum) is occupied by four thousand lamas. The structure of these monasteries clearly proves that the Buddhist monkish system is far too ancient to have been adopted from the Christian system.

But while Buddhism thus resembles Romanism in its outward forms, it manifests the spirit of Protestantism. In Asia the human mind protested in the interest of mankind against the oppression of priest-ridden Brahmanism, as the European reformers of the sixteenth century revolted against the tyranny of the Church of Rome. Brahmanism established a system of salvation by sacraments, but Buddhism revolted and founded a doctrine of personal salvation by teaching. Brahmanism was the more spiritual, as it made God everything, this world nothing; Buddhism was the more rationalistic, as it made this world everything and ignored Deity. Brahmanism is a system of fixed castes; Buddhism a system wherein the doctrine of individual freedom is asserted. Brahmanism considers the body as the soul's enemy; Buddhism accepts the laws of nature and is a religion of humanity as well as of devotion. Buddhism was a protest of nature against spirit, of humanity against caste, of personal freedom against priestly despotism, of salvation by faith against salvation by sacraments. But like other revolts, Buddhism went too far. "In asserting the rights of nature against the tyranny of spirit, Buddhism has lost God." Buddhism ignores creation and the Creator. Its tracts say: "The rising of the world is a natural case." "It is natural that the world should rise and perish." Brahmanism recognizes absolute spirit as the only reality and considers this world an illusion; while Buddhism recognizes only this world and ignores the eternal world of spirit. Nevertheless Buddhism, like Brahmanism, looks upon this life as an evil, and the aim of both systems is to escape the changes of the world and its miseries and obtain eternal repose, while both systems hold to the

STATUE OF BUDDHA.

doctrine of the transmigration of the souls of those who do not lead a correct life into other forms of animal existence until the soul is purified, when rest is obtained, according to Brahmanism, by absorption into the Divine Spirit of the universe, and according to Buddhism by entering Nirvana. Though both systems have the same aim, that of escaping the miseries and changes of existence into the absolute rest of eternity, the Brahman thinks this repose can only be obtained by mental submission and by a passive reception of what is taught by a priestcaste, while the Buddhist believes that this eternal rest can only come through a free obedience of the Divine laws. Both systems consider knowledge essential to salvation.

M. Saint-Hilaire has summed up the good and evil of Buddhism thus: Its founder proposed himself to save the human race. He did not indulge in the subtle philosophy of the Brahmans; he did not promise his followers riches, pleasures, conquests or power; but he invited them to accept salvation by means of virtue, knowledge and self-denial. We do not find such noble appeals in the Vedas or the other Brahmanic works. The Buddha's greatest glory was the unlimited charity for man which filled his soul. He devoted his life to teach man and lead him in the right way. His law was a law of grace for all. Sakya-muni, the Buddha, therefore aimed at a universal religion. He viewed man's life, regardless of rank and class, as sorrowful. He considered all alike poor and needy, and invited to come unto him all that labor and are heavy laden, offering them rest. He desired to cure the diseases of the life of the human race.

M. Saint-Hilaire remarks that in thus trying to save man, the means of Siddârtha the Buddha are as pure as his ends. He sought to persuade and to convince. He did not desire to use force. He permitted confession, and aided the weak and helpless by explanations and parables. He established habits of chastity, temperance and self-control, to guard man against evil. He employed the Christian graces of patience, humility and forgiveness of injuries. He abhorred falsehood, and reverenced truth. He forbade slander and gossip. He taught respect for parents, family, life and home.

The teaching of Gautama the Buddha, like that of Jesus the Christ, has been corrupted with doctrines which he never taught; and the forms of worship adopted in different countries vary, but principally consist in adoration of the statues of the Buddha and of his relics, he being regarded by them as that which any person may become by the four sublime truths and the ten commandments. Buddhism as a *philosophy* does not deny God; it simply ignores Him, says nothing about him. Buddhism as a *religion* is a polytheism and an idolatry, whose millions of votaries believe in a multitude of gods.

We have observed resemblances between the Buddha's teaching of charity and mercy and that of Christ's, as the fruit of the loving natures of both. Like Christianity, Buddhism was driven out of its birth-place. But M. Saint Hilaire observes that Buddhism never yet founded a good social state or a solitary good government. It failed in India, its native land, and never got a permanent hold of any Aryan race. The gloomy character of Buddhism, which looks upon all existence as an evil, with the simple motive of doing right for the sake of future reward by deliverance from a sad existence, has a corrupting influence upon duty; the idea disappears, and skepticism follows. "God is nothing; man is nothing; life is nothing; death is nothing; eternity is nothing. Hence the profound sadness of Buddhism. To its eye all existence is an evil, and the only hope is to escape from time into eternity—or into nothing—as you may choose to interpret Nirvana. While Buddhism makes God, or the good, and heaven, to be equivalent to nothing, it intensifies and exaggerates the evil. Though heaven is a blank, hell is a very solid reality. It is present and future too. Everything in the thousand hells of Buddhism is painted as vividly as in the hell of Dante. God has disappeared from the Universe, and in his place is only the inexorable law, which grinds on forever. It punishes and rewards, but has no love in it. It is only dead, cold, hard, cruel, unrelenting law. Yet Buddhists are not atheists, any more than a child who has never heard of God is an atheist. A child is neither deist nor atheist; he has *no* theology. The only emancipation from self love is in the perception of an infinite love. Buddhism, ignoring this infinite love, incapable of communion with God, aiming at morality without religion, at humanity without piety, becomes at last a prey to the sadness of a selfish isolation. We do not say that this is always the case, for in all systems the heart often redeems the errors of the head. But this is the logical drift of the system and its usual outcome."

Says Edwin Arnold concerning the Buddhist religion: "In point of age, most other creeds are youthful compared with this venerable religion, which has in it the eternity of a universal hope, the immortality of a boundless love, an indestructible element of faith in final good, and the proudest assertion ever made of human freedom."

CHINESE PAGODA.

CHAPTER XII.

ANCIENT CHINA.

SECTION I.—GEOGRAPHY OF CHINA.

HE Chinese Empire contains more than five millions of square miles, or twice the area of the United States, and has a population of almost five hundred millions, or about one-third of the number of inhabitants of the globe. China proper, inhabited by the Chinese, is about half the size of Europe, and has about four hundred millions of human beings within its limits. Of the eighteen provinces of China many contain singly more inhabitants than some of the great European monarchies.

China proper contains about one-fourth part of the territory of the empire, and three-fourths of the population. It is the portion that comprises that peculiar nation, so different from all others—the *Chinese*. China proper is bounded on the north by Tartary and the Yellow Sea; on the east by the Pacific Ocean; on the south by the China Sea, Anan, Siam and Burmah; on the west by Thibet and Tartary. It is mainly an uneven plain, though crossed by two ranges of mountains—the Peling range in the North, and the Nan-ling range in the South. The two chief rivers are the Hoang-Ho and Yang-tse-Kiang, both of which rise in Thibet; the first being eighteen hundred and fifty miles long, and the last two thousand miles.

The island of Hainan lies upon the southern coast, about eight miles from the main-land. It is one hundred and fifty miles long and seventy-five miles wide, and is very populous. A part of the people are subject to China, and a part are independent. This island produces gold, lapis-lazuli, and various curious and valuable woods.

The island of Formosa lies in the China Sea, sixty miles from the main-land. It is two hundred and forty miles long and sixty miles wide. It is traversed by mountains twelve thousand feet high, the tops of which are covered with snow most of the year. Several peaks are volcanic. The island has a temperate climate, but the seas around it are among the most tempestuous in the world; typhoons, whirlwinds and waterspouts being of frequent occurrence. Violent earthquakes also often occur. The soil is fertile, and portions of it are highly cultivated and produce grain and various fruits. The Chinese occupy only the western part, and first settled there in 1662, reducing the natives to tribute. The aborigines, who occupy the eastern part of the island, are of a slender physical frame, resembling both the Malays and the Chinese.

The Loo Choo Islands, about thirty-six in number, lie to the north-west of Formosa, about four hundred miles from the main-land. The soil and climate are fine, and the people are noted for their kind, gentle and hospitable manners. Their language is a dialect of the Japanese.

The climate of China is cold in the North, and the winters at Pekin, the capital of the Chinese Empire, are attended with deep snows and severe frosts. In the South it is hot. China lies in the same latitude as the

United States, and comprises almost the same extent upon the Pacific as our country does upon the Atlantic, so that the seasons and temperature of the two countries are very much alike. The soil of China is mainly fertile, and the whole of it is under industrious and skillful cultivation, yielding abundant crops. It produces all the fruits common to tropical and temperate latitudes. Camphor and cinnamon trees grow in the fields and gardens.

The tea shrub, or tree, grows wild in fields and hedges, but cultivation greatly improves it. It reaches a height of from four to six feet. It is usually grown in gardens. The leaves are gathered by families, and sold to merchants who trade in the article. Tea is a peculiar product of China, and the great staple of the country. Rice is grown more extensively in China than in any other country of the world, and is the main food of the people.

The silk-worm is cultivated in China, and in that country, it is said, silk was first manufactured. The various insects of China are very brilliant, and among them are many kinds of beetles and butterflies, some very large, and others beautiful. Little is known of the wild animals of China. The cattle are of the same humped species as those of India, one kind being no larger than a hog. There are not many horses. The pigs are said to be very small.

The political divisions of the Chinese Empire are China proper, Manchooria, Mongolia, Soongaria, Little Bucharia, or Chinese Turkestan, Thibet, Corea, and the islands of Hainan, Formosa and the Loo Choo group. Manchooria, Mongolia, Soongaria and Chinese Turkestan are called Chinese Tartary. Mongolia is regarded as the original home of the Mongolian race. Manchooria is the native country of the present dynasty, which has ruled the Chinese Empire for almost two and a half centuries, since A. D. 1644.

China proper is divided into eighteen provinces—Pe-chee-lee, Chang-tung, Kiang-su, Ngan-hoei, Ho-nan, Hoo-pe, Che-kiang, Kiang-si, Hoo-nan, Fokian, Quang-tung, Quang-si, Kuei-cheou, Yun-nan, Se-chu-an, Chen-si, Shan-si, Kansi, Leao-tong. The great cities of China are Pekin, the capital, with about three million inhabitants, in the most north-eastern province, Pe-chee-lee; Canton, with over two million inhabitants, in the province of Quang-tung, in the South, bordering on the China Sea; and Shanghae, Amoy, Ningpo, Nankin and Foo-choo, in the East, along the coast.

SECTION II.—POLITICAL HISTORY.

THE Chinese Empire is the oldest now existing on the face of the earth, and has until recently formed a separate world, as it were, from the rest of mankind, with a history distinctly its own and not connected with that of other nations. While great empires have successively risen and fallen in other parts of the world, China has remained the same for at least five thousand years, surviving all the great nations of Western Asia, Northern Africa and Europe. It is the only ancient empire which has continued to the present time.

While other nations have passed away, while empires have risen and fallen in other parts of Asia and the world, in accordance with the inexorable law of change which seems to govern human affairs, national as well as individual, China furnishes an example of permanence among nations. Its civilization appears to have existed without change from time immemorial, and may have existed before that of the Nile valley; and the Egyptian kings who erected the great Pyramids may have lived after the founders of the Chinese Empire. Porcelain vessels, having Chinese mottoes upon them, have been discovered in the ancient Egyptian tombs, in shape, material and appearance exactly resembling those made in China at the present time; and the great Italian antiquary of this century, Rosellini, believed them to have been imported into Egypt from China by kings who reigned in Egypt about the time of Moses or before.

China and its institutions have outlived everything else in the world. Ancient Egypt, Chaldæa, Assyria, Babylonia, Media, Persia, Judæa, Greece and Rome, have all risen, flourished, decayed and died; but China, probably more ancient than any of them, has remained the same to our own day. It has had twenty-two successive dynasties; but its customs and institutions, all that constitutes the life of the nation, have continued fixed and permanent. The present European nations, even the oldest of them, are young in comparison with the great nation of Eastern Asia. At the time when the Egyptian kings were building their Pyramids, China had a settled government and a high state of civilization, from which, if it has not materially advanced, it has not receded.

The Chinese have an extravagant chronology, making their country many thousands of years old; and their early history, like that of other Asiatic nations, is lost in the dimness of a very remote antiquity. Their fabulous chronology includes dynasties of sovereigns, each of whom reigned eighteen thousand years; but subsequently their lives dwindled to so short a period that the reigns of nine kings are embraced in forty-five thousand six hundred years. The ten ages from Tan-kou, or Pan-kwo, whom Confucius mentioned as the first man, are computed by Chinese writers to comprise ninety-six million years. But the Chinese now regard the fabulous period of their history with contempt. Kung-fu-tsee—whose name has been Latinized into Confucius—gives an account of the Chinese monarchs for a period of two thousand five hundred and sixty-two years before his time.

The Chinese were not the first inhabitants of the country, but had migrated from their original home in Mongolia to the south and south-east in the fabulous ages, and subdued or exterminated the barbarous aborigines of the country. Some remnants of these savage tribes still inhabit the mountains in Western China, where they are called *Miao*, and are perhaps of the same race as the aboriginal Thibetans.

When the Chinese first settled in the province of Shen-si, they are said to have been almost complete savages, having no knowledge of the arts of social union, or of anything which raises man above the brute. But they gradually developed a civilization; and early history speaks of sovereigns teaching their subjects every science and craft, from astronomy to agriculture, from preparing machinery for war to making musical instruments. It appears that the crown was at first elective, the people assembling on the death of a sovereign and choosing the person whom they considered most fitted to be his successor; the person so chosen being generally the prime minister of the deceased monarch.

The authentic history of China dates back almost five thousand years, but the early portion of it is wholly mythical. Chinese writers tell us that the founder of this old monarchy was FO-HI, who became Emperor about B. C. 2852. It is said that he taught his subjects how to raise cattle, instructed them in the art of writing, and introduced the institution of marriage and the divisions of the year. His successor, CHIN-NONG, invented the plow, and taught his people agriculture and medicine. The third Emperor, HWANG-TI, is said to have invented clocks, weapons, ships, wheeled vehicles and musical instruments, and to have introduced coins and also weights and measures. TI-KU, the fourth Emperor, established schools, and introduced the custom of polygamy. With his son and successor, YAU, who ascended the throne of the "Celestial Empire" in B. C. 2357, the more authentic history of China begins. He greatly advanced the civilization and wealth of his people, and constructed many roads and canals. He was succeeded at his death in

B. C. 2258 by his son SHUN, who was as good and wise a sovereign as his father. At his death in B. C. 2207, YU THE GREAT founded the Hia dynasty, which occupied the throne of the "Flowery Kingdom" until B. C. 1767. Yu the Great made himself the head of the national religion, as well as the civil ruler of the empire. His grandson, the third of the dynasty, was driven from the throne by a popular revolution, and was succeeded by his brother, CHUNG-KANG, who ruled with vigor. His death was followed by a period of civil war, which was ended by placing SHANG-KANG on the throne. He governed his empire well, and was succeeded by his son TI-CHU, the last great emperor of the famous Hia dynasty. After the death of Ti-chu, the Hia dynasty declined, and it was hurled from the throne by a revolution in B. C. 1766, when the Shang, or Yin, dynasty ascended the Chinese throne, which it held until B. C. 1122. This dynasty embraced twenty-eight emperors, who were most wicked, cruel and despicable sovereigns. In B. C. 1122 a great general named Wu-wang, headed a revolt against CHOW-SIN, the last emperor of the Shang dynasty, and reduced him to so desperate a condition that he collected his treasures and his women in his palace, and placing himself in their midst, set fire to the edifice and perished with them in the flames, as did Saracus, the last Assyrian king.

WU-WANG then ascended the Chinese throne and was the founder of the Chow dynasty, who governed China for eight hundred and seventy-three years, from B. C. 1122 to B. C. 249. Wu-wang was a great monarch, and inaugurated many wise and useful reforms for the benefit of his subjects. None of his successors possessed his ability, and their reigns were constantly disturbed by civil wars, struggles with the Tartars, and the rebellions of princes. The sovereign's power was as weak under this dynasty as it had been under any other race of Chinese emperors. During the reign of LI-WANG (B. C. 571-544), Confucius, the great Chinese moral philosopher and teacher, was born.

In B. C. 249 the Chow dynasty was succeeded by that of Tsin, whose monarchs were a far more vigorous race of sovereigns. They weakened the power of the great vassal princes, and made the emperor's power again supreme. The second emperor belonging to this dynasty was CHING-WANG, who reigned from B. C. 246 to B. C. 210, and built the "Great Wall of China" to protect his country against the inroads of the Tartars on the northern frontier of his empire. The Great Wall (*wan-li-chang*, the myriad mile wall), on the northern frontier of China proper, is the most stupendous work of defense ever erected by human hands. It was completed about B. C. 215, and is now mostly in ruins. Next to the Great Pyramids of Egypt, the Great Wall of China is the most ancient monument of human labor still remaining.

This wall bounds China proper along its entire northern frontier, along three of its provinces, and extends fifteen hundred miles from the Yellow Sea to the western province of Shen-si and far into Tartary. To procure a sufficient number of laborers for so great an enterprise, the Emperor Ching-wang ordered that every third laboring man throughout his dominions should be forced to enter his service; and these were obliged to work like slaves, without any further pay than a bare supply of food.

The wall was carried over the highest hills and through the deepest valleys, crossed upon arches over rivers, and was doubled in important passes, being supplied with strong brick towers or bastions, about a thousand yards apart. One of the highest ridges crossed by the wall is five thousand feet above the level of the sea. It greatly exceeds the sum total of all other works of the same kind, and proved a sufficient defense against the Tartars for fifteen centuries. The body of the wall consists of an earthen mound defended on each side by a wall of masonry and brick, of the most solid construction, with a terrace or platform of square bricks. The entire average height, including the parapet of five feet, is twenty feet. on a stone foundation projecting two

POLITICAL HISTORY.

feet under the brick work, and differing in height from two feet or more, according to the level of the ground. The wall is twenty-five feet thick at the base, narrowing to fifteen at the platform. The towers are forty-five feet at the base, diminishing to thirty feet at the top, and are about thirty-seven feet high.

The Emperor Ching-wang, the builder of the Great Wall, suppressed the tributary kingdoms and reduced them to their former state of dependent provinces; thus considering himself the founder of the Chinese Empire. He was the first to assume the title of *Kwang*, or Emperor. He determined that the history of China should begin with his reign; and to wipe out the memory of past events and reigns he ordered all the books recording them, including the public records, to be burned, and, it is said, also caused four hundred learned men to be buried alive, so that no knowledge of past events might be transmitted to history.

Thus a great mass of early Chinese literature perished, many of the writings of Confucius and Mencius being among them. A few fragments of their works escaped, and to them moderns are indebted for a knowledge of the principles of these great sages and of the previous history of China.

In B. C. 206 the Tsin dynasty was succeeded by that of Han, which governed China until A. D. 220. The Han dynasty

THE GREAT WALL OF CHINA.

was a race of great monarchs. The Emperor WEN-TI, who came to the throne B. C. 180, is regarded as the restorer of the ancient Chinese literature. WU-TI, who began to reign B. C. 141, was a liberal patron of science and art, and many scholars resided at his court. SIUEN-TI, who ascended the throne B. C. 73, subdued the Tartars and extended his dominion over their country westward to the Caspian Sea, thus ruling a vast dominion including all of Central Asia. During the reign of MING-TI (A. D. 58-76), Ho-shung, a Buddhist priest from

India, visited China and introduced the Buddhist religion into that country. There is a tradition among the Armenian Christians that St. Thomas also visited China and preached Christianity there during the reign of Ming-ti. The Emperor HO-TI, who reigned from A. D. 89 to A. D. 106, introduced the culture of the grape.

The famous Han dynasty came to an end in A. D. 220, when China was divided into three kingdoms. In A. D. 260 the Emperor WU-TI restored the empire by reuniting the three kingdoms, and founded the second Tsin dynasty, which held the throne until A. D. 420. The Han dynasty firmly held the Tartars in check, but these wild people established themselves in the North of China and set up an independent kingdom. Thence until A. D. 590 the South of China was governed by four successive native Chinese dynasties—the Sung, the Tse, the Ziang and the Chin. This period was marked by continuous civil war and religious dissension, which lasted until A. D. 590, when the Prince of Sui, who had conquered the Tartar kingdom in Northern China, subdued the native empire in the South also and thus reunited China into one monarchy. He became emperor and proved himself one of the wisest and best of Chinese monarchs. He devoted himself with unrelenting zeal to the promotion of literature, science, education, internal prosperity and commerce.

On the death of the Prince of Sui, in A. D. 619, the Hang dynasty ascended the throne of China which it occupied until A. D. 907. In A. D. 636 the Nestorian monk Olopen visited China and commenced the preaching of Christianity, and Nestorian inscriptions have been found in the country. The Emper KOW-TSUNG was the most celebrated sovereign of the Hang dynasty. He was a great warrior and extended his conquests westward to the frontiers of Persia. His son and successor, TAI-TSUNG, is the great hero of Chinese romance. The succeeding Hang sovereigns did not possess the vigor of the first two monarchs of this dynasty, and were the subservient instruments of the eunuchs of their court. But CHOW-TSUNG, who became emperor in A. D. 890, was a more vigorous ruler. He destroyed the eunuchs, but failed in his efforts to restore the power of the emperor. China became a prey to civil war, and the Tartars embraced the opportunity to extend their own power.

In A. D. 960 TAI-TSU restored tranquillity and founded the Sung dynasty, which occupied the Chinese throne until A. D. 1279, and liberally patronized the arts and sciences, but could not check the growing strength of the Tartars, and was obliged to seek aid from one Tartar tribe against the others. The tribes thus admitted into the country joined their countrymen, and in A. D. 1215 the Mongol Tartars, under Zingis-Khan, overran China and soon subdued the whole country. The account of this conquest and the subsequent portion of Chinese history will be related in other volumes of this book. We have carried our account of China thus far beyond the limits of ancient history in order to give a connected account up to the great Mongol conquest in A. D. 1215.

SECTION III.—CHINESE CIVILIZATION.

HE Chinese belong to the great Mongolian race, which comprises the nations of all Eastern and a great part of Central Asia—the race to which the Japanese, the Coreans, the Manchoos, the Mongols proper, the Thibetans, the Burmese, the Siamese and the Anamese belong. Compared with Christian nations they have been remarkably peaceful. In the preceding section we have alluded to the permanence of Chinese civilization—the unchangeable character of its institutions, its laws and customs. The oral language of China has remained the same for the last thirty centuries. The Great Wall is now over two thousand years old. All China was intersected by canals at a very early period, when none existed in Europe. The Great Canal, like the Great Wall, is unrivaled by any other remaining work of the kind. It is twice as long as the Erie Canal, is from two hundred to a thousand feet wide, and has many solid granite tanks along a great portion of its course. In China have been found tens of thousands of wells like the celebrated Artesian wells of Europe and America; and these were sunk in very ancient times to procure salt water. The manufacture of silk was also understood in the most remote antiquity, the cocoons of the silk-worm having been unraveled by a Chinese princess. The Chinese have been acquainted with the circulation of the blood many ages before Harvey's discovery in Europe. They innoculated for the small-pox in the ninth century, and invented printing about the same time. Their bronze money has been in use since B. C. 1100, and its form has remained the same for almost nineteen centuries. The mariner's compass, gunpowder and the art of printing, as practiced by the Chinese, were made known in Europe by Christian missionaries who had returned from China. These missionaries, coasting the shores of the Celestial Empire in Chinese junks, saw a little box with a magnetic needle, called Ting-uan-Tchen, or "needle which points to the south." They likewise observed frightful engines used by the Chinese armies called Ho-poo, or fire-guns, into which an inflammable powder was put, producing a noise like thunder and throwing stones and pieces of iron with resistless force. Father Huc says that the Europeans who entered China were as much surprised at the great libraries of the Chinese as at their artillery, and at the elegant books printed rapidly under a pliant silky paper by means of wooden blocks.

The customs of this peculiar people are entirely opposite to our own. They seem

1—33.-U. H.

our antipodes in everything. Their magnetic needle points to the south, and they say "west-north" instead of north-west; "east-south," instead of south-east. Their soldiers wear quilted petticoats, satin boots and bead necklaces, carry umbrellas and fans, and make a night attack with lanterns in their hands, as they stand in greater dread of the dark than of the enemy. They prefer to have their fireworks in the daytime. Ladies ride in wheelbarrows, and cows are driven in carriages. In China the stocks are hung upon the neck, instead of put on the feet. The family name comes first, and the personal name afterwards, so that instead of saying John Smith, they would say Smith John. In this way the Chinese name of Confucius, Kung-fu-tsee, signifies the Holy Master Kung—Kung being the family name. In mounting a horse, the Chinese get on on the right side. Their old men fly kites, while the little boys look on. They use the left hand instead of the right in greetings and farewells, and keep on the hat as a sign of respect. Their visiting cards are printed red and are four feet long. They regard the stomach as the seat of the understanding. They have villages with a million inhabitants. Their boats are drawn by men, but their carriages are moved by sails. A young and pretty married woman is a slave, but an old and withered one is most highly esteemed and beloved by the entire family. The emperor is most profoundly reverenced, but the empress-mother is far more highly esteemed. The most-highly prized article of furniture is a camphor-wood coffin, which is always kept in the best room in the house. The legal rate of interest on money is thirty-six per cent. They warm their wine. They are great epicures, and somewhat gourmands, for after dining on thirty dishes they will sometimes finish up on a duck. They toss their meat into their mouths to a tune, every man keeping time with his chop-sticks. They devour birds' nests, snails, and the fins of sharks. Their mourning color is white. They mourn for their parents three years. The chief room in their houses is called "the hall of ancestors," of whom there are pictures or tablets set up against the wall, and these are worshiped.

The most important peculiarity of China is the esteem in which learning is there held, and distinctions and rewards are bestowed upon scholarship. All the civil offices in the empire are given as rewards of literary merit. The government is a despotism, the emperor having absolute power. He is not bound by any written constitution. Nevertheless he is held to a strict responsibility by public opinion. He is under the authority of custom, as well as are his subjects. In China more than in any other country "what is gray with age becomes religion." The emperor's authority does not extend beyond governing according to the ancient usages of the country, and any persistent violation of these will bring on a revolution and result in a change of dynasty. A revolution in China, however, changes only the person who occupies the throne. The unwritten constitution of old usages continues intact. Says Du Halde: "A principle as old as the monarchy is this, that the state is a large family, and that the emperor is in the place of both father and mother. He must govern his people with affection and goodness; he must attend to the smallest matters which concern their happiness. When he is supposed not to have this sentiment, he soon loses his hold on the reverence of the people, and his throne becomes insecure." The emperor consequently tries to preserve this reputation, so as to retain the love and respect of his subjects. When a province suffers from famine, inundation, or any other calamity, he remains secluded in his palace, fasting and issuing decrees to relieve it of taxes and afford it assistance. Andrew Wilson says that "the Chinese people stand unsurpassed, and probably unequalled in regard to the possession of freedom and self-government."

The real power of the Chinese government is in the literary class. Though nominally a monarchy, the government is practically an aristocracy of learning, as the humblest and poorest man's son can reach the highest position in the empire if he has the necessary ability and merit. It is not an aristocracy of rank or birth, like that of England; nor an aristocracy of wealth, like that of the United States; nor a military aristocracy, like that of Russia; nor a priestly aristocracy, like that of ancient Egypt, and of some modern countries, as that of Paraguay under the Jesuits, or that of the Sandwich Islands under the Protestant missionaries. The Chinese aristocracy is a literary aristocracy.

The civil officers in China are called *mandarins*. They are selected from the three degrees of learned men, and all persons are eligible for the first degree, except the three excluded classes—boatmen, barbers and actors. The aspirants are examined by the governors of their own towns. Of those approved a few are selected after a second examination. These are examined a third time by an officer who makes a circuit once in three years for that purpose. They are shut up alone in small rooms or closets, with pencils, ink and paper, and are assigned a subject to write upon. Fifteen candidates may be selected out of some four hundred, and these receive the lowest degree. There is another triennial examination for the second degree, at which a small number of the highest class of learned men are promoted. The examination for the highest degree is held at Pekin, the capital, only; and then some three hundred are selected out of five thousand. These are eligible to the highest offices. Whenever a vacancy occurs, one of those who have received a degree is taken by lot from the few senior names. Several years ago there were five thousand of the highest rank, and twenty-seven thousand of the second rank, who had not been appointed to positions under the government.

The subjects upon which the candidates are examined, and the methods of these examinations are thus described: The subjects for the degree of Keujin (or licentiate) takes place at the imperial city of each province once in three years. The average number of bachelors in the large province of Keang-Nan (which has a population of seventy millions) is twenty thousand, out of whom about two hundred are successful. Sixty-five mandarins are appointed to conduct this examination and are assisted by subordinate officials. The two chief examiners are sent from Pekin. When the candidates enter the hall of examination they are searched for books and manuscripts, from which they might have gotten aid in preparing their essays. If any are detected in sly practices they are disgraced for life. Out of one hundred and forty-four successful candidates in 1851 thirteen were more than forty years old, and one under fourteen; seven were less than twenty. In order to succeed they had to know by heart the whole of the Sacred Books, and were required to be well read in history.

Three sets of subjects are assigned, each requiring two days and a night, and none is permitted to leave his small apartment until the expiration of that time. The essays must not have over seven thousand characters, and no erasure or correction is permitted. On the first day the subjects are selected from the Four Books; on the next, from the older classics; on the last, miscellaneous questions are assigned. These are some of the subjects: "Choo-tsze, in commenting on the Shoo-King, made use of four authors, who sometimes say too much, at other times too little; sometimes their explanations are forced, at other times too ornamental. What have you to observe on them?" "Chinshow had great abilities for historic writing. In his Three Kingdoms he has depreciated Choo-ko-lang, and made very light of E. and E., two other celebrated characters. What is it that he says of them?"

The utmost impartiality is observed in conducting these public examinations. The whole system of Chinese government is based upon them. Education is thus made universally desirable, as the son of the poorest man may attain the highest position under the government. Every one of the hundreds of thousands who prepare themselves to compete are obliged to know the whole system of Confucius, to memorize all his moral teachings, and to acquaint themselves with all the traditional wisdom of the country. Thus there is a permanent public sentiment in favor of existing institutions.

The highest civil offices are seats at the great tribunals or boards, and the positions of governors, or viceroys, of the eighteen provinces of China proper. The boards are Ly Pou (Board of Appointment of Mandarins), Hou Pou (Board of Finance), Lee Pou (Board of Ceremonies), Ping Pou (Board of War), Hing Pou (Board of Criminal Justice), Kong Pou (Board of Works—canals, bridges, etc.)

The members of these boards and their councilors and subordinates are twelve hundred in number. There is also a Board of Doctors of the Han Lin College, who have charge of the archives, history of the empire, etc. There is likewise the Board of Censors, consisting of the highest mandarins, whose duty is to censure anything they find wrong, whether committed by the emperor, the mandarins, or the people.

The governor, or viceroy of a province, is vested with great authority. He is likewise chosen from among the mandarins after a series of examinations. He is required to report every three years concerning the affairs of his province and give an account of his own faults; which, if he omits, and they are discovered in any other way, will subject him to punishment, such as bambooing or death. The humblest subject has the right to complain to the emperor against any officer, however high in rank the officer may be, and a large drum is placed at the palace gates for this purpose. Whoever strikes this drum has his case investigated under the eye of the emperor himself; and if he has been wronged, redress is made, but if he has complained without cause he is punished with severity. Imperial visitors, sent by the Board of Censors, may suddenly come to examine the affairs of a province at any time, and a governor or other mandarin who is detected in any wrong doing is at once reported and punished.

The emperor of China, like other Asiatic monarchs, has a number of concubines and eunuchs about the palace.

Thus the political institutions of China are built on literature. Knowledge is the way to wealth and power, to civil employment. All the talent and knowledge of the people have an interest in supporting institutions which confer upon them power and political distinction, and which give them the hope of these. These institutions have worked admirably. The Chinese are industrious, prosperous and contented, while the people in other parts of Asia are oppressed and tax-ridden by petty despots. Agriculture has been carried to greater perfection in China than elsewhere. Every piece of land except such as is devoted to ancestral monuments yields two or three crops every year, in consequence of the careful cultivation bestowed upon it. Two thousand years ago originated the ceremony of opening the soil at the beginning of the year, on which occasion the emperor officiates. Farms consist of only one or two acres, and each family raises all it needs on its farm. Each family manufactures silk and cotton, each man spinning, weaving and dyeing his own web. The division of labor is carried very far in manufacturing porcelain, the best of which is made in the village of Kiang-see, containing a population of one million. Seventy hands are frequently engaged on one cup. The Chinese display great skill in working horn and ivory. They make large lanterns of horn, transparent and perfect. Men have failed at Birmingham, in England, to cut ivory by machinery in the same manner in which the Chinese have so long been expert.

SECTION IV.—CONFUCIUS AND HIS RELIGION.

CONFUCIUS—known in Chinese as Kung-fu-tsee, (Holy Master Kung)—has been the great teacher of the Chinese nation for twenty-three centuries. He was born about B. C. 551, and lived contemporaneously with the Tarquins of Rome, with Pythagoras and Cyrus the Great. About his time the Jews returned from Babylon and Xerxes invaded Greece. His descendants have always enjoyed the highest privileges, and now number some forty thousand in China, more than seventy generations after their illustrious ancestor. His family is the oldest in the world, except the Jews, who may be regarded as a single family descended from Abraham. He has exerted greater influence on the minds of many millions of his fellow creatures by means of his writings than any other man who ever lived, excepting the writers of the Jewish and Christian Scriptures. The influence of Confucius has maintained in China that great reverence for parents, that ardent family affection, that love of order, that esteem for learning and that respect for literary men, which lie at the foundation of all the institutions of China. His minute and practical code of morals, which is studied by all the learned, and which embraces the sum of knowledge and the principle of government in China, has ever since exerted an incalculable influence on the hundreds of millions of human beings in the Celestial Empire.

This fact is abundant evidence of the greatness of the renowned Chinese lawgiver and moral philosopher. Confucius must have been one of the great intellects of the human race. He was one of the few who have devoted themselves to the moral betterment of their fellow-men. He endeavored to infuse the principles of the purest religion and the most perfect standard of morals in the character of the whole Chinese people, and was successful in his laudable efforts.

His ancestors were celebrated statesmen and soldiers in the small country of Loo, then an independent kingdom, now a Chinese province. The year of his birth, B. C. 551, was three years before Cyrus the Great became King of Persia. His father, one of the highest officers of the kingdom, and a brave soldier, died when Confucius was three years old. His mother had trained him with great care, and when he was fifteen years old he had studied the five Sacred Books named Kings. He was married at the age of nineteen, and had but one son, who died before his father, leaving but one grandson, who was the ancestor of the forty thousand descendants of Confucius now living in China. This grandson was almost as wise as Confucius, and was the teacher of the celebrated Meng-tse, whose name has been Latinized into Mencius.

In the time of Confucius, China was divided into many petty kingdoms, whose rulers were quarreling constantly, and although he held many public positions of trust, he retired to another part of the country because of the disorders then prevailing in his own kingdom. He then continued the life of a public teacher, instructing men in the simple moral truths by which he endeavored to govern his own conduct. He afterwards returned to his native kingdom of Loo, and after being out of office for some years became minister of state at the age of fifty, and his wise administration was attended with great success, and the whole people enjoyed prosperity; but finally the wild excesses of the court and the dissipation of the sovereign uprooted his wise and good laws, and Confucius resigned his office and again wandered about the country a poor man, teaching his countrymen the great moral truths which had been the rule of his life. His disciples went about the country disseminating his wise precepts. After many wanderings Confucius returned to Loo, despised and poverty-stricken, and spent his remaining years in editing the Sacred Books of China, and in writing some additions to them, and died at the age of seventy-three.

His disciples now numbered three thousand, five hundred of whom had reached official positions, seventy-two well understood his system, and ten, who were especially wise and good, constantly attended him. One of these latter was Hwuy, whom Confucius contended to have attained superior virtue, and of whom he often said in his conversations: "I saw him continually advance, but I never saw him stop in the path of knowledge." At another time he said: "The wisest of my disciples, having one idea, understands two. Hwuy, having one, understands ten." One of the chosen ten disciples, Tszee-loo, was as rash and impetuous as the Apostle Peter. Another, Tszee-Kung, was as loving and gentle as the Apostle John, and built a house near the grave of Confucius, wherein he mourned for his master after his death.

During his last years Confucius edited the Sacred Books, or the Kings, as they have been transmitted to every succeeding generation since his day. The authentic history of China dates back to B. C. 2357; but Fohi, the founder of the Chinese monarchy, was also the founder of Chinese philosophy. He began to reign about B. C. 2852. He invented the art of writing with pictured characters as a substitute for the knotty strings which had previously constituted the only means of record. He was likewise the author of the Eight Diagrams, each having eight lines, of which half are entire and half separated into two. These Diagrams, by various combinations, are believed to symbolize the active and passive principles of the universe in every essential form. Confucius edited the Yih-King, the Shoo-King, the She-King and the Le-Ke, embracing all of ancient Chinese literature as it has been transmitted to posterity. The Four Books, containing the doctrines of Confucius and his disciples, were not written by himself, but were composed by his followers after his death. One of these books, called the "Immutable Man," is designed to show that virtue consists in avoiding extremes. Another, called the Lun-Yu, or Analects, contains the conversation or table-talk of Confucius, and is very much like Xenophon's Memorabilia and Boswell's Life of Johnson.

Confucius devoted his life to instructing the Chinese people in his moral and religious principles. His system is more of a moral philosophy than a religion in the general sense of the term, yet it teaches men how they ought to live. The four things which he is said to have taught were learning, morals, devotion of soul and reverence. He counseled all to be truthful, just, loving, dutiful to themselves and others, and obedient to the ancient laws and rites of their country.

Among his sayings were the following:

"At fifteen years I longed for wisdom. At thirty my mind was fixed in the pursuit of it. At forty I saw clearly certain principles. At fifty I understood the rule given by heaven. At sixty everything I heard I easily understood. At seventy the desires of my heart no longer transgressed the law."

He says of himself: "He is a man who through his earnestness in seeking knowledge forgets his food, and in his joy for having found it loses all sense of his toil, and thus occupied is unconscious that he has almost reached old age."

"To rule with equity is like the North Star, which is fixed and all the rest go round it."

"The essence of knowledge is, having it, to apply it; not having it, to confess your ignorance."

"Formerly, in hearing men, I heard their words, and gave them credit for their conduct; now I hear their words and observe their conduct."

"A man's life depends on virtue; if a bad man lives, it is only by good fortune."

"Some proceed blindly to action, without knowledge; I hear much, and select the best course."

He was once found fault with, when in office, for not opposing the marriage of a ruler with a distant relation, which was an offense against Chinese propriety. He said: "I am a happy man; if I have a fault men observe it."

Confucius was humble. He said: "I cannot bear to hear myself called equal to the sages and the good. All that can be said of me is, that I study with delight the conduct of the sages, and instruct men without weariness therein."

"A good man regards the *root*; he fixes the root, and all else flows out of it. The root is filial piety; the fruit brotherly love."

"I daily examine myself in a threefold manner: in my transactions with men, if I am upright; in my intercourse with friends, if I am faithful; and whether I illustrate the teachings of my master in my conduct."

"Faithfulness and sincerity are the highest things."

"When you transgress, do not fear to return."

"Learn the past and you will know the future."

"The Master said, 'Shall I teach you what knowledge is? When you know a thing, to hold that you know it, and when you do not know a thing, to allow that you do not know it; this is knowledge.'"

"To see what is right and not to do it is want of courage."

"Worship as though the Deity were present."

"He who offends against Heaven has none to whom he can pray."

"If my mind is not engaged in my worship, it is as though I worshiped not."

"Coarse rice for food, water to drink, the bended arm for a pillow—happiness may be enjoyed even with these; but without virtue, both riches and honor seem to me like the passing cloud."

"Grieve not that men know not you; grieve that you know not men."

"A good man is serene; a bad man always in fear."

"There may be fair words and an humble countenance when there is little virtue."

"One of his disciples said, 'If you, Master, do not speak, what shall we, your disciples, have to read?' The Master said, 'Does Heaven speak? The four seasons pursue their courses, and all things are continually being produced; but does Heaven say anything?'"

"In the Book of Poetry are three hundred

pieces, but the design of them all may be embraced in that one sentence, 'Have no depraved thoughts.'" (This reminds us of the saying of the later Jewish Rabbis that all the 613 precepts of the Law were summed up in the words, "The just shall live by his faith.")

"If a man in the morning hear the right way, he may die in the evening without regret."

"Tsze-kung said, 'What I do not wish men to do to me, I also wish not to do to men.' The Master said, 'You have not attained to that.'"

The great principles which he taught were mainly based on family affection and duty. He advised kings to treat their subjects as fathers should treat their children. He counseled subjects to respect and obey their kings as children should respect and obey their parents. These ideas became so impressed upon the national mind that emperors are obliged to appear as governing in accordance with them, even if they do not wish to do so. Confucius taught reverence —respect for parents, respect and reverence for the past and its legacies, for the great men and the great ideas of past ages. He advised men to treat each other as brothers, and to do unto others as they would have others do unto them.

He said nothing about a personal God or a future life. He is said to have replied to one of his disciples who asked him concerning death: "While you do not know of life, how can you know about death?" His worship was directed to antiquity, to ancestors, to posterity, to propriety and usage, to the state as parents of its subjects, to the sovereign as the ruler of his people. Absolutely sincere, fully confident of all that he knew, he said and taught only what he believed. His influence and power came from the sincerity of his convictions and the perfect honesty of his soul.

Lao-tse, who was the contemporary of Confucius for twenty-eight years, and the founder of one of the three religions yet existing in China—Ta-oism—was perhaps as wise and intelligent as the great moral philosopher and lawgiver. He was, however, mainly a thinker, and made no effort to better the people; his purpose being to repress the passions and to preserve the equanimity of the soul. He taught a system like that of the Grecian Stoics. He looked upon virtue as certain of its own reward, upon everything as governed by inexorable laws. His disciples afterwards added a thaumaturgic element and an invocation to departed spirits to his system, which thus much resembles our modern Spiritualism. Lao-tse's original doctrine, as he himself taught it, was rationalism in philosophy and stoicism in morals. Confucius is said to have visited him and to have said that he could not understand him, uttering the following: "I know how birds fly, how fishes swim, how animals run. The bird may be shot, the fish hooked, and the beast snared. But there is the dragon. I cannot tell how he mounts in the air and soars to heaven."

But the great moral philosopher and lawgiver, who labored for the good of his fellow-countrymen, has exerted a far greater influence than the founder of Tao-ism; and for twenty-three centuries has Confucius been the great teacher and daily guide for one-third of mankind.

Confucius was preëminently distinguished for his energy and perseverance. He continued his noble work until death closed his eyes forever. Said he: "The general of an army may be defeated, but you cannot defeat the determined mind of a peasant." He acted in accordance with his own teachings. The following was another of his sayings: "If I am building a mountain, and stop before the last basketful of earth is placed on the summit, I have failed of my work. But if I have placed but one basketful on the plain, and go on, I am really building a mountain."

Many good things are told concerning Confucius, his courage, his humility, and other virtues. Chinese thought has received direction from his writings and his life. Though reviled and persecuted during his lifetime, he has become the patron-saint of the Celestial Empire. His doctrine has become the state religion of China, and is maintained by the whole power of the emperor and the literary aristocracy. His books are published yearly by societies organized for that purpose, and are distributed gratuitously. His forty thousand descendants are treated with the highest consideration. There are sixteen hundred and sixty temples erected to his memory, and one of these covers ten acres of ground. On the two festivals in the year sacred to his memory seventy thousand animals of various kinds are sacrificed, and twenty-seven thousand pieces of silk are burned on his altars. But his religion has no priests, no liturgy, no public worship, except on these two occasions.

The system of Confucius is, as we have said, the established religion of the state. But there are two other religions in China—Buddhism and Tao-ism—which give the Chinese the element of religious worship and teach them the doctrine of a supernatural world, not found in the Confucian system, and which are simply tolerated as adapted to weak-minded persons. Confucianism, perpetually taught by the competitive examinations, controls the thought of China. It developed from the birth of Confucius to the death of Mencius—from B. C. 551 to B. C. 313. Its second period was from the time of Chow-tsze (A. D. 1034) to that of Choo-tsze (A. D. 1200). The last of these gave the real direction to Chinese philosophy, and was one of the great men of the empire. His works are mainly commentaries on the Kings and the Four Books, and are memorized by millions of Chinese who aspire to pass the public-service examinations.

The Chinese philosophy which Choo-tsze established considers the Tae-keih, or Grand Extreme, as the highest and final principle of all existence. This principle is altogether immaterial, and the foundation of order in the universe; and all animate and inanimate nature emanate therefrom. It operates from all eternity by expansion and contraction, or by constant active and passive pulsation. The active expansive pulsation is called Yong, the passive contracting pulsation is Yin, and these are regarded as the positive and negative essences of all things. When the active expansive pulsation has attained its farthest extreme, the operation becomes passive and intensive; and all material and mortal existences arise from these vibrations. Thus creation is constantly in progress. Matter and spirit being opposite results of the same force, the former tending to variety, the latter to unity. Variety in unity is a permanent and universal law of existence. Man originates from the highest development of these pulsatory operations. Man's nature, as the ultimate perfection, is good, embracing the five elements of charity, righteousness, propriety, wisdom and sincerity. As man comes in contact with the exernal world evil follows. The holy man has an instinctive insight into the ultimate principle in its double operation, and therefore spontaneously and easily obeys his nature. Consequently all his thoughts are perfectly wise, his actions perfectly good, and his words perfectly true. Confucius was the last of these holy men. The fact that these holy men perceived instinctively the working of the ultimate principle has given their writings, the Sacred Books, infallible authority.

Confucian philosophy regards example as all-powerful, the happiness of the people as the security of the empire, the attainment of a knowledge of the essence of things as the result of constant solitary thought, and the virtue and contentment of the people as the object of all government.

The philosophy of Confucius teaches that the ultimate principle is not essentially identical with a living, intelligent and personal God. When Confucius spoke of Teen, or Heaven, he did not assert any faith in such a being. He neither asserted nor denied a Supreme Being. He simply ignored Him, as did the Buddha. The worship and prayer, according to Confucianism, does not necessarily imply such a belief. The prayer of Confucius was a prayer of reverence addressed to some sacred, mysterious, hidden power, above and back of all visible things.

He did not venture to intimate what that unknown power is. In the She-King, however, a personal God is addressed. The most ancient books recognize a Divine person. They teach that there is a Supreme Being, who is present everywhere, who sees everything, and knows everything; and that this Being desires all men to live together peaceably and as brothers. He requires right actions, pure desires and thoughts, a serious demeanor, "which is like a palace where virtue resides." He requires us to specially guard the tongue. "For a blemish may be taken out of a diamond by carefully polishing it; but, if your words have the least blemish, there is no way to efface that." "Humility is the solid foundation of all virtues." "To acknowledge one's incapacity is the way to be soon prepared to teach others; for from the moment that a man is no longer full of himself, nor puffed up with empty pride, whatever good he learns in the morning he practices before night." "Heaven penetrates to the bottom of our hearts, like into a dark chamber. We must confine ourselves to it, till we are like two instruments of music tuned to the same pitch. We must join ourselves with it, like two tablets which appear but one. We must receive its gifts the very moment its hand is open to bestow. Our irregular passions shut up the door of our souls against God."

These are the teachings of the Books of Kings, the oldest remaining productions of the human intellect. They appear to have been almost forgotten in the time of Confucius, when their precepts were entirely neglected. Confucius revised them, with additions of his own explanations and comments, and near the end of his life called his disciples around him and solemnly dedicated these Sacred Books to Heaven. He built an altar, placed the books upon it, adored God, and upon his knees humbly returned thanks for the life and health bestowed upon him to complete his undertaking.

SECTION V.—LAO-TSE AND TAO-ISM.

AO-ISM is one of the three religions of China, the other two being Confucianism and Buddhism. Tao-ism comes under three distinct forms; 1, as a philosophy of the absolute or unconditioned, in the great work of its founder Lao-tse; 2, as a system of morals of the utilitarian kind; 3, as a system of magic, connected with a belief in spirits. The Tao-te-king gives us the ideas of Lao-tse, which Chinese commentators themselves regard as very obscure and hard to understand.

The Tao, the origin of heaven and earth, cannot be named. As that which is namable, it is the mother of all things. These two are necessarily one. Being and not-being are born from each other. The Tao is empty, but cannot be exhausted. It is pure and profound, and existed before the gods. It can not be seen. It returns into not-being. It is vague, confused, obscure. It is small and powerful. It is present everywhere, and all beings return into it. It has no desires and is great. All things are born of being. Being is born of not-being.

Thus it appears that the philosophy of the Tao-te-king is that of absolute being, or the identity of being and not-being, thus corresponding with the philosophy of Hegel, twenty-three centuries later. It teaches that the absolute is the source of being and of not-being. Being is essence, and not-being is existence.

One attains to all that is not-being by identifying himself with being, which is the source of not-being. Therefore the wise man will avoid knowledge, instead of seeking it. He refuses to act instead of acting. The wise man is like water, which appears weak but is strong; which yields, seeks its lowest level, and which appears the softest thing and breaks the hardest thing. One can only be wise by renouncing wisdom. He can only be good by renouncing justice and humanity. He can only be learned by renouncing knowledge. One must have no desires, must renounce all things, and be like a new-born babe. From everything comes its opposite, the easy from the difficult, the difficult from the easy, the long from the short, the short from the long, the high from the low, the low from the high, ignorance from knowledge, knowledge from ignorance, the first from the last, the last from the first. These various antagonisms are related by the principle of Tao. Nothing is independent, or can exist without its opposite. The good man and the bad man are equally necessary to each other. To have a right desire is not to have any desire. The saint is able to do great things because he does not try to do them. The unwarlike man conquers. He who yields to others rules them. By thus denying all things we attain possession of all things. Not to act is consequently the secret of all power.

The same doctrine of opposites appears in the Phædo, in the Sánkhya philosophy of the Hindoos, and the doctrine of the Monad behind the Duad in the Zend-Avesta.

The result so far is to an active passivity. Lao teaches that not to act involves the highest energy of being, and produces the greatest results. By not acting one becomes identified with Tao and receives all its power. Here the Chinese philosopher reasoned like Gautama and Buddha. The Tao of Lao-tse is the same as the Nirvana of Gautama. The different career of each is owing to the different motive in his mind. Gautama sought Nirvana, or the absolute, the pure knowledge, to obtain a release from evil and to overcome it. Lao appears to have sought it to attain power. On this point Buddhism and Taoism disagree. Buddhism is generous, benevolent, humane, seeking to help others. Tao-ism is selfish, striving for its own. This is the cause of the selfish morality pervading the Book of Rewards and Punishments. Every good act receives its reward. This is the cause of the degradation of the system into pure magic and spiritualism.

In the Tao-te-king, the element afterwards expands in the system of utilitarian and eudæmonic ethics in the Book of Rewards and Punishments. The principle that by putting one's self into a wholly passive state one can enter into communion with the unnamed Tao, and thus obtain power over nature, leads to magic. The Tao-te-king says that he who knows the Tao needs not fear the bite of serpents, nor the jaws of wild beasts, nor the claws of birds of prey. He cannot be reached by good or evil. He does not need to have any fear of the rhinoceros or the tiger. In battle he does not need either cuirass or sword. The tiger is not able to tear him to pieces. The soldier is unable to inflict any wound upon him. He is absolutely invulnerable and secure against death.

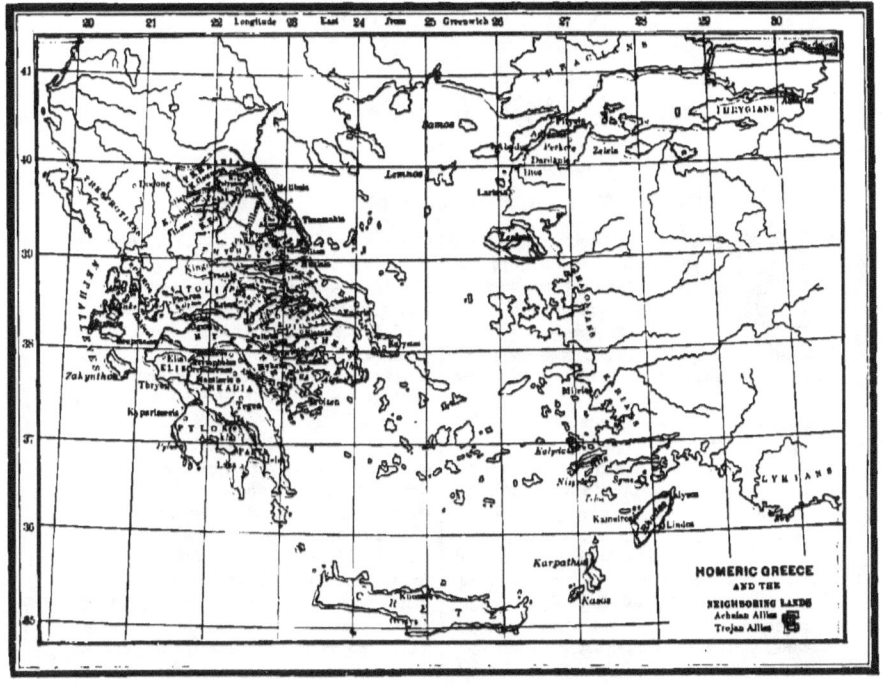

CHAPTER XIII.

ANCIENT GREECE.

SECTION I.—GEOGRAPHY OF GREECE.

ELLAS, or Greece proper, is a peninsula in the South of Europe, and is about two hundred and fifty English miles long, and about one hundred and eighty miles wide. It has been estimated to contain about thirty-five thousand square miles. It is bounded on the north by Olympus, the Cambunian mountains, and an imaginary line extending westward from the Acroceraunian promontory; on the east by the Ægean Sea; on the south by the Mediterranean; and on the west by the Ionian Sea.

The Hellenic peninsula has a number of mountains and a very irregular and extensive coast-line. Many deep bays strongly indent the shores, and long narrow promontories extend far into the sea on every side; and this is the reason for the territorial area of Greece being less than that of any other country of Southern Europe. There are many excellent harbors. The sea is not dangerous in its vicinity. There are many littoral islands of exceeding beauty and fertility off the coast. The structure of the coast-line has been favorable to maritime pursuits and to navigation, as communication between most portions of the country is easier by sea than by land, the greater mountains which intersect the peninsula in every direction being mainly lofty and rugged, and thus traversable only by a few passes, which are frequently blocked by snow during the winter.

The mountain-system of Greece may be considered a branch of the European chain of the Alps. At a point a little to the west of the twenty-first meridian of longitude east from Greenwich, the Albanian Alps give out a spur, which, under the names of Scardus, Pindus, Corax, Taphiassus, Panachäicus Lampea, Pholoë, Parrhasius and Täygetus, runs in a direction a little east of south from the forty-second parallel of north latitude to the promontory of Tænarum. A series of lateral branches project from this great chain on both sides, having a general direction from east to west, and from these project other cross ranges, following the direction of the main chain, or backbone of the region, pointing almost south-east. The chains running east and west are particularly prominent in the eastern part of the country, between the Pindus and the Ægean. There project in succession the Cambunian and Olympic range, forming the northern boundary of Greece proper; the range of Othrys, separating Thessaly from Malis and Æniania; the range of Œta, dividing between Malis and Doris; and the range of Parnassus, Helicon, Cithæron and Parnes, starting from Delphi and ending in the Rhamnusian promontory, opposite Eubœa, forming in the eastern part a great barrier between Bœotia and Attica. On the opposite side were others of the same character, such as Mount Lingus, in the North of Epirus, which extended westward from the Pindus at a point almost opposite the Cambunians; and Mount Tymphrestus in Northern, and Mount Bomius in Central Ætolia. The principal chain in the Peloponnesus extended from Rhium to Tænarum, sending off on the west Mount Scollis, which separated Achæa from Elis, and Mount Elæon, which divided Elis from Messenia; while on the east its branches were one named Erymanthus, Aroania and Cyllênê, dividing Achæa from Arcadia, and extending eastward to the Scyllæan promontory in Argolis; and another known as Mount Parthenium, separating Argolis from Laconia. The smaller important chains running north and south were Mount Pelion and Mount Ossa, which closed in Thessaly on the east; the range of Pentelicus, Hymettus and Anhydrus, in Attica; and Mount Parnon, in the Peloponnesus, extending from near Tegea to Malea.

The mountain-chains of Greece take up so much of the country that there are few plains, and these are very small. Yet there are some plains which were highly fertile. Most of Thessaly was an extensive plain, surrounded by mountains, and drained by the river Peneus. There were two large plains in Bœotia—the marshy plain of the Cephissus, of which much was occupied by Lake Copais; and the plain of Asopus, on the edge of which were the cities of Thebes, Thespiæ and Platæa. There were three chief plains in Attica—the plain of Eleusis, the plain of Athens, and the plain of Marathon. In the West and South of the Peloponnesus were the lowlands of Cava Elis on each side of the river Peneus, of Macaria, about the mouth of the river Pamisus, and of Helos at the mouth of the Eurotas. In the central region of the Peloponnesus were the elevated upland plains, or basins, of Tegea, Mantinea, Pheneus and Orchomenus. In the Eastern Peloponnesus was the fertile alluvial plain of Argos, drained by the Chimarrhus, the Erasinus, the Phrixus, the Charadrus and the Inachus.

Greece had many small rivers, most of them being mainly winter torrents, carrying little or no water during the summer. The only considerable streams were the Acheloüs, which rose in Epirus, separating Ætolia from Acarnania; the northern Peneus, which drained the great plain of Thessaly; and the Alpheus, on the banks of which was Olympia. The principal secondary streams were Thyamis, Oropus and Arachthus, in Epirus; the Evenus and the Daphnus, in Ætolia; the Spercheius, in Malis; the Cephissus and the Asopus, in Bœotia; the southern Peneus, the Pamisus, the Eurotas and the Inachus, in the Peloponnesus.

Many of the rivers of Greece disappear in subterranean passages. The limestone rocks are full of caves and fissures, while many of the plains consist of land-locked basins which seem to have no outlet. Here the streams generally form lakes, of which the waters flow off to the sea through an underground channel, some of them visible, others only supposed to exist. The Cephissus finds such an outlet from Lake Copaïs in Bœotia, and most of the lakes of the Peloponnesus have such outlets. Lakes Hylicé and Trephia, in Bœotia are believed to have similar outlets.

Greece has many small lakes. The largest is Lake Copaïs, in Bœotia, which is estimated to have an area of forty-one square miles. The next in size is probably Bœbeïs, in Thessaly, formed chiefly by the overflowings of the river Peneus. On the southern shore of Lake Pambotis, in Epirus, was the oracular shrine of Dodona. Lakes Trichonis and Conopé were in Ætolia, between the Evenus and Acheloüs. Lake Nessonis was near Lake Bœbeïs, in Thessaly. Lake Xynias was in Achæa Phthiotis. Lakes Hylicé and Trephia were in Bœotia. Lakes Pheneus, Stymphalus, Orchomenus, Mantinea and Tegea, in Arcadia.

The littoral islands of Greece were numerous and important. The largest of these was Eubœa, which lay along the entire eastern coast of Africa, Bœotia and Locris, from which it is separated by a long, narrow strait or channel. It is more than one hundred miles long, with an average width of about fifteen miles. The island next in size to Eubœa was Corcyra, off the opposite, or western coast of the peninsula, which was about forty miles long and from five to fifteen miles wide. Other islands off the west coast were Paxos, Leucas, or Leucadia, Ithaca, Cephallenia and Zacynthus (now

Zante). Off the southern coast were Œnussæ and Cythera. Off the eastern coast were Tiparenus, Hydria, Calauria, Ægina, Salamis, Cythnus, Ceos, Helené, Andros, Scyros, Peparethus, Halonnesus and Sciathus. The Cyclades and the Sporades extend in a continuous series, across the Ægean Sea to Asia Minor. On the western side, from Corcyra and the Acroceraunian promontory, the opposite coast of Italy can be seen on a clear day.

Greece is naturally divided into Northern, Central and Southern Greece. Northern Greece extends from the northern limits of the peninsula to the points where the Gulf of Malis indents the eastern shores, and the Gulf of Ambracia, or Actium, the western shores. Central Greece extends from these latter limits south to the isthmus of Corinth. Southern Greece embraces the peninsula south of the Gulf of Corinth, which peninsula was anciently known as the Peloponnesus (now the Morea).

In ancient times Northern Greece embraced the two chief states of Thessaly and Epirus, separated from each other by the lofty chain of Mount Pindus. On the eastern side of this mountain barrier were the smaller states of Magnesia and Achæa Phthiotis. In the mountain region itself, midway between the two gulfs, was Dolopia, or the country of the Dolopes.

Thessaly, the most fertile country, was nearly identical with the basin of the Peneus, being a region of almost circular shape and seventy miles in diameter. It was surrounded on all sides by mountains, from which numerous streams descended, all of which converged and flowed into the Peneus. The combined waters reached the sea through a single narrow gorge, the famous Vale of Tempé, said to have been caused by an earthquake. Thessaly was divided into four provinces—Perrhæbia on the north, along the borders of Mount Olympus and the Cambunians; Histiæotis, towards the west, on the sides of Mount Pindus, and along the upper course of the Peneus; Thessaliotis, towards the south, bordering on Achæa Phthiotis and Dolopia; and Pelasgiotis, towards the east, between the Enipeus and Magnesia. The principal towns of Thessaly were Gonni and Phalanna, in Perrhæbia; Gomphi and Tricca, in Histiæotis; Cierium and Pharsalus, or Pharsalia, in Thessaliotis; Larissa and Pheræ, in Pelasgiotis.

Epirus, the other principal country of Northern Greece, had an oblong-square shape, seventy miles long from north to south, and about fifty-five across from east to west. It was chiefly mountainous, and contained a series of lofty chains, twisted spurs from the Pindus range, having narrow valleys between, along the courses of the numerous streams.

The chief divisions were Molossis in the east, Chaonia in the north-west, and Thesprotia in the south-west. The principal cities were Dodona and Ambracia, in Molossis; Phœnicé, Buthrotum and Cestria, in Chaonia; Pandosia, Cassope, and, in later times, Nicopolis, in Thesprotia. During the entire historical period Epirus was more Illyrian than Greek.

Magnesia and Achæa Phthiotis were sometimes considered parts of Thessaly, but in the earlier period they constituted separate countries. Magnesia was the tract along the coast between the mouth of the Peneus and the Pagasæan Gulf, embracing the two connected ranges of Mounts Ossa and Pelion, with the country just at their base. It was sixty-five miles long, and from ten to fifteen miles wide. Its principal cities were Myræ, Melibœa and Casthanæa upon the eastern coast; Iolcus, in the Gulf of Pagasæ; and Bœbé, near Lake Bœbeïs, in the interior. Achæa Phthiotis was the region just south of Thessaly, extending from the Pagasæan Gulf on the east to the portion of Pindus occupied by the Dolopes. It was a tract almost square in shape, each side of the square measuring about thirty miles. It embraced Mount Othrys, with the country at its base. The principal cities were Halos, Thebæ Phthiotides, Itonus, Melitæ, Lamia and Xyniæ, on Lake Xynias.

Dolopia, the country of the Dolopes, included a portion of the Pindus range, with the more western part of Othrys, and the upper valleys of several streams which ran into the Acheloüs. It was a small region, being only about forty miles long by fifteen miles wide, and was exceedingly rugged and mountainous.

Central Greece, the tract located between Northern Greece and the Peloponnesus, contained eleven countries — Acarnania, Ætolia, Western Locris, Æniania, Doris, Malis, Eastern Locris, Phocis, Bœotia, Attica and Megaris.

Acarnania was the most western of these countries, and was a triangular tract, bounded on the north by the Ambracian Gulf, on the east by the Acheloüs, and on the south-west by the Adriatic. The northern side was fifty miles long, the eastern side thirty-five miles, and the south-western side thirty miles. Its leading cities were Stratus in the interior, and Anactorium, Solium, Astacus and Œniadæ on the coast.

Ætolia bordered Acarnania on the east and extended in that direction as far as Æniania and Doris. It was bounded on the north by Delopia, and on the south by the Corinthian Gulf. It was twice as large as Acarnania, and its area was considerably more than that of any other country in this part of Hellas. It was mainly mountainous, but contained a flat and marshy tract between the mouths of the Evenus and the Acheloüs; and further north was a large plain, in which were Lakes Conopé and Trichonis. Its chief cities were Pleuron, Calydon and Thermon.

Western Locris, the country of the Locri Ozolæ, lay along the coast of the Corinthian Gulf, just east of Ætolia. It was about thirty-seven miles long along the coast, and from two to twenty-three miles wide. Its chief cities were Naupactus, on the coast, and Amphissa, in the interior.

Æniania, or Ætæa, also lay east of Ætolia, but towards the north, while Locris adjoined it towards the south. Æniania was separated from Ætolia by the Pindus range, and was bounded on the north by Mount Othrys, and on the south by Mount Œta. It thus lay on the upper course of the Spercheius river. It was oval-shaped, and about twenty-seven miles long by eighteen miles wide. The principal town was Hypata.

Doris was located between Æniania and Western Locris. It was a small and rugged country, enclosed between Mounts Parnassus and Callidromus, on the upper course of the Pindus river, a tributary of the Bœotian Cephissus. Its greatest length was about seventeen miles, and its greatest width about ten miles. Its principal cities were Pindus, Erineus, Bœum and Cytinium, and it was on this account known as the Dorian Tetrapolis.

Malis lay north of Doris, south of Achæa Phthiotis, and east of Æniania. It resembled Doris in shape, but was smaller. Its greatest length was about fifteen miles, and its greatest width about eight miles. Its chief cities were Anticyra and Trachis, and in later times, Heraclea. The famous pass of Thermopylæ was at the extreme eastern end of Malis, between the mountains and the sea.

Eastern Locris lay next to Malis, along the coast of the Euripus, or Eubœan channel. Its political divisions were Epicnemidia and Opuntia. These in later times were naturally divided by a small strip of land regarded as belonging to Phocis. Epicnemidia extended about seventeen miles, from near Thermopylæ to near Daphnus, with an average width of eight miles. Cnemides was its principal town. Opuntia extended from Alôpé to beyond the mouth of the Cephissus, a distance of about twenty-six miles. It was about as broad as Epicnemidia. Its name was derived from Opus, its leading city.

Phocis extended from Eastern Locris on the north to the Corinthian Gulf on the south. It was bounded on the east by Bœotia, and on the west by Doris and Western Locris. It was square in shape, with an average length of twenty-five miles and an average breadth of twenty miles. The central and southern parts were very mountainous, but there were some fertile plains along the course of the Cephissus and its tributaries. The principal cities were Delphi, on the south side of Mount Parnassus, Elatæa,

Parapotamii, Panopeus, Abæ, renowned for its temple, and Hyampolis.

Bœotia was more than twice as large as Phocis, being fifty miles long, with an average breadth of twenty-three miles. It was mainly flat and marshy, but contained the Helicon mountain range on the south, and the hills known as Mounts Ptoüs, Messapius, Hypatus and Teumessus, towards the more eastern part of the country. Lake Copaïs occupied an area of forty-one square miles, or more than one-thirtieth of the surface. Lakes Hylicé and Trephia were between Lake Copaïs and the Eubœan Sea. The principal rivers of Bœotia were the Cephissus, which entered the country from Phocis, the Asopus, the Termessus, the Thespius and the Oëroë. Bœotia was celebrated for its many great cities, the chief which was Thebes. The other important cities were Orchomenus, Thespiæ, Tanagra, Coronæa, Lebedeia, Haliartus, Chæroneia, Leuctra and Copæ.

Attica was the peninsula projecting from Bœotia to the south-east. It was seventy miles long from Cithæron to Sunium. Its greatest breadth, from Munychia to Rhamnus, was thirty miles. Its area has been estimated at seven hundred and twenty square miles, about three-fourths of that of Bœotia. The general character of the region was mountainous and sterile. On the north Mounts Cithæron, Parnes and Phelleus constituted a continuous line running almost east and west. From this range three spurs descended. Mount Kerata, which divided Attica from Megaris; Mount Ægaleos, separating the plain of Eleusis from that of Athens; and Mount Pentelicus in the north, Mount Hymettus in the center, and Mount Anhydrus near the southern coast. Athens was the only important city of Attica. Marathon, famous for the first Greek victory over the Persians, was a small town twenty miles north-east of Athens. The rivers of Attica—the two Cephissuses, the Ilissus, the Erasinus and the Charadrus —were not much more than torrent-courses.

Megaris, adjoining Attica on the west, occupied the northern part of the Isthmus of Corinth, which connected Central Greece with the Peloponnesus. It was the smallest country of Central Greece, excepting Doris and Malis, being about fourteen miles long by eleven miles wide, and embracing less than one hundred and fifty square miles. Its only city was Magara, with the ports of Nisæa and Pegæ.

Southern Greece, or the peninsula of the Poloponnesus, comprised eleven countries— Corinth, Sicyon, Achæa, Elis, Arcadia, Messenia, Laconia, Argolis, Epidauria, Trœzenia and Hermionis.

The territory of Corinth adjoined Megaris and embraced the greater part of the isthmus, along with a larger tract in the Peloponnesus. Its greatest length was twenty-five miles, and its greatest width was about twenty-three miles. It had a very irregular shape, and its area was about two hundred and thirty square miles. The only important city was Corinth, the capital, whose ports were Lechæum, on the Corinthian Gulf, and Cenchreæ, on the Saronic Gulf.

Sicyon, or Sicyonia, adjoined Corinth on the west. It was situated along the shore of the Corinthian Gulf for a distance of about fifteen miles, and was about twelve or thirteen miles wide. Sicyon was its only city.

Achæa, or Achaia, was next to Sicyon, and extended along the coast for a distance of about sixty-five miles. Its average width was about ten miles, and its area about six hundred and fifty square miles. It had twelve cities, of which Dymé, Patræ (now Patras) and Pellené stand first in importance.

Elis lay on the west coast of the Peloponnesus, extending from the mouth of the Larisus to that of the Neda, a distance of fifty-seven miles, and reaching from the coast inland to the foot of Mount Erymanthus about twenty-five miles. It was one of the most level parts of Greece, comprising wide tracts of plain along the coast, and valleys of considerable width along the courses of the Peneus, and Alpheus and the Neda rivers. Its principal cities were Elis, on the Peneus, the port of Cyllêné, on the gulf of the same name, Olympia and Pisa, on the

Alpheus, and Lepreum, in Southern Elis.

Arcadia was the mountain land in the center of the Peloponnesus. It extended from Mounts Erymanthus, Aroania and Cyllene, in the north, to the sources of the Alpheus towards the south, a distance of about sixty miles. The average width of this country was about forty miles. The area was about seventeen hundred square miles. The country was chiefly a mountainous table-land, the rivers of which, excepting towards the west and south-west, are absorbed in subterranean passages and have no visible outlet to the sea. There are many high plains and small lakes, but the far greater portion of the country is occupied by mountains and narrow though fertile valleys. There were many important cities, among which were Mantinea, Tegea, Orchomenus, Pheneus, Heræa, Psophis, and in later times, Megalopolis.

Messenia lay south of Elis and Western Arcadia, occupied the most westerly of the three southern peninsulas of the Peloponnesus, and circled round the gulf between this peninsula and the central one to the mouth of the Chœrius river. It was forty-five miles long from the Neda river to the promontory of Acritas, and its greatest width between Laconia and the western coast was thirty-seven miles. The area of the country was about eleven hundred and sixty square miles. A considerable portion was mountainous; but along the course of the Pamisus, the chief stream of this country, there were some broad plains, and the whole region was fertile. Stenyclerus was the original capital, but subsequently Messêné, on the south-western flank of Mount Ithômé, was the principal city. The other important towns were Eira, on the upper Neda, Pylus (now Navarino), and Methôné, south of Pylus (now Modon).

Laconia comprised the other two southern peninsulas of the Peloponnesus, along with a considerable region to the north of them. Its greatest length between Argolis and the promontory of Malea was almost eighty miles, and its greatest width was nearly fifty miles. Its area was almost nineteen hundred square miles. The country embraced chiefly the narrow valley of the Eurotas, which was enclosed between the lofty mountain chains of Parnon and Taygetus. Hence the expression, "Hollow Lacedæmon." Sparta, the capital, was situated on the Eurotas river, about twenty miles from the sea. The other towns were Gythium and Thyrea, on the coast, and Sellacia, in the Ænus valley.

Argolis was the name sometimes assigned to the entire region extending eastward from Achæa and Arcadia, excepting the small territory of Corinth; but Argolis proper was bounded by Sicyonia and Corinthia on the north, by Epidaurus on the east, by Cynuria, a part of Laconia, on the south, and by Arcadia on the west. Its greatest extent from north to south was about thirty miles, and from east to west about thirty-one miles. Its whole area was not over seven hundred square miles. It was mountainous, like the other portions of the Peloponnesus, but included a large and fertile plain at the head of the Gulf of Argolis. Its early capital was Mycenæ. Argolis subsequently became the chief city. The other important cities were Philus, Cleonæ and Tiryns. Nauplia was the port of Argos.

Epidauria lay east of Argolis, and east and south of Corinthia. It was about twenty-three miles long from north to south, and about eight miles wide from east to west. Its only important city was Epidaurus, the capital.

Trœzenia lay just south-east of Epidauria. It embraced the north-eastern half of the peninsula of Argolis, along with the rocky peninsula of Methana. Its greatest length was sixteen miles, and its greatest breadth, without Methana, was nine miles. Its only important cities were Trœzen and Methana.

Hermionis lay immediately north of Epidauria and east of Trœzenia. It constituted the western end of the peninsula of Argolis. It was about as large as Trœzenia and its only important town was Hermioné.

Besides the littoral islands already noted, there were several others, in the Ægean Sea, deserving mention. These were Lemnos,

Imbrus, Thasos and Samothrace, in the north of the Ægean; Tenos, Syros, Gyarus, Delos, Myconus, Naxos, Paros, Siphnus, Melos, Thera, Amorgus, etc., in the Central Ægean; besides the littoral islands of Andros, Ceos and Cythnus; and Crete, to the south of the Ægean. Crete was one hundred and fifty miles long from east to west, with an average width of about fifteen miles from north to south. Its area was considerably over two thousand square miles. Its principal cities were Cydonia and Gnossus, on the northern coast, and Gortyna, in the interior. The entire island was mountainous though fertile.

The Greek islands off the coast of Asia Minor will be described in subsequent sections of this chapter.

SECTION II.—EARLY LEGENDS AND TRADITIONS.

THE early history of Greece embraces legends, traditions and fables covering the period from about B. C. 1856, to about B. C. 1100. The native Grecian sources are Homer's two great epic poems, the Iliad and the Odyssey, which, whatever their real origin may be, must ever remain the chief authority for the primeval condition of Greece. Modern criticism coincides with ancient in regarding them as the most ancient remains of Grecian literature that have been transmitted; and if their real date was about B. C. 850, as now generally believed, they must be considered as the only authority in Grecian history for almost four centuries.

Another native Grecian authority was Herodotus, who, though writing chiefly about the great Persian War, gave a sketch of previous Grecian history to the most remote antiquity, and was a reliable authority for the antiquities of his own and contemporaneous nations. Thucydides was also a great Greek authority. The opening sketch of his history gives the opinions of enlightened Athenians of the fourth century before Christ concerning the antiquities of Greece. Diodorus Siculus gathered from previous writers, especially from Ephorus and Timæus, the early traditional and legendary history of Greece, and related it in his fourth, fifth, sixth and seventh books; of which the fourth and fifth remain, the other two being lost, excepting a few fragments.

Much interesting and valuable information of primitive Grecian history is given us by the ancient geographers, especially such as Strabo, Pausanias and Scymus Chius. Plutarch's Lives treat of but one character of this early period—Theseus.

Among celebrated modern writers on ancient Greece may be mentioned the eminent Germans, Heeren, Niebuhr, Curtius and Müller; and the English authors Clinton, Mitford, Thirlwall and Grote.

The value attaching to the early historical narrative will depend on the opinion formed regarding the probability of oral traditions transmitting correctly the general outline of important national events, and likewise on the question as to what time the historical events began to be contemporaneously recorded by the Greeks in inscriptions or otherwise.

The Greeks of the historical period appear to have had no traditions concerning a migration of their ancestors from Asia. They believed their forefathers had always been in the country, though they had not always been called *Hellenes*, which was the name by which the Greeks called themselves. They called their country *Hellas*. The names *Greece* and *Greek*, or *Grecian*, were originated by the Romans. Greece had been inhabited from very early times by races mainly homogeneous and chiefly allied with their own people. These were the Pelasgi, the Leleges, the Curêtés, the Caucones, the Aones, the Dolopes, the Dryopes and others. The Pelasgi were the most important of all these early tribes. They were savages, feeding on roots and acorns, and clothing themselves with the skins of beasts. All these tribes were pure Aryans, being thus related with the Hindoos, the Medes and Persians, and the different nations of Europe, which had migrated from their primeval homes in Central Asia in prehistoric times.

The Hellenes proper had originally been but one tribe out of many cognate Aryan nations. They had inhabited Achæa Phthiotis or the country near Dodona, and had originally been insignificant in numbers and of little importance. But in the course of time they became more famous than any of the other tribes. They were consulted and appealed to for aid in times of difficulty. Other tribes adopted their name, their language and their civilization. The Hellenes developed and diffused themselves by their influence and not by conquest. They did not subdue or expel the Pelasgi, the Leleges or other tribes, but by degrees assimilated them.

The Pelasgic or ante-Hellenic period of Greece was characterized by general peace and was the golden age of the Greek poets. The general pursuit was agriculture. The Pelasgic architecture was massive and not much ornamented. The religion was simple, and there were no distinct names of gods. The national sanctuary was at Dodona.

There were only two original Hellenic tribes, the Achæans and the Dorians. The Achæans were in the ascendant in early times. They had occupied Achæa Phthiotis from a very early period, and were the most important race of the Peloponnesus before the Dorian occupation. They are said to have had three kingdoms in the Peloponnesus—those of Argos, Mycenæ and Sparta—all of which had reached a considerable degree of civilization and prosperity. The Dorians were said to have dwelt originally in Achæa Phthiotis with the Achæans; but the earliest discovered home was the region of Upper Pindus, which was called Doris until the Roman period. In this "small and sad region" the Dorians became great, increased their population, acquired warlike habits, and developed a peculiar discipline.

The Ionians were the most important Pelasgic tribe, and in early times they occupied the entire northern coast of the Peloponnesus, Magaris, Attica and Eubœa. The Æolians were another Pelasgic tribe, and embraced the Thessalians, the Bœotians, the Ætolians, the Locrians, the Phocians, the Eleans, the Pylians and others.

The Achæans, the Dorians, the Ionians and the Æolians by degrees became Hellenized, and the whole four tribes came to be considered Hellenic. A mystic genealogy was framed to express the race unity and the tribal diversity of the four great branches of the Hellenic nation Thus Hellen was the mythical ancestor of the entire Hellenic race, and his three sons were Dorus, Xuthus and Æolus. Xuthus is said to have had two sons, Achæus and Ion. Thus the Greeks supposed themselves to have been descended from Hellen through his sons, Dorus and Æolus, and his grandsons, Achæus and Ion; these sons and grandsons being regarded as the ancestors respectively of the Dorians, the Æolians, the Achæans and the Ionians.

According to the Greek traditions, some foreign elements became fused into the Hellenic nation during this early period. Thus Inachus, a Phœnician, was said to have founded Argos, the oldest city in Greece, in B. C. 1856. Three hundred years later, B. C. 1556, Cecrops, an Egyptian, was said to have founded in Attica a city which he named Athens, in honor of the goddess Athênê, or Pallas, the Minerva of the Romans.

Corinth was said to have been founded in B. C. 1520. The Egyptian Lelex is reputed to have laid the foundations of the celebrated city of Sparta, in Laconia, or Lacedæmon, about B. C. 1520. Thebes, the famous capital of Bœotia, with its celebrated citadel, the Cadmæa, was believed to have been founded about the year B. C. 1493 by the Phœnician Cadmus, who was said to have introduced letters into Greece. In the year B. C. 1485 Danaus, an Egyptian, was reputed to have arrived at Argos with his fifty daughters, and to have taught the people to dig wells. About the year B C. 1350 Pelops, a Phrygian prince, was said to have migrated to the peninsula of Southern Greece, which was thereafter named in his honor *Peloponnesus*, or the Island of Pelops.

Inachus, Cecrops, Lelex, Cadmus, Danaus and Pelops were all fabulous personages, and the accounts given of them by the early Greeks are regarded as entirely mythical. Modern authorities consider Cecrops as simply a Pelasgian hero. The accounts of Inachus and Danaus settling at Argos are regarded as pure fables. Modern writers accept the account of Cadmus coming to Thebes and teaching letters to the inhabitants as mainly true, as the Greeks evidently derived their alphabet from Phœnicia; but it is questioned whether he built Thebes or founded the Cadmea. The name and form of the Greek alphabet, and the early intercourse between Greece and Phœnicia, lend probability to the account that the Greeks derived their alphabet from the Phœnicians. Although writing was not much used for several centuries after its introduction, yet its occasional employment for public purposes was a very important check upon the strange tendencies of oral tradition, and paved the way for a more authentic record of Grecian history.

Inscriptions on the offerings in the temple, and registers of the succession of kings and priests, were some of the oldest historical documents in Greece; and though we have no positive proof that they went back to the first period, there is no evidence to contradict it, and many of the ablest historical critics believe that the Greeks used writing in public matters at this early period.

Though the civilization of the Egyptian and Phœnician settlers in Greece was higher than that of the Greeks themselves, and though some benefits were derived by the Greeks from these foreign sources, it is clearly evident that Hellenic civilization did not receive its general character and direction from these foreign influences, as the foreign colonists were comparatively few in number and were absorbed into the Hellenic nation without leaving any distinct trace of themselves upon the Grecian language, customs or religion. Thus Greek civilization was mainly an indigenous product of Hellas itself—a native development of the Hellenic race. Even the ideas adopted from foreign sources became so stamped with the Grecian character that they acquired the characteristics of originality. Thus the Greeks developed their own civilization—a civilization totally different from the Oriental or the Egyptian—a civilization stamped with ideas on the subjects of art, politics, morals and religion, which raised them far in advance of every other ancient nation, and wherein was found the first assertion of the right of man to self-government. In Greece were the first experiments in democracy made.

We will now pass to the legends and myths of early Grecian history. The fabulous characters of the Heroic Age were Hercules, the great national hero of Greece; Theseus, the civilizer of Attica; and Minos, the Cretan lawgiver. The famous *Argonautic Expedition*, undertaken by Jason of Thessaly to recover the "*Golden Fleece*," which had been carried to Colchis, and the *Trojan War*, so celebrated in Homer's Iliad, are among the great legendary events of the Heroic Age.

Hercules was celebrated among the Greeks for his wonderful feats of strength, as Samson had been among the Hebrews. Hercules was reputed to be the son of Zeus and Alcmena, the wife of Amphitryon, King of Thebes. While yet an infant in his cradle, he is said to have strangled two huge serpents which the goddess Here had sent to destroy him. The "Twelve Labors of Hercules" were the following: 1. He killed the Nemean lion by putting his arms around his neck, and wore his skin in the remainder of his exploits. He slew the Lernean hydra, a nine-headed serpent, whose heads grew on as fast as cut off, and which was destroyed when Hercules seared its neck with a hot iron. 3. He brought the Erymanthean boar upon his shoulders to Eurystheus. 4. He subdued the golden-horned and brazen-hoofed stag of Artemis, or Diana. 5. He destroyed the foul Stymphalian birds with his arrows. 6. He cleansed the Augean stables of the King of Elis, which had remained uncleansed for thirty years, by turning into them a river which flowed close by.

THE FARNESE HERCULES.

7. He tamed the furious bull of Crete. 8. He gave Diomedes to be devoured by his own horses. 9. He vanquished the Amazons. 10. He killed the three-headed, six-legged and six-armed Geryon, King of Gades, now Cadiz, in Spain, and brought his oxen to Greece. 11. He killed the hundred-headed dragon of the Hesperides, and obtained the golden apples of his garden. 12. He dragged the three-headed dog Cerberus from the gate of Hades, into which he descended twice. It is also related that Hercules separated Spain from Africa, and connected the Mediterranean Sea with the Atlantic Ocean by heaping up a mountain on each side. These mountains were named the Pillars of Hercules (now Straits of Gibraltar). Hercules killed the centaur Nessus with an arrow poisoned with the blood of the Lernean hydra, because the centaur had insulted the hero's wife, Dejanira. The dying centaur persuaded Dejanira to give a tunic dipped in his blood to her husband in reconciliation; but as soon as Hercules clothed himself in this garment he was poisoned by it, and perished in the flames of a funeral pile which he had built on Mount Œta. Zeus received him as a god, and gave to him in marriage Hebe, the goddess of youth. Hercules is usually represented as a robust man, leaning on his club, wearing the skin of the Nemean lion on his shoulders, and holding the Hesperian fruit in his hands.

In the time of Hercules, Jason, a prince of Thessaly, went on the celebrated Argonautic Expedition, so called from the ship Argo, in which he sailed. The following is the story of the Argonautic Expedition, according to the Greek poets. Phryxus, a Theban prince, and his sister Helle, being obliged to leave their native country to escape the cruelty of their step-mother, mounted the back of a winged ram with a golden fleece, to be conveyed to Colchis, a country on the eastern border of the Euxine, or Black Sea, where an uncle of theirs was king. While passing over the strait now called the Dardanelles, Helle became giddy, fell into the water, and was drowned; whence the strait received the name of Hellespont, or Sea of Helle. Phryxus arrived safely in Colchis, and sacrificed his winged ram to Jupiter, in acknowledgment of Divine protection, and put the golden fleece into that deity's temple. He was afterwards murdered by his uncle, who wished to obtain the golden fleece. It was to avenge the death of Phryxus and to secure the golden fleece

AMAZONS.

DEATH OF KING PRIAM.

THE VICTORIOUS GREEKS RETURNING FROM TROY.

LAOCOON GROUP (VATICAN).

THE WOODEN HORSE OF TROY.

EARLY LEGENDS AND TRADITIONS. 553

that Jason undertook the Argonautic Expedition. Jason obtained the golden fleece and married Media, a daughter of the King of Colchis.

The most important event of the early period of Grecian history was the famous Trojan War, the knowledge of which we derive chiefly from Homer's Iliad. The beautiful Helen, wife of Menelaüs, King of Sparta, was carried away by Paris, son of Priam, king of Troy, or Ilium, in Asia Minor. The Greek princes, indignant at this outrage, and bound by a previous promise, assembled their armies, and having appointed Agamemnon, one of their number, commander-in-chief, crossed the Ægean Sea, and laid siege to Troy (B. C. 1194). The chief of the Greek leaders besides Agamemnon, were Achilles of Thessaly and Ulysses of Ithaca. During the siege of Troy many bold exploits are said to have been performed by both. Of these exploits the most celebrated was the killing of the Trojan Hector by the Grecian Achilles. Finally, after a siege of ten years, Troy was taken by a stratagem of Ulysses. The Greeks, after having constructed a large wooden horse, filled it with soldiers, and then retiring a short distance, pretended to abandon the siege. The Trojans then brought the wooden horse into the city. During the night the Greek soldiers got out of the wooden horse and opened the gates of the city, which was then entered by the Grecian army. Troy was reduced to ashes, and its inhabitants were driven away or put to death (B. C. 1184). But the conquerors met with many misfortunes: Achilles died in Troy; Ulysses wandered about for ten years before he was enabled to reach his native shores; and Agamemnon was murdered by his own faithless wife, Clytemnestra, who had formed an attachment for another person in his absence.

THE ARGONAUTS.

In Homer's poetical narrative the gods are represented as participating in the struggle. Modern historians have doubted whether such a city as Troy ever existed, and the story of the Trojan War consequently receives little credence from them. In recent years, however, some remarkable discoveries have been made in the Troad which may perhaps aid in settling this uncertainty. A series of extensive explorations have been conducted by Dr. Schliemann upon the reputed site of ancient Troy, and his excavations have disclosed the remains of a city dating evidently more than a thousand years before Christ. These ruins lie from twenty-three to thirty-three feet below the surface of the earth, and seem to bear marks of a destructive conflagration. Many articles of domestic use, arms, ornaments, etc., have been unearthed by Dr. Schlieman. This would appear to prove at least that an ancient city existed on the site assigned by Homer to Troy, and that the ancient city to which the ruins belong was destroyed by fire, but it has not been proven beyond a doubt that the city was Troy.

Homer describes the social and political condition of Greece during the Heroic Age with very great precision. The country was not united under one general government, but was divided into many independent states, each governed by its own king.

These petty sovereigns exercised patriarchal rather than regal authority, and were responsible only to Zeus for the exercise of their power, as they claimed to be the descendants of the gods themselves, and received their authority from them.

In war the kings were the sole commanders of their respective armies. In peace they were the judges and priests of the people, administering justice among them, and offering prayers and sacrifices to the

CAPTURE OF HELEN.

Menelaus. Paris. Diomedes. Odysseus. Nestor. Achilles. Agamemnon.
HEROES OF THE TROJAN WAR.

gods. Though the kingly authority was acknowledged by the people, they required a personal superiority in the king over them as a condition of obedience to him. He was expected to display personal bravery in war, wisdom in council, and eloquence in debate. As long as he exhibited these high qualities, his right to govern them was recognized by every one, and even his caprices and violence did not encounter any opposition. When he manifested bodily or mental weakness his authority began to decline.

which they themselves cultivated. A poorer class, who were not land-owners, seem to have worked on the lands of others for pay. The seer, the bard and the herald belonged to the class of common freemen, but their attainments gave them a rank above that of their fellows, and made them respected by the nobles. The carpenters formed other classes, as only a few possessed a knowledge of the mechanical arts. The nobles only were slaveowners. There were not so many of them as in later times, and they were better treated

ULYSSES RELATING HIS WANDERINGS TO PENELOPE.

The Greeks at this early period were divided into three distinct classes—nobles, common freemen and slaves. The nobles claimed descent from the gods, as did the king. They were very rich and powerful, possessing great estates and numerous slaves. They were the leaders of the people in war. According to Homer, these chiefs did the fighting, the common soldiers being frequently only spectators of the conflict. The freemen appear to have owned the lands

at this early day than in after times. A very kindly relation at this time existed between masters and slaves.

The family relations in primeval Greece occupied a prominent place in the social system. The authority of parents was highly reverenced, and a father's curse was dreaded above everything else. All the members of a family or clan were united by the closest ties, and were bound to avenge any injury offered any individual of their clan. In the early period of Greece women held a more exalted position than in later times. The wife and mother was regarded as holding a position of great dignity and influence, notwithstanding the fact that wives were purchased by their husbands. All classes were solemnly enjoined to be hospitable. Strangers were cordially welcomed, and were given the best that the house afforded before being asked about their names or business. A stranger who sought protection had even a stronger claim upon the host, even if it brought the host into difficulty, as it was believed that Zeus would mercilessly punish any man who would not grant the request of a suppliant.

IDEAL BUST OF HOMER.

The manners of this primitive age were very simple. Labor was deemed honorable, and the kings did not consider it beneath their dignity to engage in it. Ulysses is said to have built his own bed-chamber, and to have made his raft, and boasted of his skill in ploughing and mowing. The people's food was simple, and consisted of beef, mutton, goat's flesh, cheese, wheat bread, and sometimes fruits. Wine was used, but there was no intemperance. The chiefs were proud of their excellence in cooking. The wives and daughters of kings and nobles engaged in spinning and weaving. They likewise brought water from the well, and aided their slaves in washing garments in the river.

The ancient heroes were, however, fierce and unrelenting in war. The more powerful chief plundered and maltreated his weaker neighbor. Piracy was considered honorable. Bloodshed was the order of the day. Quarter was seldom given to a vanquished enemy. The arms of the defeated foe became the trophy of the victor. The naked body of a fallen antagonist was cast out to the birds of prey. Homer represents Achilles as sacrificing twelve hundred human victims on the tomb of Patroclus.

As already said the Greeks of the Heroic Age lived in fortified cities, surrounded by strong walls and adorned with palaces and temples. The nobles had magnificent and costly houses, ornamented with gold, silver and bronze. Their dress in peace was costly and elegant. They wore highly-wrought armor in war. They were supplied with everything they did not themselves produce by the Phœnicians. The massive ruins of Mycenæ and Tiryns belong to this period, and furnish abundant proof of the strength and splendor of the cities of Greece during the Heroic Age. The arts of sculpture and design had considerably advanced. Poetry was also cultivated, but it is not very certain that writing was yet known.

Important movements of the chief races appear to have occurred near the end of the Heroic Age of Grecian history. These probably originated in the pressure of the Illyrians, perhaps the ancestors of the modern Albanians. The tribes west of the Pindus were always considered less Hellenic than those east of that range, and the Illyrian element in that region was greater than the Grecian. The Trojan War, if it actually occurred, may have been the result of Illyrian pressure upon the Greek tribes; and the Greeks may have sought a vent for an overcrowded population in the most accessible portion of Asia Minor. The same cause may have operated to produce the great movement which began in Epirus about B. C. 1200, and which caused a general migration of the populations of Northern and Central Hellas. Starting from Thesprotia, in Epirus, the Thessalians crossed the Pindus mountain-range, descended on the fertile valley of the Peneus, drove out the Bœotians, and occupied the country. The Bœotians proceeded westward over Mounts Othrys and Œta into the plain of Cephissus, drove out the Cadmeians and the Minyans, and seized the territory which received its name from them. The Cadmeians and the Minyans dispersed, and sought refuge in Attica, in Laconia, and in other parts of Greece. The Dorians at the same time left their original seats and overran Dryopis, to which they gave the name of Doris, and from which they drove the Dryopians, who fled by sea, finding a refuge in Eubœa, in Cythnus, and in the Peloponnesus.

About B. C. 1100 another movement of Grecian tribes occurred. The Dorians, overcrowded in the narrow valleys between Mounts Œta and Parnassus, formed an alliance with their neighbors, the Ætolians, crossed the Corinthian Gulf at the narrowest point, between Rhium and Antirrhium, and overspread the Peloponnesus, where they successively subdued Elis, Messenia, Laconia and Argolis. Elis was assigned to the Ætolians, and Dorian kingdoms were established in Messenia, Laconia and Argolis. The Achæans, who had previously occupied these countries, partly yielded, and partly fled northward and settled themselves on the northern coast of the Peloponnesus, expelling the Ionians, who found a temporary refuge in Attica. The conquest of the Peloponnesus by the Dorians is known as *The Return of the Heraclidæ*, because the Dorians claimed that they were recovering the territories of their great ancestor, Hercules, who had been driven from the Peloponnesian peninsula a century before.

About the year 1068 B. C., the Dorians invaded Attica and threatened Athens. The Dorians having consulted the oracle of Delphi, were told that they would conquer Athens if they did not kill Codrus, the Athenian king. When Codrus was informed of the answer of the Delphic oracle, he determined to sacrifice his life for his country; and going into the Dorian camp disguised in the dress of a peasant, he provoked a quarrel with a Dorian soldier and suffered himself to be killed. When the Dorians recognized the body as that of Codrus, they retreated from Attica and gave up the contest in despair. Out of respect to the memory of Codrus, the Athenians declared that no one was worthy of succeeding him as King of Athens; and abolishing the monarchy altogether, established an aristocratic republic, the chief-magistrates of which were called *archons*. These archons were at first chosen for life from the family of Codrus. Afterwards they were appointed for ten years, and still later a senate of archons was elected annually.

These migrations and conquests led to other movements of Grecian tribes. Finding themselves overcrowded in their small continental territories of Greece proper, some of the Greeks settled in the islands of the Ægean Sea and on the western shores of Asia Minor. The Bœotian conquest of the plain of the Cephissus led to the colonization of the island of Lesbos, in the Ægean Sea, and to the first and most northern of the Greek settlements in Asia Minor, between the river Hermus and the Hellespont, in the district of Æolis, where the Æolians founded twelve cities, of which Mitylene, in the island of Lesbos, was the chief. Many of the Ionians, who had been driven from the northern coast of the Peloponnesus, sojourned for a short time in Attica; after which they passed on to the Cyclades, and thence to the islands of Chios and Samos, and to the shores of Asia Minor directly opposite, between the Hermus and the Meander, where they founded the twelve cities in the district of Ionia. After being driven from the Peloponnesus by the Dorians, many of the Achæans migrated partly to Southern Italy, but chiefly, under Doric leaders, to the islands of Cos and Rhodes, and to the coast of Caria, in the South-west of Asia Minor, where they founded the six cities of the Dorian Hexapolis.

SECTION III.—GRECIAN MYTHOLOGY AND RELIGION.

CCORDING to Grecian theogony first came Chaos, a shapeless and formless mass of matter. This is the condition in which the Greek poets supposed the world to have existed before the Almighty power brought the confused elements into order. Chaos was the consort of Darkness; and from the union of the two sprang Terra, or Gæa, or Earth, and Uranos, or Heaven. So the obscure fiction of the Grecian poets coincides with the Hebrew account given by Moses in the following words:

"And the earth was without form and void, and darkness was upon the face of the deep. And the Spirit of God moved upon the face of the waters. And God said, Let there be light, and there was light."

Gæa, or Earth, married Uranos, or Heaven. Their offspring were Titan and Kronos, or Saturn, the god of time. Titan, the elder son, gave up his dominion to his brother Kronos, who thus became King of Heaven and Earth. Kronos married his sister, Cybele, who was also known as Rhea, or Ops.

The reign of Kronos was called the golden age. The earth yielded spontaneously subsistence for its population, and war was unknown. All things were in common, and Astrea, the goddess of justice, controlled the actions of men.

But Kronos had received his kingdom from Titan on condition that he would devour all his male children, which he solemnly promised to do. His wife, Cybele, concealed from him Zeus, Poseidon and Pluto. Titan and his giant half brothers, the Titans, then made war on Kronos. Each of the Titans had fifty heads and a hundred hands. They dethroned Kronos and took him captive. His son Zeus then took up arms against the gigantic Titans.

He assembled his brothers and the other later gods on Mount Olympus. The Titans collected their forces on Mount Othrys, opposite Olympus, and the war of the gods commenced. After the war had lasted ten years Zeus called the Cyclops to his aid, and also some powerful giants whom he had released from captivity. These assisted him in the war. Mount Olympus was now shaken to its foundation. "The sea rose, the earth groaned, and the mighty forests trembled." Zeus flung his mighty thunderbolts. The lightnings flashed, and the woods blazed. The Titans attempted, in return, to storm the skies, throwing massive oaks at the heavens, piling up the mountains upon each other, and hurling them at Zeus. But Zeus flung the giants into the abyss of the earth below, and being completely triumphant, he released his father from captivity.

But Kronos was afterwards deposed by Zeus, and found refuge in Italy, where he was highly honored, becoming King of Latium, the region in which Rome was situated. He taught his subjects agriculture and other useful arts. Kronos was represented as an old man, bent with age and infirmity, and was regarded as the god of time. In his right hand he held a scythe, and in his left a child, which he was on the point of devouring. By his side was a serpent biting his own tail, which was symbolical of time and of the revolution of the year. With the expulsion of Kronos, the ancient gods were almost forgotten, and "they seemed to retreat behind mysterious clouds and mist."

The following were the twelve great deities—six gods and six goddesses—who formed the council of the great gods on Mount Olympus, presided over by Zeus. The throne of Zeus was high on the summit of this mountain, which was also the residence of the other great gods, by whom the affairs of mortals are governed. The summit of Olympus was wrapped in clouds, and the gods were thus veiled from the sight of mortals. Far above these clouds, the Greeks supposed their deities to reside "in a region of perpetual sunshine, far above and free from the storms of the lower world." Communication was had with the earth by a gate of clouds, guarded by the goddesses of the seasons. Each god had his own dwelling, but was required to go to the palace of Zeus, or Jove, when summoned. "There they feasted on ambrosia and nectar, con-

ZEUS (JUPITER).

versed upon the affairs of heaven and earth, and listened to the music of Apollo's lyre and the songs of the Muses."

After becoming the supreme god, Zeus divided the dominion of the universe with his brothers, Poseidon and Pluto, reserving heaven for himself, and assigning the sea to Poseidon and the infernal regions under the earth, Hades, to Pluto.

The six great gods of the Olympian council, presided over by Zeus, were the following: Zeus, or Jove, called Jupiter in Latin, the Supreme god; Poseidon, called Neptune in Latin, the god of the sea; Apollo, the sun-god, and the patron of music, poetry and eloquence; Arês, called Mars in Latin, the god of war; Hephaistos, called Vulcan in Latin, the god of fire and blacksmiths; Hermês, called Mercury in Latin, the herald of the gods, and the patron of commerce and wealth. The six great goddesses of the same council were Hêrê, called Juno in Latin, the great goddess of nature, and the wife and sister of Zeus; Athênê, or Pallas, called Minerva in Latin, the daughter of Zeus, and the goddess of civilization, learning and art; Artemis, called Diana in Latin, the moon-goddess and the goddess of hunting, and the twin-sister of Apollo, the sun-god; Aphroditê, called Venus in Latin, the goddess of beauty and love; Hestia, called Vesta in Latin, the goddess of domestic life; Dêmêtêr, called Cêrês in Latin, the goddess of corn and harvests.

Zeus, the father of gods and men, is said to have been born in Crete, or to have been sent there for concealment in infancy. He was the son of Kronos, the god of Time, and of Cybele, or Rhea. He was the supreme god. Everything but the decrees of Fate was subject to him.

Besides his Latin name, Jupiter, Zeus was called Jove, or "the Thunderer." The Titans disturbed the peaceful beginning of his reign by hurling rocks and heaping mountains upon mountains. They attempted to storm the skies, so that the affrighted gods fled to Egypt to escape their fury. With the aid of Hercules, Zeus conquered the Titans and hurled them down into the abyss of the earth below.

As the Greeks inconsistently attribute all the passions and vices of human beings to the gods, they frequently represent Zeus as resorting to the most unworthy artifices to accomplish the basest designs.

The Greek poets describe Zeus as a majestic personage, occupying a throne of gold and ivory, under a rich canopy, wielding a thunderbolt in one hand, and in the other a scepter of cypress. Whenever it thundered the Greeks believed that Zeus was angry and was hurling his bolts. Whenever a cloud sailed over the sky it was believed to be the chariot of Zeus. An eagle with expanded wings sits at his feet or on his scepter. He is represented with a flowing beard, with golden shoes and an embroidered cloak. The Cretans represented him without ears to signify impartiality.

"He, whose all conscious eyes the world behold,
Th' eternal thunderer, sits enthroned in gold;
High heaven the footstool of his feet he makes,
And wide beneath him all Olympus shakes."

Poseidon, the god of the sea, was the brother of Zeus, and the son of Kronos and Ops. Zeus conferred upon Poseidon the sovereignty of the sea. When the storms raged at sea and the billows rolled, the Greeks believed that Poseidon was angry and was shaking his trident. Poseidon was also supposed to manifest his rage in earthquakes. Rivers, fountains and all waters were subject to him. With a blow of his trident, he could cause islands to spring up from the bottom of the sea. He was the god of all ships and of all maritime affairs. He could raise dreadful storms which would swallow up vessels, but with a word he could still the fury of the tempest and allay the violence of the waves. During the Trojan War, Poseidon sat upon the top of a woody mountain, in the isle of Samos, and gazed upon the conflict. Seeing the Trojans victorious, his anger was aroused against Zeus. He at once arose and came down from the mountain, which trembled as he walked. He crossed the horizon in three steps, and with the fourth step he reached his place in the depths of the sea. He then mounted his chariot, and drove so rapidly over the waves that the water scarcely touched the brazen axle of his chariot. The whales and sea-monsters all rose to do him honor. The waves shook with fear, and receded respectfully as he passed.

Poseidon desired to marry Amphitrité and sent a dolphin to persuade her to become his wife. Amphitrité was the daughter of Oceanus and Hatys. To reward the dolphin for obtaining Amphitrité's consent, Poseidon placed that fish among the stars, and it became a constellation.

Poseidon was represented as a majestic god, having a grim and angry aspect. He had black hair and blue eyes, and wore a blue mantle. He sat erect in his chariot. He held his trident in his right hand. He sometimes supported his wife, Amphitrité, in his left. His chariot was a large shell, drawn by dolphins or sea-horses. He was very generally worshiped. The Libyans regarded him as the most powerful of all the gods. The famous Isthmian Games were founded in his honor by the Greeks. He was the father of Proteus and of Triton.

Apollo, the Sun-god, was the son of Zeus and Latona, and brother of the goddess Artemis. He was born in the island of Delos, whither his mother had fled to avoid the jealousy of Hêrê, the wife and sister of Zeus. He was the god of all the fine arts, and the inventor of medicine, music, poetry and eloquence. He presided over the Muses, and possessed the power of looking into futurity. His oracles were renowned throughout the world.

Apollo destroyed all of the Cyclops, who had forged the thunderbolts with which Zeus slew Esculapius, the son of Apollo. Zeus banished him from heaven for this act, and deprived him of his divinity. During his exile he hired himself as a shepherd to Admetus, King of Thessaly, on which account he is called the god of shepherds. He raised the walls of Troy by the music of his harp, and destroyed the serpent Python with his arrows.

Apollo, as the Sun-god, was called *Sol* by the Latins. He is represented as a graceful youth, having long hair, and with a laurel crown upon his head, a bow and arrows in one hand and a lyre in the other. His head is usually surrounded with beams of light. His most famous oracle was that of Delphi. He often dwelt with the Muses on Mount Parnassus.

Arês was the god of war, and the son of Zeus and Hêrê. He was educated by the god Prispus, who instructed him in all manly exercises. He did not have many temples in Greece, but the warlike Romans bestowed on him great honors, as Mars.

The wolf is consecrated to Ares for his rapacity, the dog for his vigilance in pursuing prey, the cock for his watchfulness, and the raven because he feeds on the carcasses of the slain. He is represented as an old man, with a fierce countenance, and armed with a helmet, a pike and a shield. He sits in a chariot drawn by furious horses, called Flight and Terror by the Greek poets. His sister, Bellona, the goddess of war, conducts his chariot. Discord, in a tattered garment, holding a torch in his hand, goes before them, while Clamor and Anger follow.

Hephaistos was the son of Hêrê. He was the god of fire, and the patron of all those who worked in iron or other metals. He received his education in heaven. Zeus became angry at him and hurled him from Mount Olympus. He fell on the island of Lemnos, and was maimed thereafter. He established his abode in that island, erected for himself a palace, and built forges to work metals. He forged the thunderbolts for Zeus, also the arms for the gods and demi-gods. He made the golden chambers in which the gods resided, and also their seats and their council-table, which came moving itself from the sides of the apartment. Hephaistos created Pandora, whom the Greeks believed to have been the first woman, of clay. When she had been endowed with life, all the gods presented her with precious gifts; and Zeus gave her a beautiful box, which she was to give to the man who became her husband. Pandora carried the box to Promêtheus, who refused to receive it. Thereupon she married Epimêthus. When the box which she presented to her husband was opened, a vast number of evils and distempers issued forth from it, dispersing themselves over the world, where they have remained ever since. Only Hope remained at the bottom of the box, thus enabling the human race to bear its sorrows and afflictions.

Hephaistos became reconciled to his parents, and was restored to his place on Mount Olympus. The other gods constantly laughed at his lameness and deformity. He married Aphroditê, the goddess of beauty. His forges were supposed to be under Mount Ætna, in Sicily, and actually in all parts of the world where there were volcanoes. A temple to his honor was erected on Mount Ætna, and was guarded by dogs, who had such an acute sense of smelling that they were able to distinguish the virtuous from the wicked among the visitors to the temple. The servants of Hephaistos were called Cyclops. They had only one eye, which was in the middle of the forehead. They were of immense stature. He likewise had a son named Polyhêmus, King of all the Cyclops in Sicily, who, like them, had one eye. He fed on human flesh. When Ulysses visited Sicily with twelve of his companions, Polyhêmus seized them and confined them in his cave, devouring two of them at a meal. Finally Ulysses made the monster intoxicated with wine, put out his eye with a fire-brand, and escaped. Hephaistos is generally represented at his anvil, with all his tools about him, forging a thunderbolt, with a hammer and pincers in his hand. His forehead is represented as blackened with smoke, his arms are nervous and muscular, his beard is long, and his hair disheveled. He was considered the god of blacksmiths. The fable of this god demonstrates the high esteem in which the Greeks held the art of working in metals, as they regarded it as an occupation suitable for a god. Homer thus describes Aphroditê's visit to the work-shop of Hephaistos:

"There the lame architect the goddess found,
Obscure in smoke, his forges flaming round,
While bathed in sweat, from fire to fire he flew,
And puffing loud, the roaring bellows blew.
Then from his anvil the lame artist rose,
Wide with distorted legs oblique he goes,
And stills the bellows, and in order laid,
Locks in their chest the instruments of trade;
Then with a sponge the sooty workman dressed
His brawny arms embrown'd and hairy breast;
With his huge scepter graced, and red attire,
Came halting forth, the sovereign of the fire."

Hermês was the son of Zeus, and of Maia, the daughter of Atlas. He was born upon Mount Cyllênê in Arcadia; and in his infancy he was assigned the care of the seasons. He was the messenger of the gods, more particularly of Zeus. He was the patron of travelers and shepherds. He showed the souls of the dead the way into the infernal regions. He presided over merchants and orators, and likewise over thieves and all dishonest persons. He invented letters and excelled in eloquence. He first taught the arts of buying, selling and trading. On the very day that he was born he displayed his thievish propensity by stealing the cattle of Admetus, which Apollo tended. The divine shepherd bent his bow against him, but Hermês meanwhile stole his quiver and arrows. He afterwards robbed Poseidon of his trident, Aphroditê of her girdle, Arês of his sword, Zeus of his scepter, and Hephaistos of mechanical instruments. He is represented as an old man, with a cheerful countenance. He is likewise represented with wings fastened to his cap and his sandals. He holds in his hand the caduceus, or rod, intwined with two serpents. He could awaken those who were asleep, or put those awake to sleep by a touch of his wand.

Hêrê, the queen of heaven, was the wife and sister of Zeus, and the daughter of Saturn, and of Ops, or Rhea. She was born in the isle of Samos, where she resided until her marriage with Zeus. Her children were Hephaistos, Arês and Hebe. The nuptials of Zeus and Hêrê were celebrated with the greatest solemnity. All the inhabitants of heaven and earth were spectators. The nymph Chelone refused to attend, whereupon Hermês changed her into a tortoise, and condemned her to everlasting silence. The Greek poets represent Hêrê with a majesty fully becoming her rank as queen of the skies. Her aspect is a combination of all that is lofty, graceful and magnificent. Her jealousy of Zeus, her brother and husband, and her occasional disputes with him, caused constant confusion in heaven. Zeus suspended her from the skies by a golden chain, because of her cruel treatment of Hercules. When Hephaistos came to her aid, Zeus kicked him from heaven, and his leg was broken by the fall. The worship of Hêrê was the most solemn and universal of all the Grecian divinities. Her most renowned temples were at Argos and Olympia. Her attendant and messenger was Isis, the rainbow.

Hêrê is represented as seated upon a throne, or in a golden chariot drawn by peacocks. She holds a scepter in her hand, and wears a crown of diamonds, encircled with roses and lilies. Her daughter Hebe, the goddess of youth and health, attends upon her. Hebe was the cup-bearer of Zeus, but was discharged from office on account of having fallen down while pouring

HERMÊS (MERCURY).

out nectar for the gods at a solemn festival. Ganymede was appointed in her place. Homer thus describes the chariot of Hêrê:

"At her command forth rush the steeds divine;
Rich with immortal gold, their trappings shine;
Bright Hebe waits; by Hebe, ever young,
The whirling wheels are to the chariot hung.
On the bright axle turns the bidden wheel
Of sounding brass; the polished axle steel;
Eight brazen spokes in radiant order flame;

ATHÊNÊ (MINERVA).

Such as the heavens produce; and round the gold,
Two brazen rings of work divine are rolled.
The bossy naves of solid silver shone;
Braces of gold suspend the moving throne;
The car, behind, an arching figure bore,
The bending concave formed an arch before;
Silver the beam, the extended yoke was gold,
And golden reins the immortal coursers hold."

Athênê was the goddess of wisdom, and is said to have sprung from the brain of Zeus, fully grown and completely armed. She was at once received into the assembly of the great Olympian deities, and became the faithful counselor of Zeus. She ranked as the most accomplished of all the goddesses. Athênê invented the art of spinning, and is often represented with a distaff in her hand, instead of a spear. Arachne, the daughter of a dyer, was so skillful in working with the needle that she challenged Athênê to a trial of skill. The work of Arachne was very elegant, but it did not rival that of the goddess. In despair, Arachne hanged herself, and Athênê changed her into a spider.

Athênê's countenance was usually more indicative of masculine firmness than of grace or softness. She was arrayed in complete armor, with a golden helmet, a glittering crest, and a nodding plume. She wore a golden breast-plate. She held a lance in her right hand. In her left hand she held a shield, on which was painted the dying head of Medusa, with serpents around it. Her eyes were azure blue. An olive crown was entwined around her helmet. Her principal emblems were the cock, the owl, the basilisk and the distaff. She was worshiped universally, but her most splendid temples were in the Acropolis, the citadel of Athens. One of these temples was the Parthenon, which was built of the purest white marble. In this edifice was the statue of Athênê, made of gold and ivory. It was twenty-six cubits high, and was regarded as one of the master-pieces of Phidias. The ruins of this temple are still seen at Athens, and are admired by every beholder.

Homer describes Athênê as arming herself for the combat thus:

"Now heaven's dread arms her mighty limbs invest;
Jove's cuirass blazes on her ample breast;
Decked in sad triumph for the mournful field;
O'er her broad shoulders hangs his horrid shield;
Dim, black, tremendous! round the margin rolled,
A fringe of serpents, hissing, guard the gold.
Here all the terrors of grim war appear;
Here rages fire; here tremble fright and fear;
Here stormed contention, and here fury frowned,
And the dire orb portentious Gorgon crowned.

The massive golden helm she next assumes,
That dreadful nods with four o'ershadowing plumes,
So vast, the broad circumference contains
A hundred armies on a hundred plains."

Artemis was the goddess of hunting. She was the daughter of Zeus and Latona, and was the twin-sister of Apollo. She was worshiped on earth under the name of Artemis, but was called Luna in heaven, and was invoked in Tartarus as Hecate. Artemis avoided the society of men, and retired to the woods, accompanied by sixty Oceanides, daughters of Oceanus, a powerful sea-god, and by twenty other nymphs, of whom every one, like herself, had resolved never to marry. Artemis, armed with a golden bow and lighted by a torch kindled by the lightnings of Zeus, led her nymphs through the dark forests and the woody mountains, in pursuit of the swift stag. The high mountains were said to tremble at the twang of her bow, and the forests were said to resound with the panting of the wounded deer. After the chase Artemis would hasten to Delphi, the residence of her brother, Apollo, and hang her bow and quiver upon his altar. At Delphi she would lead forth a chorus of Muses and Graces, and unite with them in singing praises to her mother, Latona. Chione, a nymph whom Apollo loved, boldly spoke with scorn of the beauty of Artemis; whereupon the offended goddess drew her bow and discharged an arrow through the nymph's tongue, thus cruelly silencing her. Œneus, a king of Calydon, sacrificed the first fruits of his fields and orchards to the gods, but he neglected to make any offering to Artemis; whereupon she sent a fierce wild boar to ravage his vineyard.

Artemis was represented as very tall and beautiful, and attired as a huntress, with a bow in one hand, a quiver of arrows hung across her shoulders, her feet covered with buskins, and a bright silver crescent on her forehead. She was also sometimes described as sitting in a silver chariot, drawn by hinds. The emblem of Artemis was the bright moon, which cast her light over the hills and the forests. Endymion, an astronomer, was said to pass the night on some lofty mountain, viewing the moon and the heavenly bodies. This gave rise to the ancient fable representing Artemis, or the moon, descending from heaven to visit the shepherd Endymion. The temple of Artemis at Ephesus was classed as one of *The Seven Wonders of the World*. A man named Erostratus, desiring to make his name immortal, even by some bad act, set fire to this magnificent edifice, which was thus burned to the ground.

Aphroditê was the goddess of love and beauty, of laughter, grace and pleasure. She is said to have risen from the froth of the sea, near the island of Cyprus. The Zephyrs wafted her to the shore, where she was received by the Seasons, the daughters of Zeus and Themis. Flowers bloomed at her feet as she walked, and the rosy Hours attired her in divine apparel. When she was conveyed to heaven, the gods, struck with her beauty, all hastened to marry her; but Zeus betrothed her to Hephaistos, the ugliest of all the deities and the most deformed. Aphroditê's power was aided by a famous girdle called *zone* by the Greeks, and *cestus* by the Latins. It possessed the power of giving grace, beauty and elegance to the wearer of it. The goddess of Discord, in revenge for not having received an invitation to the entertainment at the marriage of Peleus, King of Thessaly, with a sea-nymph, threw a golden apple into the assembly, on which was written: "For the fairest." Hêrê, Athênê and Aphroditê all claimed this as their own. As these three goddesses were unable to decide the dispute, they referred the matter to the decision of Paris, a young shepherd, who was feeding his flocks upon Mount Ida. The three goddesses sought to influence his judgment by promises and entreaties. Hêrê offered him a kingdom; Athênê, military glory; and Aphroditê, the most beautiful woman in the world for his wife. Paris decided that the golden apple belonged to Aphroditê. In pursuance of the promise of Venus, Paris afterwards got possession of Helen, the wife of Menelaüs.

DIANA (LOUVRE).

APOLLO BELVEDERE.

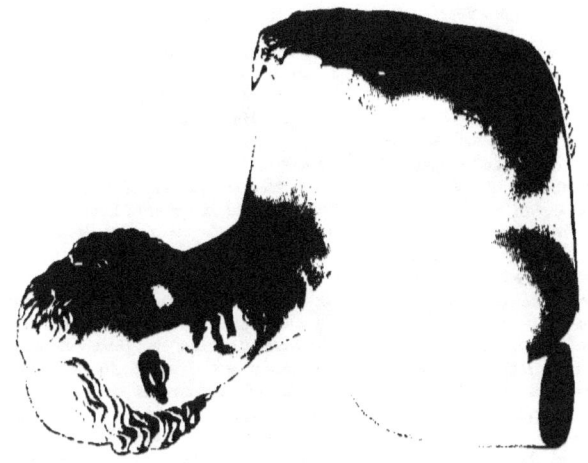

VENUS OF MILO (LOUVRE).

HERMES OF PRAXITELES.

King of Sparta, who was very renowned for her beauty. As we have seen, this produced the celebrated Trojan War.

Adonis, the son of the King of Cyprus, being killed by a wild boar, Aphroditê mourned his sad death, and changed his blood, which was shed on the ground, into the flower *anemone*. Upon hearing his dying voice, she hastened to his aid. In doing so, she accidentally ran a thorn into her foot, and the blood which flowed therefrom upon a rose changed the color of that flower from white to red. Aphroditê then prayed to Zeus that Adonis might be restored to life for six months every year—a prayer which was granted. The rose, the myrtle and the apple were sacred to Aphroditê, as were such birds as the dove, the swan and the sparrow. Aphroditê was sometimes described as traversing the heavens in an ivory chariot, drawn by doves. She was attired in a purple mantle, glittering with diamonds, and was bound around the waist by the zone. Her doves were harnessed with a light golden chain. Her son, Eros—in Latin Cupid—and a train of doves fluttered around her chariot on wings of silk. The three Graces, Aglaia, Thalia and Euphrosyne, attended her. On another occasion Aphroditê was carried through the ocean in a shell, her head being crowned with roses, while Cupids, Nereids and Dolphins sported around her. She was represented as perfectly beautiful and graceful, her countenance being expressive of gentleness and gayety. Aphroditê had many temples, the most famous being those at Paphos, Cythera, Idalia and Cnidus. Her most beautiful statue, called the Venus de Medicis, is yet admired by all who visit the gallery of Florence, in Italy. The island was supposed to be the favorite residence of Aphroditê, and her chief worshipers were at Paphos, a city of that island.

"To the soft Cyprian she graceful moves
To visit Paphos, and her blooming groves;
While to her power a hundred altars rise,
And grateful incense greets the balmy skies."

Eros, the son of Aphroditê, and the god of love, is represented as a beautiful boy, with wings, a bow and arrows, and usually a bandage over his eyes. He had wings, which denoted his caprice and his desire for change. He is described as blind, to show that our eyes are shut to the faults of those we love.

Dêmêtêr, the goddess of corn and of harvests, was the daughter of Kronos and Hestia. She was the mother of Proserpine, or Persephone, who was carried off by Pluto, the god of the infernal regions, or Hades, while she was gathering flowers in Enna, a beautiful valley in Sicily. When Dêmêtêr discovered that her daughter was missing, she sought her all over Sicily, and at night she lighted two torches by the flames of Mount Ætna, to enable her to continue her search. She finally met the nymph Arethusa, who informed her that Pluto had carried off her daughter. Thereupon Dêmêtêr flew to heaven in a chariot drawn by two dragons, and implored Zeus to order that her daughter be restored to her. Zeus consented to do this, provided Proserpine had not eaten anything in Pluto's dominions. Dêmêtêr then hastened to Pluto, but Proserpine had unfortunately eaten the grains of a pomegranate which she had gathered in the Elysian fields, and could not therefore return to earth. But Zeus, moved with compassion for the grief of Dêmêtêr, allowed Proserpine to pass six months of every year with her mother. When Dêmêtêr was searching for her daughter, she became weary with traveling, and stopping at the cottage of an old woman named Baubo, begged for a little water. The old woman gave her water and barley broth. Dêmêtêr eagerly commenced to eat the broth. Stellio, the little son of Baubo, scoffed at the goddess, whereupon Dêmêtêr threw some of the broth into his face, and the little boy was changed into a lizard.

Upon returning to earth, Dêmêtêr discovered that it had suffered greatly in her absence, from want of tillage. Attica, especially, had become very barren and desolate. Celeus, King of Eleusis, in Attica, had a son named Triptolemus, whom Dêmêtêr instructed in the arts of agriculture, in return for the hospitable reception given her by Celeus during her journey. She taught him to plough, to sow and to reap, to make bread and to rear fruit trees. She then made him a present of a chariot drawn by flying dragons, and sent him to teach agriculture to mankind. Men then fed upon acorns and roots, but Triptolemus instructed them to sow their fields with wheat, which Dêmêtêr had given him.

The most famous festivals in honor of Dêmêtêr were those celebrated at Eleusis. These were called the *Eleusinian Mysteries*, because of the secrecy with which they were conducted. Those who were admitted to these solemn ceremonies were styled "the initiated." The new members were bound by a solemn oath to maintain absolute secrecy regarding these mysterious rites, and were then dismissed. By such means were "the initiated" struck with terror, and it was considered a dreadful sin to even allude to them in the presence of "the uninitiated."

Dêmêtêr is represented as tall in stature and majestic in appearance. Her golden hair is encircled with a wreath of corn. She holds a sickle in her right hand, and a lighted torch in her left. There were numerous magnificent temples erected to Dêmêtêr, and many festivals were held in her honor. In the spring the husbandman offered sacrifices to this goddess, and also oblations of wine, milk and honey. These rustic ceremonies are described by Virgil thus:

"To Ceres bland, her annual rites be paid,
On the green turf, beneath the fragrant shade,
When winter ends, and spring serenely shines;
Then fat the lambs, then mellow are the wines,
Then sweet are slumbers on the flowery ground,
Then with thick shades are lofty mountains crowned.
Let all the hinds bend low at Ceres' shrine;
Mix honey sweet for her, with milk and mellow wine;
Thrice lead the victim the new fruits around,
And Ceres call, and choral hymns resound."

Hestia, the household goddess, was the daughter of Kronos and Rhea. She presided over the domestic hearth. Her worship was introduced into Italy by Æneas, a famous Trojan prince, and her rites at Rome varied somewhat with those of Greece.

Besides the twelve great gods and goddesses on Mount Olympus, there is a large number of other deities, infernal, marine and terrestrial. There were divinities inhabiting every field, forest and river; and all nature was believed to be working through a number of personal agents.

Amphitritê, the wife of Poseidon, has been described thus:

"Several dolphins appeared, whose scales seemed gold and azure; they swelled the waves, and made them foam with their sporting; after them came tritons, blowing their curved shells; they surrounded Amphitritê's chariot, drawn by sea-horses that were whiter than snow, and which ploughed the briny waves, and left a deep furrow behind them in the sea; their eyes flamed, and foam issued from their mouths.

"The goddess' car was a shell of marvelous form; it was of a more shining white than ivory; its wheels were of gold, and it seemed to skim the surface of the peaceful waters. Nymphs, crowned with flowers, whose lovely tresses flowed over their shoulders, and waved with the winds, swam in shoals behind the car.

"The goddess had, in one hand, a scepter of gold, to command the waves; and, with the other, held on her knees the little god Palemon, her son, who hung at her breast. Her countenance was serene and mild, but an air of majesty repressed every seditious wind and lowering tempest. Tritons guided the steeds, and held the golden reins.

"A large purple sail waved in the air above the car, and was gently swelled by a multitude of little Zephyrs, who strove to blow it forward with their breath. In the midst of the air, Æolus appeared busy, restless and vehement; his wrinkled face and sour looks, his threatening voice, his long bushy eyebrows, his eyes full of gloomy fire and severity, silenced the fierce north winds, and drove back every cloud. Immense whales, and all the monsters of the deep, issued in haste from their profound grottos to view the goddess."

Triton was the son of Poseidon and Amphitritê, and was his father's trumpeter. He is described as half man and half fish, and is usually represented as blowing a shell. He was a very powerful marine god, and was able to raise storms at sea and calm them at his pleasure.

"High on the stern the sea-green god appears;
Frowning, he seems his crooked shell to sound,
And at the blast the billows dance around."

Oceanus was an ancient sea-god, the son of Kronos and Hestia. When Zeus was King of Heaven, he deprived Oceanus of his dominion, and conferred it upon his brother, Poseidon. Oceanus married Thetis, a name sometimes used in poetry to signify the sea. He had three thousand children, and was the father of rivers. He is described as an old man, having a long flowing beard, and sitting upon the waves of the sea. He held a pike in his hand, and a sea-monster stood beside him. The ancients prayed to him very solemnly, before they started on any voyage.

Nereus was the son of Oceanus. He married Doris, and was the father of fifty sea-nymphs, called Nereides. He lived mainly in the Ægean Sea, and was represented as an old man, having azure hair. He was able to predict future events. He was frequently represented with his daughters, the Nereides, dancing around him in chorus.

The chief deity of the infernal regions, Hades, the dark and gloomy regions under the earth, was Pluto. He was King of Hell, or Hades, and the son of Kronos and Ops. None of the goddesses would marry him on account of the gloominess and sadness of the infernal regions, which were his abode; and he therefore resolved to obtain one by force. He carried away Persephone, or Proserpine, whom he saw gathering flowers with her companions in Sicily, driving up to her in his black chariot with coal black horses, compelling her to go with him, notwithstanding all her bitter tears. Vainly did the young nymph Cyone endeavor to stop the snorting horses, as Pluto struck the ground with his scepter, whereupon the earth suddenly opened, and the chariot and horses descended through the opening with Pluto and Persephone, the latter becoming the Queen of Hell.

PLUTO CARRYING OFF PROSERPINE.

Black victims, especially black bulls, were sacrificed to Pluto. The blood of the slaughtered animal was sprinkled upon the ground, so that it could penetrate to the infernal regions. The melancholy cypress tree was sacred to this gloomy god, as were likewise the narcissus and the white daffodil, because Proserpine, was gathering these when she was carried off by Pluto. Pluto was represented as seated upon a throne of sulphur, with a crown of cypress. The three-headed dog Cerberus kept watch at his feet. His wife, Proserpine sat on his left hand. He held a key to signify that when he receives the dead into his kingdom, he has the gates locked, so that they can never again return to life.

PLUTO.

Plutus was the god of riches. He was the son of Jason and Dêmêtêr. He is represented as blind and injudicious, thus showing that wicked men often acquire wealth, while good men continue in poverty. He is described as being lame, thus showing that riches are accumulated slowly. He was said to be timid and fearful, thus representing the care with which men guard their treasures. His wings signify how quickly riches may be lost.

Somnus, the god of sleep, was the son of Erebus and Nox. His palace was a dark cave, where the sun never penetrated. Poppies grew at the entrance to the cave, and Somnus himself was believed to be always asleep upon a bed of feathers, having black curtains. Dreams passed in and out through the two gates of his palace. Morpheus was his chief minister.

We will now notice the terrestrial deities Dionysus—in Latin called Bacchus—was the god of wine and drunkards. He was supposed to be an ancient conqueror and lawgiver. He was born in Egypt, and was educated at Nysa in Arabia. He taught the culture of the grape, the art of making wine from the juice of the grape, and also the way of making honey. He conquered India and other countries. He first taught nations the uses of commerce and merchandise, the art of navigation, and the method of tilling the soil. He founded cities, instituted wise laws, civilized many savage and barbarous tribes and nations, and taught them the worship of the gods.

In his youth some pirates who found him asleep in the island of Naxos, struck with his beauty, carried him off in their ship, intending to sell him as a slave. When Dionysus awoke he pretended to weep, to test the mercy of his captors, but they laughed at his distress, whereupon the ship at once stood still on the waters. Vines sprang up, twining their branches round the oars, the masts and the sails. The youthful god waved a spear, whereupon tigers, panthers and lynxes surrounded the ship. The astonished and affrighted pirates sprang into the sea, and were immediately changed into dolphins, with the single exception of the pilot, who had manifested some interest in the fate of Dionysus.

Grateful to Midas, King of Phrygia, for some service rendered him, Dionysus offered the king whatever he desired. Midas wished that everything which he touched might be converted into gold, but soon discovered that he had made a foolish request, as even his food and drink were changed into that precious metal.

The festivals of Dionysus were celebrated with drunken riots and excesses. The priestesses, styled *Bacchanates*, ran wild upon the mountains, with disheveled hair, and with torches in their hands, rending the air with their frenzied shouts, and chanting hymns in praise of Dionysus. During the celebration of these Bacchanalian rites, the people ran about the city in masks, or with the dregs of wine marking their faces.

The fir, the ivy, the fig and the pine were consecrated to Dionysus; and goats were sacrificed to him, because of that animal's propensity to destroy the vine. This god is sometimes represented as an effeminate youth, and sometimes as an aged man. He is crowned with leaves of the ivy and the vine. He holds in one hand a javelin with an iron head, encircled with leaves of the ivy and the vine. He is seated in a chariot drawn by tigers and lions, and sometimes by panthers and lynxes; his guard being a band of riotous demons, nymphs and satyrs.

Latona was the daughter of Phœbe and of Corus the Titan. She had once been a celestial goddess, but her wonderful beauty caused her to be admired by all the gods, especially by Zeus. This aroused the jealousy of Hêrê, who caused Latona to be cast out of heaven and sent the serpent Python to persecute her. Latona wandered from one place to another. The heavens refused to again receive her. The earth refused her a resting-place, for fear of arousing the anger of Hêrê. The serpent Python continually haunted her and affrighted her with his terrors. Finally Poseidon was moved with pity for the outcast goddess. The little island of Delos, which had thus far wandered about the Ægean Sea, sometimes appearing above and sometimes below the waters, became suddenly stationary when struck by Poseidon's trident, whereupon Latona flew there in the shape of a quail; and there her children, Apollo and Artemis, were born. Still Hêrê persecuted her, so that Latona was obliged to fly from Delos. She traveled over most of the world, and finally arrived at the country of Lycia, in Asia Minor, where she wandered about the fields in the intense heat of the sun. Becoming faint and dizzy, she joyfully ran towards a spring which she saw in a cool valley; but when she knelt down before the spring to quench her thirst with the cool water, some rude peasants engaged in weeding a thrush drove her away. Latona earnestly begged mercy of them.

——"Why hinder you, said she,
The use of water that to all is free?
The sun, the air, the pure and cooling wave,
Nature made free; I claim the boon she gave;
My tongue wants moisture, and my jaws are dry,
Scarce is their way for speech; for drink I die;
Water to me were Nectar."

But the peasants were unmoved by her entreaties. Latona turned around as she left the valley and called upon Zeus to punish the unmerciful peasants, whereupon they were at once all changed into frogs.

Niobe was the daughter of Totalus, and the wife of Amphion, King of Thebes. She was very proud of her fourteen beautiful children. She indiscreetly cast off Latona, and said that she herself had a better right to altars and sacrifices. Thereupon Latona asked her children, Apollo and Artemis, to punish the proud Niobe. Apollo and Artemis obeyed their mother and armed themselves with bows and arrows. Niobe's sons were pierced with Apollo's darts, and her daughters were destroyed by Artemis. The unfortunate Niobe, bereft of her children, wandered into the wilderness, weeping bitterly. The gods had compassion on her and changed her into a stone. Latona was worshiped at Argos and Delos, and her children received divine honors, being admitted into the council of the great deities on Mount Olympus.

Eos—in Latin called Aurora—was the goddess of the morning, the sister of Apollo and Artemis, and the mother of the stars and the winds. She was the daughter of Gæa, or Earth, and Titan, or, according to some, of Hyperion and Thea. She married Astræus, son of the Titans. The Greek poets represent her as seated in a golden chariot, drawn by horses as white as snow. A bright star is seen sparkling upon her forehead. She opens the gates of the east with her rosy fingers, lifts the dark veil of night, and sprinkles dew upon the grass and flowers. The stars disappear on her approach, well knowing that the rosy clouds surrounding her announce the coming of her great brother, Apollo, or the sun.

Eos, or Aurora, also married Tithonus, a Trojan prince, who prayed her to give him immortality. The goddess procured this precious gift for Tithonus, but forgot to ask for the vigor, youth and beauty which could only render immortal life desirable. Consequently Tithonus became old and feeble. Becoming tired of life, he prayed Eos to let him die. Unable to grant this prayer, the goddess changed him into a grasshopper. The Greeks regarded this insect as singularly happy and long-lived. The poet Anacreon thus says:

"O thou, of all creatures blest,
Sweet insect, that delight'st to rest
Upon the wild wood's leafy tops,
To drink the dew that morning drops,
And chirp thy song with such a glee,
That happiest kings may envy thee
Whatever decks the velvet field,
Whate'er the circling seasons yield,
Whatever buds, whatever blows,
For thee it buds, for thee it grows."

Pan was the god of shepherds and huntsmen, and the most renowned of all the rural deities. He was born in Arcadia, and was the son of Hermês. Dryope, an Arcadian nymph, was usually regarded as his mother. Pan invented the pastoral flute, with seven tubes, which he called Syrinx, whereupon a nymph so named and whom he loved fled from him, and was changed into a bundle of reeds by the gods. All strange noises heard in lonely places were ascribed to Pan, for which reason fear without cause is called a *panic*. Pan was represented as a grotesque monster, half man and half beast, having a long beard, and the horns, legs and feet of a goat. His complexion was ruddy, and his head was crowned with pine. He held a staff in one hand, and a pipe of reeds in the other. The nymphs danced around him, and the gods were cheered by his music. He taught the art of music to Apollo.

Flora was the goddess of flowers and gardens. She was described as a beautiful female who was possessed of perpetual youth. She wore a crown of flowers, and her robe was covered with garlands of roses, while she held a cornucopia, or horn of plenty.

Comus was the god of revelry and feasting. He presided over entertainments, and was generally represented as a young and drunken man, sometimes having a torch in one hand, sometimes a mask. Though standing upright, he seemed more asleep than awake, except when he was excited. During his festivals, men and women frequently exchanged dresses with each other.

Pomona was the goddess of fruit-trees, and is represented in the bloom of health and beauty, decorated with the blossoms of fruit-trees, and holding a branch loaded with apples in one hand.

Æolus was the god of the winds. He resided in one of the Æolian islands, which were named in his honor. He could foretell winds and tempests long before their appearance, and was able to raise and control them. When Ulysses visited Æolus in his island, this god gave him a bag in which were tied up all the contrary winds, so that they might not prevent his safe passage. The companions of Ulysses opened this bag to see what it contained, whereupon the winds rushed out, destroying the entire fleet, except the ship which carried Ulysses. Æolus was supposed to have been a skillful astronomer and natural philosopher, and to have invented sails, for which reason the Greek poets called him the god of the winds. He was believed to show his anger in storms and tempests.

Zephyr manifested herself in gentle breezes. Iris showed her presence in the rainbow.

Momus was the god of pleasantry and folly, and was born of Night and Sleep. He constantly laughed at the other gods and ridiculed them, for which reason they finally drove him from heaven.

Astrea was the goddess of justice. She was sometimes called the daughter of Themis, and at other times she was confounded with Themis herself; Themis being the daughter of Uranos, or Heaven, and Gæa, or Earth. Astrea dwelt upon earth in the golden age, but the wickedness and impiety of men drove her to heaven. She was represented as stern and majestic in appearance.

In one hand she held a balance, in which she weighed the actions of men, the good actions on one side of the scales and the bad on the other. She wielded a sword in the other hand to punish the wicked. She had a bandage over her eyes, to show that she would listen impartially to persons of every rank and condition.

Terminus was the god of boundaries, and his duty was to see that no one encroached upon his neighbor's land. His image was a stone head, having no feet or arms, to show that he constantly remained where he was stationed.

Nemesis was the goddess of vengeance. She was the daughter of Nox and Oceanus. She rewarded virtue and punished vice. In Attica there was a famous statue of Nemesis, sculptured by Phidias.

The Greeks believed all nature to be filled with an innumerable number of invisible deities. They supposed the dark grove, the shady vale, the cool rivulet, and every solitary scene to be the haunt of half divine beings, "more beautiful than mortals, less sacred than the gods."

In the depth of the gloomy forests lived the Dryads. The Hamadryad was born, lived and died with the oak. The Oread roamed over the mountains, pursuing the swift stag, or the young Naiad leaned upon her urn, while bending over the cool fountain reflecting her divine image.

The shepherd in wandering through Arcadia's shady groves imagined those invisible beings all around him. Their soft voices were heard in the rustling of the leaves or in the babbling brook. The hunter in pursuing the deer over the lonely mountains supposed the fleet Oread bounding past him with bow and quiver and joining the train of the huntress queen.

The discordant laugh of the half-human Satyr and the mocking Faun were heard beside the lonely rock, in the dark and gloomy recess. The superstitious peasant imagined that he saw bands of these strange beings dancing under the branches of the oak, with mocking features and with human bodies and the horns and feet of goats.

Half divine and half human creatures filled every river, grove and dale. The quiet sea-shores were populated with the green-haired Nereides, or sea-nymphs, who usually abode in the grottos and rocky caves by the coast, where altars were smoking in their honor, and where offerings of oil, milk and honey were laid by the mariner, who came to solicit their favor and protection. Their light forms were seen gliding along the shore with coral and pearls sparkling in their long tresses, and plunging into the blue waters to attend Amphitritê's car when Triton blew a blast upon his silver shell.

"At eventide, when the shore is dim,
And bubbling wreaths with the billows swim,
They rise on the wing of the freshened breeze,
And flit with the wind o'er the rolling seas."

The Muses were nine sisters, daughters of Zeus and Mnemosyne, and these were respectively named Calliope, Clio, Erato, Euterpe, Melpomene, Polyhymnia, Terpsichore, Thalia and Urania. Calliope was the Muse of eloquence and heroic poetry; Clio, of history; Erato, of eloquence or lyric poetry; Euterpe, of music; Melpomene, of tragedy; Polyhymnia, of singing and rhetoric; Terpsichore, of dancing; Thalia, of pastoral or comic poetry; and Urania, of astronomy and hymns, and sacred subjects.

The Muses chiefly resided on Mounts Parnassus, Pindus and Helicon. The Castalian spring was on the descent of Mount Parnassus. On Mount Helicon were the fountains of Aganippe and Hippocrene, the latter gushing forth below the hoof of the winged horse Pegasus.

The Muses were universally worshiped by the Greeks. Every poet began his lays by solemnly invoking the whole nine of them. They were specially esteemed among the Thespians.

The Graces were three sisters, daughters of Zeus and Eurynome, a sea-nymph; and their respective names were Aglaia, Thalia and Euphrosyne. They surrounded the throne of Zeus on Mount Olympus, and constantly attended Aphroditê, as beauty necessarily always accompanied grace.

Temples and altars were erected to the

honor of the Graces in every place occupied by the Hellenic race, and their dominion was recognized in heaven and earth. They were represented as young and dressed lightly, in a dancing attitude, with their hands joined. The Hours, children of Zeus and Themis, sometimes mingled with them in chorus.

The Sirens were three sea nymphs, daughters of the Muse Melpomene, and the river Achelöus. Their faces were like those of beautiful women, but their bodies were like those of flying fishes. They dwelt near the promontory of Pelorus, in Sicily, where their sweet voices allured to sleep all who passed by, after which they took them from the ship and drowned them in the sea and devoured them.

The Furies, or Eumenides, three in number and named respectively Tisiphone, Megæra and Alecto, were said to have sprung from the wound given by Kronos to his father, Uranos. They punished the guilty in this world by pursuing them with the pangs of remorse, and in the infernal regions by perpetual torture and flagellation. They were universally worshiped, but every one was afraid to pronounce their names or to look upon their temple. Turtle doves and sheep, with branches of cedar and hawthorne, were offered to them. They had the faces of women, but these were grim and terrible. Their black apparel was spotted with blood. They held lighted torches, daggers, and whips of scorpions. Snakes were twining around their heads and lashing their necks and shoulders.

The three Fates, Clotho, Lachesis and Atropos, were daughters of Nox and Erebus, and their power was exceedingly great, as they were entrusted with the management of the fatal thread of life. Clotho drew the thread between her fingers. Lachesis turned the wheel. Atropos cut the spun thread with a pair of scissors. Their decrees were irrevocable. They were usually described as three old women, dressed in white ermine robes, having purple borders. They wore chaplets of wool, interwoven with the flowers of the narcissus.

The three Harpies were voracious monsters, having the faces of women, the bodies of vultures, and the claws of dragons.

"At length I land upon the Strophades;
Safe from the danger of the stormy seas;
Those isles are compassed by th' Ionian main;
The dire abode where the foul Harpies reign;
Where from the mountain tops, with hideous cry,
And clattering wings, the hungry Harpies fly;
They snatch the meat; defiling all they find;
And parting leave a loathsome stench behind."

The three Gorgons were very beautiful, but their heads were covered with vipers instead of hair. Those who saw them were struck with terror and changed into stone.

The Lares, or Penates, were household gods, presiding over hospitality. Their altar was the hearth, which was regarded as a sanctuary for strangers.

The Manes were infernal deities presiding over sepulchral monuments. Sometimes by Manes only the souls of the departed are meant.

The ancients looked upon any one who by superior valor, knowledge or beneficence outranked those of the age in which he lived and by whom he was surrounded, as more than mortal, and thus deified him. His actions were often magnified by the credulity of the ignorant into deeds worthy of the gods themselves. After the death of these celebrated persons, flattery and superstition induced the people to bestow upon them divine honors, thus worshiping some as heroes and others as gods.

Truth and fiction became so mingled together in the history of these demi-gods, that the one cannot be separated from the other. These ancient heroes were viewed as beings of a higher order, born upon this earth, but having risen to the skies by their deeds and fame. Hercules, the greatest of the deified heroes of Greece, has already been alluded to, as have also the exploits of Jason and Theseus.

The Centaurs, half man and half horse, were believed to live in Thessaly. They were usually of a savage character; but one of them, Chiron, was highly accomplished. The Argonauts visited him in their expedition, and one of the Greek poets describes the scene thus:

"We entered straight a spot of gloomy twilight shade;
There on a lonely couch the Centaur huge was laid;
At length unmeasured, stretched, his rapid legs were thrown,
And shod with horny hoofs reclined upon the stone.
The boy Achilles stood erect beside the sire,
And swept with pliant hand the spirit-soothing lyre.
But when the Centaur saw the noble kings appear,
He rose and kissed and brought them dainty cheer;
The wine in beakers served; the branchy couches spread
With scattered leaves, and placed each guest upon his head."

It was widely believed that Achilles instructed Chiron in music, and a picture discovered in one of the houses of Herculaneum represents this Centaur giving lessons on the harp. The Centaurs did not all have the gentlemanly breeding of Chiron, and the poets tell us that he conquered them in a fierce conflict.

Castor and Pollux were twin-brothers, sons of Zeus and Leda. Castor was very skillful in riding and managing horses, and Pollux in wrestling. These brothers went with the Argonautic Expedition to Colchis. A frightful tempest arose during the voyage, when two flames were observed playing around the heads of Castor and Pollux, whereupon the storm at once abated. Zeus allowed them to enjoy immortality by turns, so that they alternately lived and died every month. They were drawn as two youths riding beside each other, upon white horses, armed with spears, and having a brilliant star upon their heads.

Perseus was the son of Zeus and Danae, who was the daughter of Acrisius, King of Argos. Hermês gave him a pair of wings and a diamond dagger. Pluto gave him a helmet which had the power of making the wearer invisible. Athênê gave him a shield of brass, reflecting images like a looking-glass. He cut off the head of the Gorgon Medusa, and while he was carrying it across the Libyan desert the drops of blood which fell from it produced the innumerable serpents which have infested that country ever since. When Atlas, King of Mauritania, treated Perseus with inhospitality during the latter's journey, Perseus showed him the Gorgon's head, which changed into stone all who beheld it. Atlas at once became the mountain still bearing his name, in the North of Africa. On the east of Ethiopia, Perseus saw the beautiful Andromeda chained to a rock and a sea-monster going to devour her. He showed the head of Medusa to this sea-monster, who then became a stone. Perseus then unloosed Andromeda and married her.

The winged horse Pegasus sprang from the blood of Medusa's head when it was cut off by Perseus. This horse flew to Mount Helicon, and there became the favorite of the Muses.

Esculapius, the son of Apollo and the nymph Ceronis, was a physician to the Argonauts, and after his death was worshiped as the god of medicine. He was instructed by Chiron, the Centaur. By his knowledge of the medicinal properties of herbs, he restored so many of the dead to life that Pluto complained to Zeus; whereupon Zeus struck Esculapius with thunder, and Apollo avenged the death of his son by killing the Cyclops, who forged the thunderbolts. Esculapius was represented as an old man with a long beard and a laurel crown, and leaning upon his cane. He was the father of Hygeia, who was worshiped as the goddess of health, but most writers regard her as the same as Athênê.

Promêtheus was the father of Ducalion, King of Thessaly, in whose reign the earth was submerged by a deluge. The wickedness of mankind provoked Zeus to destroy every human creature, except Ducalion and his wife Pyrrha, who were saved by entering a vessel which Promêtheus had advised his son to build.

Atlas, the brother of Promêtheus, was King of Mauritania; and was, as we have said, changed into the mountain of that name in North Africa, which is so lofty that the ancients believed it to reach to heaven. Atlas was also believed to have borne the world upon his shoulders.

Orpheus, the son of Apollo and the Muse Calliope, played so sweetly on his father's lyre that he tamed the wild beasts of the forests and stopped the rivers in their courses. The highest trees even bent down to listen to his music. His wife, Eurydice, whom he loved very affectionately, was bit by a serpent that lurked in the grass, and died of the wound. Disconsolate for her loss, Orpheus descended to Pluto's gloomy abode in Hades, determined to have her or die. The wheel of Ixion was stopped at the sound of his divine lyre, while the stone of Sisyphus stood still, Tantalus forgot his thirst, and even the Furies relented. Proserpine, the wife of Pluto, was moved by his grief, and the grim Pluto himself forgot his sternness and agreed to restore Eurydice to Orpheus on condition that he would not look at her until the light of day. Orpheus gladly agreed to this condition; but when the upper regions of the air appeared in sight, he turned back to take a look at his long-lost Eurydice, whereupon she disappeared from his view. After this, Orpheus fled from mankind forever, and his lyre remained silent. The Thracians were so enraged at him for avoiding their society that they killed him during the feast of Dionysus, and cast his head into the river Hebrus. As it was carried down into the Ægean Sea, it was heard to murmur Eurydice's name.

Amphion, also a famous musician, was the son of Zeus and Antiope. By the music of his lute, which he had received from Hermês, he raised the walls of Thebes. He is also said to have moved stones to build these massive walls. These fables are believed to signify that by the force of his eloquence he induced the wild and uncivilized Thebans of early days to build a defense around their city, as a protection against their foes.

Thus it will be seen the fertile imagination of the Greeks filled the earth, the air and the sea with a great multitude of beings endowed with more than mortal power. Every natural object, every human quality of thought or emotion, was represented among the celestial personages. The most ordinary, as well as the most remarkable, incidents of life were believed to result from the interference of the gods in human affairs. Thunder was considered the voice of Zeus, and the lightning his spear. The gentle summer breeze was believed to be the impulse given by Zephyr's wing, and the forest's echo was the voice of a goddess. Aphroditê decreed the affection of lovers, and the wound inflicted by the arrow of Eros manifested itself in the anxiety of the enamored bosom. Ares led the way in battle, while the various gods participated in the conflict, supplying their favorites with charmed arms, and bestowing upon them supernatural power and skill. On the sea Poseidon was believed to closely watch events, and when storms arose and the billows raged he was supposed to be manifesting his fury. Æolus showed his anger in the raging tempest, of which he was the author. A cloud sailing through the sky was the chariot of Zeus. The rosy-fingered Eos, or Aurora, introduced the morning. Iris manifested her presence in the rainbow. "All earth was a kind of heaven, and heaven was upon earth."

Thus Grecian mythology was formed upon poetical imagination. It was a mixture of allegory and history. The physical characteristics were more prominent in the various deities than were the moral qualities. The gods and goddesses of the Greeks were represented as participating in the affairs of mortals, frequently giving their powerful and divine aid to the furtherance of vicious and villainous projects. They were actuated by envy, malice, and all the evil passions to which human nature is subject, and readily adopted the basest measures to gratify their most nefarious purposes. Zeus, the King of Heaven, is even said to have been very profligate upon earth. Their gods and goddesses made love to each other and married. They had children the same as mortals. They also at times warred.

The Greeks were intensely religious. The story of their gods had been transmitted to them with the authority of a great antiquity, and custom had made them reverence beings who were endowed with passions and qualities which reason condemned.

The Greek mythology had been coined in the imagination of the early Grecian poets. The Grecian philosophers of later times rejected the absurd polytheism which was the popular belief; and some of them, Socrates and Plato among the number, were monotheists, believing in one Supreme and All-powerful God, who had created and who continued to rule the entire universe.

The Greeks believed in the immortality of the soul and in future rewards and punishments, according to the good or evil conduct of mortals in this life. They believed that after death the human souls descended to the shores of the dreary and pestilential river Styx, where the grim-looking Charon acted as ferryman in rowing the departed spirits across the dismal stream, which formed the boundary of Pluto's dominions.

The deceased had to be buried in order to obtain a passage in Charon's boat. Those drowned at sea, or those who were in any manner deprived of the customary rites of burial, were forced to wander about the banks of the river Styx for a hundred years, before they could cross the stream.

After leaving Charon's boat, the trembling shades of the departed spirits advanced to Pluto's palace, whose gate was guarded by the monstrous three-headed dog, Cerberus, whose body was covered with snakes instead of hair. The departed spirits were then brought by Hermês before the three judges of the infernal regions, Minos, Rhadamanthus and Æacus, who condemned the wicked to perpetual torments in Hades, or Tartarus, and rewarded the righteous with celestial pleasures in the happy islands of Elysium.

Tartarus, the place of punishment for the wicked, was the abode of darkness and terror. Tantalus, for a vile crime in his life upon earth, was in this horrible place surrounded with water, which fled from his lips whenever he sought to quench his burning thirst, while the branches laden with fruit over his head shrunk from his grasp every time his hand attempted to grasp them. Ixion was also in this horrible abode, bound with serpents to the rim of a wheel, which perpetually revolved, thus permitting no cessation of his agonies. Sisyphus was condemned to the never-ending task of rolling an immense stone up the side of a steep mountain, but as soon as he would accomplish his feat the stone would again roll down to its original place. In this dreary place were criminals writhing under the merciless lash of the avenging Furies, and other wretches were tortured incessantly with unquenchable fires.

Elysium, the residence of the righteous, was a region of indescribable loveliness and pleasure. All around were groves of the richest verdure and streams of silvery clearness. The air was pure, serene and temperate. The woods perpetually resounded with the warbling of birds, and a far more brilliant light than that of the sun was constantly diffused throughout that delightful abode, whose inhabitants, undisturbed by cares or sorrow, spent their time in the enjoyments of such pleasures as they had experienced on earth, or in admiring the wisdom and power of the gods.

The Greek worship of the gods and goddesses consisted of prayers and thanksgivings, and sacrifices, or sin-offerings, such as animals, or fruits, vines, milk, honey and frankincense. Public worship was conducted by the priests in the open air, on mountain-tops, in groves and forests, or in temples, particularly on the occasion of the great national festivals, which consisted of pompous processions, public games, dramatic entertainments, feasting, masquerading, and also drunkenness, indecency, uproar and every kind of licentiousness, as in the worship of Dionysus.

The Grecian temples were erected in the woods, in the valleys, or by the brink of rivers or fountains, according to the deity in whose honor they were set up; as the ancients attributed the management of every particular affair to some particular god or goddess, and assigned to each a special style of building, in accordance with his or her peculiar character and attributes.

But when temples were first reared, the ancients continued to worship their deities without any statue or visible representation of the divinity. The worship of idols is believed to have been introduced into Athens from the very beginning of the city. These idols were first formed of rude blocks of wood or stone, until the time that the art of engraving or carving was invented, when these rough masses were fashioned into figures resembling living creatures. Marble and ivory, or precious stones, were afterwards used in the construction of these images, and at length gold, silver, brass and other metals were used. Finally, in the refined ages of Greece, all the genius of the sculptor was employed in making those beautiful statues which have remained unsurpassed to this day.

The altars in the Grecian temples were usually lower than the statues of the gods. They were heaps of earth, ashes or stone, arranged in the form of an oblong square. Some were made of horn or brick, while others, more beautiful and splendid, were overlaid with gold. Some were designed for sacrifices made with fire. Animals were offered upon others to appease or propitiate the deity. Cakes, fruits or inanimate things were only placed upon others.

Temples, statues and altars were regarded as sacred. The privilege of protecting offenders was granted to many of them. The Greek poets often allude to this practice. Thus says Euripides:

"The wild beast is protected by the rocks,
And vile slaves by the altars of the gods."

The priests were not expected to teach lessons of morality. They only taught that the gods required slavish adulation, and an outward show of reverence for them from their worshipers, who were rewarded with the divine favor in proportion to the quantity and costliness of their offerings.

Besides the public religious services there were certain mysterious rites, performed only in secret by those who had been initiated, in honor of particular divinities. The most remarkable of these mystical observances were those already noticed as celebrated at Eleusis, in Attica, in honor of Dêmêtêr and Proserpine, and known as the *Eleusinian Mysteries*. All who were initiated in them were bound by the most solemn oath never to reveal them. It was considered a crime even to speak of them to the uninitiated. Those who were initiated in them were regarded as under the special protection of the gods.

Only Athenians could be admitted to the Eleusinian Mysteries, and they took good care to embrace their special privilege, believing that such as died without initiation would be condemned to an eternity of woe in the infernal regions. The death penalty was denounced against all who divulged these mysterious ceremonies. Nevertheless, sufficient was disclosed concerning them to prove that they mainly consisted of such mystical rites and optical delusions as were calculated to excite the superstitious veneration and dread of the alarmed votaries. Processions, gymnastic contests, music and dancing constituted a necessary part of this religious festival, as well as of others, and the nocturnal orgies of the devotees were almost as immoral and extravagant as those of the Bacchanalians.

The Greeks believed that the gods communicated with mortals, and that they made known their will and revealed the secrets of futurity by means of oracles, of which there were several in different portions of Greece. Zeus was believed to speak in the rustling of the leaves. The oldest and the most famous oracle of Zeus was that at Dodona, in Epirus. Near that place was a grove of oaks, which, according to the superstitious belief of the Greeks, chanted the message of Zeus to pious inquirers. It is also said that black pigeons frequented this grove and gave oracular responses. The oracle at Dodona is believed to have owed its origin to an artful woman, who had been stolen from the temple of Ammon in Egypt, and sold as a slave in Epirus. To release her-

INTERIOR OF THE TEMPLE OF JUPITER OLYMPUS (RESTORED).

INTERIOR OF THE PARTHENON, WITH STATUE OF PALLAS-ATHENE.

BACCHUS (ROME).

HEAD OF NIOBE (FLORENCE).

RECONSTRUCTED ALTAR ON THE ACROPOLIS OF PERGAMON.

self from the evils of slavery, this woman determined to work upon the ignorance and credulity of those among whom she had been brought, and for this purpose she stationed herself in the grove of oaks which afterward acquired such celebrity, and announced that she was inspired by Zeus and could foretell future events. This scheme was entirely successful, and the woman soon acquired a great reputation for her skill in divination; and, after her death, other artful persons readily embraced a profession rewarded with both honor and profit.

The most celebrated of all the Grecian oracles was that of Apollo at Delphi, a city built on the slope of Mount Parnassus, in Phocis. At a very ancient period it had been discovered that from a deep cave in the side of that mountain a stupefying vapor issued, with so powerful an effect as to throw both men and cattle into convulsions. The savage inhabitants of the surrounding country, unable to account for such a phenomenon, concluded that it must be caused by some supernatural agency, and they considered the incoherent ravings of those who had inhaled the noxious vapor as prophecies uttered under the inspiration of some deity. As the intoxicating exhalation arose out of the ground, it was at first supposed that the newly-discovered oracle must be that of the very ancient goddess, Gæa, or Earth; but Poseidon was afterwards associated with this divinity as an auxiliary.

Ultimately the entire credit of the oracle was transferred to Apollo. A temple was soon erected on the consecrated spot; and a priestess, called the *Pythoness*, was appointed to perform the duty of inhaling the prophetic vapor at stated intervals. To enable her to perform the office assigned her without the danger of falling into the cave, as several persons had previously done, a seat, called a tripod, because it had three feet, was constructed directly over the mouth of the crevice for her accommodation. Nevertheless the Pythoness held an office neither agreeable nor safe, as the convulsions into which the noxious vapors of the cave threw her were sometimes so violent as to produce instant death, and were always so painful that force was frequently required to bring the priestess to the prophetic seat.

The gas escaping from the crevice was believed to be Apollo's breath, and the fumes were supposed to inspire the Pythoness. She made known the will of Apollo to attendant priests, who communicated the revelation to the inquirer. The unconnected words screamed out by the Pythoness in her madness were arranged into sentences by these attendant priests, who managed to place them in such an order and fill up the breaks in such a manner as to make them express whatever was most essential to the interests of the shrine, as this was the chief object. To maintain the credit of the oracle, care was taken to generally put the responses of the oracle in such obscure and enigmatical language that the prediction might not be falsified, or might at least seem to be verified, no matter what course events might take.

The fame of the Delphic oracle soon spread far and wide; and no important enterprise was undertaken in any portion of Greece, or of its many colonies in the islands and along the coasts of the Ægean and the Mediterranean, without consulting the Pythoness. The many presents given the oracle by those who resorted to it for advice, many of whom were princes or rich and influential leaders, constituted a source of great and permanent revenue, affording the officiating priests a comfortable support, and furnishing the means for building a magnificent temple in the place of the rude structure which had been originally erected. The high veneration bestowed upon the Delphic oracle gave its directors great influence in public affairs; and this influence they sometimes exerted in a most worthy manner in sanctioning and encouraging the projects of the statesmen, legislators and warriors who endeavored to improve the political systems, reform the laws and manners, or defend the liberties, of Hellas. Like the Olympic and other games, and like the celebrated Amphictyonic Council, the Delphic oracle constituted a bond of union among the many independent Grecian communities; and, by giving the authority of the gods to measures of general public utility, it frequently repressed petty jealousies and disputes, and encouraged all to labor for the common welfare of the entire Hellenic race.

While the rest of Greece was distracted by intestine wars, Delphi, the chosen spot of Apollo, escaped the ravages of contending armies; and, in order to sufficiently secure the temple of Delphi from being plundered by warlike bands, that famous sanctuary was placed under the special protection of the Amphictyonic Council, so called from its reputed founder, the legendary Amphictyon, who is asserted by some to have been one of the early Kings of Attica. This council consisted of two deputies from each of the leading states of Greece; and it assembled twice a year, in the spring at Delphi, and in the autumn at the pass of Thermopylæ. The duties of the Amphictyonic Council were to effect a settlement of all religious and political disputes that might arise among the different Grecian states, and to decide upon proposals of peace or war with foreign nations. Each deputy took an oath that he would never subvert or injure any Amphictyonic city, and that he would oppose by force of arms any such outrage if attempted by others. He also swore that if any party in any way injured the sacred territory of Delphi, or formed designs against the temple to Apollo, he would do his utmost to bring the offenders to punishment. The Amphictyonic Council was sometimes of great advantage to the Greeks, but it very seldom exercised much influence in preventing domestic dissensions or civil wars among the Grecians.

In the process of time nearly all the states of Greece abolished monarchy and established republican governments. The division of Greece into as many independent republics as there were Grecian towns, and the almost incessant wars that distracted the Hellenic race, greatly retarded the progress of Grecian civilization. At length, Ephitus, King of Elis, having obtained authority from the Delphic oracle, instituted the *Olympic Festival*, by which the Greeks, notwithstanding their almost constant wars with each other, were enabled to meet on friendly terms once in every four years, or *Olympiad*, as such a period of time was thereafter called, at Olympia, a town in Elis. The establishment of the Olympic Festival took place in the year 776 B. C., from which date the Greeks thereafter reckoned time. To this festival all the people of Greece were invited; and in order to enable them to attend, the Delphic oracle commanded that a general armistice should take place sometime before and after each celebration. The Olympic Festival consisted of religious rites to Zeus and Hercules, and of various games, such as wrestling and boxing matches, foot and chariot races, and other contests requiring strength and agility, and of compositions in poetry and music. The victors in the Olympic Games were crowned with olive wreaths, which was esteemed by the Greeks as a very high honor.

In wrestling, the competitors were almost or altogether naked, and they appear to have exhibited great skill and agility. The presence of a vast multitude excited them to put forth wonderful efforts, and they showed no evidence of suffering, though bruised and maimed in the struggle. Leaping was performed by springing over a bar. None were allowed to enter this sport who had not practiced ten months. Boxing was a favorite sport, and seems to have been practiced much as it is now in England. No unfair advantage was taken in this or in any other contest. The slightest trick was severely punished. The energies of the most powerful men were called forth by the throwing of the *discus*, or *coit*, a round piece of stone; and the most wonderful feats were performed in hurling large weights. Running was also practiced, and the Greek writers give us accounts of the remarkable fleetness of the races. Prominent among the sports were horse-racing and chariot-racing, the latter of which was especially imposing, persons of the highest rank engaging therein. The greatest poets and musicians were assembled from all portions

OLYMPIAN GAMES (CHARIOT RACE).

FOOT RACE AT THE OLYMPIAN GAMES.

of Hellas: and a vast multitude of rich and poor, high and low, collected to witness these exhibitions, which were rendered interesting by the excitement which they produced and by the sanction bestowed upon the occasion by the national religion. There is not at the present time any public festivity, in any country, which engages the passions of men so deeply as the games of ancient Greece.

Three other great national festivals were subsequently established by the Greeks— the *Isthmian Games* celebrated near Corinth, the *Pythian Games* at Delphi, and the *Nemean Games* in Argolis. These occurred in the various years intervening between the successive festivals at Olympia; but though they acquired some celebrity, none of them reached the importance and splendor of the Olympic Games.

SECTION IV.—THE SMALLER GRECIAN STATES.

THE history of Greece after the Dorian conquest and occupation of the Peloponnesus resolves itself into that of the several states. A few general remarks may be necessary before proceeding with the history of the more important cities and states. The progress of Hellenic civilization was checked for a time and to some extent by the migrations of the different Greek races and the troubles resulting therefrom. More powerful and more enterprising, but ruder, races took the places of the weaker but more polished ones. Physical characteristics assumed a superiority over grace, refinement and ingenuity. The conquering races in comparison with the conquered ones were generally what the rough Dorians were as compared with the refined Achæans. But the political vigor of the new era compensated for this loss. "War and movement, bringing out the personal qualities of each individual man, favored the growth of self-respect and self-assertion. Amid toils and dangers which were shared alike by all, the idea of political equality took its rise. A novel and unsettled state of things stimulated political inventiveness; and, various expedients being tried, the stock of political ideas increased rapidly. The simple hereditary monarchy of the heroic times was succeeded everywhere, except in Epirus, by some more complicated system of government—some system far more favorable to freedom and to the political education of the individual."

Another natural result of the new order of things was the special dignity and importance acquired by the CITY. The conquerors naturally established themselves in some stronghold, and remained together for their better security, each such stronghold becoming a separate independent state, holding a certain portion of the surrounding territory in subjection. At the same time the unsubdued countries perceived the strength resulting from this unity, and consequently many of these abolished their previous system of village life and centralized and consolidated themselves by establishing capitals and transferring the greater part of their population to them. Such was the case with Athens, Mantinea, Tegea and Dymé. In countries occupied by one race, but divided into as many district states as there were cities, political confederations arose, sometimes resulting from a pre-existing amphictyony, but occasionally without any such previous condition. The federal tie was generally weak, and only in Bœotia did such a union constitute a permanent state of the first rank.

The division of Greece into a multitude of small states held together by no common political tie, and perpetually at war with each other, did not stand in the way of the formation and maintenance of a certain common Pan-Hellenic feeling—"a conciousness of unity, a friendliness, and a readiness to make common cause against a foreign enemy." A conviction of race identity was the foundation of this feeling, which was further encouraged by the possession of a common language and a common literature; of the same habits and the same ideas; of the same religion, with rites, temples and festivals equally open to all.

The first Grecian state attaining political importance under the new order of things was Argos. According to tradition, the first Dorian colonists forming settlements in Epidaurus, Trœzen, Phlius, Sicyon and Corinth went from Argos, and from these places Doric power was still further extended, as from Epidaurus, which colonized Ægina and Epidaurus Limera, and from Corinth, which colonized Megara. Argos, the mother of all these states, was the protectress and mistress of most of them. Her dominion extended from the Isthmus of Corinth to Cape Malea and the island of Cythera. For three or four centuries—from the death of Pheidon, about B. C. 744—Argos was the leading power of the Peloponnesus, a fact never forgotten by her, and which influenced her subsequent history.

Originally the government of Argos was a monarchy of the heroic order, the supreme power being hereditary in the family of the Temenidæ, believed to be descendants from Temenus, the Heracleid, the eldest son of Aristomachus. But before long aspirations for political liberty arose among the Argive people, the kingly power was diminished, and a government, in form monarchical but really republican, was established. This condition of affairs continued for some centuries; but about B. C. 780 or 770, on the accession of the able Pheidon, a reaction set in. Pheidon recovered all the lost royal privileges and extended them, thus becoming the first Greek "tyrant," which was the name that the Greeks applied to one who usurped powers to which he had no hereditary or delegated right. Under the able rule of Pheidon, Argos exercised somewhat of a practical hegemony over the entire Peloponnesus; and during his reign probably Argos sent forth the colonies which settled in Crete, Rhodes, Cos, Cnidus and Halicarnassus. The connection with Asia thus established induced Pheidon to introduce coined money into Greece, and also the weights and measures believed to have been identical with the Babylonian system. After Pheidon's death, the power of Argos declined, the bond uniting the confederacy weakened, the government returned to its previous form, and Argive history became almost a blank.

Before proceeding with the histories of Sparta and Athens, the two most important Hellenic states, which arose to power as Argos declined, we will take a general view of the neighboring Greek islands and of the Grecian colonies which lined the shores of Asia Minor, part of Northern Africa, the coasts of Thrace and Macedon, the shores of the Euxine, (now Black Sea), the island of Sicily, Southern Italy, and the Mediterranean shores of Spain and Gaul (now France).

After the capture of Thebes by the Epigoni, the Bœotians, expelled by the Thracian hordes, retired to Arne in Thessaly; but about the time of the great Dorian migration they returned to their native land and became united with some Æolian tribes. Monarchy was abolished upon the death of Xúthus, B. C. 1126, and the Bœotians formed a confederation of as many states as the province contained cities, at the head of which was Thebes, but with many indefinite privileges. The constitutions of the states were unsettled, and they constantly fluctuated between a lawless democracy and a tyrannical oligarchy. This great evil, along with the unsettled condition of the confederacy, prevented the Bœotians from taking a prominent part in Grecian affairs.

Acarnania, Ætolia and Locris afford no remarkable materials for history; and the most important event in the history of Phocis was the First Sacred War, described in the history of Athens. The states of Thessaly were mainly governed by arbitrary tyrants.

Corinth was the most important of the

Peloponnesian states after Sparta. At the time of the Dorian conquest of the Peloponnesus, the Corinthian throne was usurped by Alétes, whose descendants ruled the state for five generations. On the death of Telessus, the last of the Alétian dynasty, Bacchis usurped the throne (B. C. 777); and his descendants, called Bacchíadæ, governed the state for five generations longer. Telestes, the last of these kings, was assassinated, whereupon royalty was abolished, and a kind of oligarchy was established in its stead, under yearly magistrates, called *Prytanes*, chosen entirely from the family of Bacchíadæ. This family, proud of their descent and their commercial wealth, offended their subjects; and Cypselus, a wealthy citizen of Æolian extraction, assisted by the people, usurped the government (B. C. 657), and held the supreme authority for thirty years. He was succeeded at his death by his son Periander, one of the "Seven Wise Men of Greece," but many writers describe him as a rapacious, oppressive and cruel tyrant. He reigned forty years, and his life is believed to have been cut short by violence or by grief for the death of his son. He was succeeded on the throne by his nephew Psammetichus, who reigned only three years, when he was expelled by his subjects, aided by a Spartan army (B. C. 584). After this revolution the state was ruled by a commercial aristocracy, whose constitution is not definitely known, but under which Corinth was for a long time closely in alliance with Sparta. The Corinthian trade consisted mainly in the exchange of Asiatic and Italian merchandise, for which her position afforded her many special advantages. The most prosperous period of Corinth ended with the government of the Cypselids; and the loss of her colony of Corcyra, which had been kept in subjection by Periander, but which revolted after his death, was a blow to her power from which she never recovered. The first sea-fight recorded in history is the naval engagement between the Corcyrians and the Corinthians (B. C. 650).

Sicyon and the other Achæan states were distracted by revolutions like those of Corinth. After many usurpations and revolutions, all the Achæan states adopted republican constitutions, about the time that the Cypselids were expelled from Corinth.

The constitution of Arcadia became republican when the last king, Aristodémus, was stoned by his subjects for having betrayed Aristomenus and the Messenians.

Elis maintained its internal tranquillity, because of the wise laws of Iphitus, who instituted the regular quadrennial celebration of the Olympic Games. The sanctity of its soil on account of this regular festival secured it against external attack. After the abolition of royalty in Elis, two supreme magistrates called Hellanodícæ were chosen, who, besides governing the state, superintended the Olympic Games. The number of these magistrates was afterwards increased to ten, one being chosen from each of the Elian tribes; the only limit to their authority being a Senate of ninety, whose members were elected for life.

SECTION V.—THE GREEK ISLANDS.

THE revolutions of the Grecian islands resembled those of continental Greece, most of them having substituted republican constitutions for the monarchical system. After the Athenians had acquired the supremacy of the seas, the island states lost their independence, as they were treated more like subjects than like allies by Athens; but their internal constitutions remained intact. We will only notice the most important islands in a historical point of view.

Corcyra was the seat of a Corinthian colony under Chersicrates, who drove away or conquered the former inhabitants, B. C. 753. As the leader and most of his companions had been driven into exile by political dissensions, they entertained very little affection for the parent state; while the rapid growth of the Corcyrean power aroused the commercial jealousy of Corinth. This state of things resulted in open war. The Corcyrean constitution seems to have been originally aristocratic or oligarchical, like those of most of the Dorian states; but after the Persian War the rise of a democratic faction, with the support of Athens, led to the most violent internal dissensions, ending in the complete ruin of Corcyra.

Ægina, first colonized in B. C. 1358, rapidly developed by commerce and navigation into one of the leading Grecian states, even founding colonies of its own in Crete and Pontus. Ægina was for a long time the successful rival of Athens, but was finally conquered by that power under Themistocles (B. C. 485).

Many different colonies from the Grecian mainland were planted in the island of Eubœa, but its cities were not united in any confederacy, each having its own separate constitution. The Athenians conquered the island after the Persian War; but the Eubœans made several sanguinary efforts to recover their independence.

All of the Cyclades, except Delos, became tributary to Athens, when that state acquired the sovereignty of the seas.

Creté was renowned in the Heroic Age for the laws of Minos (B. C. 1300). After the death of Cleanthus, about B. C. 800, most of the chief Cretan cities adopted republican constitutions, and thereafter were independent states. The Cretans seldom engaged in foreign wars, but were almost constantly involved in mutual hostilities with each other, and this condition of things had a tendency to degrade the national character.

Cyprus was only partially colonized by the Greeks, their chief settlement being Salamis, founded by Teucer, shortly after the Trojan War (B. C. 1100). The island was in succession under the dominion of the Phœnicians, the Egyptians and the Persians. The Kings of Salamis often revolted against their Persian masters, and always maintained a limited independence. When Alexander the Great besieged Tyre (B. C. 332) nine Cypriot kings voluntarily joined him, and thereafter the island was a Macedonian dependency.

The island of Rhodes was the seat of the flourishing Dorian colonies of Lindus, Ialyssus and Cameirus. The island of Cos had a Dorian settlement of the same name within its limits.

SECTION VI.—GREEK COLONIES.

THE number and wide diffusion of the Greek colonies are very remarkable. From the Sea of Azov to the Pillars of Hercules (Straits of Gibraltar), nearly the whole coasts of the continents and the islands were studded with the settlements of this active and enterprising race. These colonies were most thickly sown towards the north and north-east, where the civilization of Hellas came in contact with that of Phœnicia, and where it successfully maintained itself against its formidable rival. Carthage and Tyre were unable to prevent the Greeks from forcing themselves into these regions, as well as in Egypt and Cyrenaica; while the Grecian race held exclusive possession of the northern Mediterranean shores, except in Spain, coming in contact with their Phœnician and Carthaginian rivals in the islands of Corsica, Sardinia, Sicily and Cyprus.

Two prominent causes led to the distribution of the Hellenic race over so many and such remote regions. One of the causes was the rapid increase of the race, which found itself overcrowded in its mother country and in its older colonies, and therefore sought a vent abroad. Thus arose those formidable *migrations* and colonizations of the Greek race, both in its native land and on foreign shores. The first of these Grecian colonizations of foreign shores were the Æolian, Ionian and Dorian settlements on the western shores of Asia Minor and the Achæan settlements in Southern Italy. The other chief cause of these Hellenic colonizations was the spirit of commercial or political enterprise, the state founding a colony desiring to extend its influence or its trade into a new region. The settlements thus founded were *colonies proper*, and these maintained at first a certain relation with their mother country—a relation not existing in the case of colonies arising from migrations of Hellenic races. Sometimes individual caprice or political disturbance led to the founding of new cities, but these instances were very rare.

In some of the Greek colonies proper the political connection with the mother country was weak; in others it was strong. The former were practically independent communities, attached to the mother country only by race affection and by certain prevailing usages, which were not obligatory nor very definite. The colony generally worshiped its original founder as its hero, and adored the same god as the parent city. It participated in the great festivals of its metropolis and contributed offerings to them. It distinguished the citizens of the mother country by special honors at its own games and festivals. It used the same emblems upon its coins. Its chief priests were in some cases drawn constantly from the mother country; and it sought a leader from the parent state if it intended to found a new colony itself. War between a parent city and its colony was considered impious, and each was regarded as under a certain obligation to aid the other in times of danger and emergency. The observance of these different usages, however, was entirely voluntary, no effort ever being undertaken to enforce them, the complete independence of the colonies being recognized.

In the other class of Greek colonies the parent state sent a body of its citizens to found a new settlement in territory which it considered its own; the colonists retaining all their rights as citizens of their mother country, and being chiefly a garrison in the new settlement designed to uphold the authority of those who sent them out. These colonies thus were absolutely and entirely dependent upon the parent state. The cleruchs were simply citizens of their mother country, who had been assigned certain special duties and granted certain benefits.

The Greek settlements of every class may be divided geographically into Eastern, Western and Southern. The Eastern colonies were those on the eastern and northern shores of the Ægean and on the northern and southern shores of the Propontis (those on the southern coast of Macedon and Thrace and on the western coast of Asia Minor), those on the western, southern, eastern and northern shores of the Euxine, or Black Sea, and on the Palus Mæotis (now Sea of Azov). The western colonies were those of Magna Græcia (Great Greece) in Southern Italy, and those of Sicily, Gaul, Spain and the neighboring islands. The Southern colonies were those of Cyrenaïca in Northern Africa, west of Egypt.

The colonies founded by the Greeks between the time of the Dorian migration and the Macedonian conquest of Greece were the most numerous and the most important established by any ancient nation, and all contributed immensely to the advancement of civilization.

We will first notice the Greek colonies along the western or Ægean coast of Asia Minor, from the Hellespont to the borders of Cilicia, in consequence of the changes wrought by the Dorian migration and conquest of the Peloponnesus. These colonies were established by the Æolians, Ionians, Dorians and Achæans; and in them arose the first of Grecian poets, Homer and Alcæus, and the first of Grecian philosophers, Tháles and Pythágoras.

After conquering the Peloponnesus, the Æolians settled at first in Thrace; but a generation later (B. C. 1124) they passed over into Asia Minor, and occupied the coasts of Mysia and Caria, naming the strip of territory which they colonized *Æolis*. They likewise colonized the islands of Lesbos, Tenedos and the group called the Hecatonnési (hundred islands). The Æolians founded twelve cities on the mainland of Asia Minor, the chief of which were Cymé and Smyrna, the others being Myrina, Gryneium and Pitané, on the coast, and Temnus, Larissa, Neonteichos, Ægæ, Cilla, Notium and Ægiroëssa, in the interior. Smyrna was destroyed by the Lydians, B. C. 600, and was not restored for four hundred years, after which it became a prosperous Macedonian colony. Mitylêné, on the island of Lesbos, was the most important of the Æolian cities in this quarter. It was the home of Pittacus, one of the Seven Wise Men of Greece. Methymna, Antissa, Eresus and Pyrrha were Æolian cities in the island of Lesbos. Cymé and Lesbos sent out colonies which settled along the shores of the Ægean to the Hellespont, thus founding the towns of Antandrus, Gargara and Assus. Sestus, in the Chersonesus, and Ænus, on the coast of Thrace, were also Æolian colonies. The Æolian towns were independent of each other. The Æolian cities of Asia Minor were finally conquered by Crœsus, the great Lydian king, in B. C. 568, and by Cyrus the Great of Persia in B. C. 554, but they afterwards became independent.

The Ionian migration, which occurred some years later than the Æolian, about B. C. 1044, was the largest that ever left Greece. The direct cause of this migration was the abolition of royalty at Athens. The sons of Codrus, unwilling to retire to private life, determined to lead a colony to Asia Minor, and were readily joined by the Ionian exiles from the northern Peloponnesus, who were overcrowded in Attica, and by large numbers of emigrants from neighboring states, who were actuated by political discontent or by the mere desire for change. They were supplied liberally with ships and munitions of war, after which they sailed to Asia Minor, landing on the Ægean coast south of Æolis. After many bloody wars with the native barbarians, the Ionians acquired possession of the lands along that coast from Milétus to Mount Sipylus.

The Ionians founded twelve cities in the new district, which received the name of *Ionia*. The twelve Ionian cities were Ephesus, Erythræ, Clazomenæ, Colophon, Myus, Milétus, Priene, Phocæa, Lebedos, Samos, Teos and Chios, of which the last three were on islands bearing their respective names. Phocæa and Milétus were by far the most important of these cities in early times. Milétus became a powerful state and for a long time warred successfully with the Kings of Lydia, but was finally subdued. As early as B. C. 780 Milétus sent colonies which settled on the shores of the Hellespont, the Propontis, the Euxine and the Sea of Azov. About B. C. 600 Phocæa became renowned as a maritime power, her sailors being the first Greeks who explored the Adriatic and the Western Mediterranean, and the only Greeks known to have ventured beyond the Pillars of Hercules into the Atlantic Ocean. The Phocæans traded with Tartessus in Spain, and founded Alalia, in Corsica; Massilia (now Marseilles) on the southern coast of Gaul; and Elea, or Velia (now Vela), in Italy. Samos became a great power about B. C. 550, under the tyrant Polycrates, and extended her dominion over many of the islands of the Ægean. The Ionian Greeks also colonized the Ægean islands of Ceos, Cythnus, Seriphus, Siphnus, Paros, Naxos, Syros, Andros, Tenos, Rheneia, Delos and Myconus.

All the twelve Ionian cities of Asia Minor and the neighboring islands were united by an Amphictyonic confederacy. Deputies from the different cities met, at stated times, in the temple of Poseidon on the promontory of Mycále, which they called Helicónean, from Helíce, the chief of the Ionian cities in the North of the Peloponnesus.

In this temple they deliberated on all matters relating to the Pan-Ionian league; but this Amphictyonic Council never interfered with the domestic affairs of the different Ionian cities. They also celebrated festivals and public games, which rivaled those of Greece proper in magnificence. In the midst of their prosperity, the Ionian cities became involved in a long and desperate struggle with the Kings of Lydia, which resulted in the gradual conquest of the several cities by the Lydian monarchs. Milétus successfully resisted all attempts at subjugation until its conquest by Crœsus in the first half of the sixth century before Christ. When Lydia was conquered by Cyrus the Great of Persia in B. C. 554, the Ionian cities of Asia Minor were also absorbed into the Medo-Persian dominion, but they afterwards became independent.

The Dorians being checked in their conquests in Greece proper after their subjugation of the Peloponnesus, many of them proceeded in detached bands to the coast of Caria and to the islands of Cos and Rhodes. This was after the Æolian and Ionian migrations. The six cities of the Dorian Hexapolis were Halicarnassus and Cnidus, on the Carian peninsula, Cos in the island of the same name, and Ialyssus, Cameirus and Lindus in the island of Rhodes. These were united thus in a sort of Amphictyony, which met in the temple of Apollo Triopius, near Cnidus. Other Dorian cities in Caria were Myndus and Phasélis.

Dorian colonies were settled in the Southern Cyclades, namely, in such islands as Melos, Pholegandrus, Thera, Anaphé, Astypalæa, Calymna, Nisyrus, Telos and Chalcia.

The Dorian colonies in Asia Minor were inferior to the Æolian or the Ionian, both in extent and importance. Occupying a narrow and unfruitful tract in Caria, south of Ionia, the six cities of the Dorian Hexapolis always continued in a condition of weakness, only Halicarnassus and Cnidus, on the mainland, in Caria, arriving at any degree of importance, while Lindus in the island of Rhodes also reached a degree of consideration. The bold navigators of Rhodes rivaled those of the most powerful commercial states. Halicarnassus eventually became the capital of a wealthy monarchy; and this city was the native place of two renowned Greek historians—Herodotus, "the Father of History," and Dionysius Halicarnassus.

The Dorian colonies were finally subdued by Crœsus, and when Lydia was conquered by Cyrus the Great they passed under the Medo-Persian dominion. A dynasty of Hellenized Carians ruled in Halicarnassus under the Persian kings.

Most of the Greek colonies on the shores of the Propontis (now Sea of Marmora), the Euxine (now Black Sea), and the Pálus Mæótis (now Sea of Azov), were founded by the citizens of Milétus during the eighth and ninth centuries before Christ. Milétus, whose commerce occupied four harbors and whose naval power amounted to almost a hundred war-galleys, owed its prosperity and greatness to its control of the northern trade. To secure this lucrative commerce, the Milésians founded numerous colonies along all the coasts of the Euxine and the Propontis, all of which became prosperous commercial marts. Their commerce was not limited to the sea-coasts. Their merchants penetrated into Scythia and advanced even beyond the Caspian to the regions now embraced in the Khanates of Khiva and Bokhara. The Phocæans also established important colonies, but they were mainly absorbed in the western trade, leaving the northern to the Milésians, who founded almost all the colonies along the shores of the Euxine.

On the eastern or Euxine coast of Thrace were a number of Greek colonies, the most important of which, beginning from the south, near the Bosphorus, were Apollonia, Mesambria, Odessus, Callatis, Tomi and Istria, all of which were Milésian settlements, except Mesambria, which was Megarian. These colonies were mainly founded in the seventh century before Christ. Odessus was once the head of a league of most of these cities. The most important of them commercially was Istria, or Istropolis.

The coasts of Thrace and Macedon were lined with flourishing Greek colonies, which were principally settled from Athens and Corinth.

The Greek colonies on the northern coast of the Ægean were Methône, on the eastern coast of the Thermic Gulf, founded about B. C. 730 by colonists from Eretria, and in Pallêné, Sithonia and Acté, which were on the three great projections of the Chalcidic peninsula. Potidæa, the most important of these in early times, was a colony from Corinth. The Chalcidian cities in Sithonia were Torôné, Singus, Sermylé, Galepsus and Mecyberna. Olynthus became a possession of Chalcedon in B. C. 480. The colonies of Eretria were chiefly in Pallêné, and the most important was Mendé. Sané was founded by Andros, near the canal of Xerxes. Acanthus, Stageirus and Argilus were on the coast between Athos and Amphipolis. Chalcedon and Olynthus arose to great power in the fifth and fourth centuries before Christ.

The Greek colonies on the coast of Thrace, between the Strymon and Nessus rivers, were Amphipolis, Eïon, Myrcinus, Apollonia, Galepsus, Œsymé, Neapolis, Datum, Scapté-Hylé and Crenides (afterwards Philippi). The earliest of these settlements were made from Thasos. Mycrinus was founded by a colony from Mitylêné about B. C. 508. Amphipolis was founded by Athens B. C. 465, and soon became a powerful and important city. It revolted from Athens B. C. 424, and was conquered by Philip of Macedon B. C. 358. The Greek colonies between the Nestus and the Hellespont were Abdera, founded by the Teians when their city had been threatened by Harpagus, the Persian general, about B. C. 553; Maroneia, a colony of Chios; Mesambria, of Samothrace; Cardia, of Milétus and Clazomenæ; Elæus, of Teos; Ænos, Alopeconnésus and Sestos of Æolis. The Greek cities of Madytus, Gallipolis and Pactya were in the Chersonésus, which became a powerful kingdom under the first Miltiades about B. C. 560, and which was held by the Persians from B. C. 493 to B. C. 419. On the Illyrian coast of the Adriatic were Apollonia and Epidamnus.

The Phocæans founded Lampsacus on the Propontis adjoining the Hellespont, having previously obtained a grant of the site of the city from one of the native princes whom they had aided in war. Lampsacus was subsequently occupied by the Milésians, under whom it became a place of vast wealth and immense commerce. Other Milésian colonies on the Asiatic coast of the Propontis were Priapus, Artacé and Cius. Proconnésus was a Milésian colony in an island in mid sea. Parium was a colony of Erythræ.

Cyzicus, a very ancient city, erected on an island connected by bridges with the coast of Asia Minor, is said to have been founded in the earliest ages by the Tyrrhenian Pelasgi, and to have been subsequently occupied by the Argonauts. About B. C. 751 it was taken possession of by the Milésians, who likewise occupied the neighboring island of Proconnésus (now Marmora). Under the Roman dominion, Cyzicus became one of the most beautiful and flourishing cities of Asia Minor.

On the coast of Thrace, just opposite Cyzicus, was Perinthus, afterwards called Heracleia, which was founded by a colony from Samos. On the European side of the Bosphorus was Byzantium (now Constantinople), named from Byzas, who founded the city in B. C. 606. Byzantium was the most prosperous of the Greek colonies in this quarter. This city commanded the entrance to the Euxine Sea, and therefore controlled the important trade which the Greeks carried on, chiefly for corn, with Thrace and Scythia. Opposite Byzantium, on the Asiatic side of the Bosphorus, was Chalcedon (now Scutari). Both Byzantium and Chalcedon were founded by Megarian colonies.

Heracleia, on the Bithynian coast, which was colonized first from Megara and afterwards from Milétus, was the first Greek colony on the shores of the Euxine. The most powerful Grecian state on the Euxine shores was Sinôpe, in Paphlagonia, founded

Greek Priestess—Greek Ladies.

Greek Peasants.

Greek Generals.

Victors in the Olympian Games—Priest of Bacchus—Greek King.

GREECE.

by the Milésians. The next best harbor on the Euxine coast, to Sinópe, was Amísus, in Pontus, also a Milésian colony. After being long under the dominion of Milétus, Amísus was seized by the Athenians during the age of Pericles, when its name was changed to Peiræǽus. In the time of its prosperity, Amísus founded a colony which soon surpassed the parent state in importance—Trapezus (now Trebizond).

Phásis, Dioscúrias and Phanagória were on the eastern coast of the Euxine, and were early Milésian colonies. During the Macedonian period Phanagória became the capital of the Greek cities on the Asiatic side of the Bosphorus. It owed its prosperity to its being the principal mart for the slave-trade, which has ever been prevalent in the countries around the Caucasus, and likewise to its being the emporium for the products brought from Central and Southern Asia by way of the Caspian Sea and the Oxus river.

The Milésians founded settlements in the Tauric Chersonésus (now Crimea), and wrested most of that peninsula from the barbarous natives. The chief of the Milésian settlements in the Tauric Chersonésus and on the neighboring coasts of Scythia were Tyras, at the mouth of the river Tyras (now Dniester); Olbia, on the estuary of the Hypanus (now Bug); Panticapæum (afterwards Bosphorus), near the modern Kertch; Phanagória, on the opposite Asiatic coast; Theudosia, on the site of Kaffa; and Tanais, at the mouth of the river Tanais (now Don). Chersonésus Heracleiotica, near the site of the modern Sebastopol, was a colony of Heracleia Pontica, on the opposite coast of Asia Minor, which was itself a colony from Megara. These colonies were mostly founded in the eighth century before Christ. The most important of the Milésian colonies in this quarter was the city of Panticapæum, which became the capital of the little Greek kingdom of the Bosphorus, and which maintained its independence until the first century before Christ, when it was seized by Mithridates the Great, the powerful King of Pontus, who there laid the foundations of his subsequent power.

On the coast of Northern Africa, west of Egypt, was the flourishing Greek city of Cyrênê, founded by a Dorian colony from the island of Théra, about B. C. 651, in obedience to the direction of the Delphic oracle. The government was at first a monarchy, the crown being hereditary in the family of Battus, the founder of the city; but the people of Cyrênê could never establish a permanent constitution, and the state was distracted by domestic dissensions until it was annexed to the Egyptian kingdom of the Ptolemies. The territory of Cyrênê was called the Cyrenaica, and other important cities besides Cyrênê were Barca and Apollonia, the latter the port of Cyrênê.

In Southern Italy there were so many Greek colonies that the country was called *Magna Græcia* (Great Greece). The earliest Greek settlement in Southern Italy was made by a colony from Chalcis, in the island of Eubœa. This colony founded Cúmæ, B. C. 1030. This city early reached a high degree of prosperity, established a powerful navy, and founded many flourishing colonies, the chief of which were Neapolis (now Naples) and Zancle (afterwards called Messana). Cúmæ had an aristocratic form of government. This constitution was subverted by the tyrant Aristodémus, B. C. 544, but his assassination restored the old constitution. Exhausted by civil dissensions and suffering severely in a war with the Etrurians and Daunians (B. C. 500), the Cúmæans were eventually subdued by the Campanians. Cúmæ was annexed to the territories of the Roman Republic B. C. 345, but on account of its harbor at Pateoli it remained important even after losing its independence.

Tarentum was founded by the Parthenii from Sparta, under Phalantus, B. C. 707. These colonists were obliged to carry on long wars against the Italian tribes in their vicinity, particularly the Massapians and the Lucanians. They triumphed over these native barbarians, and made their city one of the most flourishing maritime states in the West of Europe. But luxury ultimately rendered them weak and effeminate. To escape the grasping ambition of Rome, the

Tarentines invited Pyrrhus, King of Epirus, the greatest general of his time, into Italy. After gaining several great victories over the Romans, Pyrrhus was defeated and withdrew from Italy; whereupon Tarentum became a dependency of Rome (B. C. 277).

Croton was founded by the Achæans, B. C. 710. Even during the first century of its existence, this city became so powerful as to raise an army of one hundred and twenty thousand men. The constitution was very democratic, and so continued until the philosopher Pythágoras made his residence at Croton (B. C. 540). He established a kind of secret association among his disciples, the main purpose of which was to secure the chief political power in the hands of the Pythagoréan society. In a few years three hundred Pythagoréans held the sovereignty of Croton, and the influence of the new sect extended over all the Greek colonies of Italy and Sicily, and even over Greece proper and the isles of the Ægean. The Crotonians soon afterwards warred with the Sybarites and destroyed their city. Intoxicated with prosperity, and under the instigation of the artful and ambitious Cylon, who had been excluded from the Pythagoréan order because of his turbulent manners, the inferior men of Croton clamored for an equal division of the conquered territory of Sybaris; and when this demand was denied, as incompatible with the nature of the Pythagoréan oligarchy, these inferior Crotonians secretly plotted against their rulers, attacked them with surprise in the senate-house, put many of them to death, and drove the others into exile. Pythágoras himself soon afterwards died at Metapontum, in Lucania, having lived just long enough to see the ruin of the oligarchy to which he devoted his labors in building up. Croton never fully recovered from the effects of this ruinous civil war. It was frequently captured by the Kings of Syracuse, and it became a dependency of Rome after the departure of Pyrrhus from Italy.

Sybaris was founded by an Achæan colony, B. C. 720. The exceedingly-fertile soil, and the liberality in admitting all strangers to the privileges of citizenship, caused such a rapid increase in the population that the Sybarites are said to have raised an army of three hundred thousand men in a war against the Crotonians. Its immense wealth, obtained mainly from a vast trade in wine and oil with the people of North Africa and Gaul, made Sybaris the most populous and luxurious city in Europe during the half century from B. C. 600 to B. C. 550; and the Sybarites became notorious for their debauchery and effeminacy. The contests between the aristocratic and democratic factions produced a civil war. At length Télys, the democratic leader, obtained the supreme power and banished five hundred of the leading nobles, who sought refuge in Crotona. The Sybarites demanded these refugees, and when this demand was rejected they put the Crotonian ambassadors to death. This outrage of course produced a war between Sybaris and Croton (B. C. 510). The Crotonians defeated a far superior Sybarite army in the field, took Sybaris by storm and razed the city to the ground.

Driven from their homes, the Sybarites solicited the aid of the Spartans and the Athenians in restoring their city, and requesting them to send a colony to swell the population of the proposed new city. The Spartans refused the request of the Sybarite ambassadors, but the Athenians gladly granted them assistance (B. C. 446). An Athenian squadron of ten ships under Lampo and Xenócrates was sent to Italy with a large body of troops on board; while a proclamation was made throughout Greece, offering the protection of the Athenian fleet to all who would emigrate to the new colony. Many availed themselves of the offer; and the Sybarites, with the aid of the new colonists, soon regained their old possessions, and founded Thurium, near the site of Sybaris. But Thurium was soon torn by quarrels among its heterogeneous population, concerning who should be regarded as founders of the new city. The Delphic oracle was appealed to (B. C. 433), and the priests of that sanctuary declared Thurium to be a colony of Apollo. But the

Sybarites were not satisfied with this decision; and, believing themselves to have the best right to the country, they began to exclude, from all honors and employments, the foreign colonists whom they had invited to join them in founding the new city; but, as the new foreigners were the most numerous, this proceeding provoked a civil war, which ended in a second expulsion of the Sybarites. The Thurians then invited fresh colonists from Greece, and formed themselves into a commonwealth, choosing Charondas, of Catana, for their lawgiver. They were soon enervated by luxury; and, as they were unable to defend themselves against the Lucanians, they placed themselves under the powerful protection of Rome. This gave the Tarentines a pretext for attacking Thurium, which they captured, thus subjecting themselves to the vengeance of the Romans. After the Roman conquest of Tarentum, Thurium became a Roman dependency. The city suffered terribly in the Second Punic War; and, having become almost depopulated, was occupied by a Roman colony (B. C. 190).

The city of Locri-Epizephyrii was founded by colonists from Locri-Ozolæ (B. C. 683); but these were joined by various settlers, mainly from the West of Greece. Zaleúcus, one of their own citizens, became the lawgiver of the Locrians, and his wise institutions remained intact for two centuries. The constitution seemed to have contained a judicious mingling of aristocratic and democratic elements. The Locrians were noted for their peaceful condition, their quiet conduct and good manners, until Dionysius II., the tyrant of Syracuse, having been exiled by his subjects, sought refuge in Locri-Epizephyrii, which was his mother's native country (B. C. 357). His insolence and licentiousness, and the excesses of his followers, brought Locri-Epizephyrii to the brink of ruin; and, when he returned to Syracuse (B. C. 347), the Locrians revenged their wrongs on his unfortunate family. When Pyrrhus invaded Italy, he placed a garrison in Locri-Epizephyrii (B. C. 277); but the Locrians revolted and massacred the garrison. In revenge the King of Epirus stormed and pillaged the city. After his return to his own kingdom, Locri-Epizephyrii submitted to the Romans, and suffered terribly in the Second Punic War.

Rhégium was a Greek colony founded jointly by the Chalcidians and the Messenians (B. C. 668); but the Messenian aristocracy possessed the chief political power. Auaxilaüs subverted this oligarchy and established an absolute despotism (B. C. 494). The Rhégians sometime afterward recovered their freedom, and sought to secure tranquillity by adopting the constitution of Charondas from the Thurians. Rhégium thereafter enjoyed tranquillity and happiness, until it was captured and destroyed by Dionysius I., of Syracuse (B. C. 392). Dionysius II. partly restored the city; but during the wars of Pyrrhus with the Romans, it was so weak that it required a Roman garrison to protect it. A legion, raised in Campania, was sent to Rhégium, under the command of Décius Jubellus. These soldiers had been accustomed to a life of hardship, and they soon began to envy the luxurious ease and wealth of the citizens they had come to protect, and treacherously planned their destruction. They forged letters from the Rhégians to Pyrrhus, offering to surrender the city to that monarch; and, under this pretense, they massacred most of the citizens and drove the others into exile. The Roman Senate quickly punished this outrage, sending an army against the guilty Campanians, who had been reinforced by several bands of profligate plunderers; and, after a desperate struggle, the Roman troops obtained possession of the city, and scourged the guilty legionaries with rods and beheaded them in bands of fifty at a time. The few surviving Rhégians had their estates, their liberties and laws, restored to them. But the city was reduced to such weakness that it was unable to maintain its independence, and it therefore became subject to Rome.

The principal Greek colonies in Sicily

were Syracuse, Agrigentum, Géla, Camarína, Selinus and Megara-Hyblæa, founded by the Dorians; and Naxos, Catana, Leontini, Messana and Himéra, founded by the Ionians. Of all these cities, Syracuse was by far the most important, and its history is largely the history of ancient Sicily. Syracuse was founded by a Corinthian colony under the direction of Archytas, a nobleman of rank who had been obliged to leave his native country on account of a political dispute. Syracuse had a republican form of government for two and a half centuries, and during this period the Syracusans founded the colonies of Acræ, Casmenæ and Camarina. An aristocratic faction cruelly oppressed the citizens, but the populace threw off their yoke and drove the tyrannical nobles into exile (B. C. 485). They fled to Géla, then under the rule of Gélon, an able and ambitious usurper, who had just become sovereign of his country. Gélon raised an army, and marched to Syracuse, accompanied by the exiles, and easily obtained possession of the city.

Under the administration of Gélon, Syracuse rose suddenly to wealth and importance, while Gélon himself won such renown by his repeated victories over the Carthaginians that the Athenians and Spartans, at that time threatened by the Persian invasion, eagerly sought his aid. Gélon demanded, as a condition of such aid, that he be appointed captain-general of the allied Greeks, but the Athenians and Spartans sternly refused such a stipulation; and before Gélon could take any further steps, he ascertained that Xerxes had engaged the Carthaginians to attack the Greek colonies in Sicily and Italy, while he invaded Greece proper.

After three years of preparation, the Carthaginians sent against Sicily a vast armament, under the command of Hamilcar, numbering, it is said, three hundred thousand men, two thousand ships of war, and three thousand vessels of burden. After landing in Sicily, Hamilcar besieged Himéra, then ruled by Théron, Gélon's father-in-law. The King of Syracuse could muster only fifty thousand men for this sudden emergency, but he marched hastily to raise the siege of Himéra. On his way he fortunately intercepted a messenger from the Selinuntines to the Carthaginian general, promising to send him a stipulated body of cavalry on a specified day. Gélon led the same number of his own horsemen to the Carthaginian camp at the appointed time; and, having been admitted unsuspectedly, he suddenly attacked the enemy, who were so thoroughly disconcerted by the assault that their entire host was completely demoralized, and the Syracusans gained an easy triumph. Hamilcar was slain, and his army was cut to pieces. Carthage humbly sued for peace, which the conquering Syracusans generously granted. During the few remaining years of his reign, Gélon strenuously devoted himself to the welfare of his subjects; and after his death the Syracusans honored him as a demi-god.

Gélon died B. C. 477, and was succeeded by his brother Hiero I., whose reign was more brilliant than beneficial. He protected the arts and sciences, but he also encouraged a taste for luxury and magnificence, contrary to his more enlightened predecessor's policy. He conquered the cities of Catana and Naxos, expelled their inhabitants, and repopulated those cities with colonies from Syracuse and the Peloponnesus. He also inflicted a decisive defeat upon the Etruscan pirates off Cúmæ. These pirates had for a time been the terror of the Western Mediterranean, but after Hiero's victory over them they did not again infest the seas for several centuries. After this great achievement Hiero engaged in a war with the tyrant of Agrigentum, who was obliged to resign his power, whereupon his subjects placed themselves under Hiero's protection.

Thrasybúlus, also a brother of Gélon, succeeded to the sovereignty of Syracuse upon Hiero's death, in B. C. 459; but his tyranny and cruelty soon provoked a revolution, which ended in his dethronement and the restoration of the republican constitution. The Syracusans, however, gained little by the change. A system of secret voting, called *petalism*, was instituted, exactly like the Athenian ostracism, and most of the prominent statesmen were banished by the vote of the fickle populace. At this period the Athenians made their unfortunate attempt to conquer Sicily, whose disastrous result will be fully described in our account of the Peloponnesian War. After the utter destruction of the Athenian armaments (B. C. 413), the Egestans, who had invited the Athenians to make the invasion, solicited and procured the aid of Carthage; thus giving rise to a series of sanguinary wars, which we have already described in the history of Carthage.

Dionysius I. took advantage of the political disturbances in Syracuse by usurping the government (B. C. 405), and though he deserves the title of tyrant, his vigorous reign was signalized by triumphs over foreign foes and by internal prosperity. Most of his reign was occupied in wars with Carthage and the cities of Magna Græcia, and likewise against the ancient race of the Siculi, whose choice of party usually decided the success of these wars.

Dionysius I. was poisoned B. C. 368, and was succeeded by his youthful son, Dionysius II., who was under the guidance of the virtuous Dio. But neither Dio nor his friend, the great Athenian philosopher, Plato, was able to reform the corrupted character of the young sovereign. He banished Dio (B. C. 360), and then utterly abandoned himself to the most extravagant luxury and debauchery. Dio returned three years later (B. C. 357), and restored the republican form of government, after a long struggle, but was assassinated (B. C. 353). Syracuse was also distracted by the contests of sanguinary factions, and Dionysius II. took advantage of these to recover his throne, after ten years of exile. His tyranny, and the treachery of Icetas, the Leontine, who, when invited to aid the Syracusans, betrayed their interests to the Carthaginians, obliged the Syracusans to solicit assistance from Corinth. Timóleon, one of the truest republicans of ancient history, was sent from Corinth to the aid of the Syracusans, but with forces entirely insufficient for the emergency (B. C. 345). His abilities, however, triumphed over all obstacles. He dethroned Dionysius II., expelled Icetas, and humbled the pride of the Carthaginians by a brilliant victory. After Timóleon's death (B. C. 357), Syracuse was for a long time in a weak and distracted condition, which was terminated by the usurpation of Agathocles (B. C. 317). The wars of that usurper have been described in our account of the history of Carthage.

After the death of Agathocles (B. C. 289), the Syracusans, distracted by domestic dissensions, and hard pressed by the Mamertines and the Carthaginians, suffered the most terrible misfortunes, and were eventually obliged to solicit the aid of Pyrrhus, King of Epirus. After having conquered nearly the whole of Sicily, Pyrrhus so disgusted his supporters by his arrogance that he was obliged to retire from the island (B. C. 275). Tired of anarchy, the Syracusans at length conferred the throne on Híero II., a descendant of the ancient royal family of Gélon. Under this sovereign, Syracuse enjoyed peace and prosperity during the wars between Rome and Carthage, in which the city wisely sided with the Romans. Híero II. died of old age (B. C. 215), after a long and prosperous reign. After his death the party friendly to Carthage acquired the ascendency in Syracuse, and by the profligate use of their power so provoked the resentment of the Romans that a Roman army was sent into Sicily. After a long siege, protracted by the mechanical skill and ingenuity of the renowned mathematician and philosopher, Archimédes, the Romans took Syracuse by storm and razed the city to the ground (B. C. 212).

Most of the other Greek cities in Sicily were involved in the fortunes of Syracuse. As the Carthaginians had used Agrigentum for a naval station, the Romans seized that city as early as B. C. 262. Sicily ultimately became a Roman province, and was one of the most valuable of all the Roman possessions. It was one of the best governed of the Roman territories, in consequence of its vicinity to the heart of the Roman power, but more especially on account of its corn-harvests being considered the resource to which the Romans should look, as the agricultural productions of Italy became more and more insufficient to supply the Roman population.

The Greeks also established colonies in Gaul, Spain and Corsica. Massilia (now Marseilles), founded by the enterprising Phocæans about B. C. 600, was the most important Grecian colony on the coast of Gaul, and was famous for its trade by sea and land, its merchants visiting the interior of Gaul, and even procuring tin and lead by this route from the Scilly Isles. Her territory was rich in corn and wine. Massilia extended her colonies eastward and westward along the coast of Gaul. It planted the colonies of Olbia, Antipolis (now Autibes), Nicæa (now Nice), and Monœcus (now Monaco), to the east along the coast. To the west Massilia planted such colonies as Agatha, Rhoda, Emporiæ, Hemeroscopeium, and Mænaca, the last named near Malaga, in Spain. Commercial jealousy between Massilia and Carthage led to frequent wars between the two powers, but Massilia was always victorious. The hostility of the native Gauls and Ligurians was far more dangerous to the security of Massilia; but these troublesome foes were held in check, with the aid of the Romans, who became allies of Massilia in B. C. 218; and Massilia remained independent until the time of the Roman civil wars, when it was conquered by Julius Cæsar and annexed to Rome's dominions. Saguntum was a Greek city in Spain, whose capture by Hannibal caused the Second Punic War.

Thus it will be seen that the Hellenic race, instead of being confined to Greece proper and the neighboring islands, had diffused itself over a great portion of the ancient world, peopling the shores of the Mediterranean, the Ægean and the Euxine. Wherever the Greek language was spoken and wherever Grecian civilization was carried there was Hellas.

SECTION VII.—SPARTA UNDER THE LAWS OF LYCURGUS.

THE city of Sparta was built on a series of hills, whose outlines were varied and romantic, along the right bank of the river Eurótas, within sight of the chain of Mount Taygétum. Sparta was for centuries without walls and fortifications, relying upon the valor of its inhabitants as sufficient to protect itself against the attacks of foreign enemies. But the most lofty hill served for a citadel, and around this hill five towns were ranged, separated by considerable intervals, and occupied by the five Spartan tribes. The great forum, or public square, in which the leading streets of these five towns terminated, was adorned with temples and statues, and contained edifices in which the Senate, the Ephori, and other public bodies of Spartan magistrates were accustomed to assemble. There was likewise a splendid portico, erected by the Spartans from their portion of the spoils taken from the Persians in the battle of Platæa. The roof did not rest on pillars, but was supported by immense statues, representing the Persians attired in flowing robes. On the highest eminence was the temple of Athênê, which had the privileges of a place of refuge, as had the grove surrounding it. This temple was built of brass, as the one to Apollo at Delphi had originally been. Most of these Spartan public edifices were not distinguished by any architectural beauty, being of rude workmanship and destitute of ornamentation Private houses in Sparta were small and unadorned, as the Spartans spent most of their time in porticoes and public halls. On the south side

of the city was the Hippodromos, or racecourse, and near that was the Platanistæ, or place of exercise for youth, shaded by beautiful palm-trees.

The Dorian conquerors of Laconia constituted themselves a permanent ruling caste at Sparta, reducing most of the inhabitants of the country to a condition of vassalage, or more properly, to a state of complete slavery. During the two centuries that Sparta carried on tedious wars with Argos, the Spartan state was distracted by domestic dissensions, resulting from the unequal division of property, the ambition of rival nobles, and the diminishing power of the kings.

In the early period of Spartan history, after the Dorian conquest and occupation, the Dorian conquerors endeavored to extend their power. They were at first confined to the upper portion of the valley between the Taygétus and Parnon mountain-ranges, a region about twenty-five miles long by about twenty miles wide. The Achæans occupied the lower valley, containing the capital, Amyclæ, on the Eurótas, about two miles south of Sparta. For three centuries there was constant war between Sparta and Amyclæ, but Sparta made no progress southward. The powerful fortifications of Amyclæ held the Spartans in check and baffled every effort which they made to extend their dominion. Sparta then unsuccessfully endeavored to reduce Arcadia. She even provoked quarrels with Messenia and Argos, which led to wars of little consequence. In the eleventh century before Christ, the Dorians fully established themselves in the Peloponnesus. Sparta continued her struggle with Amyclæ for the possession of the Eurótas valley, and was confined to the upper portion of the valley by the Achæans.

During this period Sparta had been rapidly growing in power and importance. Sparta was governed by two kings, who acted as checks upon each other, and the royal power was consequently reduced to almost utter insignificance by the middle of the ninth century before Christ.

The Spartan nation consisted of three classes. The first of these was the *Spartans*, numbering nine thousand, who inhabited the capital, and who were descended from the Dorian conquerors and constituted the nobles of the state. These possessed the whole political power in the state, owned most of the land, and lived in Sparta on the rents paid them by their tenants. The second class were the *Periœci*, the free inhabitants of the rural towns and villages of Laconia, who were citizens in a certain sense, but had no political rights. They were of mingled Doric and Achæan descent, were scattered over Laconia, possessed the poorest lands, and were the only class engaged in commerce and the mechanical arts. They constituted the heavy-armed troops in the Spartan armies, but were not subject to the military discipline of the Spartans. The third class were the *Helots*, or slaves, who were originally of Achæan blood, and who were employed in cultivating the lands of their Spartan masters, to whom they paid a fixed rent of half the produce.

Towards the close of the ninth century before Christ, Sparta suddenly emerged from obscurity; and under the wise legislation of Lycurgus, her celebrated lawgiver, she became the great rival of Athens. Lycurgus was the second son of Eunomus, one of the two joint Kings of Sparta, and is believed to have flourished in the latter part of the ninth century before Christ. After the death of Eunomus, who was killed in a seditious tumult, his eldest son, Polydectes, succeeded to the throne, but died shortly afterward. Lycurgus became his successor, but reigned only for a short time. Ascertaining that a posthumous child of Polydectes would probably soon be born, Lycurgus announced his determination to abdicate the throne, if the child proved to be a son, and to continue to administer the government only as protector or regent during his nephew's minority. When the widow of Polydectes heard of the intention of Lycurgus, she told him privately that if he would marry her, no child of his brother should ever stand in the way of his possession of the throne. Lycurgus was horrified at this unmotherly proposition, but discreetly suppressed his indignation; and, to insure the preservation of the child, induced his sister-in-law to believe that he himself intended to destroy it immediately after its birth. At the same time he secretly instructed her attendants to bring the child to him as soon as it was born. Accordingly, one evening, as he was supping with the magistrates of the city, the fatherless infant boy was brought to Lycurgus, who instantly took his newly-born nephew in his arms, and, addressing the company, said: "Spartans, behold your king." The Spartans joyfully hailed the infant boy as their sovereign, and expressed the strongest admiration of the disinterested and upright course of Lycurgus in thus relinquishing the crown when he could have retained it so easily.

Although this noble act of Lycurgus raised him in the estimation of good men, it made the disappointed widow of Polydectes and her friends and adherents, his enemies. They circulated a report that Lycurgus designed murdering the infant and usurping the throne, and pursued him so relentlessly with their annoyances and persecutions that he at length retired to Crete, to study the peculiar laws and institutions of Minos, which had been instrumental in raising that island to great power and prosperity. The similarity of the system instituted afterwards at Sparta by Lycurgus to that established in Crete by Minos adequately demonstrates that the Spartan lawgiver had taken the Cretan institutions as his model. After residing for some time in Crete, Lycurgus proceeded to Asia Minor, and examined the laws, customs and manners of the Grecian cities founded in that quarter. At that time the Ionian colonies of Asia Minor far surpassed the most flourishing of the parent states of Greece. These colonies had at this early day advanced considerably in commerce and the arts, in consequence of their favorable maritime position, their fertile soil and their wise institutions. Lycurgus found there the poems of Homer, partly collected them, and subsequently introduced them into Greece proper, where they had previously been almost unknown.

During the absence of Lycurgus from Sparta, the internal disorders and factious broils which had distracted the state for so long a period reached such a degree that the laws fell into utter contempt, the authority of the kings was entirely disregarded, and anarchy and confusion prevailed. This deplorable condition of affairs convinced the Spartan people that a reform of the national institutions was absolutely essential to the welfare of the state. The eyes of the Spartans were therefore directed to Lycurgus, as the person whose experience, wisdom and integrity particularly fitted him for the work of framing a new constitution for his country. Lycurgus agreed to undertake this duty, after frequent invitations to do so; but before beginning his legislative task, he considered it advisable to procure the sanction of religion for the institutions which he intended to introduce at Sparta, in order that these institutions might receive the ready acquiescence of his countrymen. He accordingly went to Delphi, where he obtained a response from the famous oracle, telling him that he was peculiarly favored by the gods, that he was himself more divine than human, and that the system which he was about to establish would be the most excellent ever invented. Having thus secured the sanction of the Delphic oracle, Lycurgus returned to Sparta, where he cautiously began his labors by explaining his plans privately to a few of his friends. After having secured the coöperation and support of many of the leading citizens, he proceeded to summon a general assembly of the Spartan people, at which his party was strong enough to overcome all opposition, and he was therefore enabled to proceed openly in the development of his plans and the reduction of them to practice.

Lycurgus first devoted himself to the improvement of the civil and political institutions of Sparta. He retained the system of divided royalty established in the time of the twin-brothers, Eurysthenes and Procles, and he confirmed the joint possession of the throne to the descendants of these princes, though he greatly restricted the royal prerogative, transferring the executive authority to a Senate of thirty members, including the two kings, who were the official presidents of the body. The other twenty-eight Senators were selected from the wisest and most noble of the citizens of Sparta, and Lycurgus directed that the successors of these twenty-eight should ever afterward be elected by the Spartan people. The Senators were to hold their offices for life, and no person was eligible to the Senatorial office who was less than sixty years of age. The Senate was vested with deliberative as well as executive duties. The laws which it originated were afterwards submitted to the people in their general assemblies, for their approval or rejection, which each citizen signified by a single vote, without altering or even without discussing the measures brought before the people. Besides being presidents of the Senate, the kings were also the military commanders of the Spartans, and the high-priests of the national religion. They were favored with the chief seat in every public assembly, received strangers and ambassadors, and superintended the public buildings and the public highways. To guard against the kings exceeding their constitutional powers, five officers called *Ephori* were chosen yearly by the Spartan people; and these were vested with authority to bring any and all who violated any of the laws, irrespective of rank, to trial, and were empowered to punish, by fine or flogging, even the kings and Senators themselves.

After having settled the form of government for Sparta, Lycurgus directed his attention to reforming the social institutions and the manners of his countrymen. Observing the state menaced with danger in consequence of the animosity between the rich and the poor, he determined on the heroic measure of equally dividing the lands. He therefore parceled out the territory of Laconia into thirty-nine thousand lots, giving one of these to each citizen of Sparta, or free inhabitant of Laconia, or Lacedæmon. Each of these lots was only large enough to barely supply the necessaries of a single family, as Lycurgus was resolved that no person should be placed in circumstances enabling him to live in luxury. To render the state dependent only on its own territorial products, and to prevent any individual from accumulating an undue amount of wealth, he prohibited the use of any money, except an iron coin, with so small a value in comparison with its bulk and weight that the necessity of using it as the medium of exchange would make it difficult to carry on trade, especially foreign commerce. By subjecting this iron coin to a process rendering it brittle and unfit for any other use, Lycurgus endeavored to destroy every desire to hoard it as treasure. Some ancient writers tell us that this measure produced all the effects which Lycurgus hoped would result therefrom. Foreign merchants ceased to trade in Sparta, and the native artisans refrained from the manufacture of articles of luxury and ornament, because there was no longer any valuable money to offer in exchange for such wares.

Lycurgus struck a more effective blow at luxury by directing that all persons, regardless of rank or age, should eat only at public tables, and strictly forbidding any to eat at home or in private. These public tables were furnished with the plainest and least relishing food, supplied by the people, each individual being required to contribute monthly a certain portion of provisions for public use. To guard against any evasion of this law, by any person partaking of a richer fare at home or in private, regular attendance at the public meals was stringently enforced. This measure was at first violently resisted, and caused a tumult, during which a young man named Alcander beat out the eyes of Lycurgus; but the effect of this outrage was to turn the current of public feeling in favor of Lycurgus, and Alcander was delivered to the lawgiver for punishment. But Lycurgus took the young man home with him, and, by mild treatment and calm expostulation, convinced him of the impropriety of his conduct, thus converting him from a fierce opponent to an admiring supporter. All noisy conversation was forbidden at the public meals, and no person was permitted to mention elsewhere anything that had been said on these occasions. At the tables the Spartans reclined on benches without cushions; while their children, who were allowed to be present from a very tender age, were seated on stools at their feet. The regular fare was black broth, boiled pork, barley-bread, cheese, figs and dates. The drink was wine and water, served in quantities so small as to be barely sufficient to quench the thirst. A dessert, consisting of poultry, fish, game, cakes and fruits, was generally furnished at the expense of some private individual. At a later period, when the severity of the Spartan manners was relaxed, many rich and costly dainties and delicacies were added to the public meals, under the name of this dessert.

As intercourse with foreigners might corrupt the simple manners of the Spartans, all strangers were ordered to leave Sparta, and Spartans were not permitted to travel abroad. Lycurgus being a man of few words, disliked great talkers, and took great pains to introduce a short and forcible style of expression among his countrymen, in which he succeeded so well that Spartans soon became celebrated for the terseness and brevity of their speech. Such a style of expression is still called *laconic*, from Laconia, the name of the Spartan territory. All Spartans were subjected to a strict system of training from the day of their birth to that of their death. As soon as an infant was born, its father was obliged to bring it to certain public officers, who examined it; and if it was found to be sickly or deformed, it was considered of no use to the state, and was cast out into the fields to perish. Those infants whom these judges ordered to be preserved were then given in charge of nurses, provided by the state, who were instructed to rear the children in such a manner as to make them hardy in body and courageous in spirit.

At the age of seven years boys were placed in public schools for training and education. They were there divided into companies, over each of which an older boy, or a more active one, was placed as captain, and was authorized to repress disorder and punish the disobedient and rebellious. Their discipline was scarcely more than an apprenticeship to hardship, self-denial and obedience; and the only intellectual culture given them was an unconquerable spirit of fortitude and endurance, an enthusiastic love of military glory, and an unbounded attachment to their country. As the young were advancing in years they were subjected to severer privations, and were accustomed to still more trying exercises. In the most inclement weather they were forced to go barefoot, and were very lightly clothed, being permitted to wear but one garment, and this they were obliged to wear for an entire year, no matter how dirty and ragged it had become in the meantime. They were compelled to sleep on beds of reeds, and were not allowed anything that might tend to produce effeminate habits. To cultivate their love for war, they were encouraged to engage with one another in frequent combats, while their seniors looked on and applauded such as fought courageously and dexterously or did not display any outward signs of pain upon receiving the hardest blows. All their exercises were designed to make them robust in body, patient in suffering, bold in spirit, and quick and decisive in action. To make them sly and cunning, boys were encouraged to steal provisions from one another, and even from the public tables, and from the houses and gardens of the citizens. If detected in the theft, they were severely flogged, not for attempting to steal, but for not doing it carefully enough to escape detection.

Even Spartan adults were much restricted in their personal freedom, and had their respective duties assigned them by the laws, like soldiers in a camp. Every Spartan citizen was expected to consider only the public welfare, regardless of his own personal interests or pleasures, and to be prepared at any moment to sacrifice his life cheerfully, if he thus served the state. Spartan citizens were forbidden employing themselves in the mechanical arts or in tilling the soil. When not employed in military duty they were engaged in superintending the public schools, and in athletic and military exercises, in hunting, in assemblies for conversation, or in religious services. They were not permitted to take part in public affairs until they had reached the age of thirty, and even then a man of ordinary position who meddled much with political matters was considered rather forward and presumptuous. It was regarded as dishonorable for a man to spend much time with his family or to manifest a fondness for their society. The state only was regarded as deserving a Spartan's affection.

In Laconia, or Lacedæmon, the slaves were the property of the state, and were distributed, with the land, among the free inhabitants of the country. The Spartan slaves were partly descended from the original inhabitants of Laconia, and were called *Helots*, from the town of Helos, where their ancestors had made an obstinate resistance to the conquering Dorians; and to them only were assigned the duties of agriculture and the mechanical arts. They were required to follow their masters during war, and constituted a numerous light cavalry force in every Spartan army. They also officiated as domestic servants and in every other menial capacity. They were the most useful members of the Spartan community. Nevertheless, their haughty masters treated them in the most cruel and shameful manner, and frequently put them to death out of mere caprice or sport. They were required to appear in a dress denoting their bondage, such as a dog-skin bonnet and a sheep-skin vest. They were not allowed to teach their children any accomplishments which might seem to equalize them with their masters. A Spartan might flog his slaves once a day, for no other reason than to only remind them that they were slaves. They were sometimes forced to drink until they became intoxicated, and to engage in ridiculous and indecent dances, to show the Spartan youth the disgraceful and disgusting condition to which intoxicating liquors reduced men. The law did not punish any one for murdering a slave, and it was the custom for young Spartans to scatter themselves over the country in small bands, to waylay and kill the stoutest and handsomest Helots they could find, simply to exercise their prowess.

Spartan girls were trained as rigorously in athletic exercises as boys. They were regarded as the part of the state whose duty was to give Sparta a race of hardy sons. All Spartan women were generally married at the age of twenty, and although the wife enjoyed little of her husband's society, she was treated with great respect by him, and was permitted more freedom than was enjoyed by women in the other Grecian states. She was taught to take a deep interest in the honor and welfare of her country, and the high spirit of Spartan women encouraged the men to heroic deeds.

Lycurgus desired only to form a nation of able-bodied, hardy and warlike citizens; and to accomplish this result, he trampled upon every amiable and modest feeling of the Spartan women, if he could advance his favorite object. He directed that the women should give up their retired manner of living, and that they should publicly exercise themselves in running, wrestling, throwing the javelin, and other masculine diversions. He also tried to show that he had a thorough contempt for that marriage obligation which is the basis of so much of the virtue and happiness of modern society. A Spartan mother was mainly desirous that her sons should be brave warriors, and a suit of armor was considered the most precious gift which she could bestow upon them. The advice of Spartan mothers to their sons when they departed for the battle-field was: "Return with your shield or upon it." No Spartan mother would deign to look at her son who had disgraced himself by cowardice or treason to his country.

The sole object of Spartan education was to prepare the people of Lacedæmon for war, and the aim of Lycurgus was to make the Spartans a warlike race, not, however, to enlarge their territory, as he dreaded the consequences of an extension of the Lacedæmonian territory beyond the borders of Laconia. The Spartan youth were taught to be sober, cunning, persevering, brave, insensible to hardships, patient in suffering, obedient to their superiors, and unyielding in their devotion to their country. These were simply military virtues. The Spartan laws did not allow a Spartan soldier to flee before an enemy.

But the system of Lycurgus was a narrow and barbarous scheme. It destroyed personal liberty, and made every Spartan the slave of the state or community. Social independence was thus anihilated. The principle underlying the whole system and institutions of Lycurgus was—*the citizen for the state, not the state for the citizen.* The object of his code was not to make the people happy in the enjoyment of peaceful pursuits, happy in the enjoyment of the largest liberty, happy in being virtuous, happy in their homes, their families, their religion, their good fame—it was not the object of the Lycurgean system to make the Spartans happy in any of these.

The frugality and temperance of the Spartans, their grave behavior, their invincible valor, their patriotic devotion, their heroic fortitude—all these have been subjects of commendation; but the extremes to which these qualities were carried made them ascetic, harsh and unfeeling. Their love of war impelled them to an aggressive and tyrannical foreign policy, and their contempt for the peaceful arts and the quiet enjoyments of domestic life prevented them from cultivating those gentler and kindlier feelings of human nature which are practically the main sources of human happiness.

After Lycurgus had completed his code, he convoked an assembly of the Spartan people, and told them that there was yet one point concerning which he desired to consult the Delphic oracle; but that, before he departed for that purpose, he desired them to swear that they maintain his institutions, social and political, unaltered until his return. His countrymen having taken such an oath, Lycurgus proceeded to Delphi, where he obtained an assurance from the oracle that if Sparta would continue to faithfully comply with his laws it would become the greatest and most flourishing state in the world. He committed this favorable reply to writing, and transmitted it to Sparta; after which, it is said, he voluntarily starved himself to death, so that his countrymen would be forever bound by their oath to maintain his laws and institution without change. But some writers tell us that he died in Crete at an advanced age; and that, in accordance with his request, his body was afterwards cremated, and the ashes cast into the sea, so that his remains could never be conveyed to Sparta, and that his countrymen might therefore have no pretext to declare themselves relieved from their solemn obligation to abide by his laws.

The laws of Lycurgus—which the Spartans observed for five centuries—made that people the greatest warriors of Greece. But the Spartans became only a nation of warriors. They produced no philosophers, no poets, no orators, no historians, no artists.

The effects of the laws of Lycurgus upon the Spartans were soon made manifest. They became a body of well-trained, disciplined professional soldiers, at a time when scarcely any Grecian state understood the value of any kind of military discipline or training, or practiced it. Consequently Sparta became irresistible in war, and rapidly conquered the neighboring states, thus making herself supreme in the Peloponnesus. Towards the close of the ninth century before Christ she took Amyclæ and became mistress of the whole Eurótas valley, the Achæans submitting or fleeing to Italy.

In the next century the effects of the Lycurgean system upon the Spartans were still more manifest. Sparta then became a compact and organized state, spreading over the whole of Laconia, and possessing the only completely-disciplined army in Greece. She began deliberately to quarrel with the other Peloponnesian states for the apparent purpose of extending her domain. In wars with Arcadia and Argos, Sparta gained some signal advantages, Argos losing all her territory south of Cynuria.

Sparta then began a series of aggressions upon the neighboring state of Messenia, actuated partly by a desire for more territory, and partly by a dislike of the liberal policy pursued by the Dorian conquerors of Messenia towards their Achæan subjects. Hostilities soon resulted, and the contest known as the *First Messenian War* commenced B. C. 743 and lasted twenty years (B. C. 743-723). Sparta's only ally in this war was Corinth. Messenia was aided by Argos, Arcadia and Sicyon. The war was prolonged by the long defense of the city of Ithomé. During the struggle the Messenians consulted the Delphic oracle concerning the best means of securing the favor of the gods, and received as a response that they ought to sacrifice a noble-born virgin to the infernal deities. Thereupon Aristodémus, a Messenian commander, offered his own daughter as a victim; and as she was about to be sacrificed, her lover desperately endeavored to save her by the pretext that she was not fitted for the immolation. The only effect of this declaration was to excite the rage of Aristodémus, who had so greatly distinguished himself during the struggle by his valor and ability that he was elevated to the throne of Messenia. But in the midst of all his greatness and his triumphs, remorse for having sacrificed his daughter tormented him, so that he finally committed suicide upon her grave. His death was followed by the conquest of the Messenians by the Spartans, who forced the Messenians to evacuate Ithomé. Thus ended the First Messenian War, B. C. 723, Messenia being annexed to the Lacedæmonian territory. Many of the Messenians sought refuge in Argolis and Arcadia, and those who remained were reduced to slavery by the Spartans. Ithomé was razed to the ground.

After enduring Spartan oppression for thirty-nine years, the Messenians rose in revolt against their tyrannical masters; and, under the leadership of a skillful general named Aristómenes, they began the *Second Messenian War*, which lasted seventeen years (B. C. 685-668). The Messenians were aided by the Argives, the Arcadians, the Elians and the Sicyonians; while Sparta's only ally, as in the preceding war, was Corinth. The first battle was indecisive; but, with the assistance of their allies, the Messenians, under their able general, Aristómenes, defeated the Spartans in three battles. Thoroughly disheartened by their reverses, the Spartans consulted the Delphic oracle, and were told that they must obtain a leader from Athens if they wished to be victorious. In consequence of the natural jealousy between Sparta and Athens, the Spartans were reluctant to send to Athens for a leader, and the Athenians were as reluctant to furnish one, but both feared to disobey the oracle. The Athenians in derision sent the lame schoolmaster and poet, Tyrtæus, to lead the Spartan armies; but Tyrtæus proved to be as good a leader as could have been selected, as he aroused the patriotic ardor and martial spirit of the Spartans by his soul-stirring odes and lyrics that their drooping spirits were revived, and they were stimulated to redoubled exertions and speedily caused the struggle to assume an attitude favorable to them and discouraging to their foes.

The Spartans were defeated with great loss by the Messenians and their allies in a great battle at the Boar's Grave, in the plain of Stenyclerus, and were obliged to retire to their own territory; but in the third year of the war the Messenians were defeated through the treachery of Aristócrates, the king of the Arcadian Orchomenus. As a result of this defeat, Aristómenes, unable to again take the field, threw himself into the mountain fortress of Ira, where he continued the struggle for eleven years, resisting all the Spartan assaults, and frequently sallying forth from his stronghold and ravaging Laconia with fire and sword. His exploits were very brilliant. He three times offered to Zeus the Ithomates, the sacrifice called Hecatomphonsa, which could only be offered by a warrior who had slain a hundred foes with his own hand. He was at one time captured with some of his companions, carried to Sparta, and cast with them into a deep cavern, which the Spartans were accustomed to use as a receptacle for such criminals as had been condemned to capital punishment. Aristómenes escaped unhurt by the fall, but all his companions were killed. He expected to die of hunger in this dismal cavern; but on the third day, after he had lain himself down to die, he heard a faint noise, and, after rising up, he observed, by a faint light descending from above, a fox busily engaged in gnawing the dead bodies of his companions. He cautiously approached the fox and seized hold of its tail, and was thus enabled to follow the animal in its efforts to escape through the darkness, until it made its way to the outside by a small opening. With a little effort, Aristómenes widened this opening sufficiently to enable his body to pass through, and thus escaped to Messenia, where he was joyfully welcomed by his countrymen.

Notwithstanding the valor of Aristómenes, the war ended in the triumph of the Spartans, who surprised Ira one night while Aristómenes was disabled by a wound. He succeeded in cutting his way through the enemy with the bravest of his followers, and was thus enabled to escape. Taking refuge in Arcadia, he there formed a plan to surprise Sparta, but this plan was betrayed by Aristócrates, who was stoned to death by his countrymen for this treachery. Aristómenes then retired to the island of Rhodes, where he married a chief's daughter and lived the remainder of his days in ease and quiet. Many of the Messenians, not willing to submit to Sparta a second time, abandoned their country and retired to the island of Sicily, where they colonized Messana. Those who remained were reduced by the Spartans to the condition of Helots, or slaves; with the exception of the inhabitants of a few of the Messenian towns, who were admitted to the position of Periœci. Thus ended the Second Messenian War, B. C. 668; and Messenia was annexed to Laconia, and its history ceased until B. C. 369. The Messenians for a long time cherished the memory of Aristómenes, and the legends of subsequent times declared that his spirit was seen animating his countrymen and scattering ruin among their enemies, in the famous battle of Leuctra, in which the power of the Spartans was finally crushed by the Thebans.

After subduing the Messenians, the Spartans carried on a war with the Arcadians, who had been among the allies of the Messenians. The Spartans conquered the southern portion of Arcadia, but were unable to reduce the city of Tegea, which offered a successful resistance and defied the Lacedæmonian power for a century, before it was finally taken, B. C. 554.

Sparta had been the rival of Argos from the earliest times. Argos then held the entire eastern coast of the Peloponnesus under her dominion. Soon after the death of Lycurgus the Spartans wrested from the Argives all the territory eastward to the sea and northward beyond the city of Thyrea, annexing it to Laconia. About B. C. 547 the Argives began another war against Sparta to recover their lost territory, but they were defeated and their power was broken.

Sparta was for some time the most powerful state of Greece. Her own territory of Laconia, or Lacedæmon, embraced the entire South of the Peloponnesus, and the other Peloponnesian states were so completely humbled that they were unable to resist her supremacy. The Spartan influence had thus far been restricted within the narrow limits of the Peloponnesus, but about this time it began to extend into foreign lands. In B. C. 555, Crœsus, the great Lydian king, sent an embassy to Sparta, acknowledging that state as the leading power in Greece, and soliciting its alliance to resist the rising power of Persia under Cyrus the Great. The Spartans accepted the offers of Crœsus, and prepared an expedition to assist him, but before it could be sent Cyrus conquered Lydia. This alliance marks the commencement of Sparta's foreign policy, and was followed by other Spartan expeditions beyond the limits of the Greek continent. In B. C. 525 Sparta and Corinth sent a combined expedition to the coast of Asia

Minor to depose Polycrates, the tyrant of Samos, but it failed in its object. Sparta's ambition now arose to such a height that she assumed the right to interfere in the affairs of the Greek states outside of the Peloponnesus, as the champion of the cause of oligarchy. Her efforts against Attica excited the fear and hatred which the Athenians entertained for the Spartans for almost a century and a half. Sparta's influence among the states of Greece was always on the side of oligarchy or despotism, and against democracy, such as that of Athens; and the aristocracy of every Grecian city regarded Sparta as its natural champion and protector, while the democratic elements everywhere looked to Athens as their friend and supporter.

SECTION VIII.—ATHENS UNDER THE LAWS OF SOLON.

WHILE Sparta under the laws of Lycurgus was advancing in power and extending its dominion, Athens was greatly distracted and nearly brought to the brink of ruin by the contests of domestic factions, being a prey to all the evils of oligarchical oppression on the one hand and popular violence and disorder on the other.

During the early period the people of Athens were divided into four tribes—Teleontes, Hopletes, Ægicoreis and Argadeis. These were subdivided into two branches—brotherhoods and clans, and Thirdlings and Naucraries. The former division was founded upon consanguinity. The latter was upon an artificial arrangement of the state for purposes of taxation and military service. There were three classes of citizens—nobles, farmers and artisans. The nobles were vested with the whole political power, and filled all the offices in the state. The Senate, or Court of Areopagus, which held its sessions on Mars' Hill, was composed of members of this class.

The first archon of Athens after the abolition of royalty in B. C. 1068 was Medon, the son of Codrus, the last Athenian king, who had so patriotically sacrificed his life in a war with the Dorians. On the death of Alcmæon, the thirteenth archon, and the last one for life, the *Eupatrids*, or Athenian nobles, limited the archon's term of office to ten years (about B. C. 752). This dignity was still bestowed on the descendants of Codrus and Medon; but about B. C. 714 all the nobles were made eligible to the office.

In the year B. C. 683 another important change was made in the constitution by increasing the number of archons from one to nine, to be thenceforth elected annually. The first of these archons was the head of the executive power and was usually called, by way of distinction, *The Archon*, and sometimes the *Archon Eponymus*, because he gave his name to the year. He presided over the whole body of archons, and was the representative of the dignity of the state. He decided all disputes concerning the family and protected widows and orphans. The second archon was honored with the title of *The Basileus*, or *The King*, as he represented the king in his position as the high-priest of the state religion. He was the judge in every case regarding the national religion and homicide. The third archon, styled *The Polemarch*, or Commander-in-chief, directed the war department, and commanded the Athenian army in the field until the time of Clisthenes. He adjudicated disputes between Athenian citizens and strangers. The remaining six archons, called *Thesmothetæ*, or Legislators, officiated as presidents of law courts and decided all matters not specially pertaining to the first three. The whole body of archons constituted the supreme council of the state. There being no code in Athens, the decisions of the archons had the force of laws.

In addition to the archons, there was the Court of Areopagus, or Senate, which derived its name from the place of its meeting, on a rocky eminence, opposite the Acropolis, known as the Hill of Ares, or Mars' Hill. This council was composed of Eupatrids, or nobles, only; and all the archons became members of it at the end of their official terms of archonship. It was called simply the Senate or Council. Solon afterwards instituted another Senate, and the original council was named Areopagus, to distinguish it from the new body.

The nobles possessed the chief power in the state, and they used this power to oppress the people, as oligarchies generally do. The archons were vested with arbitrary powers, as there was no written code to restrain them, and they very naturally advanced the interests of their own order to the injury of the commons. In about half a century after the establishment of the yearly archons, the popular dissatisfaction reached such a height, and the general demand for a written code of laws had become so vehement, that the nobles were unable to resist any longer. The crimes and disorders of the state continued with unabated violence.

In this situation of affairs, Draco, a man of uprightness and integrity, but of a stern and cruel disposition, was elected archon (B. C. 623), and was assigned the task of preparing a code and reforming the institutions of Athens. He framed for the Athenian people a code of laws so severe that it was said that "they were written in blood instead of ink." He punished even the slightest offenses with death, saying that the smallest crimes deserved death and that he had no severer punishment for the greatest ones. The only effect of Draco's severe laws was to render them inoperative, as is usually the case with over-rigorous statutes. Men were willing to prosecute only the greatest criminals; and as a result almost all offenders escaped punishment, and were thus encouraged to continue in their wrongdoing. Draco's code placed the lives of the citizens of Athens at the mercy of the nobles, and thus increased the popular discontent. A noble named Cylon sought to turn this feeling to his own advantage by making himself tyrant of Athens, B. C. 612. He had won the olive crown at the Olympic Games, and had married the daughter of Theagenes, who had made himself tyrant of Megara. He consulted the Delphic oracle before making his attempt, and was told to seize the Acropolis of Athens "at the great festival of Jove." Cylon forgot that the Diasia was the greatest festival of Jove at Athens, and supposed that the oracle alluded to the Olympic Games; and at the next celebration of these games he seized the Acropolis, with a strong force consisting of his own partisans and of troops furnished him by his father-in-law, the tyrant of Megara. He was not supported by the great mass of the people, and was blockaded in the Acropolis by the troops of the government. Cylon succeeded in making his escape; but his followers, reduced by hunger, soon submitted to the government troops, and found refuge at the altar of Athênê. The archon, Megacles, a member of the renowned family of the Alcmæonidæ, found them at that altar, and induced them to come forth from there, by promising to spare their lives, fearing that their death there would pollute the sanctuary. But as soon as they had left the temple they were attacked and massacred. Some were even slain at the sacred altar of the Furies, or Eumenides, where they sought safety. This act of sacrilege on the part of the archons aroused fresh troubles at Athens. The entire family of the Alcmæonidæ were looked upon as tainted with the sacrilege of Megacles, and the friends of those thus massacred demanded vengeance upon the accursed race. By means of their wealth and influence, the family of Megacles were able to uphold themselves against their enemies to the end of the seventh century before Christ; but were finally banished from Attica by the decree of a council of three hundred members of their own order (B. C. 597).

The banishment of the Alcmæonidæ in B. C. 597 did not quiet the superstitious alarm excited at Athens by the sacrilege of

Megacles; and while the Athenian people were aroused by these fears a plague broke out in the city, and this was considered a punishment sent by the gods for this dreadful crime. The people consulted the Delphic oracle, which told them to invite the renowned Cretan prophet and sage, Epimenides, to visit Athens and purify the city of pollution and sacrilege. Epimenides was greatly famed for his knowledge of the healing powers of nature. He visited Athens and performed certain rites and sacrifices which the people believed would propitiate the offended deities. The plague disappeared; and the Athenians, in gratitude, offered their deliverer a talent of gold, which he refused. He would accept no other payment than a branch of the sacred olive tree which grew on the Acropolis. This purification of Athens occurred in B. C. 596.

The archons now opened their eyes to a proper sense of the perils which menaced the state. The sacrifices of Epimenides had stopped the plague, but did not end the popular discontent. The factious disturbances in the city became more and more frequent and fierce. The Athenians were now divided into three factions. The first of these consisted of the wealthy nobles, who favored an oligarchy, or a government in which all political power is vested in a few privileged individuals. The second party consisted of the poor peasantry, who favored democracy, or a government in which the masses of the people are the ruling power. The third party was composed of the merchants, who preferred a mixed constitution, in which the oligarchical and democratic elements were combined. These three factions were arrayed against each other in the fiercest animosity.

Another element of trouble adding to the distraction of the state was the hostile feeling which had grown up between the rich and the poor. Some of the citizens had acquired great wealth, while the great mass of the people had sunk into the most abject poverty, and were generally overborne with burdens entailed on them by their extravagance, and which they had no reasonable hope of ever being able to discharge. This condition of affairs was rendered more distressful by the fact that a harsh law existed in Athens, authorizing a creditor to seize the person of his debtor, and to retain, or even to sell, him as a slave. The rich only too eagerly took advantage of this cruel statute; and the poor were consequently exasperated to so intense a pitch that a general insurrection of the lower orders appeared to be on the verge of breaking out in Athens.

In this dangerous condition of affairs at Athens, the wisest men of all parties looked to Solon, a descendant of Codrus, and a person of recognized talents, virtues and wisdom, as the only person who possessed sufficient ability and influence to allay the unhappy differences which divided the people and to avert the misfortunes which threatened the state. Solon's justice, wisdom and kindness won for him the affection of the poor, while the rich were friendly to him because he was one of their class, so that he possessed the respect and confidence of every class. Influential persons encouraged him to aspire to, or rather to assume, regal power, so that he could more readily and effectually repress disorder and tumult, control faction, and force obedience to such laws as he might deem necessary to enact; but he resolutely and persistently declined to follow such advice. After some deliberation, Solon accepted the office of Archon, with special powers, which had been conferred upon him by an almost unanimous vote.

Solon was a native of the island of Salamis. His father, Execestides, although of distinguished rank, possessed only a very moderate degree of wealth, so that Solon found himself obliged to devote a great part of his youth to mercantile pursuits, to acquire for himself a competence. This proved of some advantage to him as a lawgiver, as it led him to visit foreign lands, thus affording him the best possible opportunities for studying men and manners, and for comparing the different systems of civil and political economy then existing in the various civilized countries of the ancient world. During these mercantile expeditions, Solon is said to have met and conferred with the six celebrated men, who, with himself, received the honorable title of the *Seven Wise Men of Greece*, of whom we shall hereafter give an account. Solon was a poet no less than a sage, and in the character of a poet he made his first public appearance in Athens.

At that time the Athenians had been engaged in a long struggle with the Megarians for the possession of the island of Salamis, but they had now become weary of the war, and had enacted a law that whoever should advise a renewal of the war for the recovery of Salamis should be put to death. But before long they wished this law abrogated, but fear of the penalty which it denounced prevented every one from proposing its repeal. In this juncture, Solon ingeniously devised a plan by which he was able to accomplish the desired result without any injury to himself. He had for some time pretended insanity so successfully that he deceived even some of his personal friends, and having composed a poem on the war of Salamis, he one day rushed into the market-place, and recited his verses before the assembled people with the wildest gesticulation. The citizens at first gathered about him out of curiosity, but excited by what had been recited to them, and encouraged by some of Solon's confidential friends who were present, the people repealed the obnoxious law and voted another expedition against Salamis, appointing Solon its commander. Solon led the expedition against Salamis and reduced its inhabitants to their former subjection to Athens.

But it is as a lawgiver that Solon achieved for himself an enduring fame. As the discontent of the poor was the greatest danger threatening the state, he began his reforms of the social and political institutions of Athens

He ameliorated the condition of the poorer classes by canceling all their debts, reducing the rate of interest, and by abolishing imprisonment or enslavement for debt. He also restored to freedom those debtors who had been enslaved by their creditors, and repealed all of Draco's sanguinary laws, except the one which declared murder punishable with death.

Solon next proceeded to reform the political and judicial institutions of Athens. Theseus had divided the citizens of Athens into three classes; but Solon divided them into four classes, according to the sum of their yearly incomes. The two higher or aristocratical classes were required to serve as cavalry in time of war, and were therefore called *knights* (meaning horsemen); while citizens of the two lower classes composed the infantry. The highest class held the highest offices in the state and paid the largest amount of the taxes; the second and third classes held the remainder of the offices and paid the remainder of the taxes; while the lowest class were excluded from all offices and exempt from all taxation. A Senate, or Council of State, consisting of four hundred members, elected yearly, one hundred of whom were selected by lot from the four wards of Attica, was vested with the sole power of originating all legislative measures. When Attica was divided into ten wards, each ward returned ten Councilors, thus increasing the Council of State to five hundred members. The measures proposed by the Senate, or Council of State, only became laws if they were accepted by the general assembly of the citizens of Athens, a purely democratic body, which was vested with the absolute and unlimited power of approving or rejecting the proposed measures.

The Court of Areopagus, which Solon restored, and which held its sittings on the eastern side of the Athenian Acropolis, was composed of such individuals as had worthily discharged the duties of archonship. Its members held their offices for life. This tribunal possessed paramount jurisdiction in criminal cases, and also exercised a censorship over the public morals, the affairs of religion, and the education of the people. It was empowered to punish impiety, profligacy and idleness, and also possessed the power of annulling or changing the decrees of the general assembly of the people.

Every citizen was bound to make to this court an annual statement concerning his income and the sources from which it was derived. In its judicial capacity this court sat during the night and without lights; and those who conducted the prosecution or the defense of accused persons brought before the court were not allowed to make use of oratorical declamation and were required to state plainly the facts of the case. The Court of Areopagus was long regarded with very great esteem.

Solon transferred the judicial powers previously exercised by the archons to a popularly-constituted court called the Heliæa, consisting of at least six thousand jurors, and sometimes being subdivided into ten inferior courts, each having six hundred jurors. Six of these courts were for civil cases, and four for criminal cases. Every citizen over thirty years of age, and not legally disqualified, was eligible as a juror of the Heliæa. The jurors received a small compensation for their attendance at court.

Solon established a system of rewards and punishments to stimulate virtue and to repress vice and crime. Among the rewards for faithful citizenship were crowns conferred publicly by the Senate or the people; public banquets in the town-hall, or Prytaneum; places of honor in the theater and in the public assembly; and statues in the Agora or in the streets. Foreigners were encouraged to settle in Athens, but were obliged to follow some useful occupation. The Court of Areopagus punished idleness and profligacy severely. A thief was punished by being compelled to restore twice the value of the property he had stolen.

To prevent indifference regarding the public good, Solon decreed that any one remaining neutral in civil contests should be punished with forfeiture of property and banishment from Athens. To restrain female extravagance and ostentation, he instituted measures for strictly regulating the dress of women and their conduct on public occasions. He provided for the punishment of idleness, and decreed that such parents who neglected to bring up their children to some trade or profession should, in their old age, have no right to expect aid or support from those children. He prohibited evil speaking of the dead, and provided for the imposition of a fine on those who publicly slandered the living. He forbade any father giving a dowry to his daughters, in order to discourage mercenary marriages. Solon's constitution remained in force, with slight interruption, for five centuries, and laid the foundation for Athenian greatness.

Solon was accused by his own order of having yielded too much, and by the other classes of not having granted them enough. He candidly admitted that his laws were not perfect, but that they were the best that the people would accept. The high regard in which he was held prevented any outbreak for some time.

When Solon had finished his code of laws, he exacted a solemn promise from the Athenians that they would not repeal or alter them for a hundred years. As officious persons afterwards constantly annoyed him with their suggestions of amendments for the improvement of his code, Solon concluded to retire from Athens until his countrymen should have time to become familiarized with and attached to his institutions. After obtaining the consent of the Athenians to travel abroad for ten years, and exacting from them an oath that they would preserve his laws unaltered until his return, Solon sailed to Egypt, where he frequently conversed on philosophical questions with priests and learned men of that ancient nation. He afterwards visited the island of Cyprus, where he aided a petty king, named Philocyprus, to lay out and build a city, which was called Soli, on account of the share which the great Athenian lawgiver had in its erection.

Solon proceeded from Cyprus to Asia Minor, going first to Sardis, the capital of Lydia, where he visited the wealthy and renowned King Crœsus, on which occasion occurred the conversation in which the Lydian king asked the Athenian sage and lawgiver if he did not consider him a happy man, and to which Solon replied that life was full of vicissitudes and that no one was perfectly happy in this world—a conversation for the account of which we refer the reader to the history of Lydia in the chapter on Asia Minor.

Long before the expiration of the ten years for which Solon obtained leave of absence, Athens had again become distracted by the contests of the old factions, which renewed their struggles for the ascendency. Though Solon, on his return, in B. C. 560, found his laws nominally observed, he saw everything falling into confusion. The party of the *Plain*, or the nobles, had a leader named Lycurgus; the party of the *Shore*, or the merchants, was led by Megacles; and the party of the *Mountain*, or the peasants, the advocates of democracy, was headed by Pisistratus, a cousin of Solon. These parties were actuated by the fiercest animosity to each other. Pisistratus the leader of the Mountain, or democratic party, had become a great popular favorite because of his eloquence, his generosity, his personal beauty and his military prowess. Solon clearly saw that he was an ambitious demagogue, and that by his bland and conciliatory manners, his affected moderation, and his pretended zeal for the rights of the poor, he designed to override the republican constitution and make himself master of Athens.

Solon vainly endeavored to persuade his ambitious cousin to relinquish his selfish designs. At length Pisistratus, having wounded himself with his own hand, appeared in the general assembly of the people,

SOLON BEING SHOWN THE TREASURES OF CRŒSUS.

covered with blood, and accused his political adversaries of having attacked and maltreated him. He declared that no friend of the poor could live in Athens if the people did not allow him to adopt measures for his own safety. By this artful trick he so aroused the indignation of the people that they voted a body-guard of fifty men for the protection of their favorite, whose life they had been induced to believe had been threatened. Solon earnestly endeavored to dis-

DESTRUCTION OF THE ATHENIAN ARMY IN SICILY.

suade the people from their course by telling them that the ambitious Pisistratus would use his power for the subversion of their own liberties, but all his entreaties were useless.

Solon's predictions were soon verified; as the artful Pisistratus gradually increased his body-guards until they constituted a corps of considerable strength, when he seized the Acropolis. The alarmed supporters of the constitution fiercely resisted, but Pisistratus triumphed over all opposition and usurped the government of Athens, by making himself absolute dictator or *tyrant*. The word *tyrant* was used by the ancient Greeks in a different sense from which we now use it. They called every usurper by that title, no matter how mildly and beneficently he administered the laws. Therefore Pisistratus was called a tyrant, notwithstanding that he governed the people in a merciful and enlightened manner.

After he had fully established himself in power, Pisistratus treated Solon with the greatest kindness and respect, and maintained and executed his laws, notwithstanding the opposition which the patriotic sage had persistently offered to his ambitious designs. Nevertheless Solon could never reconcile himself to his cousin's usurpation, though he sometimes gave Pisistratus the counsel and aid which he had solicited. Solon consequently retired once more from Athens, and spent the remaining days of his life in voluntary exile. It is said that he died in the island of Cyprus, in the eightieth year of his age. In testimony of the respect which they entertained for his memory, the Athenians afterwards erected a statue of the wise and good sage and lawgiver in the Agora, or place of assembly; and the inhabitants of his native island of Salamis honored him in a similar manner. In accordance with his will, his ashes were scattered around the island of Salamis, which he had saved to Athens.

For the first six years of his usurped administration, Pisistratus faithfully observed the laws of Solon. In B. C. 554 the factions of the Plain and the Shore united in driving him from Athens; but these two factions quarreled a few years afterward, whereupon Megacles, the leader of the Shore, invited Pisistratus back to his sovereignty on condition that the usurper should marry his daughter. Pisistratus accepted this offer and regained his former power in B. C. 548. He married the daughter of Megacles, in accordance with the agreement, but he did not treat her as his wife, as he had children by a former marriage, and as he did not wish to connect his blood with a family considered accursed on account of Cylon's sacrilege. Offended at this, Megacles renewed his alliance with Lycurgus, the leader of the Plain, and the two again drove Pisistratus from Athens, B. C. 547. After remaining in exile for ten years, occupying his time in raising troops and money in different portions of Greece, Pisistratus landed at Marathon with a strong army in B. C. 537; and, being joined by many of his supporters, he advanced upon Athens, defeated his foes, and again made himself master of the city.

After this second restoration to power, Pisistratus governed Athens for the remaining ten years of his life, administering Solon's laws with impartial justice, so that the people forgot their lost freedom in the fairness with which he governed them. He also distinguished himself as a patron of literature and the fine arts. He adorned Athens with many elegant public edifices, and established beautiful gardens for the accommodation of the people. He established the first public library; and caused the poems of Homer, which had hitherto existed in a fragmentary condition, to be collected and arranged properly, so that they could be chanted by the rhapsodists at the Greater Panathenæa, or twelve days' festival in honor of Athênê, the guardian goddess of Athens. By his beneficent rule, Pisistratus fully merited the opinion which Solon expressed concerning him, that he was the best of tyrants, whose only vice was his ambition. He died in B. C. 527.

Pisistratus was succeeded in the government of Athens by his two sons, Hippias and Hipparchus, who are generally known as the Two Tyrants of Athens. They ruled peacefully for fourteen years, and, like their father, governed for a time with mildness and liberality. Like him, they patronized learning and munificently encouraged men of genius, thus inducing the renowned poets, Anacreon and Simonides, to make Athens their residence. The Athenians enjoyed such prosperity under the united administration of these two brothers, and made such progress in civilization and refinement, that an ancient philosopher called that period of Athenian history a golden age. All this prosperity existed in spite of the fact that these rulers reduced the land-tax from one-tenth to one-twentieth.

Although Hippias and Hipparchus governed Athens wisely and well, their administration was cut short by a sudden and violent end. A citizen of Athens, named Harmodius, having insulted Hippias, the tyrant avenged himself by a public affront to the sister of Harmodius. This so exasperated Harmodius that he determined upon the destruction of both of the tyrants, and organized a conspiracy for that purpose with his intimate friend, Aristogiton. The two conspirators assassinated Hipparchus at the festival of Panathenæa, but Harmodius himself was slain in the tumult (B. C. 514).

Alarmed for his own safety, Hippias from this time suspected every one of being an enemy, and his character at once changed. He now became severe, and for the first time acted in such a manner as to fully deserve the title of tyrant, in the worst signification of the term. His suspicion caused him to put many citizens to death and raise vast sums by excessive taxation. In order to discover some secret connected with the death of Hipparchus, Hippias caused a woman named Leona to be put to the torture. But the woman firmly refused to reveal anything, and, in the midst of her agony, bit off her tongue and spit it in the tyrant's face. She remained firm in her refusal until death ended her sufferings. To escape the oppression of Hippias, many influential citizens now left Athens. The people of Athens became so exasperated at the tyrant that he felt that his overthrow would come sooner or later. To secure a place of refuge in such a case, Hippias cultivated friendly relations with the Medo-Persians.

The Alcmæonidæ, who had lived in exile ever since the third and last restoration of Pisistratus, now invaded Attica in the hope of expelling Hippias, but were defeated by the tyrant. Clisthenes, the leader of the Alcmæonidæ, bribed the Delphians by the gift of a splendid temple in the place of the old edifice, which had been previously destroyed by fire, and obtained a decree from the oracle, commanding the Spartans to aid in freeing Athens from the rule of the tyrant Hippias. In consequence the Spartans joined the Athenian exiles in an invasion of Attica, but were unsuccessful. In a second invasion they captured Athens and compelled Hippias to resign his powers, and banished him and his family and kin to Ligeum, an Athenian colony founded on the Hellespont by his father Pisistratus (B. C. 510).

The republican constitution framed by Solon was now reëstablished, and the memory of Harmodius and Aristogiton, who had first drawn the sword against the Pisistratidæ, was ever afterward held in the greatest veneration by the Athenians, who recorded their praises in verses regularly chanted at some of the public festivals. Clisthenes, the leader of the revolution which had delivered Athens from the rule of the family which had subverted its liberties, now became the head of the state and the leader of the popular party. He divided the Athenian people into ten tribes, which he subdivided into demes, or districts, each of which was assigned a magistrate and a popular assembly. All the free inhabitants of Attica were admitted to the privileges of citizenship, and the Senate, or Council of State, was increased to five hundred members, or fifty from each tribe.

As a precaution against any ambitious individual usurping the authority of the state in the future, Clisthenes established the celebrated institution of the *Ostracism*, by which any citizen could be banished for ten years, without trial, or even without any formal accusation, but simply by a vote of the people, each citizen writing on a shell the name of the individual whom he desired to have banished, and six thousand votes being required against a person to determine his condemnation. This institution was efficacious in the purpose for which it was established.

The measures of Clisthenes highly offended the nobles, whose leader, Iságoras, solicited the aid of the Spartans to drive out the Alcmæonidæ. The Spartans responded to his call; and Iságoras, with the aid of the Spartan king Cleómenes, proceeded to banish seven hundred families from Athens, to dissolve the Senate, and to begin other revolutionary changes. The Athenian people rose in arms, besieged Iságoras and the Spartans in the citadel, and permitted them to surrender only on condition of leaving the Athenian territory. The Spartan army then retired from Athens, Clisthenes was recalled, and his democratic institutions were restored.

In the meantime Cleómenes, the Spartan king, had been collecting a large army in the Peloponnesus, and had entered into an alliance with the Thebans and with the Chalcidians of Eubœa, for the purpose of reducing Athens and forcing her to accept the rule of Iságoras as tyrant. Alarmed at the power of their antagonists, the Athenians sought the aid of the Persians. The Persians consented to aid them on condition of their becoming tributary to Persia, but the Athenians indignantly rejected this condition and prepared to meet their adversaries single-handed. In the mean time the allied foes of Athens had invaded Attica.

Cleómenes had hitherto concealed from his Peloponnesian allies the real object of the invasion. As soon as they discovered it they refused to assist in crushing the liberties of Athens, and thus the Spartan king was obliged to relinquish his design and return home. When the Athenians were delivered from the Spartan invasion, they advanced against the Thebans and defeated them, after which they crossed over into Eubœa and chastised the Chalcidians. They formally took possession of the island and distributed the estates of the wealthy Chalcidian land-owners among four thousand of their own citizens, who settled in Eubœa under the name of *Cleruchi*, or lot-holders.

Sparta now sought to wage another war against Athens, this time to compel her to accept the rule of Hippias once more. The other Peloponnesian states declined taking part in the attempt, and Sparta was again obliged to relinquish her designs against Athens. Hippias, who was now an old man, countenanced the Spartan project. When it failed he returned to the Persian court, where he ceaselessly sought the aid of the Dorians in replacing him in power in Athens.

Thus after the expulsion of Hippias, Athens, under the patriotic statesman Clisthenes, became a pure democracy; the suffrage being extended to all classes, except slaves. Under the blessings of political equality, and impelled by patriotism, all classes, rich and poor, felt an equal interest in the welfare and greatness of the state; and Athens, under her free institutions, entered upon a new and glorious career. It is said that Clisthenes was the first victim of his own institution, the Ostracism.

SECTION IX.—EARLY GREEK POETRY AND PHILOSOPHY.

OMER, the father of poetry and the great national poet of Greece, was an Ionian Greek of Asia Minor, and flourished in the ninth century before Christ. He led a sad and wandering life, and became blind in his old age. Seven cities claimed to be his birth-place, and an English poet has said:

"Seven cities claimed the Homer dead,
Through which the living Homer begged his bread."

Modern authorities consider him a native of Smyrna. His two great epics are the *Iliad*, which describes the Trojan War, and the *Odyssey*, which recounts the adventures of Ulysses, King of Ithica, on his way home after the fall of Troy.

These celebrated epics were the great national poems of Greece, and were sung or recited at the national festivals and in the public assemblies of every Grecian state, and also related at every Grecian fireside. They were preserved by memory and from age to age, by being taught from father to son. These poems brought into prominence the unity of the Hellenic race and constituted one of the strongest ties that bound together its different branches. The Iliad opens with the beginning of the tenth and last year of the siege of Troy, and the remaining incidents and final result of the contest are described in succession with great poetical power. This forms the entire subject of the twenty-four books or sections of the Iliad; but the characters and scenes portrayed in the poem are so many as to contribute the strong charm of variety to its other beauties.

Achilles is represented as the leader of the Greeks, and many curious tales are told concerning him. He was taught war and music by the Thessalian Centaur, Chiron, and in his infancy his mother, Thetis, dipped him in the river Styx, thus making him invulnerable, except the heel by which she held him. Hector is represented as the Trojan leader, and it is said that more than thirty Greek chiefs fell beneath his powerful hand. His character, as a son, a husband, a brother and a patriot, is illustrated with wonderful skill and power, considering the rudeness and barbarism of the age. The immortal gods are represented as feeling a deep interest in the struggle and as participating actively in it; and this mingling of divine and human agency in the poem of course renders it naturally improbable. Still, aside from this objection, there is much in the Iliad to attract the attention of an inquirer into the early history of the human race.

The poem is full of descriptions and incidents which give us considerable light upon either the time of action in the poem, or the time of its composition. Heroes are represented as yoking their own cars in those days. Queens and princes are represented as engaged in spinning. Achilles is said to have killed his mutton with his own hand, and to have dressed his own dinner. Yet these tame and commonplace incidents, vulgar as they may appear when compared with the occupations of modern heroes and heroines, do not, in Homer's hands, detract in the slightest manner from the dignity and grandeur of the characters performing them. The general tone of the poem is grave and dignified, and occasionally sublime. There is often a remarkable facility in the language, so that one word will sometimes present a perfect and delightful picture to the mind.

But the strength of thought and the singular ardor of imagination displayed in the poem constitute its great merit. Says Dr. Blair: "No poet was ever more happy in the choice of his subject, or more successful in painting his historical and descriptive pieces. There is considerable resemblance in the style to that of some parts of the Bible—as Isaiah, for instance—which is not to be wondered at, as the writings of the Old Testament are productions of nearly the same age, and of a part of the world not far from the alleged birth-place of Homer."

The Odyssey has been described as resembling a poem called forth by the Iliad, and does not rank as a whole as high as the Iliad. It recounts the adventures of Ulysses, King of Ithaca, on his way home after the fall of Troy. Both poems have for more than twenty centuries continued to enjoy the admiration of mankind, and no effort in the same style of poetry has since been so successful.

HESIOD, another great Greek epic poet, lived a century after Homer, in Bœotia, where, in his youth, he was a shepherd, tending his father's flocks on the slopes of Mount Helicon, sacred to the Muses. He described the homely rustic scenes with which he was familiar, his chief poems being *Works and Days*, consisting mostly of precepts of ordinary life, and *Theogony*, which described the origin of the world, and of gods and men. Not many events of his life have been recorded, and the scanty notices transmitted to us concerning him apparently deserve little credit. He gained a public prize in a poetical contest at the celebration of funeral games in honor of a King of Eubœa. He died at a good old age, and is said to have spent the closing years of his life in Locris, in the vicinity of Mount Parnassus. Though he was of a quiet and inoffensive disposition, it was his sad fate to die a violent death. A Milésian who lived in the same house with him had committed a gross outrage upon a young woman, whose brothers wrongly suspected Hesiod of conniving at the crime, and murdered both the poet and the guilty Milésian, and cast their bodies into the sea.

In the seventh century before Christ, Grecian lyric poetry, which at first consisted of cheerful songs, took the place of the epic poetry of the earlier period, the period of Homer and Hesiod. It was called lyric poetry because it was written to be sung to the lyre. ARCHILOCHUS, a native of the island of Paros, and who flourished in the seventh century before Christ, was a great satirical poet, whose writings have nearly all perished.

TYRTÆUS, the first great Greek lyric poet, by his patriotic odes roused the martial ardor of the Spartans, whose armies he commanded in the first war against the Messenians, having been sent for that purpose by the Athenians in accordance with the decree of the Delphic oracle. He was by birth an Ionian Greek of Asia Minor, being a native of Milétus. When a young man he settled in Athens, where he became a schoolmaster. After his military campaigns he resided at Sparta, where he was highly esteemed on account of his valuable public services. Most of his productions have likewise perished, but his name is yet familiar as a household word in Greece. He was lame, and also blind in one eye.

ALCMAN, a native of Sparta, was also a
2—40.-U. H.

noted lyric poet of the seventh century before Christ. Most of his verses, which were mainly on amatory subjects, have been lost. TERPANDER, another lyric poet of the same period, was born in the island of Lesbos. He was an accomplished musician, and won several prizes for music and poetry at the Pythian or Delphic Games and at a public festival at Sparta. He improved the lyre and introduced several new measures into Greek poetry.

SAPPHO, who was born at Mitylêné in the island of Lesbos, was a celebrated lyric poetess of the sixth century before Christ. The Greeks so admired her genius that they called her "the Tenth Muse." She married a wealthy inhabitant of the island of Andros, to whom she bore a daughter, named Cleis. Sappho was short in stature, swarthy in complexion, and not beautiful by any means. She was gifted with a warm and passionate temperament, and mainly wrote poetry describing the hopes and fears inspired by love. One or two of her lyrics have been wholly preserved, namely, a *Hymn to Aphrodité* and an *Ode to a Young Lady*, both of which are so full of beauty, feeling and animation, as to fully entitle the poetess to the admiration with which her poetical genius was regarded by the ancient Greeks. Her ardent affections at last caused her to commit suicide. After her husband's death, she fell deeply in love with 'a young man named Phaon, and as all her persistent efforts failed to excite a reciprocal passion in him, she cast herself into the sea from a high rock on the promontory of Leucate. The place where she was drowned was afterwards called "Lover's Leap."

ALCÆUS, a lyric poet, contemporary with Sappho, was, like her, a native of Mitylêné in the isle of Lesbos; and is said to have been one of her lovers. Like her, he was also endowed with strong passions, uncontrolable by proper moral feeling. IBYCUS, a writer of amatory lyrics, was born at Rhégium, in Southern Italy, about B. C. 600. While a young man he emigrated to the island of Samos. He was finally murdered by a band of robbers while making a journey. Most of his poems have likewise perished.

MIMNERMUS, a famous elegiac poet and an accomplished musician, was a native of Colophon, one of the Ionian cities of Asia Minor, and flourished early in the sixth century before Christ. Only a few of his writings have been transmitted to modern times. THEOGNIS, the author of a collection of moral maxims in the form of verse, was born at Megara, and flourished about the middle of the sixth century before Christ.

ANACREON, a very celebrated lyric poet, was born at Teos, an Ionian city of Asia Minor, about the middle of the sixth century before Christ. His fame induced Hipparchus, who, with his brother Hippias, then ruled Athens, to invite him to visit that city; and Plato tells us that he sent a fifty-oared vessel to convey him to Attica. After the assassination of Hipparchus, Anacreon returned to his native city of Teos; but was again obliged to leave it, on account of the advance of the Persian army when the Greek cities of Asia Minor attempted to free themselves from the Medo-Persian dominion, in B. C. 500. He then returned to the Teian settlement at Abdera, and there died in the eighty-fifth year of his age, about B. C. 470. It is said that he was choked to death by a grape-stone while drinking a cup of wine. The remaining works of Anacreon consist of odes and sonnets, principally referring to subjects of love and wine. He was merely an inspired voluptuary, though his style is graceful, sprightly and smooth. The Athenians erected a monument to him in the form of a drunkard singing.

THESPIS, a native of Icaria, in Attica, was the first Greek dramatic poet, and flourished in the early part of the sixth century before Christ. The origin of theatrical representations has been traced to the custom of celebrating, in the grape season, the praises of Dionysus, the god of wine, by joyous dances and the chanting of hymns. To vary the hymns, or *Dithyrambics*, as they were called, Thespis, from whom the theatrical performers were called Thespians, began the custom of introducing a single speaker, whose duty it was to recite before the company for their entertainment. Thespis also invented a moveable car, on which his performers went through their exhibitions in different places. The car of Thespis was the first form of the stage. The single reciter was the first kind of actor. The persons singing the hymns or choruses continued thenceforth to be an essential part of the Grecian theater, under the designation of the *chorus*, and their duty was to stand during the performance and make explanatory comments upon it.

A fixed wooden stage in the temple of Dionysus soon took the place of the car of Thespis; when a second reciter was introduced; masks, dresses and scenery were used; and in a remarkably short space of time from the rise of Thespis, entertainments of this description had assumed the dramatic form. The incidents originally represented were mainly selected from the fabulous and legendary history of primeval Greece. The ancient theaters were constructed on a very large scale, and differed in many particulars from the modern theater. The Grecian theater was a large area, inclosed with a wall, but open above, in which nearly the whole population passed the entire day, during the celebration of the festivals of Dionysus, in witnessing the dramatic performances. The site selected for the theater was usually the slope of a hill, that the natural inclination of the ground could enable the spectators who occupied the successive tiers of seats to see the performers on the stage without any obstruction. The enclosure sometimes embraced a space so large that it could accommodate from twenty to thirty thousand people. Back of the scenes was a double portico, to which the audience was allowed to retire for shelter when it rained.

The theater opened in the morning, and the people brought cushions with them to sit on, and also a supply of provisions, so that they might not be obliged to leave their places for the purpose of obtaining refreshments while the entertainment was in progress. The daily dramatic performances embraced a succession of four plays—three tragedies and a comedy—and at the end of the representation the relative merits of the pieces performed were decided by certain judges, who awarded the theatrical prize to the favorite of the day. These public awards of honor excited emulation, which led to the production of large numbers of dramatic compositions throughout Greece, especially in Athens. It is said that the theater of Athens possessed at one time at least two hundred and fifty first-class tragedies, and five hundred second class, along with as large a number of comedies and satirical farces.

PHRYNICUS, a pupil of Thespis, is said to have invented the theatric mask. His contemporary, CHŒRILUS, was the first dramatic poet whose plays were performed on a fixed stage. Another contemporary was PRATINUS, who invented the *satyric* drama, so called because choruses were introduced into it principally by satyrs.

Greek philosophy arose in the sixth century before Christ, among the Ionian Greeks of Asia Minor. The first Grecian philosopher was THÁLES, who was born at Milétus, about the year B. C. 640, and who is regarded as the greatest of the "Seven Wise Men of Greece." His father was a Phœnician, who had settled at Milétus, and who is said to have claimed to be descended from Cadmus, the founder of Thebes. Tháles early displayed his superior talents, and was called upon to take a prominent part in public affairs. But he preferred the quiet studies of philosophy to the exciting pursuits of politics, and soon relinquished his official positions and traveled into Crete and Egypt for the purpose of conversing with the learned men of those countries, who were far ahead of the rest of the world in a knowledge of the arts and sciences.

Tháles is said to have received invaluable instructions in mathematics from the priests of Memphis, and to have taught them, in return, a method of measuring the height of the Pyramids by means of their shadows. He afterwards returned to Milétus, and there continued his philosophical studies with unrelenting zeal. Tháles would never marry, as he said he was unwilling to expose himself to the anxieties and griefs of wedded life. It is said that when his mother first advised him to take a wife, he replied: "It is yet too soon." When she gave him the same advice in his later years, he answered: "It is now too late."

His intense application to his favorite studies gave him a habit of abstraction which sometimes put him in awkward predicaments and exposed him to the ridicule of the vulgar. It is said that being absorbed one night in the contemplation of the celestial bodies, when he should have looked down at his feet, he fell into a pit, whereupon an old woman who came to assist him sarcastically asked: "Do you think you will ever be able to comprehend things which are in heaven, when you cannot observe what is at your very feet?"

Tháles died at the age of ninety, overcome with heat and pressure of the crowd at the Olympic Games, which he had gone to witness (B. C. 550). Tháles used to express his thankfulness that he was a human being and not a beast, that he was a man and not a woman, and that he was a Greek and not a barbarian. Tháles founded the Ionic school of philosophy, from which subsequently proceeded the Socratic and several other philosophical systems. His writings have all perished. From what others say of him, he seems to have supposed all things to have been first formed from water by the creative power of God.

Tháles taught that the earth is a special body in the centre of the universe, that the sun and the stars are fiery bodies nourished by vapors, and that the moon is an opaque body receiving its light from the sun. He regarded the divine mind as pervading and animating all things, and as the origin of all motion. He believed in the immortality of the human soul, and supposed that all inferior animals, and even all substances, which have motion, like the magnet, have a soul, or animating principle. He made great advances in astronomy and mathematics. He was the first Greek who predicted an eclipse of the sun, and who discovered that the solar year consists of three hundred and sixty-five days. He taught the Greeks the division of the heavens into five zones, and the solstitial and equinoctial points. He also invented the fundamental problems afterwards incorporated into Euclid's *Elements*.

ANAXIMÁNDER, the disciple and friend of Tháles, was like him, a native of Milétus, where he was born, B. C. 610. He was the first Greek who taught philosophy in a public school. He adopted some of the opinions of Tháles, but disagreed with him on different points. He taught that the sun occupies the highest place in the heavens, the moon the next place, and the stars the lowest place. He maintained that the sun is twenty-eight times larger than the earth, and that the stars are globes composed of fire and air, and inhabited by the gods. Anaximánder considered Infinity the origin of all things, and that all things must finally be resolved into this Infinity. The different parts might change, but the whole is immutable. Anaximánder made several improvements in mathematics and astronomy, and was the first to delineate the map of the earth upon a globe. He likewise introduced the Babylonian sun-dial into Greece.

ANAXIMENES, like Tháles and Anaximánder, a native of Milétus, was a disciple of the latter and his successor as teacher of the Ionic school of philosophy. He believed that *air* is God and the first principle of all things, from which fire, water and earth proceed by rarefaction or condensation.

PYTHÁGORAS, the greatest of the early Grecian philosophers, was a native of the island of Samos, and flourished about the middle of the sixth century before Christ. His father, who was a merchant, gave him an excellent education, and it is said that he manifested remarkable talents at a very early age. He visited Egypt, where he remained twenty-two years, during which he acquired a thorough acquaintance with its religious and scientific knowledge and with the three styles of writing in that famous land. After extensive travels and vast study, Pythágoras returned to Samos, where he engaged in teaching his countrymen the principles of morality, and in initiating a chosen band of friends and disciples in the mystic and abstract philosophy to which he had so long devoted his study. The Samians eagerly flocked around him to receive his instructions, and his philosophical school was in a flourishing condition when he suddenly decided to leave his native Samos.

Pythágoras passed to Southern Italy and made his residence at Croton, a city of Magna Græcia. The people of Croton were then notorious for their immorality, and as soon as Pythágoras arrived he devoted himself to the work of reforming their manners. While landing on the shore he saw some fishermen drawing in their nets which were full of fish. He purchased the fish and caused them all to be thrown back into the sea; thus seeking to impress upon the Crotonians the duty of refraining from destroying animal life. He made practical use of the art, which he had learned from the Egyptian priests, of obtaining the respect of the ignorant and superstitious by affecting mystery and assuming supernatural powers. By this means he attracted the attention of the citizens and induced them to listen to his lectures on morality. His persuasive eloquence is said to have caused the Crotonians to abandon their corrupt and licentious practices.

At the request of the magistrates of Croton, Pythágoras established laws for the future government of the community. He then opened a school of philosophy, and now became so popular that from two to three thousand persons were soon enrolled as his pupils. Pythágoras considered the sublime teachings of philosophy too sacred and valuable to be taught to ordinary men who were unable to comprehend these great truths. Every person applying for admission to his school was subjected to a rigid examination, and he only received as his disciples those whose features, conversation and general behavior gave him satisfaction, and of whose personal character he obtained a favorable account.

The school constituted a society, called *Pythagoréans*, who had all their property, and all their meals and exercises in common, and who led a stern and moral life. The pupils were subjected to years of the most rigid mental and bodily discipline. Any applicant whose patience could not endure this protracted probation, was allowed to withdraw from the society, and to take more property with him than he had contributed to the society upon entering. The Pythagoréans then celebrated his funeral obsequies and erected a tomb for him, as if he had been removed by death—a ceremony designed to signify how thoroughly the man who relinquishes the paths of wisdom is lost to society. Those applicants who passed through the appointed probation creditably were received into the body of select disciples, or Pythagoréans proper. They were admitted *behind the curtain;* and were instructed in the principles of moral and natural philosophy, after having sworn not to disclose what was taught them. They practiced themselves in music, mathematics, astronomy, morals and politics, by turns, and the most sublime speculations concerning the nature of God and the origin of the universe were communicated to them in the most direct and undisguised language. Those instructed by Pythágoras in this clear and familiar style were said to constitute the *esoteric*, or private school; while those attending his public lectures, in which the moral truths were usually delivered in symbolical or figurative style, were regarded as forming the *exoteric*, or public school.

The esoteric school at Croton had six hundred members. They lived together as one family, with their wives and children, in a public building called the common auditory. The entire business of the society was conducted with the most rigid regularity. Each day was commenced by deliberating distinctly upon the manner in which it should be spent, and was ended with a careful review of the occurrences which had transpired and the business which had been transacted. They arose in the morning before the sun made his appearance above the eastern horizon, in order that they might pay homage to that luminary, after which they repeated select verses from Homer and other poets, and enlivened their spirits to fit them for the day's duties by vocal and instrumental music. They then devoted a few hours to the study of science. After this there was an interval of leisure, usually employed in a solitary walk for the purpose of meditation. The next part of the day was devoted to conversation. The hour just before dinner was employed in different kinds of athletic exercises. Their dinner consisted mainly of bread, honey and water; as they entirely dispensed with wine after being fully initiated. The rest of the day was given to civil and domestic matters, bathing, conversation and religious ceremonies.

Pythágoras while teaching, in public or in private, wore a long white robe, a flowing beard, and, some say, a crown upon his head, always maintaining a grave and dignified manner. Besides desiring to have it supposed that he was of a nature superior to that of ordinary men, and not subject to their passions and feelings, he took care never to display any signs of joy, sorrow or anger, and to seem thoroughly calm under all circumstances.

Pythágoras visited and taught in many other cities of Southern Italy and Sicily, besides Croton. He obtained numerous disciples wherever he went, and these looked upon him with a veneration almost equal to that entertained for a god. He included politics as well as morals in his lectures, and excited the people by his denunciations of oppression and his appeals to the people to uphold their rights, thus inciting the inhabitants of several cities to cast off the yoke of their tyrannical rulers. But his active interference in politics soon aroused against him a host of foes, and finally led to his destruction. The aristocratic party throughout Magna Græcia were alarmed, and fiercely opposed the Pythagoréans. The philosopher was driven from one place to another, until he finally came to Metapontum, where his enemies excited the people against him and compelled him to seek refuge in a temple dedicated to the Muses, in which he perished from hunger.

For some time after the death of Pythágoras, his disciples were everywhere cruelly persecuted, but they subsequently recovered their former popularity. The Pythagoréan school of philosophy was restored, statues were raised in his honor, and the house in which he had lived at Croton was converted into a temple to Dêmêtêr.

Pythágoras was more than eighty years of age when he died. He left two sons and a daughter, and these three acquired considerable fame for their intellectual attainments. The sons directed their father's philosophical school, and the daughter was celebrated for her learning and wrote an able commentary on Homer's poems. It is not believed that Pythágoras committed any of his doctrines to writing, and they seem to be only gathered from his disciples.

Pythágoras appears to have taught that the Supreme Being is the soul of the universe, and the first principle of all things; that he resembles *light* in substance, and is like to *truth* in nature; that he is invisible, incorruptible, and not capable of pain. He maintained that one divine mind emanated from four orders of intelligence, namely, gods, demons, heroes and human souls. The gods were the highest of these; the demons second; the heroes, who were described as an order of beings having bodies consisting of a subtle, luminous substance, ranked as third; while the human mind comprised the fourth. The gods, demons and heroes lived in the upper air, and exercised a beneficent or maglignant influence on men, dispensing at will sickness, prosperity and adversity.

Pythágoras considered the human soul a self-moving principle, consisting of the *rational* and the *irrational*—the former a part of the divine mind with its seat in the brain, and the latter the source of happiness with its seat in the heart. This philosopher taught the doctrine of the *metempsychosis*, or *transmigration of the soul*, and his disciples therefore abstained rigidly from animal food, and were unwilling to take the life of any living creature, as they feared that in felling an ox or in shooting a pigeon they would dislodge the soul of a distinguished warrior or sage of bygone ages, or perhaps even be raising their hands against the lives of some of their own departed relatives or friends. Pythágoras even went so far as to declare that he *remembered* when he himself had passed through several *human existences* before he became Pythágoras.

Pythágoras regarded the sun as a fiery globe, located in the center of the universe, with the earth and the other planets revolving around it. He considered the sun, the moon and the stars to be inhabited by gods and demons. He taught that there are ten heavenly spheres—that of the earth, those of the seven planets, that of the fixed stars, and an invisible one called the *antichthon*, located opposite the earth. In moving through the pure ether occupying all space, these spheres emit sounds; and their respective distances from the earth corresing to the proportion of the notes in the musical scale, the tones vary in accordance with the relative distances, magnitudes and velocity of the several spheres, so as to form the most perfect harmony. In this way Pythágoras accounted for the *music of the spheres*, which his followers fabled that the gods allowed him only to hear. Pythágoras explained the eclipses of the sun as caused by the intervention of the moon between the sun and the earth, and the eclipses of the moon as produced by the interposition of the *antichthon*, or invisible sphere. Thus Pythágoras had a clearer idea of the real arrangement of the universe than any other ancient philosopher, which may be ascribed to his protracted residence in Egypt.

Pythágoras regarded musical and arithmetical numbers as vested with a mysterious importance. He is represented as teaching that *one*, or *unity*, signifies God, or the animating principle of the universe; that *two* symbolizes matter, or the passive principle; that *three* denotes the world formed by the combination of the two principles; and that *four* is the emblem of nature. The sum of these numbers is the decade, embracing all arithmetical and musical qualities and proportions.

Pythágoras, as we have seen, was himself very fond of music, and was well versed in that science. It is believed that he discovered the musical ratios, and invented the monochord, or single-stringed instrument, with moveable bridges to measure and regulate the ratios of musical intervals. He was likewise profound in geometry, and made many important additions to that science. He originated the famous demonstration in Euclid's *Elements*, the forty-seventh in the first book.

His rank as a moral teacher was very high, and the following are specimens of his many sound and excellent precepts: "It is inconsistent with fortitude to abandon the post appointed by the Supreme Lord before we obtain his permission." "No man ought to be esteemed free who has not the perfect command of himself." "That which is good and becoming is rather to be pursued than that which is pleasant." "Sobriety is the strength of the soul, for it preserves the reason unclouded by passion." "The gods are to be worshiped not under such images as represent the forms of men, but by simple lustrations and offerings, and with purity of heart."

Æsop, the noted fabulist, was an ingenious and successful teacher of wisdom. His moral lessons were veiled under an allegorical form, and were productive of durable impression. Æsop was a native of Phrygia and was born about B. C. 600. He was physically deformed. He was sold as a slave to an Athenian named Demarchus, and while at Athens he acquired an extensive knowledge of the Greek language. He was afterwards purchased by a Samian philosopher named Xanthus, and subsequently became the property of another philosopher of Samos, named Idmon, who perceived and admired his genius, and gave him his liberty, after which Æsop spent his time in traveling throughout Greece, teaching moral allegories to the people. He arrived at Athens soon after the usurpation of Pisistratus, and warned the dissatisfied Athenians, who unwillingly submitted to the usurper, as to the dangers of attempting political changes by telling them the fable of the frogs who asked Zeus to give them a king. Æsop was finally put to death by the citizens of Delphi, whose indignation he had aroused by his freedom in condemning their vices. His death is believed to have occurred about B. C. 561, when he was in his thirty-ninth year. The Athenians so esteemed his memory that they raised a statue in his honor.

The *Seven Wise Men of Greece* were the great philosopher THÁLES of Milétus, the great lawgiver SOLON of Athens, PERIANDER of Corinth, CHILO of Sparta, CLEOBULUS of Lindus, PITTACUS of Mitylêné, and BIAS of Priêné. Ancient writers mention two occasions on which these seven sages met together—once at Delphi and a second time at Corinth. The title of "Seven Wise Men" is said to have been given them from the following circumstance: Some Milésian fishermen after casting their nets into the sea, sold the expected draught of fish to some persons standing near by. But when the nets were drawn, it was discovered that they contained a golden tripod, whereupon the fishermen refused to give it to the purchasers of the draught, saying that they sold only the *fish* that might be caught in the nets. After much wrangling both parties consented to refer the matter to the citizens of Milétus, who sent to consult the Delphic oracle concerning it. The oracle ordered the tripod to be awarded to the wisest man that could be found, whereupon they offered it to their fellow-citizen, Tháles, who modestly declined it, saying that there were many wiser men than himself. Tháles next sent it to Bias of Priêné, but he likewise declined it and sent it to another. Thus this golden tripod passed in succession through the hands of all who were afterwards classed as the Seven Wise Men of Greece; after which it was consecrated to

Apollo and deposited in the famous temple of that god at Delphi.

The Seven Wise Men sought to enlighten and improve mankind by disseminating a number of moral truths and precepts in the form of maxims and proverbs. These seven sages were not only inventors of popular proverbs and moral maxims. Some of them were active politicians. One of them was a famous lawgiver, and another was a celebrated natural philosopher.

We have already given a sketch of the philosopher Tháles of Milétus, the greatest of the Seven Wise Men. The following were some of his maxims: "The same measure of gratitude which we show our parents, we may expect from our children." "It is better to adorn the mind than the face." "It is not the length of a man's tongue that is the measure of his wisdom." "Never do that yourself which you blame in others." "The most happy man is he who is sound in health, moderate in fortune and cultivated in understanding." "Not only the criminal acts, but the bad thoughts of men are known to the gods." "The most difficult thing is to know one's self; the easiest, to give advice to others." "The most ancient of all beings is God, for he has neither beginning nor end." "All things are full of God, and the world is supreme in beauty, because it is his workmanship." "The greatest of all things is space, for it comprehends all things; the most rapid is the mind, for it travels through the universe in a single instant; the most powerful is necessity, for it conquers all things; the most wise is time, for it discovers all things."

We have also given a full account of Solon, the wise and virtuous lawgiver of Athens, but we will mention an incident which transpired during his stay at Milétus, while he was visiting Tháles. Solon asked Tháles why he did not take a wife. Without giving a direct answer, Tháles introduced to Solon a person whom he said had just arrived from Athens. Solon, having left his family at home in Athens, eagerly inquired of the stranger if he had any news. The stranger, whom Tháles had advised what to say, replied that there was nothing new at Athens, except that the son of a great lawgiver, named Solon, was dead, and had been followed to the grave by a vast multitude of citizens. On receiving these sad tidings, the gentle and affectionate Solon broke out into loud lamentations. Tháles at once relieved his distinguished guest's mind by informing him that he had been deceived by a fabricated story, and remarked smilingly that he himself had been prevented from marrying and rearing a family by the dread of meeting with just such sorrows as his visitor had felt. Some of Solon's precepts are the following: "Reverence God and honor your parents." "Mingle not with the wicked." "Trust to virtue and probity rather than to oaths." "Counsel your friend in private, but never reprove him in public." "Do not consider the present pleasure, but the ultimate good." "Do not select friends hastily; but when once chosen, be slow to reject." "Believe yourself fit to command when you have learned to obey." "Honors worthily gained far exceed those which are accidental."

Periander was born at Corinth, in B. C. 665; and, as we have noticed, was the son of Cypselus, who had subverted the republican institutions of Corinth and made himself *tyrant*. Periander succeeded his father in the government of Corinth, and ruled with firmness and prudence, but with great severity. He is said to have been violent and cruel, although classed as one of the Seven Wise Men. In a fit of anger he killed his wife Melissa by a kick, and afterwards caused some women to be burned to death, having become enraged by their calumnious accusations. He banished his younger son for expressing abhorrence of him because he had murdered his wife, and is said to have committed other similar atrocious crimes. He died at the age of eighty, B. C. 584. Among his excellent precepts, many of which he never carried into practice, were the following: "In prosperity, be moderate; in adversity, be prudent." "Pleasure is fleeting; honor is immortal." "Prudence can accomplish all things." "The intention of crime is as sinful as the act." "Perform whatever you have promised."

Chilo was a Spartan, born about B. C. 630, and was one of the Ephori of that state. The following were some of his precepts: "The three most difficult things are, to keep a secret, to employ time properly, and to bear an injury." "Never speak evil of the dead." "Reverence old age." "Govern your anger." "Be not over-hasty." "The tongue ought to be always carefully restrained, but especially at the festive board." "Seek not impossibilities." "Let your friendship be more conspicuous in adversity than in prosperity." "Prefer loss to ill-gotten wealth; the former is a trouble only once endured, but the latter will constantly oppress you."

Cleobulus was *tyrant* of Lindus, in the island of Rhodes, where he was born about B. C. 634. He was noted for his personal strength and beauty, as well as for his wisdom. He visited Egypt to gain knowledge, and is supposed to have acquired in that country the taste for enigmatical writing afterwards manifested by him. He died at the age of seventy, about B. C. 564. Besides his three hundred enigmatical verses, he wrote many maxims, of which the following are samples: "Before you quit your house, consider what you have to do; and when you return, reflect whether it has been done." "Be more attentive than talkative." "Educate your children." "Detest ingratitude." "Endeavor always to employ your thoughts on something worthy."

Pittacus was born at Mitylênê, in the isle of Lesbos, about B. C. 650. He was noted for his bravery in war with the Athenians, and afterwards in the dethronement of Melanchrus, the tyrant of Lesbos. His countrymen, in gratitude for his services, placed him at the head of the state, in which capacity he served until he had fully restored order and reformed the laws and institutions of the state, after which he resigned his power and retired to private life. He died in the eighty-second year of his age, B. C. 568. The following are some of his precepts: "The possession of power discovers a man's true character." "Whatever you do, do it well." "Do not that to your neighbor which you would take ill from him." "Know your opportunity." "Never disclose your schemes, lest their failure expose you to ridicule as well as to disappointment."

Bias was a native of the city of Priênê, in Ionia, being therefore a Greek of Asia Minor. The date of his birth is uncertain. He was very generous and had a philosophical contempt for wealth. He was an able orator, and his death is said to have been caused by over-exertion while pleading the cause of a friend. He was witty as well as wise, as will be seen by the following anecdote. A scoffer having inquired of him as to his religion, he gave no reply. His inquirer desired to know the reason of his silence, whereupon he answered: "It is because you ask me about things that do not concern you." Being once in a storm at sea, the profligate sailors began to pray, in fright; whereupon Bias remarked: "Be silent, lest the gods discover that it is you who are sailing." The following were some of his maxims: "Endeavor to gain the good will of all men." "Speak of the gods with reverence." "Esteem a worthy friend as your greatest blessing." "Yield rather to persuasion than to compulsion." "The most miserable man is he who cannot endure misery." "Form your plans with deliberation, but execute them with vigor." "Do not praise an unworthy man for the sake of his wealth." "It is better to decide a difference between your enemies than your friends; for, in the former case, you will certainly gain a friend, and in the latter lose one."

SECTION X.—THE PERSIAN WAR (B. C. 499-449).

IN B. C. 502 the Ionian Greeks of Asia Minor revolted against the Persian king, Darius Hystaspes, and sent messengers to Greece to solicit aid against the Persians. It is related that the Ionian messengers had almost succeeded in inducing Cleómenes, King of Sparta, to join in the war against the Persians, when his daughter exclaimed: "Fly, father, or the ambassador will corrupt you!" Thereupon Cleómenes refused to aid the revolted Ionians. At this time Artaphernes, the Persian satrap of Lydia, at the instigation of Hippias, the expelled *tyrant* of Athens, who had applied to him for support, sent an insolent message to the Athenians, ordering them to restore Hippias to his power if they did not wish to incur the hostility of Persia. This impudent attempt at dictation so exasperated the Athenians that they at once determined to aid the Greeks of Asia Minor in their resistance to the insolent Persians, and sent a fleet of twenty ships to Milétus for that purpose. From Milétus the Athenian and Ionian fleets proceeded to Ephesus, where the land troops debarked and marched against Sardis, the capital of the Persian satrapy of Lydia, and captured and burned this city before the eyes of the Persian satrap, Artaphernes himself, who had taken refuge in the castle or stronghold of the city. But a large Medo-Persian army was soon collected, and this army defeated the united forces of the Greeks in turn. The Athenian auxiliaries returned home, and the Ionian Greeks of Asia Minor were compelled to submit to the power of the Medo-Persian Empire, after a protracted struggle.

When the Persian king, Darius Hystaspes, heard of the burning of Sardis, he became very much exasperated, and resolved to revenge himself upon the Athenians by invading their territory, and, if possible, to conquer all Greece. Shooting an arrow into the air, in accordance with the Persian custom, he prayed that Ahura-Mazda would aid him to punish the Athenians for their part in the burning of Sardis. He caused an attendant to remind him of the conduct of the Greeks every time he sat down at table, so that he would not forget his purpose. He immediately began active preparations for an invasion of Greece, and fitted out an immense armament, which, under the command of Mardonius, the son-in-law of Darius Hystaspes, proceeded across the Ægean sea towards the shores of European Greece, in the year B. C. 493. Mardonius debarked his land troops upon the coast of Macedon, after which he sailed southward with his fleet, but encountered a violent storm in sailing around the promontory of Mount Athos, by which he lost three hundred vessels and about twenty thousand men. His land force was defeated in a night attack by the Thracians with heavy loss. Disheartened by this double misfortune, Mardonius speedily returned to Asia with the shattered remnants of his fleet and army.

King Darius Hystaspes was more determined than ever upon the invasion and conquest of Greece, and raised an army of half a million men for that purpose. Heralds were sent to the Greek states to demand *earth and water* as symbols of submission. This demand was complied with by the smaller Grecian states, which feared the consequences of provoking the displeasure of the King of Persia; but Athens and Sparta indignantly refused, throwing the Persian heralds into deep wells and telling them to take thence their *earth and water*.

In B. C. 490 Darius Hystaspes sent a fleet of six hundred galleys and many transports, conveying an army of one hundred and twenty thousand men, under the command of Datis, a Median nobleman, and Artaphernes, son of the satrap of the same name, to conquer Greece, and especially to destroy Athens, and also Eretria, in the island of Eubœa, and enslave the inhabitants. Datis and Artaphernes sailed directly across the Ægean, reducing the Cyclades on the way; and, reaching Eubœa, captured Eretria, after a siege of six days, through the treachery of two members of the aristocratic party. The city was sacked and burned, and its inhabitants were placed in chains on board Persian ships. Datis then crossed the Euripus and landed at Marathon, in Attica, to wreak vengeance upon Athens.

The Athenians, greatly alarmed at this formidable invasion of their territory by the Persians, applied to the Spartans for aid; but the superstitious Lacedæmonians refused to give any assistance before a full moon; and as at the time of the application, it was still five days before that period, they delayed the march of their troops. The Athenians were therefore obliged to encounter the Persian invaders without any help, except by a heroic band of one thousand Platæans, who, grateful for the protection often extended to them by the Athenians, against the power of Thebes, hastened to assist their friends in this emergency. Besides these Platæans the Athenian army mustered about nine thousand men, with about a thousand light-armed slaves. Notwithstanding the vast numerical inferiority of the Athenians compared with the immense host of the Medo-Persians, the Athenian leaders decided, after due deliberation, that they would lead their forces against the foe in the open country.

In accordance with the Athenian custom, ten generals were appointed to command the army, one being selected from each of the ten wards of Attica, and each general being in turn vested with the chief command for a single day. But Aristides, one of these ten commanders, and a man of singular wisdom and honor, seeing the inconveniences and perils of this arrangement, resigned his day in favor of Miltíades, another of the generals, whose military talents had been fully tested. The other eight generals followed the example of Aristides, so that Miltíades was left in sole command. He thus had an opportunity to adopt such measures as were essential to insure success to his little army, and acted with a skill and prudence that fully justified the confidence reposed in him by his brother officers.

Finding the Medo-Persian host encamped upon the plain of Marathon, Miltíades took up a position on the declivity of a hill about a mile distant from the enemy. He caused the intermediate space between the two armies to be strewed with trunks and branches of trees during the night, in order to obstruct the movements of the Medo-Persian cavalry. The next day he drew up his eleven thousand troops in line of battle, putting the Athenian freemen on the right, the Platæans on the left, and the armed slaves in the center.

The Medo-Persian army numbered one hundred and ten thousand men, and was a mixed horde, consisting of levies from the many tribes and nations under the dominion of the Great King. Some of them were armed with spears, swords and battle-axes; but most of them fought with bows and arrows, darts and other missile weapons. They carried light targets of reeds or ozie in their left hands, and their bodies were in some cases covered with thin plates of metal. Their defensive armor was nevertheless inferior to that of the Athenians, and did not by any means enable the Orientals to withstand the shock of the dense Grecian phalanx. Miltíades was well aware of this, and he caused his troops to advance to the attack at a running pace, in order to give the bowmen and javelin-throwers as short a space as possible to use their missiles, and to enable the Athenian spearmen to bear down and break open the ranks of the more lightly armed Persians. This movement succeeded admirably.

At first the Grecian center, consisting of slaves, was broken by the foe; but the Athenian and Platæan freemen on the two flanks carried everything before them, after which they closed in upon the Persian troops who had broken their center, defeated them also, and remained in full possession of the field. The panic-stricken Persians fled in haste to their ships, pursued actively and slaughtered in great numbers by the triumphant host of Miltíades. More than six thousand Persians were slain in this memorable battle, while the victorious Athenians lost only one hundred and ninety-two killed, two of the ten generals being among the number. The Athenians also took seven of the Persian vessels, the rest of the fleet returning to Asia. Among the slain on the side of the Persians was Hippias, the expelled tyrant of Athens, who had sought to revenge his overthrow by joining the enemies of his country. The Spartan troops arrived the day after the battle, having left Sparta as soon as the moon was full, and having hastened by forced marches to aid the Athenians. After contemplating with great interest the scene of this glorious Athenian victory, and bestowing merited praises upon the valor of the heroic little band under Miltíades, the Spartans returned home (B. C. 490).

Such was the memorable battle of Marathon—one of the most important battles in the history of Greece and of the world. It was the first serious check ever experienced by the Medo-Persians in any quarter, and taught the Greeks the value of their disciplined valor as arrayed against the vast hosts of Asia. It gave the Hellenic race a respite in which to prepare for the decisive struggle for the preservation of their freedom and their civilization, and encouraged them to make the effort when the final and greater crisis confronted them.

Had the Medo-Persians triumphed at Marathon, not only would Greece have been enslaved, but all European civilization would have perished; and thus the whole fate of the human race and the entire course of history would have been changed. So the Greek victory at Marathon was a victory for the cause of civilization and human freedom in all time.

After menacing Athens, Datis, with the Medo-Persian fleet, returned to Asia with his Eretrian prisoners; and Greece was for the time freed from its invaders. The victory of Marathon was hailed by the Athenians with unbounded joy. Miltíades was regarded as the savior of Greece, and was received with the highest honors, being for awhile the most distinguished and beloved citizen of the Athenian republic. But soon after his great victory, his glorious career was brought to a sad end.

Even while prince in the Chersonésus, Miltíades had won the gratitude of the Athenians by annexing the isles of Lemnos and Imbros to their dominions; and he now won a greater claim to their regard by having delivered them from their most threatening danger, so that they now had unlimited confidence in him. When he therefore promised them a still more lucrative enterprise, though less glorious than the recent one against the Persians, they very readily granted his request for a fleet of seventy ships and a large supply of men and money for their use, of which he was not to render any account until his return. Miltíades at once set sail for the isle of Paros, which had furnished a trireme to the Persians during the recent invasion. He was repulsed in his attack upon Paros and received a dangerous wound. Discouraged, he relinquished the siege and returned in disgrace to Athens. Xanthippus, the leader of the aristocracy, accused him of having received a bribe from the Persians to retire from Paros. Severely wounded, Miltíades was brought into court upon a couch; and although his brother, Tiságoras, undertook his defense, the only plea that Miltíades made was in the two words "Lemnos" and "Marathon." Though the offense, if proven, was capital, the people refused to sentence the victor of Marathon to death. They commuted his punishment to a fine of fifty talents—equal to about fifty thousand dollars of our money—which being unable to pay, he was cast into prison, where he died of the wound he had received at Paros (B. C. 489). His remains were not allowed to be buried until his son, Cimon, shortly afterward paid the fine. Nevertheless the glory acquired by Miltíades by his victory at Marathon survived; and although his countrymen persecuted him while living, they ever afterward revered his memory.

The Persians had brought a block of

white marble with them, intending to erect it as a trophy upon the field of Marathon in honor of the victory which they anticipated. A half century later this marble block was carved by Phidias into a gigantic figure of the avenging goddess, Nemesis; while the brazen weapons and shields of the Persians were cast by the same artist into the colossal statue of Athênê, which was set up in the Acropolis, and which could be seen from the sea far beyond the promontory of Sunium. About the same time a picture of the battle of Marathon was painted by order of the state, and the figure of Miltíades was represented in the foreground, animating his troops to victory. The one hundred and ninety-two heroes who sacrificed their lives for their country's liberties in this celebrated conflict were buried in the field, and a mound or tumulus was raised over them.

The victory of Marathon, which saved the liberties of Greece, also contributed immensely to raise the prestige of Athens, and the commanding abilities of several of her eminent statesmen also added vastly to her power and influence. At the head of the galaxy of brilliant and talented Athenians at this period of Grecian glory were Aristídes and Themístocles, both of whom, though opposed to each other in everything else, labored alike for the greatness and welfare of their country. Aristídes was entirely devoid of personal ambition and was desirous only of the public welfare. Aristídes was, as we have seen, one of the ten generals who commanded the Athenian army on the glorious field of Marathon. He was the son of a person of moderate fortune, named Lysímachus. Themístocles was likewise descended from a respectable Athenian family. These two great statesmen were companions in boyhood, and are said to have even then manifested striking indications of the difference of their dispositions. Aristídes was calm, moderate, candid and upright. Themístocles was bold, enthusiastic, artful and plausible.

The people of Athens were still divided into the aristocratic and democratic parties. Aristídes became the leader of the aristocratic party, while Themístocles headed the democratic. Thus these two leaders were forced into almost constant opposition, both by their position and by the difference of their political views. The character of Aristídes was ranked deservedly high for wisdom and uprightness; but Themístocles, by his wonderful oratorical powers and his persuasive eloquence, was often enabled to triumph over the more honest but less eloquent Aristídes. But instead of being discouraged by such occurrences, Aristídes waited patiently until the people should arrive at a sounder opinion, exerting himself meanwhile to prevent as much as possible the evil results which he anticipated from their imprudent decisions. In the year after the battle of Marathon, Aristídes was chosen first Archon, or chief magistrate of the Athenian republic; and in this capacity he gave so many signal proofs of his uprightness and fairness that the people honored him with the surname of "the Just," and many of the citizens referred their disputes to his decision, in preference to carrying them to the ordinary courts of justice.

Jealous because of the civic honors bestowed upon his esteemed and conscientious rival, Themístocles took advantage of this circumstance to concoct and circulate an injurious rumor to the effect that Aristídes was seeking to usurp all authority, judicial as well as civil, in his own person, as a preliminary step toward making himself absolute ruler of Athens. The Athenians had not yet forgotten the usurpation of Pisistratus, who, under the mask of moderation and anxiety for their welfare, had subverted the constitution of the republic for his own individual aggrandizement. They therefore eagerly hearkened to the eloquent and persuasive voice of Themístocles; and, alarmed at the very allegation that a popular leader was once more entertaining the design of assuming unconstitutional power, they rashly condemned Aristídes to ten years' banishment by *ostracism*. While the voting by ostracism was in progress, a country voter who was unable to write came up to Aristídes, whom he did not know personally, and requested him to write the name of Aristídes upon a shell; whereupon Aristídes asked: "Did this man ever injure you?" To which the citizen replied: "No, nor do I even know him; but I am weary of hearing him everywhere called 'the Just?'" Thereupon Aristídes, without saying another word, wrote his name upon the shell, and returned it to the country citizen.

Themístocles was now without a rival at Athens, and his ascendency in the councils of the republic was undisputed; but he was destitute of that pure and unselfish patriotism which had characterized his banished rival. He had an insatiable desire for political fame, and wished to make Athens great and powerful in order that he might win for himself an imperishable renown. So great was the desire of Themístocles for preëminence that the glory won by Miltiades at Marathon threw him into a state of deep melancholy; and when asked the reason of this, he replied that "the trophies of Miltiades would not allow him to sleep." When he had won influence in the state, an opportunity for obtaining distinction soon manifested itself. The commerce of Athens had for some time suffered from the hostility of the inhabitants of the island of Ægina. Themístocles advised his countrymen to appropriate the produce of the silver mines of Mount Laurium, which had thus far been yearly divided among the citizens, to the construction of a fleet to chastise those troublesome islanders. The Athenians acted on his advice, and built one hundred galleys, with which Themístocles effectually broke the naval power of Ægina, hitherto the maritime rival of Athens. Athens thus became the leading maritime power of Greece, but Themístocles continually added to the number of its war-vessels, until they amounted to two hundred triremes, and Athens was in a short time absolute and undisputed mistress of the seas.

Themístocles was governed in his action by a belief that the Persians would renew their efforts to conquer Greece. He foresaw the importance of a well-equipped fleet for external defense in such a contingency, or as a refuge for the citizens in case of being overcome by the invaders. Events subsequently demonstrated the correctness of the anticipations of Themístocles.

Upon hearing of the defeat of his army at Marathon, King Darius Hystaspes resolved upon another expedition for the invasion and conquest of Greece on a far grander scale than the other; but a revolt in Egypt interrupted his preparations, and death soon afterward put an end to all his earthly designs (B. C. 485). His son and successor, Xerxes the Great, after crushing the Egyptian revolt, prepared to execute his father's projects for the subjugation of Greece. Persian heralds were again sent to all the Grecian states, except Athens and Sparta, which had treated the former heralds so cruelly, to demand *earth and water* in token of submission; and many of the smaller states again granted the required acknowledgment, fearing to arouse the displeasure of the Great King.

Xerxes was engaged four years in raising an army, building a fleet, and cutting a canal across the isthmus connecting Mount Athos with the Greek continent. This passage was provided for to enable the Medo-Persian army to continue their progress directly southward, instead of sailing around the dangerous promontory of Athos, where the fleet of Mardonius had been wrecked. As soon as the preparations were finished, Xerxes personally assumed command of the expedition, and marched directly for the Hellespont.

His army was the largest ever raised, and is said to have consisted of more than two millions of fighting men, of whom one million seven hundred thousand were infantry, while four hundred thousand were cavalry. The immense multitude of slaves and women who followed the army raised the vast host to more than four millions of souls. The fleet consisted of twelve hundred ships of war and three thousand transports, and carried about six hundred thousand men. It is said that, on one occasion, while Xerxes was viewing this mighty host, he was moved to tears by the thought that not one individual of all the thousands before him would be living a hundred years thereafter.

Xerxes caused a bridge of boats to be constructed across the Hellespont, between the two towns of Abydos and Sestos, where the narrow strait is less than a mile wide; but this bridge was destroyed by a furious storm, which so angered the despot that he ordered all the workmen engaged in constructing it to be put to death. He is also said to have caused the waters of the Hellespont to be beaten with rods, and fetters to be dropped into the strait, as a token of his determination to curb its violence, while his servants addressed it in this style: "It is thus, thou salt and bitter water, that thy master punishes thy unprovoked injury, and he is determined to pass thy treacherous streams, notwithstanding all the insolence of thy malice."

Another bridge, consisting of a double line of vessels, strongly anchored on both sides of the Hellespont, and joined together by hempen cables, was then constructed, and trunks of trees were laid across the decks of the vessels, the whole being smoothly covered with planks, thus affording an easy passage for the troops. The Persian hosts occupied seven days and nights in crossing this remarkable bridge; after which Xerxes marched through Thrace, Macedon and Thessaly towards the southern portions of Greece, receiving the submission of the different northern states through which he advanced; while his fleet crossed what is now known as the Gulf of Contessa and passed through the canal of Athos, and thereafter sailed southward.

In the meantime those Grecian states which had refused to submit to the advancing Persians were making vigorous preparations to resist the invaders. A congress of deputies from these different states, convened at Corinth, adopted measures for the common defense. The united Greeks exhibited extraordinary courage at this momentous crisis, not manifesting any signs of despondency for a single instant, notwithstanding the terrible odds against them. They drew upon the entire population of the confederated states for all the military force at their command to resist the immense hosts of the Medo-Persian Empire; yet with all their efforts, the Grecian forces did not exceed sixty thousand freemen and perhaps as many armed slaves. To add to the discouragement of the Greeks in this extraordinary emergency, the responses which they received from the Delphic oracle were dark and menacing. The Spartans were informed that the voluntary death of a king of the race of Hercules could save *them*, and the Athenians were answered in this style: "All else, within Cecropian bounds and the recesses of divine Cithæron, shall fall; the wooden walls alone Zeus grants to Athênê to remain inexpugnable, a refuge to you and your children. Wait not therefore the approach of horse or foot, an immense army, coming from the continent; but retreat, turning the back, even though they be close upon you. O divine Salamis! thou shalt lose the sons of women, whether Dêmêtêr be scattered or gathered!"

The Athenians were puzzled to know what was meant by the phrase "wooden walls," referred to by the oracle. Some supposed that these words alluded to the Acropolis, or citadel of Athens, which had in early times been surrounded with a wooden palisade; but Themistocles insisted that the fleet constituted the wooden walls meant by the oracle, and advised the Athenians to rely entirely upon their ships for their defense against the Persian invaders. This advice was ultimately followed; and while the Spartan king Leónidas with eight thousand confederate Greek troops took up a strong position in the narrow pass of Thermopylæ, between Thessaly and Phocis, the Athenian fleet, reinforced by the fleets of the other confederated Grecian states, sailed to the strait separating the island of Eubœa from the coast of Thessaly, and took up its station at the promontory of Artemisium, about fifteen miles from the pass of Thermopylæ.

The march of Xerxes had so far resembled that of a triumphal procession more than a hostile invasion. None had the courage to oppose his advance, and the different minor states of Greece through which he passed vied with each other in the respect which they showed the Great King and in the cordial welcome with which they greeted him and the millions of his gigantic host. But he was now to be enlightened with that unconquerable Grecian valor which had overcome the armies of his illustrious father.

When Xerxes arrived at the pass of Thermopylæ and discovered that it was defended by so small a force, he sent messengers to demand of them to lay down their arms. To which demand the heroic Leónidas replied in truly Spartan style: "Come and take them." The Persian messengers then assured the Greeks that if they would lay down their arms, the Great King would receive them as his allies and give them a country more fertile than Greece. But the brave Greeks replied that "no country was worth acceptance, unless won by virtue; and that, as for their arms, they should want them whether as the friends or the enemies of Xerxes." After giving this intrepid reply, the Greeks resumed the gymnastic exercises and the other amusements in which they had been engaged when the messengers of the Persian king arrived.

Xerxes waited four days in the hope that the Greeks would surrender. Observing that they remained as resolute as ever, he gave orders to begin the attack, and thus commenced the ever-memorable battle of Thermopylæ. But the extreme narrowness of the pass, which was only fifteen feet wide in one place and twenty-five in another, prevented the Persians from reaping the full advantage which their enormous superiority of numbers would otherwise have given them, and the undaunted Spartans repulsed with tremendous slaughter every successive column of the Persians that entered the narrow defile to force a passage. King Xerxes viewed the desperate conflict from a neighboring height; and being repeatedly startled with irrepressible emotion as he saw the bravest of his troops defeated and slaughtered, he finally ordered the discontinuance of the assault on the heroic Grecian band. The next day the combat was renewed with no better success on the part of the invaders, who, however, effected by stratagem what they were unable to obtain by force; and the treachery of a Greek named Epialtes, who was a native of Malis, led to the entire destruction of the heroic defenders of Thermopylæ.

Epialtes offered, for a large bribe, to show the Persians a secret path over the mountains, a few miles west of Thermopylæ, by which the invaders could reach the other extremity of the pass, intercept the retreat of Leónidas and assail him in the rear. The Persians eagerly accepted the offer of the Greek traitor; and the Immortals, numbering twenty thousand men, under the command of a distinguished officer named Hydarnes, started over this secret and circuitous path, in the evening. This chosen detachment marched all night, and arrived near the summit of the height about sunrise the next morning. But the invaders here found their way obstructed by a guard of Phocians, who had been assigned by Leónidas to the defense of this unfrequented mountain path.

The Persians advanced for some time without being observed, under the shadow of an oak forest covering the sides of the hill; but the Phocians were finally alarmed by the unwonted rustling among the leaves and the heavy tread of so numerous a detachment of troops, and prepared to offer a resolute resistance to the advancing foe. The Phocians, supposing that the Immortals had come to attack them, left their position in the pass and posted themselves on a rising ground where they would be less exposed to the darts of their assailants; but Hydarnes did not attack them, as they had expected he would, but, paying no further attention to them, continued his march, along the evacuated pass, towards the plain.

The gallant defenders of Thermopylæ had many secret friends in the Persian camp. The recruits which Xerxes had forced into his service during the march were not at heart enemies of Greece, and one of them managed to escape to the Grecian camp with intimation of the treachery of Epialtes, a few hours after the march of the Immortals under Hydarnes. Leónidas at once summoned a council of war, which decided that all the Greeks except the Spartans should at once retreat towards the Isthmus of Corinth, as all perceived that the pass of Thermopylæ was now untenable. But Leónidas and his heroic band of three hundred Spartans declared that, as the laws of Sparta did not allow a Spartan soldier to flee before an enemy, they would either conquer or die at their post. Seven hundred Thespians, inspired to emulation by this noble example of Spartan heroism, also announced their determination to remain at their post and share the fate of Leónidas and his gallant band.

All the Greek troops then retired from the pass of Thermopylæ, with the exception of the three hundred Spartans and the seven hundred Thespians, and about four hundred Thebans whom Leónidas had retained as hostages because of the known sympathy of Thebes with the Persian invaders who had come to destroy the liberties of the other Grecian states which the Thebans disliked. Leónidas then exhorted his brave companions in arms to acquit themselves as men who expected death and were prepared for it any moment. Said he: "Come, my fellow-soldiers, let us sit down to the last meal we shall eat on earth; to-morrow we shall sup with Pluto."

On the approach of midnight, Leónidas led his heroic little band against the overwhelming host of the Persians, who were completely surprised by this sudden and unexpected attack, and thus thrown into the greatest confusion, being unable to distinguish friend from foe in the darkness, so that in many cases they attacked each other; while the gallant Spartans and their heroic Thespian allies remained together in a compact body, fighting with the wild energy of men who had relinquished every hope of life, making dreadful havoc in the demoralized and wavering ranks of the Persians, and penetrating almost to the tent of Xerxes himself.

When the dawn of the morning disclosed to the Persians the smallness of the Spartan and Thespian bands, Leónidas led his men into the defile, whither the Persians followed him, and for a time the conflict raged with desperate obstinacy on both sides. The Spartans and Thespians fought with the courage of despair, and multitudes of the Persians fell beneath their swords. While the battle was raging the fiercest, a Persian dart pierced the heart of the brave Leonidas, and he expired; but this only aroused his gallant followers to greater fury, and the Persians began to waver, when the twenty thousand Immortals under Hydarnes were observed approaching from the other end of the pass.

The Spartans and Thespians then took their stand behind a wall on a rising ground at the narrowest point of the defile, resolved to sell their lives as dearly as possible. The Thebans cowardly begged for quarter, saying that they had been forced into the conflict against their wishes, and their lives were spared; whereupon they deserted to the Persians, by whom many of them were slain, however, before their movement was understood. The Persians now closed in upon the devoted Spartans and Thespians on all sides, some of them beating down the wall behind which the heroic defenders had stationed themselves, while others assailed them with showers of arrows. The Spartans and their allies held out heroically to the last. When some said that the Persian darts were so numerous that they obstructed the light of the sun, Dioneces, a Spartan, replied: "How favorable a circumstance! the Greeks now fight in the shade!" Finally, after performing prodigious feats of valor, the whole Spartan and Thespian band was overpowered and slain, excepting one who made his escape to Sparta to announce the fate of his heroic comrades, and who was received with contempt because he had not the courage to die at his post with those gallant companions. The dead of the Spartans and Thespians were literally covered with the arrows which their numerous Persian assailants had showered upon them.

Such was the famous battle of Thermopylæ, in which perished Leónidas and his brave band, winning for themselves an immortal fame—a fame which has grown brighter with all the succeeding ages. Two monuments were afterwards erected near the spot where they fell. The inscription on one of these recorded the heroism with which a handful of Spartans and Thespians had resisted unto death three millions of Persians. The other monument was dedicated to the memory of Leónidas and his Spartan band of three hundred, and was inscribed with these words: "Go, stranger, and tell to the Spartans that we died here in obedience to their divine laws."

While the band of Leónidas was displaying such signal proofs of its valor in defending unto death the pass of Thermopylæ, the Grecian fleet was contending with the Persians at sea with better fortune, while the elements were also on the side of Hellas. The gigantic fleet of Xerxes had anchored in the bay of Casthanæa, on the coast of Thessaly, where it was attacked by a terrific storm lasting three days, thus losing about four hundred war-vessels and a vast number of transports and store-ships, which were totally wrecked. After the subsidence of the storm, the Persians, eager to abandon a place where they found so little shelter, sailed into the strait dividing the island of Eubœa from the mainland of Greece, and anchored in the road of Aphetæ, about ten miles from the promontory of Artemisium, where the Greek fleet was stationed.

The Persian fleet was still very large, notwithstanding the great loss caused by the tempest, and the Greeks were much alarmed in consequence of its arrival in the vicinity of their own united fleet. The Greeks therefore held a council of war, which decided by a large majority that the Grecian fleet should retreat southward. The Eubœans sought to prevent the adoption of this course, as it exposed them to the vengeance of the Persians; and with this view they endeavored to induce Eurybíades, the Spartan admiral, who commanded the combined Grecian fleet, to defer its departure, at least to allow them sufficient time to remove their families and their valuable property to a place of safety. As Eurybíades remained inexorable in his decision, the Eubœans applied to Themístocles, who commanded the Athenian division of the confederated fleet, and who, in the council of war, had opposed the proposition to retreat. Themístocles reminded them that gold was sometimes more persuasive than words, and consented to prevent the contemplated retreat of the combined fleet, if he were furnished with thirty talents (about thirty thousand dollars). When the Eubœans had paid the stipulated sum, Themístocles induced Eurybíades, by means of a bribe of five talents, to countermand the orders for the retreat of the united fleet. All the officers obeyed the commands of the Spartan admiral and commander-in-chief, except Adimantus, the Corinthian admiral, who persisted in his purpose to sail away, until Themístocles bought his acquiescence in the postponement by a gift of five talents. He retained the remaining twenty-two talents for himself.

Thus the conduct of Themístocles on this occasion, by its lack of high moral principle, and the mercenary spirit manifested by the Spartan and Corinthian admirals, who could only be induced by a bribe to face the Persians, presented a striking contrast to the patriotic zeal and heroic example of the gallant defenders of Thermopylæ.

The Persian admiral now prepared for battle, and dispatched two hundred galleys with orders to sail around the eastern side of the island of Eubœa and station themselves at the southern extremity of the strait of Euripus. When the Greeks were informed of this movement by a deserter from the Persian fleet, they held another council of war, which decided to attack the Persian fleet, now weakened both by the effects of the recent tempest and by the departure of the two hundred ships. The Greek ships therefore anchored near sunset and attacked the Persian fleet. Despite the vast numerical superiority of the Persians, the Greeks soon captured thirty of the enemy's ships and sunk a larger number of them. The conflict was ended by the approach of night and by a sudden furious storm.

The united Greek fleet soon regained its former position off Artemisium; but the Persians, who were unacquainted with the narrow and intricate seas of Greece, and who were confused by the darkness and the violence of the tempest, could not determine in what direction to steer, and many of their ships were wrecked before the fleet returned to its former station at Aphetæ. The storm caused still greater havoc among the two hundred galleys which had sailed for the southern end of the strait of Euripus. These galleys were caught by the tempest in the open sea, and being unable, in the midst of the dense darkness of the night, to see a solitary star by which to direct their course, they were tossed to and fro by the merciless winds and waves, until finally the whole squadron was driven upon the Eubœan coast, where it miserably perished.

The next day the Greek admirals were informed of this last event by the crews of three new Athenian ships, which had come to reinforce the united Grecian fleet. Elated by this favorable intelligence, the Greeks renewed their attack upon the Persian fleet on the evening of the same day, totally destroying a detachment of it, called the Cilician squadron. Mortified because they had been completely beaten by a foe so far inferior in numbers, the Persian commanders determined upon a vigorous effort to retrieve their reputation, and the next morning they gave orders for a general engagement. About noon they approached the combined Grecian fleet, and a desperate struggle followed, ending in another Greek victory; the Greeks, however, losing five galleys, and many of their vessels being damaged, especially those of the Athenian division. In consequence of this circumstance and the discouraging effect of the intelligence of the destruction of Leónidas and his Spartan band at Thermopylæ, the Greek admirals decided to retreat southward, so that they might be able to give all the aid in their power to the inhabitants of Attica and the Peloponnesian states, which would be exposed to immediate invasion by the Persians in consequence of the result of the battle of Thermopylæ. The confederated Greek fleet therefore sailed southward, and, proceeding to the Saronic Gulf, anchored in the strait between the island of Salamis and the coast of Attica.

The Persian army now marched through Phocis and Bœotia into Attica, while the Persian fleet likewise moved southward, in pursuit of the Greek fleet into the Saronic Gulf. The Persian army was scarcely opposed in its march, for the Peloponnesian troops had retired within the Isthmus of Corinth, as they despaired of being able to make any effective resistance in the open country The Athenians made no effort to defend their territory, as they had been deserted by their allies, and as the chief portion of their armed force was on board the united Grecian fleet. The sacred fane of the temple of Apollo at Delphi was preserved in this time of general panic. The Delphians were intensely alarmed upon receiving intelligence that the Persians had forced the pass of Thermopylæ, and consulted the oracle as to what was necessary to do for the protection of the temple and the security of the valuable treasures contained therein. The oracle replied that "the arms of Apollo were sufficient for the defense of his shrine." The Delphians then transported their wives and children across the Gulf of Corinth into Achaia, abandoned their city, and concealed themselves in the deep caverns and among the rocky summits of Mount Parnassus. Delphi could only be approached by a steep and difficult road, winding about among the narrow defiles and steep mountain crags. When the Persian detachment marched along this road, a thunder-storm came on, arousing their superstitious fears and encouraging the Delphians, who fancied that Apollo was fulfilling his promise to interfere for the protection of his temple. Two enormous fragments of rock rolled down from the heights of Parnassus upon the heads of the affrighted Persians, either by the agency of the lightning or by the secret efforts of the Delphians, caused the precipitate flight of the invaders. The Delphians then emerged from their hiding-places and pursued the panic-stricken Persians with terrific slaughter.

When the Persian detachment returned to the main army, they apologized for their disgraceful discomfiture by telling many wonderful tales concerning the unearthly voices they had heard and the frightful forms they had beheld. The Delphic priests having an interest in crediting and circulating reports of the same nature, the belief soon became universal that the calamity which had befallen the sacrilegious invaders of the sacred shrine had been effected by supernatural agency.

Themistocles saw that there was no further hope of saving Attica when the combined Grecian fleet had arrived at Salamis. He therefore persuaded the Athenians to seek refuge in their ships, in accordance with his previous interpretation of the promise given them by the Delphic oracle that they should find safety behind their "wooden walls." They consequently conveyed their women, children and old men to the islands of Salamis and Ægina, and the sea-port town of Trœzene, in Argolis, thus abandoning their country and city to the vengeance of the Persians. But before they departed they passed a decree, at the instigation of Themistocles, recalling all their exiles for the common defense, thus obtaining the valuable aid of Aristides in this great emergency. Aristides was then residing in the island of Ægina, and as he had heard of the decree he proceeded to the general rendezvous at Salamis, generously and patriotically forgetting the injustice done him by his countrymen, and desirous only for their welfare.

The Medo-Persian army soon overran and ravaged Attica with fire and sword, taking Athens and reducing it to ashes, and massacreing the few inhabitants who had remained in it, and who had vainly endeavored to defend the citadel. The Persian fleet at the same time stationed itself at Phalerum, an Athenian sea-port, near the bay in which the Grecian navy had taken its position. The allied Greeks now deliberated upon the question of risking another conflict with the Persian fleet or retiring farther up the Saronic Gulf to assist in defending the Isthmus of Corinth, across which the Peloponnesians had raised a line of fortifications to stop the advance of the invaders. Themistocles vainly urged the council of war to remain where they then were and give battle to the Persians. Most of the Grecian admirals desired to depart, and the council of war finally decided to move the fleet at once. The council was then broken up. Themistocles, who saw that if the resolution just adopted was carried into effect, the Hellenic cause would be utterly ruined, prevailed upon Eurybiades to convene another council of war, at which he used all the persuasive powers of his eloquence to induce the Grecian admirals to revoke their weak decision. In the progress of the discussion, he said something to give offense to Eurybiades, who raised his stick as if to strike the Athenian; but Themistocles, who was only bent on persuading the admirals to remain where they then were, paid no more attention to the threatening attitude of the Spartan admiral than to say to him calmly: "Strike, but hear me." Eurybiades, ashamed of his hasty violence, requested Themistocles to proceed with his speech, giving him no further interruption. Themistocles then endeavored to convince the council of the disadvantages to which they would expose themselves and the cause of Greece by abandoning their present station, as they would thus give up a narrow channel, in which the entire Persian fleet would be unable to attack them at once, for the open seas, where they might be quickly overpowered by the superior numbers of the enemy's fleet. He likewise alluded to the cruelty of abandoning the Athenian women and children collected in the islands of Salamis and Ægina to the mercy of the invaders.

As soon as Themistocles had finished his speech, Adimantus, the Corinthian admiral, insultingly asked whether they were to be guided by the wishes of men who had no longer a city to defend, alluding to the destruction of Athens by the Persians. Themistocles replied indignantly that "the Athenians had, indeed, sacrificed their private possessions for the sake of preserving their own independence and the common liberties of Greece, but that they had still a city in their two hundred ships." He further said that "if deserted by the confederates, they would embark their wives and children, and seek a new home on the coast of Italy, where ancient oracles had foretold that the Athenians should one day found a flourishing state." He also intimated that "if the allies provoked them to adopt this course, they would speedily have cause to regret that they had driven away the only fleet which was capapable of protecting their coasts."

These words of Themistocles so alarmed the council, who feared that the Athenians might withdraw from the Grecian alliance, that it was resolved to remain at Salamis, and there give battle to the Persian fleet. Nevertheless, several of the Peloponnesian admirals soon manifested a desire to depart, and Themistocles was informed that most of them intended to sail that night. To thwart their design, he secretly sent a messenger to Xerxes to tell him that the Grecian fleet was preparing to make its escape, and that if he desired to crush his foes at once he should guard both ends of the strait in which they were stationed with his ships. Supposing Themistocles to be secretly in the Persian interest, Xerxes acted on his advice; and when the Greeks found themselves inclosed, they made a virtue of necessity by preparing for battle.

In the morning of the day on which occurred the ever-memorable battle of Salamis—October 20, B. C. 480—the Greeks chanted sacred hymns and pæans, "while, with their voices, the spirit-stirring sounds of the shrill war-trumpet ever and anon mingled." While forming themselves in line of battle under the direction of their leaders, they encouraged each other by mutual exhortations to fight bravely in defense of their wives and children, their liberties, and the temples of their gods. Every heart gave a willing response to such patriotic appeals, and under the inspiration of their righteous cause they performed prodigies of valor.

The Persians were not actuated by such worthy sentiments, but still they had strong motives for bold and active exertion. They knew that they were to fight under the immediate eye of their sovereign, as Xerxes had drawn up his army along the opposite shore of Attica, and had seated himself upon a magnificent throne on the summit of a neighboring mountain, where he watched the onset of the combatants and the progress of the battle, while around him were his guards and many secretaries, whose duty it was to record the manner in which his seamen acquitted themselves in the conflict. Persians troops lined the shores of Attica for a considerable extent, and the entire Persian army was in motion by dawn, as the soldiers were impelled by curiosity to station themselves on the neighboring heights. They chose the most commodious eminences, and every hill and elevation commanding a view of the water was eagerly sought by those desirous of viewing the impending conflict.

A shocking affair occurred in the galley of Themistocles, during this moment of anxiety and hope. While he was offering sacrifices on deck, three beautiful captive youths, said to have been nephews of Xerxes, were brought to Themistocles. The soothsayer who attended on the sacrifice took Themistocles by the hand, and ordered that the three youths be sacrificed to Dionysus, that the Greeks might be assured of safety and victory by this means. Themistocles was astonished at this extraordinary and cruel order, as no human sacrifices had been permitted among the Athenians. But the people, calling upon the god, led the youthful captives to the altar and insisted that they be offered up as victims in accordance with the directions of the soothsayer.

When a favorable breeze sprang up, the signal was given for the attack; and the Grecian fleet, composed of three hundred and eighty ships, advanced to encounter the

Persian fleet, consisting of one thousand three hundred vessels of war. The skillful assault of the Athenians soon broke the Persian line; and the Greeks gained a complete victory, after a long and desperate conflict, marked by many examples of personal valor. The Persians lost so heavily that the sea itself was scarcely visible for the many dead bodies for some distance. Many of the Persian vessels were taken or destroyed, and the remainder, utterly panic-stricken, were dispersed in different directions. The Greeks lost forty ships, but very few lives, many of those whose vessels were sunk having saved themselves by swimming to the shore.

A chosen detachment of Persian infantry had been stationed on the small island of Psyttalea, between Salamis and the mainland, to aid the Persian fleet and destroy the Greeks who might seek a refuge there while the battle was in progress. But the vigilant Aristídes led a detachment of Athenian troops, who attacked and massacred the entire Persian detachment, within sight of Xerxes himself, who, seeing his fleet dispersed and destroyed, and his select soldiers cut to pieces by the triumphant Greeks, sprung from his throne in anguish, rent his garments in paroxysms of despair, and hastily ordered the withdrawal of his army from the coast. The scattered remnants of the Persian fleet fled, some seeking refuge in the Hellespont, and others in the ports of Asia Minor, while Xerxes and his land forces beat a hasty and precipitate retreat into Thessaly.

Such was the famous sea-fight of Salamis, in which the pride of Xerxes was thoroughly humbled. The Great King was in such fear of the Greeks that he believed himself in peril so long as he remained in Europe, though surrounded with millions of his soldiers. He therefore decided upon immediately returning to Asia, and leaving three hundred thousand of his troops under Mardonius to conduct the war in Greece. Xerxes was confirmed in his decision to return to Asia by a message sent him by Themístocles, telling him that the Grecian council of war had entertained a proposition to sail at once to the Hellespont and destroy the Persian king's bridge of boats, to prevent his return to Asia, but that Themístocles had dissuaded his allies from executing this design. It is believed that the wily Athenian leader gave this intimation to Xerxes for the twofold purpose of hastening the retreat of a still formidable foe, and of securing for himself the Persian king's protection, in case any vicissitude of fortune required it. And the time when such a refuge became necessary did come to the victor of Salamis.

The retreat of Xerxes from the battle of Salamis was one of the most disastrous recorded in history. No arrangements having been made to supply the vast host of Xerxes with provisions, in the midst of the confusion and panic incident to this hasty flight, famine soon wrought frightful havoc and distress. The Persian soldiers were reduced to such extremities that they ate the leaves and bark of the trees and the grass of the fields, as they returned to their distant home. To the horrors of famine were soon added those of pestilence, and the line of retreat through Thessaly, Macedon and Thrace was everywhere strewn with heaps of dead bodies.

Sixty thousand of the chosen troops, placed under the command of Mardonius, accompanied Xerxes to the Hellespont as a body-guard. With the exception of these, who, as guardians of the monarch's person, were partly supplied with provisions, while the common soldiers were left to suffer the pangs of starvation, nearly the entire multitude which followed the retreat of their sovereign from the plains of Thessaly miserably perished before Xerxes arrived at the shores of the Hellespont, after a march of forty-five days.

The magnificent bridge of boats by which Xerxes had previously crossed over the strait had been destroyed by a tempest, and the humiliated king was glad to obtain a Phœnician vessel to transport him over to the Asiatic side of the Hellespont. Thus ended in misfortune and humiliation the most gigantic military expedition ever undertaken by man, furnishing an illustration of the evils caused by senseless vanity and immoderate ambition.

After the retreat of the Persians, the Grecian navy went into port for the winter, excepting the Athenian squadron, which, under the command of Themístocles, sailed to the Cyclades. Under the pretense of chastising the inhabitants of these islands for aiding the Persians, Themístocles extorted from them a heavy contribution, which he was accused of afterwards appropriating to his own private use, instead of putting it into the public treasury. About the same time he gave another example of his lack of principle. He told his countrymen that he had something to propose, which would inure to their benefit, but that he could not with propriety disclose it to the popular assembly. The Athenians directed him to communicate his purpose to Aristídes, and promised that if that upright statesman approved the design they would sanction its execution.

Themístocles therefore informed Aristídes that his project was to burn the united Grecian fleet while wintering in the harbor of Pagasæ, so that Athens would be the only maritime power in Greece. Aristídes reported to the people that "nothing could be more advantageous, and at the same time more unjust, than the project of Themístocles."

Upon hearing this, the Athenians rejected the proposition of Themístocles, without even inquiring as to its nature, thus attesting their boundless confidence in the wisdom and honesty of Aristídes. The Athenians were now enabled to return to their ruined city, which most of them did. But fearful that Mardonius might again force them to abandon it, many permitted their wives and children to still remain on the islands of Salamis and Ægina. The confederated Greeks passed the winter in offering sacrifices to the gods in gratitude for their deliverance from the Persian invasion, in dividing the spoils of victory, and in bestowing prizes on those who had principally distinguished themselves in the war. While these prizes were being awarded, an incident transpired, which testified to the military talents of Themístocles and to the vanity of his military colleagues.

When the commanders of the allied Grecian fleet were asked to furnish a list of the names of such as had displayed the greatest heroism and skill in the battle of Salamis, each admiral placed his own name at the head of the list, while most agreed in placing the name of Themístocles second. But the general voice of the Grecian states declared Themístocles the hero of Salamis; and the Spartans especially vied with his Athenian countrymen in the honors conferred upon him. He was invited to visit Sparta, and, upon his arrival in that city, was pompously crowned with an olive wreath, as the ablest and wisest of the Greeks. The Spartans at the same time conferred a similar mark of distinction upon their own admiral, Eurybíades, as the bravest. They likewise presented Themístocles with a splendid chariot, and sent three hundred of their noblest youths as a guard of honor to attend him to the frontier when he was on his journey home. On his next appearance in public, at the celebration of the Olympic Games, his presence excited such an interest that no attention was paid to the contestants in the arena, all eyes and minds being fixed upon the hero of Salamis who had saved Greece from the Persians.

In the meantime the Persian general, Mardonius, was not idle. He regarded the Athenians as the most formidable enemies with whom he had to contend, and therefore he sought to induce them to secede from the Grecian alliance by many liberal and tempting offers. He caused Alexander, King of Macedon, to visit Athens, and to promise in the name of the Persian king that the city should be rebuilt, the citizens enriched, and the dominion of all Greece bestowed upon them, if they would retire from the war. The Spartans had received intimation of this proceeding, and sent ambassadors to Athens at the same time to remind the Athenians of their duties to Greece, and to offer them any pecuniary aid they wished or needed, and also an asylum in Sparta for their women and children.

Under the advice of Aristídes, the Athenians answered both the Persians and the Spartans in the noblest and most patriotic style. The Athenians replied thus: "We are not ignorant of the power of the Mede, but for the sake of freedom we will resist that power as we can. Bear back to Mardonius this our answer: So long as yonder sun continues his course, so long we forswear all friendship with Xerxes; so long, confiding in the aid of our gods and heroes, whose shrines and altars he has burned, we will struggle against him for revenge. As for you, Spartans, knowing our spirit, you should be ashamed to fear our alliance with the barbarian. Send your forces into the field without delay. The enemy will be upon us when he knows our answer. Let us meet him in Bœotia before he proceed to Attica." Mardonius immediately marched upon Athens when his overtures were rejected. The confederated Greeks again shamefully left the Athenians in the lurch, not rendering them assistance in this perilous crisis. Even the Spartans, who had so recently exhorted the Athenians to stand by the general cause of all Greece, did not furnish a man to assist in the defense of Attica against the new Persian invasion; but, acting on the promptings of their selfish and coldhearted policy, seemed satisfied with erecting new fortifications at the Isthmus of Corinth, to protect the Peloponnesus.

The Athenians were consequently forced to abandon their city a second time. They again transported to Salamis such of their families as had returned to Athens, and embarking on board their ships, prepared to defend themselves to the last extremity. The patriotism which they exhibited so enthusiastically in this emergency forms a favorable contrast to the narrow and selfish behavior of the Spartans.

Upon invading Attica, Mardonius sent another messenger to the Athenians, renewing his previous liberal offers, if they would secede from the Grecian confederacy; but even the perilous situation to which they were reduced by the base and ungrateful conduct of their allies in deserting them in this dire extremity, did not cause the countrymen of Aristídes and Themistocles to abandon the common cause of Grecian independence. An example of their opposition to any concession to Persia in this perilous conjuncture is furnished by their treatment of Lycidas, a member of the Council of Five Hundred, whom they stoned to death for simply proposing that the message of Mardonius should be taken into consideration, and whose wife and children were put to death by a band of enraged women.

The troops of Mardonius now devastated Attica, and destroyed Athens a second time, after which they retired again into Bœotia, lest they should be surprised by the Greeks in the mountainous part of Attica, where their large army would be at a disadvantage, and where their cavalry would be hampered in their movements.

In the meantime, a deputation from Athens, headed by Aristídes, had gone to Sparta, to remonstrate with the Lacedæmonians and urge them to send immediate aid to the distressed Athenians. When the deputation arrived the Spartans were celebrating one of their public festivals, apparently little concerned about the fate of the Athenians; and Aristídes and his colleagues had to wait ten days before they could receive any response to their representations. Finally, when the Athenian envoys had threatened to come to terms with Mardonius, a force of five thousand Spartans and thirty-five thousand light-armed Helots, to which the Ephori added a guard of five thousand heavy-armed Laconians, was sent to the relief of Athens. While crossing the Isthmus of Corinth, this Lacedæmonian army was reinforced by the troops of the other Peloponnesian states, and when they arrived in Attica they were joined by eight thousand Athenians, and bodies of troops from Platæa, Thespiæa, Salamis, Ægina and Eubœa. As Sparta had long ranked as the leading military state of Greece, Pausánias, the Lacedæmonian general, assumed the chief command of the confederated Grecian army, which numbered almost forty thousand heavy-armed and about seventy thousand light-armed troops. The Athenian contingent was commanded by Aristídes.

The Greeks at once assumed the offensive and moved against Mardonius, who was found encamped on the banks of the Asopus, in Bœotia. Some days were passed in marching and countermarching, and in occasional skirmishing with the foe, after which the Greeks took up a position near the foot of Mount Cithæron, in the territory of Platæa, with the river Asopus in front of them, separating them from the Persians. A severe skirmish occurred, known as the battle of Erythræ, and was opened by an attack upon the Greeks by the Persian cavalry commanded by Masístius, the most illustrious Persian general next to Mardonius. His magnificent person, clad in scale-armor of gold and burnished brass, was conspicuous upon the battle-field; and his horsemen, then the most celebrated in the world for their skill and valor, severely harassed the Megarians, who were posted in the open plain. A chosen body of Athenians under Olympiodórus went to their aid, and Masístius spurred his Nisæan steed across the field to meet his antagonist. In the sharp combat that ensued, Masístius was unhorsed, and as he lay on the ground was assailed by a host of enemies; but his heavy armor, which prevented him from rising, protected him from their weapons, until, finally, an opening in his visor enabled a lance to penetrate his brain, and his death decided the conflict in favor of the Greeks.

After this victory the Greek army moved still closer to the town of Platæa, where they had a more abundant supply of water and a more convenient ground. This Greek army was the most formidable force which the Persians had thus far encountered in Greece, numbering one hundred and ten thousand men, including allies and attendants. The two armies lay facing each other for ten days without any important action, but the Persians intercepted convoys of provisions and choked up the spring which supplied the Greeks with water, while they prevented them from approaching the river by means of their arrows and javelins. Thereupon Pausánias determined to retire to a level and well-watered meadow still nearer to Platæa, followed thither by Mardonius.

A general engagement, known as the battle of Platæa, occurred on September 22, B. C. 479. The Spartans being attacked while on the march, immediately sent to the Athenians for assistance; and the Athenians, while marching to the aid of their Lacedæmonian allies, were intercepted by the Ionian allies of the Persians, and were thus cut off from the intended rescue. Pausánias, being thus forced to engage the enemy with a small part of his army, ordered a solemn sacrifice, his troops awaiting the result without flinching, in the midst of a storm of Persian arrows. The omens were unfavorable, and the sacrifices were renewed repeatedly. Finally Pausánias cast his tearful eyes toward the temple of Hêrê, beseeching the goddess that if the Greeks were destined to defeat they might at any rate die like men; whereupon the sacrifices assumed a more favorable aspect, and the order for battle was given.

The Spartan phalanx moved slowly and steadily in one dense mass against the Persians. The Persians behaved with remarkable resolution, seizing the lances of the Lacedæmonions or wresting from them their shields, while engaging in a desperate hand-to-hand contest with them. Mardonius himself, at the head of his chosen guards, fought in the front ranks, and encouraged his men by word and example. But he received a mortal wound, whereupon his followers fled in dismay to their camp, where they made another stand against the Spartans, who possessed no skill in attacking fortified places; but the Athenians, who had in the meantime beaten the Ionian allies of the Persians, now came to the aid of their Spartan allies, and completed the defeat of the Persians, scaling the ramparts and effecting a breach, through which the remainder of the Greeks entered their camp. The Persians, utterly routed, fled in all directions; but were so hotly pursued by the triumphant Greeks that their entire army was well-nigh destroyed, excepting the forty thousand Parthians under Artabazus, who had abandoned the field as soon as it was known that Mardonius was dead, and who hastily retreated by forced marches in the direction of the Hellespont. The Persians thus lost almost two hundred thousand men; and the vast treasures of the camp of Mardonius, consisting of gold and silver, besides horses, camels and rich raiment, became the spoil of the victorious Greeks.

Such was the famous battle of Platæa, which freed Greece from her Persian invaders. Mounds were raised over the heroic and illustrious dead. The soil of Platæa became a second "Holy Land," whither embassies from the Grecian states went every year to offer sacrifices to Zeus, the deliverer, and games were celebrated every fifth year in honor of liberty. The Platæans themselves were thereafter exempt from military service, and became the guardians of the sacred ground, and it was decreed to be sacrilege to attack them.

On the very day of the battle of Platæa—September 22, B. C. 479—a sea-fight occurred at the promontory of Mycalé, in Asia Minor, between the Grecian and Persian fleets, ending in the utter destruction of the latter. There a Persian land force under Tigránes had been stationed by Xerxes to protect the coast, and thither the Persian fleet retired before the advance of the Greek fleet. The Persians drew their ships to land, protecting them by intrenchments and formidable earth-works. When the Greeks discovered the sea-coast deserted, they approached so close that the voice of a herald could be heard. This herald exhorted the Ionians in the Persian army to remember that they also had a share in the liberties of Greece. The Persians, who did not understand the language of the herald, began to distrust their Ionian allies. They deprived the Samians of their arms, and placed the Milésians at a distance from the front to guard the path leading to the heights of Mycalé. After the Greeks had landed they drove the Persians from the shore to their intrenchments, and the Athenians stormed the barricades. The native Persians fought desperately, even after Tigránes was slain, and finally fell within their camp. All the Greek islands which had aided the Persians were now permitted to enter the Hellenic League, and gave solemn pledges never again to desert it.

Thus while the battle of Platæa delivered European Greece from the Persian invaders, the simultaneous land and naval battle at Mycalé liberated the Ionian cities of Asia Minor from the Persian yoke. Thus ended in disgrace and humiliation the Medo-Persian attempt to conquer the Hellenic race and subvert the liberties of Europe. The preservation of Grecian independence involved the preservation of European civilization.

SECTION XI.—SUPREMACY OF ATHENS.

LTHOUGH the great battles of Salamis, Platæa and Mycalé had freed Greece from all danger of foreign conquest, the struggle with Persia continued thirty years longer in the Medo-Persian dominions; and during this period the Greeks from being the assailed became themselves the assailants, and the Persians who had commenced the struggle on the offensive were compelled to act on the defensive; so that instead of trying to conquer the Greeks, they were now obliged to protect their dominions against Hellenic conquest.

The Persian power in the Mediterranean was so completely destroyed by the battles of Salamis and Mycalé that no Persian fleet ventured to oppose the naval power of the Greeks for twelve years. The Greeks were thus enabled to revenge themselves upon the Persians for the injuries inflicted upon them, and they did not allow their discomfited foes to rest.

The Greeks prepared a fleet of fifty vessels to deliver every Grecian city in Europe and Asia which still felt the Persian power. The Athenians furnished most of the ships, but the Spartan leader, Pausánias, commanded the fleet. Pausánias first wrested the island of Cyprus from the Persians, after which he sailed to Byzantium (now Constantinople) and liberated that city also from the Persian yoke, and established his residence there for seven years.

The Athenians determined upon recovering the colony of Sestos, which Miltíades had founded in the Chersonésus. The entire remaining force of the Persians made a final stand at Sestos, and withstood a siege so obstinate that they even consumed the leather of their harness and bedding when pressed for want of food. They ultimately succumbed to the besieging Greeks, who were gladly welcomed by the inhabitants. The Athenians returned home in triumph, laden with treasures and secured in a well-earned peace. Among the relics long seen in the Athenian temples were the broken fragments and cables of the Hellespontine bridge of Xerxes.

While Athens was thus becoming the leading state of Greece, internal changes in her constitution made her government still more democratic. The power of the people steadily increased, while that of the old archons declined until it became a mere phantom. The rulers of Athens were the people themselves, who met in a body in their general assembly in the Agora, to pass or reject the legislative measures proposed by the Senate, or Council of State. In the meantime the power of the great aristocratic families was broken; and the masses, who had borne the brunt of the hardships and the dangers of the contest with Persia, were recognized as an important element in the state. Aristídes, the leader of the aristocratic party, proposed an amendment and secured its adoption, giving the people, without distinction of rank or property, a share in the government of the republic, with no other requisites than intelligence and good moral character. The archonship, hitherto restricted to the Eupatrids, was now thrown open to all classes (B. C. 478).

Themístocles was the great popular leader in Athens. He first devoted himself to rebuilding the walls of the city, and obtained the means for this enterprise by levying contributions upon the islands which had furnished assistance to the Persians. This proceeding aroused the jealousy of the Spartans, who sent ambassadors to remonstrate against the fortification of Athens, declaring that its walls would not be able to protect it, and would only make it an important stronghold for the Persians in case of another invasion of Greece. The Athenians, unwilling to quarrel with the Lacedæmonians, or to relinquish their project of fortifying their city, adopted a temporizing policy, reminding the Spartans that the exposed position of Athens on the sea-coast made it necessary to fortify the city with walls to protect it from the attacks of pirates, but denying that they meditated the construction of such fortifications as would endanger the liberties of Greece, and promising to send ambassadors to Sparta, thus showing that they were doing nothing to give any just cause for alarm.

Accordingly Themístocles, Aristídes and Abronycus were appointed to proceed to Sparta. As the object of the Athenians was to gain time to push forward the fortification of their city, Themístocles first went to Sparta, arranging that Aristídes and Abronycus should not follow him until the walls should have been built to a considerable height. After arriving at Sparta, Themístocles stated that he was not authorized to give the promised explanations until his colleagues had arrived; and by this pretext and also by means of bribes, he managed to gain so much time that the fortifications were well advanced before the Lacedæmonians had become impatient. The Athenians labored night and day, even the women and children aiding to the utmost of their ability in the important task.

Eventually the Spartans received accounts of the exertions of the Athenians in the work of fortification. Themístocles, being unable to calm the alarm which these rumors excited, advised the Spartans not to give any credence to mere rumors, but to send some persons of rank and character to Athens to ascertain by personal observation what was actually transpiring there. The Spartans acted on his advice, but as soon as the Spartan deputies reached Athens they were arrested under the secret orders of Themístocles himself, and were detained as hostages for the safety of Themístocles and his colleagues, who had by this time also arrived at Sparta. As the fortifications of Athens were now well advanced, Themístocles boldly avowed the artifice by which he had gained time. Seeing that they had been outwitted, the Lacedæmonians dissembled their resentment, and allowed Themístocles and his colleagues to return to Athens unmolested; but they never forgave him, and their subsequent animosity contributed considerably to accomplish his ruin.

Athens thus far had no port suitable for the necessary accommodation of her vast maritime commerce. To supply this want, Themístocles now employed his fellow citizens in the construction of the commodious harbor of Piræus, a place on the Saronic Gulf, about five miles from Athens. A town was built there at the same time, and was surrounded with stronger fortifications than those of Athens itself. The walls of the Piræus were formed of large square masses of marble, bound together with iron, and were of sufficient thickness to allow two carriages to be driven abreast along the top of them. These measures gave greatly-increased facilities to the foreign trade of Athens, and the city soon became much more opulent and magnificent than it had been before the Persian invasion.

Notwithstanding all the great and important civil and military services of Themístocles, a powerful party was gradually growing in Athens against him, fostered by Spartan intrigues, and caused in a large measure by the pomp he began to display and his ostentatious references in his public harangues to the greatness of his deserts. His popularity only served to increase his peril, instead of protecting him against the machinations of his enemies. It was asserted that he wielded a degree of influence inconsistent with the security of republican institutions, and that his recent behavior gave cause for the fear that he designed to overthrow the democratic constitution and establish himself in absolute power. The people of Athens, jealous upon this point ever since the days of the Pisistrátidæ, and acting upon the principle that *eternal vigilance is the price of liberty*, banished the hero of Salamis by *ostracism*. Arístides nobly refused to join in the general clamor against his rival, and deprecated the violent proceedings of his countrymen, although he himself had been previously banished mainly through the unkind intrigues of Themístocles.

The war with Persia was still in progress. After the capture of Byzantium, the Spartan general, Pausánias, the victor of Platæa, proved a traitor to his country. After the victory of Platæa he had engraven on the golden tripod dedicated to Apollo by all the Greeks, an inscription claiming for himself all the glory of the victory. The Spartan government was offended at this proceeding and caused this inscription to be replaced by another, omitting his name entirely, and naming only the confederated cities of Greece. But the pride and ambition of Pausánias, seeing that his own country was about to retire him to private life, now sought other fields for their display and activity. Although generalissimo of the Grecian forces, Pausánias was not a Spartan king, but only a regent for the son of Leónidas. His interviews with his Persian captives, some of whom were relatives of the Great King, opened other fields to the ambition and avarice of Pausánias. His own relative, Demarátus, had relinquished the austere life of a Spartan for the luxury of an Oriental palace, with the government of three Æolian cities. The superior abilities of Pausánias entitled him to still higher dignities and honors. He therefore formed the design of betraying his country. He released his noble prisoners with a message to Xerxes, in which he offered to subject Sparta and the whole of Greece to the Persian dominion, on condition of receiving the Great King's daughter in marriage, with wealth and power suitable to his rank. Xerxes received these overtures with delight, and at once sent commissioners to continue the negotiations. Elated by his apparently-brilliant prospects, Pausánias became insolent beyond endurance. He assumed the dress of a Persian satrap, and made a journey into Thrace in true Oriental pomp, with a guard of Persians and Egyptians. He insulted the Greek officers and subjected the common soldiers to the lash. He even insulted Aristídes when the latter desired to know the reason of his singular conduct. Rumors concerning the extraordinary proceedings of Pausánias reached the Spartan government, which recalled its treacherous chief. He was tried and convicted for various personal and minor offenses, but the evidence concerning the charge of treason was not considered sufficient to convict him. He returned to Byzantium without permission from the Spartan government, but the allied Greeks banished him for his treasonable behavior. He was again recalled to Sparta, and tried and imprisoned, but escaped and renewed his intrigues with the Persians and with the Helots, or Spartan slaves, whom he promised to liberate and vest with the rights of citizenship if they would assist him in overthrowing the government and making himself tyrant.

But Pausánias was eventually caught in his own trap. A man named Argilius, whom he had intrusted with a letter to Artabazus, remembered that none of those whom he had sent on the same errands had returned. He broke the seal and discovered considerable matter of a treasonable nature, and also directions for his own death when he should arrive at the court of the Persian satrap. This letter was laid before the Ephori, and the treason of Pausánias being thus fully established, preparations were made for his arrest. He received warning, and fled for refuge to the temple of Athênê at Chalciœcus, where he suffered the penalty for his crimes. The roof of the temple was removed, and his own mother brought the first stone to block up the entrance to the building. When it was known that he was almost exhausted by hunger and exposure, he was brought out to perish in the open air, so that his death might not pollute the shrine of the goddess.

By the treasonable conduct of Pausánias, Sparta lost her ancient superiority in the military affairs of Greece, and Athens then became the leading Grecian state. When Pausánias was first recalled, in B. C. 477, the allied Greeks unanimously placed Aristídes at their head. In order to disarm all jealousy, Aristídes named the sacred isle of Delos as the seat of the Hellenic League, which, from this circumstance, was called *The Confederacy of Delos*. On this sacred island the general congress of all the Grecian states met, and here was the common treasury, containing the contributions of all the states, for the defense of the Ægean coasts and the prosecution of active hostilities against the Persians. Aristídes acted with such wisdom and justice in the assessment of these taxes that not a word of accusation or complaint was whispered by any of the allies, although he had absolute control of all the treasures of Greece. It was agreed that the allied states should annually raise among them the sum of four hundred and sixty talents (about four hundred and sixty thousand dollars), to defray the expenses of the war.

After thus laying the foundation for the supremacy of Athens, Aristídes died, full of years and honors. Although he had occupied successively many important official positions, he discharged his duties so faithfully, and with so little attention to his private interests, that he always remained a poor man, and did not leave behind him money sufficient to defray his funeral expenses. He was buried at the expense of the state, and his countrymen testified their respect for his memory by erecting a monument to him at Phalerum, bestowing a marriage portion on each of his daughters, and granting a piece of land and a yearly pension to his son Lysímachus. The character of Arístides is the most spotless furnished by antiquity, and may be compared with that of our own Washington.

After Arístides had laid the foundation for the supremacy of Athens, he retired from the active command of the allied Greek fleet in B. C. 476, and had been succeeded by Cimon, the son of Miltíades. This young noble was a man of extraordinary talent, of frank and generous manners, and of valor in war, as proven in the struggle with the Persians. He obtained immense wealth by the recovery of his father's estates in the Chersonésus, and employed it in the most liberal manner, thus contributing much to the adornment of Athens and the comfort of its poorer citizens, and adding immensely to his popularity, while his bravery and sincerity commended him to the Spartans, so that the allies considered him the most acceptable of all the Athenian leaders.

Cimon's first expedition was against the Thracian town of Eion, then occupied by a Persian garrison, and which was reduced by famine, when its governor, who feared the displeasure of Xerxes more than death, placed his family and his treasures upon a funeral pile, and setting fire to it, perished in the flames. The town surrendered to Cimon, and the garrison was sold into slavery. Cimon then proceeded to Scyrus, whose inhabitants had incurred the wrath of the Hellenic League by their piracies. The pirates were driven away, and the town was occupied by an Attic colony. The fear of Persian invasion having subsided, the ties between the allied Greeks and their chief became weaker. Carystus refused to pay tribute; and Naxos, the most important of the Cyclades, openly revolted. But the vigilant Cimon subdued Carystus and sent a powerful fleet against Naxos, which was taken after a long and obstinate siege, whereupon the island was reduced from an ally to a subject.

Cimon's victorious fleet then proceeded along the southern coast of Asia Minor; and all the Greek cities, either encouraged by his presence or overawed by his power, improved the opportunity by throwing off the Persian yoke. Cimon's force was augmented by the accession of these allies when he reached the river Eurymedon, in Pamphylia, where he found a Persian fleet anchored near its entrance, while a powerful Persian army was drawn up on the banks of the stream. The Persians were more numerous than the Greeks, and still expected reinforcements from Cyprus; but Cimon, desiring to attack them without delay, sailed up the river and engaged their fleet. The Persians fought feebly; and while being driven to the narrow and shallow portion of the stream, they abandoned their ships and joined their army on the land. Cimon seized and manned two hundred of the deserted Persian triremes and destroyed many of the others (B. C. 466).

After being thus victorious on water, Cimon's men demanded to be led on shore, to oppose the Persian army, which was arranged in close array. As the men had been fatigued with the sea-fight, it was perilous to land in the face of the numerically-superior army of the Persians, who were yet fresh and unworn, but the ardor of the triumphant Greeks overcame all objections. The land battle was more stubborn than the sea-fight. Many noble Athenians were slain, but the Greeks were ultimately triumphant, and obtained possession of the field and of a vast amount of spoils.

To crown his victory, Cimon advanced with the Grecian fleet to the island of Cyprus, where he captured or destroyed the Phœnician squadron of eighty vessels on their way to reinforce the Persian fleet in the Eurymedon, and the vast treasures which became the prize of the victors were used to increase the splendor of Athens. By these splendid victories, Cimon completely annihilated the naval power of Persia, and the Greek cities of Asia Minor were delivered from all danger of Persian supremacy. No Persian troops appeared within a day's journey on horseback of the Grecian seas, whose waters were cleared of all Persian ships. The spirit of Artaxerxes Longimanus was so thoroughly humbled that he dared no longer undertake any offensive operations against Greece. All reasonable grounds for continuing the war had now passed; but the Greeks were so elated by the great valuable spoils obtained that they were unwilling to relinquish the profitable contest, and thus continued the war seventeen years longer, not so much to humiliate Persia as to plunder her conquered provinces.

Cimon was the head of the aristocratic party in Athens, but he pursued the policy of Themistocles and executed that great statesman's designs to augment the naval power of Athens. As all danger of Persian invasion and conquest had now passed, many of the smaller Grecian states, which had a scant population, began to grow weary of the struggle, and furnished reluctantly their annual contingent of men to reinforce the allied Grecian fleet. It was therefore arranged that those states whose citizens were not willing to perform personal service should send simply their proportion of ships, and pay into the common treasury a yearly subsidy for the maintenance of the sailors with whom the Athenians undertook to man the fleet. This arrangement resulted in establishing the complete supremacy of Athens. The annual subsidies gradually assumed the character of a regular tribute, and were forcibly levied as such; while the recusant states, deprived of their fleets, which had come into the possession of the Athenians, were not able to make any effectual resistance to the oppressive exactions of the dominant republic.

The Athenians were elevated to an unexampled degree of power and opulence, and were thus enabled to adorn their great city, to live in dignified ease and idleness, and to enjoy a continual succession of the most costly public amusements, at the expense of the vanquished Persians, and also of the harshly-treated states of the dependent Confederacy of Delos. Cimon caused the fortifications of the Acropolis, or citadel of Athens, to be completed, and the way leading from the city to the harbor of the Piræus, a distance of five miles, to be protected by two long walls as strong and thick as those with which Themistocles had surrounded the town of Piræus itself; so that the whole circuit of the fortifications of Athens, including those of its port and of the line of communication between them, when completed, would measure almost eighteen miles.

As Aristides was now dead and Themistocles in exile, Cimon was the greatest and richest man of Athens. His immense wealth was liberally employed in the adornment of Athens and the pleasure of her citizens, and added constantly to his power. He did not apply to his own use the valuable share of the Persian spoil falling to him as commander-in-chief, but expended all of it for the public good, using it in the construction of magnificent porticos and the formation of shady groves, tasteful gardens, and other places of public accommodation and resort. He planted the market-place with Oriental plane-trees. He laid out walks, and adorned the Academia, afterward so celebrated by the lectures of Plato, with shady groves and fountains. He erected beautiful marble colonnades, where the Athenians delighted to congregate for social intercourse. He caused the dramatic entertainments to be celebrated with greater elegance and brilliancy. He even went so far in his liberality as to throw down the fences of his gardens and orchards, and invite all to enjoy them and partake of their produce, declaring that he regarded whatever he possessed as the property of all the citizens. He kept a free table at his own house for men of all ranks, and especially for the benefit of the poorer classes. He was accompanied in the streets by a train of servants laden with cloaks, which were given to such needy persons as were met. He also administered to the wants of the more sensitive by charities which were offered in a more delicate and secret manner. Cimon was prompted to these liberal acts, partly by the intrinsic generosity of his nature, and in some measure by a politic consideration of the necessity of courting popularity in so purely a democratic republic as Athens. With this increase of wealth the tastes of the Athenians became luxurious, and Athens emerged from her poverty and her secondary rank to become the most powerful and the most splendid of Grecian cities.

The fall of Themístocles was brought about indirectly by that of Pausánias. When the great Athenian statesman had been banished from his country, he went to reside at Argos, where he was visited by Pausánias, the Spartan leader, who unsuccessfully sought to induce Themístocles to join in his treasonable designs against the liberties of Greece. But after the death of Pausánias, some papers were discovered showing that the Athenian exile had been at least aware of the Spartan traitor's designs; and the Spartans Ephors, glad of a pretext to injure the man they hated, sent messengers to Athens to demand that Themístocles be brought to trial before the Amphictyonic Council for treason against Greece. The party led by Cimon, the son of Miltíades, was now in the ascendant in Athens, and the Athenian people, now friendly to Sparta, readily consented to this; and Themístocles was accordingly summoned to appear. But, instead of obeying the summons, he fled to the island of Corcyra, whence he crossed over into Epirus. As he found himself insecure in the latter country, he proceeded into Molossia, although he was aware that Admetus, the Molossian king, was his personal enemy. The exile, entering the royal residence when Admetus was absent, informed the queen of the dangers which surrounded him; and, in accordance with her advice, he took one of her children in his arms, and knelt before the household gods, awaiting the king's return. Admetus was so affected to pity at this sight that he generously forgave his unfortunate enemy and gave the exiled statesman his protection.

But Themístocles was not yet allowed to enjoy rest. Messengers from Athens and Sparta were sent to Admetus to demand the surrender of the fugitive, but Admetus honorably refused compliance with this demand. In order to release Admetus from any threatened hostility on the part of the allied Grecian states, Themístocles journeyed through Macedon to Pydna, a port on the Ægean sea, there embarking, under an assumed name, on board a merchant vessel, and arriving safely at Ephesus, in Asia Minor, after having narrowly escaped capture by the allied Grecian fleet at the island of Naxos, in the Ægean sea. He then wrote to Artaxerxes Longimanus, who had just succeeded his father, Xerxes, on the throne of Persia, claiming protection because of services formerly rendered to the late monarch. Artaxerxes Longimanus received his application with favor and treated Themístocles with the greatest generosity, inviting the exile to his court at Susa and making him a present of two hundred talents (about two hundred thousand dollars) upon his arrival there, telling him that, as that was the price which the Persian government had set upon his head, he was entitled to receive that sum because he placed himself into their power voluntarily.

The exiled statesman learned the Persian language so well during the first year of his residence in the Persian dominions that he was able to converse with the king without the assistance of an interpreter. His brilliant talents and his winning manners very soon made him a great favorite with Artaxerxes Longimanus, who at length assigned him an important command in Asia Minor and bestowed upon him the revenues of the cities of Myus, Lampsacus and Magnesia for his support. He passed his remaining years in Magnesia in great magnificence, enjoying all the luxuries of the East, but still feeling bitterly the persecution he had endured.

When Egypt revolted against the Persian king and was aided by Athens (B. C. 449), Artaxerxes Longimanus called upon Themístocles to make good his promises and commence operations against Greece. But Themístocles, having spent the best years of his life in building up the supremacy of Athens, could not now assist in destroying that supremacy for the benefit of the empire which he contributed more than any man then living to destroy. He only desired to escape from the ingratitude of his countrymen, not to injure them. Rather than prove a traitor to his country by assisting its enemy in conquering it, Themistocles made a solemn sacrifice to the gods, took leave of his friends, and committed suicide by swallowing poison.

The citizens of Magnesia erected a splendid monument to his memory, and bestowed peculiar privileges upon his descendants. It is said that his remains were conveyed to

PIRÆUS, THE HARBOR OF ATHENS.

2—42.-U. H.

Attica at his own request, and were there interred secretly, the laws prohibiting the burial of banished persons within the Athenian territories. The conduct of Themistocles during his public career fully bespeaks his character. His talents rank him as one of the most remarkable statesmen that ever lived, but his utter selfishness and his entire lack of integrity attest his low moral standard.

As soon as the fear of Persian conquest, which had been the only effectual bond of union among the many independent Grecian states, had been dispelled, symptoms of that unhappy disposition to civil dissensions which was the source of innumerable evils to the Hellenic race speedily commenced to manifest themselves. Old jealousies were revived and new causes of animosity were discovered or imagined. Sparta beheld the rapid rise of Athens in wealth, power and influence with envy; while the haughty and arrogant behavior of Athens toward the weaker states which she called allies, but which she really treated as vassals, was submitted to impatiently, and was repaid with secret enmity or with open but ineffectual hostility.

In this condition of Grecian affairs, the inhabitants of the island of Thasos, who regarded themselves as wronged by some measure of the Athenians relative to the gold mines of Thrace, renounced the Confederacy of Delos and sent messengers to Sparta to solicit the protection and assistance of that state. Cimon immediately led an Athenian fleet against Thasos, which speedily reduced the entire island, except the chief town, which, being well fortified and defended with obstinate valor, resisted heroically for three years, at the end of which it finally surrendered on honorable terms (B. C. 463), when its walls were leveled, its shipping transferred to the Athenians, and all its claims upon the Thracian gold mines were renounced. The Thasians were obliged to pay all their arrears of tribute to the Delian treasury, and also to engage to meet their dues punctually in the future.

In the meantime the Spartans had ardently espoused the cause of the Thasians, and were about to render them effective aid against the Athenians, when unexpected calamities absorbed the attention of the Lacedæmonians at home. In the year B. C. 464 Sparta was overwhelmed by a dreadful earthquake, whose repeated and violent shocks engulfed all the houses in the city but five, and destroyed the lives of twenty thousand of its inhabitants. Great rocks from Mount Taygétus rolled down into the streets. The shocks were long-continued, and the terror of the supposed vengeance of the gods was added to the anguish of poverty and bereavement. The anticipated vengeance soon manifested itself in human form; as the oppressed Helots, thinking that the catastrophe which had befallen Sparta furnished them with a good opportunity to strike an effective blow to recover their freedom, flocked together in bands and added another peril to the existence of the state.

It was a fearful crisis for Sparta; but her heroic king, Archidamus, was equal to the grave emergency. No sooner had the shocks of earthquake died away than he caused the trumpets to sound to arms during the first alarm caused by apprehension of the revolt. But for his prudent measures, the Spartan freeman would have paid with their lives for the oppression and cruelty which they had for many centuries inflicted upon their bondsmen. Every Lacedæmonian freeman who survived the ruin caused by the earthquake hastened to the king, and very soon a disciplined force was ready to resist the rebellious Helots who threatened to attack them. Spartan valor and discipline prevailed, and Sparta was safe for the time. The rebels fled and dispersed themselves over the country, calling upon all who were oppressed to join their standard. The Messenians rose in revolt *en masse*, seized the strong fortress of Ithomé, where their immortal hero, Aristómenes, had so long withstood the Spartan arms, fortified it afresh, and formally declared war against Sparta. A struggle of ten years ensued, which is known as the *Third Messenian War* (B. C. 464-455).

In her perilous dilemma, Sparta appealed

for aid to Athens, and two parties in the latter state entered into a bitter controversy as to the policy of assisting the Lacedæmonians. Cimon was always friendly to these people, whose brave and hardy char-

Spartans the assistance which they solicited. When others urged that it was well to allow Sparta to be humiliated and her power for mischief broken, Cimon exhorted his countrymen not to permit Greece to be crippled

ACROPOLIS AT ATHENS.

acter he had always held up as a model to his own countrymen, and he lost much of his popularity by naming his son Lacedæmonius. He therefore favored giving the

by the loss of one of her two great powers, thus depriving Athens of her companion. The generous advice of this great statesman prevailed, and Cimon himself led an Athenian army against the rebellious Helots and Messenians, who were driven from the open country and forced to shut themselves up in the citadel of Ithomé.

In B.C. 461 the Spartans again solicited the aid of the Athenians in the war with the rebellious Helots and Messenians, and Cimon led another Athenian army to their assistance. But the superior skill of the Athenians in conducting siege operations excited the envy of the Lacedæmonians, even when employed in their own defense; and the rivalry of the two powerful states again broke out into open feuds during the ten years' siege of Ithomé. The Spartans soon dismissed the Athenian auxiliaries, on the pretext that their help was no longer required. But as the Spartans retained the auxiliaries of the other Grecian states, including Ægina, the old rival of Athens, the Athenians felt the dismissal as an insult; and were irritated to such a degree that, as soon as their troops returned from before Ithomé, they passed a decree in their popular assembly for dissolving the alliance with Sparta, and entered into a league with Argos, the inveterate enemy of Sparta, and also with the Aleuads of Thessaly. The Hellenic treasury was removed from Delos to Athens, for the ostensible purpose of securing it against the needy and rapacious Spartans.

Thus were sown the seeds of rancorous enmity between the two leading states of Greece, which afterwards proved so disastrous to the interests of the Hellenic race. Cimon, who was the leader of the aristocratic party in Athens, had all the time been an enthusiastic admirer of the aristocratic institutions of Sparta, and therefore friendly to that state. The favor with which the Spartans now regarded him was his greatest crime. The Athenians had some reason to fear for the security of their democratic institutions, as the Spartans always maintained a party in Athens who were believed to be secretly conspiring against its republican constitution. However enthusiastically and sincerely Cimon supported aristocratic institutions, his countrymen, wiser and more honest, opposed him. When the Athenians therefore began to regard Sparta with enmity, his popularity rapidly declined, and the democratic opposition to him became so powerful that, when the Spartans dismissed the Athenian auxiliaries sent to their aid, the popular resentment ultimately culminated in the banishment of Cimon for ten years by *ostracism*.

Cimon's influence in Athens had for some time vastly declined. The democratic party had recovered from its temporary eclipse caused by the fall of Themístocles, as a new leader was rising to popularity and was destined to outshine all the rest of the galaxy of brilliant statesmen of the Athenian republic. This leader was Pericles, the son of that Xanthippus who had impeached Miltíades. His mother was the niece of Clisthenes, "the second founder of the Athenian constitution." Pericles was said to have nothing to contend against him except his advantages, as he was born of illustrious ancestry, and as his talents were of the very highest order, and had been carefully cultivated by the best tutorage which Greece produced. Pericles did not make any haste to enter public life, but prepared himself by long and diligent study for the part he expected to enact. He sought the wisest teachers, and acquired a skill in the science of government, while he improved his oratorical talents by training in all the arts of expression.

Anaxágoras, of Clazomenæ, the first great Grecian philosopher who announced his belief in One Supreme Creative Mind creating and governing the universe, was the special friend and instructor of Pericles, and had taught him natural and moral science, imbuing his mind with opinions far more enlarged and liberal than those prevalent at the time, so that he was as remarkable for the superiority of his intellectual acquirements as for his freedom from the prejudices and superstitions of the vulgar. To the sublime doctrines of Anaxágoras men ascribed the high tone and purity of the young statesman's eloquence.

In person Pericles was handsome, and bore

THEATRE OF DIONYSIUS AT ATHENS (RESTORED).

so striking a resemblance to Pisistratus as to deter him for awhile from taking a prominent part in public affairs, because of the superstitious jealousy with which some Athenians regarded him on that account. He was grave and dignified in manner, and affable and courteous in his intercourse with his fellow-citizens; but he never mingled in their social parties, and seldom was seen to smile, as he preferred study to amusement, and the calls of duty to the allurements of ease and idle pleasure.

After serving for several years in the Athenian army, Pericles ventured to participate in the proceedings of the popular assembly, where he soon acquired a great degree of influence. His splendid and impressive eloquence was compared to thunder and lightning, and his orations were marked by an elaborate polish and a richness of illustration, far surpassing anything of the kind previously known in Athens. His readiness and tact were equal to his eloquence. He never lost his self-possession, or permitted his enemies to betray him into an unwise manifestation of chagrin or anger, but pursued with steadiness and calmness the course approved by his judgment, regardless of the violence and abuse of his opponents.

The banishment of Cimon afforded Pericles a free field for the display of his talents and ambition, and under his leadership Athens entered upon the most glorious period of her history. That republic had now reached the height of her greatness. She wielded a power greater than that of any of the mightiest contemporary monarchs, in her capacity as head of the Grecian confederacy and as mistress of the numerous communities on the mainland and islands of Greece and on the coasts of Asia Minor, which she honored with the designation of *allies*. Athens was now virtually the capital, not only of Attica, or even of Greece proper, but of the entire civilized world; and the liberal rewards which her immense wealth enabled her to bestow on men of genius and learning had attracted to her the most distinguished philosophers, orators, poets and artists from every part of the earth.

It was an object of the most towering ambition to be the leading man in such a flourishing republic, and Pericles now perceived the way to this exalted position opening up before him. To establish and maintain his ascendency in the assembly of the people, it was absolutely necessary that he should provide a constant succession of magnificent spectacles and festive entertainments for the citizens, and as he had no large fortune, like Cimon, he was not able to afford the vast expenditure thus required. The thought that the deficiencies of his private purse might be supplied from the public treasury occurred to him; but the obstacle in the way of such a consummation was the fact that the disbursements of the public money were regulated by the Court of Areopagus, most of the members of which belonged to the aristocratic party and would have antagonized any expenditure calculated to strengthen the influence of the democratic leaders. Pericles therefore determined to begin his plans by curtailing the power of that hitherto highly-respected and influential body, and induced his colleague, Ephialtes, to carry a decree through the popular assembly to deprive the Court of Areopagus of all control over the issues from the treasury, and to transfer much of this judicial power to the popular tribunals.

Pericles next bribed the Athenian people with their own money, by augmenting the compensation of those who served as jurors in the courts of justice, and giving pay to the citizens for their attendance in the political assemblies. Large sums were also expended in adorning the city with magnificent temples, theaters, gymnasia, porticos and other public buildings. The religious festivals became more numerous and more splendid, and the citizens were daily feasted and diverted at the public expense. To obtain the funds necessary to meet this new expenditure, Pericles vastly augmented the amount of tribute exacted from the allied dependencies of Athens, so that it now amounted to a yearly revenue equal in amount to one and a half million dollars. The lines of wall begun by Cimon for connecting Athens with its ports of Piræus and Phalerum were earnestly pushed to completion under Pericles. One wall was extended to Phalerum and another to Piræus; but the difficulty in defending so large an enclosed space led to the erection of a second wall to Piræus, at a distance of five hundred and fifty feet from the first. Between these two Long Walls was a continuous line of dwellings bordering the carriage-road, almost five miles long, extending from Athens to its main harbor.

As the war with Persia furnished the only pretext for the burdensome impost, that contest was still continued. Soon after Pericles came into power, an Athenian fleet of two hundred triremes was sent to Egypt, to aid the revolted inhabitants of that country, under their able leader, Inarus, in their efforts to cast off the hated Persian yoke (B. C. 460). After a struggle of five years (B. C. 460-455), this expedition ended in humiliation and disgrace, as we shall presently see.

In the same year in which the Athenian armament was sent to aid the Egyptian rebels under Inarus (B. C. 460), civil dissensions broke out in Greece itself. A dispute between Megara and Corinth involved Athens on the side of Megara and Sparta on the side of Corinth, and thus led to a war of three years (B. C. 466-457). The war was prosecuted with vigor. The Athenians were defeated at Halæ, but soon afterward achieved a naval victory at Cecryphalía, thus more than retrieving their reputation. Ægina now came to the aid of Sparta and Corinth, whereupon an Athenian army landed on the island and laid siege to the city. A Peloponnesian army was sent to the assistance of Ægina, while the Corinthians invaded Megaris. The enemies of Athens hoped for an easy triumph, as all the forces of that republic were employed in Egypt and Ægina. But an Athenian army of old men and boys, commanded by Myrónides, marched to the relief of Megara. After an indecisive battle, the Corinthians retired to their capital, while the Athenians remained in possession of the field and erected a trophy. In consequence of the censures of their government, the Corinthian army returned twelve days after the battle and raised a monument on the field claiming the victory. But the Athenians again attacked them and inflicted upon them a decisive and humiliating defeat.

The Spartans were unable to interfere with the great and rapid development of Athenian power, as their attention was wholly absorbed in the siege of Ithomé; but their ancestral home of Doris experienced a terrible calamity in a war with the Phocians, which for a time withdrew the attention of the Spartans from their own domestic troubles. An army composed of fifteen hundred heavy-armed Spartans and ten thousand auxiliaries, sent to the relief of the Dorians, drove the Phocians from the town they had captured, and compelled them to agree to a treaty in which they promised to behave themselves in the future. The Athenian fleet in the Gulf of Corinth and the garrison in Megaris now cut off the retreat of the Spartans to their own land. But the Spartan commander, Nicomédes, desired to remain for some time longer in Bœotia, as he was plotting with the aristocratic party in Athens for the recall of Cimon from exile to power, and as he likewise wished to augment the power of Thebes for the purpose of raising up a near and dangerous rival to Athens.

When the Athenians became cognizant of this conspiracy they were aroused to revenge. They at once sent an army of fourteen thousand men against Nicomédes at Tánagra. Both sides fought bravely and skillfully; but when the Thessalian cavalry deserted from the Athenians to the Spartans, the latter began to gain ground, and although the Athenians and their allies still held out for some hours, the Spartans won the victory when the conflict was ended at daylight. The only fruit which Nicomédes reaped from his triumph was a safe return to Sparta, but Thebes thereby increased her power over the cities of Bœotia (B. C. 457).

The Athenians were aroused to greater efforts in consequence of their defeat at Tánagra. The gallant Myrónides entered Bœotia two months after that battle, and gained a most decisive victory at Œnophyta (B. C. 456). The victors leveled the walls of Tánagra with the ground. Phocis, Locris, and all of Bœotia, except Thebes, were obliged to become the allies of Athens; and these alliances were made effective by the establishment of free governments in all the towns, which were thus obliged to side with Athens from motives of self-preservation. Thus Myrónides not only conquered the foes of Athens, but filled Central Greece with garrisons or allies.

Soon after the Long Walls connecting Athens with the Piræus had been completed the island of Ægina submitted to Athens, her navy being surrendered and her walls destroyed, and this life-long rival became a tributary and subject. An Athenian fleet of fifty vessels, under the command of Tólmides cruised around the Peloponnesus, burned Gythium, a port of Sparta; captured Chalcis, in Ætolia, which was a possession of Corinth, and defeated the Sicyonians on their own coast (B. C. 455). This fleet returned by way of the Corinthian Gulf, capturing Naupactus in Western Locris, and all the cities in Cephallenia.

In the same year (B. C. 455) the Spartans ended the Third Messenian War and the rebellion of the Helots by the capture of Ithomé, the Messenian stronghold, which surrendered after a siege of ten years. This heroic defense won the respect of even the Spartans themselves. The Helots were again reduced to slavery, but the Messenians were allowed to migrate to the sea-port town of Naupactus, in Western Locris, which was presented to them by its captor, the Athenian admiral, Tólmides.

In the same year (B. C. 455) the Athenian expedition which had been sent to Egypt five years before to assist its revolted inhabitants under Inarus experienced an inglorious end. When a Persian army relieved the beleaguered Persian garrison in the citadel of Memphis, the Athenian auxiliaries retired to Prosopítis, an island in the Nile, around which they anchored their vessels. The Persians followed them and drained the channel, thus stranding the Athenian ships on dry land. The Egyptian rebels submitted, but the Athenians burned their stranded vessels and withdrew to the town of Byblus, where they were besieged by the Persians for eighteen months, until the besiegers marched across the dry bed of the channel and took the town by storm. Most of the Athenians fell in the defense of the place, only a few escaping across the Libyan desert to Cyrêné and returning home. An Athenian fleet of fifty vessels sent to their relief arrived too late, and was defeated by the Persian and Phœnician fleet.

The Athenians, who had formerly been dazzled by the brilliant victories of Cimon over the Persians and enriched by the spoils of his splendid campaigns, were becoming dissatisfied with the little glory and profit accruing to them from the petty wars waged with Sparta and her allies; and this dissatisfaction eventually manifested itself in a general desire for the recall of the exiled statesman, whose peaceful views and whose friendly feelings toward the Lacedæmonians caused him to be regarded as the person most fitted to negotiate a peace with that people. Pericles perceived the drift of public sentiment, and wisely concluding to bend to it, rather than throw himself in the way of it, he likewise expressed himself as desiring the recall of his banished rival, and accordingly proposed a decree for that purpose in the assembly of the people and carried it through successfully, thus reversing Cimon's sentence of banishment (B. C. 453).

Upon his return Cimon used all his influence in favor of peace, and after three years of negotiations Athens concluded a truce of five years with Sparta, in B. C. 451. The Athenians then directed their attention to a more vigorous prosecution of hostilities with Persia. They cast longing eyes upon the isle of Cyprus, which was divided into nine petty states and over which the Persian monarch still claimed the sovereignty, notwithstanding its previous conquest by the Spartans under Pausánias. Cimon accordingly sent an Athenian fleet of two hundred ships to seize that island, and he succeeded in effecting a landing upon it and gaining possession of many of its towns, in the face of the three hundred Persian war-vessels guarding the coast; but while engaged in besieging Citium the illustrious statesman and commander died (B. C. 449). In accordance with his direction, his death was concealed from his followers until they had achieved another glorious victory in his name, both by land and sea. The sea-fight occurred off the Cyprian Salamis—a name of propitious omen to the Athenians. A treaty of peace was thereupon concluded with Persia, thus ending the long struggle which Darius Hystaspes began against Greece, and which had lasted exactly half a century (B. C. 499-449). By this treaty Athens relinquished Cyprus and withdrew from Egypt, while the King of Persia acknowledged the independence of the Greek cities of Asia Minor.

Cimon's remains were brought home to Athens, where a splendid monument was erected to his memory. The aristocratic party at once brought forward a new leader in Cimon's brother-in-law, Thucydides, who was a man of high birth and possessed of moderate abilities as a statesman, though by no means equal in that respect to Pericles, who a few years later caused his rival to be banished by *ostracism*.

Hostilities were renewed in Greece in consequence of a slight incident. The city of Delphi, though located within the Phocian territory, claimed independence in the management of the temple of Apollo and its treasures. The inhabitants of Delphi were of Dorian descent, and were thus closely united with the Spartans. The great oracle at Delphi always cast its influence on the side of the Doric as opposed to the Ionic race, where the interests of Greece were divided. The Athenians consequently did not oppose their allies, the Phocians, when the latter seized the Delphian territory and assumed the care of the temple. The Spartans immediately engaged in what they regarded as a holy war, by which they expelled the Phocians and reëstablished the Delphians in their former privileges. Delphi now declared itself a sovereign state; and bestowed on the Spartans the first privilege in consulting the oracle, as a reward for their intervention. The Delphians inscribed this decree upon a brazen wolf erected in their city. The Athenians could not willingly relinquish their share in a power which, in consequence of the popular superstition, could frequently confer victory in war and prosperity in peace. As soon therefore as the Spartans withdrew from Delphi, Pericles marched into the sacred city and restored the temple to the Phocians. The brazen wolf was made to tell another story and to give the precedence to the Athenians.

This was the signal for a general war; and the exiles from the various Bœotian cities, who had been driven out in consequence of the establishment of democratic governments, united in a general movement, seized Chæronéa, Orchómenus and other towns, and restored the oligarchic governments which had been subverted by the Athenians. These changes produced intense excitement in Athens. The Athenian people clamored for instant war, but Pericles opposed this, as the season was unfavorable, and as he regarded the honor of Athens as not immediately at stake. But the advice of Tólmides prevailed; and that leader marched into Bœotia with a thousand young Athenian volunteers, aided by an army of allies; and the Athenians soon subdued and garrisoned Chæronéa.

The Athenian army, while on its return home, elated with victory, fell into an ambush in the vicinity of Coronæa, where it suffered an inglorious defeat, Tólmides himself, with the flower of the Athenian soldiery being left dead upon the field (B. C. 445). Many of the Athenians were taken prisoners, and the Athenian government recovered these by concluding a treaty with the new oligarchies and withdrawing their troops from Bœotia. Locris and Phocis were deprived of their free institutions and became allies of Sparta.

The oppressive exactions of the Athenians had for some time been impatiently sub-

SUPREMACY OF ATHENS.

mitted to by their dependencies; one of which, the large island of Eubœa, took advantage of the quarrel of Athens with Bœotia to assert its own independence, and other subject islands manifested signs of disaffection (B. C. 447). At the same time the five years' truce with Sparta expired, and that state made vigorous preparations to avenge its humiliation at Delphi.

Pericles, whom the people honored with increased esteem and confidence because of his warnings against the war in Bœotia, acted with energy and promptness against the revolted Eubœans. He no sooner landed on the island with a force large enough to reduce the rebellious Eubœans to submission than he was informed that the Megarians had also risen in rebellion, and that the Spartans were preparing to invade Attica. With assistance from Sicyon, Epidaurus and Corinth, the revolted Megarians massacred the Athenian garrisons, except a few in the fortress of Niscæa; and all the Peloponnesian states had united to send an army into Attica. But the energetic and politic measures of Pericles dispelled the dangers which menaced Athens. He hastened back to the mainland and defeated the revolted Megarians, and on the approach of the Peloponnesian army under the young Spartan king Plistóanax, he bribed Cleandrídes, the influential adviser of Plistóanax, to retire from Attica with his forces. No sooner had Plistóanax and his counselor Cleandrídes returned to Sparta than they were accused of having been bribed to retreat from Attica, and, rather than face their accusers, both fled from the country, thus leaving no doubt as to the truth of the charges against them. Having thus reduced the Megarians and gotten rid of the Spartans and their Peloponnesian allies, Pericles landed in Eubœa a second time, reduced the revolted island to submission, and founded a colony at Histiæa.

When Pericles afterwards gave in his account of the expenses incurred in these campaigns, he charged the sum with which he bribed the counselor of the Spartan king Plistóanax, as "ten talents" (about ten thousand dollars) "laid out for a necessary purpose;" and the Athenian people had such confidence in his integrity that they passed the article without demanding any explanation. As all parties had now become weary of the war, Athens and Sparta concluded a truce of thirty years, Athens relinquishing her empire on land, such as the foothold in Trœzene, the right to levy troops in Achaia, the possession of Megaris, and the protectorate of free governments in Central Greece (B. C. 445). But the party which began the war suffered most heavily, while the power and popularity of Pericles had reached the highest pinnacle. It was at this time that Thucydides, Cimon's brother-in-law and his successor as leader of the aristocracy, was banished by ostracism, whereupon he retired to Sparta (B. C. 444). This exiled Athenian politician must not be confounded with the great Athenian historian Thucydides, who was living at the same time.

The great popularity and power of Pericles enabled him to now unite all parties and to wield the supreme control of Athenian affairs during the remainder of his life. By the vigor and wisdom of his policy, he had obtained an honorable peace and increased prosperity for his countrymen, who were so swayed by his irresistible eloquence that they were willing to sanction any measures proposed by him. The aristocracy, who had hitherto opposed him because he was the democratic leader, now respected him as one of their own class, and became desirous of conciliating his favor, as they were no longer able to obstruct his course. The merchants and alien settlers were enriched by his protection of trade. The shippers and sailors were benefited by his attention to maritime affairs. The artisans and artists were helped by the public works which he was constantly engaged in constructing. The ears of all classes were charmed by his eloquence, and their eyes were delighted by the magnificent edifices with which he adorned Athens, such as the Parthenon, or temple of the virgin goddess Athênê, embellished by Phidias with the most beautiful sculptures, especially with

RUINS OF THE PARTHENON AT ATHENS.

the colossal statue of the goddess Athênê made of ivory and gold, forty-seven feet high. The Erechtheum, or ancient sanctuary of Athênê Polias was rebuilt; the Propylæa, constructed of Pentelic marble, was erected; and the Acropolis now received the designation of "the city of the gods."

Conscious of the peculiar strength of his position, as he was sustained by the two great parties in Athens, Pericles began to assume greater reserve and dignity, and to manifest less promptness in gratifying the wishes of the poorer classes than formerly. His power was practically as great at that time as that of any absolute monarch, although on less stable a foundation.

Only three islands in the neighboring seas now remained independent, and the most important of these was Samos. The Milésians, who had some grounds for complaint against the Samians, appealed to the arbitration of Athens, and were supported by a party in Samos itself which was opposed to the oligarchy. The Athenians very willingly assumed the judgment of the matter, and as Samos declined their arbitration they determined to subdue the island. Pericles sailed with an Athenian fleet to Samos, overthrew the oligarchy and established a democratic government in the island, and brought away hostages from the most powerful families. But he had no sooner retired from the island than some of the deposed oligarchs returned by night, overpowered the Athenian garrison and restored the oligarchy. They gained possession of their hostages, who had been placed on the isle of Lemnos, and being joined by Byzantium, they declared open war against Athens.

As soon as intelligence of this event reached Athens, an Athenian fleet of sixty vessels was sent against Samos, Pericles being one of the ten commanders. After several naval battles, the Samians were driven within the walls of their capital, where they withstood a siege of nine months; and when they were finally obliged to succumb, they were compelled to destroy their fortifications, to surrender their fleet, to give hostages for their future good behavior, and to indemnify Athens for her expenses in the war. The Byzantines submitted to Athens at the same time. Athens was completely triumphant, but the terror which she inspired was mingled with jealousy. During the Samian revolt the rival states of Greece had seriously contemplated aiding the Samians, but the adoption of this course was prevented by the influence of Corinth, which, though unfriendly to Athens, feared that such a course might furnish a precedent in case of a revolt of her own colonies.

After ten years of general peace among the Grecian states, a dispute between Corinth and its dependency, the island of Corcyra (now Corfu), led to a war which again involved the whole of Greece. Corcyra was a colony of Corinth, but having by its maritime skill and enterprise attained a higher degree of opulence than the parent city, it refused to acknowledge Corinthian supremacy and engaged in a war with her regarding the government of Epidamnus, a city founded by the Corcyræans on the Illyrian coast. Epidamnus was attacked by some Illyrian tribes, led by exiled Epidamnian nobles; and the Corinthians refused to grant the Corcyræans the aid which they solicited, because the exiles belonged to the party in power in the parent city. The Epidamnians then applied for aid to Corinth, which undertook their defense with great energy. Corcyra, in great alarm, solicited assistance from Athens. The Athenian people in their general assembly were divided in opinion as to the advisability of aiding Corcyra, but the opinion of Pericles prevailed, that statesman having urged that war could not in any event be much longer postponed, and that it was more prudent to go to war in alliance with Corcyra, whose fleet was, next to that of Athens, the most powerful in Greece, than to be ultimately forced to fight at a disadvantage.

But as Corinth, as an ally of Sparta, was included in the thirty years' truce, the Athenians decided upon making only a defensive alliance with Corcyra, that is, to render aid only if the Corcyræan territories should be invaded, but not to take part in any aggressive proceeding. The Corinthians defeated the Corcyræans in a naval battle off the coast of Epirus, and prepared to effect a landing in Corcyra. Ten Athenian vessels were present, under the command of Lacedæmonius, son of Cimon, and were now, according to the letter of their agreement, free to engage in fight with the Corinthians. But the Corinthians suddenly withdrew after the signal for battle had been given, and steered away for the coast of Epirus. Twenty Athenian ships had appeared in the distance, which the Corcyræans fancied to be the vanguard of a large Athenian fleet. Though thus deceived, the Corinthians refrained from further hostilities and returned home with their prisoners.

The Corinthians were so exasperated at the interference of Athens that they sought revenge by joining Perdiccas, King of Macedon, in inciting revolts among the Athenian tributaries in the Chalcidic peninsulas. Thus the Corinthians incited the revolt of Potidæa, a town in Chalcidice, near the frontiers of Macedon, which had originally been a colony of Corinth, but was now a tributary of Athens. The Athenians at once sent a fleet and army for the reduction of Potidæa, and this armament defeated the Corinthian general at Olynthus and blockaded him in Potidæa, where he had sought refuge (B. C. 432).

A congress of the Peloponnesian states convened at Sparta, and complaints from many quarters were uttered against Athens. The Æginetans regretted the loss of their independence; the Megarians deplored the crippling of their commerce; and the Corinthians were alarmed because they were overshadowed by the boundless ambition of their powerful neighbor. At the same time the Corinthians contrasted the restless activity of Athens with the selfish inaction of Sparta, and threatened that, if the latter state still deferred performing her duty to the Peloponnesian League, they would look for a more efficient ally.

After the Peloponnesian envoys had departed, Sparta concluded to participate in the war against Athens. Before beginning actual hostilities, the Spartans sent messengers to Athens, demanding, among other things, that the Athenians should "expel the accursed" from their presence—alluding to Pericles, whose race they affected to regard as still tainted with sacrilege. But Pericles replied that the Spartans themselves had not atoned for their flagrant acts of sacrilege, such as starving Pausánias in the sanctuary of Athênê and dragging away and massacring the Helots who had sought refuge in the temple of Poseidon during the great Helot revolt. The Athenians rejected the other Spartan demands with more deliberation, those respecting the independence of Megara and Ægina and the general abandonment by Athens of her position as head of the Hellenic League, or Confederacy of Delos. The Athenians declared that they would abstain from beginning hostilities, and would make reparation for any infringement of the thirty years' truce which they might have committed, but that they were prepared to meet force with force.

While both parties thus hesitated to commence hostilities, the Thebans brought matters to a crisis by making a treacherous attack upon the city of Platæa, which they regarded with jealousy, because it had been in friendly alliance with Athens, instead of joining the Bœotian League. A small oligarchical party in Platæa favored the Thebans, and Nauclides, the head of this party, admitted three hundred of them into the town at dead of night. The Platæans, upon waking from their sleep, found their enemies encamped in their market-place, but they did not submit, though scattered and betrayed. They secretly communicated with each other by breaking through the walls of their houses; and after they had thus formed a plan, they attacked the Thebans before daybreak.

The Thebans were exhausted by marching all night in the rain, and were entangled in the narrow, crooked streets of Platæa. Even the Platæan women and children fought against the Theban invaders by hurling tiles from the roofs of the houses. The reinforcement which the Thebans expected was delayed, and before its arrival the three hundred were either slain or made prisoners. The Thebans outside the walls of Platæa now seized such property and persons as came within their grasp, as security for the release of the prisoners. The Platæans sent a herald to inform these Thebans outside the walls that the captives would be instantly put to death if the ravages did not cease, but that if the Thebans retired the prisoners would be released. The marauding Thebans thereupon withdrew, but the Plateans violated their promise by gathering all their movable property into the town and then massacring all their prisoners. Fleet-footed messengers had already conveyed the news to Athens. These messengers brought back orders to the Platæans to undertake nothing of importance without the advice of the Athenians. But it was too late to spare the lives of the prisoners or to vindicate the honor of their captors.

Pericles viewed the impending conflict without dismay, but his countrymen were not equally undaunted. They realized that they were about to be called upon to exchange the idle and luxurious life which they had for some years been leading for one of hardship and peril, and they commenced to murmur against their great statesman for involving them in so dangerous a struggle. They did not at first possess sufficient courage to impeach Pericles himself, but vented their displeasure against his friends and favorites. Phidias, the renowned sculptor, whom the illustrious statesman had appointed superintendent of public buildings, was convicted on a trivial charge and sentenced to imprisonment. Anaxágoras, the philosopher and the preceptor of Pericles, was accused of promulgating doctrines subversive of the national religion, and was consequently banished from Athens. The celebrated Aspásia, the second wife of Pericles, was also a victim of persecution.

Aspásia was a native of Milétus. She was a woman of remarkable beauty and brilliant talents, but her dissolute life made her a reproach, as she would have been otherwise an adornment to her sex. When this remarkable woman made her residence in Athens, she attracted the attention of Pericles, who was so captivated by her beauty, wit and eloquence, that he separated from his wife, with whom he had been living unhappily, and then married Aspásia.

The Athenians generally believed that Aspásia had instigated Pericles to quarrel with the Peloponnesian states, in order to gratify a private grudge; and her unpopularity on this account caused her to be now accused before the assembly of the people of impiety and of gross immorality. Pericles personally conducted her defense, and pleaded for her so earnestly and sincerely that he was moved to tears. The people acquitted her, either because they believed the charges to be unfounded, or because they were unable to resist the eloquence of Pericles.

The enemies of Pericles next directed their attacks against the great statesman himself. They accused him of embezzlement of the public money, but he utterly refuted the charge and proved that his private estate was his only source of income. The Athenian people were fully convinced of the honesty of his administration of public affairs, because of his frugal and unostentatious manner of living. While he was beautifying Athens with temples, porticos and other magnificent works of art, and providing many expensive entertainments for the people, his own domestic establishment was managed with such strict regard to economy that the members of his family complained of his parsimony, which contrasted in a remarkable degree with the splendor in which many wealthy Athenians then lived.

After being thus vindicated by the people and confirmed in his authority by this thorough refutation of the slanders of his enemies, Pericles adopted wise measures for the defense of Attica against the invasion threatened from the Peloponnesus.

SECTION XII.—THE PELOPONNESIAN WAR (B. C. 431-404).

THE famous *Peloponnesian War*, which involved all Greece, began in the year B. C. 431, and lasted twenty-seven years (B. C. 431-B. C. 404). It is generally divided into three distinct periods—the *Ten Years' War* (B. C. 431-B. C. 421); the *Sicilian Expedition* (B. C. 415-B. C. 413); and the *Decelian War* (B. C. 413-B. C. 404).

Sparta had for her allies all the Peloponnesian states, except Argos and Achaia, together with Megara, Bœotia, Phocis, Opuntian Locris, Ambracia, Leucadia and Anactoria. The allies of Athens were Thessaly and Acarnania and the cities of Platæa and Naupactus, on the mainland, and her tributaries on the coast of Thrace and Asia Minor and on the Cyclades, besides her island allies, Chios, Lesbos, Corcyra, Zacynthus, and afterwards Cephallenia.

It was a struggle for supremacy between the Ionic races, as represented by Athens, and the Doric races, as represented by Sparta and her Peloponnesian allies. It was also a struggle between the principle of democracy, as championed by Athens, and the principle of oligarchy or aristocracy, as maintained by Sparta.

The great struggle was commenced by an invasion of Attica by sixty thousand Peloponnesian troops under the Spartan king Archidamus about the middle of June B. C. 431. As Pericles was unwilling to risk a battle with the Spartans, who were regarded as invincible by land as the Athenians were by sea, he caused the inhabitants of Attica to transport their cattle to Eubœa and the neighboring islands, and to retire within the walls of Athens with as much of their other property as they were able to take with them.

By his provident care, the city was stored with provisions sufficient to support the multitudes now crowding into it, but it was not so easy to find proper accommodations for so vast a population. Many found lodgings in the temples and other public edifices, or in the turrets on the city walls, and great numbers were obliged to seek shelter in temporary abodes which they had constructed within the Long Walls connecting the city with the port of Piræus.

Meeting with no opposition, the Peloponnesian invaders of Attica proceeded along the eastern coast, burning the towns and laying waste the country. Among the crowded population of Athens violent debates arose respecting the prosecution of the war. The people were exasperated at Pericles on account of the inactivity of the army, while the enemy was ravaging the country almost to the very gates of the city, and all his authority was required to keep the people within their fortifications.

While the Peloponnesians and their allies were desolating Attica with fire and sword, the Athenian and Corcyræan fleets were, by the direction of Pericles, retaliating upon their enemies by devasting the almost defenseless coast of the Peloponnesus. Two Corinthian settlements in Acarnania were captured, and the island of Cephallenia renounced its allegiance to Sparta and acknowledged the sway of Athens. The Eginetans were expelled from their island, which was then occupied by Athenian colonists. The desolation of the Peloponnesian coast by the Athenian navy, along with the scarcity of provisons, caused Archidamus to retire from Attica into the Peloponnesus, after an invasion of five or six weeks. He withdrew from Attica by retreating along its western coast, continuing his ravages as he retired. After returning to the Peloponnesus he disbanded his army. The Athenians then set their army in motion to chastise the Megarians, whom they regarded as revolted subjects. They ravaged the whole of Megaris to the gates of the city of Megara itself, and these devastations were repeated every year during the continuance of the war.

Early in the following summer (B. C. 430), the Peloponnesians again invaded Attica, which they were again allowed to devastate at their pleasure, as Pericles persisted in his cautious policy of confining his efforts to the defense of Athens.

The Athenians were now attacked by an enemy far more terrible than the Peloponnesian invaders. A pestilence, believed to have had its origin in Ethiopia, and which had by degrees ravaged Egypt and Western Asia, now reached Attica, making its first appearance in the town of Piræus, whose inhabitants at first believed that the enemy had poisoned their wells. The pestilence rapidly spread to Athens, where, because of the crowded condition of the city, it produced frightful havoc, carrying off vast multitudes of people. This pestilence was described as having been a species of infectious fever, accompanied with many painful symptoms, and followed by ulcerations of the bowels and limbs in the case of those who survived the first stages of the disease. It is said that the birds of prey refused to touch the unburied bodies of the victims of the plague, and that the dogs which fed upon the poisonous remains perished. The prayers of the devout and the skill of the physicians were alike unavailing to stay the advance of the disease; and the wretched Athenians, driven to despair, fancied themselves to be delivered to punishment by their gods, and particularly by Apollo, the special protector of the Doric race. The sick were in many instances left unattended, and the bodies of the dead were left unburied, while those whom the plague had not yet reached openly defied all human and divine laws by plunging into the wildest excesses of criminal indulgence.

In the anger of their despair, the Athenians vented their wrath upon Pericles, whose cautious policy they blamed as the cause of their sufferings. He still refused battle with the enemy, as he believed that the reduced numbers and exhausted spirit of his army would expose him to almost certain defeat; but, with a fleet of one hundred and fifty ships, he ravaged the coasts of the Peloponnesus with fire and sword. On his return to Athens, finding that the enemy had hastily retired from Attica from fear of the contagion of the plague, he sent a fleet to the coast of Chalcidice, to aid the Athenian land forces still engaged in the siege of Potidæa—an unfortunate proceeding, as its only result was to communicate the pestilence to the besieging army, by which the greater number of the troops were carried off.

Maddened by their calamities, the Athenians became louder and louder in their murmurs against Pericles, whom they accused of being the author of at least some of their misfortunes by involving them in the Peloponnesian War. During his absence, while he was ravaging the enemy's coasts, the Athenians had sent an embassy to Sparta to sue for peace, and when the Spartans rejected the suit contemptuously the rage of the Athenians against their great statesman increased.

Pericles justified his conduct in entering upon the war before an assembly of the people, and exhorted his countrymen to courage and perseverance in defense of their independence. He remarked that the hardships to which they had been exposed were only such as he had in former addresses prepared them to expect, and that the pestilence was a calamity which no human prudence could have foreseen or averted. He reminded his countrymen that they still possessed a fleet with which no other navy on earth was able to cope, and that their navy might yet enable them to acquire universal dominion after the present evil should have passed away.

Said he: "What we suffer from the gods, we should bear with patience; what from our enemies, with manly firmness; and such were the maxims of our forefathers. From unshaken fortitude in misfortune has arisen the present power of this commonwealth, together with that glory which, if our empire, according to the lot of all earthly things, decay, shall still survive to all posterity."

The eloquent harangue of Pericles did

not silence the fury of his personal and political enemies nor calm the alarm and irritation of the Athenian people. By the influence of Cleon the tanner, an unprincipled demagogue, the eminent statesman who had so long swayed the destinies of Athens was dismissed from all his offices and fined to a large amount. In the meantime domestic afflictions united with political anxieties and mortifications to oppress the mind of this illustrious leader, as the plague was depriving him of the members of his family and his nearest relatives one by one.

But he displayed, amid all these adversities, a fortitude which excited the admiration of all around him. Finally, at the funeral of the last of his children, his firmness gave away; and as he was placing a garland of flowers on the head of the corpse, in accordance with the national custom, he burst into loud lamentations and shed streams of tears. It was not very long before his fickle and ungrateful countrymen repented of their harshness towards their renowned statesman and reinstated him in his civil and military authority. But he soon fell a victim to the same plague which had carried his children and so many of his countrymen to their graves (B. C. 429). It is said that as he lay on his death-bed, and those around him were recounting his great actions, he suddenly interrupted them by saying: "All that you are praising was either the result of good fortune, or, in any case, common to me with many other leaders. What I chiefly pride myself upon is, that no act of mine has ever caused any Athenian to put on mourning."

Ancient writers agree in assigning Pericles the first place among Grecian statesmen for wisdom and eloquence. Notwithstanding his ambition for power, he was moderate in the exercise of that power; and it is highly creditable to his memory that, in an age and country which exhibited so little scruple in the shedding of blood, his long administration was no less mild and merciful than it was vigorous and effective. When obliged to wage war against his country's enemies, this celebrated statesman constantly studied how to overcome the foe with the least possible sacrifice of life, both on the side of his countrymen and on that of their enemies.

After the death of Pericles, the first period of the war continued seven years longer, but with no decisive advantage to either side. During the first part of this period, Cleon, the unscrupulous demagogue who had led the opposition against Pericles, directed the councils of Athens.

The second Peloponnesian raid into Attica was more destructive than the first, as the ravages extended to the silver mines of Laurium. The Peloponnesian fleet destroyed the fisheries and commerce of Athens and devastated the island of Zacynthus. During the next winter Potidæa surrendered to the Athenians, after a blockade of two years, and was occupied by a thousand Athenian colonists.

The Spartans directed their third campaign against Platæa. When Archidamus approached, the Platæans sent a solemn remonstrance, reminding him of the oath which Pausánias had sworn on the evening of the great battle before their city, making Platæa forever sacred from invasion. The Spartan king replied that the Platæans were also bound by oath to strive for the independence of every state of Greece. He reminded them of their atrocious crime in massacring the Theban prisoners; but promised that, if they abandoned the cause of Athens and remained neutral in the war, their privileges would be respected. But the Platæans would not forsake their old ally, and so the Spartans laid siege to their city.

The Platæan garrison which thus resisted the entire Peloponnesian army numbered only four hundred and eighty men, but they made up in energy for their lack in numbers. Archidamus commenced the siege by closing up every outlet of the town with a wooden palisade, then erected against this palisade a mound of earth and stone, forming an inclined plane up which his troops would be able to march. The Platæans undermined the mound, which thus fell in, and rendered useless seventy days' work of the entire besieging army. They likewise constructed a new wall inside of the old one, so that the Spartans would still not capture the city if they took the old wall (B. C. 429).

When the Peloponnesians perceived that the Platæans could only be reduced by famine, they converted the siege into a blockade, surrounding the city with a double wall, and roofing the intermediate space, thus affording shelter to the soldiers on duty. The Platæans were thus cut off from all communication with the outside world for two years. Provisions began to fail; and in the second year of the blockade almost half of the garrison escaped by climbing over the barracks and fortifications of their besiegers in the rain and darkness of a December night. The Platæans still remaining were ultimately reduced to absolute starvation. A Spartan herald was now sent by Archidamus to demand their submission, but promising that the guilty only should be punished. The Platæans thereupon surrendered. When brought before the Spartan judges, every man of the Platæan garrison was declared guilty and put to death. The town and territory of Platæa was bestowed on the Thebans, who destroyed all private dwellings, and with the materials they constructed a vast barrack to give shelter to visitors and dwellings to the serfs who tilled the land. The city of Platæa thus ceased to exist (B. C. 427).

The Athenians and their ally, Sitálces, a Thracian chief, were prosecuting the war in the North with not very much success. Sitálces, at the head of a Thracian army of one hundred and fifty thousand men, invaded Macedonia for the purpose of dethroning Perdiccas, the king of that country. The Macedonians withdrew into their fortresses, as they were unable to withstand Sitálces in the open field, and Sitálces withdrew after thirty days, as he had no means for conducting sieges. Phórmio, an Athenian commander, gained two victories in the Corinthian Gulf over a vastly larger Spartan fleet. He had twenty ships in the first battle, while the Spartans had forty-seven. In the second engagement he encountered a fresh Spartan fleet of seventy-seven vessels (B. C. 429).

In the fourth year of the war the city of Mitylêné, in the island of Lesbos, revolted against Athens. Envoys were sent to Sparta to solicit aid, which was readily granted, and the Mitylénians were received into the Peloponnesian League.

In the spring of B. C. 427 the Spartan fleet advanced to Mitylêné, but when it arrived it found the city already in the possession of the Athenians. When almost reduced by famine, the governor, acting in accordance with the advice of the Spartan envoy, had armed all the men of the lower classes for a final desperate sortie; but the result was contrary to his expectations, as the mass of the Mitylénian people preferred the Athenian supremacy to their own oligarchical government. Taking advantage of their situation, the armed Mitylénians declared that they would treat directly with the Athenians if all their demands were not granted. The governor's only choice was to begin negotiations with the Athenians himself. The city was surrendered to the Athenians, and the fate of its inhabitants was left to the decision of the popular assembly of Athens, whither the oligarchical ring-leaders of the revolt were sent.

A thousand Athenians convened in the Agora to decide the fate of their Mitylénian prisoners. Salæthus, the Spartan envoy, was instantly put to death. An animated debate ensued regarding the others. Cleon the tanner, the former opponent of Pericles, took a prominent part in the proceedings. This unprincipled demagogue, in spite of more humane and moderate counsels, obtained the adoption of his cruel proposition by the popular assembly to massacre all the men of Mitylêné and to sell all the women and children into slavery. This proposition was all the more atrocious because the great mass of the Mitylénians were friendly to Athens, while the revolt had been brought about by the oligarchy, who were the enemies and oppressors of the people. The opposition to Cleon's brutal decree had been so formidable in the Athenian popular assembly that Cleon feared a reversal of the death-sentence of the Mitylénians, and for that reason he caused a galley to be instantly dispatched to the island of Lesbos with orders for its immediate execution.

Cleon had good reasons for his apprehensions, as a sober second thought of the Athenian people after a night's reflection asserted itself, and the better class of the citizens were horrified at the inhuman decision at which they had so hastily arrived. They demanded a new assembly of the people to reconsider the matter, and although this was contrary to the law, the *strategi* gave their consent and again convened the citizens. In the second day's debate the iniquitous decree was rescinded. Every nerve was now strained to enable the vessel bearing the account of this merciful decision to overtake the messengers of the death-sentence, who were in advance a whole day's journey. The strongest oarsmen were selected for the occasion, and were urged to their greatest efforts by the promise of liberal rewards in case they should arrive in time to spare the hastily-condemned Mitylénians. Their food was given them while they plied the oars, and they were only allowed to sleep in short intervals and by turns. The weather was favorable, and they arrived just in time to prevent Paches from executing the first order. Thus the lives of the Mitylénians were spared, but the walls of their city were leveled, and their fleet was surrendered to the Athenians. The island of Lesbos, excepting Methymna, which had not taken part in the revolt, was divided into three thousand parts, three hundred of which were devoted to the gods, and the remainder were allotted to Athenian settlers. The ring-leaders of the revolt, who were the oligarchs who had been carried as prisoners to Athens, were tried for their part in the conspiracy and were put to death.

The Corcyræan prisoners who had been taken to Corinth in B. C. 432 were now sent home, in the expectation that their account of the generous treatment accorded them would lead their countrymen to abandon their alliance with Athens. They united with the oligarchical faction to effect a revolution in Corcyra, killed the chiefs of the popular party, and acquired possession of the harbor, the arsenal and the market-place; and thus, by overawing the people, procured a vote in the assembly to maintain a strict neutrality in the future. But the people fortified themselves in the higher parts of the town, and summoned the serfs from the interior of the island to their assistance and promised them freedom.

Thereupon the oligarchical faction fired the town; but while the fire was raging, a small Athenian squadron arrived from Naupactus, and its commander wisely endeavored to induce the contending parties to make peace. When he had apparently effected his purpose, a Peloponnesian fleet more than four times as large as his own arrived, under the command of Alcídas. The Athenians retired without loss, and Alcídas had momentary posession of Corcyra; but, with his habitual lack of promptness, he spent a day in ravaging the island, and the approach of an Athenian fleet larger than his own was announced by beacon fires on Leucas at night. Alcídas retired before morning, leaving the oligarchical party in the city to their fate. During the next seven days Corcyra was the scene of a reign of terror. The popular party, under the protection of the Athenian fleet, gave way to the fiercest promptings of revenge. Civil hatred outweighed natural affection. A father killed his own son. Brothers extended no mercy to brothers. The aristocratic party was well-nigh exterminated; but five hundred succeeded in making their escape, and fortified themselves on Mount Istóne, near the capital.

The sixth year of the Peloponnesian War opened amid floods and earthquakes, which added their terrors to the civil and political convulsions which distracted the land of the Hellenes. Athens was again suffering from the ravages of the plague. To appease the wrath of Apollo, a solemn purification was performed in the autumn in the sacred isle of Delos, the birth place of that god.

All bodies that had been buried there were removed to a neighboring island, and the Delian festival was revived with greater splendor. Attica escaped a Spartan invasion this year, either because of the awe inspired by the supposed wrath of the gods or by the dread of the plague. The next year, however, (B. C. 425), the Spartan king Agis I. invaded and ravaged Attica; but was recalled, after fifteen days, by the news that the Athenians had established a military station on the coast of Messenia.

An Athenian fleet under Eurymedon and Sóphocles, bound for Sicily, had been delayed by a storm near the harbor of Pylos. The commanders chose this locality for a settlement of Messenians from Naupactus, who could thus communicate with their Helot kinsmen and annoy the Spartans. The Athenian commander, Demósthenes, with five ships and two hundred soldiers, was reinforced by a Messenian detachment, thus augmenting his force to a thousand men. The wrath of the Spartans was as great as their alarm at this encroachment on their territory. Their fleet was immediately ordered from Corcyra, while Agis I., with his army, withdrew from Attica. The long and narrow island of Sphactéria, covering the entrance to the Bay of Pylos, was occupied by Thrasymélidas, the Spartan, whose ships were sheltered in the basin which it thus enclosed. While waiting for reinforcements, Demósthenes, with his handful of troops, was obliged to encounter a largely superior force. Brásidas, one of the greatest of Spartan captains, led the attack from the sea. He fought on the prow of the foremost ship, encouraging his men by word and example, but he was severely wounded, and the engagement terminated to the advantage of the Athenians. The next day the conflict was renewed and the Athenians were again successful. They erected a trophy, ornamenting it with the shield of Brásidas.

After the Athenian fleet had arrived, a still more decisive Athenian victory followed. The triumphant Athenians proceeded to blockade Sphactéria, which contained the flower of the Peloponnesian army.

The emergency was so serious for Sparta that the Ephors saw no other escape but through peace. An armistice was agreed upon, and the better spirits on both sides entertained a hope for the end of the devastating war. But the foolish vanity of Cleon and the party at his back demanded the most extreme and unreasonable conditions, which the Spartans rejected. Hostilities were renewed, with equal vexation on both sides. Fearing that his blockade would be interrupted by the winter's storms, Demósthenes determined to make an attack upon the island, and sent to Athens for reinforcements, at the same time explaining his position This report disheartened the assembly of the people, who now accused Cleon of having persuaded them to throw away the opportunity for an honorable peace. Cleon retorted by accusing the officers of cowardice and incompetency, and declared that if *he* commanded the army he would reduce Sphactéria instantly. The entire assembly burst out in laughter at this boast of the tanner, and assailed him with cries of "Why don't you go then?" The lively spirits of the Athenians at once recovered from their unusual depression, and the simple joke developed into a determination. Cleon endeavored to draw back, but the assembly of the people insisted on his assuming command. Finally he engaged, with a certain number of auxiliaries reinforcing the troops already at Pylos, to reduce the island in twenty days, and either kill all the Spartans thereon or bring them to Athens in chains.

Cleon succeeded remarkably in his undertaking. Demósthenes had made every preparation for the attack; and his prudence, along with the accidental burning of the woods on Sphactéria, rather than Cleon's military skill, was mainly the cause of the Athenian victory. The Athenians landed before daylight, overpowered the guard at the southern end of the island, and then formed in line of battle, sending out skirmishing parties to provoke the Spartans to a conflict. Blinded by the light ashes raised by the march of his troops, the Spartan general advanced over the half-burned stumps of the trees with some difficulty. His army was vastly outnumbered by the Athenians, who harassed him from a distance with arrows and compelled him to retire to the extremity of the island, where the Spartans again fought with their usual valor; but a detachment of Messenians, who had clambered over some crags generally considered inaccessible, appeared upon the heights above and decided the battle in favor of the Athenians. All the surviving Spartans surrendered, and Cleon and Demósthenes started instantly for Athens with their prisoners, arriving there within twenty days. This was one of the most important victories ever achieved by the Athenians. The harbor of Pylos was strongly fortified and garrisoned with Messenian troops, for a base of operations against Laconia.

The eighth year of the war (B. C. 424) opened with the Athenians everywhere triumphant; and the humiliated and disheartened Spartans had repeatedly solicited peace. In the early part of the year Nicias conquered the island of Cythera and placed garrisons in two of its principal towns, which were a perpetual defiance of the Lacedæmonians. He next devastated the coast of Laconia and captured some towns, among which was Thyrea, where the Eginetans had been allowed to settle after they had been expelled from their own island. Such of the original settlers who survived were taken to Athens and put to death. The brutalizing effects of the war became more apparent year after year, and these atrocious massacres were now a common occurrence.

About the same time the Spartans, alarmed at the nearness of the Messenian garrisons of Pylos and Cythera, announced that such Helots as had distinguished themselves by their faithful services during the war should be given their freedom. Many of the bravest and ablest claimed the offer. Two thousand of these were selected as deserving liberation, and were crowned with garlands and dignified with high religious honors. But several days later they had all disappeared, no one knew how but the Spartan Ephors, who were not moved from their narrow regard for the supposed interest of the state, either by honor or pity.

The Athenians were also somewhat successful in their expedition against Megaris, but their attack on Bœotia ended in disaster. The chief movement against Bœotia was managed by Hippócrates, who led an Athenian army of more than thirty-two thousand men across the Bœotian frontier to Délium, a town strongly-situated near Tánagra, among the cliffs of the eastern coast, where he fortified the temple of Apollo and placed a garrison in the works, after which he started for home. A large Bœotian army assembled at Tánagra now marched to intercept the Athenian invaders upon the heights of Délium. The battle began late in the day. The Athenian right was at first successful, but their left was borne down by the Theban phalanx. In the Athenian ranks in this battle were the immortal philosopher Socrates and his pupils, Alcibíades and Xenophon, the former afterwards celebrated as a political and military leader, and the latter renowned as a general and a historian. The arrival of the Bœotian cavalry decided the fate of the day, the Athenians fleeing in every direction, only the darkness and night saving them from total destruction. Such was the battle of Délium (B. C. 424). Délium was taken by the triumphant Bœotians after a siege of seventeen days.

Soon after these disasters in Bœotia, the Athenians were deprived of their entire dominion in Thrace. The Spartan general Brásidas had conducted a small but select army to the assistance of Perdiccas, King of Macedon, and the Chalcidian towns. The valor and integrity of Brásidas induced many of the allies of Athens to forsake her cause, and on his sudden appearance before Amphipolis, that city surrendered with scarcely an effort at defense. The Athenian party in Amphipolis solicited aid from the Athenian general Thucydides, the great historian, who commanded in that region. He was sentenced to banishment, in consequence of his failure, and passed the next twenty years in exile, during which he did more for Grecian glory by his literary work than he would have been able to accomplish in his military command. Brásidas proceeded to the most easterly of the three Chalcidic peninsulas, and most of the towns submitted to him.

The Athenians were now so depressed by their losses that they in turn asked for peace; while the Spartans, anxious for the return of their noble youths who were held prisoners in Athens, as ardently longed for a treaty. A truce of one year was accordingly agreed upon in B. C. 423, to facilitate permanent negotiations. But two days after the truce had commenced Scióne revolted from the Athenians, who demanded its restitution; and as the Spartans refused, an entire year passed without additional efforts in the direction of peace. At the end of the year Cleon proceeded to Thrace with an Athenian fleet and army, and took the towns of Toróne and Galepsus; but his attempt to recover Amphipolis resulted in a battle in which he was killed and his army defeated. Brásidas was also mortally wounded, but lived long enough to know that his troops were victorious.

Cleon's successor in the direction of public affairs at Athens was Nicias, the leader of the aristocratic party, a man of good character, though unenterprising, and a military officer of moderate abilities. By the death of Cleon and Brásidas, the Athenian and Spartan leaders, the two great obstacles to peace were removed; and in the spring of B. C. 421 a treaty for fifty years, usually known as the *Peace of Nicias*, was concluded between Athens and Sparta. Some of the allies of Sparta complained that that power had sacrificed their interests to her own, and formed a new league with Argos, Elis and Mantinéa, for the ostensible purpose of defending the Peloponnesian states against the aggressions of Athens and Sparta.

The Athenians had been excluded from the two previous celebrations of the Olympic Games, but in the summer of B. C. 420 the Elian heralds made their appearance to invite them to attend. Those who expected to see Athens poverty-stricken, because of her numerous losses, were surprised at the magnificence exhibited by her delegates, who made the most expensive display in all the processions. Alcibíades, a young man who ranked as one of the ablest citizens of Athens, entered on the lists seven four-horse chariots, and received two olive crowns in the races. His genius, valor and quickness in emergencies enabled him to become the greatest benefactor of his country, but his misdirected and uncontrolled ambition and his thorough lack of principle rendered him the cause of the greatest calamities to Athens.

Thus ended the first period of the Peloponnesian War—the period known as the Ten Years' War. It was not long, however, before the sanguinary contest was renewed. The new league alluded to in a preceding paragraph, and fresh distrusts between Athens and Sparta on account of the reluctance felt and manifested by both to relinquish certain places which they had bound themselves by treaty mutually to surrender, contributed to excite new jealousies, which were fanned into a violent flame by the artful proceedings of Alcibíades, the young Athenian just mentioned, who was now rising into political power, and whose genius and character subsequently exercised a powerful influence upon the affairs of Athens.

.Alcibíades was the son of Clinias, an Athenian of exalted rank. Endowed with unusual beauty of person and with talents of the very highest order, he was destitute of principle and integrity; and his violent passions frequently led him to conduct himself in such a manner as to bring disgrace on his memory. Even in boyhood he displayed wonderful proofs of the extent of his talents and his energy of character. It is said that on one occasion, while playing with some boys of his own age in the streets of Athens, he observed a loaded wagon approach the place where he was, and not wishing to be interrupted at that moment, he demanded of the teamster to stop; and when the teamster refused, he threw himself in front of the horses, saying to the teamster: "Drive over me if you dare!" The driver stopped his horses, and Alcibíades only allowed him to proceed when he had finished his game.

He passed his youth in a very dissipated manner among the gay companions whom his high birth, his showy and prepossessing manners, and his boundless liberality, attracted to him. Flattered by the homage paid him by one sex because of his wit, and by the other on account of his beauty—for it is said that the Athenian ladies vied with one another in their endeavors to win his affections—Alcibíades would likely have been totally spoiled, had he not been so singularly fortunate in early life as to attract the attention of the immortal philosopher Socrates.

This good man did not wish to see a youth endowed with so many brilliant and noble qualities utterly lost to virtue, and he therefore earnestly sought by his exhortations and reproofs to induce Alcibíades to relinquish his dissipated habits and to get him away from the society of his profligate associates. The philosopher succeeded to some extent; but though Alcibíades grew to love and respect the sage, and felt the full influence of his wise precepts, the impetuosity and recklessness of his disposition, the power of his passions, and the number and variety of the allurements to which he was exposed, too frequently acquired the mastery over his virtuous resolutions.

While yet very young, Alcibíades served in the Athenian army engaged in the siege of Potidæa. He was accompanied by Socrates, who saved his youthful friend's life in one of the battles, by hastening to his aid when he was wounded and about to be killed. Alcibíades afterward repaid this important service by saving the life of Socrates during the flight of the Athenian army after the battle of Délium.

When Alcibíades first took part in public affairs, which he did at an uncommonly early age, his popular manners, his unrivaled address, and his polished and persuasive eloquence, soon won for him a great degree of influence. He was at first friendly to Sparta, with which state his family had been anciently connected by ties of the strongest amity. But the Spartans did not like his dissipated and luxurious habits, and remembered in a resentful spirit the solemn renunciation which his great-grandfather made concerning his friendship toward them when they interfered in Athenian affairs in the times of the Pisistrátidæ. For these reasons the Spartans rejected the advances of Alcibíades disdainfully, and transacted all their affairs in Athens through the medium of his rival, Nicias.

Incensed at this treatment, Alcibíades became as unfriendly to the Spartans as he had previously been friendly, and he soon showed them that he could not be trifled with. Therefore when mutual distrusts arose between Athens and Sparta concerning the fulfillment of certain stipulations in the treaty of Nicias, Lacedæmonian ambassadors arrived in Athens clothed with full authority to conclude an amicable adjustment, Alcibíades managed to prevent a resumption of friendly intercourse between the two states, as he considered such a possible consummation as incompatible with his interests.

When the Spartan ambassadors announced that they were fully authorized to treat on all disputed points, he privately advised them to retract this declaration, because the popular assembly of Athens would take advantage of it to extort unfavorable terms from Lacedæmon, and he promised that, if they acted on his advice, he would support their demands before the Athenian people. The Lacedæmonian ambassadors were so weak as to follow his recommendation, and as soon as they had stated that their powers were limited, he attacked them in a fierce manner, to their utter amazement and dismay, accusing them of dishonesty and falsehood, while he cunningly took advantage of the circumstance to arouse the popular assembly against Sparta.

The Athenian people were excited with indignation at what had transpired, and were about to dissolve the league with Sparta, when the assembly was adjourned until the following day in consequence of a shock of earthquake. When the people reassembled, Nicias, observing that they were then disposed to listen to more moderate counsels, proposed that they should send an embassy to Sparta to bring about a reconciliation, before adopting any hostile measure toward that state. This proposition was accepted by the assembly; but, at the artful suggestion of Alcibiades, the Athenian ambassadors were directed to insist on such preliminary conditions as he very well knew the Lacedæmonians would never agree to. His expectations were fully realized. The Athenian ambassadors returned from Sparta without accomplishing anything, and the Athenians at once entered into an offensive and defensive league with the recently-formed confederacy headed by Argos. When Athens joined this alliance, Corinth at once seceded from it, to renew its old alliance with Sparta.

Thus the Peloponnesian War was renewed (B. C. 419), but with little spirit or energy for several years. After the vigorous prosecution of the war had recommenced, many bloody battles were fought, countless deeds of atrocity were perpetrated, and the states of Greece were for many years involved in confusion and suffering by a war begun with scarcely any cause and persisted in without any reasonable object.

Alcibiades had now attained the undisputed leadership in public affairs in Athens. Elated with his success, his taste for luxury and magnificence exceeded all bounds. He imitated the effeminacy of Oriental manners by wearing a purple robe with a flowing train, and when he personally took part in the wars he carried a golden shield, on which was represented Eros armed with a thunderbolt. The wiser portion of the people regretted his excessive love of display and his unrestrained arrogance and licentiousness; but the fickle multitude admired his brilliant talents and his exalted demeanor, while they were confirmed in their favorable disposition towards him by the feasts, games and spectacles to which he treated them.

War soon arose between Sparta and Argos in which the Spartan king Agis I. won an important victory in the battle of Mantinéa, B. C. 418. After the oligarchical party had come into power at Argos, that state renounced her alliance with Athens and entered into a treaty with Sparta. But the Argive nobles abused their power by committing brutal outrages upon the people, who effected another revolution by which they obtained possession of the city. Alcibiades came to the assistance of the Argive people with an Athenian fleet and army, at their request. Though Athens and Sparta were nominally at peace, the Athenian garrison of Pylos continued its depredations in Laconia, and Spartan privateers inflicted serious injuries upon Athenian commerce.

About this time an embassy from Sicily solicited the assistance of Athens for the city of Egesta, which was then engaged in a contest with its neighbor Selínus, which had obtained aid from Syracuse. The "war of races" had actually begun in Sicily twelve years previously, and the Athenians had repeatedly aided the Ionian cities, Leontíni and Camarína, against their Dorian neighbors, who had joined the Poloponnesian League. Alcibiades used all his influence to induce his countrymen to assist Egesta, with the hope of at once improving his ruined fortunes with the spoils of Sicily and gratifying his ambition with the glory of foreign conquest. He actually hoped not only to establish the supremacy of Athens over all the Grecian colonies, but also to subdue the republic of Carthage and all its dependencies in the Western Mediterranean.

Nicias and the entire moderate party in Athens opposed the enterprise of Alcibiades, but they only succeeded in having an embassy sent to Egesta, to ascertain if its people were actually able to fulfill their promise to furnish funds for the prosecution of the war. These Athenian envoys were thoroughly outwitted by the Egestans. They saw a splendid display of vessels in the temple of Aphrodité, apparently of solid gold, but really only silver-gilt. They were feasted at the houses of citizens, and were surprised at the abundance of gold and silver plate adorning their sideboards, unaware that the same articles were being passed from house to house and were doing repeated service in their entertainment. The Egestans paid sixty talents of silver as a first installment, and the Athenian envoys carried home with them glowing accounts of Egestan wealth.

Most Athenians seemed thus satisfied as to the resources of the Egestans; and accordingly the people voted to send an expedition under the command of Alcibíades, Nicias and Lamachus, to Sicily. Unbounded zeal took possession of all Athenians, young and old, rich and poor, all desiring to take part in the expedition; and the generals found it difficult to select from the throng of volunteers. When the armament was about to sail, a mysterious incident filled the excited masses of Athens with dismay. The *Hermæ*, or statues of the god Hermes, which stood before every door in Athens, before every temple or gymnasium, and in every public square, were found one morning thrown down and mutilated. The Athenian people, in a fit of superstitious horror, insisted upon the detection and punishment of the individuals guilty of the sacrilegious outrage. The people suspected Alcibíades, as he had once burlesqued the Eleusinian Mysteries in a drunken frolic, and was believed to be capable of committing any sacrilege. His enemies took advantage of the popular suspicion and belief to openly accuse him of the horrible deed, but he indignantly denied his guilt and demanded an immediate investigation. The people readily believed the accusers of Alcibíades, on account of his dissipated habits, and made preparations to try him at once for the impious act; but as the army seemed determined to support him, his accusers and enemies were afraid to proceed, and contrived to have the trial delayed until his return from Sicily, thus sending him out with the expedition under the burden of an unproven charge, so that they might revive it for his condemnation in case of disaster to the expedition. All his persistent demands for an immediate trial were unavailing, as his enemies obstinately refused to grant it.

On the day appointed for the sailing of the armament, almost the entire population of Athens accompanied the troops on their march at dawn to Piræus. When all were on board, the trumpet commanded silence, and the voice of the herald, in conjunction with that of the people, was lifted up in prayer. After this the pæan was sung, while the officers at the prow of each ship poured a libation from a golden goblet into the sea. At a given signal, the whole fleet slipped its cables and started at the greatest speed, each crew endeavoring to reach Egesta before the others.

The entire armament of Athenians and allies mustered at Corcyra in July, B. C. 415, and consisted of one hundred and thirty-six vessels of war and five hundred transports, carrying six thousand three hundred soldiers, in addition to artisans and a vast quantity of food and arms. When the fleet reached the coast of Italy, three fast-sailing triremes were sent to notify the Egestans of its arrival and to ascertain their present condition. These vessels rejoined the fleet at Rhégium, with the disappointing report that the wealth of Egesta was entirely fictitious, and that thirty talents more were all the aid that could be expected. The three admirals now disagreed in their opinions. Nicias desired to sail immediately to Selínus, make the best possible terms, and then return to Athens. Alcibíades proposed to look for new allies among the Greek cities, and with their assistance to attack both Selínus and Syracuse. Lamachus urged an attack upon Syracuse at once, as that was the greatest and wealthiest city in Sicily. This advice was both the boldest and the safest, as the Syracusans were unprepared for defense, and their surrender would have placed the island under the dominion of Athens; but as Lamachus was neither rich nor influential, his plan was ignored, and that of Alcibíades was adopted. The fleet sailed southward, reconnoitered the defenses of Syracuse, and took possession of Catana, which was made its headquarters.

At this point Alcibíades received a decree of the popular assembly commanding him to return to Athens for his trial. A judicial inquiry had acquitted him of the mutilation of the Hermæ, but he was still charged with profaning the Eleusinian Mysteries, by mimicking them at his own house for the amusement of his friends. The public mind was by degrees wrought up to the highest pitch of excitement by this charge, and by the rumors which the enemies of Alcibíades circulated as soon as he had sailed from Athens, to the effect that he was forming plots for the subversion of the republican constitution of the state. Some of his slaves testified to his burlesquing the Eleusinian Mysteries. This was an unpardonable crime, and those noble families which had inherited a special right from their heroic or divine ancestors to officiate in the ceremonies regarded themselves as grossly insulted. Many of the friends of Alcibíades were cruelly put to death. The public trireme which brought the summons to Alcibíades was under orders not to arrest him, but to allow him to return in his own ship. But instead of returning to Athens as ordered to do, the wily general took advantage of the courtesy extended to him to effect his escape. Landing at Thurium, he eluded his pursuers, and the messengers returned to Athens without him. In his absence from Athens the death-sentence was passed upon him, his property was confiscated, and the Eumolpidæ, or priests, solemnly pronounced him "accursed."

In the meantime the Athenians had spent three months in Sicily, effecting so little as to excite the contempt of the Spartans. Nicias, thus shamed into making some effort, circulated a rumer that the Catanæans were disposed to drive the Athenians from their city; and thus drew a large army from Syracuse to their assistance. While this army was absent from home, the entire Athenian fleet sailed into the Great Harbor of Syracuse, and landed a force which intrenched itself near the mouth of the river Anapus. On the return of the Syracusans a battle ensued, in which Nicias was victorious. He did not follow up his success, however, but retired into winter-quarters at Catana, and subsequently at Naxos, while he sent to Athens for a supply of money, and to his Sicilian allies for a reinforcement of troops.

The Syracusans passed the winter in active preparations for the struggle. They built a new wall across the peninsula between the Bay of Thapsus and the Great Port, thus covering their city on the west and the north-west. At the same time they sent to Corinth and Sparta for assistance, finding an unexpected ally in the latter city in the person of Alcibíades, who had crossed from Italy to Greece and had received a special invitation from the Spartans to come to their city, where he was received with an honorable welcome, in spite of the former animosity between him and the Spartans, and his proffered services were gladly accepted by the Lacedæmonians. At Sparta he gratified his revenge against his Athenian countrymen by disclosing all their plans and urging the Spartans to send an army into Sicily to thwart their movements.

Alcibíades exhibited a remarkable proof of his self-command while in Sparta. Aware of the simple and self-denying manner in which the Spartans lived, he relinquished his effeminate manners and his rich dress, and affected so much gravity of behavior and simplicity of attire that the Lacedæmonians could scarcely realize that he had once been the sprightly and voluptuous Alcibíades. He shaved his head, restricted his diet to the coarse bread and black broth of the public tables of Sparta, and made himself conspicuous for his austerity, even among the rigid Lacedæmonians. His speech likewise acquired that laconic style for which the Spartans were remarkable.

But the Athenians in the course of time found cause to regret that they had resorted to such harsh proceedings against their ablest leader. Under the guidance of Alcibíades, the Spartans adopted measures which led to the disastrous failure of the Athenian expedition to Sicily and caused several of the Athenian dependencies in Asia Minor and the isles of the Ægean to revolt.

Alcibíades passed over into Asia Minor to incite the Ionian cities to throw off the yoke of Athens, and he also negotiated an alliance between Persia and Sparta, through Tissaphernes, the Persian satrap of Lydia. While he was thus absent from Lacedæmon, a strong party was formed against him among the Spartan nobility, under the leadership of King Agis I., and secret orders were dispatched to the Lacedæmonian general in Ionia to put him to death; but Alcibíades received intimation as to what was in progress, and fled from the camp, seeking refuge in Lydia, where his lively wit and winning manners soon made him a favorite with Tissaphernes.

Nicias began the siege of Syracuse by the opening of the spring of B. C. 414, by fortifying the heights of Epipolæ, which commanded the city. He also built a fort at Syke and dislodged the Syracusans from the counter-walls which they were erecting. The Athenian fleet was stationed in the Great Harbor; and the Syracusans, in despair of offering an effectual resistance, sent messengers to negotiate terms for the surrender of the city. But the heroic Lamachus had been slain, and Nicias, who thus was left as sole commander of the Athenian expedition, did not exhibit sufficient activity to grasp the victory which thus seemed to await him.

Just then Gylíppus, the Spartan, reached the coast of Italy with four ships, and thinking that Syracuse and all Sicily were lost beyond recovery, he endeavored to save only the cities on the peninsula. To his great satisfaction, he ascertained that the Athenians had not actually finished their northern line of works around Syracuse. He hastened through the Straits of Messina, which he discovered were not guarded, landed at Himéra, and began to raise an army from the Dorian cities of Sicily. With these troops he proceeded directly to Syracuse over the heights of Epipolæ, which Nicias had neglected to hold. After he had entered the city, he sent orders to the Athenian general to evacuate the island within five days. Nicias payed no regard to the message, but the subsequent events attested that the Spartan commander was master of the situation. He captured the Athenian fort at Labalum, erected another upon the heights of Epipolæ, and connected it with Syracuse by a strong wall.

The towns of Sicily which had hesitated to take part in the struggle now joined the winning side. Reinforcements for the Syracusans and Spartans arrived from Corinth, Leucas and Ambracia. As Nicias was unable to continue the siege with his present inadequate force, he withdrew to the headland of Plemmyrium, south of the Great Port. His vessels needed repair, his men were discouraged and disposed to desert, and his health was impaired. He wrote to Athens, imploring for immediate reinforcements for the army and for his recall. Athens itself was at this time in a state of siege, as the Spartan king Agis I. was encamped at Deceléa, fourteen miles north of the city, in a position commanding the entire plain of Athens. The public funds were well-nigh exhausted, famine began to be felt, and the decreasing number of citizens were worn out with the labor of defending the walls day and night. But it was decided to send reinforcements to Nicias and also to harass the Spartans on their own territory. With this view, Cháricles was sent to establish a military station on the south coast of Laconia, like that of Pylos in Messenia; while Demósthenes and Eurymedon proceeded with a fleet and army to Sicily. The first enterprise succeeded, but the second was too late.

The Syracusans had been defeated in one naval engagement, but they won a thorough victory in a second sea-fight, which lasted two days, and the Athenian vessels were locked up in the extremity of the harbor. The arrival of Demósthenes with fresh troops did something toward checking the foe and encouraging the Athenians. Seeing at once that Epipolæ was the vital point, that Athenian commander used every endeavor to accomplish its recapture, but all his efforts were unavailing. Convinced that the siege was now hopeless, Demósthenes urged Nicias to return to Athens and drive the Spartan invaders out of Attica. But as Nicias remembered the bright anticipations and the magnificent ceremonies with which the expedition had started from Athens, he could not think of returning home with the humiliation of an ignominious failure. Nor would he retire to Thapsus or Catana, where Demósthenes pointed out the advantages of an open sea and constant supplies of provisions. But when large reinforcements arrived for Syracuse, the retreat of the Athenian forces became necessary, and the plans were so well arranged that it could have been easily accomplished without the enemy's knowledge.

Unfortunately for the Athenians, an eclipse of the moon occurred on the very evening of the proposed retreat. The soothsayers concluded that Artemis, the moon-goddess, the special protectress of Syracuse, was manifesting her wrath against the Athenian assailants of the city. They declared that the Athenian army must remain in its present situation three times nine days. This delay enabled the Syracusans to learn all about the intended retreat of the besiegers, and they determined to strike an effective blow before the defeated assailants should effect their escape. A land and naval battle ensued. The Athenians repulsed their assailants on land, but their fleet was completely defeated and Eurymedon was slain.

The Syracusans now determined upon the complete destruction of their enemy, and with this view they blockaded the Great Harbor with a line of ships moored across its entrance. The only hope for the Athenians was to break this line, and for this purpose Nicias made preparations for another engagement. The hills surrounding the harbor were crowded with multitudes of spectators of either party, who viewed with anxiety the conflict which was to decide their destinies. The yachts of wealthy Syracusans covered the water, prepared to offer their services whenever they might be required. The Athenians made their first attack upon the barrier ships at the entrance of the harbor, but were unsuccessful; after which the Syracusan fleet of seventy-six triremes engaged the Athenian fleet, which numbered one hundred and ten triremes. The air resounded with the noise produced by the crash of the iron prows, the shouts of the combatants, and the responding groans or cheers of their friends upon the shore. The result was in doubt for a long time, but finally the Athenian fleet commenced to retreat toward the shore, whereupon a cry of despair seized the Athenian army, which was answered by shouts of triumph from the pursuing Syracusan vessels and the citizens on the walls of the city.

The Athenian fleet was now reduced to sixty ships, and the Syracusan to fifty. Nicias and Demósthenes endeavored to induce their followers to renew their attempt to force their way out of the harbor, but they were so utterly disheartened that they absolutely refused to engage in any more conflicts by sea. The Athenian army still amounted to forty thousand men, and it was determined to retreat by land to some friendly city, where they would be able to defend themselves until the arrival of transports. If this design had been immediately put into execution it might have succeeded, as the Syracusans had abandoned themselves to drunken revelries, in consequence of their rejoicings over their victory and by the festival of Hercules, and did not for the moment think of their fleeing foe. But Hermócrates, the most prudent of the Syracusans, determined to prevent the contemplated Athenian movement. He sent messengers to the wall, who pretended to come from spies of Nicias within the city, and warned the Athenian generals not to move that night, because all the roads were strongly guarded. Nicias was thus entrapped, and lost the last hope of escape from his perilous situation.

On the second day after the battle, the Athenian army began its march in the direction of the interior of the island, leaving the deserted fleet in the harbor, the dead unburied, and the wounded to the vengeance of the enemy. On the third day of the march the road lay over a steep cliff, guarded by a detachment of Syracusan troops. The Athenians were repulsed in assaults upon this strong position for two days, and their generals resolved during the night to turn in the direction of the sea. Nicias was successful in reaching the coast with the van; but Demósthenes lost his way, was overtaken by the foe and surrounded in a narrow pass, where he surrendered the shattered remnants of his army, then amounting to only six thousand men. The victorious Syracusans then pursued Nicias and overtook him at the river Asinárus. Great numbers of the Athenians perished in their endeavors to cross the stream. Closely pressed by the army of Gylíppus, the rear of the Athenians rushed forward upon the spears of their comrades, or were hurled down the steep banks and carried away by the swift current. All discipline was at an end, and Nicias surrendered. The two Athenian generals were condemned to death by the Syracusan council. The common soldiers were imprisoned in stone-quarries, without food or shelter, thus suffering greater miseries than all that had preceded. A few of the survivors were sold into slavery, and in some cases their talents and accomplishments won for them the friendship of their masters.

Amid their private grief and public consternation, the Athenians discovered that they were being deserted by their allies. Alcibíades was inciting revolts in Chios, which, along with Lesbos and Eubœa, solicited the assistance of Sparta to deliver them from the dominion of Athens. The two Persian satraps of Asia Minor sent envoys to Sparta, seeking her aid to overthrow the Athenian dominion in Asia Minor, and pledging Persian gold for the whole expense. To the disgrace of Sparta, she concluded a treaty at Milétus, to unite with Persia in a war against Athens and to reëstablish the Persian sway over all the Greek cities of Asia Minor which were formerly thus ruled. This clause was explained in a subsequent treaty to include all the islands of the Ægean and also Thessaly and Bœotia, thus abandoning the glorious field of Platæa to the Persians and establishing the Persian frontier on the very borders of Attica. Milétus itself was at once surrendered to Tissaphernes, the satrap of Lydia.

Amid the general defection of her allies, Samos remained faithful to Athens and afforded a very important station for the Athenian fleet during the remainder of the war. The Samians, taking warning from the example of Chios, overthrew their oligarchical government, and the democracy which took its place was acknowledged by Athens as an equal and independent ally. Athens now made great preparations. The reserve fund of a thousand talents, which had not been touched since the days of Pericles, was employed in fitting out a fleet against Chios. The Athenians were now again victorious by sea and land. They conquered Lesbos and Clazomenæ, defeated the Chians, and also the Spartans in a battle at Milétus. Milétus remained in the power of the Persians and the Spartans, but these allies no longer entertained a cordial friendship for each other. The Spartans felt disgraced by their alliance with the great enemy of the Hellenic race, and Tissaphernes was now under the influence of Alcibíades, who persuaded the satrap that the true interests of Persia did not permit any power in Greece to become too powerful, but rather to let them exhaust each other in mutual hostilities, and then seize the territories of both. This advice operated mostly to the disadvantage of the Spartans, who were now so strongly reinforced that they might have soon put an end to the war. Accordingly Tissaphernes kept the Lacedæmonian fleet inactive, waiting for the Phœnicians, who were never to make their appearance; and when this pretext was no longer available, his gold was employed in bribing the Spartan commanders to cease from active operations.

Alcibíades now endeavored to bring Tissaphernes into alliance with Athens, and when he failed in this he sought to convince his Athenian countrymen at Samos that he was able to bring about such an alliance, as he only desired to be recalled to his native city. As he hated and feared the Athenian democracy, he demanded, as the price of his intercession with the Persian satrap, that a revolution should be effected in Athens by which the oligarchical government should be established. The Athenian generals at Samos agreed to his project, and Pisander was sent to Athens to organize the political clubs in favor of the contemplated oligarchical revolution.

When Pisander announced the project of Alcibíades in the popular assembly at Athens, a great tumult ensued. The people remonstrated against the surrender of their rights, and the Eumolpidæ protested against the return of a wretch who had been guilty of profaning the Eleusinian Mysteries. Pisander was only allowed to plead the exhaustion and the misery of the republic, but this plea was irrefutable, however distasteful it may have been. The people agreed to the change in the constitution with great reluctance, and Pisander was sent with ten colleagues to treat with Alcibíades. The exile was well aware that he had promised more than he could fulfill; and, to save his credit, he received the eleven ambassadors in the presence of the Persian satrap, and made such extravagant demands in his name that they broke up the conference in anger and retired.

Though these ambassadors had been deceived by Alcibíades, they had proceeded too far to recede from the contemplated revolution. Pisander returned to Athens with five of his colleagues, while the other five went about among the allies of Athens to establish oligarchies. The old offices were abolished at Athens, where a Council of Four Hundred, mostly self-constituted, ruled for four months (B. C. 411). This council was authorized to convoke an assembly of five thousand of the leading citizens for advice and aid in any emergency. As soon as these four hundred oligarchs were invested with power, they subverted every remnant of the free institutions of Athens. They treated the Athenian people with the greatest insolence and severity, and sought to perpetuate their usurped authority by raising a body of mercenary troops in the islands of the Ægean for the purpose of overawing and enslaving their fellow-citizens. When the Athenian army in the island of Samos received intelligence of the revolution in Athens and the tyrannical proceedings of the oligarchical faction, the soldiers indignantly refused to obey the new government and invited Alcibíades to return among them and aid them in restoring the democratic constitution. He complied with their request, and the troops chose him for their general as soon as he arrived in Samos. He then sent a message to Athens, ordering the four hundred oligarchs to relinquish their usurped authority at once, threatening them with deposition and death at his hands if they refused.

The message of Alcibíades reached Athens at the time of the greatest confusion and alarm. The four hundred oligarchs had quarreled among themselves and were on the point of appealing to the sword. The island of Eubœa, from which the Athenians had for some time mainly obtained their supplies of provisions, had again revolted from Athens, and the Athenian fleet which had been sent to reduce it to submission had been destroyed by the Spartans, so that the coast of Attica and the port of Athens itself were then without any defense.

In this distressing condition of affairs, the Athenian people, aroused to desperation, rose against their oppressors, overthrew the government of the four hundred oligarchs who had ruled for four months, and reëstablished their former republican institutions. Many of the oligarchs were accused of treason for their dealings with the Spartans. Most of them fled, but Archeptólemus and Antiphon were tried and executed.

The remaining portion of the Peloponnesian War was entirely maritime, and its scene of operations was on the coast of Asia Minor. By long practice and close collision with the Athenians, the Spartans had become almost equal to their great rivals in naval skill. Their attention to this arm of the service was attested by the annual appointment of the *navarchus*, an officer who for the time being exercised greater power than the kings, as he was above the jurisdiction of the Ephors.

Míndarus, the Spartan commander at Milétus, became so disgusted with the fickle policy of Tissaphernes that he sailed for the Hellespont, hoping to find the other Persian satrap of Asia Minor, Pharnabazus, more stable as an ally of Sparta. Míndarus was pursued by the Athenian fleet, under Thrasyllus, which, though smaller than the Spartan fleet, won a great victory in the strait between Sestos and Abydos (B. C. 411). Míndarus now sent for the allied fleet at Eubœa, but it was overtaken by a furious storm in passing Mount Athos and entirely destroyed. The Athenians followed up their victory by capturing Cyzicus, which had revolted from them; and several weeks afterward they won another great victory near Abydos, in consequence of the timely assistance of Alcibíades.

In the spring of B. C. 410 Míndarus besieged Cyzicus, and the Athenians resolved to relieve the town. They sailed up the Hellespont in the night and assembled at Proconnésus. Alcibíades sailed toward Cyzicus with his division of the Athenian fleet, and succeeded in enticing Míndarus to some distance from the harbor, while the other Athenian divisions stole between the Spartan fleet and the city and cut off the retreat of Míndarus. In the battle which followed Míndarus was slain, the Spartans and their Persian allies were routed, and the whole Peloponnesian fleet was captured, excepting the Syracusan vessels, which Hermócrates caused to be burned. This great Athenian naval victory restored the control of the Propontis and the trade of the Euxine to the Athenians. Ships laden with corn now reached Piræus, bringing relief to the starving poor of Athens; and the Spartan king Agis I., who still occupied the heights of Deceléa, in the forlorn hope of starving Athens into surrender, was utterly discouraged.

The Persian satrap Pharnabazus was in the meantime assisting the Spartans by all the means at his command. He fed and clothed, armed and paid their seamen, permitted them to cut timber in the forests of Mount Ida and to build their ships at his docks of Antandros. Through his aid, Chalcedon, on the Bosphorus, was able to make a defense of two years against Alcibíades, but it finally surrendered in B. C. 408; Selymbria and Byzantium being taken about the same time.

These repeated Athenian victories restored the credit of Alcibíades, who was in consequence welcomed back to Athens amid transports of joy, in B. C. 407. All the Athenian people met him at Piræus, with as much rejoicing and enthusiasm as when they had escorted him thither eight years previously, when he sailed on the fatal expedition to Sicily. Chaplets of flowers were showered upon his head, and amidst the most enthusiastic acclamations he proceeded to the Agora, where he addressed the assembly of the people in a speech of such eloquence and power that the people placed a crown of gold upon his head when he had finished, while they vested him with the supreme command of the military and naval forces of Athens. He protested his innocence before the Senate and the people. His sentence was reversed by acclamation, his confiscated property was restored to him, and the Eumolpidæ, or priests, were directed to revoke the curses which they had formerly pronounced upon him. Before he had departed with the large fleet and army now at his command, he determined to atone to Dêmêtêr for the sacrilege he had committed against her by burlesquing the Eleusinian Mysteries, celebrated in honor of that goddess. The sacred procession from Athens to Eleusis had been intermitted during these seven years, on account of the close proximity of the Spartan army. Alcibíades now postponed his departure, in order to escort and protect those who took part in the sacred ceremonies of the Mysteries.

When two new officers arrived upon the scene of war in the Ægean, the tide of battle turned against Athens. One of these officers was the younger Cyrus, the brother of the Persian king, Artaxerxes Mnemon.

RETURN OF ALCIBIADES TO ATHENS.

The other was Lysander, the new Spartan *navarchus*, who assumed the command of the Peloponnesian fleet at Ephesus. These two acted in unison in adopting measures for severe and unrelenting war against the Athenians. The Spartan admiral augmented the pay of his seamen with the gold which the Persian prince lavishly bestowed upon his ally. By this timely liberality, Lysander won over large numbers from the allies in the Athenian fleet, and rendered such as did not desert, dissatisfied and mutinous.

Alcibíades found the situation less favorable than he had hoped, upon arriving with the Athenian fleet. The Spartan troops were better paid and equipped than his own, and he resorted to levying forced contributions on friendly states, in order to raise funds. While he was absent on one of these forays he left the Athenian fleet in charge of one of his officers named Antíochus, who, contrary to express orders, engaged in battle with the Spartan fleet and was defeated with heavy loss. When the news of this event reached Athens a violent clamor was excited against Alcibíades, who was accused of having neglected his duty, and was in consequence dismissed from all his offices. Upon hearing of this, he left the fleet and retired to a fortress which he had constructed in the Thracian Chersonésus, where he gathered around him a band of military adventurers, with whose aid he engaged in a predatory warfare with the neighboring tribes of Thrace. Thus the fallen pupil of Socrates became a brigand and a pirate.

Alcibíades did not long survive his second disgrace. When he found his residence in Thrace insecure, because of the increasing power of his Spartan enemies, he crossed the Hellespont into Asia Minor and settled in Bithynia. But when he was there attacked and plundered by the Thracians, he proceeded into Phrygia, placing himself under the protection of the Persian satrap Pharnabazus. But the unfortunate chief was even followed thither by the unrelenting hostility of the Spartans, who privately urged Pharnabazus to put him to death. The treacherous Persian, in order to gain the favor of the Lacedæmonians, yielded to their wishes, and appointed two of his own relatives to assassinate the fallen chief whom he had promised to protect.

Alcibíades was then living in a small country village, when the assassins surrounded his house one night and set it on fire. Being roused from his sleep by the fire, he instantly realized the facts in the case. He hastily wrapped his robe around his left hand, grasped his dagger in his right, sprang through the flames, and safely reached the open air. His great fame for personal strength and valor deterred his assassins from resisting his attack at close quarters, or from trying to oppose his advance, but they retired a short distance and killed him with a shower of arrows. Timandra, who had accompanied Alcibíades in all his latter wanderings, was left alone to dress his body and perform his funeral obsequies.

Thus perished one of the ablest public men of ancient Greece, about the fortieth year of his age (B. C. 403). He was celebrated as a warrior, a statesman and an orator. He was noble and generous in his nature, and if he had not lacked integrity he would be worthy of our admiration. His want of principle and his ungovernable passions led him to the commission of many grievous blunders, which contributed vastly to aggravate the misfortunes which eventually overtook him.

After dismissing Alcibíades the Athenians appointed ten generals, with Conon at their head. When Conon arrived to assume command of the Athenian fleet, Callicrátidas superseded Lysander as the Spartan *navarchus* (B. C. 406). Callicrátidas was coldly received both by his own Lacedæmonian countrymen and by their Persian allies, whom Lysander had designedly prejudiced against him. Cyrus refused to see him or assist him. Callicrátidas thereupon sailed to Milétus and urged its citizens to renounce the Persian alliance. Many wealthy citizens aided him with liberal contributions of money, with which he equipped fifty new triremes and sailed to Lesbos with a fleet twice as large as that of the Athenians.

Callicrátidas engaged in a battle with Conon in the harbor of Mitylênê, in which the Athenians lost almost half of their ships and only saved the remainder by drawing them ashore under the walls of the city. The victorious Spartan commander then blockaded Mitylênê by sea and land; and the younger Cyrus, seeing his success, aided him with supplies of money. Athens made great efforts as soon as Conon's condition was known. A large Athenian fleet was sent out in a few days, and, after being reinforced by the allies at Samos, reached the south-eastern extremity of Lesbos, numbering one hundred and fifty vessels. Callicrátidas left fifty ships to continue the blockade of Mitylênê, and sailed to meet his adversary.

A long and terrible conflict ensued, but Callicrátidas was at length cast overboard and drowned, and the Athenians were victorious. The Spartans had lost twenty-seven vessels, and their fleet at Mitylênê hastily retired, leaving the harbor open for Conon to escape.

At the beginning of the next year (B. C. 405), Lysander was again entrusted with the command of the Spartan fleet. As his numbers were still inferior to those of the Athenian fleet, he avoided an engagement, but he crossed the Ægean to the coast of Attica for a personal interview with King Agis I., and then sailed to the Hellespont, where he laid siege to Lampsacus. The Athenian fleet under Conon pursued him, but did not arrive in time to save the town from capture. Conon stationed his fleet at Ægos-Potamos (Goat's River), on the northern or European side of the Hellespont, with the design of provoking the Lacedæmonian fleet to an engagement. The Athenians were upon a barren plain; but the Spartans were better situated and abundantly supplied with provisions, and were therefore in no great hurry to commence the conflict. Alcibíades, then living in his own castle in that vicinity, perceived the peril of his Athenian countrymen and advised their commanders to remove to Sestos, but his counsels were resented as impertinent. The Athenians ascribed the delay of the Lacedæmonians to cowardice, and gradually became more and more negligent of discipline.

Finally Lysander improved the opportunity when the Athenian seamen were dispersed over the country, and crossed the narrow strait with the whole Spartan force, in September, B. C. 405. Only a dozen vessels of the Athenian fleet, under the personal command of Conon, were fit for battle; and the entire fleet, excepting the flag-ship, the sacred Páralus, and eight or ten others, were captured by the Spartans without a blow. Three or four thousand prisoners, including officers and men, were massacred, in revenge for the cruelties which the Athenians had recently inflicted upon their captives. The disaster to the Athenian navy at Ægos-Potamos was the death-blow to the Athenian empire. Chalcedon, Byzantium and Mitylênê shortly afterwards surrendered to the triumphant Lacedæmonians; and all the Athenian towns, except that of Samos, submitted to the victorious foe without resistance. The Spartans everywhere subverted popular governments and established a new form of oligarchy, composed of ten citizens, with a Spartan officer, called a *harmost*, at their head.

Intelligence of the great calamity which had befallen Athens reached Piræus at night. A cry of grief and despair immediately spread from the port to Athens itself, as each person informed his neighbor of the dreadful tidings. Says Xenophon, who was then in Athens: "That night no man slept." The next morning the assembly of the people was convened to deliberate upon measures for the preservation of the city. The situation of Athens was most desperate, as her very existence was at stake. Even if no hostile force approached the city, Lysander could reduce it by starvation, as he held command of the Euxine. The number of Athenian citizens was so diminished that even criminals could not be spared from the public service. All prisoners were liberated, with the exception of a few murderers and desperate villains. Private offenses were lost sight of in the common peril, and all Athenians united in a solemn oath of mutual forgiveness.

Two months after the Athenian calamity at Ægos-Potamos, Lysander reached Ægina with an overwhelming Spartan naval force; while the Peloponnesian army at the same time encamped in the shady groves of Académia, near the gates of Athens. Although starvation was already creating havoc among the Athenians, they were still resolute in spirit; and when the Spartan Ephors offered peace on condition that Athens should consent to the destruction of her Long Walls, an Athenian Senator was imprisoned for simply discussing the acceptance of such terms. When the Athenians finally sent offers of surrender, three months were consumed in useless debate before the terms were agreed upon. The Thebans and the Corinthians insisted upon an unconditional surrender, and that the very name of Athens should be extinguished, the city to be entirely destroyed, and the Athenian people to be sold into slavery. The Spartans, more generous, refused to "put out one of the eyes of Greece," or to enslave a people who had performed such great services to the entire Hellenic race in the great emergency of the Persian invasion.

It was ultimately agreed that the Long Walls and the fortifications of Piræus should be destroyed, that the Athenian ships of war should be surrendered, that all Athenian exiles should be restored to citizenship, and that Athens should relinquish all her foreign possessions (B. C. 404). These severe conditions were enforced with unnecessary insolence. Lysander himself presided at the demolition of the walls; and the work, which was difficult on account of the solidity of the walls, was turned into a kind of festal celebration. A chorus of flute-players and dancers, wreathed in flowers, encouraged and enlivened the workmen engaged in the task; and as the stupendous walls built under the auspices of Pericles fell, stone by stone, the army of destruction sent up shouts of triumph, as they regarded this day as the dawn of the liberties of the Grecian states which had so long been held under the domination of Athens.

Thus ended the Athenian supremacy in Greece (B. C. 404), after a continuance of seventy-three years from the date of the formation of the Confederacy of Delos (B. C. 477–B. C. 404). The power which had been conferred on Athens for the common defense against the Persians had in some instances been exercised by her in an oppressive manner over her subject allies, and her later history is disgraced by many cruel acts. Though the political ascendency of Athens thus ceased to exist, her intellectual dominion has remained imperishable; as her art, poetry, oratory and philosophy have continued to reign supreme in the civilized world to the present time for a period of over two thousand years.

SECTION XIII.—SUPREMACIES OF SPARTA AND THEBES.

SPARTA, in alliance with Persia, became the leading state of Greece after the downfall of the Athenian ascendency by the capture of Athens by Lysander. All the Grecian cities yielded to the influence of Lacedæmon by abolishing their free governments and establishing oligarchies in their stead. Athens herself abolished her democratic constitution, and her government was entrusted by the Spartans to thirty officers, whose oppressive, rapacious and sanguinary administration ere long obtained for them the title of the *Thirty Tyrants*, by which designation they have always been known in history.

Critias was the leader of these unjust and cruel rulers, who unscrupulously put to death all whom they suspected of being friendly to free institutions, or who had wealth that might be confiscated. As Critias had been formerly banished from Athens by a vote of the people, he now wreaked his revenge with the utmost cruelty upon the best and noblest citizens. Blood was the order of the day; and imprisonments, fines and confiscations were of hourly occurrence. By the advice of Therámenes, who headed a more moderate party, three thousand citizens were selected from the partisans of the Thirty Tyrants, whose sanction was indispensable to important proceedings. But all, except this enfranchised class, were placed beyond the protection of law and were liable to be put to death at any moment at the word of the tyrants, without even the form of a trial. A list was made of those who were destined to be put to death, and any of the ruling party were allowed to add such names to this list as either avarice or hate suggested. The wealthiest citizens were the first victims, as the estate of the murdered man reverted to his accuser. Therámenes, in his turn, was offered a wealthy alien to assassinate and plunder, but rejected the proposition with indignation. This refusal implied a protest against the reign of terror, for which he paid with his life. He was denounced as a public enemy, his name was stricken off from the role of the Thirty Tyrants and also from that of the Three Thousand, and he was sentenced to immediate execution. He sprang to the altar in the Senate-House; but there was no longer any fear of divine vengeance, nor any humanity or justice, in the rulers of Athens. He was taken to prison and condemned to drink the poison hemlock. The executions in Athens were so numerous that more Athenians perished during the eight months in which the Thirty Tyrants ruled than during the severest ten years of the Peloponnesian War. Multitudes of Athenians fled from their blood-stained city and sought refuge in Bœotia and other neighboring Grecian states.

The reaction had already set in, both in ill-fated Athens and throughout Greece. In her humiliation, Athens no longer excited the fear or jealousy of her former allies; while Sparta was setting up a new empire in Greece far more oppressive than that of her fallen rival, instead of proceeding in such a manner as to deserve the title of "Liberator of the Greeks." Even in Sparta itself, Lysander's pride and harshness aroused discontent, and the Thirty Tyrants of Athens were regarded by every one as the instruments of his scheming ambition.

A small band of Athenian exiles in Thebes at last resolved upon striking a blow for the deliverance of their countrymen, and placed themselves under the leadership of Thrasybúlus, an able Athenian general, then also living in exile in Bœotia, and seized the fortress of Phyle, in the mountain barrier of Attica, on the road to Athens; and this fortress at once became the rallying-point for the friends of Athenian freedom. Thrasybúlus soon found himself at the head of seven hundred men. The Thirty Tyrants, with the Spartan garrison in the Acropolis and the Three Thousand, marched out to attack them, but were repulsed with vigor, while a snow-storm interfered with their purpose to lay siege to the fortress, and they were obliged to retire to the city. Perceiving the doom of their power, the Thirty now committed another horrible atrocity, in order to secure for themselves a place of refuge. They caused all the inhabitants of Salamis and Eleusis capable of bearing arms to be brought as prisoners to Athens, while the towns were occupied with garrisons in their own interest; after which they filled the Odeon with Spartan soldiers and the Three Thousand, and extorted from this assembly a vote for the instant massacre of the prisoners from Salamis and Eleusis.

The repulse of the force which the tyrants had sent against Thrasybúlus encouraged many Athenian citizens to flock to his standard, and he soon found himself strong enough to attempt the deliverance of Athens itself. Supported by the popular indignation at the brutal tyranny of the Thirty, Thrasybúlus marched with a thousand men to Piræus, seized the port without opposition, and fortified himself upon its castle-hill, Munychia. The entire Spartan party in Athens marched against him, but was defeated with heavy loss, Critias himself being slain. This unexpected success of Thrasybúlus filled the Thirty and their unscrupulous adherents with consternation; and shortly afterward the citizens of Athens, emboldened by the repulse of the tyrants in their attack upon Thrasybúlus, rose in open revolt, deposed the Thirty, who had reigned only eight months, and appointed a *Council of Ten* in their stead, to administer the government of Athens provisionally and to effect an understanding with Thrasybúlus and his followers in Piræus.

But the Council of Ten had no sooner been entrusted with authority by the Athenian people than its members began to show a disposition as antagonistic to popular rights as that exhibited by the Thirty Tyrants; and, instead of seeking to bring about a reconciliation of parties, they sent ambassadors to Sparta to solicit assistance to crush the insurrection of Thrasybúlus. Messengers also arrived at Sparta with a like request from the deposed Thirty Tyrants, who, after their overthrow, had retired to Eleusis. The Lacedæmonians readily complied with the requests made to them, and sent Lysander with an army to force the Athenians to submit to the government of the Thirty Tyrants. While Lysander entered Athens with a Spartan army, his brother blockaded Piræus with a Lacedæmonian fleet.

Lysander would probably have compelled Thrasybúlus to surrender, had not a party hostile to him obtained the ascendency in Sparta in this critical emergency. This party was anxious to prevent Lysander from acquiring the glory of conquering Athens a second time, and for this reason they appointed Pausánias to the chief command of the Lacedæmonian army in Attica, whither he instantly proceeded at the head of a large army. After being first repulsed, Pausánias defeated Thrasybúlus. As soon as Pausánias had arrived at Piræus he showed an indisposition to continue the war began for the purpose of replacing Lysander's partisans in an authority which they had so grossly misused, and, with his sanction, a treaty was concluded between the Athenians in the city and those holding possession of Piræus.

This pacification provided for a general amnesty for all past offenses, except those of the Thirty Tyrants and their eleven cruel executioners, and those of the Council of Ten; while the democratic institutions of Athens were to be reëstablished. The exiles were restored, and Thrasybúlus and his comrades marched in solemn procession from Piræus, to present their thank-offerings to Athênê on the Acropolis. An assembly of the people afterwards annulled all the acts of the Thirty Tyrants, restored the archons, the judges, and the Senate, or Council of Five Hundred, and ordered a revised code of the laws of Draco and Solon. Thrasybúlus and his party were rewarded with olive wreaths for their deliverance of Athens.

With a clemency which the Thirty Tyrants had never shown to others, those blood-thirsty monsters were permitted to reside safely at Eleusis. But these wretches, ungrateful for the leniency thus shown them, soon plotted for the subversion of the popular government at Athens. When the Athenians ascertained that these bad men were raising a body of mercenary troops to be employed against the liberties of the people, they marched to Eleusis and put the deposed tyrants and their chief supporters to death.

Athens, under her restored democracy, though fallen from her former greatness, rejoiced in the restoration of her old laws; while the city, the temples, and all the old customs and beliefs were regarded with increased veneration. This regard for the past displayed itself in its worst form in the condemnation and death of the immortal Socrates, the wisest, the most virtuous, and the most celebrated of Grecian philosophers. He did not belong to any political party, and opposed the extreme measures of both the aristocracy and the democracy. He had served the republic in civil capacities and had fought against its enemies on many battle-fields. He had ever used his power as a citizen on the side of justice and mercy. Critias, the leader of the cruel and tyrannical Thirty, had been his pupil, but when in power he hated and persecuted his former tutor. He was now accused by the restored democracy of despising the gods of Athens, of introducing religions innovations, and of corrupting the morals of the young.

Socrates was born at Athens in B. C. 470. His parents were in humble circumstances. His father, Sophroníscus, being a statuary of little reputation, while his mother was a midwife. In his youth, Socrates aided his father in his profession, but he subsequently relinquished the chisel and devoted himself to the more important duties of a public teacher. He received a good education, in spite of his father's limited means.

He began his career as a public teacher in a plain and unpretentious manner, which contrasted remarkably with the affected mystery and the ostentatious display of learning with which many of the Grecian tutors endeavored to win the attention and respect of the people. He went about without shoes and attired in a poor cloak at every season of the year; and, instead of confining himself to splendid halls and porticos, he passed the entire day in the public walks, the gymnasia, the market-place, the courts, and other places of general resort, reasoning and conversing on moral or philosophical questions with every one whom he met, rich or poor, learned or ignorant.

Wherever he went he was followed by a circle of admiring disciples, who acquired from him the spirit of free inquiry and were inspired with some of his zeal for the greatest good, for religion, for truth, and for virtue. Among the most famous of his disciples were Crito, Alcibíades, Xenophon, Plato, Aristíppus, Phædon, Cebes and Euclid. He taught them in ethics, politics, logic, rhetoric, arithmetic and geometry, and he read with them the works of the leading poets and pointed out their beauties.

He pointed out the difference between religion and impiety. He explained what constituted justice and injustice, reason and folly, courage and cowardice, the noble and ignoble. He spoke of systems of government and the qualities essential in a magistrate. He taught on other subjects with which every honorable man and every good citizen should be familiar. He gave a practical turn to all his inquiries, as he maintained that virtue is the object of all knowledge.

He sincerely believed in the existence of an omnipotent, omniscient, omnipresent and benignant God, the original cause and the ruler of the entire universe. The entire field of nature, and particularly the wonderful structure of the human body, appeared to him as furnishing abundant evidence of an intelligent Creator. He considered it rash to speculate upon the substance of this Great Being, and regarded it as sufficient to point out his spiritual nature in an intelligible light.

Although he believed in one God, the Supreme Ruler of the entire universe, he also recognized the existence of other deities whom he appears to have considered as subordinate intelligences, possessing a certain amount of influence over human affairs and deserving reverence and worship. He always spoke respectfully of the national religion of Greece and observed its prescribed rites with regularity.

Socrates was distinguished above every other Grecian philosopher for the unruffled serenity of his mind. He permitted no calamity to unbalance his temper. His wife, Xantippe, was noted for her violent temper. He was nevertheless extremely kind to her, and sought to smooth the roughness of her temper; and when he found all his efforts of no avail, he considered her frequent scoldings as an indispensable discipline, calculated to teach him patience and self-control.

Socrates always treated his body as though it were a servant, and inured it to privations of all kinds. Moderation became an easy virtue to him, and he retained his youthful vigor of body and mind to old age. He was ever ready to discharge his duties as a citizen, however they might conflict with his favorite studies and his professional work as a public instructor. He served in the armies of his country on three different occasions. First, at the age of thirty-nine, he took part in the siege of Potidæa, where he surpassed his fellow-soldiers in the ease with which he withstood the hardships of a winter campaign, distinguished himself by his bravery, saved the life of his young friend, Alcibíades, and subsequently, with commendable generosity, relinquished in his favor the prize of honor which his own valor had deserved. Seven years later Socrates bore arms the second time, and was one of the last to retreat from the field after the disastrous battle of Délium. During this retreat he saved the life of Xenophon who was severely wounded, and who, in gratitude for this service, wrote the life of his preceptor and benefactor, and transmitted to posterity the maxims of this great philosopher. Socrates would himself have been slain in this retreat, had it not been for the opportune aid of Alcibíades, who was thus enabled to repay the like service which his tutor had rendered him at the siege of Potidæa.

Socrates subsequently served the Athenian republic in a civil capacity. In his sixty-fifth year he became a member of the Council of Five Hundred, and attained the dignity of president—a position which none could fill for more than one day. On the day in which he exercised this duty, he obtained the acquittal of ten innocent men, who had been falsely accused by an angry party of citizens, who clamored for their execution; but no threats or violent language had the least particle of influence upon the inflexible justice of Socrates.

In the time of Socrates there was a class of teachers in Athens called *Sophists*, who deduced correct conclusions from false premises and were ready to defend vice as well as virtue. It was to destroy the influence of these Sophists that Socrates discoursed with the people in the streets and in the workshops of Athens. The great and good philosopher exposed the false reasonings and the pernicious doctrines of the Sophists, who professed to teach every branch of human knowledge, declaring that they *knew everything* and were familiar with law, politics, philosophy, the fine arts, etc. They frequently endeavored to embarrass and confound the great mind of Socrates himself, by means of their miserable quibbling and playing upon words. His eminent disciple, the philosopher Plato, has transmitted to us an amusing account of one of these disputations, in which two Sophists tried to prove to Socrates that he was able to speak and remain silent at the same time, that he had a father and had *no* father, that a dog was his father, and that his father was everybody's father.

The right and vigorous judgment of the great philosopher was too much for the subtleties of the Sophists, and in his contests with them he always succeeded in exposing the fallacies involved in their arguments and in drawing forth the truth from the errors and absurdities under which they had hidden it in so artful a manner. In his disputations with the Sophists, Socrates used with success his favorite and singular mode of arguing, by asking them a series of questions and leading them by degrees to make such admissions as proved fatal to their side of the question. By such means he overcame his opponents and really forced them to refute themselves with their own mouths. Socrates did not teach any system of philosophy; but, by enforcing the maxim "Know Thyself" upon his pupils, he sought to induce them to discover the truth for themselves.

Notwithstanding the great services which Socrates had rendered to his country and to the great cause of truth and virtue, he was destined to endure the full weight of popular ingratitude. The closing period of his life happened to fall in that unfortunate time for Athens when that state had sunk into a condition combining the worst evils of anarchy and despotism, consequent upon the calamitous results of the Peloponnesian War. Amid the general immorality then prevailing in Athens, in consequence of the revolution in the government, hatred and envy discovered opportunities to carry out their nefarious designs. A base faction, under the leadership of a young Milésian, accused Socrates before the assembly of the people of having introduced new gods and of denying the old deities of the state, alleging that by this and other practices he had corrupted the minds of the young. The enemies of the great philosopher endeavored to support their accusations by perverted statements of his language and by expressions detached from the connection which modified them. Conscious of his moral purity, Socrates disdained to make a labored defense of his character. He had no fear of death nor any respect for his judges. With brevity and noble dignity, he showed that the charges against him lacked any foundation whatever, and alluded to the services which he had rendered to the republic. But the boldness and freedom with which he spoke only tended to excite his ignorant and prejudiced judges against him, and he was condemned, by a majority of three voices, to die by drinking poison.

Socrates was then led to prison to await the day on which he was to meet his death. His mind continued tranquil and undisturbed, and he was still consoled by a clear conscience and by religious and moral feeling. The execution of the death-sentence was delayed by an accidental circumstance. The day after his condemnation was the one on which the sacred vessel, Páralus, sailed on its annual mission from Athens for the sacred isle of Delos, with offerings to the god Apollo; and, in accordance with ancient usage, no execution could take place until this consecrated ship's return. The great philosopher thus obtained a respite of thirty days, which was an important delay for him and his disciples. His friends assembled in his apartment every morning, and he conversed with them, as was his habit to do. He encouraged them in the path of virtue, instructed them in the subjects which he had investigated, and, by his own example, showed them that real happiness followed obedience to his precepts. In his hours of solitude he composed a hymn to Apollo and arranged in verse several of Æsop's fables. The resignation of Socrates contrasted remarkably with the grief of his friends, at the thought of his approaching death. They contrived a plan for his escape and bribed the jailor, but the consent of Socrates himself was necessary to the success of the project. From his known principles, his friends feared that the philosopher would not sanction their scheme, but they resolved to make the effort. Crito, his old and tried friend, sought to persuade him to agree to their plans.

Early in the morning of the next to the last day, Crito visited Socrates with this end in view. As the good man was still asleep, Crito sat down gently beside his bed and waited until he awoke, when he was informed by Crito concerning the unanimous request of his friends, urging every motive suggested by the singular circumstances of Socrates, especially the care of his family, to induce him to save his life, if possible. After Crito had finished, Socrates thanked him for this evidence of his affection, but declared that he could not reconcile flight with his principles.

Finally the fatal day arrived when he was to drink the poison. His family and friends gathered early to pass the last hours with him. His wife, Xantippe, was intensely affected, and expressed her grief by loud cries. Socrates made a signal to Crito to have her removed, as he desired to pass his last moments in tranquillity. The philosopher then talked with his friends, first respecting his verses; then regarding suicide, of which he disapproved in strong terms; and lastly, in reference to the immortality of the soul—a doctrine in which he firmly believed. He passed most of the day in these interesting discussions, and spoke with such feeling and confidence of his hopes of enjoying the happy society of the good and the great in the next world that he seemed to his friends to be already more like a glorified spirit than a dying man.

The approach of daybreak at length warned him that the fatal hour had arrived.

He asked for the cup of poison hemlock; and when he took it into his hand his friends were overwhelmed with such grief that they burst into tears and loud lamentations. Socrates alone was calm and composed. He slowly drank the hemlock, and then consoled his friends as he walked up and down the apartment. When he found it difficult to walk, he lay himself down upon his couch; and, before the vital spark had left him, he exclaimed: "My friends, we owe a cock—the emblem of life—to Esculapius." This reference to the god of medicine evinced his desire to honor the religious usages of his country in his final moments. He then covered his head with his cloak, and passed away in the seventieth year of his age (B. C. 399).

Soon after his death, his fickle countrymen repented of their harsh treatment towards him, acknowledged his innocence, and considered their calamities a punishment for their injustice towards him. They reversed his sentence, put his accusers to death, banished others who had plotted his destruction, and erected a brazen statue in his honor. His memory was so revered that the different philosophical sects which afterwards arose, all claimed to have originated from his school, and were proud to be honored by his name, even while they rejected or misrepresented his doctrines.

History has preserved an affecting incident in connection with the death of Socrates. A Spartan youth who heard of his fame and wisdom so anxiously desired to see the philosopher that he traveled to Athens on foot for that purpose. Upon arriving at the gates of the celebrated city, he inquired for Socrates; and upon being informed that the great and good man had died by the decree of his own countrymen, his grief and horror knew no bounds. The sorrowing youth turned from the city and inquired for the tomb of Socrates, going thither and bursting into tears as soon as he had reached the spot. He slept upon the tomb that night, and the next morning started on his sad journey back to Lacedæmon.

As we have already observed, the immediate result of the Peloponnesian War was to transfer to Sparta the political ascendancy previously exercised in the affairs of Greece by Athens; and for some years the Lacedæmonians exercised an almost unlimited supremacy over the other Grecian states.

The Elians were the first to feel the unrestricted power of Sparta. As guardians of the sacred grove at Olympia, where the Olympic Games were celebrated, they had excluded the Spartans from the national games at the time when the Athenians appeared with such magnificence under the direction of Alcibiades, and they had likewise borne arms against them, as allies of the Argives and the Mantinéans (B. C. 420–B. C. 416). They had capped the climax of their insults by ejecting the Spartan king Agis I. from their temple when he had come with sacrifices to consult the oracle. Agis now demanded satisfaction, and when the Elians refused to give it, he invaded Elis with a large Lacedæmonian army, but retired in superstitious alarm upon the occurrence of an earthquake (B. C. 402). The next year he recovered his courage; and with a large number of allies, among whom were even the Athenians, he overran and plundered the sacred land and performed by forcible means the sacrifice which he had not been permitted to offer peaceably. This victorious expedition encouraged the Spartan king to direct his vengeance against the Messenians who had been settled in the Laconian territory or upon the adjacent islands, and he drove away or enslaved all of them (B. C. 401).

King Agis I. died the following year (B. C. 400), and was succeeded in his crown by his brother Agesilaüs, who was brave, honest and energetic—virtues which the circumstances of his reign demanded. The alliance between Sparta and Persia and the pecuniary assistance which the Persians had rendered to the Spartans contributed largely to the Lacedæmonian triumph over Athens in the Peloponnesian War, as that aid enabled the Spartans to pay and provision the large army and navy which they were obliged to maintain. But the countenance and aid which the Lacedæmonians gave to the younger Cyrus in his unsuccessful attempt to wrest the Persian crown from his brother, King Artaxerxes Mnemon, in B. C. 401, brought on a renewal of the old hostility between the Greeks and the Persians.

In compliance with the request of Cyrus for Spartan aid in his revolt against his brother, the Lacedæmonians requited him for the assistance he had extended to them against Athens in the Peloponnesian War, by sending him a detachment of eight thousand heavy-armed troops and ordering their admiral on the Ionian coast to coöperate with the fleet of Cyrus and to act in obedience to his orders. The Spartans also granted Cyrus permission to raise recuits in every part of Greece, so that he soon had a force of about thirteen thousand Grecian mercenaries, over ten thousand of whom were heavy-armed, and the remainder targeteers. At Sardis, the capital of Lydia, the Greek auxiliaries joined the main body of the army of Cyrus, composed of a hundred thousand Asiatics; and soon afterward the entire army, led by this Persian prince in person, began its famous march towards the heart of the Medo-Persian Empire.

Xenophon, a young Athenian who had been a pupil of Socrates, and who afterwards became so renowned as a historian, accompanied the expedition of Cyrus as a volunteer, and afterwards wrote an account of it, which is yet preserved, under the name of Xenophon's Anábasis, and which is universally recognized as one of the most masterly and beautiful pieces of narration ever produced. After advancing over fifteen hundred miles without any serious opposition, the army of Cyrus, numbering one hundred and ten thousand men, of whom thirteen thousand were Greek mercenaries, encountered the army of his brother, King Artaxerxes Mnemon, numbering, according to Plutarch, nine hundred thousand men, but according to Ctesias, only four hundred thousand, on the plain of Cunaxa, about fifty-seven miles from Babylon; as we have seen in the history of Persia, where the battle has been fully described. The advantages which were gained by the victory of the Greek auxiliaries in the army of Cyrus over that portion of the army of Artaxerxes Mnemon opposed to them were lost in consequence of the death of Cyrus, who was slain in his imprudent eagerness to kill his brother. His severed head was exposed to the view of both armies, and this so disheartened his troops that they retired from the field, thus abandoning the conflict.

The Greek auxiliaries, who had pursued the defeated left wing of the army of Artaxerxes Mnemon for a distance of some miles, did not hear of the death of Cyrus until the day after the battle. Flushed with recent success, they were unwilling to relinquish the enterprise in which they had engaged with high hopes, even after they had ascertained that they had lost their leader; and they therefore sought to induce Ariæus, on whom the command of the Asiatic troops of Cyrus now devolved, to continue the war against Artaxerxes Mnemon, by promising him an easy triumph and the Medo-Persian crown as his reward. But Ariæus was very well convinced that all hopes of bringing the enterprise to a successful end had departed with the life of Cyrus, and he therefore declined the flattering offers of the Greek mercenaries, at the same time inviting them to accompany him in the retreat which he at once began in the direction of Asia Minor. The Greeks consented with reluctance, and the retreat was accordingly commenced, the route selected extending almost directly northward along the banks of the river Tigris. By the command of King Artaxerxes Mnemon, Tissaphernes, one of the Persian satraps of Asia Minor, soon afterwards solicited a conference with the Grecian leaders, and offered to give them a safe conduct to the coast and to supply them with provisions during the journey, if they would refrain from any further hostile acts and return home as hastily as possible. Tissaphernes also entered into a secret negotiation with Ariæus, and, by menaces and

THE RETURN OF THE TEN THOUSAND UNDER XENOPHON.

promises, induced him to renew his allegiance to Artaxerxes Mnemon and to aid in the king's project for harassing and destroying the Greek auxiliary force. At length, when the retreating army had arrived at the banks of the Zabatus, a tributary of the Tigris, the perfidious Tissaphernes executed the atrocious designs which he had for some time contemplated.

The treacherous satrap first enticed into his tent Cleárchus, the Greek commander-in-chief, along with four other Grecian generals and many inferior officers, under the pretext of holding a conference; after which he caused them to be apprehended and their attendants who remained outside to be massacred. He then sent Ariæus to inform the Greeks that Cleárchus had been put to death for having violated the treaty with the King of Persia, but that the other generals were safe. The fate of these unfortunate officers remained a mystery for a long time, but it was finally ascertained that Tissaphernes had sent them to Artaxerxes Mnemon, who caused them all to be put to death.

The Greeks were thrown into the utmost dismay at being thus deprived of their leaders, in the midst of a hostile people, at a distance of two thousand miles from home; but the difficulties and perils which surrounded them awakened the energies of Xenophon, who, although having no authority in the army, assumed the command in this emergency, assembled the remaining officers, exhorted them to act with a vigor and decision worthy of the Grecian name, reminding them of the heroic exploits of their brave ancestors in circumstances equally as discouraging. His eloquent address powerfully influenced all who heard it. New officers were chosen at once to supply the places of those who had been the victims of the treachery of Tissaphernes, and Xenophon was elected commander of one of the divisions. The troops were formed into a hollow square, with the baggage in the middle, and commenced the celebrated march which history has recorded under the title of *The Retreat of the Ten Thousand.*

The pursuing Persians for some time hung upon the rear of the retreating Greeks as they slowly marched toward the distant shores of the Euxine, and harassed them with their skirmishing parties; but their fear of Grecian prowess prevented them from venturing upon a general engagement, notwithstanding their overwhelming numerical superiority over the Greeks. After having endured great hardships from want of provisions, from the attacks of the barbarous tribes occupying the countries through which their line of retreat led them, and from the intense severity of an Armenian winter, the Greeks at length arrived at Mount Theches, from which the Euxine is visible, although more than fifty miles distant. Weary with their long and perilous journey, the soldiers, upon reaching the summit of this mountain and contemplating the cheering prospect presented to them, burst out into a simultaneous and enthusiastic shout of the "The sea! the sea!" They embraced each other and wept for joy at the bright hopes of returning to their homes and their friends.

A few days later they reached the Greek city of Trapezus (now Trebizond), on the southern shore of the Euxine, after having marched more than a thousand miles through a hostile and naturally-difficult country with remarkably little loss. At Cerasus, another Grecian city at which they soon arrived, their forces were mustered, which showed that eight thousand six hundred men of the original ten thousand heavy-armed still survived. From Cerasus they proceeded, partly by land and partly by water, to Byzantium. Instead of returning to their respective states in Greece, these gallant survivors of the Retreat of the Ten Thousand became adventurers, first entering the service of Seuthes, a Thracian prince, and afterwards joining the Spartan army in Asia Minor.

King Artaxerxes Mnemon did not readily forget or forgive the aid afforded his brother Cyrus by the Greeks. After harassing, to the extent of his ability, the retreat of the auxiliaries under Xenophon, the Persian satrap, Tissaphernes, in accordance with his sovereign's orders, led his forces against the Greek colonies in Asia Minor, to take revenge upon them for the hostile conduct of the parent states in European Greece. Sparta, as the chief abettor of the designs of Cyrus, and as the virtual master of all Greece in consequence of her triumph over Athens in the Peloponnesian War, was naturally the chief object of the jealousy and resentment of the Persian king. While Sparta's elevation to the first rank in Greece rendered her a prominent mark for the enemy, it also brought along with it the means of resisting foreign aggression, which the Spartans very soon put in force. When they received information of the predicament in which their Asiatic allies and dependencies were placed, they instantly dispatched an army to Ionia, under the command of Thimbron, who was joined by Xenophon, with a portion of the remnant of the Ten Thousand.

The Persian satrap Tissaphernes now endeavored to drive the Greeks from all their cities on the coasts of Asia Minor. Though Thimbron succeeded in regaining possession of Pergamus and several other Greek cities, he was speedily recalled, and Dercyllidas was appointed to command the Lacedæmonian forces in Asia Minor. The new Spartan commander for some time conducted the war with ability, but was also soon recalled, though not disgraced. The third Spartan commander was the renowned Agesilaüs, one of the greatest Spartan kings and generals.

Agesilaüs had become one of the joint Kings of Sparta upon the death of his predecessor and elder brother, Agis I., to the exclusion of the late king's son. He was small in stature and afflicted with lameness, but was admirably adapted to guiding the helm of state in those eventful and troublous times. He was possessed of great vivacity of temper and energy of spirit, of powerful talents and invincible resolution, being at the same time gifted with a submissive gentleness and docility of temper, a power of bearing reprimand and listening to reason, which delighted his friends and his followers as much as his bold vehemence awed his foes in the council or in the field. Such was the character of the prince who assumed the management of the Spartan war against Persia in B. C. 396. Upon arriving in Asia Minor, Agesilaüs established his headquarters at Ephesus, and in this city he wintered his troops during the several ensuing campaigns. After the Spartan army had arrived at Ephesus, in B. C. 396, they spent the winter in busy preparations, which thus gave the wealthy city the appearance of one vast arsenal. In the spring of B. C. 395, Agesilaüs advanced upon Sardis and put the Persian cavalry to flight. The Persians were defeated in every encounter, while the triumphant Spartans enriched themselves with the plunder of the Persian camp and ravaged the country almost under the very eyes of the satrap Tissaphernes. The Spartan leader had not only to contend with his enemies in the open field, but he likewise had to be on his guard against the artful diplomacy of Tissaphernes, who, aware of his inability to cope with Agesilaüs in war, sought to allure him by pretended proposals of peace. Agesilaüs was not thus easily deceived. He proceeded in his military operations with equal caution and boldness, and signalized his second campaign by an important victory over his enemies on the banks of the river Pactolus. This defeat eventually cost Tissaphernes his life, as his irritated and ungrateful sovereign caused him to be put to death soon after the engagement.

The unfortunate Tissaphernes was succeeded in the command of the Persian forces in Asia Minor by the other Persian satrap, Pharnabazus, who was just as unable to cope with the able Spartan leader. But the brilliant military career of Agesilaüs in Asia Minor was at length brought to a termination by causes beyond his control.

Well knowing the influence of gold over the proceedings of the Grecian states, the Persians were unceasing in their efforts, by means of bribes and diplomacy, to arouse discontents against Sparta and to subvert her interests among the other Grecian states, while Agesilaüs was conducting his brilliant and destructive campaigns in Asia Minor. Venal hirelings were easily found, to undertake the task of disseminating dissensions among the allies of Sparta. Thebes, Corinth and Argos were the first Grecian cities to manifest hostility to Sparta. An offensive league was formed against the Lacedæmonians, and Athens was ere long induced to join this alliance against the power which had destroyed her supremacy. The Spartans made vigorous preparations to oppose their new enemies.

The Lacedæmonians raised a large army, and entrusted the chief command of it to Lysander, the conqueror of Athens. This great and experienced commander led his forces into the Theban territories, in order to end the struggle by a decisive blow; but he was surprised under the walls of Haliártus by the Thebans, his army being routed and himself slain (B. C. 395).

Pausánias, who arrived on the field too late to give the necessary aid to avert the defeat, did not dare to return to Sparta with the defeated army, but took refuge in the temple of Athênê at Tegea; and, as his countrymen had sentenced him to death, he spent the rest of his life in that sanctuary. His son, Agesípolis, succeeded him as one of the joint Kings of Sparta.

The Theban victory at Haliártus confirmed the courage of the four allied Grecian states and encouraged many of the minor states to join the league against Sparta. Thus Athens, Corinth, Argos and Thebes were strengthened in their alliance by the addition of Eubœa, Acarnania, Western Locris, Ambracia, Leucadia, and Chalcidice in Thrace. The allies assembled a large army at Corinth in the spring of B. C. 394, and it was proposed to march directly upon Sparta and "burn the wasps in their nests before they could come forth to sting." But the Spartans had advanced to Sicyon by the time that the allies arrived at Nemea, and the latter found themselves obliged to fall back for the protection of Corinth, where they were attacked and defeated by the Spartans (July, B. C. 394).

The situation of affairs had become so alarming to Sparta after the Spartan defeat at Haliártus that messengers were sent to Agesilaüs in Asia Minor, asking him to return at once to the defense of his country. Though in the midst of such triumphs as induced him to contemplate the subversion of the very throne of Persia, the Spartan king instantly obeyed the order for his return (B. C. 394), declaring that "a general only deserved the name when he was guided by the laws of the country and obeyed its magistrates." In one month Agesilaüs made his way across the Thracian Chersonésus and the plains of Thessaly until he reached the Bœotian territories, taking the very route which had detained the effeminate Xerxes an entire year. When Agesilaüs heard of the Spartan victory at Corinth, he exclaimed: "Alas for Greece! she has killed enough of her sons to have conquered all the barbarians."

The approach of so great a warrior as Agesilaüs did not alarm the Thebans and their allies. They advanced to meet him; and at Coronæa, thirty miles from Thebes, a fierce battle was fought. The Thebans were at first successful, and after they had routed the Orchomenians they pressed to their camp in the rear, which they plundered; while Agesilaüs had in the meantime triumphed along the remainder of the line and routed the allies, compelling them to seek refuge upon the slope of Mount Helicon. The Thebans were thus surrounded and were obliged to sustain the entire weight of the Spartan assault; and no other battle like this had ever been fought by Grecians. The Thebans finally succeeded in rejoining the defeated and routed hosts of their allies; but the victory belonged to the Spartan king, as he remained master of the field (B. C. 394).

While the Lacedæmonians had thus won the two victories of Corinth and Coronæa on land, in the year B. C. 394, their navy suffered a most disastrous defeat at Cnidus about the same time. After his calamitous defeat at Ægos-Potamos, just before the close of the Peloponnesian War, Conon, the Athenian admiral, retired to Cyprus, where he passed seven years in a kind of honorable exile, under the protection of Evagoras, the friendly and virtuous king of that island. Though Conon lived here peacefully and happily, his patriotic spirit lamented unceasingly the fate which had overtaken Athens. But Evagoras was not sufficiently powerful to furnish the essential means for the restoration of the Athenian republic to its former grandeur, even though a favorable opportunity seemed to present itself while Sparta was engaged in her wars in Asia Minor against the Persians.

In these circumstances, Conon determined to apply to the Persian king for assistance. Being supplied with recommendations to Artaxerxes Mnemon by Evagoras, who was the Great King's tributary, the patriotic Athenian passed over to Asia and had a personal interview with the Persian monarch, who supplied him with money sufficient to enable him to equip a powerful fleet which was manned principally by the Greeks of Rhodes and Cyprus. In pursuance of an agreement, Conon and the warlike Persian satrap Pharnabazus were jointly placed in command of this fleet.

Thus Conon now reappeared in alliance with the old enemy of Greece against the bitter foe and rival of Athens. Seeing the antipathy beginning to be felt among the Grecian states against the growing power of Sparta, the King of Persia had sent envoys to all the leading cities of Greece to combine them in a league against the arrogant Lacedæmonians.

Desirous of retrieving the honor lost by him at Ægos-Potamos, Conon scoured the seas in quest of the fleet by which the Spartans maintained their sway over the Greek cities of Asia Minor. In command of his fleet, Conon was soon blockaded at Caunus by the Spartan fleet under Pharax; but when the Persians were reinforced, the blockading Lacedæmonian squadron retired to Rhodes. The inhabitants of that island had long reluctantly submitted to the dominion of the Spartans. They arose against Pharax, forced him to withdraw and placed themselves under the protection of Conon, who at once sailed to Rhodes and took possession of the island, after which he repaired to Babylon, where he obtained a still more liberal supply of money from the Persian monarch for the active prosecution of the war against Sparta.

With the assistance of Pharnabazus, who was now joined with Conon in command, the latter equipped a formidable fleet and offered battle to Pisánder, the Spartan admiral, off Cnidus, in Caria, in the South-west of Asia Minor. The Persian fleet, consisting mainly of Greeks and Phœnicians, was superior from the beginning, and especially when Pisánder was deserted, during the progress of the battle, by his Asiatic Greek allies. Nevertheless he fought with Spartan valor until his death ended the conflict. More than half the Spartan fleet was either taken or destroyed, more than fifty galleys falling into the hands of Conon and Pharnabazus (B. C. 394). In consequence of this Lacedæmonian defeat, the Spartan empire fell more rapidly than it had risen eight years before. Conon and Pharnabazus sailed from port to port, being hailed as deliverers by all the Asiatic Greeks. The Spartan *harmosts* everywhere fled before their arrival, and only Abydos and the Thracian Chersonésus withstood the power of Athens and Persia.

The next spring (B. C. 393). the united Athenian and Persian fleet under the joint command of Conon and Pharnabazus crossed the Ægean, ravaged the eastern coasts of Laconia, and placed an Athenian garrison in the island of Cythera. By gold and promises, the Persian commander assured the Greek allies whom he met at Corinth of his unfailing support of them against Sparta. Through the zealous efforts of Conon, who labored unceasingly for the welfare of Athens, the Persian king disbursed a large sum from his treasury to rebuild the walls and fortifications of Athens. By the enthusiastic labors of the Athenians and the assistance of the crews of the combined fleets of Athens and Persia, the Long Walls of Athens and the fortifications of Piræus were rebuilt; and Athens was restored to something like its former strength and splendor in a very short space of time. Conon's recent services more than effaced the memory of his former disasters, and his countrymen hailed him as a second founder of Athens and restorer of her greatness.

The war was thereafter prosecuted in the territory of Corinth, and the chief object of the allies was to guard the three passes in the mountains extending across the southern part of the Corinthian isthmus. The most northerly of these passes was defended by long walls, running from Corinth to Lechæum; the other two by strong garrisons of the allied troops. The Spartans were at Sicyon, whence they could easily ravage the fertile plain and plunder the countryseat of the wealthy Corinthians. The aristocratic party in Corinth already complained and longed for the old alliance with Sparta, but the dominant democratic faction invited an Argive company into the city and massacred many of the aristocracy, who avenged themselves by admitting Praxítas, the Spartan leader, inside their long walls; and a battle ensued within this confined space, in which the Corinthians were defeated. The victorious Spartans destroyed a large portion of the walls, after which they marched across the isthmus and captured two Corinthian towns on the Saronic Gulf.

The Athenians were so alarmed at the way thus opened for a Spartan invasion of Attica that they marched to the isthmus with a force of masons and carpenters and assisted the Corinthians in rebuilding their walls (B. C. 392). But they were building for their enemies, as Agesilaüs, with the Spartan fleet, gained possession of the walls and the port of Lechæum. Several other towns on the Corinthian Gulf, with a vast amount of spoils and numerous captives, likewise came into his possession. The Lacedæmonians now surrounded Corinth on every side; and the Thebans, despairing of success for the allies, sent envoys to solicit peace with Sparta.

While these envoys were still in the presence of Agesilaüs, he received intelligence of an unprecedented and mortifying Spartan disaster. The Athenian Iphícrates had been for two years drilling a troop of mercenaries in a new system of tactics designed to unite the advantages of heavy-armed and light-armed troops. He had demonstrated their efficiency in several experiments, and was now prepared to test them upon the Spartan battalion, which was likewise regarded as well-nigh invincible. The Spartans while returning to their camp at Lechæum, after having escorted their Amyclæan comrades some distance on their way homeward to celebrate a religious festival, were attacked in flank and rear, with arrows and javelins. Encumbered with their heavy armor, the Lacedæmonians were unable to cope with their agile adversaries, and their long pikes were of little avail against the short swords of the *peltasts*. In consequence, the Spartans at length broke their ranks in confusion, many being driven into the sea, and pursued by their victorious foes, who wrestled with them and slew them in the water (B. C. 392).

In Asia Minor hostilities were prosecuted with varying success. Thimbron, the Spartan general, was defeated and killed by the Persian leader, Struthas, his entire force of eight thousand men being cut to pieces (B. C. 390). About the same time an Athenian squadron, on its way to aid Evagoras against Persia, was captured by a Spartan fleet. Thrasybúlus was then sent with a larger Athenian naval force, with which he reëstablished Athenian supremacy in the Propontis and reimposed the toll which Athens had formerly collected on all vessels passing out of the Euxine; but Thrasybúlus was slain in the midst of this expedition. By renewed efforts, the Spartans again became masters of the straits; but Iphícrates, with his *peltasts*, surprised the Spartans among the passes of Mount Ida and won a decisive victory, thus restoring the Athenian supremacy in that region.

The Spartans in the meantime had been seriously alarmed at the rebuilding of the walls and fortifications of Athens. In their anxious councils held on this occasion, they discussed the question of detaching Persia from its alliance with the Grecian enemies of Sparta, as the only way of stopping the proceeding so detrimental to the interests of Sparta. They felt that they could only regain the friendship of Artaxerxes Mnemon by abandoning for a time, if not permanently, all hope of recovering their possessions in Asia Minor, considering such a sacrifice a less evil than the restoration of the power of Athens. They accordingly sent successive embassies to the Persian court, imploring peace on the most humble terms, the only condition which they made being the withdrawal of the Persian monarch's support from Athens. Though Antálcidas, the principal Spartan envoy, was a person of remarkable address and cunning, he would not probably have induced Artaxerxes Mnemon to accede to the requests of Sparta, had not Conon prematurely betrayed his real object in his dealing with Persia, by endeavoring to induce the Ionian Greeks of Asia Minor and the isles of the Ægean to once more acknowledge the supremacy of Athens by representing Athenian power and influence as fully reëstablished after the rebuilding of the walls and fortifications of the celebrated city. Although this effort of Conon was sought to be made in secrecy, it did not escape the ears of Antálcidas, who made an ample and dexterous use of the circumstance at the Persian court, so that Conon was put to death on arriving there as the Athenian envoy, while King Artaxerxes Mnemon acceded to the petition of Antálcidas; and thus was concluded the *Peace of Antálcidas* (B. C. 387).

The Persian Monarch furnished the means to enforce the terms of this treaty; and a large Spartan and Persian fleet, commanded jointly by Antálcidas and Tiribazus, visited the Hellespont and threatened Athens with famine by cutting off the supplies of corn from the Euxine. All the Grecian states were now ready to listen to terms, and in a congress of deputies from the various states Tiribazus presented the following propositions: "King Artaxerxes thinks it just that the cities in Asia and the isles of Clazomenæ and Cyprus should belong to him. He thinks it just to leave all the other Grecian cities, both small and great, independent, except Lemnos, Imbros and Scyros, which are to belong to Athens as of old." The Thebans at first objected to these conditions, but were soon induced to take the oath, in consequence of the warlike threats of the Spartans. These terms of peace, which thus prostrated Greece at the feet of the Medo-Persian Empire, were engraven on stone tablets and set up in every Grecian temple.

The humiliating Peace of Antálcidas constitutes an epoch in the decline of the Grecian states. It soon became apparent that in proposing the ruinous concessions of this treaty, Sparta had acted wholly with a view to her own selfish interests, and that to serve these she had willfully and permanently sacrificed the general welfare of Greece. She had abandoned the Greek cities of Asia Minor because experience had taught her that in contending for them, Athens had, and always would have, the advantage, because of her maritime situation. The provision in the treaty for the freedom and independence of the minor communities in Greece from the supremacy of the larger and more powerful states was introduced by Sparta to place her in the light of a general liberator, and she thus artfully won the confidence of the parties apparently benefited through her intervention. The consequences of this stroke of policy displayed themselves soon after the treaty went into operation. The Spartan Senate became the common referee on all occasions of petty dispute among the minor Grecian states, and decided all differences in a manner most favorable to their own ambitious designs, which comprehended the virtual subjection of all Greece to the sway of Sparta. Perceiving themselves deprived of all opportunities of foreign conquest, the restless and warlike Lacedæmonians had directed their thoughts to recovering and perfecting their ascendency in Greece itself; and in this spirit their artful ambassador, Antálcidas, had drawn up the conditions of the treaty of peace bearing his name. The result answered his purpose, as Sparta was now at the height of her power, being for a time the virtual arbiter of the destinies of Greece.

The Spartan hatred of Thebes did not cease with the return of peace. To annoy the Thebans, the Spartans caused Platæa to be rebuilt and as many of its citizens as possible to be brought back. Sparta exercised her supremacy in an arrogant manner toward the minor Grecian communities. The city and republic of Mantinéa, in Arcadia, was the first victim of the Spartan schemes of aggression and acquisition. Upon the pretext that the Mantinéans had furnished supplies of corn to the enemies of Sparta during the recent struggle, the Spartans sent an army against Mantinéa in B. C. 386, and after an obstinate and protracted defense the city was compelled to surrender and to acknowledge the supremacy of its Lacedæmonian conquerors. A like fate overtook the little republic of Phlius, which was obliged to become a submissive dependent of Sparta by the mere dread of the power of her arms, without any attempt at resistance. But another design of the ambitious Lacedæmonians, which they attempted to carry into execution about the same time, was not so easy of accomplishment, and was more important in its consequences.

Olynthus, the chief city in Chalcidice, had suddenly risen into wealth and power at a time when Athens and Sparta were too busily engaged with other matters to regard it with either jealousy or cupidity, and had become the center of a powerful and flourishing league in the southern parts of Macedonia and Thrace. But there was no lack of malcontents in a country possessed of so much general freedom without general intelligence. Although Olynthus had treated the states composing the powerful confederacy which it headed with an unusual liberality, two cities of the league, Acanthus and Apollonia, considered themselves justified in taking offense at some part of the Olynthian policy, and sent an embassy to Sparta, soliciting protection from what they styled "the dangerous ambition" of the Chalcidian capital. Nothing could have been more agreeable to the wishes of the Spartans than this request, as Olynthus had recently given deep offense by entering into, or at least by seeking for, an alliance with Athens and Thebes, at this time the two great objects of Lacedæmonian hatred and jealousy. The Spartan Senate accordingly voted ten thousand men to assist Acanthus and Apollonia, or, in reality, to subjugate Olynthus (B. C. 382). The two brothers, Eudámidas and Phœbidas, were ordered to lead this Spartan army against Olynthus, Eudámidas to take the field at once with such forces as were in readiness, and Phœbidas to follow with the remainder of the troops when collected. Accordingly Eudámidas marched with a force of two thousand Spartans to the Chalcidian district, and won some important successes over the Olynthians in the first campaign; but when he afterwards approached Olynthus too recklessly, he was intercepted and slain, while his army was irrevocably dispersed.

Agesilaüs, who was still one of the joint Kings of Sparta with Agesípolis, next sent his brother Teleútias with ten thousand men to conduct the Olynthian war. Teleútias defeated the Olynthians in several engagements; but when, like Eudámidas, he had advanced too near the walls of Olynthus, he and his army met a like fate, the courage of the citizens appearing to be fully aroused when danger menaced their household gods. The Spartan king Agesípolis conducted the next campaign with powerful reinforcements, and ravaged the Olynthian territory, but was seized with a fever called *calenture*, which carried him to his grave. Polybíades, who was appointed his successor in the command of the Spartan army, proved to be an able general and was successful in forcing the Olynthians, who were now shut up in their capital and exhausted by four years of warfare, famine and distress, to surrender. Sparta required absolute submission in peace or war on the part of the conquered city as the condition of capitulation.

On this occasion the Spartans introduced the barbarians, as they were called, of Macedon into the field of Grecian politics; as they accepted assistance from the Macedonian king, Amyntas, and rewarded him at the close of the war with a part of the territory wrested from Olynthus—a very dangerous proceeding, as the subsequent history of Greece fully proved.

We have stated that, at the beginning of the Olynthian war, Phœbidas was to follow his brother with the remainder of the Spartan troops destined for service against Olynthus. Phœbidas actually marched with eight thousand men for the seat of war, but was incidentally led to employ his army in a different object from the one originally designed, and this circumstance gave rise to a new struggle which shook Greece to its very center.

While marching northward to assist in the operations against Olynthus, Phœbidas halted in Bœotia and encamped in the vicinity of Thebes. As the city of Thebes had not been exposed to the long and severe drainage which had exhausted the resources of Athens and Sparta, it had gradually risen in wealth and importance, until it had become equal to any Grecian state in means, spirit and influence. But although the Thebans did not fear injury from without, they were distracted by internal dissensions on account of the strife of factions for supremacy. The democratic party, which was headed by the archon Isménias, struggled for ascendency with the adherents of aristocracy, whose leader was the archon Leontíades. The democracy had for some time been supreme in the state, and the aristocracy habitually looked to Sparta for aid in recovering their lost power. When therefore Phœbidas arrived with his troops in the vicinity of Thebes accidentally, the Theban aristocrats, seeing the favorable opportunity thus thrust upon them, resolved to call upon the Spartan commander for assistance against their democratic antagonists. Leontíades, the aristocratic leader, accordingly presented himself to Phœbidas and offered him possession of the Cadmæa, or Theban citadel—an offer which the Spartan general very readily accepted. The time for this enterprise was the most auspicious that could have been selected; as it was the season of one of the festivals of Dêmêtêr, when Theban matrons performed their devotional ceremonies in the citadel, no males being present at these rites.

When Phœbidas received the gate-keys of the Cadmæa from Leontíades, he hastened from his encampment to the citadel, which he at once seized, without encountering any resistance. The Theban people were struck with surprise and consternation; and, although Leontíades assured them of the peaceful intentions of the Spartans, four hundred of the leading citizens fled to Athens when they saw Isménias dragged into the citadel by the Lacedæmonian invaders. When he had accomplished his nefarious design, Leontíades hastened to Sparta and easily persuaded the Spartan Senate of the propriety of having a Lacedæmonian garrison in Thebes. The Theban aristocracy, thus protected and aided by Sparta, inaugurated a reign of terror in their city; and the confiscations, banishments and executions which followed were almost unparalleled in Grecian history. The aristocratic party, supported by the Spartan garrison in the Cadmæa, reveled in the blood of their democratic adversaries. But the oppressed Theban people soon found deliverers.

Among the many Theban exiles resident at Athens, one of the most distinguished was Pelópidas, a youth of noble birth, brilliant talents and ardent patriotism. Animated with a desire to deliver his countrymen from their oppressors, he acted in concert with a few comrades to effect that purpose. The other Theban exiles at Athens, glad to embrace this opportunity to take vengeance on their tyrants, warmly supported the plot of Pelópidas and joined his standard.

Pelópidas was the ardent friend of Epaminóndas, a Theban venerable in years and exalted in virtue. Epaminóndas at first held back from the conspiracy formed by Pelópidas and the Theban exiles at Athens, because its execution required deceit and the possible shedding of innocent blood. He was a strict Pythagorean, and his principles were so pure that he was never known to trifle with truth, even in jest, or to sacrifice it for any interest.

Phyllidas, the secretary of the oligarchical government of Thebes, was in the plot against his masters and took a prominent part in its execution. He invited the two *polemarchs*, Archias and Philippus, with the principal Spartan leaders, to a sumptuous banquet on a certain night; and when they were sufficiently stupefied with eating and drinking, he proposed to introduce some Theban ladies. Before these entered the apartment, a messenger brought a letter to Archias and requested his attention to it, as it contained a warning of something serious that was to happen; but the careless voluptuary, intent only on indulgence in wine and other excesses, thrust the letter under the cushions of his couch, with the remark: "Serious matters to-morrow!"

Pelópidas and his friends, who had arrived in the city in the disguise of hunters, thereupon entered the banquet-room shrouded in female garb. The half-intoxicated guests greeted them with a boisterous welcome, and they scattered themselves, with seeming carelessness, among the company. As one of the Spartan lords attempted to lift the veil of the person who was speaking to him, he received a fatal wound; and this was the signal for a general attack. Swords and daggers were drawn under the silken apparel, and were thrust into the hearts of the two *polemarchs* and the Spartan leaders, so that none of the tyrants escaped alive. The traitor Leontíades perished with the rest. The prisons were now opened and five hundred captive friends of liberty were freed from their chains, and these joined the armed force of the revolutionary conspirators. To the profound joy of the wondering citizens of Thebes, the voices of the heralds were heard in the dead of the night, summoning them to the standard of freedom, and proclaiming: "The tyrants are no more!" On the morrow crowds of the Theban youth flocked to the standard of the emancipators; democracy was reëstablished; and in a few days the Spartan garrison, seeing that its enemies were reinforced by a strong force of Athenian auxiliaries and returned Theban exiles, capitulated, and were allowed to evacuate the Cadmæa.

Thus, after enduring an oppression of three years from their tyrannical oligarchs, the Theban people were liberated by a successful revolution begun and ended in one night (B. C. 378)—a revolution, which for righteousness of cause and energetic vigor of execution, stands almost without a parallel in the world's history.

The Spartans, though having no right to complain of this catastrophe to their garrison in the Cadmæa, saw that it might furnish a dangerous example to other subject states, and as soon as they received intelligence of the event they resolved to go to war for the recovery of Thebes. Active military preparations were at once entered upon, and thus arose a war between Sparta and Thebes which raged with great violence for seven years, and which contributed largely to the final downfall of the celebrated republics of ancient Greece.

The Spartan king Cleómbrotus led an army into Bœotia, and Athens was called upon to account for having furnished an asylum to the Theban exiles. Feeling themselves unprepared to enter into a war with Sparta, the Athenians agreed to sacrifice their two generals who had rendered the most efficient aid to the Theban revolutionists. One of these generals was executed, and the other, having fled from Athens, was sentenced to banishment. The Thebans feared that they would be left without allies to contend against the Lacedæmonian power. For the purpose of forcing Athens to come to their assistance, they bribed Sphódrias, the Spartan general, to invade the Athenian territory. He accordingly entered Attica in the night and perpetrated various ravages, but retired the following day. The Spartan government disclaimed all knowledge of this affair, and brought Sphódrias to trial for it; but he was acquitted, through the influence of Agesilaüs. Athens at once entered into an active alliance with Thebes and declared war against her old enemy and rival.

A new league of Grecian states was now formed against Sparta, on the plan of the Confederacy of Delos. This league included seventy cities in its most prosperous period. Athens was at the head, but the independence of the various members of the league was carefully guarded. A congress at Athens regulated the share of each state of the confederacy in the general expenditure. The fortifications of Piræus were completed, new war-vessels were constructed, and all the allies hastened forward their military contingents. Thebes raised a Sacred Band—a heavy-armed battalion, consisting of three hundred chosen citizens of the noblest families, united by the most intimate bonds of friendship. Thebes had two great leaders. One of these was Pelópidas, the illustrious liberator of his country, and a man of high character and abilities. Still more eminent was his intimate friend and associate, Epaminóndas, who, as we have seen, was imbued with the highest virtues by nature and education. Though Pelópidas was *bœotarch*, Epaminóndas was most prominent in drilling and disciplining the troops.

Epaminóndas did not covet wealth or fame, though he affected no undue contempt for either. He only followed a public life because his country required his services. He conducted himself in such a manner in his command as to do more honor to the dignities with which he was invested than they conferred upon him. When circumstances no longer required his exertions he retired to private life, in order to indulge in those philosophic studies which had given his mind its calm strength and magnanimity. Though he excelled all his compeers in eloquence, it was said respecting him that no man knew more and spoke less. Besides being one of the most accomplished soldiers of his time, he was one of the wisest statesmen and one of the best of citizens.

Epaminóndas and Pelópidas entertained the most perfect and disinterested friendship for each other—a friendship rare under such circumstances, and exceedingly creditable to both.

Agesilaüs, who still directed all the councils of Sparta and controlled its destinies, now perceived the necessity of taking more energetic measures. He took the field in person, at the head of an army of eighteen thousand foot and fifteen hundred horse, and conducted two campaigns in Bœotia, devastating the country and harassing Thebes and its dependencies; but the skill of Pelópidas and Epaminóndas and their able Athenian ally, Chabrias, prevented him from winning any decisive success (B. C. 378–B. C. 376).

Phœbidas, the former captor of the Cadmæa, whom Agesilaüs had left in command in Bœotia when he returned to Sparta, was defeated and slain by the Thebans. The repeated injuries inflicted upon the territories which supplied the Thebans with provisions now caused them to suffer from famine, and all the efforts to obtain supplies by sea from Eubœa were foiled by the Spartan garrison established on that island. In this emergency the Eubœans rose in revolt, drove the Lacedæmonian garrison from the island, and Thebes was afforded effectual relief. But Thebes was shortly afterwards menaced with a more serious calamity. Sparta and her allies fitted out a fleet of sixty large vessels for the purpose of transporting troops into the vicinity of Thebes and cutting off all her communications by sea. In this crisis Thebes was saved by Athens. Chabrias, who was as able a commander by sea as by land, was entrusted with the command of a powerful Athenian fleet, and inflicted a most decisive defeat upon the Spartan fleet near the isle of Naxos, which left the trade of Thebes and Athens perfectly free and restored the maritime empire of Athens in the East. In the western seas, Corcyra, Cephallenia, and the neighboring tribes on the mainland, joined the Athenian alliance. The Thebans were as victorious on land, and the Bœotian cities submitted to their control during the two years that they were free from Spartan invasion. In B. C. 374 all Lacedæmonians were expelled from Bœotia; free governments were established in all the Bœotian cities, except Orchómenus and Chæronéa; and the Bœotian League was revived. The triumphant Thebans now proceeded to avenge themselves on the Phocians for having invited the Spartans into Central Greece twenty years before, and to seize the treasures of Delphi; but the Phocians escaped this threatened vengeance by the timely assistance of the Spartan king Cleómbrotus.

The Athenians now had reasons for a hostile attitude toward Thebes, and they sent messengers to Sparta with proposals of peace, which the Lacedæmonians gladly accepted; but the negotiations were broken off by the inopportune restoration of the Zacynthian exiles by Timótheus, Conon's son, and hostilities between Athens and Sparta were renewed. The Athenian fleet under Timótheus scoured the western seas and routed the Spartan fleet under Nicólochus (B. C. 374). Iphícrates, the successor of Timótheus in command, continued his predecessor's successful career by vanquishing a third naval force which the Lacedæmonians had collected from Corinth, Syracuse and other allied states and dependencies.

The Thebans were so elated with their prosperity at this stage of the war that they rejected a proposal of the King of Persia, who sought their aid in suppressing a rebellion against his authority in Egypt, and who for this reason interposed his mediation between the contending powers of Greece (B. C. 374). The Thebans, in their hour of triumph, also outraged the feelings of humanity by razing to the ground several hostile cities of Bœotia, among which was Platæa, the little republic so long the friend and ally of Athens, which received the homeless Platæan citizens and expressed the most intense indignation against their Theban persecutors. The effect of this harsh behavior of the Thebans brought them to reason, as they shortly afterward agreed to a congress of the Grecian states, which was held at Sparta, to consider the question of a general pacification, as the states were by this time weary of the struggle (B. C. 371).

The treaty which this congress negotiated was called the *Peace of Callias*, from Callias, the principal Athenian envoy. Agesilaüs represented Sparta, while Epaminóndas was the leading Theban plenipotentiary. It was agreed that the Spartan garrison should be withdrawn from every Grecian city, and the independence of every Grecian state, large or small, was acknowledged. Athens and Sparta, weary of the struggle, signed the treaty very readily; Athens and her allies signing separately, but Sparta taking the oath for the whole Lacedæmonian confederacy. Here was the rock on which the whole negotiations between Sparta and Thebes split; as Epaminóndas declared with boldness and justice that he could not and would not agree to the treaty unless he were allowed to sign in the name of the whole Bœotian League. He defended his attitude in an eloquent speech, claiming justly that Thebes was as rightfully the sovereign city of Bœotia as Sparta was of Laconia. The arrogance of Sparta in refusing to concede this point shows that her domineering pride had not been tamed by calamity. While claiming the right to an irresponsible authority over the cities around her, she was unwilling to concede the same privilege to any other power. Epaminóndas firmly adhered to his position, asserting the right of Thebes to hold an equal position with any other Grecian state. As Agesilaüs obstinately persisted in his arrogant refusal, the congress broke up, leaving Sparta and Thebes at war, while peace had been concluded between all the other states.

Thebes, thus deserted by her allies, was now in a dangerous and difficult situation, as Sparta was supported by her former allies. The rest of the Greeks appeared to look upon the resolute courage of the Thebans in this perilous crisis as utter madness, and expected in a very short time to see Thebes utterly crushed by the overwhelming power of Sparta and her allies. But Thebes was saved in this dangerous emergency by the military talents of Epaminóndas, who proved himself the greatest general that Greece ever produced. Conscious of his own power and the value of the new tactics which were soon to take the place of the Spartan system, he revived the failing spirit of his anxious countrymen, invented good omens to counteract the discouraging influence of their evil ones, and in his personality he sustained the spirit of the entire nation by the greatness of his soul.

The Spartan king Cleómbrotus, the colleague of Agesilaüs, was already in Phocis, with a confederate army of twenty-four thousand foot and sixteen hundred horse. The Thebans could not muster much more than half that strength, but in discipline and valor they far excelled the motley host under Cleómbrotus. The Sacred Band, consisting of three hundred chosen men of tried fidelity and bound together by inviolable bonds of friendship, was under the command of Pelópidas, and always fought to conquer, until it fell before the Macedonian arms many years later.

Cleómbrotus began the campaign with energy by seizing Creusis, on the Crissæan Gulf, with twelve Theban vessels which lay in the harbor, thus providing at the beginning a base of supplies and a line of retreat. He then marched along the Gulf of Corinth into Bœotia, and within a few months after the congress at Sparta encamped at Leuctra (B. C. 371). Three of the seven Theban *bœotarchs* were so greatly alarmed that they proposed to retreat upon Thebes and send their wives and children to Athens for safety, but they were overruled in their purpose. Epaminóndas and Pelópidas were vigilant and cheerful. Though his troops were numerically inferior to those of his enemy, Epaminóndas was confident in the spirit with which he had been chiefly instrumental in inspiring them. He so arranged his army as to be always superior at the actual point of contact, instead of engaging all at the same time, which had previously been the uniform practice in Grecian warfare. The Theban left was a dense column, fifty feet deep, led by the Sacred Band under Pelópidas. The famous battle of Leuctra was begun by this Theban left wing, which attacked the Lacedæmonian right, which contained the select troops of Sparta led by Cleómbrotus himself; while the Theban center and right, which faced the allies of Sparta, were kept out of the engagement. There had never been any fiercer fighting on any Grecian battle-field. The Spartans sustained their ancient valor, but the onset of the Theban left was irresistible, and the whole Lacedæmonian army was thrown into confusion, of which Epaminóndas availed himself by performing an evolution which decided the fate of the day. He formed the attacking column into a wedge, which he hurled impetuously through the demoralized lines of the Lacedæmonians, spreading death and disorder all around. The Spartans and their allies never recovered from the shock, and, in spite of their desperate resistance, were completely routed. Cleómbrotus himself was mortally wounded, and his shattered army fled for refuge to its strong encampment, which Epaminóndas prudently left unassailed. The Thebans erected a trophy on the plain of Leuctra in honor of their splendid victory. The allies of Sparta, many of whom were in the battle through fear rather than choice, inwardly rejoiced at the result of the battle.

All Greece was intensely astonished at the issue of the battle of Leuctra—the first pitched battle in which a Spartan army had been overcome by inferior numbers. On the day when the bad news reached Sparta, its inhabitants were engaged in celebrating festival games and invoking the favor of the gods for the coming harvest. When the Ephors were informed of the terrible calamity they communicated the names of the slain to their relatives, and also commanded the women to abstain from all signs of mourning, excepting those whose relatives survived the defeat. On the following day the friends of the slain appeared in their best attire in the public places and congratulated each other on the bravery of their kinsmen, while the friends of the survivors of the disastrous defeat looked sorrowfully forward to the sentence of eternal disgrace which the state passed upon every citizen who fled before an enemy. In this instance, however, the doom of ignominy was dispensed with. Actuated either by a spirit of charity or by the consciousness that Sparta, in her exhausted condition, could not afford to lose more of her citizens, Agesilaüs moved in the Senate that the rigor of the laws should be mitigated on this occasion. Said he: "Let us suppose the sacred institutions of Lycurgus to have slept during one unfortunate day, but henceforth let them resume their wonted vigor!" The prudent counsels of Agesilaüs were adopted.

The disastrous battle of Leuctra was the greatest calamity that had ever befallen Sparta. Spartan influence was destroyed, even over the Peloponnesian cities. The Spartan dependencies north of the Corinthian Gulf were lost, some being seized by the triumphant Thebans, and the others by Jason, tyrant of Pheræ, in Thessaly. The Spartan ascendency in Greece, which had continued thirty-three years from the time of the capture of Athens by Lysander, in B. C. 404, was now superseded by the Theban supremacy, which lasted nine years, from B. C. 371 to B. C. 362.

In the meantime the intelligence of the Spartan defeat at Leuctra had produced an unexpected effect at Athens. The Thebans were so desirous of propitiating the favor of the Athenians that they sent a special courier to Athens to announce the event; but the Athenians, jealous of the growing power of Thebes, coldly received the messenger. Though unwilling to promote the prosperity of Thebes, the Athenians at the same time endeavored to extort every possible advantage to their own affairs from the depressed condition of Sparta.

Disappointed in their hopes of support and aid from Athens, the Thebans sought the alliance of a prince at this time more powerful than the Athenian republic, namely Jason of Pheræ, who at this time ruled all Thessaly. Jason was a man of extraordinary talents and unbounded ambition, and aimed at the sovereignty of all Greece. Besides being endowed with all the personal qualities of the old kings of the Homeric period, from whom he claimed to be descended, he possessed the military skill and the political ability of his own maturely-developed epoch. Such a personage was well calculated to rise to power in a country like Thessaly, where the primitive habits of a pastoral life were only partly intermingled with more refined customs, derived from the neighboring states of the ancient Grecian confederacy. Jason, who was originally simply a citizen of Pheræ, a considerable town in the South of Thessaly, acquired so much influence and popularity by his talents and conduct that, under the title of captain-general, he exercised the full extent of royal power in his native country.

Jason's mind was capable of the loftiest designs. He saw how easily his numerous and hardy mountaineers, whom he had trained to an almost unparalleled degree of discipline, could win for him the ascendency over the exhausted states of Central Greece and the Peloponnesus. He even meditated conquests beyond Greece, like those afterwards realized by Alexander the Great. As a preliminary step in his policy, he diligently sought to acquire a friendly influence over the Grecian republics. He visited the most important of them on several occasions, and, by specious address and semi-barbaric splendor, gained considerable favor among them. He entered into an alliance with Thebes, though its most eminent citizen, Epaminóndas, spurned all his advances and disdainfully rejected his presents. Yet Epaminóndas was probably the poorest citizen who ever became distinguished as a soldier and a statesman among the republics of ancient Greece.

Entertaining such views, Jason of Pheræ, as Prince of Thessaly, at once accepted the invitation of the Thebans to join their army and to give them the support which Athens refused. While both the triumphant Thebans and the vanquished Spartans still lay encamped near the famous battle-field of Leuctra, Jason, at the head of two thousand light horse, joined the Theban army and was gladly welcomed by his allies. But conscious that his ultimate designs concerning Greece would be better advanced by his appearance in the character of a mediator between the belligerent powers than as an ally of either of them, Jason counseled peace, and, acting as negotiator himself, he soon succeeded to such an extent as to bring about a truce (B. C. 370).

On the conclusion of this truce, all parties at once retired from the field, the Lacedæmonians returning home in such haste as to imply a lack of confidence in this sudden pacification, as well as their dislike of the unexpected mediator. All the Grecian states seem to have felt at this time a considerable degree of alarm regarding Jason, whose proceedings, after he had returned to Thessaly, were calculated to confirm their worst anticipations. He openly declared his intention to be present at the ensuing celebration of the Pythian Games at Delphi, and to claim the right to preside there as an honor due to his descent, his piety and his power. He collected about eleven thousand cattle of different kinds, for the sacrifices of the oracle; thus amply indicating the number of the followers with which he designed making his appearance.

But in this crisis of such ill omen to Greece—when the ambitious purposes of the Prince of Thessaly were apparently approaching consummation—his career was ended forever by assassination. After reviewing his cavalry, he sat to give audience to supplicants, when seven youths, under the plea of stating some point on which they disagreed, approached him and murdered him (B. C. 370). The reason for this act has ever remained a mystery. The friendly welcome given by the Grecian cities to the five assassins who escaped fully indicates the feeling with which the Grecian states received the intelligence of Jason's assassination. This tragedy saved Greece from conquest by powerful northern neighbors for a period of thirty-three years.

In the meantime the Mantinéans took advantage of the perilous situation in which the great catastrophe at Leuctra had left Sparta to avenge their former wrongs, and solicited the aid of Epaminóndas. Blinded by their jealous animosities, Sparta and Thebes, with their respective allies, soon recommenced hostilities. The year after that in which Jason lost his life was characterized by several proceedings of some importance on the part of the rival states of Greece. Arcadia, then in alliance with Thebes, was invaded and ravaged by Agesilaüs; and Epaminóndas retaliated by leading an army of seventy thousand men, consisting of the youth of Bœotia, Acarnania, Phocis, Locris, Eubœa, Argolis and Elis, into Laconia, and advanced upon Sparta itself, which had not felt the heavy hand of a hostile invader for several centuries (B. C. 369). During all this time the Spartan women had never beheld an armed foe, and the defenseless city was filled with consternation. But the energetic and venerable King Agesilaüs was equal to the emergency. He abandoned Arcadia, on the approach of the Thebans, and went to the relief of his native city, which, by his consummate skill, valor and prudence, he succeeded in preserving from the inroad of a hostile foe far outnumbering his own forces. Agesilaüs repulsed the cavalry of Epaminóndas, who retired down the Eurótas valley, burning and plundering the rich and defenseless territory of Laconia, thus wreaking the hostility which the genius of Agesilaüs had warded off from its capital.

The chief objects of the expedition of Epaminóndas were yet to be fulfilled. He desired to organize and strengthen the union of Arcadian towns already formed. To guard against mutual jealousy and rivalry on the part of the existing cities, the new city of Megalópolis was built, and peopled by colonists from forty towns. This new city became the capital of the Arcadian League, and here a congress of deputies, called *The Ten Thousand*, was to be regularly convened; while a standing army of deputies from the different cities of the league was likewise raised.

Epaminóndas likewise contemplated a

project for the restoration of the Messenians. For three centuries this valiant people had been exiled from their native land, which was held in possession by the Lacedæmonians. The letters of Epaminóndas now recalled the Messenian exiles from the shores of Italy, Sicily, Africa and Asia, and they enthusiastically flew to arms to recover the land of their heroic ancestors. They fortified the citadel of Ithomé anew, and rebuilt the destroyed city of Messéne upon the western slope of the mountain and protected it with strong walls. The Messenian territories extended southward to the gulf bearing their name, and northward to Elis and Arcadia. Epaminóndas was actuated by motives of humanity in restoring the exiled Messenians, as well as by a desire to raise a powerful rival to Sparta in the Peloponnesus.

King Agesilaüs took advantage of the disfavor with which Athens had looked upon the Theban victory at Leuctra by sending to that republic able and cunning emissaries, who, with the assistance of the ambassadors of Corinth and Phlius, succeeded in inducing the Athenians to take up arms, not to restore Spartan supremacy, but to establish that general peace which had been agreed to at the congress at Sparta by every state, excepting Thebes. The existing war appeared, in the eyes of the other Grecian states, to proceed entirely from the obstinacy of Thebes; and, under color of this specious argument, Athens now participated in the war as an ally of Sparta.

An Athenian army of twenty thousand men under Iphícrates marched to Arcadia, for the purpose of diverting Epaminóndas from his campaign in Laconia. The great Theban general had just perfected the humane and politic proceeding of restoring the Messenians to the land of their ancestors, when he heard of the movement of the Athenians under Iphícrates. He immediately evacuated Laconia; and Iphícrates at once retired from Arcadia, as if the object of the campaign had been accomplished. Watching each other's movements, the two generals withdrew in the direction of their respective homes, which they reached without any hostile collision. This pacific end of the campaign caused Epaminóndas to be accused of misconduct; but he defended himself in so forcible and dignified a manner before the assembly of the Theban people that the factious endeavors of his enemies to injure him simply added to his honor and popularity. The most important result of the campaign was the revival of the Messenian commonwealth, as it permanently deprived Sparta of almost half her long-held territory.

The Thebans had gained other advantages, and they were prepared to enter the field the next spring with undiminished confidence, though the Lacedæmonians, in concert with the Athenians under Chabrias, had fortified the Isthmus of Corinth, for the purpose of closing the passage into the Peloponnesus against another Theban invasion. But Epaminóndas forced one of the Spartan posts and devastated the Corinthian territories (B. C. 369). Sicyon deserted the cause of Sparta and entered into an alliance with Thebes. The Thebans were in turn defeated in an attack upon Corinth, and their foes were reinforced by a squadron which arrived at Lechæum, from Dionysius I., the tyrant of Syracuse, conveying two thousand auxiliaries from Gaul and Spain.

But here the campaign ended. Instead of marching into the Peloponnesus, Epaminóndas retired with his forces and returned to Thebes. This retreat for a time injured his popularity. The Spartans under Archidamus, son of Agesilaüs, next expelled the Theban garrisons which had been introduced into the different cities of Laconia. In the meantime the Arcadians, elated by their newly-acquired power, aspired to share the sovereignty with Thebes, as Athens did with Sparta. Under their leader Lycomédes, who had first proposed the league, the Arcadians gained several advantages in the West and inflicted the final death-blow to Spartan power in Messsenia. Archidamus, at the head of a Spartan army, afterwards invaded Arcadia and won a signal victory over the valiant Lycomédes. In this battle the Arcadians suffered frightful slaughter, while the Spartans did not lose a man (B. C. 368). When intelligence of this victory reached Sparta, the venerable Agesilaüs and all the assembled people wept for joy. As no Spartan mother had to lament for the loss of a son, this engagement was styled, in the Spartan annals, the "Tearless Battle." By fortifying their frontier in accordance with a plan suggested by Epaminóndas, the Arcadians put a stop to Lacedæmonian incursions for a time. The Thebans did not regret this defeat of their allies, as it curbed their pride and showed their need of protection from the sovereign state.

In the meantime Pelópidas was sent into Thessaly with a strong force to restore quiet to that region, then disturbed by the tyrant Alexander of Pheræ, Jason's brother and third successor on the throne of Thessaly. When the Thebans arrived in Thessaly, the frightened despot implored their clemency and submissively bound himself to fulfill every stipulation dictated to him, both those relating to his own possessions and those respecting the Theban dominions. Pelópidas organized a league among the Thessalian cities and entered into an alliance with Macedon. Among the hostages sent from the Macedonian court was the young prince Philip, son of Amyntas, then fifteen years of age, who was destined to act an important part in the later history of Greece.

During the years B. C. 367 and B. C. 366, the Persian court became more and more the theater of Grecian negotiations, or, more properly, intrigues; all the belligerent states of Greece desiring at least the pecuniary assistance of King Artaxerxes Mnemon. Pelópidas was the Theban embassador sent to Susa, and he faithfully and skillfully fulfilled the objects of his mission. The Persian monarch was so charmed by the noble appearance and the commanding eloquence of Pelópidas that he distinguished him above all the rival envoys from the other Grecian states and ratified a treaty with him of a most advantageous character for Thebes. This treaty was designed for the general pacification of Greece, and by its provisions the Great King recognized the Hellenic supremacy of Thebes and the independence of Messéne and Amphipolis, decided a dispute between the Arcadian and the Elians in favor of the latter, and required Athens to reduce her navy to a peace footing, and Sparta to acknowledge the independence of Messenia, under the pain of bringing down upon both these powers the joint vengeance of Persia and Thebes in case of refusal.

These peace propositions demanded the full consideration of all the parties concerned. Accordingly, as soon as Pelópidas had returned home and informed his countrymen of the favorable result of his negotiations, the Thebans dispatched ambassadors to all the states of Greece, inviting them to appear by their representatives at Thebes, to deliberate, in full congress, upon the conditions of the proposed treaty. The minor Grecian states very generally obeyed this summons, but Athens and Sparta seem to have received it with silent contempt. But the Thebans did not meet with the success they expected in convincing the assembled deputies as to the propriety of the propositions submitted to them for their approval. Lycomédes, the Arcadian envoy, courageously told the Thebans that their city was not the place for the sitting of such a congress, and that Arcadia, at least, did not care for, nor need, the alliance of the Great King. Other deputies expressed similar sentiments, and the congress broke up without reaching any decision. Though the alliance of Persia and Thebes on this occasion involved no such degrading consequences to Greece as the treaty which Antálcidas had negotiated for Sparta, the motives of Thebes were the same as those of Sparta had been—namely, to establish for herself an ascendency over the other Grecian states. The just and virtuous Epaminóndas stood aloof from all participation in these political and diplomatic intrigues.

When Pelópidas was shortly afterwards called to the North a second time, to mediate in the affairs of Macedon, and had placed the legitimate heir to that kingdom on his throne, the ungrateful Alexander of

Pheræ, tyrant of Thessaly, seized him by surprise as he was on his way home with a small train, and cast him into a dungeon. The Thebans at once sent an armed force to rescue or avenge their ambassador. But unfortunately Epaminóndas was at this time degraded from his command, and the Theban army was defeated and almost totally destroyed. The great victor of Leuctra had joined the expedition as a private soldier, but, long before the enterprise was completed, he was called to his old station as head of the army by acclamation of the troops. He safely led the defeated and shattered army home, but immediately received the command of a second expedition which succeeded in releasing Pelópidas.

Epaminóndas again led a Theban army into the Peloponnesus in B. C. 366, and, having rapidly reduced Achæa, he restored order in that country and bound its people by oath to join the standard of Thebes. But the Achæans did not long observe this engagement, partly because the Thebans, after Epaminóndas had returned home, sent commissioners to reverse much that he had wisely done, thus highly exasperating the party in Achæa which favored Sparta and which finally acquired the ascendency in the state. The result was that the Achæans and the Lacedæmonians jointly ravaged Arcadia, which was still the ally of Thebes, though habitually jealous of any effort undertaken by that state to acquire an undue elevation. Nothing else of importance marked the progress of the war for awhile, although the two chief states concerned in it had lost none of their animosity toward each other. But the secondary or subordinate parties engaged in the struggle were weary of the constant sacrifices they were called upon to make, without even the hope of any advantage to themselves. Thoroughly disgusted with their allies, Athens and Arcadia contracted an alliance for their mutual welfare and protection. Corinth, Achæa and Phlius—communities which had been the faithful allies of Sparta, in adversity as well as in prosperity—petitioned that republic either to agree to the pacification recently proposed by Thebes, or, at least, if Sparta could not with honor consent to the cession of Messenia, to allow them to conclude a separate treaty with the latter state for themselves. But instigated by the ardent eloquence of Archidamus, the son of Agesilaüs, the Spartans, though their cause and fortunes were declining and being deserted, haughtily replied that they would never acknowledge the independence of Messenia, but that their allies might act as they thought best. At first Thebes would only agree to a treaty with Corinth, Achæa and Phlius on condition that they would join the league against Sparta; but the three states asking for peace would not consent to this proposition, and Thebes finally saw proper to grant them the neutrality which they so ardently desired. By this proceeding Sparta was deprived of all her influential and powerful allies except Dionysius the younger, the reigning tyrant of Syracuse, who, about this time, in accordance with his father's engagements, sent a considerable force to the aid of Lacedæmon, which seems to have been so far humbled by adversity as to think only of the defense of the Peloponnesus, which then was not threatened with any Theban invasion.

Alexander of Pheræ, Prince of Thessaly, the perfidious tyrant who had formerly been curbed in his cruelties and oppressions by Pelópidas and Epaminóndas, had in the meantime regained the power which he had lost, and again tyrannized over the frontier cities of Thessaly and Bœotia with such a degree of severity that the Thebans again found themselves obliged to interfere. Pelópidas was accordingly sent with ten thousand men into Thessaly, where he was joined by many of those who had been victims of Alexander's cruelty and tyranny. Alexander, at the head of twenty thousand men, was defeated by Pelópidas in a battle at the foot of the mountains of Cynoscéphalæ (B. C. 363). But rage at the sight of his old enemy and captor overcame the prudence of Pelópidas, and the heroic and patriotic leader of the conquering Thebans fell a victim to his own gallantry. Dashing forward impetuously and rashly, Pelópidas challenged the Thessalian tyrant to a single combat. The cowardly oppressor sought protection behind his guards, who poured a shower of javelins on Pelópidas, slaying him before his friends could come to his rescue. Though the Thebans were victorious in another battle with Alexander of Pheræ, the death of their favorite leader seems to have prevented them from following up their successes to such advantage as they might otherwise have done; for we see that, at the end of the war in Thessaly, they were satisfied to leave the tyrant Alexander in undisputed possession of his own original dominion of Pheræ, although Theban supremacy was established throughout the rest of Thessaly.

In the meantime the Peloponnesus was not at peace, though the Thebans had their hands too full of other employment to prosecute the war across the Isthmus of Corinth at this time, in consequence of the occupation of their arms in Thessaly, and a dangerous outbreak of the aristocratic faction in Thebes itself, ending in the destruction of the city of Orchómenus.

We have observed that the Arcadians, although allies of Thebes, were as jealous of Theban supremacy as of Spartan ascendency. The confederated cities of Arcadia had become ambitious as they advanced in power, and they aided Thebes against Sparta only for the purpose of establishing their own absolute domination in the Peloponnesus, upon the ruins of the Lacedæmonian power. Actuated by this selfish motive, the Arcadians took the field against Elis. The peaceful Elians, finding themselves unable to repel the invaders of their territory, solicited the aid of Sparta. The Lacedæmonians readily granted the desired assistance; but the Arcadians continued their aggression upon Elis, seizing one Elian town after another, until they obtained possession of the city of Olympia with its sacred grove, which they seized during the year of the festival celebrating the one hundred and fourth Olympiad, when vast multitudes from every portion of Greece were present, as usual on such occasions, and when hostilities had always been suspended.

The festive celebration was disturbed by an act of sacrilege. The conquering Arcadians deprived the Elians of their supervision of the games and installed the Pisatans in their place. A large army of the Arcadians and their allies was present to enforce this irregular proceeding. The Elians and their allies, the Achæans, attempted to surprise their Arcadian conquerors in an unguarded moment in the midst of the games, and a battle occurred on the sacred ground. The temple of Zeus was used as a fortress, and the gold and ivory statue of that great god fashioned by Phidias seemed to gaze upon a scene of sacrilegious strife. Some of the Arcadian leaders, from motives of avarice, seized the rich treasures which centuries of superstition had collected around the Olympian shrine. Other generals were shocked at this sacrilegious act. The Mantinéans refused to share in the spoils, and were therefore proclaimed traitors to the Arcadian league; but the majority of the confederated cities of Arcadia participated so strongly in the feeling of horror at this spoliation that they decreed the restitution of the sacred treasures, and even of the sacred city itself, to the Elians, whom they invited to send a deputation to Tegea with the view of concluding a treaty of peace. The fear of calling down upon their heads the vengeance of the gods was the reason for this turn of affairs, which was as agreeable to the people of Elis as it was distasteful to the persons sharing in the plunder of the Olympian shrine. Among those who shared in this spoliation was the commander of the Theban garrison at Tegea, where the deputies of Arcadia and Elis met to negotiate the terms of peace.

After having agreed upon a peace, the deputies sat down, in accordance with custom, to an entertainment prepared for them: and when everything indicated an appearance of unity and concord, the unsuspecting representatives of Arcadia and Elis were suddenly seized by a band of armed men and cast into prison. The chief actor in this proceeding was the Theban captain, who had been instigated by others in a similar predicament with himself regarding the sacred treasures of the Olympian shrine. The Arcadian cities assumed such a threatening attitude in consequence of this act that the Theban captain was intimidated into speedily releasing his prisoners; but he found it more difficult to repair the injury which his imprudent outrage had caused his country. The outrage just alluded to alienated the good will of half of Arcadia from Thebes, especially when the Thebans refused to discountenance the act of the Theban garrison at Tegea when applied to for redress of the wrongs thus inflicted, but instead threatened to send an army to restore order. The Arcadians were so exasperated at this haughty and menacing course of Thebes that they solicited aid from Athens and Sparta, and made vigorous preparations to defend their territories against their recent powerful ally.

In the summer of B. C. 362, Epaminóndas invaded the Peloponnesus for the fourth and last time, leading a large allied army, consisting of Bœotians, Thessalians and Eubœans, into Arcadia, and halting at Tegea, where he expected to be joined by some of his old fellow soldiers of Arcadia; but in this anticipation the hero of Leuctra was disappointed. Nevertheless, he was bold in his operations and confident of the issue of the impending struggle. Upon ascertaining that the Spartans under the venerable Agesilaüs were advancing to join the Arcadian league at Mantinéa, Epaminóndas decamped in the night-time and made a dash at Sparta, which was saved from total ruin by the conduct of a Cretan deserter, who informed Agesilaüs of the Theban general's design in time for the old king and his son to return to the defense of his capital and his household gods. After a battle in the very streets of Sparta, the Theban invader was obliged to retire. Thus foiled in this enterprise by the betrayal of his design and by the desperate valor of the Spartans, Epaminóndas, determined to perform some deed worthy of his renown, then marched to surprise Mantinéa, eluding the Arcadians and their allies, who had moved to the relief of Sparta, by his rapid evolutions. Thus left unprotected by the withdrawal of the Spartan army, Mantinéa must have fallen into the possession of the Thebans, at a time when its citizens and their slaves were employed in the harvest-fields, had not a strong detatchment of Athenian cavalry reached the city a few hours before the arrival of Epaminóndas. Though weary and hungry, the Athenians, by their determined valor, saved Mantinéa by repulsing the Theban invaders.

The Arcadian allies soon afterwards returned to their position at Mantinéa; and Epaminóndas, anxious to efface the memory of his recent failures, resolved upon risking a great battle with the enemies of Thebes. His preparations for this engagement and his conduct during its progress have been considered by all historians as indicating wonderful military skill. The elevated plain between Tegea and Mantinéa was the place destined for the final struggle between Sparta and Thebes. When the Thebans arrived on the field they laid down their arms, as if preparing to encamp; and the Spartans, supposing that they did not intend to fight, scattered over the field in some confusion, some tending their horses, some unbuckling their breast-plates. After thus deceiving the Spartans and their allies by pretending to decline an engagement, Epaminóndas suddenly formed his Bœotian troops into a wedge-like phalanx, as at Leuctra, and fell upon the enemy before they had time to resume the arms which they had laid aside so rashly. A most sanguinary conflict ensued. The Spartans fought with their accustomed valor; but under the disadvantage always occasioned by disorder, they were powerless to recover themselves on the instant. Epaminóndas took advantage of the situation by hurling a body of his chosen troops upon the enemy's center, whereupon the Spartans and the Mantinéans fled. But in the midst of the struggle the heroic Epaminóndas fell pierced by a javelin, thus receiving a mortal wound. He was carried aside by his friends, whereupon his followers stood paralyzed with dismay, and were unable to follow up the advantage for which he had prepared the way. At the end of the battle the Spartans asked permission to bury their dead, but both armies claimed the honors of the day and erected trophies of victory. Such was the famous battle of Mantinéa, in which Epaminóndas bought his second great victory over the Spartans with his life (B. C. 362).

Epaminóndas lived for a short time after the tumult of battle had ceased, the javelin still sticking in his breast. His friends feared to remove it, lest he should die the instant it was withdrawn. The illustrious Theban chief bore the agony of his wound until he was assured that his army was triumphant, whereupon he exclaimed: "Then all is well!" In reply to the sorrowing spectators who lamented that so illustrious a warrior and statesmen died childless, Epaminóndas exclaimed: "I leave you two fair daughters—Leuctra and Mantinéa!" He then drew the fatal spear-head from his wound, and, with the rush of blood which followed, his life ebbed away, and "he died calmly and cheerfully, in the arms of his weeping countrymen, leaving behind him a name second to none in the annals of Greece." "Epaminóndas was a pure, unselfish patriot; a refined, moral and generous citizen." Cicero regarded him as the greatest man that ancient Greece ever produced. No Greek at any time more truly deserved the title of "Great." Many of the worthiest who came after him selected him for their model. Like the Chevalier Bayard, Epaminóndas was truly "a knight without fear and without reproach."

The glory and preëminence of Thebes began and ended with the public career of Epaminóndas; and after the battle of Mantinéa, that state sank to her former position among the republics of ancient Greece. The glory of Hellas had departed forever. Exhausted by her intestine struggles, caused by the mutual jealousies among the several states, Greece rapidly declined, and her ultimate ruin was hastened by the Social War and the Sacred War, which soon followed; so that, demoralized and disunited, this renowned land finally lay prostrate and ready to fall a prey to the arms of the despoiler—and this despoiler soon made his appearance in the person of Philip of Macedon.

Under the auspices of the King of Persia, who still desired to levy men for his service in Egypt, overtures for a general peace were again made to the Grecian states. Sparta alone refused to agree to the new treaty, because it recognized the independence of Messenia. Apparently incensed at the course of King Artaxerxes Mnemon, Agesilaüs, although an octogenarian, crossed the sea at the head of one thousand heavy-armed Lacedæmonians and ten thousand mercenaries to assist Tachos, King of Egypt, who had sought Spartan aid in his revolt against the dominon of Persia. The appearance of this little, lame old man, without any royal retinue or magnificence, excited ridicule among the Egyptians; but when he abandoned the cause of Tachos and joined the standard of Nectanabis, who had risen in arms against Tachos, the Egyptians were able to comprehend the full importance of the decrepit little Spartan king, as he placed Nectanabis upon the Egyptian throne. But Agesilaüs died at Cyrênê on his way home, in the eighty-fourth year of his age and the forty-first of his reign (B. C. 361). His body, embalmed in wax, was conveyed with great pomp to Sparta. An ancient oracle had foretold that Sparta would lose her power under a lame king—a prophecy which was now verified through no fault of the king. Agesilaüs had all the virtues of the Spartans, without their common failings of avarice and deceit. He likewise had a warmth and tenderness in friendship seldom possessed by his countrymen. He has been styled "Sparta's most perfect citizen and most consummate general, in many ways, perhaps, her greatest man."

In the meantime Athens carried on wars in the North, by sea against Alexander of Pheræ, and by land against Macedon and the princes of Thrace. The second period of Athenian greatness culminated in the year B. C. 358, when Eubœa, the Chersonésus and Amphipolis were once more reduced under the dominion of Athens. The allied dependencies of Athens had long and patiently borne the system of exaction which she formerly practiced, but the patience of these dependencies finally became exhausted. In B. C. 358 the isles of Chios, Cos, Rhodes, and the city of Byzantium, acting in concert with several minor communities, and after having duly prepared themselves for the consequences, transmitted a joint declaration to the Athenian government, that, "as they now needed and derived no assistance or protection from Athens, the tribute hitherto paid in return for such countenance could no longer be required." This message aroused great indignation at Athens, which at once sent a fleet to check the rebellious spirit of the dependent allies.

The principal instigator of this measure was Chares, a man of profligate character, and one of the leading abettors of the oppressive impositions which had occasioned the revolt. The conduct of the *Social War*, as this contest was styled, was committed to this popular favorite. The two ablest commanders then in Greece, Timótheus and Iphícrates, were passed over, because of their known desire for conciliatory measures in preference to hostile proceedings in this instance. Chabrias was the only man of note or ability on board the Athenian fleet, and the expedition was productive of honor only to him, though he lost his life through the acquisition of it. Upon the arrival of the Athenians at Chios, their commander, Chares, found himself unable to take his fleet into the harbor, on account of the vigorous resistance of the rebellious allies, who had assembled in force on the island. Chabrias alone entered the little bay with but one ship entrusted to him; but when his men found themselves unsupported by the rest of the fleet, they leaped into the sea and swam back to the other vessels, leaving their brave leader, who preferred death to dishonor, to fall by the enemy's darts. The subsequent operations of Chares met with no better success than this attack upon Chios.

A new fleet was dispatched to his aid, under the command of Mnestheus, the son of Iphícrates, and the son-in-law of Timótheus, both of whom acted as his counselors, though neither of these two veterans held any important official station in the expedition. When the two Athenian fleets were united, it was resolved to besiege Byzantium, for the purpose of calling the entire strength of the revolted confederates to the defense of that city. The project succeeded. The revolted allies united all their naval forces and appeared before Byzantium. But a fierce storm rendered it unadvisable and impracticable, according to the view taken by Timótheus and Iphícrates, for the Athenians to confront the foe. Nevertheless Chares confidently insisted on assailing the allied rebels, notwithstanding the risk of shipwreck and other obstacles feared by his companions, but his opinions were overruled.

Chares at once sent messengers to Athens branding Timótheus and Iphícrates with all the opprobrious epithets which he could think of, and those two commanders were at once recalled and tried for neglect of duty. Timótheus was condemned to pay a fine of one hundred talents (about one hundred thousand dollars) to the state—a sentence which sent this worthy son of Conon and descendant of Miltíades into exile. Iphícrates, who was less scrupulous than his fellow-victim, filled the court with his armed friends and thus overawed the judges and forced an acquittal. He, however, like Timótheus, retired from his ungrateful native city; and neither of these eminent leaders ever afterward participated in public affairs.

Having thus rid himself of his colleagues, Chares roamed over the seas, attended by bands of singers, dancers and harlots, without concerning himself any further about the prosecution of the war. He finally brought down upon his country the wrath of the Persian king by hiring himself and his troops to assist the project of Artabazus, the rebellious Persian satrap of Ionia. A threatening message from King Artaxerxes Ochus so alarmed the Athenians that they recalled their fleet, thus practically permitting the revolted allies the enjoyment of the independence for which they had contended (B. C. 355). Athens was also induced by other causes to submit quietly for the time to this humiliating diminution of her dominion and her resources.

Thus the Social War was generally inglorious and exhaustive to Athens, and her power rapidly declined thenceforth. During the four years that this war had been in progress (B. C. 358-355), Philip of Macedon had been able to seize all the Athenian dependencies on the Thermaic Gulf and thus to extend the Macedonian power to the Peneus.

SECTION XIV.—RISE OF MACEDON UNDER PHILIP.

MACEDON, or Macedonia, was the country lying immediately north of Thessaly, between Mount Scardus on the west and the maritime plain of Thrace on the east. It was bounded on the north by Pæonia. Its greatest length from north to south was about ninety miles, and its width from east to west averaged seventy miles. Its area was probably almost six thousand square miles, about half that of Belgium. The country is divided by high mountain-chains, capped with snow, into a number of distinct basins, some of which have a lake in the center, while others are watered by rivers, which flow eastward into the Ægean, with a single exception. The basins are of such extent as to present the appearance of a succession of plains. The more elevated regions are mostly richly wooded, abounding with sparkling rivulets, deep gorges and numerous waterfalls; but in some places the country seems dull and monotonous, the traveler passing for miles over a series of bleak downs and bare hill sides, stony and without shrubs.

The chief mountains of Macedon were the Scardian and other branches from the chain of Hæmus; Pangæus, famous for its rich gold and silver mines; Athos, jutting into the Ægean sea, forming a remarkable and dangerous promontory; and Olympus, partly belonging to Thessaly. Most of these, especially the Scardian chain and Mount Athos, were richly wooded, and the timber produced by them was highly valued by ship-builders. The chief rivers of Macedon emptying into the Adriatic were the Panyásus, the Apsus, the Laüs, and the Celydnus; those flowing into the Ægean were the Haliácmon, the Erigon, the Axius, and the Strymon.

The soil of Macedon was fruitful; great abundance of corn, wine and oil being especially produced on the seacoast; while most of the mountains were rich in mineral treasures. Macedonia was noted for its excellent breed of horses, and thirty thousand brood mares were kept in the royal stables at Pella. Macedonia was said to contain one hundred and fifty different nations, each of its cities and towns being at one time regarded as an independent state. The western part of the country was inhabited by the barbarous Taulantii, in whose territory was the city of Epidamnus, founded by a Corcyræan colony, and whose name the Romans changed to Dyrácchium, now called Durazzo. In this same region was the city of Apollonia, founded by the Corinthians. South of the Taulantii, but also on the Adriatic, was the territory of the Alymiótæ, whose chief cities were Elyma and Bullis. East of these was the little inland district of the kingdom of Oréstes, where the son of Agamemnon is said to have settled after the murder of his mother. Macedonia proper was the south-eastern portion of the country, and contained the city of Ægæa, or Edessa, the cradle of the Macedonian kingdom, and Pella, the favorite capital of its most powerful monarchs. The districts of Macedonia proper bordering on the sea were called Piéria, and were consecrated to the Muses. These districts contained the important cities of Pydna, Phyllace and Dium. North-east was the region of Amphaxitis, bordering on the Thermaic Gulf, and its principal cities were Therma, afterwards called Thessalonica, now Salonica, and Stagíra, the birth-place of Aristotle. Chalcidice, or the Chalcidian peninsula, between the Thermaic and Strymonian Gulfs, has its coasts deeply indented with bays and inlets of the Ægean sea, and contained many important trading cities and colonies, the chief of which were Pellênê, in the headland of the same name; Potidæa, a Corinthian colony; Toróne, on the Toroanic Gulf; and Olynthus, celebrated for the many sieges sustained by it. In the region of Edonia, near the Strymon river, was Amphipolis, a favorite Athenian colony, Scotussa and Crenídas, the name of the latter being changed to Philippi by Philip of Macedon.

According to the Greek tradition the Macedonian kingdom was founded by Hellenic colonists from Argos under Cáranus, who were said to have been conducted by a flock of goats to the city of Edessa, which was easily stormed and taken (B. C. 813). The Macedonian people were not Hellenes, but belonged to the barbarous races, differing very little from the Greeks in ethnic type, and being most nearly related with the Illyrians in race. The Argive colony was hospitably received, and gradually acquired power in the region of Mount Bermius; and, according to Herodotus, Perdiccas, one of the original Argive emigrants, was acknowledged as king. Other ancient writers mention three kings before Perdiccas, whose combined reigns embraced a period of about a century. The period following is very obscure, little being known except the names of the kings. PERDICCAS I. is said to have reigned almost fifty years, from about B. C. 700 to B. C. 650. He was succeeded by his son, ARGÆUS, who reigned about thirty years, from B. C. 650 to B. C. 620. Argæus was succeeded by his son, PHILIP I., who likewise reigned about thirty years, from B. C. 620 to B. C. 590. Philip I. was succeeded by his son, AEROPUS, who reigned about twenty-five years, from B. C. 590 to B. C. 565. Aeropus was followed by his son, ALCETAS, whose reign lasted twenty-eight or twenty-nine years, from B. C. 565 to B. C. 537. Alcetas was followed by his son, AMYNTAS I., who was king at the time when the Persian expedition under Megabazus invaded the country and reduced it to tribute B. C. 507.

In B. C. 507 Amyntas I. submitted to Darius Hystaspes; and fifteen years afterward, during the first expedition of Mardonius, Macedonia became a mere province of the Medo-Persian Empire, the native kings being reduced to tribute. After the retreat of Xerxes, in B. C. 480, Macedonia recovered her independence, and began to extend her conquests eastward along the northern coast of the Ægean, meeting two rivals, the new Thracian kingdom of Sitacles upon its eastern frontier, and the Athenian power in the Greek cities of the Chalcidic peninsulas. PERDICCAS II., on ascending the throne, in B. C. 554, found his kingdom exposed to attacks from the Illyrians and the Thracians, while the Athenians encouraged his brother to contest the crown with him, which caused him to aid Sparta in the Peloponnesian War. The short but brilliant reign of ARCHELAUS I. (B. C. 413-B. C. 399) laid the foundation of Macedonian greatness. He improved the country by the construction of roads, strengthened it by forts, and introduced a better discipline in the army. He made Pella his capital and liberally patronized literature and art, inviting Socrates to his court and munificently protecting Eurípides when he was exiled from Athens. Archelaüs was assassinated by Cráteras, one of his favorites (B. C. 400); and his death was followed by forty years of civil wars and sanguinary revolutions, which are of no interest or importance.

When PERDICCAS III., who owed his elevation to the aid received from Pelópidas the Theban, was slain in battle with the Illyrians, he left to his infant son, Amyntas, a kingdom occupied by enemies and weakened by internal dissensions; but in this emergency, Philip, the late king's brother, who had escaped from Thebes, whither he had been sent as a hostage at the age of fifteen, asserted his nephew's rights, in opposition to several pretenders, who, according to custom, took advantage of the troublous times to claim the sovereignty. Philip was not swayed from his purpose by danger or difficulty. Naturally gifted with very superior mental powers, his residence in Thebes in his boyhood, as a hostage, had given him the opportunity of enjoying the instruction of Epaminóndas, in whose house he is said to have been brought up, and whose military skill he had the opportunity of witnessing. Frequent visits to the leading Grecian republics had added to the advantages which he so early possessed, by enabling the Macedonian prince to examine the most civilized institutions and to form a personal acquaintance with the greatest philosophers and warriors of the time. As Philip was in the bloom of youth, agreeable in appearance and winning in manners, it is not surprising that he so speedily won the affections of the Macedonian people from his half-barbarous rivals.

The pretenders to the Macedonian throne were, however, supported by the Thracians, who had invaded Macedon on the east after the death of Perdiccas III., while the Pæonians and the Illyrians had entered the kingdom from the north. Philip managed to disarm the hostility of all these foes by bribes, promises and flattery—means which he always used with skillful care, and for which he had always been noted. In B. C. 360 or 359 he was elevated from the regency to the throne, as PHILIP II., the people considering the precariousness of an infant reign as not adapted to the circumstances of the time.

Athens was the quarter whence Philip was threatened with new troubles. Having acted as an auxiliary only during the Grecian war which ended with the battle of Mantinéa, while Sparta and Thebes had put forth and exhausted their entire strength and resources, the Athenian republic had again found itself in the ascendency among the Grecian states at the close of the war, both respecting population and means. But with the return of prosperity to Athens, the pride and profligacy of its citizens likewise returned; corruption holding sway in the court, the Senate and the assembly of the people; the property of the good and innocent at home being confiscated to gratify the craving vices of the masses; while the tributary allies of the republic were oppressively and unscrupulously taxed to supply the same insatiable demands.

Such was the condition of the prosperous but miserable Athenian republic at the death of Perdiccas III, who had deeply incensed the Athenians by disputing their claim to Amphipolis, a city which the general council of Greece acknowledged as their dependency. Having this reason for disliking Perdiccas III., the Athenians continued their hostility to his brother and successor and sent an embassy to aid Argæus, the chief pretender to the Macedonian throne. Philip defeated and killed his rival in battle and took his Athenian allies prisoners. On this occasion Philip gave the first exhibition of that artful policy to which his long career owed its splendor and success. Instead of manifesting indignation against his Athenian captives, he treated them with the greatest kindness and respect, restored their property and sent them all home without ransom, and filled with admiration for his character and conduct. This politic and generous behavior produced the effect for which it was intended. When Philip's ambassadors presented themselves at Athens with peace propositions, the republic at once agreed to a treaty. As Philip had thus adroitly rid himself of one enemy, he next directed his attention to his northern neighbors, the Pæonians, whose king died at this crisis without heirs. Taking advantage of this situation, the Macedonian monarch led an army into Pæonia and easily reduced its inhabitants to subjection, annexing their territory to his own. After augmenting his military strength and his influence by this acquisition, Philip invaded Illyria and severely chastised its people for their recent incursion into Macedonia, compelling them to humbly beg for peace. Thus in the space of two years, the remarkable activity and address of this youthful Macedonian monarch restored internal tranquillity to his own kingdom, and elevated it to a far more vigorous and healthy condition than it had ever previously enjoyed.

After thus mastering his barbarous neighbors and securing the northern frontiers of his kingdom, Philip directed his attention to the south; and while Athens was engaged in the Social War, he began those aggressions which were destined to ultimate in his conquest of the whole of Greece.

His first movement was as cunning as that of a fox. Olynthus and Amphipolis, the most important of the confederated republics lying between Macedon and the sea, naturally attracted his first attention. To prevent the opposition of the Athenians, who claimed Amphipolis, until his designs were accomplished, Philip deceived them with the belief that he was about to subdue the city for them; and the Athenians, occupied in the Social War, allowed themselves to be thus duped. He also detached Olynthus from its alliance with Amphipolis. The Amphipolitans resisted his attack with great valor, but were eventually forced to surrender at discretion (B. C. 358). Philip treated the vanquished with equal policy and magnanimity, banishing only a few of the most violent leaders and instigators of the resistance to his arms, and dealing mildly with the remainder of the citizens. The city was incorporated with the kingdom of Macedon, to which it formed a valuable acquisition, on account of its maritime situation. After this conquest, Philip diligently cultivated the friendship of the Olynthians, feeling that their aid would enable him almost to defy the utmost wrath of the Athenian republic, which he would not be able to deceive much longer with regard to his actual designs. But the Athenians were still too much occupied in other directions to examine into the real character of the young monarch who continually gratified their vanity with conciliatory messages and flattering promises, while his actions had assumed a very ambiguous, if not a very menacing aspect. In addition to retaining Amphipolis, the Macedonian king captured the Athenian fortresses of Pydna and Potidæa and sent their garrisons home, expressing his polite regret that his alliance with Olynthus necessitated such a proceeding in one who entertained the profound respect for the Athenians which he did. Fully profiting by the toleration with which Athens still treated his actions, Philip invaded Thrace, annexing to his kingdom that part of the country containing valuable gold mines.

Philip next entered Thessaly and liberated that country from the cruel despotism of three tyrants, the brothers-in-law, and also the assassins, of Alexander of Pheræ. The Thessalians were so grateful for this deliverance that they made Philip their sovereign in everything except in name, ceding to him a large portion of their revenues and placing all the conveniences of their harbors and shipping at his command. The Macedonian king well knew how to make permanent this valuable grant. He contrived to extract from the Thracian gold mines about a thousand talents (equal to a million dollars) annually.

The triumphant King of Macedon now sought a consort for his throne. In one of his excursions from Thebes, he had formerly seen and admired Olympias, the daughter of Neoptólemus, king of the little territory of Esoire, on the western frontier of Thessaly. He now went thither to woo this fair princess, and before long he had the pleasure of presenting her to his court at Pella. While engaged in the festivities attending this event, Philip was suddenly again called to take the field, in consequence of intelligence sent to him by some of his emissaries, to the effect that Illyria, Pæonia and Thrace were jointly preparing to release themselves from the yoke which he had imposed upon them.

Philip sent Parménio, one of his ablest generals, to Illyria, and personally took the

2—46.-U. H.

field against the Pæonians and the Thracians. Both these enterprises succeeded, and the rebellious provinces were reduced to submission. Before Philip returned home, he received intelligence that his horses had gained the chariot-race at the Olympic Games; an occurrence which highly delighted him, as it measurably brought him within the pale of Grecian citizenship. Almost at the same instant he received the still more gladsome news that his queen had given birth to a son at Pella. A letter which Philip wrote to Aristotle indicates the gratification which the king felt on this occasion, as well as the high regard which he entertained for the philosopher, whose acquaintance he had made at Athens. Said Philip in this letter: "Know that a son is born to us. We thank the gods not so much for their gift, as for bestowing it at a time when Aristotle lives. We assure ourselves that you will form him a prince worthy of his father, and worthy of Macedon." Fourteen years after this letter was written (B. C. 356), Aristotle became the tutor of Philip's son; and, undoubtedly, much of the future glory of Alexander the Great may be attributed to the lessons of this renowned philosopher.

The dominion of the King of Macedon now extended from the Adriatic sea on the west to the Euxine sea on the east, and from the Hæmus mountains on the north to the southern limits of Thessaly on the south. Over this vast range of territory Philip's influence predominated, though he permitted a nominal sovereignty to continue in the hands of others in some quarters, at least temporarily. In Eastern Thrace, Kersobleptes, son of the deceased Cotys, held the title of king, and in Byzantium the Athenian influence still predominated, notwithstanding that city's share in the advantages and independence resulting from the Social War. Philip found it necessary to act cautiously in assuming dominion in Byzantium, because of the jealous care especially extended by Athens to her interests and commerce in that quarter. His desires were, however, steadily fixed upon the possession of that great commercial city; and his designs upon both Byzantium and Olynthus, as well as the ulterior objects to which the acquisition of these cities was only preliminary, were furthered by a new war which broke out in the center of Greece about this time.

This new struggle in Greece was known as the *Sacred War*. It began in B. C. 458, four years after the battle of Mantinéa and in the same year in which commenced the Social War between Athens and her dependent maritime allies. The Sacred War originated in certain proceedings of the Amphictyonic Council, the body which in early times had exercised so much influence in Grecian affairs, and which, after its rights had for a long time lain dormant, had begun to reassert them vigorously, supported mainly by the influence of Thebes. Instigated by the Theban representatives, the Amphictyons imprudently revived the old subject of the seizure of the Theban citadel by Phœbidas, and imposed a fine of five talents (about five thousand dollars) on Sparta for that transaction. The Lacedæmonians ignored this decree, and neither the Amphictyons nor the Thebans possessed sufficient power to enforce it by violent means.

Incited in the same manner by the Thebans, the Amphictyonic Council sentenced the people of Phocis to pay a heavy fine for having cultivated certain lands consecrated to Apollo and belonging to that deity's famous temple in the sacred city of Delphi, where the Amphictyons then held their sessions. The Thebans appeared to have been actuated by mercenary, ambitious and revengeful motives in urging these measures. The preponderance of Thebes in the Amphictyonic Council would have enabled her to pervert to her use the sums paid in as fines, had the decrees of the council been complied with. If, on the contrary, the fines remained unpaid, the religious prepossessions of all Greece would most likely have been shocked by the unconcern manifested by the Spartans and the Phocians to the sacred edicts of the Amphictyonic Council, and a plausible pretext would be furnished to war on the Phocians at least, in defense of the pretended rights of Apollo. Contemporary orators did not hesitate to declare that Thebes designed replenishing her finances from the rich treasures of the temple of Apollo, the only way to which lay through Phocis.

If these views were really entertained by the Thebans, they were only partially fulfilled. The exorbitant amounts of the fines insured their non-payment by the Spartans and the Phocians, and the Amphictyonic Council consequently declared the delinquents to be public enemies, whom every Grecian state that hoped for divine favor was bound to aid in forcing to compliance and submission. But the general public opinion of Greece paid no heed to the voice of the once-powerful Amphictyonic Council. Only the Thebans and the Locrians, with a few minor states who were actuated by private motives, obeyed the summons to punish the violators of law and the contemners of religion. Before the attempt to enforce obedience to the sacred council's decrees was made, the Phocians, who were destined to receive the measure of punishment, had made such ample preparations for resistance as to convince their enemies that they were not to be intimidated or coerced so easily. After receiving secret supplies of money, with assurance of additional support, from the Spartans, to whom they naturally appealed for sympathy in this emergency, the Phocians, without waiting to be attacked, anticipated their enemies by striking the first blow, encouraged to this course mainly by the advice of Philomélus, an ambitious and daring character among them, and the head of one of their wealthiest and most popular families. After cunningly preparing the minds of his countrymen for the exploit, Philomélus led a strong force hastily to Delphi and easily got possession of the sacred city, which had hitherto been solely and effectually protected by the powerful influence of superstition (B. C. 355). The Phocians were convinced by their leader that they were not guilty of any sacrilege, as a certain passage in Homer named them as the true guardians of the Delphic shrine.

After having successfully completed his enterprise, Philomélus was very careful to acquaint all Greece of the grounds on which he had expelled the Amphictyons from Apollo's sacred city, and had taken possession of the shrine in the name of his country; and no general feeling of horror or indignation appears to have been aroused in Greece by the tidings of this event. No new parties acceded to the contest in consequence of it, but the animosity of those engaged in, or about to engage in, the contest was not lessened by the seizure of Delphi. Nevertheless the Sacred War eventually involved most of the Grecian states, and was chiefly instrumental in subverting their independence, as already remarked.

Thebes seems to have been unprepared for the general unconcern with which the other Grecian republics viewed the decrees of the Amphictyonic Council and the action of the Phocians. Even the immediate dependencies of Thebes were not easily aroused to action, and the Phocians for a time proceeded unopposed in their bold conduct. Under the energetic leadership of Philomélus, and with the assistance of a powerful body of mercenaries, the Phocians invaded the territory of the Locrians and grievously harassed these allies of Thebes. When the Thebans, after the expiration of a season, were enabled to take the field, fortune forsook them. The Phocians triumphed in almost every battle during the two campaigns following the capture of Delphi.

But the Phocians at length experienced a great loss in the death of their valiant leader, which, from its circumstances, induced the Thebans to ascribe it to divine vengeance on account of their sacrilegious conduct. He was wounded in battle and was driven by the enemy to the verge of a precipice, from which he jumped, being thus dashed to pieces. He was probably impelled to this act by fear of a death by torture, as this war was characterized by circumstances of peculiar barbarity; no quarter being given to the Phocians, because of their impious crimes, and they treating their foes in the same manner, in self-defense.

Philomélus was succeeded in command of the Phocian army by his brother, Onomárchus, who was as able as his predecessor, but less scrupulous in the means which he employed to advance the interests entrusted to him. He made an unsparing use of the Delphic treasure in coining money for enlisting recruits for his army, and for bribing the allies of Thebes to desert her cause. For a time the cause of Phocis appeared to be invigorated with a fresh spirit, and Onomárchus took advantage of every favorable circumstance. In command of a large and well-equipped army, he ravaged Doris and Locris, and finally entered Bœotia and took by storm several of the dependent cities of Thebes. He likewise sent his brother Phayllus into Thessaly at the head of seven thousand men, to aid the party which had espoused the cause of Phocis in that country, in opposition to the powerful counter-interest of Macedon. But the Macedonian king led a powerful army against Phayllus, defeated him and drove him out of Thessaly in humiliation. Onomárchus was thereupon obliged to evacuate Bœotia and to advance against Philip of Macedon. In the battle which followed, the Phocian commander, by his skillful tactics, gained a decisive advantage over his new foe, compelling him to retreat back into his own kingdom to recruit his military strength. Onomárchus then returned to Bœotia with a considerable force of Thessalian auxiliaries in addition to his former army. But as soon as he was ready to make a fresh attack upon the power of Thebes, Philip of Macedon reëntered Thessaly, so that the Phocian general was once more called to defend that country and his allies there. In the sanguinary battle which ensued, the Phocians were utterly defeated and routed by the Macedonian king, Onomárchus and six thousand of his troops being slain, while three thousand of them were made prisoners and never afterward returned to their native land, some writers saying that they were cast into the sea by order of the triumphant Philip.

The King of Macedon might at this time have easily completed the ruin of Phocis had such been his object. He desired to perpetuate the internal dissensions of Greece, and not to strengthen any one state at the expense of another. He therefore remained satisfied for the time in having defeated the effort of the Phocians to wrest Thessaly from his own possession. He was somewhat obliged to pursue this policy, as he very clearly perceived that any attempt on his part to invade any Grecian state would instantly alarm them into the organization of a general league, against which he would at this time be powerless. Inspired by such motives, the wily Macedonian king again devoted himself to such projects of gradual and limited conquest which he perceived would furnish the most certain way to that absolute dominion on which he had set his heart.

Olynthus and Byzantium now began to see more clearly the designs entertained against them by Philip of Macedon, and to feel the results of his continued intrigues. In order to effectually resist his power, these two commercial cities entered into a new alliance with Athens, which republic clearly saw the ultimate drift of Philip's policy.

Philip was for some time obliged to remain in a state of inactivity, in consequence of a wound which he had received in one of his recent battles, and when he recovered from this accident his attention was again drawn to the Sacred War. Phayllus, the Phocian commander, the brother of Onomárchus, had instigated his countrymen to renew the struggle (B. C. 352); and by further plundering the Delphic shrine, he obtained sufficient means to raise an army of mercenaries, equal numerically to any other that had entered the field in the same cause. Athens furnished five thousand auxiliaries for this force, and Sparta furnished one thousand.

As soon as Philip heard of these preparations, he determined to seize the opportunity to enter Phocis, thinking that, by assuming the role of conservator of Apollo's shrine against its desecrators, the Phocians, he would inspire the leading Grecian states

DEFEAT OF THE THRACIANS BY THE MACEDONIAN PHALANX.

with such pious awe that they would permit him to pass Thermopylæ without opposition. His many emissaries among the different Grecian republics flattered him into the conviction that this would be the case. Accordingly he led a large army toward Phocis, but Greece was saved from the Macedon king's ambition, in this crisis, by the patriotic course of Athens. Upon receiving information of Philip's march, the Athenians instantly took the alarm, entered their ships, and placed a strong guard in the pass of Thermopylæ before the ambitious invader was able to reach the spot. Chagrined at finding the avenue to Central and Southern Greece impregnably closed against him, as well as at finding his purpose thus easily understood, Philip had no other alternative than to retire by the way he came, leaving the Thebans and their allies to prosecute the war against the Phocians without his assistance.

The Athenian people were elated because of the success of this first decisive movement against the King of Macedon, and immediately thereafter they convened in full assembly to take action in regard to their future course. This assembly became memorable in consequence of the first appearance of the illustrious orator, Demosthenes. This remarkable man was the son of a respectable Athenian citizen, of whose care he was deprived at the early age of seven years. The guardians to whose charge the youth was afterwards assigned did not prove faithful to their trust, and one of the first acts of Demosthenes, when he arrived at manhood, was to accuse them in public of having defrauded him of a part of his property.

This was the first essay of this celebrated orator in public speaking, and though he was successful in recovering some of his embezzled inheritance, his oratorical abilities were not considered of a very high order. He labored under a weak habit of body and other personal disadvantages, while his voice was exceedingly defective. But oratory was then the only way by which an ambitious man might reach power in Athens, or by which a patriotic soul might gain the influence essential to an efficient service of the republic. Demosthenes had both these characteristics, and was impelled thereby to a course of severe and incessant application, ending in his overcoming fully every obstacle thrown by nature in the way of his acquisition of oratorical skill and distinction.

Demosthenes is said to have overcome the impediment in his speech by putting pebbles in his mouth; to have cured himself of an unseemly habit of shrugging up his shoulders by suspending a sharp-pointed sword above them; and, by declaiming upon the seashore, to have accustomed himself to address calmly the most tumultuous of popular assemblies. The most brilliant success attended these diligent and persevering exertions of the young orator, who is said to have made his first speech on public questions when he was twenty-eight years of age. Two years later when he had acquired a large degree of popularity, he presented himself before the public assembly referred to, and uttered the first of a series of impassioned invectives against Philip of Macedon, in consequence of which that monarch ultimately acknowledged that "Demosthenes was of more weight against him than all the fleets and armies of Athens." These invectives, styled *philippics*, have been regarded ever since as models of popular eloquence, being truly as described by a historian, "grave and austere, like the orator's temper; masculine and sublime, bold, forcible and impetuous; abounding with metaphors, apostrophes and interrogations; producing altogether such a wonderful effect upon his hearers that they thought him inspired."

The great orator directed all his mighty powers in his first philippic to the duty of fully acquainting his Athenian countrymen with the real character of the King of Macedon, and of inciting them to a vigorous resistance to his designs. Demosthenes made a permanent impression upon the Athenian democracy; but the aristocracy advocated a different policy. The leaders of this opposite party were Phocion, an eminent leader and statesman, and Isocrates, an orator of great reputation and a man of spotless integrity. Phocion and Isocrates used all their influence to bring about a reconciliation between the Macedonian monarch and the Athenian people, as they were fully convinced that such was the only method of securing peace and reviving Grecian glory. These leaders considered their countrymen too feeble to oppose the growing power of Macedon, and consequently regarded it as the best policy to win the friendship of Philip. They also contended that Persia, which had deprived Greece of all her colonies in Asia Minor, was the foe always to be most dreaded. They likewise asserted that Philip was the only general of the time that was able to humble the Oriental barbarians and to lead the Grecian armies to victory on the fields consecrated by the valor of their illustrious ancestors. They looked upon him as the only leader capable of recovering the lost Hellenic colonies. Phocion and Isocrates were perfectly sincere and disinterested in these opinions, and a number of other influential Athenians regarded matters in the same light and entertained the same views. But the gold of the Macedonian king had more influence with the adherents of this passive and peaceful policy among the Athenian populace than all the efforts of Phocion, Isocrates and their partisans. Not only were the ignorant and the lower classes corrupted by Philip's emissaries, but many talented and distinguished individuals became the unprincipled hirelings of the artful monarch, and the ablest and most active of these was Démades, an orator who rivaled Demosthenes himself.

The advice of Demosthenes was not at once acted upon. The Athenians only partially raised the auxiliary force which he urged them to send to Olynthus and other allied states that were seriously menaced by Philip, and even this appears never to have been sent. For two years the Macedonian king remained seemingly inactive, for the purpose of again lulling to sleep the vigilance of the Athenians, which had been aroused by his attempt to pass Thermopylæ. Nevertheless, he was secretly occupied in distributing his gold among the Athenian dependencies in Eubœa and in making preparations to realize his long-contemplated designs upon Olynthus. His intrigues won vast numbers of the Eubœans to his interest; and in B. C. 349 his adherents in the island and those remaining faithful to Athens came to blows. Philip sent a Macedonian detachment to the island for the protection of his partisans, while the Athenians sent a force under Phocion to uphold their friends. The Athenian leader's prudence caused the hasty and complete overthrow of the Macedonian party in a pitched battle; and after Phocion had settled the affairs of the island, he returned to Athens, being triumphantly received by his rejoicing countrymen.

Though Philip was disappointed by the failure of his party in Eubœa, he was not thereby alarmed into any abandonment of his ambitious designs; but he took the field in person against the Olynthians, distinctly informing them that either they must leave Olynthus or he must leave Macedon. The Olynthians sent ambassadors to Athens imploring instant aid, as soon as Philip had entered their territory, and while he was occupied in the preliminary task of reducing the minor towns in the district. Sharp debates arose in Athens concerning the propriety of granting the Olynthian request. Démades and other supporters of the Macedonian interest counseled its utter rejection; but Demosthenes once more, in one of his most vigorous orations, advised his countrymen to provide for their own security by defending their allies against the ambition of Philip. The Athenians, swayed between two opposing forces, ultimately decided upon such half measures as were worse than total inactivity. They sent their favorite, Chares, a man calculated to charm the mob, but not adapted to military command, with a small force to the relief of Olynthus. Chares did nothing whatever for the Olynthians. He made a descent upon the coast of Thrace to fill his own coffers and to gratify the plundering spirit of his troops, and soon afterwards returned to Athens to expend the proceeds of his expedition in entertaining the populace with shows and feastings. Thus opposed by the Athenians, Philip invested Olynthus with his army and besieged the city. The Olynthians again sent ambassadors to Athens, and Demosthenes again lifted his eloquent voice in behalf of the distressed republic, imploring the Athenian people to prove themselves worthy of their heroic ancestors by coming to the rescue of their imperiled ally.

This second Olynthian embassy to Athens was no more successful than its predecessor. The Athenians sent four thousand foreign mercenaries, under the command of Charidemus, a man of the same character as Chares, to the relief of the beleaguered city. When this force reached Olynthus, it conducted itself in so unworthy a manner as to annoy and encumber the Olynthians, rather than to help them. Philip conducted the siege with vigor, but the resolute resistance of the Olynthians allowed them time to send a third embassy to Athens. On this occasion Demosthenes made another eloquent plea in behalf of the distressed city, and with better success than previously. He thoroughly aroused the Athenians to a sense of the dangers with which the ambition of the King of Macedon threatened Greece, and they decreed the instant arming of the citizens to assist Olynthus. But, unfortunately, this resolution came too late; as Philip got possession of Olynthus before it could be put in force, mainly in consequence of the treachery of two Olynthian commanders. The triumphant Macedonian monarch demolished the walls of the conquered city and carried its inhabitants into captivity (B. C. 348). Though Philip profited by the treachery of the two Olynthian generals who betrayed their city into his hands, he showed his contempt for the infamous traitors by the terrible punishment which he inflicted upon them. The spoils of the vanquished city vastly enriched the Macedonian treasury, and the entire district of Chalcidice was annexed to Philip's dominions, while the northern ports of the Ægean sea were open to his fleets. These acquisitions were celebrated by the splendid festival held at the Olympian town of Dium, lasting nine days. It was even visited by Athenians, and all were delighted with the affability of the wily Philip and his zeal to do honor to learning and the Muses.

During Philip's retreat from Thermopylæ, the Phocians and the Thebans were left alone to continue their causeless and barbarous war against each other, none of the larger Grecian states furnishing any effective assistance to either of them. Though Athens and Sparta were still nominally allies of Phocis, they were already tired of a contest which was attended with no benefit to themselves, and but feebly aided their ostensible allies.

Phayllus, the third Phocian leader in the Sacred War, died of consumption soon after he had succeeded to the command; and his countrymen entertained such profound reverence for the memory of his brothers and himself that they appointed his son Phaleucus, who was then a mere youth, to lead their forces. In several succeeding expeditions neither party gained any decisive advantage. They alternately ravaged each other's frontiers, and alternately boasted of victories which excited little attention in the rest of Greece. Even a Theban invasion of the Peloponnesus excited little notice, except in Arcadia, the country thus invaded. The Spartans and the Phocians ultimately forced the Thebans to retire, and Phocis and Bœotia again became the theater of petty and indecisive hostilities.

But after the capture of Olynthus by Philip of Macedon, a change occurred in the situation of affairs. Elated by his recent successes, Philip determined to make himself master of the pass of Thermopylæ, usually styled "the Gates of Greece," as one of the next steps to the general supremacy at which he aimed. The pass of Thermopylæ lay near the Phocian territories, and Philip for some time meditated upon the best plan of seizing these territories. Perceiving that the alliance between Athens and Phocis was a great obstacle in the way of his projects, he sent emissaries to detach Athens from the alliance. He also sent a squadron to invade and ravage the Athenian dependencies of Lemnos and Imbros, in order to draw the attention of the Athenians to their own affairs and to make them feel the demands of the Sacred War more annoying.

This Macedonian armament fully succeeded, as it surprised the islands of Lemnos and Imbros, and even made a descent upon the coast of Attica itself, where several rapidly-collected detachments of Athenian cavalry were defeated and routed. Philip sent another expedition to Euboea, to drive the Athenians from that island. He likewise succeeded in this enterprise, chiefly through the aid of the powerful party which his continued intrigues had raised among the inhabitants. He permitted the island to enjoy a nominal independence for some time, in order to color over this proceeding measurably to the Athenians.

But the unhappy fate of the Olynthians, in addition to these recent injuries, naturally aroused the indignation and jealousy of the Athenians, who were at first inclined to appeal to arms and take vengeance on the Macedonians, but the wily Philip soon changed the tone of the fickle Athenian populace. He pretended that everything which he had done had been forced upon him by the necessity of protecting his friends and allies, and professed the most ardent wish to be on amicable terms with the Athenian republic; and when certain influential Athenian citizens appeared in his presence to make complaint concerning the injuries received from Macedonian soldiers, he redressed their grievances, lavished kindness and presents upon them, and sent them home filled with admiration for his affability and generosity. These individuals presented themselves before the assembly of the Athenian people at a critical time, and gave such an account of Philip's friendly feeling towards the republic that the Athenians changed their warlike attitude, suspended their military preparations, and decided to send an embassy to the Macedonian court at Pella to deliberate on terms of peace with Philip.

Demosthenes and his greatest oratorical rival, Æschines, were two of the ten ambassadors sent on this peace mission to the court of Pella (B. C. 348). Demosthenes had for a long time seen through Philip's schemes, as his orations fully proved; and this mission was not an agreeable one to the orator, after all that he had said, but he was obliged to accept a share in it by the general demand of the Athenian people. Demosthenes conducted himself in a very unworthy manner throughout this embassy, partially on account of the embarrassment of confronting a man whom he had so often denounced before his countrymen, and partially because of the lack of personal courage characteristic of this orator. The majority of the other envoys were rather friendly disposed towards Philip, who therefore found it easy to dupe them by fair and flattering utterances. The result of the mission was the return of the embassy to Athens with the mere announcement that the King of Macedon was willing to enter into an alliance with the Athenian republic. As soon as the ambassadors had taken their departure from Pella, Philip instantly showed what reliance could be placed on his professions.

With the promptitude characteristic of all his military movements, the Macedonian monarch dashed upon Thrace, made its king, Kersobleptes, prisoner, and took possession of the entire country, including the cities of Serrium, Doriscus and others on the Thracian coast tributary to Athens. By this military expedition, Philip likewise got possession of the important passage of the Hellespont, one of the great barriers against Oriental or Scythian inroads into Greece. The Athenians sent a messenger to Philip to complain of these hostile acts, but he returned a cold and haughty reply. His position was then so formidable that the Athenians saw that their own security absolutely demanded the instant conclusion of a treaty of peace with him, notwithstanding the wrongs which they had suffered from him. Accordingly the ten ambassadors went to Pella a second time, and a treaty of peace was ratified.

But being resolved to obtain possession of the pass of Thermopylæ, Philip managed to entirely ignore the Phocians in this treaty, upon the pretext that, as he had promised to aid the Thebans in their quarrel with Phocis, it would be unbecoming in him openly to assume a friendly attitude towards the latter state. He, however, assured the ambassadors, at the same time, that he hated the Thebans, and would rather chastise them than the Phocians. All the Athenian ambassadors, except Demosthenes, had been bribed with Philip's gold; and they left Pella with every indication of absolute confidence in the Macedonian king's promises. But no sooner had they departed than Philip again showed what amount of dependence could be placed upon his word. He led an army towards Thermopylæ, marched through the pass unopposed, and shortly entered the Phocian territory. The unhappy Phocians, thrown off their guard by the accounts which they had received from Athens immediately after the return of the ambassadors, were duped into the belief that the Macedonian monarch was their friend, and they cordially welcomed him. Philip for a time concealed his designs, until he had convened the Amphictyonic Council at Delphi.

When the great council convened, in B. C. 347, only the deputies of Thebes, Locris and Thessaly were present, all these parties being intensely antagonistic to Phocis. The fate of that republic was sealed from that very moment. Under the directing influence of the ambitious King of Macedon, the council decreed that the cities of Phocis should be dismantled and reduced to the condition of villages with only sixty houses each—a proceeding amounting nearly to depopulation; that the arms and houses of the inhabitants should be sold; that they should pay a heavy annual fine; and that they should be excluded from the Grecian confederacy and from the Amphictyonic Council. The council passed a number of other decrees against the unfortunate Phocians. Philip was appointed to preside at the Pythian Games, and the two votes in the Amphictyonic Council which Phocis had lost were given to Macedon, which thus became an Amphictyonic state.

The news of these harsh edicts, which the Macedonians rigorously enforced, produced consternation and horror at Athens. The Athenians now reproached themselves for their want of vigilance which permitted Philip of Macedon to reach such a dangerous degree of power and influence; but they regarded it as utterly useless for them then to assume an aggressive attitude; and when the decree incorporating Macedon with the Hellenic body by making it an Amphictyonic state was presented to them for their approval, they offered no objection, though they do not seem to have acknowledged Philip's claim to be an Amphictyon. Even Demosthenes approved of peaceful measures under the existing circumstances; and the virtuous Isocrates, in accordance with his previous views, addressed a discourse at this time to Philip, exhorting him to a firm union with the Grecian states and to the direction of their united power against the Medo-Persian Empire. While making these concessions, the Athenians welcomed the expatriated Phocians, allowing them to settle in Attica and other possessions of the Athenian republic.

With the end of the Sacred War came a brief period of peace for Greece. But most of the states were either engaged with their own private quarrels, or were restless and chagrined at the terms upon which peace had been obtained, which was consequently a hollow and deceptive truce. Nevertheless, Philip was as diligent as ever in the prosecution of his ambitious schemes. After he had returned from Delphi with eleven thousand Phocian captives in his train, he visited Thrace, in which country he founded the two cities which he named respectively Philippopolis and Cabyla, which he peopled with most of his captives.

Some time afterward Philip led an expedition into Illyria to strengthen his power in that country (B. C. 344). While he was absent there, an embassy arrived at Pella from the Persian king, Artaxerxes Ochus, with offers of friendship to the King of Macedon. Philip's son Alexander, then a boy only twelve years of age, entertained the Persian envoys in his father's name, and excited their wonder at his extraordinary intelligence and dignified behavior. The embassy resulted in nothing of any consequence.

On returning from Illyria, Philip received a very welcome message from the Thebans, requesting him not to suffer their allies of Arcadia and Messené to be trampled upon by the domineering Spartans. The King of Macedon instantly perceived how easy it would now be to establish his influence in the Peloponnesus, and he accordingly obtained a decree from the Amphictyonic Council authorizing him to protect the aggrieved Arcadians and Messenians against the arrogant Lacedæmonians. Armed with this decree, and in spite of the most powerful eloquence of Demosthenes, who now exerted himself to his utmost against the ambitious designs of the king, Philip sailed to the coast of Laconia without being observed, and, after landing, he ravaged the Spartan territories and reduced the countrymen of Lycurgus and Leonidas to submission. The triumphant Macedonian king, in his ostensible capacity of mediator, but really that of dictator, settled the boundaries of the Peloponnesian states and composed their differences; after which he marched triumphantly to the city of Corinth, being welcomed along the route with the highest honors. He returned to Macedon, after witnessing certain festivals at Corinth.

Philip appears to have now regarded the Athenians with a certain degree of contempt, because of their fickle and vacillating character. His next proceedings seem to indicate such a feeling toward the people whom he was once so careful to cajole and flatter. He seized upon Halonnésus, an island on the Thracian coast belonging to Athens, while he also supported and encouraged the enemies of that republic in the Thracian Chersonésus, a measure calculated to do serious injury to the interests of the Athenian colonies in that region.

These proceedings, and others of a similar character, aroused the Athenians to energetic action; and they sent a strong force under Diópithes, a brave and skillful commander, and a devoted friend of Demosthenes, to protect their colonies in the Tracian Chersonésus. Diópithes made an irruption into Philip's Thracian territories, carrying away a vast amount of plunder and captives, without encountering any opposition on the part of Philip, who was then occupied in Upper Thrace. But the Macedonian king made loud complaints at Athens through his emissaries, who induced the people to bring the accused commander to trial. Demosthenes defended his friend in a vigorous oration and obtained his acquittal, and the Athenians were consequently encouraged to yet greater efforts.

They accordingly fitted out a fleet which plundered the coasts of Thessaly, seizing many Macedonian vessels. Another Athenian force, which was sent to Eubœa, drove the Macedonians from that island. But Philip, who had laid siege to Perinthus, indulged in remonstrances, until the obstinate defense of the Perinthians induced him to abandon the siege, when he led his army against Diópithes and utterly defeated him. Philip's fleet also captured some Athenian ships laden with corn for the relief of Perinthus—a circumstance which enabled the Macedonian king to execute a masterly stroke of policy. He sent vessels back to Athens, with letters assuring the citizens that he was fully aware that they were friendly to him, but that some mischievous leaders were his enemies.

This letter failed to have the desired effect, because Demosthenes exposed the trick and induced his Athenian countrymen to continue their protection to those cities which Philip was endeavoring to conquer. Phocion being sent with a new force of auxiliaries for this purpose, found the Macedodian king engaged in the siege of Byzantium, and forced him to abandon that enterprise. Phocion then made the most judicious preparations for the future protection of the allies and tributaries of Athens in Eastern Thrace and returned home, where he was welcomed with the utmost enthusiasm (B. C. 340).

The reason why Philip so readily submitted to the humiliation of being thwarted in his design on Byzantium was that his attention was called in a new direction at the time, thus affording him a plea to retreat with credit from the attempt in which he was engaged. Some time previously, Atheas, king of a Scythian tribe occupying the region between the western shores of the Euxine and the Danube, solicited Philip's assistance against some troublesome neighbors, promising, as a reward, that the King of Macedon should be declared heir to the throne of this Scythian tribe. Philip's ambition was tempted by this proffer, and he sent a considerable force to aid Atheas, who, however, had vanquished his enemies before the arrival of the Macedonian troops. The triumphant Atheas received his Macedonian allies with the most ungrateful coldness; and when these returned to their king, Philip was occupied in the siege of Byzantum; but he resolved to abandon the siege and have revenge on Atheas. The disciplined Macedonian soldiers easily overcame the Scythian barbarians; and, after a satisfactory campaign, Philip returned laden with booty, principally horses and herds, and with twenty thousand captives. Philip's son, Alexander, still a mere youth, accompanied his father on this expedition, and saved his life in battle, after he had received a wound which made him lame for the rest of his life.

While Philip was thus employed in the Scythian country, quarrels again broke out among the Grecian states. The citizens of Amphissa, a town in Locris, about eight miles from Delphi, had tilled a plain which had been some time previously devoted by the Amphictyonic Council to perpetual sterility in honor of Apollo. The Amphictyons, in their next meeting, denounced the Locrians of Amphissa as guilty of sacrilege and caused their lands to be laid waste and their houses to be burned. The Locrians were so enraged at these proceedings that they attacked the Amphictyons on their return from the spot, and the council afterwards raised a military force to avenge this outrage. The Locrians likewise appealed to arms and defended themselves against their assailants with success, until the council decided to solicit the assistance of Philip of Macedon, in his character of General of the Amphictyonic Council.

The deputation from the Amphictyonic Council met Philip just after he had returned from his Scythian campaign. He readily accepted the charge assigned to him, and was soon on his way by sea to the coast of Locris. He eluded certain Athenian vessels stationed in that region by the stratagem of throwing fictitious letters in their way, and effected a safe landing; after which he marched upon Amphissa, receiving a force of Theban auxiliaries on the way. When the Athenians were informed of Philip's disembarkment and march, they were so dreadfully alarmed that they sent ten thousand mercenaries to the defense of Amphissa. But the Macedonian king defeated and routed this force, and immediately afterwards easily took Amphissa by storm.

Ater he had garrisoned the unfortunate city with Macedonian troops, Philip followed up his success by a new measure, as bold as it was judicious. As he had some doubts as to the permanent friendship of the Thebans, whose territories were very important as lying in his way to those of Athens, he determined upon seizing the city of Elatéa, a strong fortress upon the frontier between Phocis and Bœotia, and distant from Attica only two days' march. Philip perceived that the possession of this strong post would enable him to keep the Thebans on terms of friendship through fear, and would likewise afford him a position from which he would, at any opportune moment, be able to make a dash upon the towns and cities of Attica. Accordingly, Philip led his army to Elatéa, and, with his usual good fortune, he soon obtained possession of the city (B. C. 338). Elatéa was located on a rocky eminence, at the base of which flowed the river Cephissus, opening a navigable route from that spot into Attica. The Macedonian monarch vastly added to the natural strength of the city by erecting new walls and other fortifications, after which he remained in his new stronghold for some time, getting ready for a formidable effort to acquire the ultimate mastery of Greece.

Nothing that had thus far signalized Philip's career so alarmed the Athenians as did his capture of Elatéa. When they received intelligence of that event, they were stricken with dismay. An assembly of the people was convened, and the eloquent voice of Demosthenes was again heard in denunciation of the enemy of Grecian liberty. The great orator's words had the effect of arousing his degenerate countrymen to a full sense of the perils of this crisis; and though the Athenians were then more licentious than at any other period of their history, they still showed that they could be aroused to noble exertions in the cause of their country's freedom. Following the advice of Demosthenes, the Athenians raised a large army to confront the Macedonian king, while they also sent ambassadors to Thebes and other Grecian republics, requesting them to arm and unite in the defense of their common independence. Demosthenes himself went on this mission to Thebes, and that republic was aroused by his vehement eloquence to a sense of its duty to the cause of Grecian freedom. The Thebans openly renounced their alliance with Macedon and prepared to unite with Athens in the struggle for the preservation of Hellenic independence.

Before long a formidable allied army, consisting mainly of Athenians and Thebans, but also including Corinthians, Achæans, Eubœans and other Grecian confederates, in all numbering about thirty thousand men, marched into the plains of Bœotia to expel the common enemy from the soil of republican Greece. Philip, now fully prepared for the impending conflict, led an army of thirty-two thousand men to Chæronéa, which he considered the most desirable place to encounter his antagonists. The allied Grecian army also proceeded to Chæronéa, and on the plain around that city was fought the battle which decided the fate of Greece.

The Macedonian king himself confronted the Athenians with one portion of his army, while he assigned his youthful son Alexander to the command of that portion facing the Thebans. In the early part of the bloody struggle these two divisions of the Macedonian army suffered different fortunes. Although Alexander was then only eighteen years of age, he conducted his operations with such prudence and valor that the Thebans were entirely routed with frightful slaughter, and their valiant Sacred Band was entirely cut to pieces. The Athenians made their first attack with such impetuosity that they gained a temporary advantage over Philip's division, driving all before them for a time. But the incompetency of the Athenian commanders, Lysicles and Chares, enabled Philip to retrieve the fortunes of the day. His adversaries followed up their success without order or discipline, urged on by Lysicles, who arrogantly exclaimed: "Let us drive the cowards to Macedon." But then Philip suddenly led his celebrated phalanx to the summit of a hill and dashed down with steady and irresistible force upon the Athenians, who were so overpowered by the shock that they were unable to recover their ranks. Most of them, Lysicles among the number, saved themselves by fleeing from the field, thus presenting a dishonorable contrast to the heroic conduct of the valiant but ill-fated bands of Thebes. When Philip perceived that his victory was complete, he at once ordered the slaughter to be discontinued. The survivors among his vanquished foes acknowledged themselves defeated, in accordance with custom, by requesting permission to bury their dead. Before this could be done, Philip insulted the memory of the slain by appearing on the sanguinary field in Bacchanalian triumph, after a banquet given in honor of the great victory of the day. For the moment he was tamed to pity by the sight of the Theban corpses, but he soon lost this feeling. Such was the battle of Chæronéa, which was the death-blow to Grecian independence (B. C. 338).

The triumphant Macedonian monarch treated the people of Thebes with the most remarkable severity, rigorously punishing those opposed to him in that republic, putting his adherents in all its offices, and garrisoning the city with Macedonian soldiers. But he treated the Athenians with kindness, as he had a more refined and more powerful people to deal with; and, instead of doing injury to Athens or its inhabitants, he offered them peace on certain conditions, one of which was that they should surrender the isle of Samos, the great bulwark of their maritime power; but they were allowed to retain their democratic form of government and to remain in undisturbed possession of Attica. Altogether, the terms which Philip offered to Athens were more favorable than they could have expected, and a treaty of peace was concluded.

Thus the famous battle of Chæronéa put an end forever to the republican glories of ancient Greece. The history of the decline and overthrow of these remarkable states should ever serve as a lesson to nations. When the Greeks were united in one firm league, they were able to cope with the most powerful and the most remote empires; but when they became divided, they ultimately fell a prey to a comparatively-small and semi-barbarous tribe in their own immediate vicinity. The isles, colonies, dependencies and tributaries, upon which much of the early power of the Hellenic states depended, had already been lost to them, one by one, in consequence of their own internal quarrels. The battle of Chæronéa left them with scarcely any of their possessions, excepting those that lay within and around the walls of their own cities. Nevertheless, as shown by a circumstance which occurred in the year after the battle, had all the Hellenic states made common cause with each other, Philip would not have been able to conquer them.

In B. C. 337 the conquering King of Macedon convened a general congress of the Amphictyonic states at Corinth, from which only the Spartans remained absent. Those who were present made a calculation of the forces which they were able to jointly raise, and it was discovered that an army of two hundred and twenty thousand infantry and fifteen thousand cavalry could be brought into the field by the Grecian republics. With such an available force at their command, they would not have been obliged to submit to the yoke of a half-civilized despot, had they been sufficiently united in the cause of Grecian freedom.

Philip's motives for assembling this general Grecian congress at Corinth were of the same ambitious character as those which had previously directed all his actions. He had from the beginning aimed at universal dominion, and had always considered the conquest of Greece as only a step to the conquest of Asia, which he very well knew could only be accomplished by the friendship and aid of the Grecian states. These ulterior designs undoubtedly afforded a sufficient reason for the leniency with which he treated the Grecian republics after his decisive victory at Chæronéa, and for his allowing them to retain their old democratic institutions and their nominal independence. The Macedonian king found a sufficient pretext for asking the aid of the assembled states at Corinth, in the cruel oppression which the Greek colonies of Asia Minor had endured from the Persian government, as administered by its appointed satraps; and he urged upon the Greeks to retaliate upon the Persians for the invasions of Greece in the times of Darius Hystaspes and Xerxes.

The Grecian congress at Corinth entered into Philip's designs with apparent readiness, and named him generalissimo of the Græco-Macedonian armies, while the din of military preparations again resounded throughout Greece. The king was prevented from immediately entering on his Eastern expedition by disturbances in Illyria and domestic dissensions in Macedon. Alexander quarreled with his father for mistreating his mother Olympias, and ultimately, in a moment of irritation, threw himself into the arms of the dissatisfied Illyrians. The king attacked and subdued the Illyrians, and, by the employment of all his art, finally succeeded in soothing Alexander.

The transactions just related occupied so much time that Philip's career and life were ended before he had an opportunity to prosecute his schemes of Asiatic conquest. In B. C. 336—two years after his subjugation of Greece by his victory at Chæronéa—Philip of Macedon was assassinated by Pausánias, a Macedonian nobleman. Some asserted that the assassin was bribed to this deed by the Persians; but there is good reason for believing that Alexander only put forth this imputation to justify his invasion of the dominions of the great king, or to clear himself and his mother Olympias from the suspicion which was entertained by very many that they were accessories to the crime. Aristotle, who was present at Pella at the time, attributed the deed to motives of private revenge on the part of Pausánias, who was seized and put to death immediately after he had committed the act. As may well be supposed, the republican Greeks, and especially the Athenians, rejoiced at the death of the man who had subverted the liberties of their country.

Philip's character has been differently estimated by historians. His contemporaries and posterity, friends and foes, have all acknowledged the greatness of his abilities; but the motives by which he was actuated have been viewed in extremely-opposite lights. No one who views his career impartially can doubt that he was ambitious of power and dominion, and unscrupulous as to the means of acquiring these. He began his career as the sovereign of a poor and unimportant kingdom, but, by the force of his own talents, he had made himself the virtual ruler of a hundred principalities before his death.

He obtained his extended dominion by the force of arms when the occasion required it, but his most potent instrument was his artful policy. In all the annals of history, no prince ever carried the arts of diplomatic intrigue to the same degree as did King Philip II. of Macedon; and though we must not forget that the contemporary writers who delineated his character were his avowed and inveterate enemies, there is little reason for believing that they have misrepresented him in ascribing *bribery* as at the foundation of his entire policy. His first step, on all occasions when he desired to subject any community to his influence or his dominion, was to discover and win over to his side its factious and dissatisfied citizens and leaders, who, if unable to accomplish his ends for him by secret intrigue, might, at any rate, injure and check the efforts of his antagonists in the same community, and make an open military conquest much more easy.

Though Philip was unscrupulous in the use of the basest instruments to assist him in his acquisition of power and dominion, he exhibited, in numerous instances, sufficient mental greatness to use the power which he thus acquired with nobleness and generosity. His treatment of the Athenians after the battle of Chæronéa was magnanimous and humane, even if he was partially prompted thereto by a view of ulterior interest. When his generals, on that occasion, advised him to attack Athens, he calmly responded: "Have I done so much for glory, and shall I destroy the theater of that glory?"

Historians have recorded other sayings of his, of a like character, and uttered under similar circumstances; and from these we may fairly infer that Philip's ambition for power and dominion was largely mingled with the love of performing great deeds.

The combination of good and evil elements in Philip's character is yet more forcibly exemplified by his conduct in other capacities than those of the warrior and the statesman. Though almost constantly occupied in the bustle of war and politics, he had a love for polite learning and for all those studies which refine and adorn human nature. This feature of his character is fully shown by his letter to Aristotle on the birth of Alexander; and we have additional evidence of it in his constant anxiety to attract to his court all who were renowned throughout Greece for learning and literary ability. He personally corresponded with various celebrated philosophers of the Grecian schools, and his letters are reputed to have been remarkable for their elegance and good sense. He was usually kind and generous to his friends to the highest degree, and he administered justice to his subjects in a paternal and impartial manner.

A vice by which Philip frequently, if not habitually, disgraced himself was his excessive indulgence in wine; and it is said that when, on one occasion, while intoxicated, he had given judgment against an old woman, in a case brought before him, she exclaimed: "I appeal from Philip drunk to Philip sober." He also disturbed the domestic peace of his family by his unfaithfulness toward his wife, Olympias.

SECTION XV.—LITERATURE, PHILOSOPHY AND ART.

SIMÓNIDES, a highly-eminent elegiac poet, was born in the isle of Ceos, about the year B. C. 560. Upon reaching manhood he opened a school and for some time taught singing and dancing, but grew weary of this occupation and passed over into Asia Minor, where he wandered from city to city, writing, for pay, poetical eulogiums on the victors in the public games. He visited Athens during the rule of Hippias and Hipparchus, and afterwards sailed to Sicily, where his poetical talents won for him the friendship of Híero I., King of Syracuse, who was distinguished for his liberal patronage of men of learning and genius. At the court of this enlightened sovereign, Simónides spent most of the remaining years of his life, and it was there that he composed some of his chief poems. Simónides was renowned for his wisdom, as well as for his poetical genius. When Híero asked him concerning the nature of God, Simónides asked to be permitted to think upon the subject before giving a reply. At the end of the time he requested two days more, and thus continued asking, always doubling the number of days demanded, until Híero inquired in astonishment for the reason of such delay. Simónides replied that the longer he reflected upon the subject the more difficult it seemed. Being once asked whether knowledge or wealth was most desirable, he replied that it must be wealth, as he daily saw learned men waiting at the doors of rich men. This answer was intended as a reflection upon sycophancy. Simónides mainly excelled in elegiac poetry, but he likewise attempted other kinds of poetical composition with success. His songs celebrated the heroes of Marathon, Thermopylæ, Salamis and Plataea, and were greatly admired. For the first of these pieces he gained a prize in a contest with Æschylus, the tragic poet. Simónides was unrivaled in tenderness and plaintive sweetness, and one of his works, styled *Lamentations*, is particularly mentioned by ancient writers as a poem of such touching pathos that it was impossible to read it without shedding tears. Simónides is said to have perfected the Greek alphabet by the addition of four letters to it, and to have invented what is styled *artificial memory*. He preserved his faculties until he was very well advanced in years, and won a prize for poetical composition in his eightieth year. He died in Sicily at the age of ninety. Only a few verses of his many poems yet remain.

PINDAR, of Thebes—the illustrious contemporary of Simónides—was the greatest Greek lyric poet, and celebrated the triumphs of the victors in the Olympic Games, but likewise wrote hymns, dirges and pastoral songs. Pindar's lyrical poems have been objects of general admiration in ancient and modern times. He was born at Cynoscéphalæ, near Thebes, about the year B. C. 520. Pindar's first poetical efforts were not appreciated by his countrymen, the Bœotians, but the rest of Greece at once testified their admiration of his genius. Hiero I., King of Syracuse, and Theron, King of Agrigentum, bestowed their friendship and patronage upon him; while princes and states vied with each other in honoring him. The Delphic oracle ordered a seat to be placed for him in the temple of Apollo, where he might sing the verses composed by him in praise of that god. The oracle also declared that a portion of the first fruits offered in the temple should be set apart for his use. He offended his countrymen by lauding the Athenians in one of his poems, and was heavily fined in consequence; but the Athenians at once presented him with a sum of money twice the amount of the fine imposed upon him. Pindar's lyrics abound in moral and elevating sentiments, while being characterized by such originality of thought and vigor of expression that he is deservedly considered the greatest lyric poet of Greece. Many of his poems have been lost, and all that remain are four books of odes celebrating the victors at the Olympian, Pythian, Neméan and Isthmian Games. Pindar died suddenly in the fifty-fifth year of his age, while sitting in the public theater. The esteem in which he had been held in life was increased by his death. His memory was regarded with such veneration that when Alexander the Great took and destroyed Thebes, he spared the house and family of Pindar.

Dramatic poetry was raised to a great height by the three great Athenian tragic poets—ÆSCHYLUS, EURIPIDES and SOPHOCLES—all of whom were in some way connected with the battle of Salamis. Æschylus fought in the battle; Sóphocles, at the age of fifteen, danced to the choral song of Simónides in honor of the victory; and Eurípides was born in Salamis on the day of the battle. Æschylus was the first eminent Grecian dramatist. He was born at Eleusis, in Attica, B. C. 520. He was deservedly designated as "The Father of Tragedy," because of the many improvements which he effected in the Athenian theater, and because of the force and dignity of his tragic compositions, which elevated and refined the infant drama. Æschylus was without a rival in dramatic composition until his fifty-sixth year, when he was defeated in a theatrical contest by Sóphocles, a young competitor of merit and genius. He was unable to endure the mortification of seeing his rival's works preferred to his own, and therefore retired from Athens, going over into Sicily, where he was welcomed by Híero I., King of Syracuse, at whose court the lyric poets Simónides and Pindar, and the comic writer Epicharmus, were then living. Æschylus wrote almost a hundred dramas, but only seven have been preserved. His works are characterized by a boldness and originality which have rarely been rivaled; but, in trying to be concise and forcible, he sometimes became abrupt and obscure; and his language, though usually grand and sublime, is frequently of a bombastic style. Æschylus died at Gela, in Sicily, in the sixty-ninth year of his age. A singular account is given of the manner of his death. It is related that, while he was one day walking, bareheaded, in the fields, an eagle, mistaking his bald head for a stone, dropped a tortoise upon it, thus killing him on the spot. The inhabitants of Gela buried Æschylus with great pomp and erected a monument over his grave.

SOPHOCLES, the successful rival of Æschylus, was born at Colonos, in the vicinity of Athens, about the year B. C. 497. His father, Sophilus, although a blacksmith by trade, seems to have been an individual of some importance and in easy circumstances. Sóphocles was given a good education and was early distinguished for his rapid progress in his studies. At the time of the battle of Salamis he had reached his sixteenth year, and, on account of his personal beauty and his musical skill, he was selected to lead the chorus of noble youths who danced around the trophy erected by the Greeks to commemorate that great naval victory. The dramatic achievements of Æschylus had early won the admiration and aroused the ambition of Sóphocles, who, upon reaching manhood, directed all his mental energies to the composition of tragic poetry. After he had spent considerable time in preparation, he ventured, in his twenty-eighth year, to compete with Æschylus for the dramatic prize. Encouraged by the decision of the judges in his favor, Sóphocles continued to write dramas, and is said to have produced about one hundred and twenty tragedies, of which only seven have been transmitted to modern times. He likewise composed many elegiac and lyric poems and a prose work on dramatic poetry. Sóphocles was a warrior and a politician as well as a poet. He served under Pericles in one of the wars with the Spartans, and was subsequently associated with him in the command of an army sent by the Athenians against the island of Samos. He led the forces which took Anæa, an Ionian city, near Samos; and, after his return from his campaigns, his grateful countrymen chose him for chief Archon of the republic. His popularity continued to the end of his life. He always made his appearance in the theater when any of his dramas were to be performed, and on these occasions he was always greeted with the enthusiastic plaudits of the audience, and the crown of victory was conferred upon him by the judges twenty times. He suffered many afflictions. When he had arrived at an advanced age, his undutiful children, actuated by a desire to obtain possession of his property immediately, affected to believe him fallen into a condition of mental weakness, and sought legal authority to deprive him of the management of his affairs. But Sóphocles had no difficulty in proving that his mind remained unimpaired, notwithstanding his advanced age. He produced the tragedy of *Œdipus Colonêus*, which he had just composed, and then asked if a person of an imbecile mind could produce such a work. The judges, filled with admiration for his genius, refused the application of his children and censured them severely for their base and unfilial conduct. Sóphocles received many invitations to visit foreign lands, but his attachment to his native country prevented him from leaving it, even for a short time. Sóphocles has been classed in the front rank of tragic poets, both by his contemporaries and by all succeeding ages. Sóphocles died in his ninetieth year (B. C. 407). It is said that his death was caused by the excess of his joy at receiving the prize for a drama which he had produced at that advanced age. At the time of his death Athens was besieged by the Spartans, and that rigid people so highly esteemed his poetic genius that their general, Lysander, granted an armistice until his funeral obsequies should be performed. His countrymen, who loved him for his mild, amiable and upright character, as much as they admired him for his brilliant talents, erected a monument to his memory.

EURIPIDES, the third great Athenian tragic poet, was born at Salamis, on the day of the great sea-fight there, as already noticed. His father, Mnesarchus, seems to have been a person of respectable rank; and it is said that his mother, Clito, was of noble birth, although the comic poet, Aristóphanes says, in one of his dramas, that she was a vender of pot-herbs. In the general distress resulting from the Persian invasion of Attica, the parents of Eurípides may have been obliged to follow an humble calling to obtain a livelihood; but such can only have been the case for a brief period, as they were certainly able to give their son such an education as only persons in affluent circumstances could do in those times. The Delphic oracle having predicted that Eurípides would become an object of general admiration and be crowned with the victor's wreath, his parents fancied that he was destined to excel in gymnastic contests. For this reason they had him carefully trained in athletic exercises, but they did not neglect his mental culture. His teachers were the celebrated philosopher, Anaxágoras, and the accomplished rhetorician, Pródicus. Besides philosophy and oratory, he studied music and painting, especially the latter, in which he reached great eminence.

When Eurípides had arrived at the age at which he became his own master, he abandoned the exercise of the gymnasium, which he apparently never relished, and applied himself with more than his usual zeal to his favorite philosophical and literary studies. Profiting by the fate of his tutor Anaxágoras, who was banished from Athens for promulgating opinions subversive of the established religion, Eurípides prudently determined to adopt a less dangerous profession than that of correcting popular errors, and thus commenced writing dramas in his eighteenth year. Thenceforth, until he left Athens for Macedonia, in his seventy-second year, he continued his dramatic labors, and wrote seventy-five, or according to some, ninety-two plays. He composed a number of his tragedies in a gloomy cave in his native island of Salamis, to which he retired for that purpose at times from the noise of Athens. He wrote slowly, because of the great care he took to polish his works; and it is said that, having once related that he had taken three days to compose three verses, a brother poet boasted that he had written a hundred in the same space of time. To this Eurípides replied: "That may be; but you ought to remember that your verses are destined to perish as quickly as they are composed, while mine are intended to last forever." In his seventy-second year Eurípides accepted an invitation from Archelaüs, King of Macedon, and retired to that monarch's court, where resided many other eminent characters from the Grecian republics. Thus, by retiring to Macedon, Eurípides had the satisfaction of living in the society of many distinguished and talented men, among whom were Zeuxis, the celebrated painter; Timótheus, a skillful musician; and Agatho, an able tragic writer.

The dramas of Eurípides are less sublime, but more tender, than those of Æschylus and Sóphocles. They are deservedly admired for the moral and philosophical sentiments with which they abound, as well as for their exquisite beauty of versification; but Eurípides has been criticised for lack of skill in forming his plots, and the Athenians believed that they detected impiety in some of his expressions. He married twice, and unhappily in both instances, and this was perhaps the cause of that severe treatment of the female sex in his works, for which reason he was called "the woman-hater." Eurípides died at the court of Macedon, in the seventy-fifth year of his age and the third of his residence in that country (B. C. 405). It is said that he was torn to pieces by the hounds of King Archelaüs while walking in a wood. The Macedonian king honored his remains with a pompous funeral and erected a monument to his memory.

As tragedy in ancient Greece arose from the dithyrambic verses at the feasts of Dionysus, the god of wine, so comedy originated in the phallic hymn which was chanted by the processions of worshipers during the same festivals. The earliest comic performances were scarcely more than simple mountebank exhibitions. SUSURION, who is usually alluded to as the first comedian, was an individual who wandered through the villages of Attica with a company of buffoons, reciting ludicrous compositions on a temporary stage. EPICHARMUS, a native of the island of Ceos, but who lived most of his time in Sicily, whither he was taken by his parents when he was only three months old, is usually regarded as the first comic poet. He flourished about the middle of the fifth century before Christ, and composed fifty-two comedies, every one of which has perished. He was banished from Sicily for alluding disrespectfully to the wife of Hiero I., King of Syracuse. He lived almost a hundred years. Other comic poets, contemporary with Epicharmus, were CRATINUS and EUPOLIS, natives of Athens, both of whom composed many comedies, none of which have been preserved.

ARISTOPHANES, the most celebrated of the Grecian comic poets, was likewise a native of Athens. The date of his birth is not definitely known, but he introduced his first comedy during the fourth year of the Peloponnesian War (B. C. 427). He was very popular, and wrote comedies for many years. His plays, like those of the early comic poets, consisted of caricatures and ludicrous representations of living men and manners. He composed fifty-four plays, of which only seventeen remain.

Greek historical writing arose in the fifth century before Christ. The only records of the past prior to this period were the legends and fables of the poets and the uncertain accounts transmitted from age to age by tradition. HERODOTUS, the first Greek historian—called "the Father of History"—was born at Halicarnassus, in Asia Minor, B. C. 484. After reaching manhood he removed to Samos, where the elegant Ionic in which Homer's poems were composed was the prevailing dialect. Herodotus soon completely mastered this dialect, and his works are said to exhibit it in greater perfection than those of any other Greek writer. After forming the design of writing history, he traveled for materials into Egypt and Italy and also into different parts of Asia, acquiring much valuable information in this way concerning nations previously unknown and manners and customs never described before. After giving an account of all that he had seen and learned, in nine books, he read parts of it to the Greeks assembled at the Olympic Games, and thus acquired a wider and more immediate fame than he could have obtained otherwise in times when there was no art of printing to multiply copies of literary productions. We are indebted to Herodotus for our knowledge of a very large and important portion of ancient history. He is believed to have spent the latter period of his life at Thurium in Magna Græcia, and to have died there at the age of more than seventy years (B. C. 413).

THUCYDIDES, another renowned Greek historian, was born at Athens in the year B. C. 470. His father, Olorus, was one of the noblest and wealthiest citizens of Athens, and claimed to be a descendant of the kings of Thrace. Thucydides received an excellent education, having been instructed in philosophy by Anaxágoras, and in oratory by Antiphon, a famous rhetorician. When about fifteen years of age, he accompanied his father to the Olympic festival, where he heard Herodotus recite a part of his history amid the applauses of the assembled Greeks, and on this occasion he was so strongly animated with a desire to emulate the honored historian that he burst into tears. Herodotus observed this, and is said to have congratulated the father of Thucydides upon having a son who manifested so ardent a love for literature at so early an age. Thenceforth Thucydides regarded the writing of history as the great object of his ambition. When the Peloponnesian War broke out in b C. 431, Thucydides, rightly believing that a series of important events were about to transpire which would afford him ample materials for an interesting history, commenced taking notes of all that occurred, and continued this practice during the greater portion of that protracted struggle. From these notes he afterwards produced an excellent and highly-polished historical work. In the early portion of the contest Thucydides resided in Athens, and personally witnessed the ravages of the pestilence, which he has described in a graphic and striking manner. He subsequently removed to the island of Thasos, in the Ægean, near the coast of Thrace, the country of his ancestors, where he owned extensive estates and valuable gold mines. He afterwards traveled, and is believed to have died about B. C. 410. His history, written in the Attic dialect and consisting of eight books, is much admired for its vigorous and lively descriptions, its scrupulous regard for truth, and the spirit of frankness and impartiality pervading the entire narrative.

The next renowned Greek historian was XENOPHON, who was born at Athens in B. C. 450, and was a disciple of Socrates. He lived in comparative obscurity until he was fifty years of age, when he was invited to Sardis, the Lydian capital, by a friend who desired to introduce him to the younger Cy-

HERODOTUS READING HIS HISTORY TO THE ASSEMBLED GREEKS.

rus, the brother and rival of the Persian king Artaxerxes Mnemon. Xenophon was persuaded to go thither, and he consequently joined the Greek auxiliaries through whose assistance Cyrus sought to acquire his brother's crown. The expedition, which the historical part of Xenophon's work relates in full, met with disaster, and was followed by the celebrated Retreat of the Ten Thousand, under the leadership of Xenophon, who subsequently became the historian of this famous march. As his Athenian countrymen proscribed him, King Agesilaüs of Sparta provided him with a safe retreat at Eléa, where he passed many years with his family in an agreeable country-seat and wrote most of the historical and philosophical works which have given him his fame. In consequence of war breaking out between the Spartans and the Eléans, Xenophon was obliged to relinquish his delightful retirement and seek refuge in Corinth, where he died at the advanced age of ninety years. His chief works are his *Memorabilia* (Memoirs of Socrates); *Cyropædia* (Institutions of Cyrus the Great); *Anábasis* (Expedition of the younger Cyrus); *Hellénica* (a continuation of Thucydides' unfinished history of Greece); besides Treatises on Economics, Tyranny, Taxes, Hunting and other subjects; his view of the Spartan and Athenian republics, and several other interesting works. Xenophon was called "the Attic Bee," because of his clear, natural and graceful style. As a philosoper Xenophon was a most worthy pupil of Socrates. For some time after Xenophon's death there was no regular Grecian historian to take up the chain of events at the point where he had left off; but the deficiency was largely supplied by the numerous oratorical productions of the age of Philip of Macedon and Alexander the Great.

CTESIAS, a Greek historian ranking far below the three great ones just named, was the contemporary of the latter two, and was for seventeen years the court-physician of the Persian king Artaxerxes Mnemon, and wrote histories of Assyria, Babylonia, Media and Persia, contradicting those of Herodotus on nearly every essential point; but the authority of Herodotus has been accepted in preference by the majority of the most eminent modern historians. Ctesias returned from Persia to Greece in the year B. C. 398.

The Athenians, having had a government correctly styled "the extreme of democracy," were very naturally the first people to cultivate public speaking. The whole administration of government was exercised by the general assembly of the people, and there was no more certain way to fame and fortune than the winning of their favor by the charms of eloquence. The Athenian populace was not, however, a mere mob, whom fluent nonsense could captivate, or who preferred a howling demagogue to the refined statesman. They possessed a finer and more delicate organization than the people of more northern climates. Their musical taste was cultivated, and their perception of the beauties of style was strengthened by the musical and literary contests at the public festivals. The more laborious employments were filled by slaves, thus giving the citizens leisure to attend to the affairs of state; and the comic writers give us very amusing accounts of the absolute rage for legislation, pervading all classes of citizens in Athens. There was therefore "a great demand for orators in the market, and consequently there was a corresponding supply."

PERICLES was the first great Athenian orator, as well as the greatest Athenian statesman. His style of speaking, and his character, to some extent, resembled that of the great English statesman and orator, George Canning, whom modern writers have frequently compared with him. The power possessed by Pericles in Athens was wholly attributable to his brilliant talents, but he died too early for his own fame and for his country's welfare. The funeral oration delivered by him over those who fell at Nisæa has been recorded by Thucydides in his own peculiar style, and consequently cannot be quoted as a specimen, but it perhaps contains the essence of what he actually said, and may therefore serve to give us some remote idea of those powers which "wielded at will the fierce democracy."

We have observed how greatly inferior ALCIBIADES was to his renowned uncle, though he seemed intended by fortune to act a similar part. But his fame as a statesman and orator is very trifling, and his intellectual power without the guidance of moral principle produced a lamentable effect, and his misdirected talents and misapplied industry were the cause of sore evils to his country.

The orations of LYSIAS and ISÆUS are fine specimens of Grecian legal oratory, rather than of public eloquence. Both these are distinguished for their elegant style and their harmonious sentences. The former is simple, the latter is more energetic; but the age in which they flourished, at the end of the Peloponnesian War, was not favorable to the development of oratorical talents.

An ancient philosopher has said that "great occasions produce great men." The beginning of the great struggle between Macedonian supremacy and Grecian independence was the most important crisis in Grecian history. "The coming events were casting their shadows before." Demosthenes appeared at this period to arouse Athenian patriotism by his fervid eloquence.

The age of Demosthenes produced an abundance of orators, who were brought forward by the busy excitement of the time. The speeches of most of them have been lost, but the historians tell us sufficient concerning them for us to form an opinion of their characters. DÉMADES was originally a common sailor, possessing strong natural powers, but these were unpolished by education and unregulated by moral principle. His habits in private life were coarse and brutal, and these qualities likewise tinctured his eloquence, but his rude bluntness often produced a greater effect in the public assemblies than the polished elegance of more refined speakers.

HYPÉRIDES was a speaker of a very opposite kind, as he possessed an exquisite taste, a delicate sense of harmony, and a richly-cultured intellect, but his delicate sensibility made him weak and timid. He lacked energy and boldness sufficient to encounter the tumults of the public assemblies, but at the courts of law he was an able and pleasing advocate. PHOCION and LYCURGUS appeared to have been more indebted to their virtuous characters for their influence than to their oratorical talents. They were always listened to with respect, as the people knew that they spoke from conscientious conviction, and they were therefore more esteemed as statesmen than admired as orators. DINÁRCHUS is only known as the accuser of Demosthenes on the charge of having taken a bribe from the fugitive Hárpalus to engage the Athenians to protect him from Alexander's vengeance. The truth of the charge is extremely doubtful, but it is urged in the invective of Dinárchus very artfully and spiritedly. The merits of the oration are, however, lessened by the virulence and violence of the attack.

The rhetorical compositions of ISOCRATES, who was born B. C. 436 and was one of the most illustrious contemporaries of Demosthenes, likewise contributed immensely to the same subject. Isocrates was usually classed as an orator, but his discourses invariably came before his countrymen in a written form, as the weakness of his frame and voice made him incapable of the exertion of delivering them before a public assembly. Isocrates was, however, fully conversant with the principles of oratory, and taught them to the noblest youths of Athens and Greece for a long period with the most remarkable success. His discourses are of a very high order of composition, and in these he sometimes addressed himself to political and likewise to moral subjects. In his political discourses he regularly advocated the cause of Philip, in opposition to the counsels of Demosthenes; and although the eloquence of his opponent was irresistible, Isocrates always succeeded in winning the respectful attention and the applause of his fellow-citizens. A few of the orations of Isocrates yet remain, one of the most admired being an address to Philip of Macedon himself.

ÆSCHINES, the greatest of the oratorical rivals of Demosthenes, was a supporter of the Athenian aristocracy and the Macedonian supremacy as against the democracy and the opposition to Macedonian ascendency as led by Demosthenes. Though lacking the boldness and vehemence of his illustrious opponent, the style of Æschines was more varied and ornamented. Said Quinctilian, the great Roman rhetorician: "Æschines has more flesh and muscle, Demosthenes more bone and sinew." His style is flowing and harmonious; his periods are exquisitely polished; and his ridicule is very spirited and graceful. He would in all likelihood have reached the highest distinction at any other period, but he was borne down by the superior talents of his renowned rival. At first Æschines was, like Demosthenes, a most vigorous opponent of Philip of Macedon. His subsequent desertion of the democratic and patriotic party made him exceedingly unpopular, and induced him to cultivate the favor of his audience by rhetorical artifices, rather than exalted sentiments, which he actually sometimes pretended to ridicule as forced and affected.

The career of DEMOSTHENES, the most distinguished of Athenian orators, constitutes a portion of Grecian history, and, as such, has already been detailed. His discourses, nevertheless, deserve more special attention than has been given them in the preceding section. When asked what qualities were essential to effective speaking, Demosthenes is said to have replied that three things were requisite; and, in fuller explanation, said that these qualities were "action—action—action." This forcible exposition of his views of eloquence enables us to anticipate the characteristics of his own style of oratory. We therefore discover that vehement delivery was the chief characteristic of Demosthenes' style of speaking. But if an equal power of forcible expression had not been combined in him with the power of energetic action, he would not have been the very foremost of all orators, as he has always been acknowledged to be. Those orations which were called *Philippics*, because they were uttered against Philip of Macedon, are usually pointed to as the most effective specimens of Demosthenes' oratory. A number of others remain, of almost equal eloquence, and among these are especially the orations for the Olynthians and the orator's defense of himself against Æschines. All of these discourses constitute important additions to the historical records of the periods in which they were uttered.

DEMOSTHENES.

The two original schools of Grecian philosophy were the *Ionic*, founded by Tháles, and the *Italic*, or *Pythagorean*, founded by Pythágoras. These two systems gave rise to several others towards the end of the fifth century before Christ, known respectively as the *Socrátic*, the *Eleátic* and the *Heraclitéan*, the last two being modifications of the Italic. The first sprang from the school of Tháles, in the doctrines of which its founder, Socrates, was initiated by his teachers, Anaxágoras and Archelaüs, who were pupils of Tháles.

The founder of the Eleatic sect, so called from its seat at Eléa, an Ionian city in Asia Minor, was XENOPHANES, a native of the Ionic city of Colophon, also in Asia Minor. This philosopher lived to the great age of one hundred years, and is supposed to have died about the middle of the fifth century before Christ. He at first professed the Pythagorean philosophy, but he afterwards modified it with so many of his own doctrines that he came to be considered the founder of a new school. There is some uncertainty respecting the exact nature of his philosophical system, as none of his writings have been preserved. But it is believed that he taught that the universe is eternal, maintaining that if there ever had been a time when nothing existed, nothing could ever have existed. He is also believed to have taught that there is one God, incorporeal, eternal, intelligent and all-pervading, and that there are innumerable worlds in the universe.

PARMÉNIDES, a disciple of Xenóphanes, and his successor as teacher in his philosophical school, was born at Eléa, in the early part of the fifth century before Christ. Like his master, Xenóphanes, Parménides held that the universe is eternal and that there is an all-pervading and animating principle called God. He taught that the earth is a sphere and located in the center of the universe; that there are two elements, fire and earth; and that all things, animate and inanimate, have been produced by the action of the animate upon the inanimate.

ZENO, usually called "the Eleatic," to distinguish him from the philosopher of the same name who founded the sect of the Stoics, was a native of Eléa and a pupil of Parménides, whom he afterwards succeeded as teacher of the Eleatic philosophy. Zeno zealously defended the rights of the people, and is said to have been put to death with the most cruel torments by the tyrant of his native city, in punishment for having formed a conspiracy against his authority. None of Zeno's writings remain, but it is believed that his philosophical doctrines varied very little from those of his predecessors in the same school. He taught that nature does not admit of a vacuum; that there are four elements, namely, heat, moisture, cold and dryness; that man's body is formed of earth and his soul of an equal mixture of the four elements. Zeno was an able logician, and delighted to display his dialectic powers by indifferently supporting either side of a question, so that there is doubt respecting his actual views on some subjects. He maintained that motion is impossible, and Seneca asserted that he even went so far as to question the existence of the material world.

LEUCIPPUS, a disciple of Zeno, originated the *atomic theory*, which was subsequently extended by DEMOCRITUS, "the laughing philosopher." Leucíppus asserted that all things consist of very minute individual atoms, which, in themselves, possess the principle of motion, but that the universe was formed in consequence of these atoms falling into a vacuum. Demócritus was born at Abdera on the Thracian coast of the Ægean in B. C. 460, and was one of the most celebrated Greek philosophers. After having traveled through Egypt, Chaldæa and other Oriental lands, he returned to Abdera, where he devoted himself to philosophical studies. His grand axiom was that the greatest good consists in a tranquil mind. He has been called the "laughing philosopher," in contrast to HERACLITUS, "the weeping philosopher." Demócritus died in B. C. 357.

Heraclítus founded the sect of the Heraclitéans. He was a native of the Ionic city of Ephesus, in Asia Minor, and flourished in the early part of the fifth century before Christ. He was so much respected for his wisdom that his fellow-citizens requested him to become their ruler; but he refused to do so, giving as his reason that their minds were so perverted that they could not relish or appreciate good government. When Heraclítus appeared in public, he went about ostentatiously bewailing the wickedness of mankind. On one occasion he played at dice in public with a number of boys, to show his contempt for the ordinary occupations of men; and when the citizens gathered about him in surprise, he addressed them thus: "Worst of men, what do you wonder at? Is it not better to do this than to govern you?"

Being at length unable apparently to endure the society of his fellow men, Heraclítus retired to a mountain solitude, where he lived on herbs and roots, like the hermits of later times. When he became dropsical, in consequence of this poor diet, he returned to Ephesus to ask for medical advice. But even when his life was at stake, he was unwilling to live like other people, and therefore, instead of plainly stating his case to the physicians, he asked them enigmatically, "whether they could make a drought of a shower." Seeing that they could not comprehend his meaning, and disdaining to explain himself any further, he retired to an ox-stall, where he lay down on a heap of dung, hoping, we are told, that its warmth would draw the watery humors out from his body. He there died in the sixtieth year of his age, a victim to his own cynical nature and his extreme love of singularity.

Heraclítus left behind him several works which were highly esteemed by his disciples. He studied to write as well as to speak in an obscure manner, so that great acuteness and great pains were required to comprehend his meaning. It is said that the tragic poet Eurípides, having lent Socrates a copy of a treatise produced by Heraclítus, afterwards asked him what he thought of the work, when Socrates replied, that "the things which he understood in it were excellent, and so, he supposed, were those which he did not understand; but they required a Délian diver."

EMPÉDOCLES, a famous Grecian philosopher of the Pythagoréan sect, was a native of Agrigentum, in Sicily, and flourished about the middle of the fifth century before Christ. Like many other followers of Pythágoras, Empédocles engrafted some of his own opinions upon the Pythagoréan system. He maintained the Pythagoréan doctrine of the existence of an active and passive principle; the latter being matter, and the former an ethereal and intelligent fire, which produced and pervades and animates all things. He likewise believed in the doctrine of the metempsychosis, or transmigration of the soul, and accordingly taught the principle of refraining from killing or eating animal flesh.

ANAXÁGORAS was the first teacher of the Ionic school of philosophy, on whom the ancients bestowed the remarkable designation of *Mind*, either because of the peculiar vigor of his intellect, or on account of the fact that this philosopher was the first who described God as an incorporeal intelligence, separate from, and entirely independent of, matter. He was born in the Ionic city of Clazomenæ, in Asia Minor, in the year B. C. 500. Anaxágoras was a resident of Athens for many years, during which period he had several pupils who afterwards became renowned, such as Socrates, Eurípides and Pericles. He was finally brought to trial for impiety, because he taught that the sun was a fiery stone, and not the god Apollo, as was popularly believed. He was banished from Athens, and passed the remainder of his life in teaching philosophy at Lampsacus, on the Asiatic side of the Hellespont. Anaxágoras, as we have said, was the first of the ancient philosophers who taught that God is independent of matter, and not merely a spiritual or fiery essence pervading the universe as its *soul* or animating principle, which was the pantheistic doctrine taught by Pythágoras and a few other philosophers.

ARCHELAUS, the last teacher of the Ionic school, was a native either of Athens or of Milétus, it is not definitely known which. He was a disciple of Anaxágoras, and accompanied him in exile. On the death of Anaxágoras, Archelaüs succeeded him in the charge of his school at Lampsacus; but afterwards returned to Athens where he opened a school of philosophy, which had many pupils.

SOCRATES, the greatest and best of all the Grecian philosophers, has been alluded to extensively in a preceding section of this work, where the circumstances of his teaching and his martyrdom have been fully narrated. We have there stated that it was to destroy the pernicious influence of the Sophists that Socrates discoursed with the people in the public thoroughfares and in the workshops of Athens. He did not really teach any system of philosophy, but, by enforcing the maxim "Know Thyself," upon his pupils, he sought to lead them to discover the truth for themselves. It was his virtues and his efforts to improve the morals of his countrymen that aroused his enemies, who finally succeeded in having him condemned to death by drinking the poison hemlock, as already related. As Socrates himself left nothing in writing, our knowledge of his doctrines is derived from his illustrious disciples, Plato and Xenophon. The six schools of Grecian philosophy which afterwards arose all traced their sources to the teaching of the immortal Socrates.

PLATO—called *the Divine*, and one of the

LAST HOURS OF SOCRATES.

greatest of Athenian philosophers — was born in the island of Ægina, B. C. 430, but was of Athenian descent. He was the founder of the *Academic* school of philosophy, so called because he delivered his lectures in the shady groves of Académus, near the gates of Athens. Plato was the most illustrious of all the disciples of Socrates, and, in his *Dialogues*, he represents himself as conversing with his famous teacher.

When very young, Plato gave the most promising indications of his genius, devoting himself mainly to the cultivation of poetry and the fine arts. Before he had arrived at the age of twenty-five he had produced epic and dramatic poems of considerable length, but he cast these into the fire when he had heard Socrates delivering a discourse.

From that moment Plato determined to devote himself entirely to the study of philosophy, and for eight successive years he attended the lectures of Socrates. When that wise and good man became a victim to persecution, Plato was at his side in his latter days, and subsequently embodied in the dialogue called *Phædo* those beautiful thoughts on the Immortality of the Soul which the martyred philosopher expressed in his last moments. After his preceptor's death, Plato retired from Athens to Megara, then traveled into Italy, Egypt and other countries, filling his mind with the philosophic lore to be found in each, after which he finally returned to Athens to open a new school for the instruction of youth. He selected as the spot for this purpose the shady grove which had been the property of a citizen named Académus, from whom it was thenceforth called the *Academy*. Multitudes of the most distinguished youths of Greece were soon attracted to Plato's school by the philosopher's genius and learning, and even females were often present at his lectures in disguise.

The fame of Plato's wisdom circulated far and wide, and many kings and communities solicited his aid to improve the political constitution of their governments. King Dionysius I., the tyrant of Syracuse, succeeded in persuading Plato to visit his capital, but the tyrant's character was too mean and vicious to enable him to profit by the philosopher's teachings, and Plato was actually obliged to flee from the court of Dionysius to save his life. Plato continued teaching philosophy in Athens, with few intervals, until his death, which occurred in the seventy-ninth year of his age. His personal character appears to have been worthy of the genius displayed in his writings.

Plato's writings embody the views designated as the Platonic philosophy, and comprise thirty-five dialogues and thirteen epistles. These works include so immense a variety of subjects, ethical, physical, logical and political, that it is impossible to give any connected view of them as a whole, in a limited compass. Like many of the ancients, Plato conceived of two principles, *God* and *Matter*, as having an eternal coexistence in the universe. He considered the Deity as an Intelligent Cause, the origin of all spiritual being, and the creator of the material world. Plato's writings abound with many fine thoughts, but the whole is pervaded with a fanciful spirit of theory. No other ancient philosopher had the honor of attracting so many followers, so brilliantly did his genius shine forth in all his writings.

ARISTOTLE, the founder of the *Peripatetic* sect, was born B. C., 384, and was a native of Stagira, a town of Thrace, on which account he has frequently been called the Stagirite. He was initiated into the elements of knowledge at an early age, and at seventeen he went to Athens, where he commenced to study under Plato. That distinguished philosopher was not long in discovering the wonderful talents of his pupil, and was accustomed to calling him "the Mind of the School." Aristotle went to Macedon to become the tutor of Alexander the Great, in accordance with the promise made, at that prince's birth, to his father, King Philip. Alexander was about fourteen years old when Aristotle undertook his education (B. C. 343). Their connection lasted eight years, during which period the teacher

734 ANCIENT HISTORY.—GREECE.

gained the regard of his pupil so thoroughly that Alexander was accustomed to say that "Philip had given him life, but Aristotle had taught him to live well."

When Alexander ascended the Macedonian throne, and began his career of conquest, Aristotle returned to Athens and opened a school in the shady grove called the *Lyceum*. On account of his practice of walking there when delivering his lectures to his pupils, his followers were called *Peripatetics*, or walkers. Aristotle, however, continued corresponding with his royal pupil; and, at his teacher's request, Alexander employed several thousand persons in Europe and Asia to collect specimens of the animal kingdom and sent them to Aristotle, who was thus enabled to write a History of Animated Nature in fifty volumes, of which only ten yet remain.

ARISTOTLE AND HIS PUPIL, ALEXANDER.

Aristotle wrote on a great many subjects, and the most acute intellects of succeeding ages have readily adopted his opinions. His History of Animated Nature has been admired for its accurate descriptions. His other works are remarkable for the wonderful acuteness of mind therein displayed. Aristotle was one of the giant intellects of the world, and his system of mental philosophy prevailed for two thousand years, when his deductive system was superseded by Bacon's inductive system. Aristotle's lectures attracted throngs of listeners from all the great cities of Europe and Asia.

ANTISTHENES, a famous Athenian philosopher, born B. C. 420, was the founder of the sect called the *Cynics*, who maintained that man attained the greatest earthly happiness by renouncing all worldly pleasures. He was also a pupil of Socrates, and was distinguished by his severity of manners, remarkable even among the pupils of that simple and unassuming teacher. Socrates disapproved the raggedness which Antisthenes delighted to display in his apparel. Said the immortal preceptor: "Why so ostentatious? Through your rags I see your vanity."

DIOGENES, an eccentric philosopher and the most celebrated of the Cynics, carried the doctrines of that sect to the wildest extreme, renouncing all the pleasures, comforts and conveniences of life. He was a Greek of Asia Minor, being a native of Sinopé, in Paphlagonia, and was born B. C. 418. It is said that he went in rags, begged his bread in order to be insulted, and sat in the eaves of the houses under the rain. We are also told that he embraced snow statues in winter, and usually lived in a tub. He did all this, it is said, to inure himself to all hardships, to prepare himself to endure all vicissitudes of fortune, and to counteract the advance of luxury by his example. He did not wish to possess anything which he considered superfluous, and his only worldly possessions were a rugged garment to cover his nakedness, a wooden staff for walking, a wooden bowl for drinking, and a tub for shelter. One day observing a boy drinking from the hollow of his hand, the philosopher dashed his wooden bowl to pieces, saying: "Behold! That boy has taught me that I still have something that I can do without!"

Being at one time seen with a lighted lantern in midday in the streets of Athens, and being asked what he was hunting, Diogenes replied: "An honest man." On another occasion, seeing the officers of justice in Athens carrying off an individual for stealing a trifling article, the philosopher remarked: "The big thieves have caught a little one." Diogenes was rude and merciless in his speech. He employed sarcasm as his great weapon to teach mankind. There is, however, a noble meaning in some of his sayings, which comprise the best exposition of the Cynical philosophy.

A profligate person having written over the door of his dwelling, "Let nothing evil enter here;" Diogenes said: "Which way, then, must the stranger go in?" Seeing a young man blush, the philosopher said: "Take courage, friend, that is the color of virtue." In answer to a person who asked him at what hour he ought to dine, Diogenes said: "If you are a rich man, when you will; if you are poor, when you can." Said some one: "How happy is Calisthenes in living with Alexander;" to which Diogenes replied: "No, he is not happy; for he must dine when Alexander pleases."

Hearing some one complain that he should not die in his native land, Diogenes said: "Be not uneasy; from every place there is a passage to the regions below." Being presented at a feast with a large goblet of wine, he threw it upon the ground; and upon being blamed for wasting so much good drink, he replied: "Had I drunk it, there would have been double waste; I, as well as the wine, would have been lost." Being asked what benefit he reaped from his laborious philosophical studies and his search for wisdom, Diogenes answered: "If I reap no other benefit, this alone is sufficient compensation, that I am prepared with equanimity to meet every sort of fortune."

When he had reached a good age, Diogenes was captured by pirates at sea and sold as a slave in Crete, where he was purchased by a wealthy Corinthian, who was struck with the reply the captive philosopher gave to the auctioneer who put him up for sale. Said the vender: "What can you do?" To this Diogenes replied: "I can govern men; therefore sell me to some one who wants a master." He thereafter passed much of his life in Corinth, and became the teacher of his master's children, and likewise exercised the office of a censor of the public morals. At that place he was visited by Alexander the Great, who found him, at the age of eighty, sitting in his tub. Said Alexander to the philosopher: "Can I do anything for you?" To which Diogenes replied: "Yes, you can get out of my sunshine." The young king was so well pleased with this answer that he said: "Were I not Alexander, I would be Diogenes!"

DIOGENES.

Diogenes did not always have the advantage in sharp speaking. Some one, observing him embrace a statue covered with snow, inquired if he did not suffer from the cold. "No," answered the philosopher; whereupon the stranger responded: "Why, then, I can see no great merit in what you are now doing." One day he entered Plato's neatly-furnished house and trampled a fine carpet under his feet, saying: "Thus I trample upon the pride of Plato." To this Plato justly replied: "And with a greater pride of your own." On another occasion, hearing that Plato, in one of his lectures in the Academy, defined man as a "two-legged animal without feathers," Diogenes stripped a fowl of its feathers, and, carrying it into the Academy, exclaimed: "Behold Plato's man!" Plato was in the habit of calling Diogenes a mad Socrates, alluding to the combination of wisdom and extravagant folly constituting his character.

Diogenes had a supreme contempt for the whole human race. He went barefoot even when the ground was covered with snow. His father had been a banker at Sinopé, and was banished from that city for counterfeiting. Diogenes himself had been guilty of the same offense before he became a Cynic, and was also exiled, whereupon he came to Athens and visited Antisthenes, who treated him with great contempt and would have driven him away with his staff, because he did not wish to have any more disciples; but Diogenes, who was neither surprised nor intimidated, bowed his head and said: "Strike, you will never find a stick hard enough to drive me off as long as you speak." Antisthenes, overcome by his obstinacy, allowed Diogenes to become one of his disciples.

ZENO, a native of the island of Cyprus, born B. C. 362, founded the sect of the *Stoics*, who practiced the strictest virtue and morality, and sought happiness by an absolute indifference to all the vicissitudes of life. The Stoics resembled the Cynics in general, but did not carry their self-denial to the same extreme limits in regard to dress and habits. But while the Stoics were as austere in their morals as the Cynics, they endeavored to introduce novel principles into speculative philosophy. The Stoical philosophy teaches the existence of two principles in nature, by which, and out of which, all things have been formed. One of these principles is active, consisting of pure ether or spirit, which dwells on the surface of the heavens, and which is God, or the creative spirit of the universe. The passive principle is matter, which is in itself destitute of all qualities, but is capable of receiving any impression, or being moulded into any form.

Zeno's father was a Cyprian merchant and sent his son to Athens, when he was about thirty years old, with a cargo of Phœnician purple, which was lost by shipwreck on the coast of Piræus. But Zeno arrived safely at Athens, and, as he had already received an excellent education, he continued his studies and finally resolved to open a school of philosophy. He selected a public portico called the *Stoa*, as the scene of his lectures, and hence the term *Stoic*, as applied to Zeno's followers. They were also sometimes called "the Philosophers of the Porch." On this portico, or Stoa, Zeno taught successfully for a long time, exhibiting in his own life a perfect example of the stern morality which he inculcated on others. He was frugal in his diet and in all his expenses, grave and dignified in his manners, and his dress was always plain, though scrupulously neat. Zeno committed suicide when he was ninety-eight years of age, in consequence of having broken one of his fingers, a circumstance which he regarded as rendering him unfit for earth. Said he: "Why am I thus importuned? I obey the summons." He accordingly strangled himself when he reached home, influenced to the act by a miserable superstition.

ARISTIPPUS of Cyrênê, another pupil of Socrates, founded the sect of the *Cyrenâcis*, who ran into the opposite extreme, holding that pleasure was the only good and pain the only evil, a principle which opened the way to every kind of licentiousness. EPICURUS, a disciple of Aristíppus, adopted the same principle, but endeavored to correct its dangerous tendency by teaching that virtue was the real source of pleasure, and vice of pain; but his followers did not accept his reasoning in regard to vice, especially as he denied the doctrine of the immortality of the soul, by which his teaching could only be sustained. The sect of the *Epicuréans*, named after Epicúrus, whom they regarded as their founder, therefore considered luxury and the gratification of the appetites as the chief end of existence.

Epicúrus was born at Gargetus, a small town in the vicinity of Athens, B. C. 344. At the age of eighteen he went to study at Athens and remained there for a considerable time. He afterwards made his residence successively at Mitylênê and Lampsacus, in both of which cities he opened a school for the instruction of others in his philosophical doctrines. But he was not long satisfied with a provincial reputation; and in his thirty-eighth year he returned to Athens, where he purchased a garden, in which he began to teach his system of philosophy, therefore often called "the Philosophy of the Garden." As his opinions were an agreeable contrast to the doctrines of the Cynics and the Stoics, which were then prevalent, Epicúrus soon became exceedingly popular. Epicúrus himself was noted for his temperance and continence and endeavored to impress upon his pupils the necessity of restraining all the passions, in order to lead a happy life.

PYRRHO, a native of the Ionic city of Eléa, in Asia Minor, born B. C. 340, founded the sect of the *Skeptics*, who regarded everything as uncertain, some even going so far as to doubt their own existence. It is said that Pyrrho's friends found it necessary to attend the philosopher in his walks, lest his doubt about the existence of a precipice or an approaching wagon or carriage might result in ending all his mortal doubts at once. Like many of the other Grecian sages, Pyrrho reached a good old age. He died at ninety, and was honored with a monumental statue by the Athenians, as well as by the Eléans. Pyrrho's followers first called themselves the *Pyrrhonic School*, but were finally named *Skeptics*.

The *New Academics*, founded by CARNÉADES and ARCÉSILAS, adopted the principles of the Skeptics to some extent, and consequently introduced the worst doctrines of the Sophists. Several minor sects were founded on modifications of these doctrines, but it is not necessary to enumerate them in this work.

The fine arts commenced at so early an age that their origin is not recorded.

Though they were cultivated with much success in very early times, especially by the Egyptians and the Phœnicians, the Greeks were the first to give them their ineffable beauty and to raise them to a degree of perfection which the world had never before known and which succeeding ages have never been able to surpass. The Hellenic race seem to have possessed an exquisite sense of the grand and the beautiful; and their fine taste stimulated and guided their brilliant genius and enabled them to confer all the charms and dignity of poetry on arts which had at first been simply mechanical. The fine climate, the bright sun, the azure skies, the fair and blooming vales, the majestic hills, and the romantic shores and islands of Greece and the other lands bordering on the Ægean and Mediterranean seas, doubtless exercised a vast amount of influence over the imaginations of the naturally ardent and excitable people who occupied those favored regions, and contributed to direct their attention to studying and improving those arts which imitate nature.

Ionia was the scene of the earliest triumphs of Grecian art, as well as the birthplace of Grecian philosophy and poetry. While the civilization of the mother land was retarded by an unceasing series of revolutions and internal dissensions, the Hellenic colonies on the fertile shores of Asia Minor were making rapid progress in wealth and prosperity, and were finding leisure to cultivate art, science and literature. So we discover that as early as the eighth century before Christ, when European Greece had not yet emerged from its primitive barbarism, the Ionian cities of Asiatic Greece had already become the seats of refinement and taste. There originated the Ionic style of architecture, and there painting and sculpture were first practiced by the Hellenic race.

But, along with its poetry and philosophy, the arts of Ionia by degrees reached European Greece, as well as the flourishing Grecian colonies in Italy and Sicily. At the time of the Persian invasion Greece is said to have had a hundred ivory statues of the gods, every one of which was of colossal size, and many of which were elegantly gilded. At this time Greece had likewise many magnificent temples and other splendid public edifices, constructed of the finest marble.

After the Persian invaders had been driven out, Greece ceased to follow its colonies and itself began to lead in the cultivation of the arts, as well as in literature and philosophy. Athens, which the barbarian host of Xerxes had reduced to a heap of smouldering ruins, soon arose out of its ashes; and under the wise and liberal policy of Themistocles, Cimon and Pericles, in the remarkably short period of forty years, it became the most magnificent city in the world, and was enriched with the most elegant specimens of ornamental art ever produced by any age or nation.

It was during the period after the Persian Wars, in the days of Athenian greatness and glory, that Greek art reached its highest degree of perfection, in those masterpieces of architecture and sculpture which the greatest genius of the modern world has not even been able to approach.

The *Parthenon*, which was erected during this period, yet remains whole, after the lapse of about twenty-three centuries, and affords abundant evidence as to the truth of the accounts transmitted to us from the ancient authors concerning the elegance and grandeur of Grecian architecture. This splendid temple was dedicated to Athênê, the tutelary goddess of Athens, and was constructed of beautiful white marble. It is of the Doric style of architecture, and is two hundred and seventeen feet long.

Fergusson, in his History of Architecture, says the following concerning the Parthenon: "In its own class it is undoubtedly the most beautiful building in the world. It is true it has neither the dimensions nor the wondrous expression of power and eternity inherent in Egyptian temples, nor has it the variety and poetry of the Gothic cathedrals; but for intellectual beauty, for

THE PARTHENON, ATHENS.

perfection of proportion, for beauty of detail, and for the exquisite perception of the highest and most recondite principles of art ever applied to architecture, it stands utterly and entirely alone and unrivaled—the glory of Greece, and the shame of the rest of the world."

Not only in Athens were there such splendid examples of the perfection of Grecian architecture, though it was there that they were seen crowded in vast numbers. There were temples in Elis, Delphi, Corinth, Eleusis, Argos and many other Grecian cities, rivaling in size and majestic grandeur those of Athênê's favored city.

The area of the Acropolis, or citadel of Athens, in which the Parthenon stands, was in ancient times adorned with many magnificent porticos and other public structures, and the whole of its extent, which was over six miles in circumference, was so diversified with works of painting and statuary that it is said to have exhibited a continuous spectacle of elegance and beauty. Under the administration of Pericles (from B. C. 458 to B. C. 429), sculpture and architecture reached their perfection in Athens. It was during that period that the renowned PHIDIAS, the greatest sculptor that the world has ever produced, adorned the city with the works of his genius. Above all the numerous temples and statues on the rocky height of the Acropolis towered the colossal bronze statue of Athênê, with its glittering helmet and spear, visible far out at sea, as if the goddess were guarding the city bearing her name. The most admired of the works of Phidias was the ivory statue of Athênê in the Parthenon, thirty-nine feet high, and having also about forty talents' worth of gold in its composition.

The great temple of Zeus at Olympia, in Elis, was two hundred and thirty feet long and sixty-eight feet high. This vast edifice was of the Doric style of architecture, and was surrounded with a splendid colonnade, adorned with the most elaborate sculpture. A gigantic statue of Zeus, about sixty feet high, was in the interior. This colossal figure was the masterpiece of the renowned Phidias, and was made of ivory draped with gold. It represented Zeus seated on a lofty throne of ivory and ebony, inlaid with precious stones, and ornamented with the most beautiful sculptures and paintings, exhibiting some of the most striking and poetical adventures of the gods. The head of the colossal image was encircled with an olive crown. An emblem of victory was in the right hand, and a burnished scepter was in the left. The flowing robes were embellished with flowers and figures of animals wrought in gold.

Other temples were much larger than that of Olympia, if not so richly adorned. The temple of Dêmêtêr and Persephone at Eleusis, built about the same time, was capable of containing thirty thousand persons. Besides the Olympian statue of Zeus, Phidias executed many beautiful figures of gods and heroes to adorn the principal temples of Greece. The works of Phidias have excited the admiration of the world, and succeeding artists have endeavored to rival them in vain.

We have already alluded to the origin of the three styles or orders of architecture, which are yet recognized by builders—the Doric, the Ionic and the Corinthian—the principal difference being in the character of the column. The Doric is the oldest, being the style used by the ancient Dorians, as its name implies. Though plain and massive, it was graceful in proportions. The column is generally without a base, and the capitals are not ornamented. The finest specimen of this style is the Parthenon. The remains of the great temples of Pæstum, in southern Italy, present some fine examples of the ancient Doric style. The great temple of Apollo at Delphi, and that of Hêrê at Samos, the largest temples ever seen by Herodotus, were built in this style. The latter temple was about three hundred and fifty feet long, and one hundred and ninety feet wide.

The Ionic style, as the name implies, had its origin among the Ionian Greeks of Asia Minor; and its main characteristics are lightness, gracefulness and tastefulness of ornament. The shaft of the column, which is slender, is supported by a base; and spiral volutes adorn the capital. The great temple of Artemis at Ephesus, begun about B. C. 600, was of the Ionic order; and was four hundred and twenty-five feet long, and two hundred and twenty feet wide. The Corinthian style, which is a modification of the Ionic, is distinguished for its graceful ornamentation. It is said that its capital was suggested to the mind of the famous sculptor, Calímachus, by seeing a basket covered by a tile and overgrown by the leaves of an acanthus. The earliest structure in the Corinthian style was the monument of Lysícrates, sometimes styled "the Lantern of Demosthenes," which was erected B. C. 335. This style was generally selected for edifices requiring special elegance and delicacy, as temples dedicated to Aphroditê.

Like architecture, sculpture or statuary owed its origin to religion. The first statues, which are very rude and uncouth, are those of the gods. Preceding the sculpture of detached figures was the adornment of the temples by figures in relief, of which there yet remains an example in a figure of the two lions over the gateway of the ancient city of Mycenæ. It was only in the period of Athenian glory and greatness following the Persian War that this beautiful art reached its perfection, under the great master, Phidias.

It is acknowledged that the Greeks reached absolute perfection in sculpture. The finest specimens of Grecian sculpture yet remaining are the figures that adorned the pediments and friezes of the Parthenon, most of which were taken to England by Lord Elgin, and are now in the British Museum. Most of them are in a mutilated condition, but they embody the very perfection of loveliness, majesty and power. These works were executed by the school of artists under the direction of Phidias, during the period of Athenian supremacy immediately following the Persian War. The immortal works of these sculptors are distinguished for their absolute purity and repose, which is entirely lacking in the productions of the later sculptors, which the uninstructed consider more beautiful.

Painting did not reach perfection among the Greeks so early as sculpture, yet it made considerable progress in this period of Grecian history; and the great painters—POLYGNOTUS, PARRHASIUS and ZEUXIS—embellished Athens with numerous pictures, and aided in making her the glory of Greece.

Grecian art maintained its preëminence during the Macedonian period. The most eminent sculptors of the fourth century before Christ were PRAXITELES, of Athens, and LYSIPPUS, of Sicyon; and the most illustrious painter was APELLES, of Ephesus. The success of Apélles was owing to his constant application. His maxim was: "No day without a line." Lysíppus was celebrated for his bronze works. The statues of Aphroditê by Praxíteles combined feminine grace with intellectual dignity, and have never been surpassed. Alexander the Great ordered that only Apélles should paint his picture, and that only Lysíppus should represent him in bronze.

Other famous painters of this time were TIMANTHUS, PAMPHILUS and EUPOMPUS. The most celebrated pictures of Zeuxis are those of Hercules strangling the serpents, of Hêrê, and of Jupiter surrounded by the other gods. The most celebrated painting of Timanthus is his Sacrifice of Ephigenia.

Among Greek sculptors, Praxíteles excelled in the soft and beautiful, as Phidias did in the grand and sublime. The principal works of Praxíteles were kept at Athens, but the Aphroditê of Cnidus was the most famous of all the productions of his chisel, and for a long time attracted visitors from every part of the world. This statue was executed in Parian marble, and stood, according to the account of a spectator, in a temple dedicated to the same deity. According to this description the sculptor seems not only to have presented a form of exquisite symmetry, but to have also given the stone something resembling the softness of flesh.

POLYCLETUS, CAMACHUS and NAUCIDES

were also great sculptors of the age of Praxíteles and Lysíppus. These sculptors combined to fill the temples and public edifices of the Grecian cities with models of beauty and grace, sometimes executed in marble, and sometimes in bronze. The most celebrated work of Polyclétus was a colossal figure of the Argive Hêrê, composed of ivory and gold.

The Greek paintings were in water colors or in wax, as oil colors were unknown. Polygnótus devoted himself to the adornment of many of the public edifices of Athens; and the Stoa, or painted porch, where Zeno afterward taught his principles of philosophy, was one of his works. Polygnótus was the first Grecian painter of fame, and was contemporary with Phidias, during the flourishing period of Athenian greatness and glory.

Painting reached a higher degree of perfection under Zeuxis and Parrhasius, as an interesting incident concerning these two artists shows. In a trial of skill Zeuxis painted a bunch of grapes so naturally that the birds came and picked at them. Thereupon Parrhasius said: "Now draw aside the curtain that covers my picture." When Zeuxis attempted to do so, he found that the curtain was the picture, and he immediately acknowledged the superiority of his rival. Said Zeuxis at one time: "I paint slowly, but I paint for eternity."

The Greeks carried the various arts of design to a high degree of perfection, and in all of these they exhibited a highly delicate and refined taste, furnishing a standard for posterity in many things. Greek art was not only illustrated in sculpture and architecture, but in the internal decorations of their houses, their elaborately-painted walls and ceilings, their ornamental tiling, their tastefully-constructed furniture, their beautiful vases, and other vessels both for use and ornament. The Greeks displayed a genius in all these for the invention of beautiful forms which has yet remained unsurpassed.

SECTION XVI.—GENERAL VIEW OF GREEK CIVILIZATION.

THE ancient Greeks belonged to the Aryan, or Indo-European branch of the Caucasian race, and were therefore kindred with the Sanskritic, or Brahmanic Hindoos, the Medes and Persians, the Romans and other Latin nations, and the modern nations of Europe and America. They were a finely-formed race, and their women were generally very beautiful. The characteristics of the Grecian face were dark complexions and black hair and eyes. Excepting the Spartans, the Greeks were lively, cheerful, ardent, volatile and fond of gay and showy amusements. They had some of the higher gifts of mind in a degree unsurpassed by any other nation. For this reason they made such advances in philosophy, in the science of government, in elegant literature, and the arts of painting, sculpture and architecture. Many of their works of art are yet models throughout the civilized world.

In the Oriental nations the only government was despotism. There was an absolute lord, whose subjects were virtual slaves, without any political rights whatever. The Greeks were the first people to develop democracy—government of the people, by the people and for the people. It was owing to their political freedom that the Greek civilization was the highest of antiquity, and that the Greeks surpassed all other ancient peoples in art, literature and philosophy.

The Greek states had no hired or standing armies, but relied for their defense on a militia, composed of citizens and armed slaves, which was called to the field in time of war. The poems of Homer inform us that in early times many of the Greek chieftains and warriors fought in chariots drawn by horses; but at a later period chariots were wholly dispensed with. The officers and the upper classes fought on horseback, and the common soldiers on foot. The regular cavalry were armed with swords and spears. The infantry were composed of two classes, respectively known as the heavy-armed and the light-armed. The heavy-armed infantry usually consisted of citizens, while the light-armed were made up of slaves or of freemen of the lowest rank.

The heavy-armed foot soldiers wore helmets of brass or iron upon their heads, and cuirasses and greaves of the same metals upon their breasts and legs. They grasped the sword or spear with the right hand, and carried the buckler or shield on the left arm. They usually fought in a close body, called a phalanx, in which the file was sometimes eight men in depth, and at other times sixteen. The light-armed troops used bows and arrows, javelins and slings, and were considered of so little importance, in comparison with the heavy-armed, that the ancient writers, in describing battles, often said nothing about the light soldiery, in giving the number of troops engaged.

The Greeks advanced to meet the enemy at a quick but regular pace, and with a silence only sometimes broken by the sound of the trumpet or the Spartan flute, until the mortal combat was announced by the clash of arms and the groans of the dying. Every citizen between the ages of twenty and sixty was subject to being summoned to the defense of the state, but those of advanced age were exempted from foreign service. The Athenians were accustomed to appointing ten generals to every army, one being taken from each of the ten wards of Attica. At first each of these officers was successively entrusted with the sole command for one day, but the evils in consequence of so injudicious a custom becoming at length apparent, the practice was modified, so far as one of the ten was appointed to the actual command, while the other nine accompanied him as counselors, or remained at home with the honorary title of generals.

The Grecian towns were fortified with walls, towers and fosses, or ditches, which made it very difficult to take them by siege in those times, although the places then considered and proved impregnable would have been reduced in less than an hour by our modern artillery. Although the engines of war used by the Greeks were impotent as compared with modern cannon, they had machines by which they were enabled to harass, and frequently to take by storm, places which were very strongly fortified. The chief of these engines were the battering-ram, the moving-tower, the tortoise, the catapult and the balista.

The battering-ram was a very large beam of wood, having at the end an iron head, shaped so as to partially resemble that of a ram. Some of these machines were suspended from the roof of a wooden building erected to screen the men who worked them from the missiles of the besieged; while others, smaller in size, were carried in the arms of men. They were used to batter down walls, and are said to have been sometimes dreadfully effective. For the purpose of deadening their blows, the besieged were in the custom of lowering bags of wool before those parts of the walls against which they were directed.

The moving-tower was a wooden building in the form of an obelisk, and was set on wheels, by means of which it could be pushed forward to the fortifications which were the objects of attack. These towers were from thirty to forty feet square at the base, and were higher than the ordinary walls of fortified towns. They contained a battering-ram in the lower story. In the middle portion they had a drawbridge, which could be lowered in such a way as to enable the assailants to pass over from the tower to the walls. At the top they were filled with soldiers, who hurled javelins and discharged arrows at the defenders of the walls.

The tortoise was a kind of wooden house, about twenty-five feet square and twelve feet high. Like the moving-tower, it was set on wheels, by means of which it could be moved forward to the walls. It was

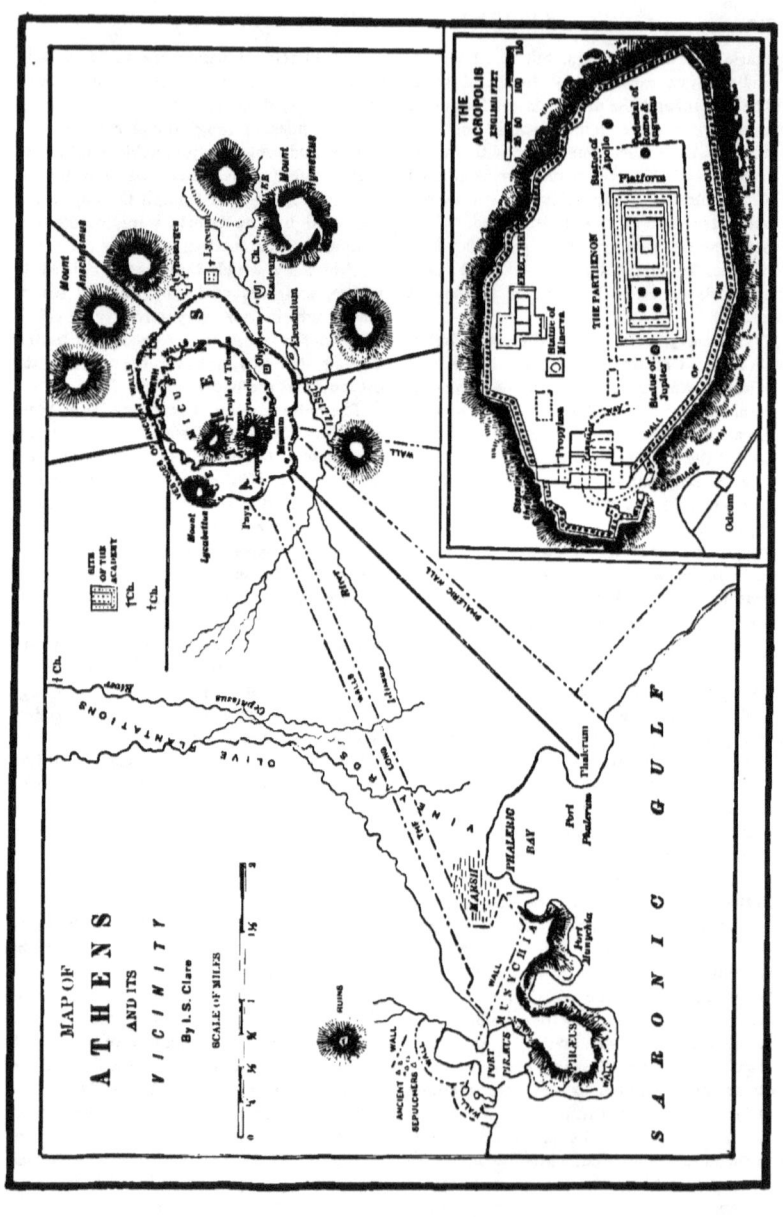

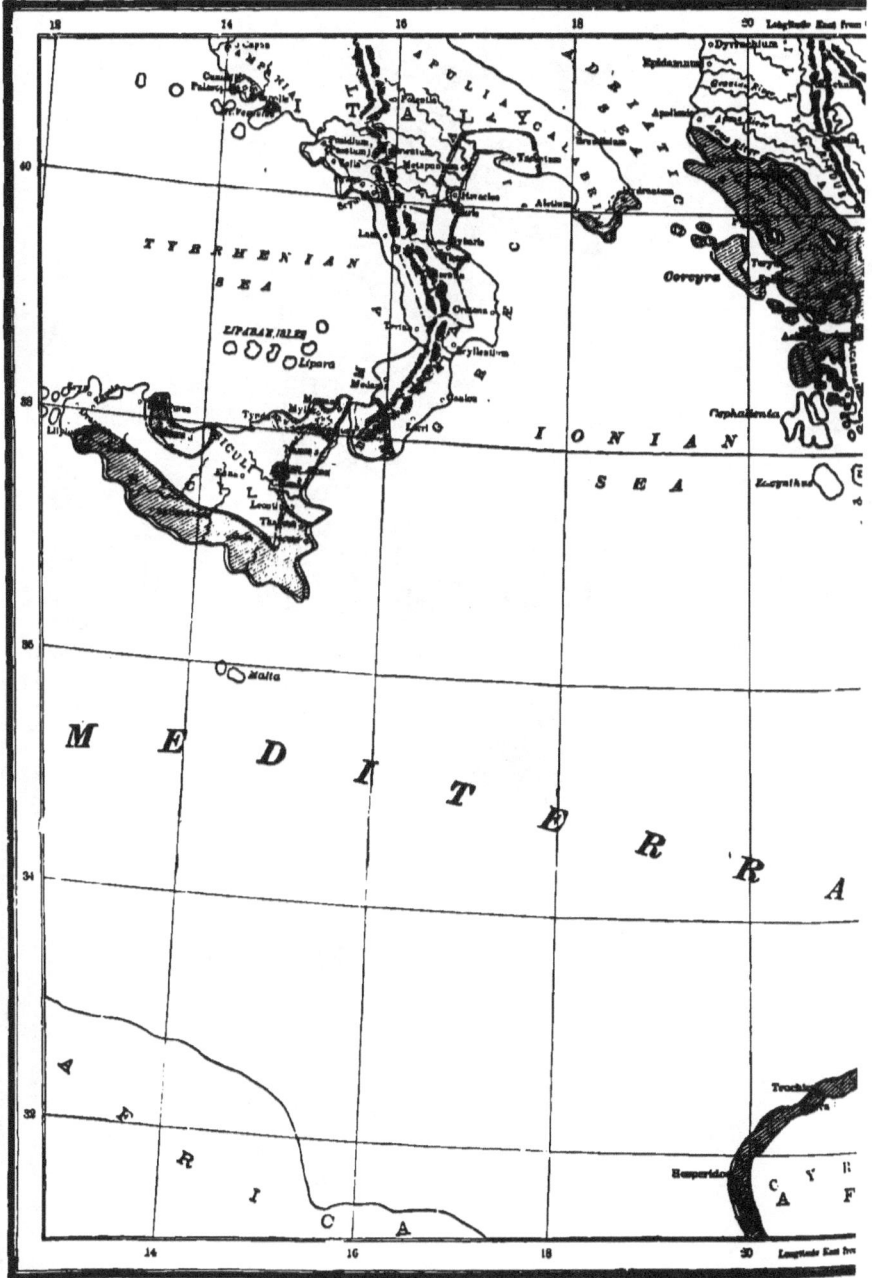

covered with strong hides, which had been steeped in certain drugs to make them fireproof. It was called a tortoise because of its immense strength, which rendered those inside of it as safe as a tortoise in a shell. It was used as a covering for the protection of persons employed in filling up the ditches and sapping the walls of fortified towns.

The balista and the catapult were machines used to hurl showers of darts and stones, and are described as having to a great extent resembled the modern crossbow, but were proportionately of immense size.

In Homer's time the Greek ships of war were large open boats capable of carrying from fifty to one hundred and twenty men. A sail was hoisted when the wind was fair and moderate, but these vessels were ordinarily propelled by oars. At that early period the rowers sat in a single line along each side of the vessel, but afterwards the Corinthians invented a kind of galley, called the *trireme*, which had three tiers of rowers, and which was decked like the largest of modern vessels.

The largest triremes usually carried a crew of about two hundred men, composed partly of sailors and partly of soldiers, or, as moderns would call them, *marines*. In sea-fights these marines occupied the deck of the vessel and attacked the foe with darts or javelins; and when the vessels approached very closely to each other, they fought hand to hand with sword and spear. The trireme was the largest war-vessel in most common use, but there were many larger galleys. There were many ships of four or five tiers of oars, and sometimes vessels of enormous size had thirty or forty tiers of rowers, but these latter were built more for show than for use.

The prows of Grecian ships were generally ornamented with sculptured representations of gods, men or animals, like the figure-heads of modern vessels. A piece of wood, armed with a brass or iron spike, and called the *beak*, projected from the lower part of the prow. This was of great service in damaging or sinking an enemy's vessel, as it was an important part of an ancient commodore's tactics to endeavor to strike his ship's beak against the side of the hostile ship and thus run it down. Very often another maneuver was resorted to, for the purpose of forcing an engagement, namely, bearing down upon the enemy's line, so as to break the oars of his ships, and thus make them unmanageable. The ships were then brought close to each other, and the fortune of the day was decided by the personal conflict which followed.

No other country in the world ever produced such magnificent and durable public buildings as did ancient Greece. The Grecian temples and public edifices have long been deservedly classed among the wonders of human art. They were constructed of polished stone or of the finest marble, and displayed the admirable proportions and beauty of the three styles of Grecian architecture—the Doric, the Ionic and the Corinthian. Though now in ruins, they are still objects of imitation to nations of the most refined taste. The modern architect congratulates himself upon being able to copy their characteristic excellences, without hoping to excel them.

The private houses of the mass of the Grecian people in the cities were built of clay or unbaked bricks, and were arranged in irregular lines along the sides of narrow streets. The wealthy, however, had large and elegant mansions. Their dwellings were divided into several apartments, having two or more stories, ascended by staircases. A large gate was in front; and outside of this was a heap of manure left there by the horses and mules, and a number of dogs and pigs were accustomed to gather there.

Thus the houses of the Greeks were generally as plain as their temples and public edifices were magnificent. The floors were of stone, and the walls were white until the time of Alcibiades, who ordered them to be painted in Athens. The houses generally stood away from the street A laurel tree or altar sacred to Apollo was often placed in front of houses. Often an inscription was marked on the door as a good omen. In the interior were apartments surrounding an open court, about which were porticos for exercise; while in the center was an altar on which sacrifices were offered to the household gods. The women's chambers were wholly separate from those of the men, and the girls were kept in a remote room under lock and key. The slaves were sheltered in an upper story, to which they ascended from steps on the outside of the house. The roofs of the houses were flat, and served as places of promenade in the cool of the day. Curtains were sometimes used instead of doors. Houses were heated by means of fire-places; and, as chimneys were unknown, the smoke escaped through openings in the ceilings. Roses and violets were planted side by side with onions. The first rooms seen upon entering the house were decorated with paintings. The houses of the wealthy were profusely embellished with paintings, sculptures, vases and ornamental works of art. The walls were plastered, and finished with joiner's work. The walls and ceilings were adorned with paintings. The furniture was set off with gold and ivory. Screens of rich tapestry were likewise in use.

The articles of Grecian household furniture were chairs, beds of geese feathers, bedsteads, bedsteads with mosquito-nets, sheep-skin-blankets, tables, candelabras, carpets, footstools, lamps, chafing-dishes, vases of different forms, baskets, basins, bellows, brooms, cisterns, ovens, frying-pans, hand-mills, knives, soup-ladles, lanterns, mirrors, mortars, sieves, spits, and most of the articles now in use, or substitutes for them. Dishes and other vessels were of pottery, metal or wood. Variously-formed and beautifully-designed lamps were used.

The Greeks ate three daily meals, reclining on couches, and using neither table-clothes nor napkins. In primitive fashion, they used neither knives nor forks, but spoons were in common use. They washed their hands before and after each meal. Among the common people dried fish and barley bread, with dates, were the principal food. Animal food and many delicacies of cookery were also partaken of. The wealthy, of course, indulged in all sorts of luxuries. After dinner came the *symposium*, when host and guests drank goblets of wine, mixed with hot or cold water. The master of the feast was chosen by lot. This drinking bout was enlivened by varied conversation, music, dancing, and all sorts of games and amusements. Guests invited to a banquet were met by slaves, who removed their sandals, washed their feet, and furnished them with water for their hands.

Before going to a feast, the Greeks washed their bodies and anointed them with oils; and when they arrived, their host welcomed them either by taking their hands or by kissing their lips, hands or feet, according as he desired to show them more or less respect. Before a repast was begun, a part of the provisions on the table was set apart for the gods, and a hymn was generally sung at the close of the meal. Before they quaffed their wine, the Greeks often poured some of it on the ground in honor of any god or absent friend whom they desired to remember. This was called a *libation*.

The Greeks had some notions of propriety. They considered long nails, dirty teeth, wiping the nose at meals, spitting upon the waiter at table, etc., as offensively vulgar. One who talked much about himself was regarded as a *bore*. Seeking to sit near the host at a ceremonious feast was looked upon as foppery; as were also bragging about taking a child to Delphi to deposit his hair; saying that one had taken care to have a black footman; placing garlands before a door when one offered sacrifice; erecting a monument to a lap-dog, etc.

The climate of Greece being one of the mildest in the world, the dress of the people was light and simple, being designed more as a graceful covering for the body than as a protection against the inclemencies of the weather. The dress of the Greeks was nearly the same for both sexes. Their garments were made of wool, linen, and later of cotton. The Greek dress consisted of an inner *tunic* and an outer robe or shawl called the *pallium*. The tunics of the men extended down to the knees, while those of

A GREEK SYMPOSIUM.

the women descended in flowing folds to the heels. The women bound their tunics at the waist by a broad sash; and their palliums, which were usually saffron-colored, were confined at the waist by a broad ribbon. Both these garments were bordered at the bottom by an edging of different color. In later times the Athenian women wore long loose dresses with flowing sleeves. Only travelers and workmen had their heads covered; all other men and all the women having no covering for their heads. The flapped hats, which were worn by workmen and travelers, were tied under the chin. The better classes of Greeks wore sandals and shoes on their feet out of doors, and these were bound with thongs. The lower orders always went barefooted.

The Greek women braided and curled their hair in a very tasteful manner, and set it off with golden grasshoppers. They also wore golden ear-rings and bracelets; and in the days of Athenian luxury and splendor, the ladies of Athens had a custom of painting their cheeks and eyebrows, sprinkling their hair with yellow-colored powder, and encircling their heads with wreaths of flowers. When they went out of doors they always wore a veil over the face.

The Greek women were kept in a state of seclusion and restraint, similar to that of the Turkish women and the women of other modern Oriental nations. They were closely confined to the house, except during solemn festivals and other public ceremonies, and employed their time in spinning, weaving, baking bread and superintending the labors of their female slaves. When they appeared in public, they walked in procession, with downcast eyes, with their slaves and attendant maidens around them, or went directly and without ostentation to the place to which they had been called by business. But the lower classes were not practically exempted from such restrictions, and females of rank even resorted to many contrivances

TYPES OF GREEK WOMEN.

to evade them. The Spartan women also conducted themselves differently, as the laws of Lycurgus required them to exhibit themselves in public. These women did not mourn the loss of their husbands or sons who died the death of heroes in battle, but appeared in public with every indication of joy after such an occurrence, and only seemed sorrowful when those with whom they were connected had disgraced themselves by returning home unhurt from an unsuccessful battle with their country's enemies.

Thus Greek women were virtual slaves, and led secluded lives in their homes, both before and after marriage, devoting themselves to weaving, spinning and domestic duties. They took care of the sick and had charge of the servants, who were slaves. The *Hetæræ*, chiefly foreigners, were a class of women who enjoyed greater social privileges, living in their own houses, and receiving guests of both sexes. These were generally noted for their personal beauty and grace of manners, and also for literary accomplishments, and are said to have been "the most witty and brilliant talkers of Athens." The famous Aspásia, who became the wife of Pericles, belonged to this class.

The Greeks were divided into two great classes, freemen and slaves. We have observed that in Sparta the slaves performed all mechanical, agricultural and menial labors; while the free citizens employed themselves in war and military exercises, in superintending the public schools, in conversation, or in religious services. But in Athens and the other Grecian republics the citizens engaged in mechanical employments, as well as in the more lucrative pursuits of commerce; while the slaves engaged in various handicrafts, as well as agricultural and menial duties.

The Greeks had slaves of all classes and grades, such as domestic servants, agricultural laborers, and artisans. The rich families had many slaves, while the poor citizen had only one. The governments of the various Grecian states employed slaves upon the public works. These slaves, generally foreigners, the Greeks called barbarians. Many Asiatics and Thracians sold their children into slavery, and the buying and selling of slaves was a regular business at Athens and in other parts of Greece. Children born of slave women were doomed to slavery. Menial slaves were at the mercy of their masters and mistresses. Slaves were often tortured, to make them confess their own guilt or the guilt of their masters.

The Greeks worked mines of silver, copper and iron, and obtained marble and other building stone from the quarries. They engaged in spinning and weaving, pottery, and the manufacture of arms and armor, gold and silver ornaments, hardware and furniture. Besides the large numbers employed in industrial arts were the merchants, shopkeepers, tradesmen and agriculturists. Piræus was the sea-port of Athens; but the wholesale trade, and most of the retail trade, were conducted in the market-places.

In ancient Greece were leather bottle-makers; bankers; barbers, some of them females; barber surgeons, whose shops were lounging-places; basket-makers; butchers; blacksmiths; carpenters; coppersmiths; cotton manufacturers; curriers; dyers; enamelers; factors; farmers; fishermen; flax-dressers; founders; fresco painters; fullers; gilders; goldsmiths; gardeners; weighers; papermakers; perfumers; pilots; tutors; quack doctors; shepherds; tanners; weavers, etc.

In Athens many of the citizens had no private occupation, but lived on the pay they obtained for attending the political and judicial assemblies, on the provisions made to them at the public festivals, and on the money occasionally granted them from the public treasury or from the coffers of wealthy citizens. Their pastimes were conversation, or listening to the orators in the Agora, or market-place, walking in the public gardens, attending the lectures and disputations of the philosophers and assisting in the many processions, games and festivities, which were held in honor of the gods.

Writing was done with ink made from soot, on prepared skins, bark, papyrus, or with a sharp-pointed instrument on thin sheets of lead or layers of wax. During the glorious days of Athens many private persons had large libraries. The Greeks very carefully attended to the education of the young. The Spartan system of training, as we have seen, consisted only of exercises calculated to discipline the mind to fortitude and to strengthen the physical powers; as the study of the arts and the sciences, and the pursuits of literature, were considered unworthy the attention of a Lacedæmonian citizen. But the Athenians, and other Grecians who imitated the usages and institutions of Athens, gave their youths a far more liberal education. Boys only went to school. The schoolmaster was the *grammaticus*, or grammarian. The sons of wealthy parents had a *pedagogue*, or private tutor, who watched over them when out of school, and who was generally selected from the slaves. The elementary branches, such as reading, writing, grammar, music, recitation, and later, philosophy and oratory, were taught. Passages from the works of the poets were committed to memory. The music taught consisted of singing, playing on the lyre, and reciting compositions in poetry. In early manhood the sons of the wealthy attended lectures on philosophy, oratory etc., in the Lyceum, the Academy, or some other institution. There were many schools; while attendance upon the public debates, where the first and greatest orators in the world were heard, was general.

Gymnasia, provided at the public expense, were much resorted to for pastime and exercise; and there the body was rendered supple by running, leaping, boxing, wrestling, throwing the discus, the javelin, or the quoit, shooting with the bow and arrow, etc. The gymnasium was a part of Greek education, and was the training school for the Olympic Games. In later years the porticos became the resort of philosophers, rhetoricians and Sophists, who publicly discussed moral and metaphysical questions.

The Greeks were fond of music and played on stringed-instruments, such as the harp and the lyre, and on wind instruments, such as the double and the single pipe. The Athenians highly prized musical accomplishments, and female musicians were hired at feasts and social gatherings to heighten the enjoyment of the guests.

Marriages among the Greeks were generally arranged by the parents, and dowries were expected. The Athenian marriages were generally formed at an early age, the Grecian women being marriageable when they were in their fourteenth year. Nuptial engagements were entered into with many formalities, yet they were dissolved very easily, as all that was required for that purpose was that the parties should furnish the Archon with a written certificate of their agreement to separate from each other. The Spartan marriages were of a singular character, like all the other Lacedæmonian institutions. After a Spartan had obtained the consent of the lady's parents, he was obliged to carry off his destined spouse, as it was regarded as very unbecoming in a lady to *consent* to be married. Even after they had become married, the young husband and wife were extremely careful to avoid being seen in each other's society; and when there happened to be no children, years sometimes passed before it was generally known that the parties were married, so secret were they in all their associations with each other.

The Greeks celebrated their funerals with great pomp and ceremony. The corpse was first washed, anointed, and dressed in a costly garment; after which it was laid out in state, for one, two, or sometimes even three days. A wreath of flowers was placed on its head, and in its hand was set a cake of flour and honey as an offering to Cerberus, the three headed watch-dog of Hades. The Greeks believed that before the remains of the dead were buried the soul wandered about in Hades without rest, not being permitted to cross the river Styx into Elysium. Immediately after death a small coin, called an *obolus*, and equal in value to about a penny and a half of English money, was placed in the mouth of the deceased to pay the ferryman

Charon for taking his spirit across the dark river Styx. Between the time of death and the funeral the body was constantly surrounded by relatives and friends as mourners, with hired women making loud lamentations, and with a chorus of flute-players. On the funeral day the corpse, enclosed in a cypress coffin, was put on a chariot and conveyed to the place where it was to be finally disposed of. The funeral proccession accompanying the remains was arranged in the following order: First came musicians, playing or chanting mournful tunes; after which advanced the male relatives and friends in black attire; next followed the coffin, and behind it walked the women. In accordance with the directions of the deceased or of the family, the corpse was either buried in a grave, vault or tomb, or burned upon a funeral pile. Piles of wood, called *pyræ* (meaning pyres), were used for burning a corpse, and oil and perfumes were cast into the flames. When the pyræ had burned down, the remains were extinguished with wine, and the bones were gathered, washed with wine and oil, and deposited in urns, which were sometimes made of gold. Bodies which were buried were first put in coffins usually made of baked clay or earthenware. Vases and other articles were laid in the grave with the dead. Libations of wine were made at the same time, or a sacrifice was offered to the gods, prayers were said, and the name of the deceased was invoked aloud. The ceremony was ended with a funeral banquet, and it was customary to erect a monumental stone or statue over the grave. At stated times sacrifices were performed at the tomb, and the grave was decorated with flowers.

Religious rites and ceremonies mainly devolved upon the priests, but the people attended at the services in the temples, and furnished their finest cattle and their choicest products as offerings. No business was undertaken without consulting the gods by religious ceremonies.

There were three principal gymnasia, which were places of public exercise near Athens, and there the philosophers and rhetoricians delivered their lectures. The most famous of these was the Academy, which was so named because it had been the country-seat of the wealthy Académus, who spent most of a large fortune in ornamenting this delightful site. It was here where Plato delivered his lectures, for which reason his followers were named Academics. On the opposite side of the city, near the river Ilyssus, was the Lycéum, with its shady groves in which Aristotle lectured to his pupils. Cynosárges, about a mile from the Lycéum, was the residence of Antísthenes, the founder of the sect of the Cynics.

The whole country about Athens, especially the long road to Piræus, was ornamented with various kinds of monuments, particularly with tombs of eminent poets, statesmen and warriors. This road was enclosed by a double wall, called the Northern and Southern walls, erected during the administration of Themístocles. This double wall was almost five miles long on both sides, and enclosed the two harbors called respectively Piræus and Phalerum. The walls, which were constructed wholly of freestone, were more than eighty feet high and so wide that two baggage wagons could pass each other. Piræus and Phalerum were really small cities, with public squares, temples, market-places, etc. The crowd that enlivened the quays of Piræus gave that chief harbor a livelier appearance than Athens itself. The port of Munychia lay to the east of Piræus, and, like both Piræus and Phalerum, was formed by the bays of the coast. Munychia was a place of great natural strength, and the Spartans garrisoned it after they had conquered Athens.

Athens was located in a plain, which, on the south-east, extended for about four miles toward the sea and the harbors, but was enclosed by mountains on the other side. Several rocky hills arose in the plain, of which the largest and loftiest was fortified by Cecrops as the *Acropolis*, or citadel of Athens, and was sometimes named Cecropia. Most of the buildings were erected around this citadel, spreading toward the sea. The summit of the hill was almost level for a space of about eight hundred feet long by four hundred feet wide, as if Nature herself had designed the site for those masterpieces of architecture which displayed the splendor of Athens at a distance. The only road leading to the Acropolis passed through the Propylæa, a magnificent gateway adorned with two wings and two temples filled with the finest samples of sculpture and painting. This gateway was erected by the architect Mnesicles, during the administration of Pericles, and was decorated with elegant sculptures by Phidias. Through these splendid portals was an ascent by steps leading to the summit of the hill, which was crowned with the temples of the guardian deities of Athens. On the left stood the temple of Athênê, the protectress of cities, containing a column which fable represented as having fallen from heaven, and an olive-tree believed to have sprung spontaneously from the ground at the decree of the goddess. The temple of Poseidon was beyond that of Athênê. On the right side towered the Parthenon, sacred to the virgin Athênê—"the glory of Athens, and the noblest triumph of Grecian architecture." The Parthenon, raising its lofty head above the city and the Acropolis, was the first object which caught the eyes of the traveler, whether he approached by land or sea.

At the foot of the Acropolis, on one side, stood the Odéum, or music hall, and the theater of Dionysus, where were celebrated the tragic contests on the festival of that god. On the other side stood the Prytanéum, where the chief magistrates and the most worthy citizens were honorably entertained at a table furnished at the public expense. A small valley named Cœlé (*the hollow*) lay between the Acropolis and the hill on which the Court of Areopagus had its sittings. This valley also separated the Areopagus from the Pnyx, the small rocky hill on which the people met in their general assemblies. The simplicity of the furniture of the Pnyx contrasted remarkably with the grandeur of the neighboring edifices. On this spot the renowned orators of Athens addressed the assembled masses. This spot can still be seen, as it is cut in the natural rock, and has in the present century been cleared of its rubbish, and the four steps by which it was ascended.

The Ceramícus, or pottery-ground, containing the market-place, lay beyond the Pnyx. The market-place was a large square surrounded on every side with public buildings. On the south was the Senate-house and the statues of the Eponymi, ten heroes from whom the tribes of Athens derived their respective names. On the east stood two splendid Stoai, or porticoes—that of the Hermæ, or statues of Hermes, bearing inscriptions of the names of the citizens, allies and slaves, who had distinguished themselves in the Persian War; and that of the Poëcilé ornamented with numerous elegant paintings, especially one representing Miltíades at the battle of Marathon. Under this *Stoa* Zeno lectured to his pupils, wherefore the disciples were called *Stoics*.

SECTION XVII.—CONQUESTS OF ALEXANDER THE GREAT.

HE condition of Greece at the time of the assassination of Philip of Macedon is sufficiently clear from the circumstances attending the general congress of the Grecian states at Corinth, where every Amphictyonic state, excepting Sparta, virtually acknowledged, through its representatives, the supremacy of Macedon. Philip's views in convening that congress were fully shared by his son Alexander, who prepared to carry them into effect as soon as he had ascended his father's throne. Before he became securely seated on the Mace-

donian throne, Alexander encountered some little opposition from his first cousin, the son of Philip's brother; but the young king soon overcame this opposition. His qualifications rendered it extremely difficult for any pretender to dispute his claims. Alexander was calculated to win his way to a throne amid a multitude of rival competitors, as he was in the flower of youth, possessed of a handsome and active though slight person, and also of a countenance full of manly beauty, and winning manners, and as he was already famed for his military skill and his chivalrous valor. Alexander was only twenty years of age when he ascended his father's throne.

Frequent allusion is made to a remarkable instance of his extraordinary readiness of judgment. One day a fiery horse was brought out before Philip and his courtiers, when it was discovered to be impossible for any one to mount the beast, until Alexander came forward and easily accomplished the task, after he had discovered that the direct cause of it being unmanageable was that its head was turned to the sun. This royal youth was the only one present who had sufficient penetration to perceive this. This animal became the celebrated war-horse which carried Alexander through many of his campaigns, and was named Bucéphalus. This remarkable quickness of intellect had all the advantages of culture through the care of Aristotle.

The young king first devoted himself to measures for the preservation of the Macedonian ascendency in Grecian affairs. He made a journey to Corinth for this purpose, and received the submission of the states of Thessaly on his route thither. When he reached Corinth he convened the deputies of the Amphictyonic republics, took his seat among them as an Amphictyon, and easily obtained from them his appointment as generalissimo, or captain-general of the Græco-Macedonian confederacy, the post so recently occupied by his father.

Philip's designs on Asia by the conquest of the Medo-Persian Empire, which had formally been approved by the Grecian congress at Corinth, were revived by the youthful Alexander, and the congress again promised the assistance of the Grecian republics (B. C. 335). The young monarch then returned to Macedon, where his presence was demanded; as the Illyrians, the Triballi, the independent Thracian tribes, and other nations bordering on Macedon, had risen in arms against that suddenly-risen power and menaced it with serious calamities; but Alexander, by his military skill and his valor, subdued the hostile tribes very easily, and proved to his barbarian neighbors what he had told his subjects in a different spirit when he became sovereign, namely, that "the king's name only was changed; but the king remained the same."

Alexander likewise gave a terrible proof of his equal ability with his father, soon afterward, in his treatment of the Grecian states. While he was occupied in Illyria, a rumor of his death was circulated. The democratic party at Athens was elated by the news, and Sparta once more thought of becoming supreme in Greece; but the report excited the greatest sensation at Thebes. That city beheld a humiliating memorial of departed freedom, in the Macedonian garrison which Philip had placed in the Cadmæa. When intelligence arrived that the youthful Macedonian sovereign was dead, a favorable opportunity seemed to have arisen for casting off the Macedonian thralldom. The democratic party in Thebes, which had opposed the interests of Alexander, now arose and put to death Amyntas and Timolaüs, the commanders of the Macedonian garrison in the citadel, but who did not reside in it.

Seeing the necessity of decisive measures to nip this revolt in the bud, Alexander immediately led his army against Thebes, which he reached in the remarkably-short space of fourteen days. He desired to give the rebels an opportunity for peaceful submission, but they sallied from the city with rash impetuosity and attacked his troops; and the consequence was that Alexander took Thebes, and utterly destroyed the city, in punishment for the revolt. A vast multitude of the inhabitants were slain, and about thirty thousand were carried into captivity. The walls and houses of the celebrated city which had given Greece such an illustrious poet as Pindar and such renowned warriors as Pelópidas and Epaminóndas were leveled with the ground, and Thebes ceased to exist forever. Amidst this merciless destruction, Alexander displayed several traits of generous and honorable feeling. His veneration for literary genius prompted him to spare from the general ruin the house which had been the residence of the bard Pindar. A band of Thracians had invaded the house of a noble lady named Timocléa, who had been subjected to the grossest violence by the Thracian leader. When this brutal leader afterward requested the lady to show him where her treasure was hidden, she conducted him to a well, and, as he was stooping over it, she pushed him into it, and overwhelmed him with stones. She was instantly seized and taken into the presence of Alexander, who was so struck by her majestic appearance that he asked: "Who are you, that can venture to commit so bold a deed?" She replied: "I am Timocléa, the sister of Theágenes, who fell at Chæronéa, fighting at the head of the force he commanded, against your father, for the liberties of Greece." This courageous reply only won the admiration of Alexander, who accordingly spared Timocléa and her children from the doom of slavery, to which the patriotic Thebans had been reduced, regardless of age, sex or rank, excepting a few individuals who escaped in the tumult to Athens.

A feeling of awe was excited by the destruction of Thebes which was most favorable to Alexander's influence among the Grecian states; all of which, excepting Sparta, which still maintained an appearance of gloomy indifference to passing events, sent addresses of congratulation to Alexander when he had returned to Macedon. On this occasion Alexander gave Athens a sharp and unpleasing answer, thus showing that he was fully aware of the animosity of a great party there to his cause. He demanded of the republic that Demosthenes and nine others, whom he mentioned as the principal instigators of disorders in Greece, be given up. In reply, the Athenians displayed an obsequious willingness to comply with his demand, but humbly asked that the parties be left to be dealt with in accordance with the ordinary course of law. The young monarch acceded to their request, and before long was too closely engaged with more important matters to concern himself much about the punishment of a few Athenian politicians, who in this way escaped his wrath.

Soon after he had returned to Macedon, Alexander started upon his long-contemplated invasion of Asia. At this time the vast Medo-Persian Empire, which still reached from the borders of India on the east to the western shores of Asia Minor on the west, thus including all of Western Asia except Arabia, had fallen into decay, in consequence of the corrupting influence of wealth and luxury, which the Persians had enjoyed for two centuries. Darius Codomannus had just ascended the throne of Persia in the very year in which Alexander became King of Macedon (B. C. 336). He was personally the best of the successors of Cyrus the Great, but was unfitted for the difficult crisis in which he found himself.

Alexander started from Pella in the spring of the year B. C. 334 at the head of an army of thirty thousand infantry and almost five thousand cavalry. Twelve thousand of the foot soldiery were furnished by the Grecian republics, but five thousand of these were mercenaries. Twelve thousand of the infantry were furnished by Macedon itself, while the remainder were obtained mainly from Thrace and Illyria. Macedon, Thessaly and Thrace, being always better supplied with horses than the republics of Greece, provided Alexander with his cavalry.

The whole Græco-Macedonian army crossed the Hellespont at Sestos, in galleys and transports, and thus stood upon the soil of Asia, in the dominions of the Persian king, who was all the while perfectly aware of the designs and movements of Alexander's army, but left the task of opposing the invaders to his satraps in Asia Minor. These officials made formidable preparations for the defense of their provinces; and with the standing armies of Lydia, Phrygia, Cappadocia, Bithynia and Ionia, they advanced toward the Hellespont to encounter Alexander's army soon after it had landed on the Asiatic shore.

The Persian satraps, headed by Memnon of Rhodes, took a position on the eastern bank of the little river Granícus, about thirty miles from the Hellespont, where they determined to oppose the further progress of the invader. Alexander also advanced to the Granícus, after having visited Troy and sacrificed to the gods there. The Macedonian king made a skillful disposition of his troops, and then attempted to cross the river in the face of the enemy. He himself led the cavalry across the little stream, leaving Parmenio to follow with the infantry. The Persians resisted bravely and drove the Macedonians back into the river, but Alexander encouraged his troops with word and gesture and succeeded in landing safely on the opposite side of the stream. In the battle of the Granícus, which followed, the young Macedonian monarch, who was conspicuous by his shining armor and his position in front of his followers, performed prodigies of valor, slaying with his own hands Mithridátes, son-in-law of King Darius Codomannus, and also piercing the heart of Ræsaces, another Persian noble of high rank. Alexander's reckless courage would have cost him his life, had not Clitus, one of his father's old officers, come to his rescue and cut off the arm of a Persian whose cimeter was about to descend upon Alexander's head.

When the Macedonian phalanx and the remainder of Alexander's infantry under Parmenio had succeeded in crossing the Granícus, the victory was soon decided in favor of the invaders. It has never been ascertained how many Persians were slain in this engagement, but it is said to have been large, while Alexander lost only thirty of his infantry and eighty-five of his cavalry. Several satraps and other dignitaries of high rank among the Persians were slain. After the battle the triumphant Macedonian king exhibited much humanity to his captives, and likewise to the wounded of his foes, as well as to those of his own troops who were suffering from wounds. Among his prisoners were a large body of Greek mercenaries who served in the Persian ranks, and these he punished for fighting against their country and kindred by sending them to work in the mines of Thrace.

Alexander, with consummate policy, made the Grecian states share in his victory, by sending to Athens three hundred suits of Persian armor to be placed in the temple of Athênê, with this inscription: "Alexander, son of Philip, and the Greeks—excepting the Lacedæmonians—offer these, taken from the barbarians of Asia."

The consequence of the battle of the Granícus was the death-blow to Persian authority in Asia Minor, of which Alexander was now virtual master. After this first victory, Alexander proceeded to deliver the Greek cities on the Mediterranean coast of Asia Minor from Persian thralldom. He marched to Sardis, the Lydian capital, which opened its gates to him and implored and received his favor and friendship. He then visited Ephesus, the Ionian capital, and also treated its inhabitants generously, assuring them of his assistance to secure them against Persian exaction in the future, and aiding them to rebuild their famous temple to Artemis, which was one of the Seven Wonders of the World.

Milétus and Halicarnássus, the capitals of Caria, presented closed gates to Alexander; but both were taken after being vigorously besieged, although Halicarnássus made a heroic and vigorous defense, the garrison being under the command of Memnon of Rhodes, one of the ablest of the Persian generals. Memnon managed to shut himself up in a strong castle, which Alexander did not consider of sufficient account to waste any time in assailing. Alexander

VICTORY OF ALEXANDER THE GREAT ON THE GRANICUS.

demolished Halicarnássus, as a war measure, to prevent it from affording a post of vantage to the foe in the future.

This was almost the first instance in which the young Macedonian king had thus far committed the slightest injury to private or public property. He had bestowed benefits wherever he had made his appearance; and by his generous treatment of the inhabitants of the conquered provinces, and by his wise regard for established customs and institutions, Alexander secured their attachment to his cause. He restored the democratic institutions of the Greeks, and allowed the Asiatics to retain their own hereditary laws, being thus as generous to the native races as to the descendants of the Hellenic colonists. As winter overtook him at Halicarnássus, he spent a part of the season in that vicinity, employing himself in establishing the government of the maritime provinces which he had subdued. He allowed such of his troops as had recently married to return to Macedon to spend the winter in their own homes. This was one of those acts of kindness and indulgence which won for him the affections of his soldiers.

Before starting out on his invasion, Alexander had a powerful fleet collected to support his operations on land; but he now found it to be thoroughly useless, because of the superior numbers of the Persian ships, and he accordingly ordered its dispersion, saying to his generals that he would make himself master of the sea by conquering on land, as every harbor that surrendered to him would diminish the enemy's naval resources. This gave him an additional reason for limiting his early operations to the coast; and he therefore passed some time in Caria, where he was welcomed with exceeding hospitality. He preferred a frugal diet and unostentatious fare, although he was greatly urged to partake of the luxuries of the place.

From Caria, Alexander passed to Lycia, a large maritime province, which contained more than thirty large and important towns and sea-ports. After he had received the submission of these places, he proceeded to Pamphylia, the next maritime province in the line of his advance eastward. He found himself obliged to use stringent measures in dealing with Aspendus, the Pamphylian capital, whose inhabitants seemed disposed to trifle with him. While he was in Pamphylia, Alexander decided to depart for a time from his course along the sea-coast, and to march northward into Phrygia, where he expected reinforcements from Greece, and to unite with his army the detachment under Parmenio, who had been sent to secure the Macedonian king's interests in that province. After overcoming some trifling obstruction from an inland tribe named the Posidians, Alexander effected this junction of his forces and arrived at Gordium, the early capital of Phrygia, where an occurrence transpired, which was regarded as prophetic of his future conquest of Asia.

In the citadel of Gordium there was a very ancient consecrated chariot, which had of old afforded a savior to Phrygia in an important emergency, when the people were ordered by an oracle to look for one such a chariot. The chariot had been preserved with reverent care from that time, being suspended by the yoke to a wall and fastened with a knot constructed in so intricate a manner from the rind of a carnol-tree that no eye was able to discover where the knot commenced or ended. It had for a long time been said that an oracle had declared that whoever should untie this complicated knot should win the dominion of Asia. Alexander visited the consecrated chariot; and, according to some writers, finding himself unable to unfasten the intricate knot, he cut it with his sword; but, according to the statement of his general, Aristobúlus, who witnessed the affair, Alexander wrested the pin from the beam, saying that that was sufficient to make him lord of Asia. Whatever he did, his army and the multitude of the time believed him to have succeeded in unfastening the *Gordian Knot*, and a storm of thunder and lightning, occurring at the time, confirmed the impression. Alexander countenanced this opinion by performing a splendid sacrifice in gratitude for the future glory which had been thus decreed for him.

Alexander met Parmenio in Phrygia, in accordance with expectation, and likewise obtained there a reinforcement of new troops from Greece, accompanied by those troops who had been allowed to pass the winter at their homes. The new recruits numbered a little over a thousand infantry and five hundred cavalry. The smallness of this reinforcement was mainly attributable to the powerful check which the Persian fleet under Memnon the Rhodian exercised upon all the coasts and isles of the Ægean.

While Alexander was in Phrygia, he heard of Memnon's death, and of the subsequent retirement of a great part of the marines, or land troops serving on board, from the fleet. This circumstance caused him to order Antipater to raise another fleet in Greece. After he had completed his purpose in Phrygia, the Macedonian king directed his attention to the provinces of Paphlagonia and Cappadocia, as the possession of them was essential in order to make him master of all Asia Minor. He found this an easy task, as Paphlagonia was not governed by a Persian satrap, but by a native prince who had been a vassal of Persia, and who was willing and glad to acknowledge Alexander as lord-paramount, instead of Darius Codomannus. The Macedonian monarch therefore made a treaty with the Paphlagonians; after which he directed his attention to Cappadocia, which was a Persian satrapy at that time without a satrap, the recent occupant of that office having lost his life in the battle of the Granicus. Accordingly the Macedonians found it very easy to overrun this vast province, and to subject it to their king's dominion.

Alexander was as prudent in securing his conquests as he was active in making them. In all the provinces through which he passed, wherever he discovered an existing power friendly to him, he did not disturb it; and wherever there was a vacancy in such authority, he placed some of his own trusty followers in the vacant office, assigning them a military detachment to aid them in executing the duties of their station and to strengthen their power as firmly as he was well able to do.

In the spring of B. C. 333 Alexander left Cappadocia, advancing southward, with the prospect of having soon to engage in the severest conflict he would have to encounter in Asia. He had some time previously received intelligence that Darius Codomannus was raising a vast host on the plains of Babylon to drive the Macedonian invaders from his empire. The Persian king had the most unworthy reasons for not appearing sooner in the field personally. He had at first hoped and tried to relieve himself of his enterprising foe by the treacherous means of private assassination; and, on one occasion during Alexander's career in Asia Minor, just related, he almost accomplished his base design. A Macedonian noble, Alexander, the son of Æuropus, whom the young Macedonian king had loaded with bounties, was prevailed upon, by the offer of ten thousand talents, to plot against the life of his royal benefactor; but the treason was detected in time to prevent its execution. These were the means by which the Persian monarch at first endeavored to get rid of his adversary; and he did not entirely relinquish the ignoble design of suborning the followers of his antagonist, even after he had recourse to the more manly and more honorable method of leading an army to expel the invaders from his dominions. The fact that Darius Codomannus had now an army of about seven hundred thousand men, with which to confront his foe, made these nefarious schemes the more disgraceful.

With this immense host, Darius, accompanied by his family, in accordance with Persian custom, and surrounded by all the trappings of Oriental splendor, moved slowly from the plains of Babylonia into Syria. Alexander likewise led his army from Cappadocia into Syria, but first made himself master of Cilicia, the only remaining province of Asia Minor, which had not until then submitted to his arms. While at Tarsis, the capital of Cilicia, Alexander fell into a dangerous illness, in consequence of

2—49.-U. H.

imprudently bathing in the cold waters of the Cydnus, at a time when his body was heated by violent exercise. His condition was considered alarming by all his attendants, excepting Philip the Acarnanian, an eminent physician, who acquired celebrity in consequence of his connection with a certain incident arising from this illness. While Philip was handing a potion to the king, the latter received a letter from Parmenio, warning him that the physician had been bribed to poison him. When Alexander had raised the potion to his lips, he handed the letter to Philip, and observing that there was no change in his countenance while reading it, drank the liquid without saying a word. His confidence was well placed. The physician calmly assured him that the charge was utterly false, and the result proved the truth of his words, as Alexander recovered hourly from the time that he drank the potion given him by the physician.

The mountains separating Syria from Cilicia were only passable by an army at two points, one called the Syrian Gate, and the other named the Amanic Gate. His confidence in the devotion and valor of his troops, and his eagerness for a decisive encounter, induced Alexander, upon his recovery, to lead his army through the Syrian Gate into the plains of Syria. As soon as he had done so, he learned to his surprise and satisfaction that Darius had withdrawn from the open country of Syria, and had moved into Cilicia through the Amanic Gate, almost at the very moment that the Macedonian king had conducted his army through the Syrian Gate.

Alexander assembled his followers and eagerly pointed out to them the error committed by the Persian king in withdrawing his army from the open Syrian plains and taking up a new position in a hilly country, where his cavalry, the most efficient portion of his vast host, could be of but little avail. This and other circumstances so encouraged the Græco-Macedonian soldiers that they requested to be led to battle immediately. Their enterprising leader soon gratified their military ardor. He retraced his course to the Syrian Gate, repassed it, and soon reached the river Pinarus, on the plain of Issus. The vast Persian host was posted on the opposite bank of the stream. Alexander took charge of the right wing of his army, leaving the left wing under the conduct of Parmenio.

On the approach of Alexander's army, Darius Codomannus posted his Greek mercenaries, the part of his army upon which he himself mostly relied, in the front, opposite to the Macedonian phalanx. These Greek mercenaries were a very powerful body of troops numbering altogether thirty thousand. The Persian king flanked these choice troops with his heavy-armed barbarians, but the greater part of his unwieldy host was left behind in a condition of absolute inutility, because the confined nature of the ground would allow of no better disposition of them.

Upon reaching the bank of the Pinarus, Alexander dashed boldly into the river and safely landed on the opposite side. The barbarian hosts composing the right and left wings of the Persian army fled in confusion before the young Macedonian monarch, but the Greek mercenaries of the King of Persia for a while gallantly held their ground. After an obstinate contest they gave way, and the Persians on all sides followed their example. A force of the Persian cavalry remained on the field longest, and gave their king an opportunity to save himself by flight. The retreating troops of Darius Codomannus were cut down in vast numbers, and one hundred and ten thousand are said to have been left dead upon the field. The battle of Issus ended in a complete victory for Alexander, but his own loss, principally in the struggle with the Greek mercenaries, was severe. The historians have given us no exact account of the number of the Græco-Macedonian slain, and the number of his troops in this engagement is uncertain, as it is only known that he had recently received some reinforcements from the Greek cities of Asia Minor to the force which he had originally brought with him from Macedon.

King Darius Codomannus fled from the field in the midst of the battle; and his camp, with all its treasures, and his family, consisting of his mother, Sysigambis, his wife, Statira, his daughters and his infant son, fell into the hands of the triumphant Alexander. The Macedonian king, contrary to the ancient custom, treated his royal captives with the greatest kindness. The wife of Darius, who was considered the most beautiful woman in Asia, died soon after her capture, and received a most magnificent burial from the king of Macedon. On hearing of this, Darius is said to have exclaimed: "If it be the will of heaven that I am to be no longer King of Asia, may Alexander be my successor!"

The negotiations then ceased, and Alexander pursued his march along the coast of Phœnicia. At Damascus a vast amount of treasure belonging to the King of Persia fell into Alexander's possession. The famous Phœnician seaport of Sidon and other cities, the emporiums of commerce between Asia and the Mediterranean for many centuries, very readily submitted to the conqueror; but Tyre, the greatest and the most flourishing one of them all, refused him its allegiance and prepared for a resolute resistance. Although the Tyrians had sent ambassa-

ALEXANDER'S VICTORY AT ISSUS.

Such was the famous battle of Issus, which made Alexander the Great master of most of Syria and Phœnicia (B. C. 333). Alexander followed up his victory by marching along the coast of Syria, which everywhere submitted on his approach, into Phœnicia. While marching thither, Alexander received a deputation from the unfortunate Persian king, who had escaped safely to Susa, and who now made propositions for a treaty of peace and friendship with his young conqueror. Fully conscious of his power, and irritated at the lordly terms in which Darius Codomannus still considered proper to address him, Alexander replied that he could

dors to the Macedonian king, declaring themselves ready to yield to his orders, they boldly told him, when he announced his intention to visit their city and offer sacrifice to Hercules, that they would admit neither Persian nor Macedonian within their walls.

The strength of Tyre's position encouraged its inhabitants to thus brave the Macedonian power. Old Tyre, as a colonial settlement of the Sidonians, had been built upon the mainland (B. C. 1252); but after its destruction by Nebuchadnezzar, the great Babylonian king, its people sought refuge upon a neighboring island, about half a mile from the mainland, where New

Tyre rapidly arose, becoming more powerful and flourishing than the older city. Relying upon the depth of the surrounding waters, and upon the gigantic wall, more than a hundred feet high, and proportionately thick, which enclosed New Tyre, its inhabitants now ventured to deny an entrance to Alexander, whom they knew to have no fleet at command, and whom they accordingly hoped to resist with success.

But the Tyrians did not comprehend the indomitable energies of the young Macedonian king. He clearly perceived the danger of allowing such a nucleus of naval power to continue in alliance with Persia; and he therefore determined to obtain possession of the island city at whatever cost. His followers, whose efforts had thus far been unbaffled, zealously adopted his views; and the siege of Tyre began in earnest. For the purpose of opening a passage for his army, Alexander undertook to construct a great mole between the insular city and the mainland, as other modes of access to New Tyre were beyond his reach. He defended his men, while they were laboring at this work, by means of wooden towers and other contrivances; but the Tyrians galled them severely and retarded their operations by means of ignited darts, projectiles of different kinds, and fire-ships. But the mole advanced slowly and surely, until one night the besieged Tyrians towed a large hulk filled with combustibles to the mole, and, setting fire to it, succeeded in destroying completely the result of many weeks' labor. This disaster convinced Alexander of the necessity of having the aid of a fleet in his attack upon the city, and he was so fortunate as to soon obtain what he needed.

Sidon and other Phœnician maritime cities sent all their war-galleys to assist Alexander in his siege of Tyre, and these were reinforced by the squadrons from the islands of Cyprus and Rhodes, which had been tributaries of Persia, but which now determined to cultivate Alexander's favor. When he had received these valuable auxiliaries, Alexander recommenced siege operations by sea and land with redoubled vigor. The mole was reconstructed, and the apparently-impregnable city of Tyre was finally taken by storm, after a siege of seven months (B. C 332). It would seem that the final and successful assault was made from both the mole and the besieging fleet, and that it lasted two days, the Tyrians defending themselves with the most determined obstinacy. They emptied on their assailants vessels of boiling tar and burning sand, which penetrated to the bone, and exhausted every means suggested by patriotism or despair to save their city. But at length breaches were made in the walls of the city by the battering rams and other engines of the besiegers, and Tyre was carried by storm. The Tyrians suffered a heavy punishment for their obstinate defense of their city, eight thousand of them being slain and thirty thousand sold into slavery. Alexander is said to have lost four hundred men in the siege.

During the siege of Tyre, Alexander received a second letter from King Darius Codomannus, offering his daughter in marriage to the conquering Macedonian monarch, along with all the region between the Euphrates and the Mediterranean for her dower, as the basis of a treaty of peace and amity; but Alexander's haughty answer to this proposition caused its failure. It is said that Parmenio said to Alexander when this offer was made by the Persian king: "I would accept the terms." To this Alexander is said to have replied: "So would I, were I Parmenio."

After the capture of Tyre, Alexander marched toward Jerusalem to chastise its inhabitants for refusing to furnish him with provisions during the siege; but his wrath against them was disarmed when, upon nearing the city, he was met by a deputation of the people, headed by the High Priest, who had come to him to offer their submission. The High Priest was attired in white robes, and Jehovah's name was inscribed on his miter. Alexander advanced with great respect and bowed reverently before the High Priest, thus exciting the surprise of his officers, but the young conqueror said: "It is not the priest whom I adore, but the God whom he serves."

After having taken Tyre and obtained the submission of Jerusalem, Alexander directed his course southward and besieged and took the Philistine city of Gaza, which had refused to acknowledge his sway. The conqueror on this occasion departed from his accustomed magnanimity and inflicted a heavy punishment on the captured city, massacring the entire garrison of one thousand men, and causing the governor, Bœtis, to be dragged around the city behind his chariot-wheels, in barbarous imitation of Achilles, who dragged Hector around the walls of Troy. The fall of Gaza completed the conquest of Palestine by Alexander the Great (B. C. 332).

After the reduction of Gaza, Alexander advanced into Egypt for the purpose of bringing that country under his authority. The Macedonian conqueror was joyfully received by the people of Egypt, who were tired of Persian oppression, and they gladly submitted to his sway; so that Alexander's career in Egypt was one continued triumphal march. Sabaces, the Persian satrap of Egypt, having been slain in the battle of Issus, the land of the Nile was governed by a subordinate official, who made no resistance to the conquering Macedonian king, but, on the contrary, united with the Egyptian people in welcoming him and hailing him as their lord and sovereign. Alexander proceeded to Memphis, the Egyptian capital, where he held a magnificent festival, and still further won the affections of the Egyptians by joining them in their worship of the old bull-deity, Apis.

From Memphis, Alexander passed down the main branch of the Nile to the city of Canopus, at the mouth of that branch. Observing with surprise that a region so fertile and so rich in commercial resources had no suitable harbor, he determined to found a maritime metropolis which should give Egypt one everlasting memorial of his name and dominion—a purpose which he fulfilled in the founding of the city of *Alexandria*, named in his honor (B. C. 332).

The site of this new city was so well chosen that it rapidly attained the condition of a flourishing commercial emporium. For many succeeding ages Alexandria continued to be the center of the world's commerce and civilization, and it has remained a city of the highest importance to Egypt to the present day.

After Alexander had projected this monument of his name and his sagacity, he proceeded to the Libyan desert, accompanied by a small escort, for the purpose of seeing the temple of Ammon, and consulting the oracle of that deity, as his illustrious ancestors, Perseus and Hercules, had done many centuries before him. The temple of Ammon was located in the oasis of Siwah, to the south-west of Alexandria, and about one hundred and fifty miles from the sea-coast. Alexander admired the enticing beauty of this fertile spot in the barren sands of the desert. He received a most favorable response from the oracle of Ammon, after which he returned to his army at Memphis.

In the meantime King Darius Codomannus had assembled a new army in Assyria, consisting of more than a million men, gathered from the Eastern provinces of his empire. Alexander arranged the government of Egypt, putting some of his own trusty followers in the most important offices; and in the spring of B. C. 331 he led his army directly from Egypt toward the very heart of the Medo-Persian Empire, declaring that "the world no more admitted of two masters than of two suns." He crossed the Euphrates and the Tigris and advanced against the Persian king, whose immense hosts he encountered near the Assyrian town of Arbéla, on the plain of Gaugaméla, east of the Tigris, where was fought the battle that decided the fate of Asia.

Alexander's army had been increased, by recent reinforcements from Europe and from his newly-acquired Asiatic dependencies, to forty-seven thousand men, of whom almost one-seventh part consisted of cavalry. The lowest estimate of the Persian horsemen makes them number forty thousand, and their strength was increased by fifteen elephants and two hundred scythe-armed chariots. Darius Codomannus did not on this occasion have so powerful a body of Greek mercenaries as he had at Issus, though his army was now a more efficient one in other respects. His forces were not now composed of the effeminate guards and standing troops of Persia, but consisted mainly of Parthians, Bactrians, Hindoos, Hyrcanians and others from the central East—troops which were hardy and courageous, if they were undisciplined.

Such were the characters and numbers respectively of the Græco-Macedonian and the Medo-Persian armies that contended with each other in the vicinity of Arbéla for the the dominion of Asia. In the evening the Macedonians ascended an eminence from which they first beheld the widespread army of the Persian king, drawn up in good order on the plain of Gaugaméla; Darius having seen, but too fatally, the disadvantages of a confined position with his immense force of cavalry. Both armies lay quiet for the night. The next morning Alexander led down his troops, in two heavy-armed phalanxes of sixteen thousand men each, into the plain of Gaugaméla. The Persians began the battle by a charge of the Scythian cavalry on the right wing of the Macedonian army, but after a desperate contest they were forced back, and Darius ordered his lines to advance. Alexander broke the lines of the enemy by suddenly pushing his phalanxes in between the left wing and the centre of the Persian army. This movement threw the Persians into disorder, and in a great measure decided the battle in favor of Alexander. From that moment the scene was more of a massacre than a battle, excepting in one point, where a powerful force of Parthian and Indian horse maintained an obstinate struggle, but were finally routed by the Thessalian cavalry, thus terminating the battle in the utter defeat of the Persians. A destructive pursuit of the flying Persian hosts by the triumphant Macedonians completed the disasters of the army of Darius. The loss of the defeated Persians was about forty thousand in killed, while the Macedonians lost only about five hundred. Such was the famous battle of Arbéla, which put an end to the great Medo-Persian Empire after an existence of two centuries, thus making Alexander the Great lord of Asia at the early age of twenty-five years(B. C. 331).

After the battle Darius Codomannus fled to Ecbatana, the capital of Media, and the summer capital of the Medo-Persian Empire, accompanied by a few followers, resolving, if Alexander pursued him thither, to retire still farther to the eastward, and seek refuge in Bactria. Though determined, if practicable, to obtain possession of the person of Darius Codomannus, for the purpose of depriving the Central Asian tribes of a rallying point in the future, Alexander found himself obliged to first devote his attention to the consolidation of his power in the provinces which his decisive victory in the battle of Arbéla had placed in his power.

From Arbéla, Alexander therefore led his army southward to the opulent city of Babylon, the winter capital of the Medo-Persian Empire, where a large part of the accumulated wealth of the Persian monarchy fell into his hands. He was accordingly enabled to distribute ample pecuniary rewards to every one of his soldiers. After arranging the government of Babylonia, Alexander proceeded to Susa, the capital of Susiana, and the chief capital of the Medo-Persian Empire, where he received a still greater accession to his treasury, a sum equal to about fifty million dollars of our money coming into his possession at this place. While at Susa, Alexander exhibited a remarkable instance of his humanity by settling the family of Darius Codomannus in the royal palace of their ancestors, and also displayed a great deal of prudence in appointing a native chieftain to the government of Susiana. He had pursued the same prudent and liberal policy at Babylon, thus securing the affections of the people. From Susa, Alexander marched to Persepolis, the capital of Persia proper, where still greater accessions of wealth came into his possession.

During his stay at Persepolis, which lasted several months, the conqueror gave one of the first indications of his having been overcome by excessive prosperity. At a magnificent banquet, Alexander, heated with wine, gave his assent to a proposition offered by one of his companions that a bonfire should be made of the old palace of the early Persian kings. The Macedonian conqueror soon repented of having given his assent to this mad outrage, but most of the palace was destroyed before the fire could be extinguished.

After arranging the government of Persia proper, Alexander left Persepolis and proceeded to Ecbatana, with the view of obtaining possession of the Persian king, who was still at the Median capital, whither he had fled after the battle of Arbéla. On the approach of the Macedonian conqueror, King Darius Codomannus fled to the mountainous region of Bactriana, whither he was hastily pursued by Alexander, who, on reaching Ecbatana, heard that his intended prey had escaped only five days before. After following upon the footsteps of the fugitive king to the eastward, in a long and toilsome march, performed with wonderful celerity, Alexander came near the object of his pursuit upon the frontiers of Bactriana. But Alexander was here apprized that the treacherous Bessus, the Persian satrap of Bactriana, who had accompanied the Persian king, had thrown off his allegiance to the unfortunate Darius Codomannus, and had kept him bound as a prisoner. The Macedonian monarch continued his pursuit with increased speed, and at length discovered the fugitive party fleeing before him. As he was going onward in hot pursuit, Alexander, to his deep and sincere affliction, beheld Darius Codomannus dying by the roadside, having been stabbed by two Persian nobles in attendance on Bessus, for the purpose of stopping the pursuit or of facilitating their own flight (B. C. 330). The generous Macedonian king honored the remains of his unfortunate rival with a magnificent burial in the tombs of his illustrious ancestors at Pasargadæ, the original capital of Persia proper, and treated the family of Darius Codomannus with all due respect. Alexander had never sought the life of the fallen king, and he now pursued the assassins with a spirit of the keenest resentment. Bessus and the two assassins afterwards fell into Alexander's hands, and he punished them with a most cruel death, in imitation of the barbarous customs of the East.

The provinces of Bactriana, Ariana and Sogdiana—comprising an important part of the vast region of Central Asia, anciently known as Scythia, but now called Tartary and Turkestan—were subdued by Alexander the Great, only after great exertions and sacrifices on his part, and after a campaign of almost three years. The people of these regions are said to have expostulated with Alexander, and to have asked him this question: "Have you furnished yourself with winged soldiers?" This allusion to the impregnable character of their country aroused the pride of Alexander, and he resolved to conquer the country at any cost. Nowhere else, during his wide career of conquest, did Alexander display so many of the qualities of the warrior as upon the plains of Scythia, not being deterred from his purpose by heat or cold, hunger or thirst, danger or toil, wounds or disease. Soldiers who have a commander who can bear all these casualties can accomplish anything. But the gallant Macedonian warriors, who had defied sword and lance on many a sanguinary field, narrowly escaped perishing from hunger and fatigue.

Before the close of his Scythian campaign, Alexander married the beautiful Roxana, "the Pearl of the East," a Bactrian princess, whom he had taken prisoner at the capture of a Scythian fortress. Alexander's love of conquest did not deter him from devoting some attention to the civilization and durable welfare of the countries which he had subjugated. Four new towns, named Alexandria, in his honor, became the centers of the caravan trade, and diffused the Grecian civilization among the people of Central Asia. Parmenio and other officers had been engaged meanwhile in the subjugation of Hyrcania and Parthia, which, with the reduction of Bactriana, Ariana and Sogdiana, completed Alexander's conquest of the Medo-Persian Empire (B. C. 327).

But Alexander's fair fame was tarnished by several brutal acts. Elated by his conquests, he had assumed the pomp and dress of an Oriental monarch, and had thus offended some of his officers. Philótas, the son of Parmenio, the ablest of Alexander's generals, had made some disparaging remarks upon the change in the king's manners and habits, and was put to death on an unproven charge of conspiring against his sovereign's life. Parmenio himself was executed for alleged complicity in the same pretended conspiracy.

The next year (B. C. 327), while in winter-quarters in Bactriana, Alexander committed a deed which has left an indelible stain upon his memory, and which showed that he was by degrees deteriorating under the corrupting influence of success. He had originally been noted for his temperate habits, but now he began to indulge occasionally to excess in wine and to claim the ceremony of prostration and divine honors from his followers. On one occasion, during a feast held in Bactriana, in honor of Castor and Pollux, at which Alexander was present, the conversation turned upon the comparative brilliancy of his own exploits and those of Dionysus, the god of wine, who is said to have also conquered Asia. Many of those present conceded the superiority to Alexander, and for this they were rebuked by Clitus, the old officer who had saved Alexander's life in the battle of the Granícus. As all were heated with wine, the discussion grew animated, and at length Clitus censured the king severely for allowing himself to be compared to the gods. Intoxicated with the rest of the party, Alexander was so irritated with the reproof that he arose and advanced in an angry manner to Clitus, who was thereupon forced to leave the room by some of the more prudent of the party. But Clitus returned, and, being still exasperated, again reproached the king in severe terms, whereupon Alexander, losing all self-control, killed Clitus with his sword. This crime had no sooner been committed than it caused Alexander much bitter repentance; and so profound was his remorse that he did not eat or drink, nor leave his chamber, for three days, until his faithful and sorrowing followers succeeded in their entreaties to induce him to return by degrees to his usual manner of living.

While Alexander the Great was pursuing his conquering career in Asia, the general peace of the Grecian republics was disturbed by a revolt of the Peloponnesian states, with Lacedæmon at their head, which attempted to shake off the hated yoke of Macedonian supremacy. Sparta, as we have seen, had been maintaining a sullen neutrality during the agitations of the Grecian confederacy in the later years of Philip's reign preceding his conquest of Greece, and had also declined to participate in Alexander's campaigns in Asia. Three years after Alexander had started on his career of Oriental conquest, and while his viceroy, Antipater, was occupied in Thrace, the Spartan king Agis II. took advantage of the apparently-favorable opportunity to head a revolt of the Peloponnesian states against the Macedonian power; but the effort ended in a signal failure, Agis II. being defeated and killed in battle with Antípater, who had returned to Greece; and the haughty Spartans humbly begged for peace, which Alexander, when applied to, magnanimously granted to them.

About the same time there was an oratorical contest in Athens between Demosthenes and Æschines. These renowned orators engaged in a trial of strength, before the assembly of the Athenian people, on the results of which depended the best interests of the one or the other. Demosthenes came forth triumphant from this oratorical contest, and Æschines was condemned to exile. To the lasting honor of Demosthenes, he treated his fallen rival with exceeding generosity, giving him a purse of gold to support himself in his misfortune. Æschines showed that he also was noble-hearted and magnanimous. Upon his banishment from

Athens, he retired to the island of Rhodes, and there established a celebrated school of eloquence. When he read to his pupils the masterly oration of Demosthenes which had made himself a homeless wanderer, they were unable to refrain from giving the most vehement applause, whereupon Æschines said to them: "Ah! what would you have said, had you heard the wild beast himself roaring it out?"

About this time Alexander sent to Athens the statues of the tyrannicides, Harmódius and Aristogíton, which he had taken at Susa, whither Xerxes had carried them. By these kindly and politic donations, along with the share in his glory accruing to the republic through the auxiliaries furnished him by Athens, which was then the ruling power in Greece outside of Macedon, Alexander kept that state in a friendly and peaceful attitude during the entire period of his conquering career.

Antípater managed to weaken the anti-Macedonian party in Athens by procuring the banishment of the orator Demosthenes, the life and head of the party. Harpalus, one of Alexander's captains, had incurred his master's displeasure, and fled from Asia to Athens in consequence, hoping to purchase an asylum there with his peculated gold—an expectation in which he was not disappointed, as the favor of many leading Athenians was to be bought with a price. Phocion and Demosthenes were the only ones who discountenanced Harpalus; but, ultimately, even Demosthenes was said to have accepted a bribe. Whether this charge was true or false, it finally procured the banishment of the illustrious orator. A threat from Antípater forced the Athenians to quickly expel Harpalus from their city, and to impeach those who had taken his presents or espoused his cause. A heavy fine was imposed on Demosthenes, as one of this number; and, as he was unable to pay it, he was obliged to retire in exile to the island of Ægina.

After this nothing transpired to agitate the public mind in Greece until Alexander caused a proclamation to be issued by his representatives at the Olympic Games, declaring "that all the Grecian cities should immediately recall and receive those persons who had been expelled from them, and that such cities as refused to do so should be forced to compliance by the Macedonian arms." When this decree was issued, there were at least twenty thousand exiles from the various Grecian republics. Most of the states regarded this decree as a piece of despotic insolence, as they were thus called upon to receive into their society persons whom the public voice had expelled as guilty of the most enormous crimes. Athens, especially, felt intense indignation at this imperious edict, but failed in her efforts to awaken a spirit of resistance among some of the other Grecian states.

Ambitious of further conquests, Alexander the Great, in the year B. C. 327, invaded India with a powerful army composed of European and Asiatic soldiers. He had been frequently reinforced during his last campaigns by fresh contingents from Europe, which was very necessary in order to leave small detachments behind him to secure his conquests. Large numbers of Scythians likewise enrolled themselves under his standard, on his conquest of their country. Thus he entered upon his Indian campaign with a powerful army. This campaign was mainly confined to the Indus valley and the Punjab.

Alexander's progress was vigorously opposed by the warlike tribes inhabiting those regions, while the natural difficulties of the ground were likewise very troublesome. He passed the celebrated city of Nysa, fabled to have been founded by Dionysus, the god of wine, after which he crossed the Indus in the upper part of its course, and continued his advance amidst its widening tributaries. Alexander pushed forward to the Hydaspes, one of the tributaries of the Indus, on the opposite bank of which a powerful Indian prince, Porus, King of the Punjab, had assembled an army of thirty-four thousand men, with many armed chariots and elephants, to dispute the passage of the river by the Macedonian army. Alexander perceived the impossibility of crossing with prudence in the face of the enemy, and he therefore resorted to the expedient of lulling to rest the vigilance of Porus, who exhibited both valor and activity.

Alexander succeeded in crossing the Hydaspes, and, in a fierce engagement, he defeated Porus and took him prisoner. When brought into the presence of Alexander, the conqueror admired the loftiness and majesty of person of his royal captive. Said Alexander: "How shall I treat you?" Porus calmly replied: "By acting like a king?" Thereupon Alexander responded, smiling: "That I shall do for my own sake; but what can I do for yours?" Porus repeated that all he desired was contained in his first request; and Alexander was so well pleased with the profound sense of what was great and becoming in a sovereign, as exhibited in the captive monarch's words, that he not only gave Porus his liberty and restored him to his throne, but afterwards made him viceroy of all the Macedonian conquests in India.

Alexander founded two new cities on the Hydaspes, Nicæa and Bucéphala, the former meaning *city of victory*, and the latter named in honor of Alexander's celebrated warhorse, Bucéphalus, which died near the spot. After besieging the city of Sangala, Alexander found himself master of the entire region drained by the tributaries of the Indus, and above the point where their confluence makes the Indus one mighty stream. The conqueror then marched eastward to the Hyphasis, and was preparing to add the fertile region drained by the Ganges to his empire, when his soldiers, seeing no end to their toils and hardships, positively refused to follow him any further; and Alexander was obliged, with great reluctance, to abandon his career of conquest and to return to Persia.

After marching back to the Hydaspes, Alexander resolved upon returning by a new route, along the coasts of the Erythræan (now Arabian) Sea and the Persian Gulf; and, with this end in view, he procured all the vessels he could find and built new ones, to convey his army down the Indus. The passage of the army down the river occupied several months, on account of the opposition from the barbarians on the banks of the stream. Upon reaching the ocean, Alexander is said to have sat upon a rock near the shore, gazing at the wide expanse of waters, and to have wept bitterly that there were no more worlds to conquer. Disembarking his land troops, Alexander marched along the sea-coast with his main force, leaving his admiral, Neárchus, to pursue his way to the Euphrates by sea. The toils and hardships of this march were extremely severe. Three-fourths of the army perished in the deserts of Gedrosia (now Beloochistan) from hunger, thirst, fatigue, and from the miseries of the climate. Alexander cheered his troops in their march by magnanimously sharing in all their privations. Upon reaching the shores of the Persian Gulf, Alexander's army was rejoined by the fleet under Neárchus. The march of Alexander's army through the fertile district of Carmania (now Kerman), a province of Persia, resembled a triumphal procession; and the soldiers, once more in a friendly country, believed their hardships over, and abandoned themselves to enjoyment. Alexander himself imitated in public the conduct attributed to Dionysus, the god of wine, who was said to have sung and danced with his companions all over Asia.

After his return to Persia, Alexander punished the governor of Persepolis, who had been tempted to assume independent authority during the conqueror's absence. Alexander now devoted his attention to the organization of a permanent government for the extensive empire which he had established. He aimed at uniting the Medes and Persians with the Greeks and Macedonians into one great nation, possessed of the institutions and the civilization of Greece; and during his stay at Persepolis, the Macedonian customs permitting polygamy, Alexander married Statira, daughter of the murdered Darius Codomannus, and ten thousand of his officers and soldiers married Median and Persian women. Alexander's mild and generous treatment of the con-

DEFEAT OF PORUS BY THE MACEDONIANS.

quered people made him as much respected and beloved by the Persian nobility and people as if he had been their native, legitimate prince. During the last years of his life, Alexander's mind was occupied with schemes, which, to his credit, were directed to the durable improvement of the countries which he had subdued. He opened the navigation of the Euphrates, founded many towns, and marked out commercial depots to connect the trade of the Nile, the Euphrates, the Tigris and the Indus.

While planning schemes for fresh conquests, Alexander the Great met with a premature death from the effects of his dissolute and intemperate habits. After visiting Susa and Ecbatana, and projecting important improvements in those cities, Alexander proceeded toward Babylon, which city he intended to make the capital of his vast empire. He was reluctant to enter Babylon, on account of various prophecies announcing that spot as destined to prove fatal to him; but grief for the death of Hephæstion, the intimate friend of his youth, at Babylon, determined him to visit that city.

Upon reaching Babylon, the conqueror was attacked with a sudden illness, caused by his excessive indulgence in strong drink, which carried him to his grave, at the early age of thirty-two years, and after having reigned over Macedon and Greece twelve years (June 28, B. C. 324).

During the progress of his illness, his soldiers, as on various other occasions, of sickness, hung about him in a state of indescribable anxiety and grief. When his condition became desperate, his favorite soldiery were allowed to enter his room, when an unparalleled scene transpired. The dying conqueror, pale and speechless, but thoroughly conscious, beheld his gallant warriors enter one by one, weeping bitterly, to take a last look at the chieftain who had so often led them to battle. He had sufficient strength to hold out his arm; and each soldier, in passing by, kissed the beloved hand which had on so many occasions waved them on to victory. When asked, just before his death, to whom he left his vast empire, Alexander replied: "To the most worthy." He, however, gave his signet-ring to Perdiccas, but said: "I am afraid my obsequies will be celebrated with bloody ceremonies." The remains of Alexander the Great were conveyed to Alexandria, in Egypt, where they were interred.

The character of this wonderful man will be best understood by a reference to his deeds. Although he was a scourge to many nations, he accomplished much permanent good among them. He awakened millions of mankind from the sleep of barbarism, and diffused among them the arts, the institutions and the civilization of Greece. On the wide extent of his conquests he founded at least seventy cities, whose sites were generally so well selected that they redounded to the commercial greatness and civilization of the countries in which they were located. In his other measures of general polity, Alexander was solicitous for the welfare of the nations which he had conquered.

In his private character, Alexander seemed to have been constitutionally liberal, generous and humane. Though his remarkable good fortune brought errors and vices in its train, he was guilty of fewer odious actions than most other conquerors. The tone and temper of his time furnish the only excuse for his insatiable ambition and his disregard of human life. Although Alexander's thirst for power seems almost insane to us, we must remember that the great philosopher Aristotle "nursed in Alexander's boyish breast the spirit which blazed forth so fiercely in his manhood," and that the wisest men of his time looked upon his career with approval and admiration. Other blemishes upon Alexander's character, such as his excessive indulgence in wine, which brought him to a premature grave, and his murder of his friend and benefactor, Clitus, were peculiarly his own.

The death of this man, whose word and will constituted the law of most of the then-known world, produced the most important consequences, which, of themselves, afford the most convincing evidence of Alexander's wonderful personal ability. While he lived, the many commanders who served under him, and who had constantly before them the most enticing example of successful ambition, seem ever to have instinctively felt and recognized the presence of a master, and to have cherished no thought of aiming at the possession of independent power. No sooner, however, had the mighty conqueror breathed his last, than each of these officers, in looking around among his fellows, discovered none to whose claims he was willing to yield his own, and therefore all began to put forward pretensions to a share of dominion.

The great and permanent result of Alexander's conquests was the Hellenizing of all Western Asia and Egypt—that is, the diffusion of Grecian civilization, ideas, language and literature, over this vast region; and thus preparing the way for the birth and development of Christianity, a religion which arose from the commingling of the Greek and Hebrew civilizations in Judæa. On the other hand, Greece became influenced by Oriental habits; Grecian patriotism and public spirit declined; art and literature decayed; and the Greeks became a nation of pedants and adventurers.

www.ingramcontent.com/pod-product-compliance
Lightning Source LLC
Chambersburg PA
CBHW030542300426
44111CB00009B/834